THE OLD REGIME AND THE REVOLUTION

ALEXIS DE TOCQUEVILLE

THE OLD REGIME
AND THE
REVOLUTION

VOLUME ONE
THE COMPLETE TEXT

EDITED AND WITH AN
INTRODUCTION AND CRITICAL APPARATUS BY
François Furet and Françoise Mélonio

TRANSLATED BY
Alan S. Kahan

THE UNIVERSITY OF CHICAGO PRESS
CHICAGO AND LONDON

FRANÇOIS FURET (1927–1997) was the leading
French historian of the Revolution and, according to the
New York Times, "one of the most influential French thinkers of the
post-war era." FRANÇOISE MÉLONIO is the editor of Gallimard's
critical edition of Tocqueville's works. ALAN KAHAN is associate
professor in the Department of History at Florida International
University and author of *Aristocratic Liberalism.* He is also translating
the second volume of *L'Ancien Régime et la Révolution,* to be
published by the University of Chicago Press.

The University of Chicago Press, Chicago 60637
The University of Chicago Press, Ltd., London
© 1998 by The University of Chicago
All rights reserved. Published 1998
Printed in the United States of America
07 06 05 04 03 02 01 00 99 98   1 2 3 4 5

ISBN: 0-226-80529-8 (cloth)

The French text on which this translation is based has been licensed
to the University of Chicago Press by Éditions Gallimard
and is protected by French and international copyright
laws and agreements. © Éditions Gallimard.

Library of Congress Cataloging-in-Publication Data

Tocqueville, Alexis de, 1805–1859.
[Ancien régime et la Révolution. English]
The Old Regime and the Revolution / Alexis de Tocqueville ; edited
and with an introduction and critical apparatus by François Furet
and Françoise Mélonio ; translated by Alan S. Kahan.
p.   cm.
Includes index.
ISBN 0-226-80529-8 (cloth : alk. paper).
1. France—History—Revolution, 1789–1799—Causes.   I. Furet,
François, 1927–   .   II. Mélonio, Françoise.   III. Title.
DC138.T6313   1998
944.04—dc21   97-43814
CIP

♾ The paper used in this publication meets the minimum
requirements of the American National Standard for Information
Sciences—Permanence of Paper for Printed Library Materials,
ANSI Z39.48-1984.

Contents

Translator's Foreword / *ix*

❧

INTRODUCTION
by François Furet and Françoise Mélonio
The Genesis of *The Old Regime and the Revolution* / 1
The Structure of the Work: Book One / 12
The Structure of the Work: Book Two / 20
The Structure of the Work: Book Three / 41
The Evolution of the Work / 54
Tocqueville's Files, Manuscripts, and Proofs / 75
Note on This Edition / 79

❧

Preface / *83*

BOOK ONE

CHAPTER ONE
Contradictory Opinions about the Revolution at Its Birth
93

CHAPTER TWO
That the Fundamental and Final Objective of
the Revolution Was Not, as Has Been Thought,
to Destroy Religion and Weaken the State
96

CHAPTER THREE
How the French Revolution Was a
Political Revolution Which Acted Like
a Religious Revolution, and Why
99

CHAPTER FOUR

How Almost All of Europe Had Come to
Have Identical Institutions and How These
Institutions Fell into Ruin Everywhere

102

CHAPTER FIVE

What Did the French Revolution Really Accomplish?

105

✿

BOOK TWO

CHAPTER ONE

Why Feudalism Was Hated by the
People in France More Than Anywhere Else

111

CHAPTER TWO

How Administrative Centralization Is an
Institution of the Old Regime, and Not the Work of
Either the Revolution or the Empire, as Is Said

118

CHAPTER THREE

How What Is Now Called Government
Paternalism Is an Institution of the Old Regime

124

CHAPTER FOUR

How Administrative Justice and the Immunity of
Public Officials Are Institutions of the Old Regime

132

CHAPTER FIVE

How Centralization Had Been Able to
Introduce Itself among the Old Powers and
Replace Them without Destroying Them

135

CHAPTER SIX

On Bureaucratic Habits under the Old Regime

138

CHAPTER SEVEN

How France, of All the Countries of Europe, Was
the One Where the Capital City Had Already Acquired
the Greatest Domination over the Provinces, and
Consumed the Entire Country

145

CHAPTER EIGHT

That France Was the Country
Where People Had Become Most Alike

149

CHAPTER NINE

How Such Similar Men Were More Divided than
Ever Before, Separated into Small Groups That Were
Estranged from and Indifferent to One Another

152

CHAPTER TEN

How the Destruction of Political Liberty
and the Division of Classes Caused Almost All
the Ills of Which the Old Regime Perished

163

CHAPTER ELEVEN

Of the Kind of Freedom That Existed under
the Old Regime and Its Influence on the Revolution

171

CHAPTER TWELVE

How, Despite the Progress of Civilization, the
Condition of the French Peasant Was Sometimes
Worse in the Eighteenth Century Than It Had
Been in the Thirteenth

180

❦

BOOK THREE

CHAPTER ONE

How Around the Middle of the Eighteenth Century
Intellectuals Became the Country's Leading Politicians,
and the Effects Which Resulted from This

195

CHAPTER TWO

How Irreligion Was Able to Become a
General and Dominant Passion among the French of
the Eighteenth Century, and What Kind of Influence
This Had on the Character of the Revolution

202

CHAPTER THREE

How the French Wanted Reforms before They Wanted Freedoms

209

CHAPTER FOUR

That the Reign of Louis XVI Was the Most
Prosperous Period of the Old Monarchy, and How
This Very Prosperity Hastened the Revolution

217

CHAPTER FIVE

How Efforts to Help the Masses Radicalized Them

225

CHAPTER SIX

Some Practices Which Helped the Government
Complete the Revolutionary Education of the Masses

230

CHAPTER SEVEN

How a Great Administrative Revolution
Had Preceded the Political Revolution, and
the Consequences That This Had

234

CHAPTER EIGHT

How the Revolution Came Naturally from What Preceded It

241

APPENDIX

On the *Pays d'états,* and in Particular on Languedoc

249

Tocqueville's Notes / 257

Notes and Variants / 317

Glossary / 435

Index / 439

Translator's Foreword

"Make a strong effort to avoid as much as possible, in
all these chapters, the *abstract* style, in order to make myself fully
understood and, above all, read with pleasure. Make a constant effort
to contain abstract and general ideas in words which present a precise and particular picture. . . . One writes in order to please,
and not to attain an ideal perfection of language."
—From a note by Tocqueville

When I first approached *The Old Regime and the Revolution* with the
intention of translating it into English, I was almost stopped by the difficulty of translating its wonderful opening paragraph. I persevered, and
it is for the reader to judge the result. In the pages that follow I have
tried to recreate the multiple layers of Tocqueville's meaning and, at the
same time, to preserve the beauty and elegance of Tocqueville's highly
nuanced style. Yet the effort to reproduce the author's "intention" cannot meet with lasting success, for even a translator's own estimate of success changes as the translator's interpretation of the author changes. My
rendering bears the mark of my own interpretation of Tocqueville, with
which some will disagree.[1]

This translation also bears the mark of François Furet, perhaps the best
reader Tocqueville has ever had. Furet helped inspire this project, encouraged its completion, and, along with Françoise Mélonio, wrote the Introduction that appears in the following pages. His untimely death in the
summer of 1997 was a grievous loss.

No preface could hope to justify the myriad decisions a translator
is called upon to make, but some explanations here may prove useful.
A word that bedevils many translators of French texts is *peuple,* whose

1. See Alan S. Kahan, *Aristocratic Liberalism: The Social and Political Thought of Jacob Burck-
hardt, John Stuart Mill, and Alexis de Tocqueville* (New York: 1992).

literal and often inaccurate English rendering would be "people." In nineteenth-century French, *peuple* usually had a much more limited meaning, particularly when used by those of Tocqueville's political convictions. I have therefore usually translated it as "lower classes" or, more rarely, "masses," depending on Tocqueville's meaning. Another troublesome term is *moeurs,* a word Tocqueville uses frequently and with varying though usually broad meaning. It can include practices, ideas, morals, customs, feelings, and habits. Tocqueville himself felt the need to explain his use of the word in *Democracy in America:* "I here intend the term *moeurs* to have its original Latin meaning; I use it not only for *moeurs* in the strict sense, what one might call habits of the heart, but also for the different notions men possess, the various opinions that hold sway among them, and the sum of ideas that form their mental habits."[2] I have most often translated *moeurs* by "mores," a word that has both the flaws and the virtues of unfamiliarity for many readers but which I found was the only English equivalent with the same range of meanings. Finally, I have made occasional adjustments in paragraphing to avoid multiple very short paragraphs.

Decisions have also been called for with regard to the organization of this volume by comparison with the French edition published by Gallimard in the Pléiade series. Whereas the French edition separates the "critical apparatus" from the "historical notes," these elements are here combined as "Notes and Variants" for the reader's convenience. Also included in the "Notes and Variants" are certain materials that will appear in the second volume of the French edition; being closely related to the text of *The Old Regime* as published here, we have drawn them into our volume one. Finally, a "Historical Glossary" has been added to the American edition to aid the nonspecialist reader in deciphering unfamiliar terms and references. Glossed terms are indicated by daggers in the text. A translation of volume two, which consists of Tocqueville's drafts and notes for the projected continuation of his history, is in preparation.

Translating Tocqueville has been a strenuous pleasure. The translator's craft is one of ill repute—the translator is a betrayer, say the Italians—but translation is also a form of emancipation. Montesquieu, perhaps the chief influence on Tocqueville, says in *The Spirit of the Laws* that it is impossible to be free without law, that the essence of freedom, for both the individual and the state, lies in being bound by rules. Similarly, the trans-

---

2. Alexis de Tocqueville, *De la démocratie en Amérique,* in *Oeuvres complètes* (hereafter cited as *OC*), v. 1, t. 1, edited by J.-P. Mayer (Paris, 1961–), p. 300.

lator is bound by the author's meaning, yet is free to change the words. I have found the experience liberating.

In making this translation I have benefited from the assistance of many. Keith Baker helped originate this project. Financial assistance from Florida International University and from a Translation Grant by the National Endowment for the Humanities speeded its completion. François Furet and Françoise Mélonio provided invaluable aid in many regards. John Tryneski of The University of Chicago Press has been an unfailing source of good humor and encouragement. In addition I would like to thank the Press's anonymous readers and all those who have provided comment and commentary over the years. But most of all I would like to thank my wife, Sarah Bentley. She is the co-translator of the Introduction, and throughout this work her contribution extends beyond my capacity to translate it into appropriate language.

Alan S. Kahan

Introduction
Françoise Mélonio and François Furet

The Genesis of *The Old Regime and the Revolution*

For Tocqueville, history was the continuation of politics by other means. He did not share Chateaubriand's gloomy affection for ruins, Greek temples, or Gothic churches; he was not captured by the poetic charms of the Middle Ages, as were Scott, Guizot, Augustin Thierry, Michelet, and Barante. A disinterested taste for the past seemed frivolous to one who saw democracy running at flood tide: "Basically, only things of our time interest the public and really interest me. The greatness and uniqueness of the spectacle presented by our contemporary world absorbs too much of our attention for us to attach much importance to those historical curiosities which are enough for learned and leisured societies," he wrote to Kergorlay, 15 December 1850, at the very moment when, in the midst of writing his *Recollections,* he was looking for the "great subject of political literature" that would become *The Old Regime.*[1] The questions Tocqueville raised about the history of his time or of the preceding centuries were political questions, always the same ones, questions that cropped up throughout his writings and his political career: Why did France's transition to democracy assume a revolutionary form? How can we guarantee freedom in an egalitarian society?

Tocqueville had found the origin of these questions in his family inheritance. He liked to recall that he was the great-grandson of the famous Malesherbes. In 1835 when writing on democracy, in 1836 when writing on the state of France before 1789, and later when writing on the old regime, Tocqueville cited the *Remonstrance of the Cour des Aides* of 18 February 1771, in which Malesherbes was the first, according to Tocqueville, to defend the general rights of humanity and those of the nation. It was to Malesherbes that Tocqueville owed the idea of continuing administrative

---

1. Tocqueville to Kergorlay, 15 December 1850, *OC* (see p. x, n. 2, above), v. 13, t. 1, pp. 230–31.

centralization in France since Philip the Fair (1285–1314), and the corresponding weakening of the principle of representation. Since the fourteenth century, "the nation has been, so to speak, *forbidden,* and given guardians."[2] But filial piety did not prevent Tocqueville from denouncing what was missing from Malesherbes's liberalism due to Malesherbes's ignorance of the real principles of representation, and to his confusing privilege with freedom.[3] Malesherbes certainly bequeathed to Tocqueville the desire for freedom, but not the recipe for preserving freedom in an age of equality.

The Terror had tinged the family history with tragedy: Tocqueville's mother, saved by Thermidor from the scaffold on which Malesherbes perished, renounced her grandfather's taste for the Enlightenment while retaining his undying attachment to Louis XVI. To the child Alexis she sang laments about the king's death, and "everyone wept, not over all the personal hardships we had suffered, nor even over so many relatives that we had lost during the civil war and on the scaffold, but over the fate of that man who died more than fifteen years ago."[4] Tocqueville's father, Hervé, a devoted servant of the Restoration, which made him first prefect, then peer of France, was the author of a memoir on the Terror. He later published *A Philosophical History of the Reign of Louis XV* (1847) and then a *Survey of the Reign of Louis XVI* (1850):[5] both works blamed the blindness of the kings on the spirit of the times and the aristocracy's obsession with its privileges, but they remained subject to what Alexis called the aristocratic view of history, which assigned to the Court and to famous persons a major role in the course of events. Tocqueville owed little of his understanding of the old regime to his father, but he inherited from his parents their anguish over the aristocracy's tragic destiny and

---

2. *Remonstrances,* cited by Tocqueville in *Democracy in America,* v. 1, note K, relating to chapter 5. In this essential note we already see the outline for the development of *The Old Regime.*

3. A draft of book two, chapter eleven, reads: "The beautiful remonstrances of M. de Malesherbes at the entry of the Seven Years' War are full of truths, but of irrelevant truths. It was only through arbitrariness and folly that the monarchy succeeded in hiding the parlement's flaws as a political body from the eyes of the people, and making that court popular." Notes and Variants, p. 373.

4. Tocqueville to Lady Lewis, 6 May 1857, *Oeuvres complètes,* edited by Gustave de Beaumont (1865), v. 6, p. 384. Hereafter cited as *OC* (Beaumont).

5. *Histoire philosophique du règne de Louis XV* (Paris, 1847) and *Coup d'oeil sur le règne de Louis XVI depuis son avènement à la couronne jusqu'à la séance royale du 23 juin 1789* (Paris, 1850). A portion of the latter ("Survey of the Reign of Louis XVI") has been translated by R. R. Palmer in *The Two Tocquevilles* (Princeton, 1987), pp. 39–144.

over the revolutionary passions that his entire historical work was an attempt to explain.[6]

For Tocqueville the revolution not only weighed painfully on his family memories: he thought he was reliving their misfortune in 1830, and then again in 1848–51. The recurrence of revolution drove his thought. The revolution of July 1830, which returned Hervé to private life, eliminated all chance of a career in the judiciary for the young Alexis. Against his family's wishes, Tocqueville took the oath of allegiance to the new regime—"an unpleasant moment"—all the while looking for general historical causes and political remedies among the family disappointments: in 1831 he traveled to the United States to study the art of accommodating democracy while avoiding revolutions; in 1836 he sought, as a historian, to explain "The Social and Political State of France before and after 1789."[7] In 1848–51 he saw the frightened nation throw itself into the arms of a dictator; starting in 1850, he put on paper his political *Recollections* of the Second Republic; then, through a reversal of past and present, he began a search for the roots of the French people's inveterate taste for servitude. *The Old Regime* (1856) was the first part of that search, which was to be continued by a work on the Revolution and the Empire that remained unfinished. The history of France, according to Tocqueville, was always the tragic history of a nation frantic for equality. And it was always a political and engaged history through which, by explaining the failures of the author and his nation, Tocqueville sought to prevent the repetition of those failures. In Tocqueville's historical inquiry, as in his social investigations pursued in America, England, and Algeria, the search for a diagnosis was inseparable from the sought-for cure.

Tocqueville's first historical text was born from just such a political aim. On 11 June 1835, John Stuart Mill had asked Tocqueville for an article on France to educate English readers of the *London Review* about "questions of high politics." Mill thus hoped to spread "democratic doctrines" among the English aristocracy. By 12 September Tocqueville had changed the subject: "I fear," he wrote, "that, despite all my efforts, my country's present situation could not be well understood in England if I did not first make known what the situation was immediately before the French

6. See his "Correspondance anglaise: Conversations et correspondance avec Nassau Senior," in *OC,* v. 6, t. 2, p. 412.

7. "L'Etat sociale et politique de la France avant et depuis 1789," *OC,* v. 2, t. 1, pp. 31–68; translated by John Stuart Mill as "On the Social and Political Condition of France," *London and Westminster Review* 25 (April 1836): pp. 137–69.

Revolution, and if I paint that picture, whose colors are bound to be a little faded, I fear I shall not sufficiently interest the reader." [8] From 1836 on, therefore, history for Tocqueville was a necessary detour on the way to understanding the present. Erudition had little place in it. Without much regret, Tocqueville gave in to his "too-pronounced tendency toward general ideas," excusing himself by the nature of the subject, for "there is no other which makes one reflect more about the general rules found in human societies." [9]

At this time Tocqueville was not trying to understand the specificity of the history of France or the mystery of the Revolution. For him, the revolutionary phenomenon was nothing more than the sudden acceleration of a movement towards equality that was at work in the whole western world. The French had merely precipitated and radicalized the end of the aristocratic social state, which was inherent in the evolution of the nations of Europe. French history, however revolutionary it may have been, had been novel only in "form, in development, not in principle or in substance. All that the Revolution did would have been done, I have no doubt, without it; it was nothing but a violent and rapid process by means of which we adapted the political situation to the social situation, facts to ideas and laws to mores." [10] This was a way of repeating what Guizot had stated in his lectures of 1820–21 at the Sorbonne: that "the shake-ups we call revolutions are less the symptom of what is beginning than the declaration of what has already happened." [11] French ideas were in fact universal ideas. The French had opened the road to equality in philosophical theory and social practice. Furthermore, the history of France that Tocqueville painted with broad strokes in 1836 illustrated the fundamental idea of *Democracy in America:* "When we turn the pages of our history, we do not meet, so to speak, any major events of the past seven hundred years that have not furthered equality." Since the Middle Ages, the impoverishment of the nobility and the corresponding enrichment of the Third Estate constituted in France, as elsewhere, a first "revolution," which was hidden from the actors. The inegalitarian appearances were false. The nobility, stripped of its political power, cultivated imaginary distinctions by way of compensation. The victorious Third Estate lacked only a "tool" to strike down the nobility: the kings offered themselves before they were overthrown as well. In the 1836 article, politics played only a secondary

8. Tocqueville to Mill, 12 September 1835, *OC,* v. 6, t. 1, p. 296.
9. Tocqueville to Mill, 10 February 1836, *OC,* v. 6, t. 1, p. 307.
10. "L'Etat social" (see n. 7 above), pp. 65–66.
11. François Guizot, *Essais sur l'histoire de France* (1823), pp. 15–16.

role. Tocqueville thus affirmed the primacy of social determination, after Guizot and before Marx. Everything was accomplished before 1789. After the Revolution, democracy having been achieved, history ended. The French hardly changed between 1789 and the time Tocqueville was writing. Tocqueville thus shared with his contemporaries the illusion of an end of history and a belief in the uniform course of universal civilization. This is why, rather than writing an account of the France of 1830, as Mill had suggested, he devoted himself to the second volume of *Democracy in America,* a picture of the pure type of democracy, of which France was only an empirical variation.

The Revolution of 1848 at first seemed to justify Tocqueville in his vision of universal history. Events had confirmed the findings of *Democracy in America,* that "solemn warning which reminded men that society had changed shape, humanity had changed its circumstances, and new destinies were in store," as Tocqueville wrote in the preface to the new edition of 1848. America had shown the way to peaceful equality; France, depending on whether it chose freedom or democratic tyranny, would experience the fate of "the whole civilized universe." In less than two years, this hope for a peaceful republic had soured. In 1848–51 Tocqueville believed he was reliving the events of 1789–99. First he saw the Constituent Assembly repeated in April 1848, when he was triumphantly elected by universal suffrage; then the June insurrections mimicked the Terror—though a much mitigated Terror, which threatened freedom chiefly through the desire it inspired in the stunned bourgeoisie and nobility for law and order, and which hastened the bewildered nation towards dictatorship. In 1850–51 Tocqueville's correspondence abounds in metaphors to describe his dejection: "I understand neither how this can last nor how it can end, I find myself without a compass, without sails or rudder on a sea whose shores I cannot see, and, weary of useless activity, I lie down at the bottom of the boat and await the future," he wrote on 19 June 1850.[12] All Tocqueville's later work was the result of this desire to find a harbor. Through history, Tocqueville sought the means of leading democracy to port. The *Recollections* begun in June 1850 were an attempt to draw lessons from his experience as a deputy and minister in 1849; but in vain. The present yielded no explanation for the failure of the Second Republic, since the personality of Louis Napoleon Bonaparte seemed too insignificant to be elevated to the dignity of a historical cause. And that is why Tocqueville sought to understand how it was that such a mediocre pretender—here Tocqueville

---

12. Tocqueville to Mme de Circourt, *OC,* v. 18, p. 34.

was being unjust—managed to come to power: How was the tolerance of the French for despotism to be explained? Why did "very analogous principles and similar political theories" lead to a peaceful democracy in the United States and to recurrent revolutions in France? [13]

The initial project of *The Old Regime* was therefore a continuation of *Democracy in America:* Tocqueville was looking for landmarks in the troubled world into which equality had thrown humanity and was trying to make sense of the present by studying its "point of departure." The first mention of the project, in December 1850, clearly shows Tocqueville's intention to affirm the continuity of his ideas since 1835: "The thing that would be most original and most in accord with the nature and habits of my mind would be a collection of thoughts and insights about present times, a broad judgement on our modern societies and the prediction of their probable future. . . . I need to find a solid, firm base in facts for my ideas. I cannot find that except by writing history, by focusing on a period whose discussion will give me the opportunity to depict the men and affairs of our century and allow me to make a general picture out of all these individual portraits. Only the long drama of the French Revolution can provide me with this period." [14] The history that Tocqueville undertook was therefore a philosophical history which, by hunting down analogies, sought in the past the germs of the present. Here Tocqueville was following in the steps of Augustin Thierry and Guizot, who made the entire history of France the prefiguration of the Revolution. But Tocqueville reversed the direction of this project. The liberal historians of the Restoration had shown the rise of freedom through history, absolving even absolutism insofar as it was a necessary condition for leveling the great. The failure of the Second Republic led Tocqueville to reject this optimism. The past was condemned in the name of its Bonapartist posterity, so that the entire history of France seemed to be a highway to servitude. Tocqueville wrote the history of a failure, a penitential history without innocents, except for the poor, the eternal oppressed. Was his only intention to construct a "bridge of sighs," as Barbey d'Aurevilly claimed? Tocqueville was not a man for sterile regrets. He hated the spineless submission of an Adolphe Thiers to the laws of history. To wager on men's greatness, to desire their emancipation—that was the vocation of the statesman. For Tocqueville, writing history was an insurrection of the soul, which sought in past misfortune the reasons for hope and action. "I am not, thank God,

13. *L'Ancien régime et la Révolution, OC,* v. 2, t. 2, p. 337 (note relating to the 1856 book).
14. Tocqueville to Kergorlay, 15 December 1850, *OC,* v. 13, t. 2, p. 231.

among those who think that the disease we suffer from is incurable,"
wrote Tocqueville.[15] He would look everywhere for reasons to hope: in
the unbridled desire of the aristocrats of the old regime for a freedom
they confused with privilege; in 1789, the "time of immortal memory"; in
the Estates of Languedoc; and even in the French national temperament,
a nation "never so free that one must despair of enslaving it, nor so en-
slaved that it cannot still break the yoke." The portrait was certainly conventional; it was a concession to the "false taste" of the times, by the
author's own confession, but the encouragement was necessary.

From the outset, therefore, *The Old Regime* was intended to bring
aid to a people in distress. From the past, Tocqueville drew a lesson into
which he condensed the whole of his political thought: "There is nothing
less independent than a free citizen." Thus the divergence from the *Recollections,* which ironically retold the present. An unsuccessful politician,
Tocqueville there unveiled the cunning of history: "The fate of this world
is determined by causes and effects, but often contrary to the desires of
all those who produce them, like the flying banner spread by the opposite
action of wind and tether."[16] *The Old Regime* again used irony, showing
the Revolution surging from the cunning of history, from the blindness of
kings and nobles. But this irony was integrated into a tragic plot—a modern tragedy in which the hero was overwhelmed not by Providence or by
the laws of history but by his own consent to servitude and his unconscious desire for a master.

If the political intention and position of Tocqueville's philosophical
text was therefore clear from the outset in 1850, his method of inquiry
was not. The erratic genesis of *The Old Regime* recalls that of the second volume of *Democracy in America.* Tocqueville, to whom everything
seemed simple at first, altered the balance of his work through a series of
changes of direction, a drift that derived from his point of departure.
Once he had decided not to write a conventional narrative history like
that of Thiers, Tocqueville deprived himself of the support of traditional
chronology. Abandoning chronological order for the order of ideas,
simple narration for the puzzling-out of causes, he was forced to invent a
chronology and a technique of inquiry. In 1850, Tocqueville was thinking
"of the Empire, that unique act of the still-unfinished drama that we call
the French Revolution."[17] Two years later, oscillating between research

---

15. See Notes and Variants, note to p. 86, line 26.
16. "Souvenirs," *OC,* v. 1, p. 50.
17. Tocqueville to Beaumont, 26 December 1850, *OC,* v. 8, t. 2, pp. 343–44.

on the old regime, on the Revolution, and on the Directory, he was uncertain: "Basically I still don't know if I have a subject. But I am searching
for it with desperate energy."[18] In spite of himself, because he was looking
for causes, Tocqueville would go progressively back in time as he discovered unforeseen analogies between the past and the present. As Tocqueville looked in vain for the moment that demarcated the old and new, he
wrote, "Nothing has changed."

Let us examine the circumstances of this march into the past. In July
1852, from the Tocqueville château, Tocqueville studied what the lower
classes had gained from the Revolution, in order to explain their persistent hatred for absolutism, which created fertile ground for the success
of both Napoleons. As early as December 1852 he had to conclude that
"nothing or almost nothing had changed" since 1780. Nevertheless, he had
not decided to write a history of the *longue durée.* "You would laugh," he
wrote to his correspondent, "if you saw a man who had written so much
about democracy, surrounded by the works of feudal lawyers and bent
over old registers of feudal dues or other powdery documents. . . . The
boredom this study causes me is added to all the reasons I already had
to dislike the old regime, and will end up by making a real revolutionary
out of me."[19]

Another stroke of fate was required for the birth of *The Old Regime;*
not the least of the book's charms are the successive encounters between
intellectual project and expediency that marked Tocqueville's progress.
On 1 June 1853, having fallen ill, Tocqueville had to move to a village
near Tours, which boasted a mild climate, a learned doctor (Bretonneau),
and a large collection of archives of the former generality[†] which were
then being catalogued by a young archivist, Charles de Grandmaison.
There he would work until May 1854, discovering the richness of the
administrative archives of the eighteenth century, leery, at first, of seeming lost in them: "It would be a great mistake to be concerned only with
depicting the old regime," he wrote to Freslon on 9 June 1853.[20] A "short
chapter of thirty pages" would be enough. A plan of June 1853 still leads
the reader in five chapters from the general shape of the Revolution to the
18th Brumaire. On 10 August, after two months of study, an abrupt
change occurred: in the government administration of the eighteenth century Tocqueville had discovered the prefiguration of modern bureau-

18. Tocqueville to Beaumont, 1 July 1852, *OC,* v. 8, t. 3, p. 58.
19. Tocqueville to Freslon (unpublished letter copied by Beaumont), 7 September 1852.
20. Unpublished.

cracy. "Up to the present I was ignorant enough to believe that what we call administrative justice was a creation of Napoleon. It is *purely the old regime preserved. . . .* In reading the correspondence of the ministers of Louis XV and their subordinates, we seem to see a crowd of little embryos moving about, destined to become the professors of imperial administrative law, Cormenins, Macarels, Boulatigniers in germ. It is so true that if we knew the old regime better, we would find that the Revolution was far from having done all the good and all the evil it is said to have done, and that it stirred up society much more than it changed it."[21] So, on 1 December 1853, when Tocqueville began to write, his purpose had changed, or rather he had imagined a new chronology: the Revolution, whose birth, according to conventional wisdom, could be dated, although it was impossible to date its death, was rooted in the *longue durée* of the old regime, which constituted a "first revolution." The years of reform from 1770 to 1780 already displayed the shape of the Revolution.

Nevertheless, we should not exaggerate the change in Tocqueville's plan between 1850 and 1853. He had considerably expanded his original project but had not altered its spirit, putting off until a second volume the study of the Revolution and the Empire, which in his eyes still constituted the heart of his work. In 1836 he had made 1789 the end of history. In 1856 he presented the mystery of the Revolution, the break it created, and hence the story it called for. In February 1856, when he had just finished writing, his persistent hesitations about the title show his fidelity to his original project: he tended first towards "The Revolution"—that was too flat. On 17 February 1856, on the advice of his publisher Levy and his friend Ampère, Tocqueville decided for "The French Revolution," a title "vague and not very new but . . . true."[22] Beaumont thought "The Spirit of the French Revolution" or, better, "Democracy and Freedom in France" would have been more appropriate.[23] Between the first and the sixth of March, a sudden shift occurred, and Levy's catalogue appeared with an insert announcing the publication of *The Old Regime and the Revolution*. We do not know who suggested this title, but we do know that Tocqueville cherished the idea of going back to his original one, closer to the overall project for which the volume that appeared in June 1856 was merely a long introduction.[24] The title of the English edition

21. Tocqueville to Freslon (unpublished), 10 August 1853.
22. Tocqueville to Beaumont, 17 February 1856, *OC,* v. 8, t. 3, p. 370.
23. Beaumont to Tocqueville, *OC,* v. 8, t. 3, pp. 372–73.
24. Tocqueville to Beaumont, 17 and 22 March 1856, *OC,* v. 8, t. 3, pp. 379, 384.

was more explicit than the French.[25] *The Old Regime* was not a picture of the old society but an inquiry into the "causes" of the French Revolution and, more generally, into the "point of departure" for the disordered democracy of nineteenth-century France.

Tocqueville's method of inquiry also resulted from his desire to illuminate the present by means of the past. In *Democracy in America,* he had affirmed the primacy of mores over laws. Consistent with his previous work, *The Old Regime* was not a history of institutions. "I am very much convinced," he wrote to Corcelle, "that political societies are created not by their laws but by the feelings, beliefs, ideas, the habits of heart and mind of the men who compose those societies, by that which nature and education have made them, have prepared them to be."[26] Absolutism was less a doctrine of divine right, or a system of institutions, than layers of practices and a body of often unconscious representations. Hence, to his own regret but prompted by theoretical necessity, Tocqueville slowly became initiated into the scholarly methods so foreign to him. General history was interested only in the royal annals. The administrative history or the rural history of the old regime was not an unexplored field, but it remained the affair of compilers or scholars like Cheruel or Raudot. Tocqueville's political understanding of the past would lead him to change the arrangement of his sources: "I think," he wrote, "that we are in a better position today than we were twenty years ago to understand the vast object of the Revolution as a whole, to measure it, to judge it; we are close enough to see it clearly, to understand the ideas and feelings that filled the hearts and minds of those who threw the world into this terrible adventure, through a sort of internal reaction that still makes itself felt in our minds and hearts, and far enough from them so that it is not impossible to appreciate their acts and to discover the reality of their work."[27] Onto the old regime, so close in time, Tocqueville would be able to transpose his methods as a sociologist and parliamentarian, oral inquiry and the manipulation of government files, and to reason by analogy and comparison.

Around 1850 one still could have direct contact with the Revolution. In his youth, Tocqueville had already questioned the aged Royer-Collard; in Normandy in 1852, he sought facts from his overseer and the may-

---

25. *On the State of Society in France before the Revolution of 1789, and on the Causes Which Led to That Event.*

26. Tocqueville to Corcelle, 17 September 1853, *OC,* v. 15, t. 2, p. 80.

27. Tocqueville to Mme de Circourt, 18 September 1852, *OC,* v. 18, p. 85.

ors of the surrounding villages who had information or documents about the end of the eighteenth century. There were even a few survivors— quite old, of course—of the Revolution: these included a Monsieur Cordhomme, who had been a member of the city council of Valognes in 1793, and an old Benedictine monk, who could testify about the mores of the past. Better still, Tocqueville could witness the last spasms of the old regime, in Germany. In 1831 he had visited the United States to observe the possible future of France; at Bonn, from 19 June to 21 August 1854, he studied its archaeology. The voyage in space was a voyage in time: "For a man who has seen American society," Tocqueville wrote to Circourt, "which, so to speak, is leaving modern Europe to head for the future, there is nothing more novel or more interesting than to see the societies that are outside modern Europe on the side of the past."[28] At Bonn, ju- rists and bureaucrats helped Tocqueville, as the Americans had done, to understand German political culture, to better understand similarities and differences from the French old regime. "For it is one of the particu- lar weaknesses of our mind to be unable to judge objects, to see them clearly and in full light, if another object is not placed alongside," wrote Tocqueville to Freslon on 30 July 1854.

In addition to oral questioning, Tocqueville read pamphlets and bu- reaucratic documents, as he had done in the United States. Evidence of this enormous labor survives in folders full of pages covered with im- patient handwriting about roads, police, subsistence, feudal dues. Here Tocqueville sought to understand, through the bureaucracy's incessant discussions, "the old regime in full life, its ideas, its passions, its preju- dices, its practices."

The reader will be conscious of all this oral inquiry and archival inves- tigation only through the limited extracts from his notes that Tocqueville placed at the end of his book, and through the "Notes and Variants" in- cluded in this volume. In 1856 as in 1840, he wanted to be brief and clear in order to keep the educated public interested.[29] There is no in-depth description of a generality: "All this is jargon," noted Tocqueville in the margin of an attempt at description.[30] The intended public's taste was not

28. Tocqueville to Circourt, 30 June 1854, *OC,* v. 18, p. 181.
29. See Tocqueville to Lewis, 13 August 1856: "It was necessary to seize my country's atten- tion, something very difficult in this time of moral and intellectual decline. For that it was nec- essary to be brief and to write a book which could be read by everybody. For this reason I had to lighten my load of all the weight of detail." *OC,* v. 6, t. 3 (forthcoming).
30. See Notes and Variants, note to p. 120, line 26.

the only reason. The examples in *The Old Regime* are simple illustrations, most often lacking any indication of source or even date. They were written and added at a late stage, to ease comprehension for uninformed readers. It is the way arguments are arranged that furnishes the proof, not the mere accumulation of facts and references. Tocqueville is a "classic," Boutmy would say fifty years later: he shakes off the facts to get rid of them before writing, "like a traveler shaking off the dust from the road before appearing in decent company." "The 'petty facts' have value merely as points of reference during research, and then as *specimens,* as striking lessons from things that help one to make a lively and substantial picture. This last point may have disturbed the austere thinker's conscience; Tocqueville may have feared that increased liveliness of description would be taken for increased power of evidence, and that the reader would think, because he found more color and relief in the picture, that there was more strength and solidity in the proof. According to Tocqueville's rules of judgment, particular facts were comparable to testimony by children or servants, nearly always the most interesting, closest to the reality to be understood, but too often partial, injudicious, and mixed with hearsay. The court accepts them as information but denies them the legal value of testimony and takes them into account only if they are confirmed by their agreement with the general circumstances of the case."[31] This remark, true of *Democracy in America,* is still true, although to a lesser degree, of *The Old Regime,* whose scholarly basis was long ignored. We can regret, along with Taine, Boutmy, and many others, Tocqueville's extreme modesty with regard to displaying his erudition, and his tendency to deploy all facts in accord with deductive rigor. At the same time, his classical or "literary" concern to subordinate everything to a single design gives *The Old Regime* both its depth and its clarity of exposition.

The Structure of the Work: Book One

Unlike *Democracy in America,* in which the sequence of chapters often appears arbitrary, especially in the second volume, *The Old Regime* is clearly organized. It treats three major topics sequentially. First, it examines the nature, or character, of the French Revolution, in form and substance, attempting to define what makes this event so memorable in French and European history. Second, it probes the remote origins of the Revolution, at the crossroads of absolutism and aristocratic society.

---

31. E. Boutmy, *Eléments d'une psychologie du peuple américain* (Paris, 1911), pp. 11–13.

Third, it discusses the reasons for the Revolution's sudden outbreak at the end of the eighteenth century.

Tocqueville begins by comparing what the French wanted to do in 1789 with what they actually did. They wanted passionately to break with their past, but they ended up reinvesting the mores and ideas of the old regime in the new. To explain their Revolution demands a double effort of the historian, who must simultaneously grasp how, contrary to common sense, the idea of a blank slate, a tabula rasa, could take shape within a nation; and how it was nevertheless covered by the weight of habit. This double issue led Tocqueville to distinguish two phases within the course of the Revolution.

Tocqueville focused first on the novelty of the French Revolution, at once extraordinary, incomprehensible, repulsive, and fascinating in the eyes of its contemporaries. Though not immediately visible, this novel character quickly became obvious to the most perceptive observers, from Burke to Maistre, who were dumbfounded by so unprecedented a spectacle. Its originality was in striking contrast with the results expected from it. But behind the event that broke with the past was a long-term continuity. This paradox was presented in the first two chapters of part one and enlarged upon in the last three. It was clearly of prime importance to Tocqueville to explain it.

The novelty of the French Revolution lay in its desire to be "universal," like certain religious revolutions, even though it was social and political in nature. For many, the Revolution did become a new kind of religion, born of social equality, a religion that could engender such powerful forces that it was imitated even by its enemies. Tocqueville was reminded of Christianity, whose universal appeal had triumphed over the local religious cults of the Greek polis. He compared democratic abstraction with Christian abstraction without deducing the former from the latter but, rather, showing democracy in the fullness of its paradoxal charm. By making the regeneration of humanity their goal, the French of the late eighteenth century sought to realize in this world an ambition that Christians seek to achieve only in the next. The Revolution inspired hopes and aroused passions comparable to those of religion, while providing only a political arena for them, thus inventing that "new kind of religion" which is revolutionary politics. Along with Michelet—whose *History of the Revolution* he must surely have read, though he never referred to it—Tocqueville understood that a new type of collective psychological investment appeared in 1789. Not that revolutionary messianism lacked precedents in earlier movements up through the High Middle Ages. But, on the one hand, those movements never triumphed, and, on the other, they remained rooted in sacred texts, thus in religion. Nor did any of them ever receive as warm a welcome as did French ideas at the end of the eighteenth century. The Revolution of 1789 immediately raises the question of the general intellectual receptiveness to its universalist credo.

Like Michelet, Tocqueville perceived the extraordinary originality of this faith, and its power over the imagination. Unlike the republican Michelet, however, Tocqueville also understood its strangeness. It was a faith comparable to a religious feeling and yet of a political nature; a faith in humanity, yet incarnated in a single nation; an abstract faith in the future, yet linked to a history. This is why the Revolution at all costs had to exorcise the curse of the past and keep a constant watch over the boundary separating this past from the revolutionaries' work. The Revolution had to keep affirming its right to inaugurate the great re-creation of society. A prisoner of history, revolution is a form of activity haunted by the project of negating history. "In 1789," Tocqueville wrote in his preface to *The Old Regime,* "the French made the greatest effort ever undertaken by any people to disassociate themselves from their past, and to put an abyss between what they had been and what they wished to become." Thus Tocqueville explained why the French wanted to imagine their past only as the inverse of their new condition, and why they spared nothing "to disguise themselves."[32] What they called the "old regime," a phrase they invented in order to separate themselves totally from their entire past, represented the other side of the revolutionary rupture in the chain of time.

It is this "other side," the old regime, that had to be investigated, for it embodied, in condensed form, all the strangeness of the revolutionary belief system. Through this search, Tocqueville explored once again one of the leading ideas of his American journey a quarter of a century earlier: the idea that American democracy lacked a revolutionary character because it had no "old regime" to fight against or overcome, whereas French democracy had to defeat an aristocratic society before it could prevail. The Americans did not have to become democrats because they already were democrats when they occupied the land that would become their republic: their voyage across the Atlantic was their way of breaking with their past. So what they called their revolution, at the end of the eighteenth century, was merely a repetition of their original choice; break-

32. Preface, p. 83.

ing the bond with the English monarchy was inherent in the Americans' experience of freedom and in their egalitarian society. The contractual founding of the United States was truly the birth of a new nation, resulting from the will of its freely associated citizens. To achieve this end, the Americans were not compelled to condemn their past, exorcise their history, or accept the revolutionary fiction of the tabula rasa. They only had to consult their tradition and even their memories.

The French at that time faced the opposite situation. To reestablish their community on the basis of natural rights, they had to condemn their tradition and forget their memories. It was this moral and political position that Tocqueville saw as the basis of the French situation, as contrasted to the American; and it was this position that defined, in his eyes, its revolutionary character. The idea of a radical break with the past took hold in the French mind and provided the novel spectacle of a people collectively detesting its own history. Tocqueville thus revived the theme of the "abstraction" of the French Revolution, so dear to Romantic criticism of the Enlightenment. Such abstraction did not stem solely from the use of philosophical principles to resolve a political crisis. It was so thorough and complete because it hid a tremendous effort of negation. A desperate effort, if it is true that nations cannot escape from their past any more than individuals can; but the inevitability of their failure added one more mystery to the creation of this astonishing collective desire. Tocqueville set himself the task of understanding how, at the end of the eighteenth century, France's rejection of its national history was brought about by this very history—in other words, how hatred of the "old regime" was a product of the old regime.

Tocqueville was thus led to distinguish the French form of democracy from the American, and he devotes the first part of his book to explaining this difference. But if the Anglo-American social state is relatively easy to decipher, both because it is recent and because it is simple (in the sense of being derived from only one principle), that of eighteenth-century France is infinitely less so. This is the case not only because French society is rooted in a very ancient past, elements of which were inherited by and became part of the absolute monarchy, but because the French themselves, with the Revolution, did everything possible "to disguise themselves." They wanted to start from the beginning; they erased their tracks for fear of retracing their steps, they were at pains to obliterate everything that could relate them to their ancestors or to earlier generations. So much so that those who did not want to accept the new identity had no alternative but this "old regime," defined by the date of its death, and found themselves deprived of a future. Such was the strength of the revolutionary idea, inseparable from its fragility.

Far from opposing strength to fragility, Tocqueville sought to understand these two aspects of the Revolution as complementary. He described its strength as its universal appeal, comparable to that of Christianity. Its fragility, however, is that it differs from religion, for the Revolution's only judge is history, which it has rejected from the outset. If the Revolution "works" in the mind like a religious belief, it claims to work only on and in this world, where the historian awaits it. Having described the magnitude of revolutionary feeling, Tocqueville devotes the last two chapters of his introduction to the balance-sheet of revolutionary action.

The best way to understand what the French Revolution destroyed was to look outside France, towards a Europe that had shared its major historical characteristics since the fall of the Roman Empire. At the end of the Middle Ages, European feudal institutions resembled each other so closely that Tocqueville could easily speak of an "old constitution of Europe." In 1854, faithful to his comparative method, he traveled to Germany in search of confirmation; he already knew some English history from his youth. "From the borders of Poland to the Irish Sea," he wrote, "the manor, the lord's court, the fief, the services to be performed, the feudal dues, the corporations, everything was similar."[33] By the eighteenth century these institutions were more or less moribund, depending on the location—a little more in England, a little less in Poland—but everywhere, even in eastern Europe, in the Slavic and Germanic lands, they were in decline.

This decline must be understood both objectively and subjectively. It affected all the powers of the Middle Ages as if they had been afflicted with lethargy: they had lost their psychological basis, lost what had made them live in people's hearts. Even the dominant personalities of the system, the lords and nobles, had lost the will to make the institutions work and allowed their political liberties to fade. What, then, of the dominated, those who had no privileges to defend? Nothing prevented them from approving the actions of the prince-sovereigns, who gradually emancipated them from the neighboring castle in the name of "civilization." Like Guizot, Tocqueville used this vague, scholarly word to express many different things at once—material progress, improved communications, the softening of mores, the emancipation of individuals, and that mysterious

---

33. Part one, chapter four.

divinity known as "the spirit of the times." In a mind pervaded as Tocqueville's was by the certainty that European history had a providential meaning, the word "civilization" came closest to expressing the body of characteristics by which this "meaning" was manifested. Not the least of these characteristics was the way succeeding generations understood the progress of civilization.

For Tocqueville, historical epochs come to a close less because they themselves fall apart than because they are discredited in people's minds. *
Witness what happened, in modern Europe, to any "feudal" or "gothic" survivals; the premature devaluation implied by these adjectives indicates how much former times had been devalued by public opinion even before the disappearance of the institutions with which they were associated. In the eighteenth century, a passion for new things was moving minds and *
social groups everywhere, beginning with the upper classes. The general contempt for anything related to the Middle Ages became even more pronounced as what remained of the period lost vitality. Tocqueville announced one of the central ideas of his book quite casually, almost as an aside: that the hatred aroused by the remnants of feudalism was inversely proportional to the importance of those remnants.

The English case, on the other hand, remained different as always. Tocqueville's lifelong interest in the English exception is apparent in his last book, in which English history is frequently cited, by way of contrast, to explain the French old regime. In the 1830s, when he wrote *Democracy in America,* England provided him with an aristocratic reference point.[34] Twenty years later, at the end of the chapter under discussion, Tocqueville spoke of England as a country that manifested the "old constitution of Europe" only on the surface, for in reality it was completely modern, governed by new principles. Modernity, however, had slipped inside feudal forms. The two views are not necessarily contradictory, since the second leaves open the possibility of a renewed aristocracy. Nevertheless, if many ancient traditions had survived with a new spirit, it was because they were not so outworn in everyday life, so dead in people's minds, or even so hated. Even the English revolution in the seventeenth century did not make them disappear. In describing a totally modern England grafted onto the dead tree of feudalism, Tocqueville undoubtedly wanted to refute Burke, whose *Reflections* he always kept in mind. But he stopped short of trying to explain the survival of the English "constitution," which

34. Seymour Drescher, *Tocqueville and England* (Cambridge: Harvard University Press, 1964), chapter three.

his predecessor had contrasted to the revolutionary tabula rasa of the French. Tocqueville was not finished with Burke, who continued to accompany him throughout *The Old Regime.*

Aside from England, Europe in the eighteenth century offered the same spectacle as France, but in varying degree: medieval institutions were dying everywhere, universally discredited and sometimes actually hated—a feeling that extended to the lower classes. Yet it was these dying institutions, already dead in the minds of many contemporaries, that the French Revolution sought to liquidate, to root out. Not that it was an easy job: these institutions were so entwined with everything in society and government that their eradication certainly deserves to be called a revolution. A new social order evolved, uniform and egalitarian. But in the final analysis this radical elimination merely abolished a dying world, condemned to disappear everywhere. The Revolution was just the French form of a larger movement, by which modern equality founded its empire on the ruins of feudal society. Thus it was the opposite of a chance event or an unforeseeable creation: it was the crowning moment of two centuries of work (ten generations, says Tocqueville, which brings us to the juncture of the sixteenth and seventeenth centuries). If the Revolution had not taken place, the old regime would have fallen anyway, little by little, just as it did elsewhere, whereas in France it was destroyed at one blow and in its entirety.

This analysis was sufficient to refute Burke's diagnostic. Burke was astonished that France broke with "the old common law of Europe" when this old law had already fallen apart everywhere, even, unbeknownst to him, in his own country. Tocqueville, however, in his effort to understand the French Revolution as part of this spectacular consecration of a historical moment, laid himself open, as Guizot had done before him, to misunderstanding the extraordinary complexity of the event and the originality of the form of political action that it inaugurated. But Tocqueville always detested the simplifications of historical "fatalism."[35] He knew that there were several revolutions in the Revolution, so that he could not describe only a single one that emerged, fully formed, out of the old regime. Besides, Tocqueville had just written that the event, while predictable, was unplanned; and that it brought about new hopes and new behavior because it imported into modern politics ideas and emotions borrowed from religion. Although the French Revolution was not new because of *what* it did, it nonetheless invented an extraordinary way of

---

35. Cf. *Democracy in America*, v. 2, part one, chapter twenty.

doing it. Burke had seized upon the wrong object for his astonishment and indignation.

The issue Tocqueville grappled with in his last work was not the why but the how. The old regime was condemned to disappear sooner or later in any case, since the Revolution merely finished what was already begun. Its destiny was written in that great, mysterious law of the coming of democracy, of which only the consequences, not the causes, were within the grasp of human intelligence, according to Tocqueville. That which was original and even unique to France was the proper material for historical investigation: this radical destruction, accompanied by condemnation without appeal and by an intransigent passion for rupture, could only have had its causes in what preceded it. The collective fiction, the idea of a discontinuity in the chain of time, could only have arisen from prior decay. But precisely because it detested the old regime the Revolution hid it. Wanting to abolish the old regime, the Revolution concealed its reality, having inherited it in spite of itself.

The formidable French event, enthralling people's imaginations even fifty years after its occurrence, had first to be approached from this double enigma, which revealed what was totally new about the Revolution. How and why did the idea of beginning human society afresh take root in one of the oldest nations of Europe? What, in spite of its implausibility, caused this idea to be accepted as true, to be fervently celebrated or passionately hated? Where did the French come up with the religious idea of breaking with the chain of time, and why did they think of themselves as the universal nation? This bundle of questions evokes the same conundrum: a history that flourishes in the negation of itself.

This very negation, so strongly felt and demanded by the actors of the period, obscured the other side of the event, by which the Revolution completed the work of the preceding centuries—Guizot's Revolution, after Michelet's Revolution. For if the Revolution is examined in terms not of its intentions but of its real consequences, it is not what it claimed to be; it "innovated much less than is generally supposed."[36] Although it surprised its contemporaries, it merely concluded an evolution begun well before, which finally led to the annihilation of the old social structure—an evolution visible everywhere in Europe but which only France completed by the extraordinary spectacle of an old nation sealing a new social contract. The entire question of the Revolution thus involves the particular character of the former society's history and the manner of its

36. *Old Regime*, book one, chapter five.

disappearance in France; the secret of the Revolution may be found in the connections between these two phenomena. We here rediscover Tocqueville's oldest conviction, the one that had taken him to America: although the origin of democracy's forward march is incomprehensible to human intelligence, its variations and its consequences can still be studied, understood, and even mastered. The author of *Democracy in America* may have lost hope on this last point, in what concerned his own country; but he was all the more determined to understand why.

The Structure of the Work: Book Two

The second and main part of *The Old Regime* concentrates on the earlier French society in order to explore the difference between the events in France and the general evolution of Europe. The third part bears on public opinion's radical condemnation of the old society at the end of the eighteenth century, and what can be learned from it. In the first editions of the work, there was no break between books two and three, but Tocqueville introduced the division as early as the third edition (1857), unfortunately without explaining why. It is unlikely that he was merely attempting to distribute the chapters more evenly into three parts. The division clearly corresponds to an internal structure of ideas, periods, and subjects: book two seeks the origins of French particularity in Europe, while book three focuses on the revolutionary passions at work in the old regime, from the middle of the eighteenth century on. The title of the first chapter of book three, "How Around the Middle of the Eighteenth Century Intellectuals Became the Country's Leading Politicians, and the Effects Which Resulted from This," shows well enough by its theme and its time period that the author was beginning a new development of his analysis: if the "men of letters" had become his country's political mentors, then revolution was not far away.

By contrast, book two tackles questions more distant and also more general. Half (chapters two through seven) is devoted to the development of administrative centralization, and half (chapters eight though eleven) to the effects of this phenomenon on the state of society, as if the secrets of what the men of the Revolution baptized "the old regime" could be found here. This twofold analysis is framed, at beginning and end, by two chapters that seem to be outside the central theme: chapter one concerns the particularly odious character of feudal rights in France, and chapter twelve emphasizes the unhappiness and even the deterioration of the peasant's condition during the eighteenth century. Why frame book two, the core of the proof, with these two studies of the rural world?

Examination of the first chapter shows that Tocqueville was interested less in the rural world per se than in the problem of feudal rights, taken as a general introduction to the crisis of the old regime in France. He starts with a comparison with Germany and England to discover what is particularly French in this respect—namely that feudal dues were most hated where they had least survived. Almost everywhere in Germany in the eighteenth century, elements of the old serfdom were retained, and manorial jurisdiction had maintained its rights: witness the law code prepared by the Frederick the Great and promulgated by his successor. Nothing like this was accomplished in France, where serfdom, with rare exceptions, had ceased to exist between the thirteenth and fifteenth centuries. Furthermore, the French peasant had early on become a landowner—a very small landowner, it is true, but master of his plot and thus consumed by the passion to enlarge it and jealous of any other authority over his little domain. This situation was found neither in Germany nor in England, where the large aristocratic or bourgeois estate was typical, local political power also remained in the hands of the chief landowners. In France, on the contrary, these powers had increasingly been taken from the lords by the agents of the royal government, and little was left of them by the eighteenth century.

The intention of this analysis was to show the peculiar fate of "feudal institutions" in French history. "Feudal institutions" was a term used by Tocqueville for a system of government based on landownership.[37] One factor that contributed to this peculiar fate was the French peasant's long experience as a landowner and his passion for expansion and independence. Another was that the peasant's emancipation from the lord's sway had been facilitated by the growth of a central administrative authority interested in reducing the lord's jurisdictional prerogatives. Hence feudalism remained in the French old regime "the greatest of all our civil institutions while ceasing to be a political institution."[38] The same historical movement consolidated feudalism in civil life and destroyed it as a political power. The jurists of the monarchy confirmed and codified the par-

37. This very vague definition may fit feudalism proper, inseparable from the lord's domain and a pyramid of dependencies, or the local powers of the English gentry. Here Tocqueville has the former in mind, which he studied through the German example. But in his eyes the English example represented a postfeudal adaptation of aristocratic domination.

38. Part two, chapter one.

ticular rights derived from feudal society; its agents fought and destroyed the political relationship implied by those rights. The French peasant saw only oppression, without deriving any useful benefit from it. Buttressed by his land, the cradle of his freedom, he saw in "feudal dues" only the residual signs of a former subjection: this explained his anger and hatred, which were not found elsewhere, where feudalism remained largely intact. In France, the lord's power had not only been uprooted by the king's agents but had been delegitimized in the peasant's heart, at the very moment when the peasant wanted to be liberated from it as the owner of his land.

Tocqueville here embarks on the most profound part of his definition of the old regime. In his mind, the phrase "old regime" related not to a social state but to the crisis of a social state, not to the old feudal or aristocratic society but to a late period of this society when it was already being torn apart by contradictory principles. The principal characteristic of the French old regime was the disassociation of the civil order from the political order. Civil inequality (left over from feudalism or reinvented by the aristocracy) was combined with political equality (since all the king's subjects were equally subject to him). In some sense this was an inversion of the later dilemma of the liberals, who between 1815 and 1848 strove to reconcile civil equality and political inequality. Tocqueville never believed in the lasting character of this attempt.[39] He looked with equal pessimism at the old regime and at the limited-suffrage regimes of the nineteenth century—the former as a corruption of the aristocratic principle, the latter as a denial of the democratic principle. At the end of his life he applied his simultaneously deductive and comparative method, freely borrowed from Montesquieu, more than ever: it was in France that revolution broke out because it had already begun there, concealed behind the name of the old regime.

Thus the first chapter in book two treats a subject much broader than its title implies. In looking for reasons why feudal dues were particularly hated by the French peasant, Tocqueville presents the essence of his argument: that the old regime was the first revolution, before *the* Revolution. He is saying not merely that the feudal principle was in decay, or dying, in old-regime France, since this was true of other countries in

39. Tocqueville to Kergorlay, 29 June 1831: "I can't help but think that Louis XVIII's charter was necessarily a short-lived work; he had created aristocratic institutions in political law, and left in civil law a democratic principle so active that it must soon destroy the bases of the structure which he was creating." *OC,* v. 13, t. 1, p. 233.

Europe, but that feudalism in France was the object of hostile passions extending to everything "aristocratic." What was targeted was not the already moribund social order, of which the feudal principle was the cornerstone, but the acceptance it had enjoyed for so long. In France, obedience broke down with the legitimacy of the aristocratic order.

Having introduced these ideas, Tocqueville begins his analysis of administrative centralization, which he sees as the old regime's distinctive character; this allows him to date the old regime to roughly the last two centuries of the monarchy. The Revolution had assigned the old regime a date of death but no birthday, combining a vast period of time—the eras of feudalism and of absolute monarchy—under a single condemnation. Tocqueville, however, applied the name "old regime" only to the period of absolutism, when administrative centralization developed—a new way of saying that the revolutionary formula had historical reality only for a relatively short period, from Louis XIII to Louis XVI.

In this respect, Tocqueville changed the view of the national past that he had presented to the English public in his 1836 essay. There, to be sure, he had emphasized the centralization of power in the king's hands, its gradual extension to all areas of government, the abolition of the local political prerogatives of the aristocracy, as characteristic of France before 1789. But he had portrayed these as so many consequences of the progress of "democracy," and had analyzed them (in the second half of the essay) only as a follow-up to his study of democratic progress. When Tocqueville wrote that first study of the old regime, he had just realized the link between democracy and centralization: it was one of the ideas he had brought back from his second trip to England in 1835, an idea he derived from observing the implementation of the 1834 Poor Law Amendment.[40] Tocqueville applied it to the French historical context by associating aristocracy with local power, democracy with centralization. The decline of the aristocracy and the rise of democracy, however, remained the central points, as if the transformations of civil society determined political and institutional change.

Twenty years later, Tocqueville abandoned this approach, based as it was on the idea of the social state as the source that nourishes historical change. No doubt he had inherited that idea from Guizot, who taught

40. He noted in his travel diaries: "Centralization, a democratic instinct, the instinct of a society which has pulled itself out of the medieval system of individualism." *OC*, v. 5, t. 2, *Voyages en Angleterre, Irlande, Suisse et Algérie*, p. 49. See Drescher, *Tocqueville and England*, chapter five.

him so much of what he knew about prerevolutionary France. The outline of the 1856 book is very different, for here the study of administrative centralization precedes that of social transformation, as if Tocqueville had inverted the causal link between the two orders of phenomena. This crucial shift from the 1836 essay to the 1856 book was clearly a lesson drawn from experience.[41] When writing *The Old Regime,* Tocqueville had just lived through the revolution of February 1848 and the coup d'état of 2 December 1851. In this rapid alternation of several very different regimes, the effects of a social state which itself had not changed, or had changed only slowly, could not be seen. Tocqueville was faced by the same problem as Guizot or Marx: how to explain a succession of political revolutions within the same social state. But he did not, as they did, make class struggle the dominating factor of historical causality. Tocqueville had more freedom to rediscover in French events the tyranny of a revolutionary tradition, itself rooted in the omnipotence of a centralized government. The Republic of February 1848 was not the victory of one class over another but an imitation of the French Revolution. The coup d'état of December was made possible by the combination of a prestigious name and a bureaucratic state that was independent of society.[42] Through the history of this bureaucratic state, Tocqueville began his inventory of the old regime.

According to Tocqueville, it was an error to believe that the bureaucratic state was a product of the Revolution. On the contrary, it was characteristic of the two centuries that preceded and prepared it: the bureaucratic state was more recent than the monarchy but older than the Revolution; it gradually rose above aristocratic society, simultaneously dominating and transforming it. Tocqueville assigned no precise date to this history, for it was a gradual process, made up of new practices as well as improvised institutions that became permanent over the course of time. But the prominence Tocqueville assigns to fiscal administration and to the intendants makes it plain that Tocqueville's old regime had Louis XIV as its center and symbol. The eighteenth century merely displayed the crisis of the type of monarchical government instituted by the Sun King, an unstable mix of tradition and modernity, which the Revolution exploded

41. This idea is developed in François Furet, *Penser la Révolution française* (Paris, 1978), pp. 190 ff.

42. There are several very Tocquevillian pages on the coup d'état of December 2nd in Marx, in "The Eighteenth Brumaire of Louis Napoleon." See F. Furet, *Marx et la Révolution française* (Paris, 1986), p. 97.

like a bomb without realizing that it had inherited many of its ingredients.

By placing himself within a short chronology, Tocqueville also shows that he is not going to discuss the genesis of the old regime. What interests him is not its source but its course; he is concerned not with understanding what caused it but with analyzing what made the old regime simultaneously so powerful and so fragile, and what led it to the revolutionary blank slate. From the outset—from book two, chapter two, where his study really begins—Tocqueville presents the vast central bureaucracy as fully formed, composed of men controlled by the king, with agents everywhere in charge of overseeing everything—taxes, public order, roads, aid for the poor, encouraging agriculture, and so forth. Tocqueville makes no mention of the religious wars of the sixteenth century, which led, by reaction, to the Bourbons' desire for unification in the seventeenth century. Nor does he mention the European wars which demanded the centralization of strength and resources. No, the subject of his book lies elsewhere, in the nature of this form of governance and in its effects.

Tocqueville worked on few sources other than eighteenth-century ones. Occasionally he followed a source farther back in time, but only to contrast an institution's origin with what it later became. The periods prior to the bureaucratic monarchy he knew through the great historians of the Restoration, above all Guizot. Beyond this, he imagined them through the ideal type of aristocracy that governed his intellectual life. But Tocqueville's documentary study proper deals only with the later period, when the agents of the king of France had penetrated the very pores of the old society. Tocqueville privileged the study of administrative documents, which showed this innovation best. He sifted through the F series (central government) of the national archives, and he was interested primarily in documents left by the intendants, the principal actors in what he wanted to understand. He reflected at length on the commentaries Turgot left on his experience in the Limousin. He worked for months on the documents of the intendancy of Tours. And we can clearly see what he was looking for and found: traces and proofs of the many-tentacled grasp of a bureaucracy directed from Versailles by the bureau of finance, ruling over the vast territory for which it was responsible. The intendant was its pivot, taking orders from the minister, overseeing their implementation through his little army of subordinates, and making reports on resistance and success. It was not the *lettre de cachet*,[†] not arbitrary authority, that Tocqueville saw as typifying the French old regime. On the contrary, it was this daily, organized, rational desire to be involved in everything and to have everything under control. Commenting on a *lettre de cachet* of 1785 found among the intendant's papers, Tocqueville characteristically wrote in the margin: "This is indeed raw power, plain to see. When we take a closer look, however, we see that it was not the exercise of this rarely used power, which was hampered or made odious by publicity, that most prepared the nation's spirit for what we see, but the hidden, petty, bureaucratic despotism that made itself felt in all things, everywhere and every day. It was not tyranny but paternalism that made us what we are. Liberty can take root and grow in the former but cannot be born or develop in the latter. The former can create liberal nations, the latter can only make servile and revolutionary peoples."[43]

This, then, is the major thread of the analysis: the royal government's extension of paternalistic authority over the French; the exercise of a protectorate over the towns through the sale of municipal offices that had previously been elective; the tutelage of villages and even the smallest parish, whose syndics were reduced to mere tools of the subdelegate, and hence of the intendant, and hence of the state. Even justice, supposedly in the hands of independent magistrates since they owned their positions, often fell under the government's thumb through the game of evocations and exceptional proceedings; the judicial irresponsibility of the state's agents was a tendency of the old regime before characterizing article 75 of the Constitution of the Year VIII. In brief, a "spirit" of the old regime was at work everywhere in the very century in which it supposedly disappeared. Those who wanted to see its traits in unvarnished form had only to look at Canada in the same period; that distant colony, to which the French old regime was exported but that lacked a feudal predecessor, imported the old regime's elements without mixing them with earlier ones. As a result, Canada, organized under Colbert, offered a preview of Algeria under Louis-Philippe! By Contrast, the immigrants who populated the Thirteen Colonies imported from the other side of the ocean the libertarian spirit of English institutions, extending and deepening its influence in creating the American Republic. In the long note that he devoted to Canada as a window on French centralization, Tocqueville rediscovered the inspiration for his first book.[44]

In France, of course, the old regime was able to hold sway only by superimposing itself on an earlier social and political situation. Although

---

43. From the notes entitled "Prisons—1 October 1853" in the Tocqueville manuscripts.
44. Note 20, "How It Is in Canada That One Can Best Judge the Administrative Centralization of the Old Regime."

the bureaucrats of the eighteenth century were very similar to those of the nineteenth, before the Revolution they were dealing with a different society, whose tradition was unfavorable to them since it favored the local powers of the aristocracy. The bureaucrats of the old regime managed to defeat the aristocracy so completely only by allowing it to survive on a nonpolitical level, a stratification deposited by the centuries and gradually covered over by history. The most paradoxical trait of the Tocquevillian old regime is that it was already part of a revolutionary dynamic: everything that the Enlightenment brought in terms of progress, wealth, and new innovations—everything that Tocqueville, following Guizot and many others, calls the movement of "civilization"—was fuel for the central government's machinery. People's feelings, the intellectual excitement, the raising of hopes, the multiplication of needs acted as spurs to the enterprises of the centralized state. Government in accord with reason was one of the great images of the nation's forward march. And the mission of government in accord with reason was to take care of everything. Centralization did not perish in the Revolution, for it was itself the beginning of the Revolution.

Tocqueville saw clearly, however, that centralization remained imperfect under the old monarchy, not only because it allowed a society organized according to older principles to persist beneath it, but because the old monarchy itself was blinded by visions of power and failed to understand how laws were limited by mores. Jurist that he was, Tocqueville knew well the extraordinary legislative and regulatory activity of the legislators of the old regime. But he also knew that the same texts were often reiterated by the Versailles officials because they hadn't been obeyed. Further, he knew local history too well, through the intendant and his subdelegates, to ignore the distance that separated law from fact in a period still marked by a great diversity of men and things. The image of an old regime characterized by administrative centralization must be tempered by a fairly substantial limitation: the uncertain application of laws and regulations. Quoting a letter from an intendant who was pleading with the minister for a tax exemption, Tocqueville comments: "this is the old regime in a nutshell: a rigid rule, lax implementation." And he adds, as if to soften the impact of the preceding chapters: "Anyone who judged the government of those times by the list of its laws would make the most foolish errors."[45]

The government's "prodigious activity" was struggling against the na-

---

45. Part two, chapter six.

ture of things. Attempting to regulate the lives of the French in detail, aspiring to legislate on topics too diverse, the government exposed the law to discredit by repetitions and exemptions at the very moment when it was making law the exclusive instrument of public authority: that was the price paid for the confusion between government and administration. And what a price! On the one hand, the law was weakened by the desire for uniformity with which it was invested, for it had to be evaded by the very people whose job it was to see that it was applied everywhere. On the other hand, it prepared people for submission or subversion, if not for both: a person hemmed in by the law in his daily life, obeying only through fear of the policeman, was all the more disposed to overthrow the government if he believed he could take possession of the source of law. Let the law control him, or let him control the law—that was all there was to it. Inseparable from a proliferation of texts intended to guide its agents' actions, administrative centralization favored belief in the state's omnipotence without enforcing the obedience the state was owed.

In other words, centralization prepared citizens for revolution, which depends precisely on this dual mental disposition. Here Tocqueville discovered what, at the deepest level, linked the old regime to the conditions of its disappearance. Absolute monarchy had not only separated the state from feudal society; through a centralized administration it had reinvented a social link for its own profit. It united to itself all the French people, who had become its subjects, in a vertical relationship of dependence and resentment; by habituating them to expect everything from the state, it also made them fear everything from the state, opening the way, without realizing it, for the great revolutionary passions. The government had "replaced Providence." [46] Politics had adorned itself with the hopes of religion. It mattered little whether the government was uninspired or poorly obeyed as long as everyone saw it as capable of everything: merely changing leaders would suffice to ensure society's happiness. And the omnipotence of Paris made this change of sovereignty feasible when public opinion could be led to see its salvation in it.

From here on, Tocqueville changes the angle of his analysis. In chapters two through seven of book two he looks at the growth of the bureaucratic state and its characteristics. The remaining chapters (eight through twelve) are concerned with the consequences of this phenomenon for society, beginning with the two principal ones: a tendency to make individu-

---

46. Part two, chapter six.

als alike, and a reinforcement of the passions that separated them. On the one hand, the French became more and more similar to each other. On the other, they were more and more separated into mutually impervious castes: microsocieties jealously surveying their boundaries, their sense of exclusivity the stronger, the more recent or fragile the boundaries. The Revolution of 1789 smashed these boundaries in a night that has remained famous, revealing the nakedness that they hid: a social mass more uniform than in any other country in Europe.[47]

First, Tocqueville discusses the theme of similarity from a dual perspective, of provinces and of people. The monarchy created national unity by progressively eliminating the uniqueness of the various provinces, by uniform legislation, and by greatly increasing legislative or regulatory texts intended for the whole kingdom. At the end of the eighteenth century, this unifying spirit nourished both royal edicts and ideas for reform. It had become a social need. The other aspect of similarity was the growing resemblance among people. Tocqueville was not referring to *all* the French, for he knew only too well that the peasants still formed an immense, separate class at the time; he was referring to the French of the upper classes—the nobility and the rich or well-off bourgeoisie, separated from each other by the most characteristic barrier of the old social order, yet becoming more and more alike. Why?

The nobility was growing poorer and the bourgeoisie richer, in a revolving-door movement. Tocqueville speaks of an evolution extending over several centuries, which ended up putting the majority of landed property into the hands of the bourgeoisie but some also into the peasants' hands. While maintaining and even reinforcing its privileges, the nobility lost (or sold) much of its land. As it lost its political power, it lost its land: an interesting political interpretation of an economic and social phenomenon like the distribution of landownership. Tocqueville probably meant that the nobility, deprived of its political prerogatives by royal power, distanced itself from the land, which was the basis of political power. Henceforth useless to the peasants and attracted by the kings, the richest members of the nobility went to the city, where they lived like bourgeois. Still more quickly the poorest nobles sold their land, which no longer brought with it jurisdiction over people, while retaining their

---

47. The night referred to is the famous night of 4 August 1789, when the representatives of the clergy, nobility, and the Third Estate joined in abolishing all the particular privileges of caste and region.—Trans.

feudal dues and rents. Thus nobles lost wealth and power—or, rather, power and wealth—to the profit of the bourgeois, sometimes richer than the nobles.

There was thus a long movement towards equalizing conditions, to use Tocqueville's words. It was an economic equalization, which hid an equalization of another sort, even more essential: once deprived of his special political rights, linked to the manor, the noble was no different from the bourgeois with respect to the royal government. Both were subjects. Power was abstracted from society and was henceforth outside it—a necessary separation for society to exist as *civil* society, as against the *political* society ranged above it. It was this dissociation between politics and civil society that gave rise to equality of rank, because it destroyed at its very roots the aristocratic principle that linked political power to hereditary social status. It left the king faced only by subjects. The growing equality of wealth was merely a consequence of this development.

The exception that proved the rule was English history, which in the *Old Regime* Tocqueville constantly contrasted with French history, at the cost of going back on what he had thought twenty years earlier when writing *Democracy in America.* Tocqueville's first great work was articulated around the contrast between France and America and between the French Revolution and the American Revolution; France and America were two democratic societies very different from one another yet belonging to the same egalitarian family, while England remained aristocratic. On the contrary, in the *Old Regime* the American reference disappears almost completely, for lack of relevance, while the comparison with English history, as in the writings of Madame de Staël and Guizot, often returned to Tocqueville's pen and never left his mind. England's particularity was to have remained aristocratic under a monarchy, whereas the French monarchy had emptied the aristocratic principle of its content. Why? Because, as Tocqueville explains in the following chapter, the English aristocracy was no longer, properly speaking, a nobility, that is to say, a caste, entry to which was protected by judicial boundaries. Tocqueville was referring not to the English titled aristocracy but to what historians have called the gentry, that class open to the money of landowners equipped with local authority. The English gentry was an example of a new kind of nobility, in which new families attached themselves to what remained of old ones in order to benefit both from land rent and from the concomitant political rights guaranteed by custom. In England, time served to link past with present; in France, time served as an element of division: the monarchy was separated from the society that had engendered it and in which it had taken root for so long; the nobility was separated from the land and from feudal political prerogatives. This separation became a dual source of social homogenization: on the one hand, French society was defined as a whole, as opposed to an "abstract" state, and, on the other hand, French society consisted of individuals who had all lost political liberty and were less unequal to one another in wealth, especially in land.

This new similarity had other sources, derived to a greater or lesser extent from the same basic development. Henceforth both nobles and bourgeois tended to live in the city most of the time. There they all read the same books by the great writers of the Enlightenment; there they all received the same education, "literary and theoretical"; there they were all impregnated by the same dominant influence, that of Paris, which had become the inevitable national reference. Increasingly, they acquired the same tastes, the same ideas, the same pleasures, and soon the same mores. Differences in manners separated them longer, for these were the slowest to be erased, but for how long? Here Tocqueville rediscovered an idea he had developed in *Democracy in America* but now applied to old-regime France: a society of individuals, deprived of their traditional links of mutual dependence, separated from one another, tends towards homogeneity and even towards conformism in habits and opinions. Only the exercise of political freedom, as in the United States, can be a counterweight to this tendency, because it simultaneously recreates a place for autonomy and a place for solidarity. But the France of the old regime was under the government of a single individual, which deprived its subjects of both autonomy and solidarity. The old regime made "people alike, and made them mutually indifferent to each other's fate."[48]

It is the second qualification that Tocqueville analyzes in the following chapter (chapter nine); its title summarizes the apparent contradiction: "How Such Similar Men Were More Divided Than Ever Before, Separated into Small Groups That Were Estranged from and Indifferent to One Another." The old regime was not exactly a democratic social state, in which people tend to be similar yet isolated, but rather a hybrid type of society, for people were becoming more and more similar but were not individually isolated by retreat to their private concerns: instead, they were separated by belonging to mutually estranged and even hostile social groups. On the one hand, they were already "democratic"; on the other hand, they were still "aristocratic"—a deplorable combination, since it

48. Part two, chapter eight.

was also the sign and the means of their subjection to the state. Between the aristocratic social condition and the democratic social condition, Tocqueville here outlines the concept of an intermediate social state,
born of the corruption of the two principles; this new condition may be
called "absolutist," to give full importance to the role played by the bureaucratic state, incarnated by the "absolute monarchy."

This intermediate social condition was characterized by what Tocqueville called "collective individualism," to contrast it to the organic solidarity of aristocratic societies and to the individualism proper to democratic
societies. In this intermediate condition, everyone was linked to a social
group. The tax base, for example, consisted not of individuals but of communities; yet these groups, instead of being united by a chain of reciprocal
obligations, made up a social fabric fragmented into small societies absorbed by their own corporate interests and incapable of collective feelings other than distrust or hatred of the neighboring community. Tocqueville found the model for this society of "collective individualism" in the
relationship between the nobility and the bourgeoisie; it then permeated
the whole social body from top to bottom.

At the end of the Middle Ages, the noble and the bourgeois still participated jointly in administering the kingdom's affairs, both national and
local. Tocqueville refers particularly to the Estates-General and to the
provincial estates of the fourteenth century, through which the three orders of the kingdom often jointly affirmed their will, in the face of a royal
authority needing their support. By the seventeenth century, however, all
this was over. Nobles and bourgeois no longer deliberated or acted together; the king alone decided. For lack of any contact in public life, they
became mutually independent and also mutual strangers—soon mutual
enemies.

How and why did the French move from estrangement to hostility?
The absolute monarchy was built simultaneously on the dispossession
and the maintenance of the aristocracy. The monarchy built its undivided
political domination on the ruins of the nobility's power, but it maintained and even consolidated the exclusivity of the nobility in civil society.
Squeezed by financial needs, the monarchy kept levying new taxes but
gave the nobility increasingly glaring exemptions; indeed, with regard to
the payment of the chief of these taxes, the *taille,* the bourgeoisie itself
largely succeeded in separating itself from the lower classes. For the same
reasons, the king of France sold access to nobility by all sorts of means:
by creating hereditary officials in justice, in finance, and in municipal government; by patents of nobility; by frequent measures of reform of the no-

bility intended to force usurpers of titles or those who were declared such to pay for them; and so forth. Unlike the English merchant who purchased an estate, the French buyer did not thereby acquire a local political prerogative or a defined right to participate in public affairs; on the contrary, when the city council was formed only of officials who owned their positions, it lost its connection with the population and its role of spokesperson and intermediary power. In the old regime, what was purchased with nobility was privilege: it was a title to be separated from one's fellow citizens. The mutual isolation of individuals affected by egalitarian passions in democratic society had its way paved by the bureaucratic monarchical state, which reduced aristocracy to a passion for privileges and distinctions. Vanity, as Stendhal would say, was the subjective link which, at heart, united the French of the old regime with revolutionary democracy.

Here too we should note Tocqueville's important clarification of his use of the word "caste." The French nobility failed to become an English aristocracy. French nobles had been transformed by the state's actions into a caste, that is, a closed group deprived of political power (which would have united them with the rest of the French) and possessing privileges that separated them from others. As always in Tocqueville's sociological vocabulary, the term "caste" refers not only to objective reality but to a particular society's representation of reality. Under the circumstances the nobility/caste was not, as the word normally implies, defined by birth, since admission could be purchased. Nor did nobility derive solely from the notion of privilege, for many other social groups had privileges, even if they were by definition different. What made French nobility into a caste was its separation from the nation through the enjoyment of exclusive rights that were purely civil; but the nobility became even more of a caste by imagining itself as separate and by making this separation its essence; by cultivating its gilded ghettoization; by adoring that which condemned it to the nation's resentment; by drafting with its own hands that decree of exclusion with which Sieyès would attack it in 1789.

This dynamic of social differentiation, in which nobility lost its principle, blood, and its function, public service, made the nobility subject both to money and to the state, constantly dividing it from within. The only means left to it for recapturing its ever more problematic identity was to overplay its distinction from the rest of society, and in this game the most recent nobles, who were at the same time the least sure of themselves and the most interested in maintaining the value of a recently acquired title, were also the most intransigent. Those who were living proof that the nobility was not a caste created by birth also had the most interest in putting the maximum distance between their recent elevation and the bourgeoisie they had just left. They possessed a caste's social imagination par excellence. "At no point in our history," commented Tocqueville, "was nobility so easily acquired as in 1789, and never were the bourgeois and the noble so estranged from one another."[49]

This attitude, which enclosed the kingdom's elites in vanity and resentment, had repercussions all along the social scale. It created a model of behavior that fragmented society, outside of the vast peasant world, into hostile little rival groups, caught up in constant competition for "rank," of which the bureaucratic state was the sole judge. The noble or the recently ennobled despised the bourgeois, and the lowest urban petty bourgeois despised the peasant. Between these two extremes extended the vast field of social jealousy, dominated by the state, distributor of honorific or real privileges, of which the former were not the least important. Every profession, every social group, possessed its own statutes along with its prerogatives, guaranteed by the king and frequently renegotiated for hard cash. All offices, and there were thousands of them, included the means to distinguish those who had bought their rights and duties. Thus were constituted the very numerous "corps" of the urban bourgeoisie, separate from both the nobility and the lower classes, jealous of one and despising the other, and in the clutches of the servile agitation caused by the passion for government jobs, a passion the old regime would bequeath to the Revolution.

The absolute monarchy, then, had a dual impact on French society in the old regime. The monarchy, so to speak, constituted French society as a civil society, a world outside political power. To the monarchy, equal obedience was due from all—the condition of uniform law. On the other hand, the monarchy kept reconstituting aristocratic society according to its own needs, by increasing differences in status in return for money. It destroyed the principle of nobility by creating an even greater number of nobles. The monarchy repressed all the king's subjects while selling them exemptions from its laws. It constantly recreated equality and inequality, fortifying each of the two passions by its opposite. It created the conditions for the tabula rasa of '89.

The society of the old regime thus remained an incomplete civil society, less because it bristled with multiple castes than because it was not *free*. Its fundamental vice, which explains its potentially revolutionary

---

49. Part two, chapter nine.

character, was the absence of freedom: with Tocqueville we always come back to this point. Freedom would have given society a means to eliminate, or compensate for, its fragmentation into closed and hostile groups to which the monarchy had reduced it. With freedom, society would have been allowed reconciliation, and soon solidarity, through discussion of the public interest. In a note that clearly expresses the basis for his judgment, Tocqueville comments, "I am convinced that only a government looking for strength solely within itself, and always taking men separately, like that of the old regime, could have maintained the ridiculous and senseless inequality that existed in France at the time of the Revolution; the slightest contact with "self-government" [Tocqueville uses the English word.—trans.] would have changed it profoundly and would quickly have transformed or destroyed it." [50]

The old regime, according to Tocqueville, could thus be defined both socially and politically, these dual aspects being intertwined. This is the subject of book two, chapter ten. On the one hand, Tocqueville sees a society in the grip of what he called "collective individualism," forerunner of the simple individualism of democracy. On the other hand, he sees a state also separated from society but creating its resources from the manipulation of social status and government positions, with no *political* link to society but only a relationship marked by a dialectic of subservience and revolt. In short, Tocqueville reveals an old regime which was no longer aristocratic, although it maintained and even reinforced judicial barriers between classes, and therefore not democratic, although in relation to the state the French were more and more equal in the absence of political participation. The system maintained itself through the growth of the state's needs in combination with the subjects' vanity, and the passion for government positions that substituted for public debate. The nation watched over its investments (offices, loans) rather than its freedom; it saw the state only in terms of its interests. In other words, in its relations with the state, the nation constituted merely an assembly of private interests, without existing as a political body. The Revolution would be the history of the constitution of the French into a political body, but at the cost of the exclusion of a "class," the nobility—such was the mutual class hatred transmitted from the old regime to the Revolution.

To the pessimism of this picture, which Tocqueville himself may have thought excessive, or, at least too rigid, too determinist (an aristocratic-despotic old regime opening the way to a "failed" democratic revolution),

---

50. *L'Ancien régime, OC,* v. 2, t. 2, p. 340 (note 26).

Tocqueville added the breath of fresh air of chapter eleven: "Of the Kind of Freedom That Existed under the Old Regime and Its Influence on the Revolution." It was a theme he had already dealt with in 1836, in his essay "The Social and Political State of France before and after 1789." Towards the end of that essay he contrasted two concepts of liberty. The first concept, aristocratic liberty, exalts independence the more because it emerges from a world of dependence. It endows its possessor with a sense of escaping from the hierarchical obedience of which the social order is composed, and hence an energy derived from an affirmation of the self as superior. In exceptional circumstances this energy can even be cultivated by a dominant people, such as that of ancient Rome, which felt that it alone had the right to be independent. By contrast, the second concept, the democratic idea of freedom, extends the benefit of independence to each person, independence becoming a universal human right; each individual is assumed to be sovereign, and the political body is legitimate only to the extent that it organizes the sovereignty of each individual on a collective level; in obeying the law, citizens are still obeying only themselves.

Of these two ideas of liberty, only the second, according to Tocqueville, is "just," because it is universal. Yet this very universality deprived independent of its passion and even its exaltation by comparison with aristocracy. It exposed freedom to the risk of a prosaic exercise, limited to the private sphere of existence, making room for a despotism of a doubly new type: freedom risked finding its defenders isolated and without energy at the very moment when obedience had lost the moral status it had possessed in an aristocratic society.

The old regime, however, did not succumb to this eventuality. It was characterized, here again, by the temporary coexistence of aristocratic freedom and democratic freedom, at the watershed of time when history combined both types of psychological structure. The French of the eighteenth century had retained a medieval perception of their freedoms, freedoms in the plural, as so many privileges that were immemorial, or granted by the kings in the course of time. But at the same time they were ever more imbued with the idea that each of them ought to enjoy freedom as an indefeasible right because it was founded in reason. For a while, therefore, instead of fighting each other, the two ideas of freedom joined forces to create a "public opinion" in society whose power served as a brake on the enterprises of authority.

An early analysis from the 1836 essay appears in book two, chapter eleven, of the 1856 book as a counterpoint to the picture of society's subjection by the monarchy. Indeed, we could hardly expect the society that Tocqueville has just described in such dark colors to become the cradle of an act of emancipation as spectacular as that of 1789, which is why Tocqueville reintroduces, just as he did twenty years before, the mutilated but still powerful life of freedom. It was a double inheritance from aristocracy, embodied in both institutions and mores. The monarchy, in its centralizing effort, had to permit local and customary practices to survive; these were outflanked rather than destroyed. Even the new positions invented by the monarchy to raise exceptional revenues were ramparts of independence for their beneficiaries, since so many of them were purchased. The nation's mores remained stamped with a spirit of resistance to central authority, thanks to the particular rights, inherited or acquired, possessed by each individual or group. The tone was set by the nobility, divided between nostalgia for its former role and the desire to rediscover its prerogatives through judicial oversight by the government. The clergy, however, cannot be ignored; it formed a rich, powerful, independent body, involved in secular matters. Even the bourgeoisie had a share in this desire for independence, for it too was the owner of its public offices and its privileges.

Aristocratic freedom had penetrated all the nonrural classes of the old regime. No doubt it was intermittent, irregular, and circumscribed by the limits of class and privilege. But it had the merit of stamping the public spirit of the age, which was then gathering strength, with daring and passion. There was still no sign of the obsession with material well-being and the congenital flabbiness of bourgeois civilizations. Obedient or disobedient, faithful to their king or recalcitrant with his agents, the French of this period still displayed to the world they were entering the virtues of the one they were overthrowing. "Thus reduced and deformed," concludes Tocqueville, "freedom was still fruitful. It was freedom that, in the very era when centralization worked more and more to equalize, to bend, and to tarnish all characters, preserved their native originality, their color, and their shape for a great many individuals, nourished self-respect in their hearts, and often made the desire for glory predominant over all other passions. Freedom alone educated those vigorous minds, those bold and proud geniuses whom we will see appear, and who will make of the French Revolution the object of the simultaneous admiration and terror of generations to come. It would be very strange if such manly virtues had been able to grow from a soil where freedom no longer existed."[51]

51. Part two, chapter eleven.

In this way, according to our author, the notorious dual character of the French Revolution, liberal and illiberal, can be explained. This duality has underlain interpretations of the Revolution and controversies over these interpretations. For the Revolution proper, the one that began in 1789, included two parts of unequal duration and of very different nature. The first was limited to the year 1789 and concluded, at latest, with the *journées* of October: it was the revolution of freedom against despotism, accomplished by the nation. Starting with the rebellion of the parlements, it culminated with the meeting of the Estates-General, the budding of a national public spirit, the Declaration of the Rights of Man. Tocqueville described it as a spectacle of incomparable beauty. The second was the very opposite, for it was the Revolution of class hatred and unbridled egalitarian passion at the price of political freedom. It covered a much longer period, beginning in the fall of 1789 and crowned just ten years later by the arrival of Bonaparte. The coup d'état of 18 Brumaire told the truth about the dictatorial decline of the egalitarian Revolution, which had previously known the terrorist regime of the Year II.[52]

In so describing the Revolution, Tocqueville rediscovered a classic distinction made by the liberal historiography of the Revolution, but he changed the reasons for it. For the liberal historians of the Restoration, the Revolution was a theater of class struggle. The bourgeoisie won its stripes as the dominant class against the nobility, but in the battle it was temporarily forced to cede ground to the popular classes, which were little inclined towards freedom. Tocqueville interprets the contradictory character of revolutionary events in a quite different light. His interpretation is based on an analysis of absolutism, or of the French social state as it was constantly subverted and reworked by the bureaucratic monarchy. It was absolutism that paved the way for democracy, the destiny of modern societies. Similarly, equality was imposed on French history from above, by a first revolutionary destruction of aristocratic hierarchies; the Revolution was lived with such passion because society was atomized into rival groups by a caste spirit nourished and upheld by the monarchy's actions. Its deadly legacy was simultaneously egalitarian and despotic. The old regime, however, also revealed the remains of a society imbued with the aristocratic spirit; and this legacy, combined with a universal demand for individual rights, briefly interposed its effects between absolutism and revolutionary centralization.

52. See Alan Kahan, "Tocqueville's Two Revolutions," *Journal of the History of Ideas,* v. 46 (October, 1985), pp. 585–96.

The mysterious part of the French Revolution was not the dictatorship of the Year II or the eventual omnipotence of the Napoleonic prefect, since this part was foreshadowed in the old regime before being aggravated by the radical destruction of the aristocracy. The enigma of the Revolution was, rather, the brief, beautiful period in 1789, when the ancient tradition of freedom, half-hidden, resurged in a new version, extended to all humanity. As for the Revolution's principal course, which made French democracy into a society with such an uncertain, fragile relation to political freedom, its origins had to be sought in centralizing absolutism. The Tocqueville of 1856, living in the internal exile to which his opposition to the second imperial despotism relegated him, despaired that the consequences could be overcome.

The principal secrets of the political history of the Revolution were to be found in the evolution of the upper classes. But Tocqueville wanted to end book two with a synthesizing chapter that would take into account the whole of French society in order to understand the general social upheaval of 1789. In book two, the backbone of the work, the first chapter aims to answer the question, Why did the Revolution break out in France? The following chapters attempt to disentangle the characteristics assumed by the Revolution, preceded as it was by the effects of administrative centralization on political mores and on minds. The final chapter of book two grapples with the rural masses of the old society in order to understand not only why they were poor and oppressed but, even more important, why they were isolated, set apart from everything. The peasants evidenced the kind of generalized anomie into which the social world had fallen; individuals, like classes, no longer understood what linked them together.

The peasant of the old regime doubtless paid less in feudal dues than his medieval counterpart. But those that remained were even more odious to him, as we have seen, because of the obsolescence of these burdens, which no longer brought anything in return. Most often, the lord's absence showed clearly that the feudal relationship had lost its substance. If the lord stayed in his castle, it was because he was too poor to live in town or at Court; but towards the peasant he was as harsh as a banker toward a debtor. The loudest voice in the countryside was elsewhere: it was the state and its taxes. When the rural community needed a representative, it was to respond to the state's demands, to determine the share of taxes each person owed. This syndic, moreover, chosen each year largely at random, was more a rival from whom one had to hide one's paltry possessions than a delegate to whom one confided one's interests. Each time the peasant crossed paths with a demand from the state—for taxes, corvée labor, conscription—he had to hide from his neighbors in order to shelter himself from the king's agents. He was free and a landowner, yet he lived apart from his fellowmen in a countryside abandoned by the educated classes: how could he not be bitter about his situation?

His fourteenth-century ancestor may well have been more oppressed, but he was never isolated and despised to this extent. In understanding emotions and political passions, Tocqueville, who read Rousseau avidly, always perceived the despair born of comparison. Peasants in the eighteenth century "remained without technology in the midst of prodigies of the arts, and uncivilized in a world shining with enlightenment."[53] They constituted an isolated and discredited social universe, already landowners and yet almost primitive, set apart from the great movement of civilization of which their contemporaries were so strongly aware. What was worse, the peasants were held in such contempt as to render them alien, incomprehensible creatures to the upper classes. In this respect the bourgeoisie imitated the nobility, fleeing the countryside which had so often been their cradle, disowning the peasants from whom they sprang, doing all they could to make others forget that they had been part of this "people" who were referred to only in terms of animal husbandry, in order to better hide their roots. This distancing was done so much and so well that on the very eve of the Revolution the upper classes had no idea of the vast social upheaval rumbling at their feet.

It is difficult not to find in chapter two of book two an echo of the events Tocqueville had just lived through, which put an end to his political career. During the period when he was writing, the rural classes' contribution to the success of the coup d'état of 2 December was a subject of general reflection. Karl Marx, in his commentary written in the heat of the event, proposed his famous description of the French peasant as the principal support of the Bonapartist dictatorship.[54] Tocqueville himself treats the French revolutions of 1789 and 1848 in the same context. In that of 1789, the peasants intervened immediately, like a vast force, blind and independent, to which the urban bourgeoisie gave its share of the spoils from the Catholic Church; attached to the new order of things by material gain, the peasants judged all regimes in regard to it and loved Napoleon as the guarantor of their piece of land. In 1848, with the es-

53. Part two, chapter twelve.
54. Karl Marx, *The Eighteen Brumaire of Louis Napoleon*, section 7.

tablishment of universal suffrage, they became supporters of the party of order, in which they rediscovered the large landowners in a renewed alliance of the whole agricultural population. But this alliance turned out to be brief, since Bonaparte's nephew, with the large landowners' help, managed to confiscate freedom for his own benefit. Thus rural French society twice affirmed its deplorable collective isolation in the nation's midst. Neither the aristocracy nor the bourgeoisie was ever able to channel the peasantry's strength to serve free institutions, not at the end of the eighteenth century, and not in the middle of the nineteenth. The permanence of revolutionary culture was nourished by this reciprocal impotence between classes, inherited from the old regime before becoming a product of the Revolution.

The Structure of the Work: Book Three

Book three, devoted to the more immediate causes of the French Revolution, goes back only as far as 1750. It opens with the most classic and controversial issue in this vast subject, that of revolutionary ideas and their inventors, who are not yet called intellectuals but men of letters. After the fall of Robespierre it was a commonplace to blame the Revolution on the philosophy of the Enlightenment in terms made famous by Gavroche: "It's Voltaire's fault," "It's Rousseau's fault." The Revolution caricatured as a "plot" figured in the Jesuit Abbé Barruel's *Mémoires,* which appeared in 1796:[55] it was a constant theme in counterrevolutionary thought, in which the affirmation of the rights of religion against philosophy held such a prominent place. But it also played a major role in the liberal critique of the Revolution, from Benjamin Constant to the Doctrinaires, and even among antiliberal authors such as Saint-Simon or Auguste Comte. There was no Romantic writer who did not pay tribute to it.

Tocqueville lived his life in this intellectual atmosphere. The milieu in which he was raised was typical of the French nobility, full of guilt feelings for having listened too much to Voltaire and his imitators under the old regime. We notice this remorse here and there in the *Philosophical History of the Reign of Louis XV,* written by Tocqueville's father.[56] Tocqueville was no less convinced, though he had ceased to believe in God during his adolescence, of the indispensable character of religion as the foundation

---

55. Abbé Barruel, *Mémoires pour servir à l'histoire du jacobinisme* (London, 1797–98).
56. Hervé de Tocqueville, *Histoire philosophique du règne de Louis XV* (Paris, 1847).

for individuals and societies, and still more so if these individuals and societies belonged to a democratic age.[57] He was not the last to regret that
the ideas of the French Revolution developed as a break with the Church
and Catholic tradition. Nonetheless, he remained one of the few great
writers of the Romantic generation—along with Stendhal—to retain a
weakness for the eighteenth-century philosophy on which he had been
raised; no one had better assimilated the ideas of Montesquieu and Rousseau than he. He loved the Enlightenment not only for its great authors
but also for its enthusiasm for natural rights, its intellectual energy, its
historical optimism. In this respect, Tocqueville shows no traces of the
counterrevolutionary mind; if the new ideas replaced religion rather than
superimposing themselves on it, it was less the fault of their intrinsic nature than of the circumstances in which they found themselves. The same
argument had been propounded in 1801 by Mounier against Barruel.[58]

Tocqueville was quite familiar with this debate through a contemporary treatment by the great jurist Portalis,[59] which inspired him, though
he didn't admit it, to write his own version of the debate. That the authors
of the eighteenth century wanted to improve or transform the social state
by simplifying it through rules founded on reason was not in itself an exceptional ambition: from the time of the Greeks that ambition had been
found in literature and philosophy. What was surprising was that, from
the mid-eighteenth century on, this idea became a principal theme for
writers and was warmly received by the public. The reason for its popularity among writers lies in the contrast between the outdated and even
bizarre character of social relations, and the desire of men of letters to
substitute simple and natural arrangements—a desire heightened by the
fact that most of these writers lived in the world of the imagination and
of conversation, deprived in both cases of real political experience. Here
Tocqueville rediscovers the thread of his analysis, since administrative
centralization led both to the extravagances of rank and to the simplifications of abstract thought in defining society in relation to the state.

Here also we see the reason for society's celebration of its men of letters, whose frustrations and political inexperience it shared. In the absence of a true aristocracy, whom else could society follow? The remains

---

57. He described this period in his intellectual life in a letter to Madame Swetchine of
26 February 1857. See *OC,* v. 15, t. 2, pp. 313–16.

58. J.-J. Mounier, *De l'influence attribuée aux philosophes, aux franc-maçons et aux illuminés
sur la Révolution de France,* rev. ed. (Paris, 1822), pp. 106–23.

59. Jean-Etienne Marie Portalis, *De l'usage et l'abus de l'Esprit philosophique pendant le dix-
huitième siècle* (Paris, 1827), 2 vols.

of the aristocracy, subdued by power, reduced to quarreling over precedence, also followed literary opinion, which, furthermore, was formed in aristocratic salons. Even the men who participated in one way or another in government—ministers, administrators, magistrates—did not know how to think about reforming the state. They knew the details of government, since that was their profession, but they were ignorant of the art of politics, which consists of foreseeing, deciding, persuading, for this art assumes the practical exercise of freedom. Here Tocqueville was thinking of Turgot and his physiocratic friends who were simultaneously men of power and reformers; when they proposed to the young Louis XVI, in 1775, to gather around himself each year a representative assembly of the kingdom, they saw such an assembly as having a purely advisory role, relating exclusively to taxes and public works.[60] They totally missed the nation's underlying desire, which was political, as 1789 would reveal.

For lack of an outlet in institutions or regular activity, the desire for political participation found intellectual satisfaction in literature, a French predilection of long standing. A literary politics was created for want of a true political life; it centered on a substitute literary aristocracy for want of a true aristocracy. Hence the abstraction of the debate on public affairs, so often remarked upon by critics of the French Revolution. Tocqueville recognized it in the vocabulary of official texts under Louis XVI. Its secret was not a mysterious "French mind," which since the beginning of time had tended towards general ideas, but the encounter of a literary civilization with a type of government. The Revolution, having consecrated that encounter, would pass it on to contemporary France.

In the second volume of *Democracy in America,* Tocqueville had already discussed the taste for general ideas as a natural trait of democratic peoples.[61] In centuries of equality, all men are independent, separate, and weak, and they tend to imagine their history not as if moved by certain individuals but as the product of a collective force or of a cause acting equally on all. They don't have time to become involved in the details of particular cases; nor do they have to, since historians provide them with general interpretations. Tocqueville diagnosed this tendency among the Americans as early as 1840; but it was counterbalanced in the United

60. Edited by Dupont de Nemours but not put into practice, the "Report on Local Government" of 1775 foresaw a pyramid of assemblies—from village governments to a "Royal Municipality"—composed of landowners, with one vote per property bringing in 600 livres of income. The powers of these assemblies were related to apportioning taxes and to public works.

61. *Democracy in America,* v. 2, part one, "Influence of Democracy on the Intellectual Movements in the United States." See also ibid., chapters three, four, and twenty.

States by the daily practice of local democracy, whereas in France it was encouraged by the coexistence of a democratic social state and political-bureaucratic paternalism. What Tocqueville's 1856 analysis added to that of 1840 was his introduction of a third element, the existence of a great number of writers capable of responding to the strong social demand for literature born during the preceding centuries. These intellectuals made themselves the representatives of a society without representation, at the price of a massive change in the nature of their work. The great authors of the century of Louis XIV had all avoided politics. All those of the Enlightenment were political writers, carrying the spirit of literature and philosophy into politics. Deprived of freedom, they were deprived of experience, condemned to abstraction or utopia even when they knew the business of government.

Was it in the same vein that they attacked religion? Christianity, in this period, was generally on the retreat all over Europe, according to Tocqueville, especially among the upper classes. But France was the only country where Christianity was attacked directly, violently, and in the name of unbelief. It was as if a new, special passion had arisen in France, fixated on the elimination of the Christian religion with no attempt to substitute another—hence the dual mystery of the fanaticism of this passion without foundation in another faith. Tocqueville is reminded of ancient paganism which Christians had reduced to the memory of a superstition, or of the European wars of religion, when the Protestants had drawn their boundaries against the Catholic Church. In the eighteenth century, however, the page of Protestantism seemed to have been turned: the memory of persecution, still so close, still fueled hatred for the Church while no longer encouraging religious proselytizing. Tocqueville raises this question indirectly rather than discussing it; his old regime, unlike Quinet's,[62] is strangely silent on the revocation of the Edict of Nantes, as it is on Jansenism, that aborted Protestantism which was so quickly incorporated into political polemics. But this indifference to the religious history proper of old-regime France does not prevent Tocqueville from looking at Voltaire and his imitators with the same perspective as Quinet: If the Church and religion were no longer fought in the name of another God, or of a higher claim to fidelity to the same God, what was the meaning of the fight?

---

62. See F. Furet, *La gauche et la Révolution au milieu du 19e siècle: Edgar Quinet et la question du Jacobinisme 1865–70* (Paris, 1986), chapter three.

The question was all the more pressing for Tocqueville because he regarded religion as a necessary moral foundation for humanity, in harmony with natural feeling. Its forms might vary, and certain religions might die while others would take their place, but the fact of religion was inseparable from human nature, as a need for hope, an exorcism of mortality. In America, religion constituted an opinion common to all citizens, endowing democratic equality with divine sanction while allowing its effects to be limited; it unified ideas and softened the mores of a social world stirred by money and individual passions. In Europe, on the contrary, in a Europe that was not yet democratic but in which the old feudal spirit was dying out everywhere, Christianity was in retreat, to the profit of unbelief.

In France this phenomenon assumed a brutal and massive character among the entire educated public. This public followed the writers, who had become its representatives by default, and the writers attacked the Church as an obstacle to their abstract reconstruction of society. Criticism did its undermining work less within the sphere of faith than at the conjunction of politics and religion; or, if you will, the former aspect was merely a consequence of the latter. Religion was discredited by means of the attack on the Church. Following the intellectuals, opinion was led to see the Catholic Church as merely a beneficiary of the old regime's abuses, a figure of tradition, an incarnation of the past, while the spirit of the times was to reconstruct according to reason alone. Writers above all had reason to hate the Church, for the Church was in charge of overseeing writing and policing ideas—a responsibility it exercised enough to be hated but not enough to be feared. No one understood better than Tocqueville to what extent the volume of protest against the old regime was proportional to the residual character of its capacity for arbitrary action. Writers were harassed but not silenced. In mobilizing its heavy procedures against some of them, the Church brought them to the attention of their readers and increased their success, while condemning itself to public contempt. It manufactured its own rejection, both as authority and as tradition; its death as a faith was preceded by its disqualification as a power or as part of the old regime.

It is with respect to religion, then, that Tocqueville underlines the difference between France and the rest of Europe. Among the upper classes, irreligion was making progress everywhere, but hatred for the Church was the favorite literary theme only among the French. Hume was as irreligious as Voltaire, but only Voltaire made war on the Church and on religion. The French public of the Enlightenment was carried away from

the moral foundation natural to every individual; it substituted belief in
the regeneration of society for vanished religious faith. This foreshadow-
ing of revolutionary passion, which Tocqueville did not hesitate to compare to a "new kind of religion," was the source of extraordinary actions but also of political men of a previously unknown type, emancipated
from all moral scruples.[63] And even though, according to our author, religion in the nineteenth century had gradually regained its hold over souls,
that breed of men ready to sacrifice everything for politics had survived
the French Revolution and was swarming throughout the whole civilized
world.

Here Tocqueville returns to the theme outlined at the beginning of *The
Old Regime,* according to which the Revolution acted like a religious revolution yet lacked religious content. But this theme, though he develops
it, remains obscure. What is a nonreligious religion? The idea gains nothing in clarity if the mental dispositions it seeks to define—for example,
absolute devotion to a cause, the spirit of sacrifice—must outlast the
Revolution among some people while religion proper has regained possession of the majority. The political situation in France in the nineteenth
century did not allow Tocqueville to regard the revolutionary break between the Catholic Church and democracy as a crisis that was past, a
closed wound. To explain this break by the particularities of the French
old regime made it difficult to interpret the decline of Christianity at the
European level; but the survival of the confrontation in postrevolutionary
France made it still more difficult to see it as an accident. If the American
Republic deployed a sort of preestablished harmony between Christianity
and democracy, the French Revolution manifested a lasting antagonism
between the two.

Tocqueville failed to solve this contradiction not only because he was
silent on the division between Catholics and Protestants, so fundamental
for so many authors.[64] He also was trapped by the ambiguities of his ideas
about religion.[65] On the one hand, he saw in religion a spiritual reality
inseparable from human nature—invincible, inexpungible, since religion
has its universal seat in the soul. Even the French Revolution, despite its
professions of faith, could have no lasting impact against religion. But be-

---

63. Part three, chapter two.
64. Most great historians of the French Revolution date the birth of the revolutionary spirit
to Protestantism—whether to congratulate themselves or to complain about it—for example,
Guizot, Buchez, Louis Blanc, and Quinet.
65. See Pierre Manent, *Tocqueville et la nature de la démocratie* (Paris, 1982), chapter eight:
"La démocratie et la religion."

lief in God is also caught in time, linked to given institutions, inserted into a particular society; in this respect religion is subject to the vicissitudes of history. With regard to religion's secular existence, America and France offered two opposite versions: Christianity respectively as friend and as enemy of democracy. Which was more real, more lasting? Tocqueville wanted to believe it was the American version, since he saw it as offering the better future, both for society and for religion. But he was not sure.

The insertion of religion into the social world could be more determining than the religious phenomenon as such, even for a type of faith as abstract and as universalist as Christianity. In America, the Christian sects were seminal elements of democratic equality. In France, the Catholic Church joined hands with the king. What made the Church independent of the king—its riches, its lands, and its feudal rights—was also what associated it with the hated old regime. It lost the public's esteem both by its submission and by its privileges. Free in the midst of a society of equals, the American churches remained the most influential of civil institutions. In postrevolutionary France, the Catholic Church, uprooted from its property, retained from the past only servility towards authority; it remained more than ever what it had become in the eighteenth century, a plaything and a scapegoat, instead of being the guardian of morals and the geometric center of opinion. Thus the destiny of Christianity in democracy was not as assured as the young author of *Democracy in America* had been able to claim in 1835. Indeed, five years later, in the second volume, the same author spoke of *pantheism* as a philosophical tendency natural to democratic man.[66] This observation, drawn from the background of French Romanticism, recurs in the 1856 work. And what if the revolutionary spirit was only a particularly acute form of this democratic pantheism?

* * *

As we have seen, the revolutionary spirit was in place very early on, in its political form, as a product of centralization. In the brew of ideas and feelings that led up to the Revolution, Tocqueville singled out and devoted a whole chapter to the hold on the French imagination of the ambition to reform the entire social structure, starting with the state. We have seen to what extent the *idea* of the state, even more than its reality, dominated the daily practice of public affairs. But to an even greater ex-

66. *Democracy in America,* v. 2, part one, chapter seven: "What Makes Democratic Nations Incline Towards Pantheism."

tent it invaded the French vision of the future. It also provided the French with a method of reform whereby, without their realizing it, reform became revolution.

To retrace this mental route, Tocqueville invoked the physiocrats, whom he had read with care, as his notes testify.[67] The "economists," as this sect was called in the eighteenth century, offered him the combination of a cult of the state and bureaucratic hyperrationalism that was typical of the French reforming mind, even more so as Quesnay and his disciples had been advisers to the ruler. Here were men who had devoted their time and thought to the public good, taking their inspiration from an ideal society in which the state would rule over all individuals in the name of reason. They had no concern whatsoever for tradition or for human passions. Their sole objective was to reestablish government on true principles, substituted for the errors of the past. For lack of a model in time, they invented a model in space, namely China, where the educated, a meritocracy recruited through competitive examinations, were the instruments of the natural order! Thus, in the midst of the old regime, the physiocrats imagined a sort of democratic despotism—a "rational," all-powerful state, uniform rules, the equality of individuals. They were describing many features of the socialist idea. But above all they bequeathed to the Revolution an essential part of its inspiration.

Not that their great theoreticians, or their disciples either, played an important role in the Revolution. On the contrary, the former were dead, and even the latter, such as Dupont de Nemours, looked like refugees from another age, for the tabula rasa of 1789 dominated public opinion. But Tocqueville perceived the posthumous life of ideas after the death of their inventors and the disappearance of the particular circumstances of their emergence. He clearly saw that in 1789 the sect's theories had long been dead in the public mind as far as their prescriptive if not dogmatic character was concerned. Yet these theories had left deep traces; although the doctrine had fallen into disuse, the modern philosophic cult of the state, which agreed so well with the nation's historical experience, remained. In commenting in his working notes on a letter from Dupont de Nemours to Jean-Baptiste Say, Tocqueville remarked that despite the unpopularity into which the physiocrats fell under the Revolution, their ideas "are nevertheless very deserving of study, because they show the ideas which, derived peacefully and naturally from the nation's state of

---

67. See Tocqueville's notes, especially those on Turgot, in the Notes and Variants to this volume and in the second volume of *The Old Regime.*—Trans.

mind, institutions, and mores, from its education, its history, from what was most powerful in the impressions and memories of the old regime (before it was violently jolted and thrown off course by the revolutionary movement), were bound to mingle with all the new institutions and to remain the permanent basis of our political instincts, a basis from which we have eliminated (only in part) the need to use freedom to destroy the old regime, but to which we naturally returned as soon as the old regime was destroyed." [68]

This note illustrates once again Tocqueville's concern to interpret the Revolution in its contradictory aspect, successively favorable and hostile to freedom. By tracing the course of the old regime in search of the two sources of the Revolution, Tocqueville pays the price of oversimplification. In fact, it is not certain that in the eighteenth century "the idea and the desire for political freedom proper presented themselves last, as they were the first to disappear." [69] After all, *The Spirit of the Laws,* which appeared in 1748, predated the writings of the physiocrats, and the campaigns of the parlements against absolutism began even earlier. The physiocrats themselves, at the period of their greatest power, watered their wine: their champion Turgot, once he had become controller-general, was a semidissident in relation to orthodoxy, for he was liberal in politics as well as in economics. It was he who reestablished the parlements, which had been dissolved by Maupeou in 1771. Tocqueville saw this measure as signaling a change in public opinion rather than as stemming from personal conviction. The two are not incompatible, but the former is less evident than the latter: the popularity of the parlements was well rooted in the eighteenth century.

In Tocqueville's analysis, this change marked the intersection of the desire for a radical reform of government with the people's desire to perform such a transformation themselves. The revolutionary idea was born in the confluence of these two feelings, equally strangers to the meaning of compromise. It superimposed the sovereignty of the people, copied from that of the king, onto the desire to wipe the slate clean, which attached itself like a parasite to the promises of reform. Among a people totally unprepared for political freedom, the ambition to remake the entire social machine could only lead to catastrophe. All in all, "an absolute ruler would have been a less dangerous innovator"—a sentence so extraordinary, from the pen of an unconditional lover of freedom, that it is

---

68. *L'Ancien régime, OC,* v. 2, t. 2, p. 369.
69. Part three, chapter three.

immediately followed by an explanation: ". . . when I consider that that same revolution, which destroyed so many institutions, ideas, and habits opposed to freedom, also, on the other hand, abolished so many others which freedom can hardly do without, I am inclined to believe that perhaps if the revolution had been accomplished by a despot, it would have left us less unfit to become a free nation, some day, than the revolution made in the name of the people, and by them."[70]

What augured ill for the success of the Revolution of 1789 was its merging of a belated love of liberty with a project for the general reconstruction of society that was typical of absolutism. It would have been better if the administrative monarchy could have been taken to its logical conclusion, and could itself have destroyed aristocratic society and finally benefited from a really "absolute" (in the sense of "despotic") power. Such an evolution would have preserved the possibility of a global dismemberment of the regime thus created; freedom would then have attacked all its parts. History illustrated another scenario: the people overthrew the monarchy as the heirs/continuators of what had already been accomplished. The people carried on the old regime's work and were therefore incapable of making the passion for freedom survive, the passion that was at the very source of their uprising.

At the end of book three, chapter three, Tocqueville imagines *another* history of the Revolution, beginning with Bonaparte and ending with the Constituent Assembly! This hypothesis is not very consistent, because it turns things around to put 1789 at the end of the Revolution. From that perspective, it becomes difficult to conceive of the previous overthrow of the absolute monarchy by a "despot," unless one is to imagine an uprising inspired solely by antiaristocratic sentiments and provided with a credible candidate for the role of leader. In such a case, it is hard to see where the "despot" in question would find justification in the eyes of the nation for replacing the old dynasty in order to complete its work, before being chased out himself in the name of freedom. To reverse the Tennis Court Oath and the 18 Brumaire makes both events lose much of their probability. But the idea is still brilliant insofar as it breaks with the determinist prejudice that so often accompanies studies of the French Revolution, and it is essential to understanding Tocqueville. In his view, the passion for liberty rediscovered by the French at the end of the eighteenth century was always mixed with the French habit, almost a desire, for bureaucratic paternalism, in which they saw a guarantee of equality. Seventeen-eighty-

70. Ibid.

nine displayed their hatred of despotism but did not extinguish their tendency to subordination, to which the destruction of the aristocracy gave new scope. So much so that the Revolution displayed, almost immediately, the essential character of modern France, which consisted of "mix[ing] together unlimited government centralization and a dominant legislative body: administration by officials and government by the voters. The nation as a body had all the rights of sovereignty, each particular citizen was confined to the strictest subjection: from the one, they demanded the experience and virtues of a free people; from the other, the qualities of a good servant."[71]

In Tocqueville's eyes, this contradiction guided the whole course of the following century, for the Revolution gave it irresistible power and unforgettable shape. The French never ceased to revive and even to cherish its constraints, while Tocqueville, on the contrary, deplored their renewal. His book was an attempt to date these constraints and to understand them, as a consolation for the oppression into which France fell on December 2, 1851; Tocqueville freely stated this intention in the next paragraph. Since it defines the entire work, the paragraph is here quoted in full: "It is this desire to introduce political liberty among ideas and institutions which are foreign or opposed to it, but for which we had already acquired the habit or conceived the taste, that for sixty years has produced so many vain attempts at free government, followed by such disastrous revolutions. Finally, fatigued by so many efforts, put off by a task so laborious and so sterile, the French abandoned their secondary objective to return to their primary one. Many of them were reduced to thinking that to live as equals under a master still had, after all, a certain attraction. Thus today we find ourselves infinitely more like the physiocrats of 1750 than our fathers of 1789."[72]

The absence of freedom, however, so characteristic of the nation's modern history, produced different effects in different periods. Under Louis XIV, it played an even greater role than war in bankrupting the country, as Vauban had already remarked. Tocqueville accepted the testimony of this great witness for the prosecution from the Sun King's reign. On the other hand, he suspected as biased the vast literature of the following century that depicted the kingdom in bleak colors; he believed it representative of a changed state of mind rather than faithful to the social reality it claimed to describe. It was a type of observation Tocqueville

71. Ibid.
72. Ibid.

makes frequently, which relates testimony to the observer more than to that which is observed. If so many eighteenth-century authors, coming from so many different backgrounds, whined about the state of France, it was because they all shared a state of mind that tended to censure or, conversely, to reform. Under the great king the country was ruined, but silence was general: writers practiced literary genres other than social criticism, and the few who risked it masked their intentions. During the Enlightenment, writers of every stripe, even the least talented, sought to reform the conduct of public affairs. The omnipresence of this desire created the impression that everything was getting worse and worse, though what was really happening was that public opinion was daily becoming more politically sensitive.

Tocqueville did not paint the eighteenth century with the dark colors of a Michelet. He did not believe in that general decadence of the kingdom generally described by the men of letters and intendants. For lack of statistical evidence, which he made no attempt to assemble, he imagined France as growing in population and wealth, and, indeed, his retrospective "optimism" is confirmed by the economic and social history of the twentieth century. The movement accentuated after 1750, irrigated by the passion for material well-being that accompanied the forward march of "civilization." Here Tocqueville borrows from the writers of the Enlightenment one of their favorite words, a word invented during that period to describe the whole of material progress, the softening of mores, and the feeling, so characteristic of modern man, that the future must be better than the past. To the beginning of this story the state itself added its contribution, led by the social machine, despite its archaisms, and by public opinion, even though the state pretended to be above everything. Its bureaucrats also worshiped at the altar of progress.

Throughout the nation a mental upheaval was taking place, which Tocqueville saw as the "march towards revolution." The turmoil of 1787–89 was provoked not by stagnation or poverty but, on the contrary, by change and relative prosperity. As evidence, Tocqueville claimed that the regions where this turmoil was most pronounced were also those where change had been the most rapid, such as the Generality of the Ile-de-France; conversely the West, where the war of the Vendée and the Chouan uprisings of Brittany and Lower Brittany would break out, remained caught up in the old regime. Here Tocqueville gave in to the illusory precision of teleological reasoning, which goes backward from observable effects to supposed causes: he was far from certain that feudal or postfeudal institutions were much more alive in the Vendée than anywhere else. But the interest of his thesis lies elsewhere—in the idea that in the old kingdom, which was subject to profound change, the expectations of the French moved even faster than the transformations of French society. Imagination, that ambiguous blessing of modern democracy, took hold of people's minds; it bathed them in the pleasures of equality and the hope of social perfection. As the government's abuses became ever more onerous, people were simultaneously attracted by the future and fearful of the present. Inasmuch as the monarchy mobilized the savings of individuals for its own use, and used money to constantly remodel aristocratic society, the monarchy of the old regime appeared even more archaic because in other respects it encouraged the movement of civilization.

Indeed, far from standing still, the monarchy was a workshop of reform. It participated in the philanthropic spirit that had seized the whole nation. It wanted to alleviate what it called the people's wretchedness without realizing that it was spreading the very language that would be used against it during the Revolution; but nobody yet knew what a revolutionary lower class was. The documents of the period describe this lower class, sometimes idyllically as the object most worthy of the government's attentions, sometimes contemptuously as a primitive race; both ways in which the lower classes were caricatured completed their revolutionary education. The former put the poor at the center of the state, while the latter incited their revolt. The combination of arbitrariness and weakness exemplified by authority prepared people for the violent overthrow of the laws.

Absolute monarchy destroyed the basis of its own power two years before the Revolution: the edict of 17 June 1787 established—alongside the intendant in the *pays d'élection,* which comprised almost three-quarters of France—a hierarchy of provincial assemblies, with a doubling of the number of representatives of the Third Estate, charged with allocating and collecting taxes. Tocqueville saw this measure as the dismemberment of the old regime by the creation of elected assemblies with the power to govern.[73] The system had been in practice from time immemorial in the *pays d'état;* but its extension throughout the kingdom, along with the doubling of the Third Estate, made the newly elected powers coexist in the *pays d'élection* with the intendant, who, though displaced, was nevertheless charged with helping and supervising the assembly. There was no better way to turn the whole kingdom topsy-turvy. Assemblies combining

---

73. He probably exaggerated the practical implications. See P. Renouvin, *Les Assemblées provinciales de 1787* (Paris, 1921).

landowners of all three orders were not best qualified to administer a tax system that was unequal, particular to each order; and their mission by its very nature implied constant conflict with the intendant or his subdelegates. It was the end of the administrative constitution of old-regime France, the prelude to the overthrow of its political constitution, since the former was more fundamental than the latter, as proved by the revolutions of the nineteenth century. The originality of the French Revolution—by comparison, for example, with the English Revolution of the seventeenth century—was to have churned the national soil to its depths. And it was the monarchy, faithful to its subversive genius, that started it all, before abandoning its pursuit to the people.

Hence the Revolution's apparent suddenness in France and its extraordinary openness to any innovation whatsoever: the old regime well and truly created a political and social void, open to all experiments. Burke made the mistake—for in the end Tocqueville returned to his preferred author—of believing in a stable old regime that was partly constitutional in the old sense of the word, so that the rupture of 1789 became incomprehensible. In reality, the old regime was a first revolution before *the* Revolution; the phrase designated a social and political state in constant dissolution and reconstitution, a monarchy too democratic for what it retained of aristocracy, too centralized for what it retained of feudalism, a bastard system whose reputation and authority would not long resist the ambiguity of its principles. Less than a century after Louis XIV, the Sun King had left neither a government nor a society but simply ideas in whose name he was replaced. The revolutionaries' tabula rasa was his work.

The Evolution of the Work

In the genesis of *The Old Regime,* the political aim and bias of a philosophical study of history was paramount, the scholarship secondary. Tocqueville was a self-taught historian who reluctantly forced himself to dig through archives for answers to new questions.

In December 1850, while writing his *Recollections* at Sorrento, Italy, Tocqueville took stock of his initial ideas in a letter to his friend Kergorlay. At that time he envisaged, in the vein of *Democracy in America,* "a broad judgment on our modern societies and the prediction of their probable future," which would be supported by "a solid and steady base" of historical facts: "the ten years of the Empire, the birth, development, decline, and fall of that enormous enterprise." "My doubts," he added, "bear much less on the choice of this subject than on the way in which to treat it."[74]

To any student of Napoleon, the obvious model was Thiers, whose *History of the Consulate and the Empire* was published with great success in nine volumes between 1845 and 1862. "My first idea was to redo Thiers's book in my own way," wrote Tocqueville. "To write *the same history* of the Empire but to avoid extensive treatment of the military aspect, which Thiers on the contrary discussed with so much self-satisfaction and with a ridiculous claim to really understand the military profession."[75] The history of the Empire, with all its battles and glory, seemed destined for retelling. Bonaparte himself had set the example through his bulletins and the memoirs he had dictated or inspired. But as Tocqueville himself realized, he had no particular gift for narrative history. Worse, it ran counter to his political purpose. Glorifying military achievements and detailing the succession of new laws meant hiding the bureaucratic despotism of the Empire, so that Bonaparte, having imposed his personal despotism on the French, would continue to impose the despotism of his memory on the historian. In 1836, Tocqueville had abhorred Thiers's inability to make moral judgments in his *History of the French Revolution* (1823–1824).[76] Thiers's history of the Empire seemed even more abhorrent: "It is too long and too detailed, yet nonetheless incomplete," wrote Tocqueville. Bonaparte, who had repressed anarchy and covered France with glory, had killed even the desire for freedom: "He surrounded France with a web of centralization which smothered all individual effort and all collective and individual resistance, and prepared the way for the despotism of an assembly or an emperor." Since Thiers had analyzed none of this, Tocqueville concluded that "the history of the Empire and of the emperor remain to be written."[77] By distancing himself from Thiers and rejecting narrative history from the outset, Tocqueville broke free from the idolatry of success and made possible a critical history of the despotic tradition in France.

74. Tocqueville to Kergorlay, 15 December 1850, *OC*, v. 13, t. 2, pp. 229–34.

75. Tocqueville to Kergorlay, 15 December 1850, *OC*, v. 13, t. 2, p. 231.

76. See Tocqueville's notes on Thiers's *French Revolution* in *OC*, v. 16, pp. 537–40. He declared that Thiers was "the most perverse and the most dangerous of all men," "incapable of distinguishing good from evil and of understanding general ideas." Tocqueville to Royer-Collard, 6 December 1836, *OC*, v. 11, p. 29.

77. *Correspondance anglaise: Conversations et correspondance avec Nassau Senior*, 19 August 1850, *OC*, v. 6, t. 2, pp. 286–87.

Once he had decided to "judge the facts rather than recite them," Tocqueville ran up against the great example of Montesquieu. In 1835, *Democracy in America* had seemed to update *The Spirit of the Laws*. In 1850, Tocqueville took Montesquieu's *Considerations on the Causes of the Greatness and Decline of the Romans* as his model. "There we pass through Roman history without stopping, so to speak; and yet we understand enough of that history to want to hear the author's explanations and understand them."[78] Kergorlay provided a good summary of Tocqueville's project: it was the making of a "history with blank spaces" in order to highlight the author's "intellectual and reflective nature" through the holes, or missing elements, in the work.[79]

At first sight, after the enormous effort made to publish historical documents inspired by Augustin Thierry and Guizot, this return to the old philosophical history seems to be a regression. Tocqueville's originality lay in applying the viewpoint of philosophical writing to recent history, which was too close to be easily discerned in its total perspective, and in subordinating the entire discussion to a new examination of the origins of despotism in France. In his effort to understand the origins of the French taste for servitude, Tocqueville would pass from a ready-made subject, the Empire, to a new construct, the old regime. In 1850, for lack of a method he thought he was holding firmly to a subject. Once the method was chosen, it was the subject that escaped him.

The state of the manuscripts bears traces of the constant give-and-take between Tocqueville's basic ideas and the documents he was reading. Just as he did on the second volume of *Democracy in America,* Tocqueville proceeded by successive reformulations: the accumulation of pages tirelessly recopied and modified by light touches were preserved even when they bore the inscription "to be burned," "to put aside," or "little to save." He started by writing down a few basic ideas or outlines, sometimes trying them out on his correspondents. Then, setting aside his contemporaries' books, he took "incredible pains to find the facts [by himself] in the documents of the time" and to classify these facts under headings that related to his basic ideas (despotism, centralization, the abstraction of the philosophes, and so forth). "This harvest thus laboriously gathered," wrote Tocqueville, "I close myself in, as if in a tight space, and I examine very carefully, in a general review, all the ideas that I have acquired on my own. I compare them, connect them, and then create the law to describe

---

78. Tocqueville to Kergorlay, 15 December 1850, *OC,* v. 13, t. 2, p. 233.
79. Kergorlay to Tocqueville, 19 January 1851, *OC,* v. 13, t. 2, p. 237.

the ideas that have come to me spontaneously in the course of my la-
bors."[80] In this final phase of exposition, Tocqueville was still searching
for himself. He would first write in a narrow column and then fill the
margins with additions, corrections, or references to notes. Sometimes he
added a supplementary page while deploring his "uncertainty" or his "in-
decision." For example, when he spoke of the similarity among the people
of the eighteenth century, he was afraid of giving "a description [that was]
if not exaggerated, at least too absolute, which could give rise to considerable criticism, and in any case diminish the effect I want to produce."
In August 1855, attempting to analyze the irreligion of the men of letters,
he invited himself to return to the question when his mind was re-
freshed—a "question I have been unable to resolve to my satisfaction."
Kergorlay raised a series of objections to this section, hedged as it was
with "howevers," and "althoughs": "One must avoid tiring [the reader]
by tormenting him with too many nuances and perspectives within the
same passage. Much must be conceded to the desire to fully satisfy the
reader by the charm of the writing style." To which Tocqueville replied:
"The first draft is often much preferable in form to anything that reflection adds afterward. But the idea itself gains by being churned up and
handled over a long period of time, written and rewritten, turned over
and over in my mind in every way."[81] Part of the work's attraction comes
from the author's debate with himself, pursued with the reader. After
1850, as in 1835, Tocqueville could not stop being an "examining machine,"
"a reasoning machine, a kind of syllogism incarnate," but a syllogism with
an open conclusion, which immediately generated new chains of logic.[82]
Let us follow Tocqueville in his long endeavor to understand French political culture through history.

* * *

Until 1852, Tocqueville let himself be seduced by the false glitter of analogy. At Sorrento, from December 1850 to April 1851, he tracked down
the resemblances between the great Napoleon and his nephew, who was
still only prince-president. As early as December he drafted an initial outline devoted to the great "act" of the Empire within the "strange play"
that was the French Revolution.[83] On his return to Paris he was at first

80. Tocqueville to Duvergier, 1 September 1856, OC (Beaumont), v. 6, p. 331.

81. Tocqueville to Kergorlay, 28 August 1856, OC, v. 13, t. 2, p. 309.

82. Tocqueville to Alexandria Batavia (unpublished), 25 July 1831, at Yale University. On this
aspect of Tocqueville's writing see Eduardo Nolla, "La démocratie ou le livre fermé," Revue
Tocqueville, 1997, 1.

83. See this plan in OC, v. 2, t. 2, pp. 301–4.

absorbed by the projected revision of the constitution, which could have forestalled Louis Napoleon's coup d'état; he then finished his *Recollections*. On 22 December, writing to his friend Nassau Senior, he traced a parallel between the coup of 2 December and the 18 Brumaire: both events led to military tyranny. But whereas Napoleon Bonaparte had the support of the educated classes, Louis Napoleon had only that of rogues: he was a cut-rate Napoleon.[84] In the dejection provoked by his voluntary retreat from public affairs, Tocqueville regarded work, or even a semblance of work, as a distraction.[85] He spent a few hours each day in the Royal Library, then in the archives to consult the register of the Directory's deliberations. In June he moved to Tocqueville and put his books in order, and then in July and August he wrote two chapters of allusive history: "How the Republic was Ready to Receive a Master" and "How the Nation, While no longer Republican, Had Remained Revolutionary."[86] He was depicting not only the Directory but also the year 1851, when despotism was already rumored, one of those "moments when the world resembles one of our theaters before the curtain is raised. We know we are about to see a new show. We already hear the preparations being made on stage."[87] This historical analogy with the French Revolution, common to Tocqueville, Marx, and many others in those years, was not without danger. In the belief that they were replaying the great revolutionary drama, people acted under the illusion that the outcome was fixed. Guizot's failure, followed by that of Lamartine in 1848, had already shown the problem of obsession with the past. Half-clever politicians who were always too slow during a revolution were "like those highly educated doctors who, very knowledgeable about ancient illnesses of the human body but still ignorant of the new and particular illness from which their patient suffers, never fail to kill him with learning."[88] The march to the coup d'état repeated the lesson.

In any case, Tocqueville did not permit himself to abuse historical analogy, and his two chapters were merely "a draft and an essay, a way of set-

84. *OC,* v. 6, t. 2, p. 375.

85. See Tocqueville to Beaumont, 1 February 1852, *OC,* v. 8, t. 3, p. 21: "I lose my concentration every minute and I don't have any desire to do what I'm doing. Paris is as hard to bear as the devil." See also Tocqueville to Beaumont, 18 February 1852 and 7 March 1852, *OC,* v. 8, t. 3, pp. 26, 32.

86. *OC,* v. 2, t. 2, pp. 269–92. [To appear in volume two of this translation.—*Trans.*]

87. *OC,* v. 2, t. 2, p. 291.

88. Speech to the annual public meeting of the Academy of Moral and Political Sciences, 3 April 1852, *OC,* v. 16, p. 231.

ting the tone."[89] He indulged himself in the pleasure of describing "almost contemporary emotions," but this essay was not the beginning of the future book, perhaps not even meant to be a part of it. "I don't really know if I have a subject yet. But I am desperately searching for it. For without the resource of a great book to write, I truly do not know what would become of me," wrote Tocqueville while beginning his chapters.[90] After he finished writing, his doubts increased still more.[91]

Starting in April 1852, Tocqueville undertook new research on the spirit of the Revolution—on both the intellectual origins of the event and on the passions it had aroused among the mass of the peasantry. He was looking for the Revolution's intellectual origins only in the ten years that preceded 1789, but he quickly moved beyond them in both time and space. From the outset he cast France's mental agitation in European terms, one that could not be understood without a comparative study of the Germans and the French. At this date Tocqueville was ignorant of almost everything about the Germanic world; as was his habit, he inquired of experts—his Germanophile friends Gobineau (in April) and Circourt (in May), who proved a real resource for Tocqueville, though not a very selective one.[92] In January 1853, Tocqueville consulted the great German political writer and theologian Bunsen, to whom he specified the purpose of his research:

> I am trying to put myself at the time of the [Revolution's] birth and to get a clear idea of the first impressions, the first thoughts, that the still indistinct view of that great movement suggested to foreigners. I would like to find records of the various judgments made about it from the outside, during the years 1787, 1788, '89, '90, '91, and '92, by the important people of the times, the writers,

89. Tocqueville to Beaumont, 24 August 1852, *OC,* v. 8, t. 3, p. 71.

90. Tocqueville to Beaumont, 1 July 1852, *OC,* v. 8, t. 3, p. 71.

91. See also Tocqueville to Beaumont, 24 August 1852, *OC,* v. 8, t. 3, p. 71.

92. Gobineau to Tocqueville, 29 April 1852, in response to a lost letter from Tocqueville asking where to look for sources of the new ideas in Germany. Gobineau suggested glancing at the polemical writings of Luther and Erasmus for the sixteenth century; Leibniz for the seventeenth; Mendelssohn, Lessing (above all the play *Emilia Galotti*), and the biographies of Schiller and Goethe for the eighteenth. *OC,* v. 18, pp. 195–96. Tocqueville responded that he was only interested in the end of the eighteenth century. In a letter of 21 May 1852, in response to questions from Tocqueville about preparatory work for the Revolution during the second half of the eighteenth century, Circourt alerted Tocqueville to Barruel; Voltaire's correspondence; the works of Bourgoing, Jovellanos, Minano, Condorcet, Voyer d'Argenson, Helvétius, Raynal, Diderot, Mably, and Servan; the complaints of the parlements in 1771; Saint-Martin and the two guides of Montjoie and Lefranc on freemasonry; the memoirs of Custine on Germany; and various works on Italy. *OC,* v. 18, pp. 72–74. Tocqueville seems to have paid little attention to this varied list.

the statesmen, the rulers; what they thought about it in advance, what they concluded from it or what they believed they could draw from it for use in their
own countries; the influence they believed it exerted on the general course of
European affairs; the advantages they thought they could reap from it. Unfortunately, to my great regret, I do not know Germany. I have lived until now
almost exclusively in the English world.[93]

The reading of the memoirs, collections of letters, and diplomatic documents that were suggested to Tocqueville nourished both the first chapter
of *The Old Regime* ("Contradictory Opinions about the Revolution at Its
Birth") and a chapter of his never-completed book on the Revolution.

In the summer of 1852, Tocqueville had run into another question
"along the way." In June he had moved to his château in Normandy. It
was a good place to understand the virulence of the peasants' hatred for
the nobles, and their corresponding fondness for the Napoleons, who
in their eyes were protecting the conquests of the revolution; in 1837,
Tocqueville had been defeated for election to the National Assembly to
the cry of "Down with the Nobles." On 22 July 1852, he described to
Kergorlay the two crucial questions that he could not answer for lack
of knowing what documents were available. "What did the lower classes
materially gain during the Revolution? In other words, how can one estimate the value of the confiscated lands that were given to them, the feudal
dues that were abolished, the burdensome or offensive taxes that were destroyed, and finally the debts or leases that were paid in a fictitious manner with the help of the assignats."

What was the state of landownership in 1789? "I think that in a large
part of France the lower classes were already landowners to a much
greater extent than is commonly imagined. And that the number of these
impoverished small landowners, who today are such a hub of socialism,
was already a major element in the Revolution."[94]

Kergorlay was not encouraging: "It would take an army of Benedictines to discover those unknown times, just as if they were among the most
obscure periods of the Middle Ages; but you have other things to do than
to be one of those indefatigable researchers, and, furthermore, you would
be the only one."[95] According to Kergorlay, it would be better for Tocque-

---

93. Tocqueville to Bunsen, 2 January 1853, *OC*, v. 7, p. 328. In his response of 21 April 1853
(unpublished, Tocqueville Archives), Bunsen suggested the *Cours de lectures sur la Révolution
française* by Niebuhr (1829), and the works of Arndt, Johannes Müller (letters), and Droysen
(*Freiheitskriege* [Wars of liberation]).

94. Tocqueville to Kergorlay, 22 July 1852, *OC*, v. 13, t. 2, pp. 243–44.

95. Kergorlay to Tocqueville, 2 August 1852, *OC*, v. 13, t. 2, p. 247.

ville to limit himself to a few generalities on the emancipation of industry and trade by the Revolution, and on the nationalization of the émigrés' property. Tocqueville, who shared his friend's contempt for scholars who "were knowledgeable in exact proportion to the uselessness of the studies they pursued," resigned himself to "patching together" a modest investigation, using his privileges as a former deputy to have archival collections opened to him and to take notes on them.[96] Folders O and A of Tocqueville's research notes, in which the results of his efforts are collected, testify to an intense exchange of letters and somewhat erratic readings, which show clearly the then embryonic character of eighteenth-century studies, halfway between oral memory and history. Tocqueville consulted his friends who were lawyers or economists (Freslon, Hippolyte Passy), landowners and politicians (Lepeletier d'Aunay, Duparc, Kergorlay), scholars from Paris or Normandy (Léopold Delisle; Leroux de Lincy; Dubosc, archivist of the department of the Manche; Gallemand, a rich landowner from Valognes); he questioned his overseer on changes in agricultural wages; he examined his childhood memories. Did he study the law about salvage? "Someone once told me about a cask of excellent wine that was drunk at the château in this connection." And then he plunged into varied written sources: indemnities paid in Normandy to émigrés according to the law of 1825—a law he had studied as a young attorney;[97] notaries' archives and registers; the historical treatises on feudal rights by Edmé de Freminville, Renauldon, and Henrion de Pansey; sectional registers established in 1791, 1792, and 1793, whose creation the Constituent Assembly had ordered in 1790 to serve as the basis for the land tax it created. Tocqueville, who could borrow the registers from the neighboring towns of Saint Pierre Eglise and Fermanville, considered these documents "excellent": "Nothing could be more interesting. We find in them the whole subsoil of the field we have been cultivating for sixty years," he wrote to Freslon.[98] A self-taught historian, Tocqueville reasoned by analogy about the old regime, relying on his experience as a landowner. Was it necessary to estimate the value of feudal dues? "Let us suppose," he wrote, "a parish like Tocqueville under the old regime, and myself as the lord." What would be the relations with each of the neighboring small landowners, and who would be required to grind flour at Tocqueville's mill, bake in his oven, and so forth? In the months during 1852 when he initiated himself into scholarship, Tocqueville sometimes

96. Tocqueville to Z. Gallemand, 28 August 1852, *OC,* v. 10, p. 569.
97. See *OC,* v. 16, pp. 38 ff.
98. Unpublished, 7 September 1852.

suffered "intellectual indigestion." "It is the ocean for a hundred leagues all around" he wrote.[99] Worse, he was well aware that nothing could prove that the example of Normandy was generalizable.[100] One must, however, admire the articulation between the problem posed and the choice of sources. In his notes, Tocqueville strictly limited himself to discussing what in residual feudalism explained the hatred between nobles and common- ers. What he undertook was not a rural history, nor a history of social classes, but a history of revolutionary passions as they had been aroused by absolutism. In 1856, *The Old Regime* would develop what he had dis- covered in 1852: "Feudalism had remained the greatest of all our civil in- stitutions while ceasing to be a political institution. Thus limited, feudalism aroused much more hatred, and it is correct to say that the partial destruc- tion of medieval institutions had made them a hundred times more hateful than they would have been if left intact."[101] Thus feudalism had only one vice, but it was unforgivable: it had become uselessly burdensome in a France where absolutism had monopolized all political functions.

At the end of his stay in Normandy in September 1852, Tocqueville was still not sure of his subject. "[I do not know] how to direct myself in this ocean of the French Revolution. I study, I try, I attempt to squeeze more out of the facts than I believe has been attempted up to now, in order to extract from them the general truth that they contain. I have not yet decided on a plan, and have not yet written anything that I could call the beginning of a book," he wrote to Mme de Circourt on 18 Septem- ber.[102] In any case, he had decided to study the administrative practices of absolutism and provisionally to abandon his work on the Directory, the Consulate, and the Empire. A note from December 1852 marks the turning point: "I returned Thibeaudeau's memoirs of the Consulate to the library without having read them; to be taken up again when I return to that period."

Some notes and letters dated March and April 1853 allow us to follow the new direction then taken by his Paris researches: he continued his

---

99. Tocqueville to Kergorlay, 20 August 1852, *OC,* v. 13, t. 2, p. 252.

100. Tocqueville to Freslon (unpublished), 7 September 1852: "In what concerns the burdens that feudalism laid on the French and in particular on the argicultural class in 1789, with much loss of time and intellectual indigestion from documents that are very heavy and have little sub- stance, I will arrive at a very clear and fairly exact idea of the nature of these burdens and of their weight, where they were still borne. But as for knowing where they were borne and by consequence acquiring a real idea of the general effect they could have produced, that is impos- sible. For they varied still more according to place than they differed among themselves."

101. Book two, chapter one.

102. Tocqueville to Mme de Circourt, 18 September 1852, *OC,* v. 18, p. 85.

work on landed property by reading the articles published by Lavergne in the *Revue des deux mondes* on the division of land in England and France.[103] And, more particularly, he threw himself into the study of government under the old regime: "I want to try to understand what was, in truth, the France of the old regime at the moment when it was surprised by the Revolution, the situation of individuals, the customs of public administration, for there was little else but custom."[104] In March he took notes on the government of rural parishes and villages and on the provincial administration of Upper Guyenne; Lepeletier d'Aunay advised him to read the *L'Administration des finances de la France* by Necker, and the article "Election" in Diderot's *Encyclopédie*.[105] In April he worked at the Hôtel de Ville on the papers of the generality of Paris. Having abandoned the study of the intellectual origins of 1789 for that of administrative customs, he had temporarily lost interest in the Revolution, which had not yet had time to put its innovations into practice; at the head of his notes he remarks that after 1787 "the old administrative constitution changes profoundly, and we enter into the brief and not very interesting period that separates the administrative old regime from the system of government created by the Consulate, which still rules us."[106] Although he had a clearer idea of the direction his introductory chapter on the old regime should take, he still found it difficult to find points of reference among the wide variety of absolutist practices; here too, however, he tried to proceed by analogy and by relying on his own political experience.[107] To Beau-

103. *Revue des deux mondes*, 15 March and 15 April 1853 (notes from folders K and L).

104. Tocqueville to Beaumont, 8 April 1853, *OC*, v. 8, t. 3, pp. 102–3.

105. Unpublished, 28 March 1853. Le Peletier also recommended reading le Tellier's work on the project on municipal government (1778).

106. Tocqueville's reading notes, file 43, folder I.

107. See Tocqueville's research notes from 1852–53, folder K, "Various Ideas." Tocqueville, unable to find any rules of municipal administration, wrote:

> The best way of seeing what happened in the countryside therefore seems to me to be, not to look a priori at what then were the organs and the rules for municipal administration, but to take all the things which today constitute the chief acts of that administration one by one, and to see what then existed for each one of these acts.
>
> The principal acts of municipal government today are:
>
> 1) The administration of communal property, sale, purchase, rental, and legal actions resulting from them
> 2) The maintenance of the church
> 3) The school
> 4) Local roads
> 5) The poor, public charity
> 6) The rural police
>
> Here, it seems to me, are the chief acts of civic life properly speaking.

mont he confessed his discouragement: "I am lost in an ocean of research, and in the midst of it all I am sometimes overcome by fatigue and discouragement. It is discouragement not only with myself but with mankind, as I become daily more aware of the small number of things that we know, of their uncertainty, of their constant repetition in new words for three thousand years; finally the insignificance of our species, of our world, of our fate, of what we call our *great* revolutions and our *great* affairs."[108] Tocqueville's stay at Tours (1 June 1853 to the end of May 1854) would offer him the sources and the method necessary to answer the questions he asked himself.

*   *   *

At Tours, Tocqueville was looking primarily for a more pleasant climate than the Cotentin for someone suffering from tuberculosis; he took up residence at Saint Cyr, at Les Trésorières, in a spacious, sunny house, sheltered from the north wind, very close to the famous doctor Bretonneau. Les Trésorières was two and a half miles from Tours, close enough that Tocqueville could go to the archives on foot but far enough away that he could escape the curiosity of local high society. Thus, partly by chance, partly by choice, Touraine became the chief example of a generality studied in *The Old Regime*. Tocqueville moved there with two work projects, contained in plans made in June 1853.[109] The first was to think about the nature of the Revolution. It was an event that initially seemed "of moderate importance" but soon aroused "a kind of religious terror." What, then, was this Revolution, and why did it begin in France rather than elsewhere? This is the basic idea of book one of *The Old Regime*.

But this new project remained part of an older, larger project that Tocqueville detailed on 26 June 1853: "First chapter, general description of the Revolution. Second chapter, the Republic from inside. Third chapter, the Republic from outside. Fourth chapter, how towards the end of the Republic France was ready to receive a master. Five, the 18 Brumaire." In June 1853 the investigation into absolutism was still only the beginning of the projected work. Yet Tocqueville, with the boldness of great discoverers, at first wanted to go back to Louis XI.[110] The archivist Charles de Grandmaison advised him to limit his efforts to Louis XIV

---

108. Tocqueville to Beaumont, 23 March 1853, *OC,* v. 8, t. 3, p. 95.

109. Tocqueville's research notes, folder K, folio 43.

110. On several occasions *The Old Regime* dates the appearance of the French disease from the fifteenth century. But these are only secondhand remarks, supported by very little documentation.

and his successors.[111] Grandmaison, a very young archivist Tocqueville had had the good fortune to chance upon, was a fine representative of the new generation of professional archivists educated by the Ecole des Chartes, founded in 1830 and reorganized in 1846. Charles de Grandmaison had been named to Tours after two years of internship at the Bibliothèque nationale in 1850–52, where he had met Tocqueville. Grandmaison had found the collection of Tours in "chaos." Archival technique was still in its infancy. Absolutism, where law was founded on tradition, had never known a document that was out of date solely because of its antiquity, one that never left the storage room. It was the Revolution that had invented the very idea of an archive, making old titles and charters irrelevant, and concentrating in enormous collections the papers that were, in principle, available to the public. But if the Revolution had invented the principles, it had left the task of applying them to succeeding generations. At Tours, Grandmaison busied himself accordingly with establishing the first inventory of collections from the old regime. Since he had little sympathy for the Empire, he eagerly placed his competence at the service of the notorious opposition figure Tocqueville. We may imagine Tocqueville in those months of 1853, hastening daily to the archives, armed with the black morocco portfolio of a former deputy, then reaching Grandmaison's office, a "narrow gallery" opening onto the prefecture's vegetable garden. And there, "with the patience and scrupulousness of a Benedictine"—without a research assistant to make notes for him, to Grandmaison's dismay—he covered several hundred pages, going through folder after folder of documents from the eighteenth century.[112] These notes reveal almost to the day the way in which Tocqueville went about studying the "functioning of social relations and government in old-regime France."[113]

In the history of the generality, Tocqueville started with the relations with central authority; he studied this in two sections between July and September—the general instructions contained in ministerial letters addressed to the intendants and, in the opposite direction, the relations of the intendant with the minister during the last thirty years of the old regime. But Tocqueville was far more interested in the daily management

111. See Charles de Grandmaison, *Alexis de Tocqueville en Touraine, notes et souvenirs intimes* (Paris, 1893).

112. Ibid., p. 12.

113. *Correspondance anglaise: Conversations et correspondance avec Nassau Senior*, 13 February 1854, *OC*, v. 6, t. 2, p. 408.

of the generality than in broad instructions. Under the old regime the rules were harsh, but the practice was sometimes arbitrary, sometimes pusillanimous. Tocqueville studied all the acts of the administration: business relating to printing, to the draft and to raising troops; police; prisons; taxes; roads; food; and, above all, the administration of the towns. On 30 November he began to analyze the edicts of August 1764 and May 1765 by which the controller-general, Laverdy, reorganized the municipal government of towns of more than 4,500 inhabitants in order to destroy the influence of the great bourgeois families who held venal offices. Before making these edicts, Laverdy had asked the intendants to initiate a major investigation of the functioning of municipal institutions. On the folder of his notes concerning this inquiry Tocqueville wrote the description: "Some of the most important and instructive work that I have done in the Tours archives." Indeed, it was in these folders that there appeared to Tocqueville clear evidence of the progressive displacement of elected officials by bureaucrats and the owners of venal offices. Not that the kings had deliberately planned this act of oppression: it was the need for money, which Tocqueville called "financial robbery," that induced the kings— and Louis XIV more than any other—to sell public offices and to crush the lower classes with taxes. Furthermore, absolutism was not the sole guilty party in French history. The notables, by letting the poor be taxed in their place and by gladly watching them stripped of power, had encouraged the king's vices. For the lower classes, taxed to the hilt, life remained precarious, poverty inevitable. An occasional revolt was quickly suppressed by the bailiff's men. Peasants are like mules, spoiled by rest, according to Richelieu's *Political Testament:* "I have heard exactly the same things said about the Arabs by the generals of the army of Africa," noted Tocqueville.[114] The chapter in *The Old Regime* on the abandonment of the peasants owed much to the archives of Tours.

There remained to discover what there was in absolutism that still limited the government's excesses. Tocqueville did this by examining the conflicts between the government and judicial bodies; in October he studied the decrees of the Royal Council (1600–1789); in November, the struggle of the Royal Council with the parlements after 1770 and the functioning of the courts in the generality of Tours. This research was immensely significant. In 1835, in *Democracy in America,* Tocqueville had judged that one of the chief contributions of America to political science was to submit the state to ordinary courts and the common law. "The right to sue

114. Tocqueville's reading notes, folder H.

the government's agents before the courts," he wrote in 1845, "is not a part of freedom, it is freedom itself, freedom in what is clearest and most tangible"; it is "a very precise scale of liberalism." [115] Without going so far as to praise the venality of offices, as other liberals had done, Tocqueville was not far from sharing Constant's opinion in his *Principles of Politics* (chapter 19) "that a removable or revocable judge is more dangerous than a judge who has bought his position. To have bought one's position is less corrupting than to always have to fear losing it." Hence Tocqueville's extreme disapproval of the intrusions into justice of a government organ like the Royal Council. Hence also his praise of the parlements, in the tradition of Malesherbes, though he did not share Malesherbes's illusions. For the parlements too were condemned by the very progress of civilization, which led to ever more centralization. In discovering in embryonic state in the old regime the very principle of administrative justice which he thought had been invented by the Empire, Tocqueville concluded that the Revolution "had stirred up society rather than change it." [116]

The discovery of continuity did not, however, make Tocqueville underestimate the mental upheaval that occurred during the last decades of the eighteenth century. "It is interesting to see," he wrote to Freslon, on 23 September 1853,

> to what degree the government of 1780 is already different from that of 1750. The laws are the same: in appearance there are the same rules; in the abstract there are the same principles; it is the same on the surface. Fundamentally there are already different methods, different habits, another spirit. Rulers and ruled are no longer recognizable. We did not fall from the excess of evil into revolution, but from progress into revolution. Having reached the middle of the staircase, we threw ourselves out the window in order to get to the bottom more quickly. And afterwards almost the whole world did the same.

Because the movement affected minds more than it affected laws, Tocqueville was not content merely to sift through administrative archives; he read reports and projects for reform in order to understand the principle of discontent that was the seed of 1789—reports full of complaints about the lower classes, such as those of a large tenant-farmer from the Soissonnais and the writings of the physiocrats. In July 1853 he borrowed from the library the writings of the elder Mirabeau, and read the collection of physiocratic texts that Daire had published in 1846;

---

115. Article of 16 February 1845, in Tocqueville's newspaper *Le Commerce, OC,* v. 3, t. 2, pp. 156–57.
116. Tocqueville to Freslon (unpublished), 10 August 1853.

in October he analyzed the summary of the cahiers; in November he went through the transcripts of the provincial assembly of Lower Normandy, the last attempt at reforming the monarchy (November–December 1787).[117]

At the end of October, Tocqueville considered his long Benedictine novitiate complete; it was time to stop reading and to start writing. Furthermore, the cold weather made the daily walk to the archives unwise. We now see Tocqueville "at the edge of the great moat,"[118] weighed down by a mountain of notes, and full of doubts: "I am less and less able to see the basic new idea which ought to be found among this mass of papers," he wrote to Ampère.[119] A self-taught historian with no taste for the petty facts that delight scholars, Tocqueville found it difficult to orient himself in the old documents despite the explanations dispensed by Charles de Grandmaison. Yet he was more of an expert than he thought. He had read the late eighteenth-century archives as a former county councillor and deputy and could distinguish rules from practices, discern the language of interest and power beneath the official verbiage. At the obvious risk of some anachronism, Tocqueville's research notes, far from being an unformed "mass of papers," already offered an interpretation of the old regime, with attempts at formulation, political judgments, and a constant back-and-forth between the past and the present, each throwing light on the other. In reading the projects for education described in the cahiers of the clergy, Tocqueville already saw "the state as maker of men" of which the Convention dreamed: "Isn't this typical? Where is the real support for freedom of the individual in this nation ready to revolt against all authorities? Show it to me!" Precursors of the Convention, the clergy of the old regime surpassed them in their desire for freedom, a desire lost by the Ultramontane and Bonapartist priests who were Tocqueville's contemporaries. "What immense retrogression during the past sixty years!" complained Tocqueville.[120]

Having read the archives as a politician, Tocqueville had little difficulty in drafting the first part of his book, which dealt with the general character of the revolution. In January he drafted the first chapter, and

---

117. Tocqueville to Beaumont, 1 July 1853, *OC*, v. 8, t. 3, p. 132; Tocqueville to Mrs. Grote, *OC*, v. 6, t. 2, p. 410.

118. Tocqueville to Ampère, 18 November 1853, *OC*, v. 11, p. 227: "I have sent back to the Paris libraries all the books they had lent me, and, in order not to succumb to the temptation of reading more, I have made no new requests for books. So here I am, this time, at the edge of the great moat."

119. Tocqueville to Ampère, 2 October 1853, *OC*, v. 11, p. 223.

120. Tocqueville's research notes, folder K, folio 43.

on 20 May 1854 he wrote Ampère that he had "at least half a volume *almost* finished. All the chapters have been outlined." [121] At that date the drafts show that Tocqueville had indeed sketched out the five chapters of book one. It was then that he came up against the "mountain of notes" relating to administrative history gathered for book two. Here he had to illustrate general ideas by presenting precise examples, and discuss the actual practices rather than the general political character of the Revolution. Tocqueville had still not fully grasped the administrative characteristics of the French old regime; he therefore returned to the comparative method with which he had been familiar since his trip to America.

* * *

The comparative perspective had been present at the very beginnings of Tocqueville's project, for it was born of his astonishment at the irreducible gap between the liberal tradition of the Anglo-Americans and the revolutionary tradition of continental Europe. While sifting through the archives in 1853, Tocqueville had reread Blackstone, whom he had studied twenty years earlier,[122] and had read the history of England by Macaulay, to whom he posed further questions.[123] For studying the history of France, however, English history offered inadequate help, for the kings of France had destroyed the old aristocratic constitution as early as the fourteenth century, so that the two histories diverged. Besides, to understand absolutism one had to look at other absolutisms, in Russia and Germany. In the autumn of 1853, Tocqueville read Haxthausen's *Etudes sur la situation intérieure de la vie nationale et les institutions rurales de la Russie,*[124] and he put the notes he took on it in his files on the old regime.[125] For although Russia in the 1850s was already "a terribly democratic society," it still exhibited and even accentuated the traits of old-regime France: in Russia, as in France, the absenteeism of the notables facilitated oppression by a bureaucracy that was so far away that its administration was as inefficient as it was expensive.[126] So Tocqueville returned to the

121. Tocqueville to Ampère, 20 May 1854, *OC,* v. 11, p. 241.

122. Tocqueville to Senior, 2 July 1853, *OC,* v. 6, t. 2, pp. 160–61. Tocqueville judged Blackstone "a fairly mediocre intelligence, without an open mind, without real breadth of judgment, in a word, a *commentator* and a *lawyer,* not what we understand by the words *jurist* and *political writer.*"

123. See the correspondence between Tocqueville and Macaulay in 1853, *OC,* v. 6, t. 2, pp. 160–63.

124. [Studies on the domestic situation and the rural institutions of Russia.—Trans.] 2 vols. (Paris, 1847–52).

125. See his notes in *OC,* v. 16, pp. 562–68.

126. Tocqueville to Beaumont, 3 November 1853, *OC,* v. 8, t. 3, p. 164.

contrast between American liberalism and Russian despotism that he had analyzed in a famous passage of 1835. If Grandmaison is to be believed, Tocqueville even wished he were young enough to travel to Russia to write a book that would have been the complement to *Democracy in America.* Since Tocqueville, on principle, never resorted to secondhand reports, he could only rarely use the comparison with Russia in his work.

There remained Germany, which was similar to France, but a France delayed on the highway of civilization. Tocqueville had visited Germany briefly in 1849, but his visit was cut short by his entry into the cabinet. In the summer of 1853 he laboriously began to study German, "almost indispensable" for his task.[127] In October 1853 he read the memoirs of Frederick the Great to learn about the work of centralization in eighteenth-century Prussia. Then, following his habit, he forced himself to link the study of the past with that of the present: along with Beaumont, he subscribed to the *Kölnische Zeitung* from October 1853 until June 1854. In this newspaper he gleaned some news about French politics that slipped by the censors, but mainly he was attempting to compare the rise of socialist passions and the progress of centralization in the two countries. He also read reviews of the work of German historians.[128] It was a useful prelude to the on-site investigation which for Tocqueville was a methodological necessity. He decided on a stay at Bonn, a university town endowed with an excellent library and where he already knew a few professors who could correct his knowledge of Germany, so far gained solely from books.[129] He planned then to travel through Westphalia to Dresden and Berlin to encounter some aristocratic debris from the antediluvian world of the old regime.[130]

Having arrived at Bonn on 19 June 1854, Tocqueville rented a small apartment on the banks of the Rhine and resumed the investigative methods he had used in America. His notes reveal no deep study of German philosophy. Two small notebooks about places and people are largely copied from the *Etudes sur la révolution en Allemagne* by Saint-René Taillandier, which appeared in 1853. In this conservative author, Tocqueville

---

127. Tocqueville to Kergorlay, 28 July 1853, *OC,* v. 13, t. 2, pp. 255–56.

128. Notably the review by Heinrich von Sybel on 13 January 1853. Tocqueville's notes on the *Kölnische Zeitung* are included in the research notes for *The Old Regime* in folder Q. Sybel wrote seven anonymous articles on *The Old Regime* for the *Augsburger Zeitung* (10 July–31 August 1856).

129. Tocqueville to Gobineau, 22 July 1854, *OC,* v. 9, p. 216.

130. Tocqueville to Circourt, 30 June 1854, *OC,* v. 18, p. 181. On the trip to Germany see K. J. Seidel, "Tocquevilles Forschungsaufenthalt in Bonn 1854," *Rheinische Vierteljahr-Blätter* 41 (1977): pp. 283–97.

found something to comfort him in his contempt for Hegelians of both
the left and the right, whom he condemned collectively, without even
reading their works, as so many fatalist, anti-Christian, and materialist
philosophers. The interest of Tocqueville's notes lies not in this summary
of the history of ideas but in his insightful reading of works on the history
and law of Prussia and Württemberg, and in the many conversations he
had that allowed him to test his hypotheses. As early as 16 July, Tocqueville could write to Beaumont: "I see with a certain satisfaction that the
ideas I had of [Germany] without knowing the country, purely from
abstract reasoning, attempting to discover why the Revolution had happened among us rather than in Germany, appear to me to be fully confirmed by the factual details." [131] Tocqueville, however, could not touch
"the living old regime" in Germany as he had wished. Mme de Tocqueville had always had a contrary nature: on 6 August she suffered an attack
of rheumatism in her right wrist. Goodbye to Dresden, Westphalia, Berlin: Tocqueville had to leave on 17 August for Wildbad, a small spa in the
Black Forest with no scholarly resources whatsoever. The trip was "totally
spoiled and rendered almost useless for me," lamented Tocqueville.[132] It
was the rancor of an impatient husband. Despite the brevity of the trip,
Germany would be the constant point of comparison with France in *The
Old Regime.*

Back in France in September, Tocqueville moved to Compiègne (September 1854–3 April 1855). After some supplementary reading in October and November (the digest of old laws, the histories of the Estates-
General by Ratherie and Boullée), he made a general index of his notes in
December in order to start writing the draft he called the "Rubbish." A
page from this period filed in the "Rubbish" gives an outline for the whole
of book two, which in 1856 Tocqueville would divide into two separate
books for the third edition:

1. How the feudal system had left fewer traces in France than elsewhere,
and yet become more odious there than anywhere else.

2. The public administration was already more centralized in France before
the Revolution than in any other country in Europe.

3. How France, of all the countries of Europe, was the one where the capital
had acquired the most domination over the provinces and most absorbed national life.

131. Tocqueville to Beaumont, 16 July 1854, *OC,* v. 8, t. 3, p. 224.
132. Tocqueville to Ampère, 4 August 1854, *OC,* v. 11, p. 251.

4. That France was the country in Europe in which men had already become the most similar among themselves, and at the same time the country where they were the most isolated into small groups that were indifferent to one another.

5. How in eighteenth-century France the peasant was more isolated from the other classes, more abandoned, and, in certain respects, in a worse condition than he had ever been in during the preceding centuries and than he still was in throughout most of the countries in Europe.

6. How the absence of all public life favored the birth and hastened the development of the philosophical doctrines which produced and characterized the French Revolution.

7. On the influence that the philosophes' opinions on religious matters exercised over the character of the Revolution.

8. How public prosperity, which for thirty years increased rapidly despite the flaws in the constitution and the government's efforts to correct those flaws, hastened the Revolution.

9. How the idea and the desire for political freedom manifested themselves only late in the eighteenth century and only at the approach of the Revolution.

The first five headings already display the entire structure of the present book two: one chapter on feudal dues; a study of centralization, at first a single chapter divided into three sections but later divided into four separate chapters (the present chapters two to five); an analysis of bureaucratic mores, of which only the chapter on Paris appeared in this first plan; and then a section on individualism ultimately divided into two very harsh chapters on the eighteenth century, which would be balanced by the chapter written in February 1855 on the kind of freedom that existed in the old regime. The whole terminates with a portrayal of the peasants' condition. The number of subdivisions gives the reader the feeling that the thesis has been chopped up into small pieces. But here the structure of the book imitates the process that led towards revolution, which resulted from multiple independent causes.[133]

*   *   *

133. See this outline on a separate page in a file of the Rubbish from the chapter on the bureaucratic revolution:

It marches all by itself without men. One of its characteristics. The character of all *true* revolutions, those which are not accidents.

Still more, everyone contributes to it. Some because of what they do for it, others because of what they do against it, some by acting, others by doing nothing. So that we successively assign it the most contradictory causes. The cause is the deepest. It is that which forces all these acts to contribute to the same end.

When he left Compiègne in April 1855, Tocqueville had drafted the whole work except for the last four sections about the approach of the revolution. Further, he had put on paper several sketches on the philosophes, unfinished for lack of enthusiasm and uncertainty about what line to follow. These last chapters were for Tocqueville the most "political," the hardest to write. He was hesitant about how to interpret the Enlightenment: Ought he to stress the demand for freedom or the despotic tendencies of the reformers? He had at first thought of integrating the study of the physiocrats into the discussion about "the kind of freedom which was found under the old regime," which he drafted in February 1855. But he decided to postpone the discussion of the physiocrats until the portrayal of the final years before the Revolution in order to stress the reformers' indifference to public freedom. As to the philosophes, Tocqueville hesitated still longer; he had written a first draft in the spring of 1855; he then rewrote it in August and yet again in the autumn: a chapter "written without enthusiasm," he noted on the folder of his notes, "although originally the subject stimulated my mind greatly and attracted me very much." Tocqueville knew he was walking on very thin ice here, for "perhaps what remains most alive of the original spirit of the Revolution lies in literature." Above all, he wanted to bring a balanced judgment to bear:

> In this chapter I did not want to put the ideas of the eighteenth century on trial, or, at least, the just, reasonable, applicable portion of those ideas, which are, after all, my own. I only wanted to show the unique effects that must have been produced by a politics which, even though it contained good ideas, was professed solely by people who had no idea of the way in which those ideas could be implemented: the whole aim of my book is to present the innumerable abuses which condemned the old regime to death; I therefore do not wish to blame those who wanted to destroy it but, rather, the way in which they attacked it, and the mental disposition that their lifestyle and their inexperience produced in them in that necessary destruction.[134]

These chapters written, Tocqueville proceeded "obstinately, passionately, and sadly" to finish the volume.[135] At the end of April 1855 he had completed the last two chapters and the conclusion, which, in the author's own opinion, "concludes nothing. It limits itself to once again gathering up all the things spread out in the book which were intended to explain why the Revolution came about naturally from everything which has just

---

134. Tocqueville to Beaumont, 24 April 1856, *OC*, v. 8, t. 3, p. 395.
135. Tocqueville to Ampère, 27 December 1855, *OC*, v. 11, p. 304.

been said." [136] The real conclusion could only be the story of the Revolution—which is why readers blamed Tocqueville for not concluding, that is, for lack of partisan blame or praise. [137]

A decision had to be made about which notes were indispensable. Tocqueville was unwilling to interrupt the narrative's flow, since the effect of the whole seemed to him more important than erudition. So he resolved to put the notes at the end of the book and to keep them sparse. He did not even agree with Beaumont's suggestion that he give references for his quotations. To parry objections, however, Tocqueville published long extracts from his reading notes, which were marginal reflections, not citation of sources. [138]

Tocqueville gave special status to his studies on Languedoc. [139] He had at first thought of devoting a chapter to the *pays d'états* following the one on centralization, so impressed was he by the decline of the provincial estates and the flaws in their constitution. The decision to put the study of the estates of Languedoc in an appendix and to devote a long discussion to them rested on epistemological necessity as well as political purpose. [140] Tocqueville used comparative history to evaluate the weight of absolutism. Languedoc, like England, exemplified the slow transition from aristocracy to equality, but with the difference that Languedoc had the same history as all of France, the sole variable being the absence of absolutism's grip. The history of Languedoc, a *pays d'états* where local life was flourishing, "could have been" that of the whole of France if it were not for the despotic tendency of the kings. The history of Languedoc was thus a fictitious history, an imaginary history of France, which by means of comparison allowed one to disentangle what was specific to the culture produced by absolutism. It was a history not without political virtue since it gave flesh to the dreams of those who did not possess the reality of freedom. Like the American experience described in *Democracy in America,* Languedoc at the end of *The Old Regime* offers the French a picture of happiness, which can be read as the ideal liberal society that Tocqueville desired for France. In the last pages of the book, Tocqueville thus offers a lesson in political hope.

*   *   *

136. Tocqueville to Beaumont, 25 April 1856, *OC,* v. 8, t. 3, p. 397.

137. Tocqueville to Mme Swetchine, 13 August 1856, *OC,* v. 15, t. 2, p. 28.

138. Tocqueville to Beaumont, 26 March 1856, *OC,* v. 8, t. 3, p. 386.

139. See Beaumont's comments, *OC,* v. 8, t. 3, p. 405.

140. Tocqueville took notes at the National archives and on the published laws of Languedoc in May 1855 and January 1856—the last documentary work he did for *The Old Regime.*

By the beginning of June, the book was printed. It was published by Michel Levy, the preferred publisher of the old Orleanists, in a print run of two thousand copies. Publication was delayed for a week by the death of Tocqueville's father and took place on 16 June. By August the first edition was sold out, and in October Levy hastily printed two thousand more copies, without giving Tocqueville the time to make any corrections beyond the division of book two into two books, which clarified the new spirit that animated the thirty years directly before the Revolution. A third edition of two thousand copies appeared in July 1857 and was sold out by December 1858, the date at which a fourth edition appeared. Public demand remained strong until the end of the century: 23,600 copies were sold before 1900. After the turn of the century, however, the book was almost forgotten until 1934.[141] The initial success surprised Tocqueville himself, who saw it as signifying the political revival of the Empire's opponents. In fact, this success was unusual in the category of what a contemporary called "thinker's books," especially for a book that wounded political passions. Tocqueville annoyed the democrats by revealing the antiquity of peasant proprietorship and the economic prosperity of the eighteenth century, thus minimizing the break made by the revolutionaries; he saddened the legitimists by denouncing the misdeeds of absolutism. Nevertheless, he changed everyone's interpretation of absolutism by showing the desire for servitude inherent in reverence for the state, which was born in old-regime France and prospered in modern France.

For a long time Americans were not very interested in a history so unlike their own; after an edition in 1856 and another in 1876, no American edition was published until after World War II. But a good number of German, Russian, and English historians and reformers reinterpreted European history in the light of Tocqueville's analyses, just as the French had done. European in conception, founded as it was on the constant comparison of France, Germany, England, and even, to a certain extent, Russia, *The Old Regime* has been a European book in its reception as well, since Europeans have found in it a lasting means of understanding the revolutionary tradition among nations that have known absolutism.

Tocqueville's Files, Manuscripts, and Proofs

The files relating to *The Old Regime* preserved in the private archives at Tocqueville contain five types of documents: Tocqueville's research notes;

---

141. On the work's reception see Françoise Mélonio, *Tocqueville et les Français* (Paris, 1993), chapter three.

plans, sketches, and drafts grouped by Tocqueville under the heading of "Rubbish" [Tocqueville used the English word.—Trans.]; the handwritten manuscript; the printer's copy with considerable handwritten corrections; and the galleys and proofs with handwritten corrections and remarks by Beaumont.

Tocqueville divided the notes into eighteen categories, using hand-marked folders. They are usually written on one type of paper, in black ink, and have few cross-outs. Tocqueville wrote on both sides of each sheet, in a single column, and made additions in the margin. These notes, written between 1836 and 1856 (with a few additions made even later), are very heterogeneous; they include simple collections of quotations as well as sections incorporated word for word in the final text. Tocqueville reclassified all the notes and put almost all the pages in files in 1856, probably to make them simpler to consult while he wrote the projected sequel to his work. The notes are found in the following order:

A. "Feudal Dues." Forty-nine numbered folios.

Unnumbered folder. "Rubbish, Work of M. Macarel. Notes on administrative law (1845)." This is the incomplete manuscript of Tocqueville's speech to the Academy of Moral Sciences on Macarel's course on administrative law.

B. "Turgot." Forty-eight numbered folios.

C. "Analysis of the Cahiers: Work on the cahiers done in 1836"; "analysis of the summaries of the cahiers (October 1853)"; "Studies done in the National Archives (1856)," without any numbering of the folios.

D. "Economists." Notes on Letrosne, Quesnay, Mercier de la Rivière, Baudeau, in folios numbered from 24 to 51. The first twenty-three folios would correspond with the notes on Mirabeau, lost, of which there remains a copy by Beaumont.

E. "M. Dareste." "Extract from the report on the state of the agricultural classes" by Dareste de la Chavanne, and notes on the other reports addressed to the Academy of Moral and Political Sciences for the same competition in 1853. Twenty-eight numbered folios.

F. "Notes taken on the Collection titled: General Collection of Old French Laws." Seventy-one numbered folios.

[There is no G.—Trans.]

[H]. "Notes taken at the Tours Archives 1853." One hundred sixty-six numbered folios.

I. "Notes taken in the files of the former Generality of Paris at the Hôtel de Ville." Twenty-two numbered folios.

J. "Miscellaneous." One hundred twenty-five numbered folios. Notes on: Necker; "the extract made by M. Droz of a manuscript existing in the Besançon archives and titled political instructions of M. de Serilly"; D'Argenson's memoirs; the reports of the intendants ordered by the Duc de Bourgogne (1698) made by the Comte de Boulainvilliers; Edme de Freminville; Mollien; grievances about the high taxes borne by the lower classes by Gaultier de Biauzat (1788); Boncerf; the *Encyclopedia* article on "franc fief"; the transcripts of the provincial assembly of upper Vienne 1779, 1780, 1781; the same of Berry 1778–79; various decrees of the Royal Council rendered in 1750 and in 1785; various notes on centralization and the bureaucracy of the old regime.

K. "Various ideas." About fifty pages without continuously numbered folios, consisting of unconnected ideas written down between 1836 and 1856 with a brief classification made after the first volume was finished.

L. "Studies on England." Thirty-four numbered folios on Blackstone; Macaulay and Lavergne's studies on agriculture.

M. "Foreigners' Judgments about the Revolution." Without foliation for the whole, contains notes on Burke, the memoirs of Heinrich Steffens, and *Briefe aus Paris zur Zeit der Revolution,* by Heinrich Campe (Brunswick, 1790). (Notes made in June–July 1858.)

N. "M. Arthur Young." Twenty numbered folios.

O. "Statistical Facts and Other Work at Tocqueville." Fifty-four numbered folios containing the study made in 1852 on "landownership before 1789. The environs of Tocqueville"; various documents received by Tocqueville; notes titled "finances of the old regime" and "administrative inquiry on the unity of weights and measures (1764)."

P. "Legislative and Executive Power of the Courts." Thirty-nine numbered folios.

Q. "Studies on Germany." Two notebooks and 192 numbered folios. Includes two small notebooks in portfolios titled "notebooks containing observations on *places* and on *people,*" containing notes taken in alphabetical order on Taillandier's work. Then files titled "Germany, Work on Germany done in Germany in June, July, August, and September 1854," including conversations and notes on the Prussian agrarian legislation; the "Works of Frederick the Great"; "Goethe's memoirs of 1792"; "the Cologne gazette in 1854"; and various documents sent to Tocqueville. Finally, notes on the "constitution of the agricultural class in Russia" (notes on Haxthausen).

R. "Various Notes." Partially foliated. Mainly notes on the administration of the estates; the venality of offices according to Henrion de Pansey; the Estates-General; Voltaire and "Philosophes or irreligious writers who were precursors or contemporaries of Voltaire outside of France."

The second category of documents is the box of "Rubbish." It is entirely in Tocqueville's handwriting except for five letters Tocqueville received between 1852 and 1856 suggesting sources, and a note from Grandmaison, the archivist at Tours. The pages, much crossed out, on the same paper as the reading notes, are written in black ink in a single column on both sides of each sheet. The file was neither put in folios nor systematically classified and appears as a mass of handwritten folders containing pages omitted at various stages of writing: an index and summary of notes, "preparatory work," "rubbish," "residue from the last review" of 1856. For each chapter there are only documents with many omissions.

The handwritten manuscript of *The Old Regime* is composed of pages on the same type of paper as used for the notes and the rubbish, written on both sides of each sheet in a single column in black ink, and included in a folder inscribed: "Manuscript of *The Old Regime and the Revolution* (1856). Here are the variants and notes which I might usefully review in case of a second edition." The pages were grouped by Tocqueville in his handwritten folders according to the order of the chapters in the final text, and are foliated by folder. The manuscript contains many corrections, and gives only an incomplete text or an early draft for certain chapters.

The fourth document is the printer's copy, made and paginated by the printer, which bears the handwritten title "The Old Regime and the Revolution. Manuscript returned by the printer." Tocqueville wrote in the margin or between the lines for minor corrections, and added pages for major changes. Chapter ten of book two—"How the Destruction of Political Liberty and the Division of Classes Caused Almost All the Ills of Which the Old Regime Perished"—is entirely in his handwriting. Part of the notes are missing (the notes on feudal law and analyses of the cahiers of the clergy that Tocqueville later reclassified in his research notes; and the analysis of the cahiers of the nobility reclassified in the Rubbish).

The final file contains the two sets of galleys and three sets of proof, with Tocqueville's numerous handwritten corrections (incomplete throughout).

During Tocqueville's lifetime, *The Old Regime* went through four editions (June 1856, October 1856, July 1857, and December 1858). It was for the second edition that the original twenty chapters of book two were divided into twelve chapters for book two and eight for book three. The third edition only introduced minor stylistic revisions. The complete list of corrections was published by J. P. Mayer in his edition of the *Oeuvres complètes,* pp. 325 ff. Only important changes have been included here.

Note on This Edition

The present text is that of the last edition (the fourth) that appeared during Tocqueville's lifetime, similar to the third edition revised by Tocqueville. Tocqueville's research notes, being for the most part not drafts or variants but documentary notes, have been included in the present edition under "Notes and Variants." The "Notes and Variants" also include the most significant information from the "Rubbish," the manuscript, and the printer's copy.

This Introduction was translated by Alan S. Kahan and Sarah Bentley.

THE OLD REGIME AND THE REVOLUTION

Preface

This book is not a history of the French Revolution, whose story has been too brilliantly told for me to imagine retelling it. It is a study of that Revolution.

In 1789 the French made the greatest effort ever undertaken by any people to disassociate themselves from their past, and to put an abyss between what they had been and what they wished to become. In pursuit of this aim they took all kinds of precautions to bring nothing old into the new order—they put themselves under strict constraint to make themselves different from their ancestors. They overlooked nothing in their effort to disguise themselves.

I have always believed that they were less successful in their unique enterprise than observers have thought, or than they themselves thought at first. I am convinced that, despite themselves, they retained from the old regime most of the feelings, habits, and even ideas which helped them make the Revolution that destroyed it. Unintentionally, they used the debris of the old regime to construct the framework of their new society. Thus, in order to properly understand the Revolution and its work, one must forget for a moment the France of today and ask questions of a France that no longer exists. That is what I have attempted to do in this book; but it has been a more difficult task than I expected.

The first centuries of the monarchy, the Middle Ages, the Renaissance, have all given rise to great works and been the object of very extensive research, which has taught us not merely the facts about what happened, but about the laws, the customs, the spirit of the government and the nation during those different periods. But up to now no one has done the same for the eighteenth century. We think we know eighteenth-century France very well because we see its glittering surface so clearly, because we know all the details about its celebrities, because clever or eloquent critics have made us familiar with the works of its great writers. But we have only confused and often mistaken notions about the manner in which business was conducted, the real practices of institutions, the exact relations between classes, the condition and feelings of those who could not make themselves seen or heard, about the real basis of ideas and mores. I have tried to see into the heart of the old regime, so close to us in years, but hidden from us by the Revolution.

In order to get there, I have not just reread the famous books produced by the eighteenth century; I wanted to study many works deservedly less well-known, which, however poorly written, reveal still better perhaps the true instincts of the times. I have worked to understand all the public records where the French were able to display their opinions and desires on the eve of the Revolution. The transcripts of the proceedings of the provincial Estates, and later of the provincial assemblies, have furnished me with much information on the state of affairs. Above all, I have made great use of the cahiers [†] written by the three orders in 1789. These cahiers, whose originals fill many manuscript volumes, shall remain the testament of the former French society, the supreme expression of its desires, the authentic manifestation of its last wishes. They are a unique historical document. But even they have not sufficed.

In countries where the government is powerful, there are few ideas, needs, sufferings, interests, and passions that do not sooner or later come before the authorities in their true colors. In visiting the archives of such a country one acquires not merely a good idea of its procedures, one sees the entire country revealed. If today one gave a foreigner all the secret correspondence which fills the files of the Interior Ministry and the prefectures, he would soon know more about us than we know ourselves. In the eighteenth century the government was already, as one can see in reading this book, very centralized, very powerful, and extremely active. It was constantly helping, hindering, permitting. It could promise much and give much. Already it influenced things in a thousand ways, not only public affairs, but the fate of families and the private lives of every individual. Furthermore, there was no publicity, so that no one was afraid of telling the government their secret problems. I have spent a long time studying its surviving records, in Paris and in the provinces.[1]

There, as I expected, I found the old regime in full bloom, its ideas, its passions, its prejudices, its practices. In those records everyone spoke his own words freely, and exposed his inmost thoughts. I thus ended up learning many things about the old society of which its contemporaries were unaware, because I had before me documents which they never saw.

As I progressed in this research, I often encountered to my surprise many traits of modern France in the France of the old regime. I rediscovered there a mass of feelings that I thought had been born of the Revolution, a crowd of ideas that up to then I had thought derived from it, a thousand habits that pass for having been created by the Revolution alone. Everywhere I found the roots of present society deeply implanted in the past. The closer I got to 1789, the more I saw the spirit which made the Revolution sprout and grow. Little by little I saw the whole shape of the Revolution unveiled before my eyes. Already it displayed its temperament, its spirit, its very self. In the old regime I found not only the source of what the Revolution would do at the start, but still more what it would do in the end; for the Revolution had two very distinct stages. In the first the French seemed to want to abolish their entire past, in the second they seemed to take up again a part of what they had left behind. Many laws and political practices of the old regime disappeared in 1789 only to return a few years later, like some rivers that go underground only to reappear a few miles further on, the same stream between different banks.

The object of this book is to understand why this great revolution, which was simultaneously taking shape all over Europe, broke out in France rather than elsewhere, why it was so natural a product of the society it was going to destroy, and how, finally, the old monarchy could fall so suddenly and so completely. In my mind, this is not the end of the work. My intention is, if I have the time and energy, to follow the Frenchmen of the old regime with whom I have lived so intimately through the upheavals of the Revolution; to see how they were changed and transformed in the course of events, yet never changed their nature, always reappearing with slightly different faces, but always recognizable.

I will begin by examining them during the first stage of '89, when equality and liberty shared their devotion; when they wanted to create not only democratic institutions but free ones; when they sought not only to destroy privileges but to honor and recognize rights. It was a time of youth, enthusiasm, pride, a time of generous and sincere emotions, whose memory, despite its mistakes, will always be preserved by humanity, and which, for a long time to come, will trouble the sleep of all those who wish to corrupt or enslave France.

While rapidly following the course of that revolution, I will try to show what events, what errors and miscalculations, made those same French abandon their original course and, forgetting liberty, desire nothing more than to become the equal servants of the master of the world. I will show how a stronger government, much more absolute than that which the Revolution had overthrown, arose and concentrated all power in itself, suppressed all the freedoms so dearly bought, and put vain idols in their place. I will show how this government called the votes of electors who could neither inform themselves, nor organize, nor choose, "the sovereignty of the people"; how it called the assent of silent and servile assemblies "free taxation." I will show how—while taking away the nation's ability to govern itself, destroying the chief guarantees of law, the freedom to think, speak, and write, that is, the most precious and noble of the conquests of '89—the government continued to adorn itself with the halo of the Revolution.

I will stop at the point where the Revolution seems to me to have just about finished its work and given birth to modern society. I will then consider the new society itself; I will try to figure out in what respects it resembles that which preceded it, and in what it differs, what we have lost in this immense transformation of everything, and what we have gained. I will finish by trying to see into our future.

Part of this second work is sketched out, but it is still not ready for publication. Will I be able to finish it? Who can say? The fate of individuals is still more hidden than that of nations.

I hope I have written the present work without prejudice, but I do not pretend to have written it without passion. It would hardly be possible for a Frenchman to feel nothing when he speaks of his country and ponders his times. I admit that in studying our old society in all its aspects, I have never entirely lost sight of our modern society. I wanted to discover not only what illness killed the patient, but how the patient could have been cured. I have acted like a doctor, dissecting every organ in order to discover the laws which govern the whole of life. My purpose has been to paint a picture both accurate and instructive. Whenever I encountered in our forefathers any of those manly virtues which are most necessary in our times and which have almost disappeared, I have highlighted them: true independence of mind, high ambition, faith in ourselves and in a cause. I have also taken care to cast light on the vices which, having devoured the old society, continue to gnaw at our own, so that in seeing the evil they have done, we can better understand the evil they can still do. To attain this goal, I have not refrained from offending anyone; whether individuals, classes, opinions, or memories, however respectable they may be. I have often done it with regret, but always without remorse. May those whom I have thus displeased pardon me in consideration of my sincere and disinterested purpose.

Some may accuse me of displaying too strong a taste for freedom, which, I am assured, is hardly of concern to anyone in France today. I ask those who reproach me thus to take into account that in my case this habit is very old. It was almost twenty years ago that, speaking of another society, I wrote almost exactly what I am now about to say.

In the midst of the shadows of the future we can already perceive three clear truths. The first is that today humanity is driven by an unknown force which we can hope to moderate, but not to defeat, which sometimes gently urges and sometimes shoves us towards the destruction of the aristocracy. Second, of all forms of society, the one where aristocracy does not and cannot exist is just the one which will have the most difficulty escaping absolute government for long. The third truth, finally, is that nowhere does despotism produce such pernicious effects as in just this kind of society; for, more than any other kind of government, despotism favors the development of all the vices to which such societies are especially prone, and thus pushes them in the direction in which they are already inclined to go.

People today, no longer attached to one another by any ties of caste, class, guild, or family, are all too inclined to be preoccupied with their own private interests, too given to looking out for themselves alone and withdrawing into a narrow individualism where all public virtues are smothered. Despotism, rather than struggling against this tendency, makes it irresistible, because it takes away from citizens all common feeling, all common needs, all need for communication, all occasion for common action. It walls them up inside their private lives. They already tend to keep themselves apart from one another: despotism isolates them; it chills their relations; it freezes them.

In these kinds of societies, where nothing is fixed, everyone is constantly tormented by the fear of falling and by the ambition to rise. Money has acquired an astonishing mobility, ceaselessly changing hands, transforming the status of individuals, raising or lowering families, and at the same time becoming the chief means by which to distinguish between people. Thus, there is virtually no one who is not constantly compelled to make desperate efforts to keep it or to make it. The desire to enrich oneself at any price, the preference for business, the love of profit, the search for material pleasure and comfort are therefore the most widespread desires. These desires spread easily among all classes, even among those previously most distant from them, and if nothing stops them they soon succeed in demoralizing and degrading the entire nation. But it is the very essence of despotism to favor and extend them. These debilitating passions help despotism, they occupy men's minds and turn them away from public affairs, while making them tremble at the very idea of a revolution. Despotism alone can furnish these passions with the secrecy and shadow which make greed feel at home, and let it reap its dishonest profits despite dishonor. Without despotism these passions would have been strong, with it they are all-powerful.

Liberty alone can effectively combat the natural vices of these kinds of societies and prevent them from sliding down the slippery slope where they find themselves. Only freedom can bring citizens out of the isolation in which the very independence of their circumstances has led them to live, can daily force them to mingle, to join together through the need to communicate with one another, persuade each other, and satisfy each other in the conduct of their common affairs. Only freedom can tear people from the worship of Mammon and the petty daily concerns of their personal affairs and teach them to always see and feel the nation above and beside them; only freedom can substitute higher and stronger passions for the love of material well-being, give rise to greater ambitions than the acquisition of a fortune, and create the atmosphere which allows one to see and judge human vices and virtues.

Democratic societies that are not free can be wealthy, refined, even splendid, powerful because of the weight of their homogeneous mass; one can find there private virtues, good family men, honest merchants, and very worthy squires; one will even see some good Christians, for their country is not of this earth and the glory of their religion is to bring them forth amidst the greatest corruption of mores and under the worst governments: the Roman Empire in its greatest decadence was full of good Christians. But what will never exist in such societies are great citizens, and above all a great people, and I am willing to state that the average level of hearts and minds will never cease to decline as long as equality and despotism are combined.

This is what I said and thought twenty years ago. Since then nothing has happened to make me change my mind. I proclaimed my high opinion of liberty when it was in fashion, and one can hardly think badly of me for maintaining it when it is no longer in style. Indeed, in my love of freedom perhaps I differ less from my opponents than they imagine. What person could be naturally base enough to prefer dependence on the caprice of one man, rather than follow laws which he himself has helped to make, if he thought his country had the virtues necessary to make good use of freedom? I don't think such a person exists. Despots themselves don't deny that freedom is a wonderful thing, they only want to limit it to themselves; they argue that everyone else is unworthy of it. We do not differ over whether freedom is worthwhile, but over the higher or lower opinion we have of people. Thus one can state that the preference that one shows for absolute government is in direct proportion to the contempt that one has for one's country. I hope I may wait a while longer before converting to that opinion of France.

Without praising myself, I think I can say that this book is the product of considerable labor. There is one short chapter which alone has cost me more than a year of research. My pages could have overflowed with notes; I have chosen to insert only a few of them at the end of the book with references to the relevant pages in the text. There one will find examples and proofs. I could provide much more upon request if anyone thinks it worthwhile to ask.

Book One

CHAPTER ONE

Contradictory Opinions
about the Revolution at Its Birth

There is nothing more suited to instilling modesty in philosophers and statesmen than the history of our Revolution. Never was such a great event, with such ancient causes, so well prepared and so little foreseen.

Frederick the Great himself, despite his genius, did not predict the Revolution. He sensed it without seeing it. Furthermore, he acted in accordance with its spirit before it happened; he was its precursor and even its agent; but he did not recognize its approach. When the Revolution finally appeared, the new and extraordinary features which distinguished it from the innumerable crowd of revolutions remained hidden at first.

From abroad, the Revolution was the object of universal curiosity; throughout the world it gave rise to a sort of hazy notion that a new era was beginning, to vague hopes of change and reform; but no one yet suspected what the French Revolution would be. The kings and their ministers lacked even the confused feeling which moved the masses. At first they considered it one of those occasional fevers to which all peoples are subject, whose only effect is to create new opportunities for their neighbors. If by chance they spoke the truth about the Revolution, it was despite themselves. True, the chief rulers of Germany, meeting at Pilnitz in 1791, proclaimed that the danger which threatened royalty in France was common to all the old powers of Europe, that they were all menaced; but at bottom they did not believe it at all. Their secret records reveal that these were only the pretexts behind which they hid their plans or dressed them up for the eyes of the crowd.

As for themselves, they thought that the French Revolution was a mere fleeting local accident to be taken advantage of. In this light they conceived their plans, made their preparations, and formed their secret alliances; they already fought among themselves over the prospective booty, made agreements, broke them. They were prepared for everything except what actually happened.

The English, who were endowed with more experience and better understanding by the memory of their own history and their long experience of political liberty, discerned the approach of a great Revolution as if through a thick veil; but they could not make out its shape. The influence it would soon have on their own destiny and on the world's remained hidden. Arthur Young, who foresaw an imminent revolution, and who traveled through France just before it broke out, was so ignorant of its meaning that he wondered whether the result would not be an increase of privileges: "As for the nobility," he said "if the revolution gives them still more weight, I think it will have done more evil than good."

Burke, whose mind was stimulated by his hatred for the Revolution from its birth, even Burke was briefly unsure about it. At first he thought it meant that France would be weakened and virtually destroyed. "One must believe," he said, "that the military power of France has been destroyed for a long time to come; it is possible that it is permanently eliminated, and that the generation to come may say as Caesar did: Gallos quoque in bellis floruisse audivimus—we have heard that the Gauls too were once famous warriors."

The event was no better judged at home than abroad. In France, on the eve of the Revolution, people still had no clear idea of what it would do. Among the mass of cahiers, I could find only two which showed any fear of the populace. People were anxious about the power retained by the monarchy, by the Court, as it was still called. The weakness and the short duration of the Estates-General[†] worried them. There was fear that the Estates-General would be intimidated. This particularly worried the nobility. "The Swiss," said many cahiers, "must take an oath never to bear arms against the citizenry even in case of riot or revolt." Give the Estates-General their freedom and all abuses would easily be eliminated; the reform to be accomplished was immense, but it was simple.

However, the Revolution followed its course. As the monster raised its head, it showed its unique and terrible face. After destroying the political institutions of France, it abolished the civil institutions; after changing the laws, it altered the mores, customs, and even the language. After it had destroyed the fabric of government, it uprooted the foundations of society, and finally seemed to want to challenge God himself. Soon the Revolution overflowed the boundaries of France by previously unheard-of means: a new tactic, murderous maxims (armed opinions, as Pitt called them), an enormous power which breached frontiers, toppled thrones, crushed nations, and, oddly enough, at the same time won them to its cause. As these things happened, viewpoints changed. That which at first had appeared to rulers and statesmen like an ordinary event in the life of Europe, now seemed a fact so new, so contrary to the whole previous course of history, and yet so universal, so monstrous, so incomprehensible, that in regarding it the mind lost its bearings. Some thought that this unknown power, which nothing seemed to help or hinder, which could not be halted and could not stop itself, was going to force human society to its complete and final dissolution. Many considered it the visible work of the devil: "The French Revolution has a satanic character," said de Maistre, in 1797. Others, on the contrary, found in it the benevolent hand of God, who wished to renew not merely France but the whole world, and who was creating a new human race. Many writers of the time betray something of that pious terror that Salvian experienced at the sight of the barbarians. Burke, thinking along the same lines, wrote: "Without its former government, or rather without any government at all, it seemed that France was a fit subject for insults and pity, rather than the scourge and terror of the human race it became. From the tomb of the murdered monarchy came forth a huge, inchoate being, more horrible than any that had ever afflicted the human imagination. This strange and hideous beast headed straight for its goal, without being frightened by dangers or hindered by remorse; contemptuous of common sense and ordinary methods, it brought low those who could not even understand how it came to exist."

Was the event really as extraordinary as it appeared to contemporaries? As tremendous, as earth-shattering, and as rejuvenating as they supposed? What was its real meaning, what was its real character, what were the permanent effects of this strange and terrible revolution? What exactly did it destroy? What has it created?

It seems that the time has come to answer these questions, and that today we are situated at just the right place to best see and judge this great thing. We are far enough from the Revolution to feel only faintly the passions of those who made it, but we are close enough to understand and empathize with the spirit that led them to it. Soon this will be impossible, for great revolutions which succeed make the causes which produced them disappear, and thus become incomprehensible because of their own success.

CHAPTER TWO

That the Fundamental and Final Objective of the Revolution Was Not, as Has Been Thought, to Destroy Religion and Weaken the State

One of the first acts of the French Revolution was to attack the Church, and among the passions born of the Revolution the first lit and the last extinguished was this passion against religion. Even when enthusiasm for liberty had evaporated, even after people were reduced to buying peace at the price of servitude, they continued to revolt against religious authority. Napoleon, who was able to defeat the liberal spirit of the Revolution, made fruitless efforts to quench its anti-Christianity. Today, too, we have men who think they can make up for their servility towards the pettiest government officials by their insolence towards God, men who while abandoning all that was most free, most noble, and proudest in the doctrines of the Revolution, pride themselves on remaining true to its spirit because they are still unbelievers. Yet today it is easy to convince oneself that the war against religion was only an incident in the Revolution, one of its striking but fleeting aspects, a transitory product of the ideas, passions, and particular circumstances which preceded and prepared the Revolution, and not part of the Revolution's own spirit.

The philosophy of the eighteenth century is rightly considered one of the principal causes of the Revolution, and it is certainly true that that philosophy was deeply irreligious. But one must carefully distinguish between two very different aspects of that philosophy. In one part we find all the new or reinvigorated ideas about society and the principles of civil and political law, such as the natural equality of men, the abolition of caste, class, and professional privileges, and in consequence of this the sovereignty of the people, the omnipotence of the social power, and uniformity of rules. All these doctrines are not only causes of the French Revolution, they are its substance; they are the most fundamental of its works, the most lasting, and in the long run the most valid.

In the other part of their doctrines the philosophes† of the eighteenth century were filled with a kind of rage against the Church. They attacked its clergy, its hierarchy, its institutions, its dogmas. They wanted to tear Christianity up by the roots. But this part of eighteenth-century philosophy, derived from the situation which the Revolution destroyed, ought to gradually disappear, buried by the Revolution's triumph. I will add only a few words here to make myself understood, because later on I want to take up this important subject again: it was much less as a religious doctrine than as a political institution that Christianity aroused these furious hatreds. The priests were not hated because they claimed to regulate the affairs of the other world, but because they were landowners, lords, tithe collectors, and administrators in this one; not because the Church could not take its place in the new society that was being created, but because · it occupied the strongest and most privileged place in the old society which was being ground into dust.

Consider how the course of time has brought this truth to light and demonstrates it daily: to the extent that the Revolution's political work has been consolidated, its antireligious work has been destroyed. Thus to the extent that all the old political institutions that the Revolution attacked have disappeared, to the extent that the powers, influences, and classes which were particularly odious to it have been irreversibly defeated, and that as the final sign of their defeat the very hatreds that they once inspired have dissipated, to the extent, finally, that the clergy has separated itself from all that fell with the old regime, we have gradually seen the power of the Church rise and strengthen itself in people's minds. And do not think that this is restricted to France: there is hardly a Christian church in Europe which has not revived since the French Revolution.

To believe that democratic societies are naturally hostile to religion is to commit a great mistake: nothing in Christianity, nothing even in Catholicism, is absolutely contrary to the spirit of democratic societies, and many things are very favorable. History shows that the most vital root of religious instinct has always been planted in the heart of the masses. All the religions that have died found their last refuge there, and it would be very odd if those institutions which tend to make the ideas and passions of the masses dominant had the necessary and lasting effect of leading the human mind to impiety.

What I have just said about religion, I will repeat with still stronger reason about society. When one saw the Revolution simultaneously overthrow all the institutions and practices which had previously maintained a hierarchy in society, and kept people in order, one might assume that its result would be not only to destroy a particular social order, but all order, not a particular government, but government itself: one would have had to conclude that the Revolution's nature was essentially anarchic. And yet, this was true only in appearance.

Less than a year after the Revolution began, Mirabeau wrote secretly to the king: "Compare the new order of things with the old regime; from this comparison is born consolation and hope. Most of the acts of the National Assembly[†] are clearly favorable to the monarchy. Is it nothing to be without parlements,[†] without *pays d'états,*[†] without the assembly of the clergy, without privileges or nobility? The idea of having only one class of citizens would have pleased Richelieu; equality facilitates the exercise of power. Several reigns of absolute government would not have done as much for royal authority as this single year of revolution has done." That was how a man capable of leading the Revolution understood it.

Since the goal of the French Revolution was not only to change the old government but to abolish the old kind of society, it had to simultaneously attack all the established powers, eliminate old influences, wipe out traditions, transform mores and practices, and in a way to empty the human mind of all the ideas on which obedience and respect had previously been based. From this came its singularly anarchic character. But now clear away all the debris: you will see an immense central power, which has devoured all the bits of authority and obedience which were formerly divided among a crowd of secondary powers, orders, classes, professions, families, and individuals, scattered throughout society. The world had not seen a similar concentration of power since the fall of the Roman Empire. The Revolution created this new power, or rather this power seemingly recreated itself amid the wreckage made by the Revolution. The governments which were founded by the Revolution are more fragile, it is true, but they are a hundred times more powerful than any that it overthrew; more fragile and more powerful for the same reasons, as will be discussed below.

Through the wreckage of the half-demolished old regime Mirabeau already perceived this new concentration of power. Despite its size, it was still invisible to the eyes of the crowd, but time has gradually made it plain to all. Today, monarchs are especially fascinated by it. Not only those rulers whom the Revolution created, but even those most opposed to it, regard it with envy and admiration; they all attempt to destroy the privileges and immunities within their realms. They mix ranks, equalize status, substitute government officials for aristocrats, uniform rules for local liberties, and centralized government for a diversity of powers. They work long and hard at this revolutionary task. And if they encounter any obstacle, they sometimes borrow the Revolution's methods and justifications to remove it. Thus one can see them when necessary inciting the poor against the rich, the bourgeois against the noble, the peasant against his landlord. The French Revolution has been at once the scourge and the teacher of princes.

CHAPTER THREE

How the French Revolution Was a Political Revolution Which Acted Like a Religious Revolution, and Why

Every political and civil revolution has taken place within the borders of a single country. The French Revolution did not have a territory of its own; further, to some extent its effect has been to erase all the old frontiers from the map. It has united or divided people despite their laws, traditions, characters, and languages, turning compatriots into enemies, and strangers into brothers; or rather it established, above all particular nationalities, a common intellectual homeland where men of all nations could become citizens.

In all history you will not find a single political revolution which has had this character. You will find it only in certain religious revolutions. The French Revolution must be compared to a religious revolution, if you want to find an analogy to help in understanding it.

Schiller justly remarks, in his history of the Thirty Years War,[†] that the great Reformation of the sixteenth century brought together nations which hardly knew each other, and united them through their new feelings. Indeed Frenchmen fought Frenchmen while Englishmen came to their aid, and men born at the furthest extreme of the Baltic penetrated the heart of Germany in order to protect Germans whom they had never heard of before. All foreign wars took on something of the character of civil wars; in all civil wars foreigners appeared. Every country's old interests were forgotten for new interests; questions of territory gave way to questions of principle. All the rules of diplomacy were mixed up and confused, to the great astonishment and dismay of the statesmen of the time. This is precisely what happened to Europe after 1789.

The French Revolution is therefore a political revolution which acted like and began to look like a religious revolution. Observe the characteristic traits which make it resemble one: not only is it widespread, but, like a religious revolution, it is spread by preaching and propaganda. It is a

political revolution which inspires conversions, and which preaches as
ardently to foreigners as it acts passionately at home: think what a new
sight this is! Among all the unheard-of things that the French Revolution
presented to the world, this was certainly the newest. But let us not stop
here; let us try to proceed a little further and see if this resemblance of
effects does not derive from some hidden resemblance in their causes.

Religions usually consider man in himself, without regard for what the
laws, customs, and traditions of a country have added to the common
base. Their principal purpose is to regulate the relationship between man
and God, and the general rights and duties of men toward each other,
independently of the form of society. The rules of conduct which religions
prescribe relate less to the man of a particular country or time, than to
the son, the father, the servant, the master, the neighbor. These rules are
based on human nature itself; they can be equally accepted by all men
and they are equally applicable everywhere. Thus it can be seen that religious revolutions have often had vast scope and are rarely limited, like
political revolutions, to the territory of a single people, or even to a single
race. And if one examines the subject still more closely, one finds that
the more a religion has the abstract and general character which I have
just described, the more it spreads, despite differences of laws, climate,
and men.

The pagan religions of antiquity, which were all more or less linked to
the political constitution or the social state of each people, and which
preserved even in their dogmas a certain national and often municipal
appearance, were ordinarily confined to the limits of a territory, which
they rarely left. They sometimes gave birth to intolerance and persecution; but conversion was almost entirely unknown to them. Thus there
were no great religious revolutions in the West until the arrival of Christianity. Christianity conquered in a short time a great part of the human
race, easily crossing the barriers that had halted the pagan religions. I do
not think it is lacking in respect for that holy religion to say that it owed
its triumph in part to the fact that it, more than any other, was separate
from all that might be particular to one people, to one form of government, to one social state, to one time or one race.

The French Revolution operated, with respect to this world, in precisely the same manner that religious revolutions have acted with respect
to the other world. It considered the citizen in an abstract manner, outside of any particular society, the same way that religion considers man in
general, independently of time and place. The Revolution did not only

ask what the particular rights of French citizens were, but what were the general political rights and duties of men. Because it always went back to that which was least particular, in other words to that which was most natural with respect to social state and government, the French Revolution was able to make itself accessible to everyone and was immediately imitable in a hundred different places.

Because the Revolution seemed to be striving for the regeneration of the human race even more than for the reform of France, it lit a passion which the most violent political revolutions had never before been able to produce. It inspired conversions and generated propaganda. Thus, in the end, it took on that appearance of a religious revolution which so astonished its contemporaries. Or rather, it itself became a new kind of religion, an incomplete religion, it is true, without God, without ritual, and without a life after death, but one which nevertheless, like Islam, flooded the earth with its soldiers, apostles, and martyrs.

Furthermore, one must not think that the procedures which the Revolution employed were absolutely unprecedented, and that all the ideas which it brought to light were entirely new. In all eras, even in the High Middle Ages, there have been agitators who, in order to change particular customs, have invoked the general laws of human society, who attempted to oppose the natural rights of man to the constitution of their country. But all these efforts failed. The same spark which set Europe afire in the eighteenth century was easily put out in the fifteenth. Indeed, in order for this kind of argument to produce a revolution it is necessary for certain changes to have already taken place in conditions, customs, and mores, which prepare the human mind to accept it.

There are times when men are so different from one another that the idea of one law applicable to all seems incomprehensible. There are others when it is enough to show them, as in a glass darkly, the image of such a law, for them to immediately recognize it and run towards it. The most extraordinary thing was not that the French Revolution did what it did, or that it came up with the ideas that it produced: the great novelty was that so many nations had reached a point where such practices were so effectively employed, and such principles so readily accepted.

CHAPTER FOUR

How Almost All of Europe Had Come to Have Identical Institutions and How These Institutions Fell into Ruin Everywhere

The peoples who overthrew the Roman Empire and in the end formed the modern European nations differed from each other by race, national origin, and language; they resembled each other only in their barbarism. Once established on the Empire's soil, they long fought among themselves in the midst of an immense confusion, and when they finally achieved stability, they found themselves cut off from each other by the destruction that they had wrought. Civilization being almost extinct and public order destroyed, social intercourse became difficult and dangerous, and the larger European society became fragmented into a thousand separate and hostile little societies which lived in isolation from each other. And yet from the midst of this incoherent mass suddenly emerged uniform laws.[2]

These new institutions were not imitations of Roman law; they were so alien to it that later on Roman law was used to reform and abolish them. Their form was original and distinguished them from all other laws that men have made for themselves. They corresponded to each other symmetrically, and they formed a body composed of parts so well joined that the articles of our modern law codes are no more closely linked; they were sophisticated laws designed for the use of a half-savage society.

How could such legislation have formed, spread, and finally become general throughout Europe? It is not my task to find out. What is certain is that in the Middle Ages it was found more or less throughout Europe, and that it reigned in many countries to the exclusion of all other laws.

I have had occasion to study the political institutions of medieval France, England, and Germany, and as I progressed in my work, I was astonished at the sight of the incredible similarity to be found among their laws. How could such different and separate peoples have given themselves such similar laws, I wondered? Their laws varied constantly and almost infinitely in detail, according to place, but they had the same foundation everywhere. When I found in the old German legislation a political institution, a rule, a power, I knew in advance that by looking hard I would find something substantially similar in France and England, and in fact I always did. Each of the three peoples helped me better understand the two others.

Among all three, government was conducted according to the same principles, political assemblies were formed from the same elements and given the same powers. Society was divided in the same way, and the same hierarchy was displayed between the different classes: the nobility occupied an identical position in each society; they had the same privileges, the same appearance, the same character. These were not different men, they were very much the same everywhere.

The constitutions of the towns resembled each other and the countryside was governed in the same way. The peasantry's condition varied little; the land was owned, inhabited, and farmed in the same way, the farmer subjected to the same burdens. From the borders of Poland to the Irish Sea, the manor, the lord's court, the fief, the services to be performed, the feudal dues, the corporations, everything was similar. Sometimes the names were the same, and, what is even more remarkable, a single spirit animated all these analogous institutions. I think one may suggest that in the fourteenth century the social, political, administrative, judicial, economic, and literary institutions of Europe resembled each other perhaps even more than they do today, when civilization seems to have taken care to open all roads and break down all barriers.

It is not part of my story to tell how the ancient constitution of Europe gradually became weakened and run-down; I will limit myself to the statement that by the eighteenth century it was half-ruined everywhere.[3] In general the decline was less marked in eastern than in western Europe, but everywhere the age and often the decrepitude of the old regime was visible.

The gradual decadence of the institutions proper to the Middle Ages can be followed in their archives. We know that each manor possessed registers called terriers, in which, down the centuries, were listed the boundaries of fiefs, the fees due, the services to be performed, the local customs. I have seen terriers of the fourteenth century which are masterpieces of method, clarity, organization, and intelligence. They become more obscure, undigested, incomplete, and confused as they become more recent, despite the general progress of education. It is as though political society was falling into barbarism at the same time that civil society was completing its enlightenment.

Even in Germany, where the old constitution of Europe had kept more of its original characteristics than in France, everywhere some of the institutions that it had created had already been destroyed. But it is less in considering what was missing than in observing the condition of what remained that one can judge the ravages of time. The municipal institutions which in the thirteenth and fourteenth centuries had made the chief cities of Germany rich and enlightened little republics, still existed in the eighteenth century; but they presented only a hollow facade.[4] Their laws seemed to be in force; the magistrates they established bore the same names and seemed to do the same things; but the activity, the energy, the communal patriotism, the fertile and manly virtues which they had inspired had disappeared. The old institutions had shrunk without changing shape.

All the medieval powers that still existed were struck by the same illness; they all displayed the same weakness and dilapidation. Still more, all that was associated with the ancient constitution without exactly being part of it, and preserved its forms, immediately lost its vitality. From this the aristocracy contracted a senile incapacity; political liberty itself, which had filled the Middle Ages with its works, seemed struck by sterility everywhere that it retained a medieval character. Where the provincial assemblies preserved their old constitutions unchanged, they hindered the progress of civilization more than they helped. They were foreign bodies virtually closed to the new spirit of the age. The hearts of the people deserted them and were attracted to the rulers. The antiquity of these institutions did not make them more respectable; on the contrary they discredited themselves every day by getting older; and oddly enough they inspired more hatred as they seemed to have less power to injure in their decadence. "The existing state of things," says a German writer, a contemporary and friend of the old regime, "seems to have become generally offensive to everyone and sometimes contemptible. It is strange to see how nowadays one judges everything that is old unfavorably. These new feelings exist even within our families, and trouble their peace. They extend to our housewives, who can no longer bear their old furniture." And yet in Germany, as in France at the same period, society was extremely active and daily more prosperous. But look carefully; this stroke completes the picture: everything that lived, acted, and produced was of recent origin, and not merely new, but in contradiction with the old.

It was the monarchy, which no longer had anything in common with the medieval monarchy, which now possessed different powers, had another place, another spirit, and inspired different feelings; it was the state administration which everywhere extended itself over the wreckage of the local powers, it was the hierarchy of government officials which more and more replaced the government of the nobility. All these new powers acted according to procedures and followed principles unknown to, or rejected by, the men of the Middle Ages; they were actually related to a new social state, of which the men of the Middle Ages had not had the faintest idea.

In England, where one would have initially said that the ancient constitution of Europe was still in vigor, it was the same. If we forget the old names and disregard the old forms, we find, from the seventeenth century on, the substantial abolition of the feudal system, the mixing of classes, a displaced nobility, and an open aristocracy. Wealth has become power, there is equality before the law, equal taxation, a free press, open debate; all these are new principles of which medieval society was ignorant. But these new things are exactly what, gradually and skillfully introduced into the old feudal order, reanimated it, without risking its dissolution, and filled it with fresh strength while leaving the ancient forms intact. Seventeenth-century England was already a completely modern nation which had merely preserved within itself, as if embalmed, a few medieval relics.

This brief glance outside France was necessary in order to understand what follows; for whoever has seen and studied only France will never understand anything about the French Revolution.

CHAPTER FIVE

What Did the French Revolution Really Accomplish?

The only purpose of the preceding chapters has been to throw light on this subject and facilitate the solution of the question that I posed at the beginning: What was the real purpose of the Revolution? What, in the end, was its true character? Exactly why was it made? What did it do?

The Revolution was certainly not made, as some believe, to destroy religion. Despite appearances, it was essentially a social and political revolution, and in comparison with others of its kind it did not at all tend to perpetuate disorder, to make it somehow permanent, to make anarchy into a method, as one of its principal adversaries said, but rather to in- ♪ crease the rights and power of political authority. It did not have to change the character of our civilization, as others have thought, halting its progress, nor even to fundamentally change any of the basic laws on which human society in our West has rested. When we detach the Revolution from all the accidents which briefly altered its appearance at different times and in different countries, in order to consider it in its own right, we clearly see that the Revolution's only effect was to abolish the political institutions which for several centuries had reigned unopposed among the majority of European peoples, and which we usually call feudal institutions. It did so in order to replace them with a more uniform and simple social and political order, one based on social equality.

This was enough to make an immense revolution, for independently of the fact that the old institutions were still interwoven with almost all the religious and political laws of Europe, they had inspired a mass of ideas, feelings, habits, and mores which were strongly connected to them. It required a frightful convulsion to destroy them and suddenly to extract from the social body a part which was connected to all its organs. This made the Revolution appear even bigger than it actually was. It seemed to destroy everything, because what it did destroy was related to everything and in some sense was embedded in everything.

However radical the Revolution was, it innovated much less than is generally supposed, as I will show later on. What one can say is that it entirely destroyed, or is in the process of destroying (because it is still in progress), everything that derived from aristocratic and feudal institutions in the old society, everything that was in some way connected to them, everything that bore, in the least degree, their smallest imprint. It preserved from the old world only those things which had always been foreign to the old institutions, or which could exist without them. The Revolution was least of all an accident. True, it took the world by surprise, and yet it was the result of a very long process, the sudden and violent climax of a task to which ten generations had contributed. If it had not taken place, the old social structure would nevertheless have collapsed everywhere, here sooner, there later, with the only difference that it would have continued to fall apart piece by piece instead of collapsing all at once. The Revolution finished off quickly, by a feverish and convulsive effort, without transition, without precautions, without regard for anything, what would have been done anyway, little by little, in the long run. This was its effect.

It is surprising that what seems so easy to see today was at that time so muddled and so hidden from the eyes of the most farseeing. "You want to correct the abuses of your government" says Burke to the French; "but why create something new? Why not return to your old traditions? What keeps you from recovering your ancient liberties? Or, if it is impossible for you to rediscover the long-lost shape of your ancestors' constitution, why not look to us? Here you would have found the old common law of all Europe." Burke does not realize that what stands before his eyes is the revolution which will abolish the old common law of Europe; he does not understand that this is its sole purpose.

But why did this revolution, ripening everywhere, threatening everywhere, break out in France rather than somewhere else? Why did it have certain characteristics among us which did not appear anywhere else, or did so only partially? This second question surely deserves to be asked; its examination will be the subject of the following books.

Book Two

Why Feudalism Was Hated by the People in France More Than Anywhere Else

At first glance it is surprising that the Revolution, whose real purpose was to abolish what remained of medieval institutions, did not break out in the countries where those institutions, better preserved, oppressed the people most, but, on the contrary, in those lands where the people were least oppressed: their yoke seemed least bearable where it was actually lightest.

In almost no part of Germany, at the end of the eighteenth century, was serfdom completely abolished, and in most parts the people remained attached to the soil, as in the Middle Ages.[5] Almost all the soldiers who composed the armies of Frederick the Great and Maria-Theresa were true serfs. In the majority of the states of Germany in 1788 the peasant could not leave the manor, and if he left it he could be pursued wherever he went and returned by force. He was subject to manorial justice, which watched over his private life and punished his intemperance and his laziness. He could not rise in rank, nor change his profession, nor marry without his master's consent. A great part of his time had to be given to the master's service. Several years of his youth had to be spent in the domestic service of the manor. The seigneurial corvée[†] existed in full strength, and could extend, in certain countries, up to three days a week. It was the peasant who rebuilt and maintained the lord's buildings, brought his produce to market and sold it, and was charged with carrying the lord's messages. The serf could, however, own land, but his title was always very insecure. He was required to cultivate his field in a certain way, under his lord's supervision, and he could neither sell it nor mortgage it at will. In certain cases he was required to sell its produce; in others he was forbidden to sell it: he was always required to farm his land. Even his children's inheritance did not go to them intact: a portion was ordinarily kept by the manor. I don't have to search obsolete laws for these rules, I find them even in the law code prepared by Frederick the

Great and promulgated by his successor, at the very moment when the French Revolution had just broken out.[6]

Nothing similar had existed in France for ages: the peasant came and went, bought and sold, made contracts and worked as he wished. The last vestiges of serfdom remained only in one or two of the recently conquered eastern provinces; everywhere else they had entirely disappeared, and even their abolition went back to a time so distant that its date was forgotten. The learned research of our time has shown that from the thirteenth century serfdom was no longer to be found in Normandy.

But yet another revolution had been made in the people's condition in France: the peasant had not only ceased to be a serf, he had become a *landowner*. This fact is still so poorly understood today, and it has had, as we will see, so many consequences, that I may be allowed to stop a moment to consider it.

We long believed that the division of the land dated from the Revolution and had been produced by it alone; the contrary is proved by all kinds of evidence. At least twenty years before the Revolution, one finds agricultural societies which already deplored the over-division of the soil. "The division of inheritances," says Turgot around this time, "is such that what was enough for a single family is divided among five or six children. These children and their families can no longer subsist solely from the produce of their land." Necker said, a few years later, that there was in France an *immensity* of small rural properties.

In a secret report made to an intendant[†] a few years before the Revolution, I found: "Inheritances are divided in an equal and disturbing way, and, everyone wanting to have a little of everything, pieces of land are infinitely and incessantly subdivided." Could one not believe that this was written today? I have made great efforts to partially reconstruct the land survey of the old regime and I have sometimes succeeded. According to the law of 1790 that established the land tax, each parish had to make a list of the properties then existing within its boundaries. These lists have mostly disappeared. Nevertheless, I found them in a number of villages, and, in comparing them with contemporary tax rolls, I saw that in those villages the number of agricultural proprietors reached half, often two-thirds, of the present number; which seems really remarkable when one remembers that the total population of France has increased by more than a quarter since then.

Already, as in our day, the peasant's love for the land was extreme, and all his passion to possess the soil afire. "Today lands are always sold for more than their value," says an excellent contemporary observer; this is "a result of the passion of all the inhabitants to become landowners. All the savings of the lower classes, which elsewhere are placed in banks and in government debt, here in France are devoted to the purchase of land."

Among all the new things which Arthur Young saw among us when he visited us for the first time, there was nothing which struck him more than the great division of the soil among the peasants; he states that half the land of France belonged to them. "I had no idea," he often says, "of such a state of affairs"; and, in fact, such a state of things then existed nowhere but in France or in its near vicinity.

There had been peasant proprietors in England, but they were already to be found much less frequently. In Germany one had always seen, everywhere and in all eras, a certain number of free peasants who possessed some bits of land in full ownership.[7] The special and often bizarre laws which govern peasant proprietorships are found in the most ancient Germanic feudal codes; but this kind of property had always been unusual, and the number of these small proprietors very few. The regions of Germany where, at the end of the eighteenth century, the peasant was a proprietor and almost as free as in France were mostly situated on the banks of the Rhine;[8] it is also there that the revolutionary passions of France spread the most quickly and have always been the most lively. The portions of Germany which have been, on the contrary, longest impermeable to such passions are those where nothing similar has yet occurred. A fact worth noting.

To believe that the division of the land in France dates from the Revolution is therefore to make a common mistake: the fact is much older than the Revolution. The Revolution did, it is true, sell all the lands of the clergy and a large part of the lands of the nobility; but if one wishes to consult the records of those sales, as I have occasionally had the patience to do, one will see that most of these lands were bought by people who were already landowners. Thus, if property changed hands, the number of proprietors was increased much less than is thought. There was already in France an *immensity* of proprietors, to repeat Necker's theatrical but accurate phrase.[9]

The Revolution's effect was not to divide the land but briefly to liberate it. The small proprietors in fact had been greatly hindered in their use of their land, and had borne many burdens which they were not allowed to eliminate. These burdens were doubtless heavy, but what seemed unbearable to the peasants was precisely the circumstance which ought seemingly to have eased their lot: these same peasants had been liberated from the government of their lords more than anywhere else in Europe; another revolution not less great than that which had made them landowners.

Even though the old regime is still close to us, since every day we meet people who were born under it, it already seems lost in the night of the past. The radical revolution which separates us from it has produced the effect of centuries: it has hidden what it has not destroyed. Today there are few who can give an accurate reply to this simple question: how was the countryside governed in 1789? And in fact no one would know how to answer precisely and in detail, without having studied, not the books, but the government records of that time.

I have often heard it said: the nobility, which had long ceased to take part in the government of the state, kept until the end the administration of the countryside; the lord of the land governed the peasants. This seems to be a mistake.

In the eighteenth century, all parish business was conducted by a certain number of officials who were no longer the agents of the manor and no longer chosen by the lord. Some were named by the intendant of the province, others were elected by the peasants themselves. It was up to these authorities to divide the taxes, repair churches, build schools, convoke and preside over the parish assembly. They supervised the common lands and regulated their use, brought and defended lawsuits in the name of the community. Not only did the lord no longer control the administration of all these local matters, he no longer supervised them. All the parish officials were under the administration or control of the central authority, as will be shown in the following chapter. Furthermore, one almost never sees the lord any longer acting as the king's representative in the parish, as the intermediary between the king and its inhabitants. It is no longer he who is charged with applying the laws of the state, with assembling the militia and levying the taxes, making known the commands of the prince and distributing his aid in time of need. All these rights and duties belong to others. In reality the lord is but an inhabitant whose immunities and privileges separate and isolate him from everyone else; his rank is different, not his power. In their letters to their subdelegates, the intendants take care to say that *The lord is merely the first citizen.*

If you leave the parish and consider the canton, you will find the same picture. Nowhere do the nobles govern together, no more than they do separately; this was unique to France. Everywhere else this characteristic trait of old feudal society had been partly conserved; the ownership of the land and the government of its inhabitants were still linked.

England was administered as well as governed by the principal land-owners. In the very parts of Germany where the princes had best suc-ceeded in escaping the tutelage of the nobility in state affairs, as in Prussia and Austria, the nobility had largely retained the administration of the countryside, and even if, in certain regions, the princes had gone so far as to supervise the lord, nowhere had they yet taken his place.

Indeed, the French nobility had long had contact with public admin-istration in only one respect: justice. The greatest among them had kept the right to have their own judges decide certain cases in their own name, and they still from time to time made police regulations within their do-mains. But the royal authority had gradually curtailed, limited, and sub-ordinated manorial justice, to the point that the lords who still exercised it considered it less a power than a source of income.

It was the same with all the special rights of the nobility. The political part had disappeared; the financial portion alone remained, and some-times had greatly increased.

For the moment I only want to consider those useful privileges which went par excellence by the name of feudal dues, because these were the privileges that most affected the lower classes. Today it is difficult to say what those dues still consisted of in 1789, because their number was im-mense and their diversity great, and many of them had already disap-peared or been transformed. The meaning of the words which designated them, already confused for contemporaries, has become very obscure to us. Nevertheless, when we consult the books of the feudal lawyers of the eighteenth century, and when we look carefully at local customs, we see that all the dues that still existed could be reduced to a few principal kinds; other types existed, it is true, but only as isolated examples.

Almost everywhere the traces of the manorial corvée had largely van-ished. The majority of tolls on roads had been lowered or abolished, yet there were few provinces where several did not still exist. In all provinces, the lords levied taxes on fairs and markets. We know that throughout France they enjoyed exclusive hunting rights. In general, they alone had dovecotes and pigeons; almost everywhere they forced the peasant to grind his grain at their mill and press his grapes in their press. A universal and very burdensome tax was that of "*lods* and *ventes*"; that is, a tax which was paid to the lord every time land was bought or sold within the boundaries of his manor. Throughout the country, finally, the land was burdened with rents and fees and dues payable in cash or in kind, which were owed to the lord by the proprietor, and which the proprietor could not buy out. Across all the variations, one common trait is present: all these dues were more or less connected to the land and its produce; all fell upon the farmer.

We know that clerical lords enjoyed the same advantages; for the Church, which had a different origin, a different purpose, and a different nature than feudalism, had nevertheless finally become deeply enmeshed with it. Even if it was never entirely incorporated into that foreign body, it had penetrated so deeply within it, that it was as if it was encrusted there. Thus bishops, canons, and abbots possessed fiefs or subfiefs in virtue of their ecclesiastical functions; the convent usually had the lordship of the village in which it was situated. The Church had serfs in the one part of France where they still existed; it employed the corvée, levied dues on fairs and markets, had its oven, its mill, its winepress, its stud bull. More than anywhere else in the world, the French clergy possessed the right to collect tithes.† 10

But what interests me here, is that in all of Europe the same feudal dues, *exactly the same ones,* existed then, and that in most countries on the Continent they were much heavier. I will cite only the example of the seigneurial corvée. In France, it was rare and light; in Germany it was still universal and heavy.

Furthermore, many of the dues of feudal origin which most upset our ancestors, which they considered not only unjust, but uncivilized: the tithe, the permanent agricultural dues, the perpetual payments, the lods and ventes, all that they called, in the rather dramatic language of the eighteenth century, *the enslavement of the land,* all these things were then found in part among the English; several still exist in England even today. They do not prevent English agriculture from being the most advanced and the most productive in the world, and the English people barely notice their existence.

Why, therefore, did these same feudal dues arouse in French hearts a hatred so fierce that it has even survived its object, and therefore seems inextinguishable? The cause of this phenomenon is, on the one hand, the fact that the French peasant had become a landowner, and, on the other, the fact that he had entirely escaped from his lord's government. There were doubtless many other reasons as well, but I think that these were the chief ones.

If the peasant had not owned the land, he would not have noticed the burdens which the feudal system placed on agricultural property. What does the tithe mean to someone who is not a farmer? It is only levied on the farmer's produce. What does the tax on land mean to someone who has none? What do even the hindrances to the land's use matter to someone who farms the land for somebody else? On the other hand, if the French peasant had still been governed by his lord, feudal dues would also have appeared much less unbearable to him, because he would have seen them as a natural consequence of the constitution of the country.

When the nobility possesses not only privilege but power, when it governs and administers, its special rights can be both greater and less noticed. In the feudal era, we looked at the nobility in more or less the same way as we regard the government today; one bore the burdens it imposed in consideration of the guaranties that it offered. The nobles had offensive privileges, they possessed burdensome rights, but they assured public order, dispensed justice, executed the law, came to the help of the weak, and ran public affairs. To the extent that the nobility ceased to do these things, the weight of its privileges seemed heavier, and finally their very existence seemed incomprehensible.

Imagine the French peasant of the eighteenth century, or rather the French peasant of today, for he is still the same: his condition has changed, but not his feelings. Look at him as the documents I have cited depict him, so passionately in love with the land that he devotes all his savings to buying it at any price. To acquire it he must first pay a fee, not to the government, but to some other local landowners, as foreign to him as they are to public affairs, almost as powerless as himself. Finally, he owns it; he puts his heart into it with his seed. The little piece of dirt that belongs to him in this vast universe fills him with pride and independence. However, there remain the same neighbors who tear him from his fields and force him to work elsewhere without pay. If he wants to defend his crops against their game, these men forbid it; the same men wait for him at the ford to demand a toll. There they are again at the market, where they sell him the right to sell his own crops; and when he returns home, and wants to use what remains of his wheat for himself, the wheat that has grown under his eyes and by his hands, he cannot do so without having it milled in the mill and baked in the oven of these same men. Part of the income of his little property must be used to pay their fees, and these fees are permanent and irredeemable.

Whatever he does, he encounters these troublesome neighbors everywhere. They disturb his pleasure, hinder his work, eat his produce; and when he has finished with them, still others appear, dressed in black, who take the best of his harvest from him. Imagine the situation, the needs, the character, the passions of this man and calculate, if you can, the amount of hatred and envy stored within his heart.[11]

Feudalism had remained the greatest of all our civil institutions while ceasing to be a political institution. Thus limited, feudalism aroused much more hatred, and it is correct to say that the partial destruction of medieval institutions had made them a hundred times more hateful than they would have been if left intact.

CHAPTER TWO

How Administrative Centralization Is an Institution of the Old Regime, and Not the Work of Either the Revolution or the Empire, as Is Said

I once heard a speaker, back when we had political assemblies in France, who said of administrative centralization: "That great conquest of the Revolution, which Europe envies us." I wish that centralization was a great conquest, I admit that Europe envies us for it, but I maintain that it was certainly not a conquest of the Revolution. On the contrary it was a product of the old regime and, I will add, the only part of the old regime's political constitution which survived the Revolution, because it was the only one which could adapt to the new social state which the Revolution created. The reader who has the patience to read this chapter carefully may find that I have proved my point overabundantly.

Let us leave aside what are called the *pays d'états,* that is, those provinces which governed themselves, or rather still had the appearance of partly governing themselves. The *pays d'états,* situated at the extreme boundaries of the kingdom, contained barely a quarter of the total population of France, and among them there were only two where provincial freedom really existed. I will return to the *pays d'états* later on and show to what extent the central power had subjected even them to the common rules. I want to concern myself principally with what in the official language of the time were called the *pays d'élection,*† although there were fewer elections there than anywhere else. These provinces completely surrounded Paris; they were geographically compact and formed the heart and most of the body of France.

When we first look at the former administration of the kingdom, there seems everywhere to be a variety of rules and authorities, a confusion of powers. France was covered with administrative bodies or isolated officials who were independent of one another, and who participated in government by virtue of an irrevocable right that they had purchased and that could not be taken away from them. Often their functions were so intermixed and so similar that they interfered with each other's work while doing their own.

The courts took part indirectly in the legislative process; they had the right to make official rules which had force within the limits of their jurisdictions. Sometimes they collided with the administration proper, harshly censuring its measures and issuing writs against its agents. Local judges made police regulations in the towns and villages where they presided.

The towns had extremely varied constitutions. Their magistrates bore different names, or took their powers from different sources: here a mayor, there consuls, elsewhere syndics. Some were chosen by the king, some by the old lord or by a prince of the royal house; there were some who were elected for a year by their fellow citizens, and others who had bought the right to govern them in perpetuity.

These were the remnants of the old powers; but gradually there was established among them something that was comparatively recent or transformed, which has yet to described. A uniquely powerful administrative body had developed at the center of the kingdom, near the throne, which united all powers in a new way: the *conseil du roi* or Royal Council.

It was old in origin, but most of its functions were of recent date. It was everything at once. It was a supreme court, since it had the right to overrule the decisions of all ordinary courts; it was a superior administrative tribunal—all special jurisdictions were ultimately subordinate to it. As government council, it also possessed, at the king's pleasure, legislative power. It debated and proposed laws, fixed and distributed taxes. As chief administrative council, it was up to it to establish general rules to guide government agents. It decided all important matters and supervised lesser authorities. All roads led to the Royal Council, and from it came the impulses that guided everything. In itself it did not have any authority, however. It was the king alone who decided, even when the Council appeared to decree. Even when it seemed to dispense justice, it was composed only of *advisers,* as the parlement said in one of its remonstrances.

This Council was not composed of great lords but of people of low or mediocre birth, former intendants and other people with experience in practical affairs, all serving at the king's discretion. The Council usually acted quietly and secretly, always with less pretension than power. Also, it had no fame in itself; or rather it was lost amidst the splendor of the nearby throne. It was so powerful that it affected everything, and at the same time so obscure that history has barely noticed it.

At the same time as the entire country's government was directed by a single body, almost all control of internal affairs was given to a single agent, the controller-general. If you open an almanach of the old regime, you will find that each province had its own special minister; but when we study the government and its files, we soon see that the minister of the province acted merely on a few unimportant matters. The ordinary course of affairs was directed by the controller-general; gradually he had gained control of everything which had to do with money, i.e., almost all public administration. We see him act successively as minister of finance, interior minister, minister of public works, and minister of commerce.

At the same time as the central government had, in reality, only one agent at Paris, it had but a single agent in each province. In the eighteenth century we still find great lords who bear the title of Governor of the Province. Often hereditary offices, these were the old representatives of the feudal monarchy. They were still given respect, but they no longer had any power. In reality the intendant controlled the government.

The intendant was a man of common birth, always a stranger to the province, young, a man with his career still to make. He did not exercise his powers by virtue of election, birth, or purchase. He was chosen by the government from the junior members of the Council and was always subject to dismissal. When away from the Council, he represented it, and that is why in the official language of the time he was called a *commissionnaire départi,* a "detached" commissioner. Almost all the powers possessed by the Royal Council itself were combined in his hands; he exercised them in the first instance. Like the Council, he was both administrator and judge. The intendant was in contact with all the ministries; he was the sole agent of the government's will in his province.

Beneath him, and appointed by him, an official removable at his discretion was placed in each canton: the subdelegate. The intendant was usually a recently ennobled man; the subdelegate was always a commoner. Nevertheless, he represented the entire government in the little area to which he was assigned, as the intendant did in the larger region. He was under the intendant as the intendant was under the ministry.

The Marquis d'Argenson tells us, in his memoirs, that one day Mr. Law said to him: "I would never have believed what I saw when I was controller of finance. Know that the kingdom of France is ruled by thirty intendants. You have neither a parlement, nor estates, nor governors; it is thirty subordinate officials, detached for duty in the provinces, on whom the happiness or misfortune of those provinces, their prosperity or their poverty, depend."

These all-powerful officials were, however, eclipsed by the remnants of the old feudal aristocracy and virtually lost in the radiance the aristocracy still projected. That is why, even in their own time, they were hardly noticed, although their fingers were already everywhere. In society the nobles had the advantage of rank, of wealth, and of the respect which was still given to old things. In government, the nobility surrounded the king and made up his court; they commanded the fleets, directed the armies; they were, in short, that which most struck contemporaries' eyes and too often monopolizes posterity's attention. One would have insulted a great lord by suggesting he be named an intendant; the poorest gentleman of rank would have generally refused to accept the position. The intendants were in their eyes the representatives of an interloping power, new men, appointed to govern the bourgeois and peasants, and, furthermore, not the kind of person one would wish to associate with. Nevertheless these men ruled France, as Law said and as we will see.

Let us start with the right of taxation, which to some extent contains all other rights. We know that part of the taxes were farmed out. For those, it was the Royal Council which negotiated with the financial companies, set the terms of their contracts, and fixed the mode of payment. All other taxes, like the taille, the capitation† or the vingtièmes,† were established and levied directly by the agents of the central government or under their all-powerful supervision.

By a secret decision every year, the Council fixed the total amount of the taille and its numerous parts, and also divided it among the provinces. The taille thus increased from year to year without anyone being warned of it in advance by any publicity. Since the taille was an old tax, its basis and raising had formerly been assigned to local agents, who were all more or less independent of the government, since they exercised their powers by right of birth or election, or by virtue of a purchased office. It was the lord, the parish collector, the "Treasurers of France," the "élus" who had previously administered the taille. These authorities still existed in the eighteenth century, but some no longer had anything to do with the taille, and others dealt with it only in a very secondary and completely subordinate way. Even then, all power was in the hands of the intendant and his agents; he alone, in reality, apportioned the taille among the parishes, guided and supervised the collectors, and granted delays or rebates.

With other taxes of recent date, like the capitation, the government was no longer bothered with the leftovers of the old powers; it acted alone, without any interference from the governed. The controller-general, the intendant and the Council fixed the amount of everything.

Let us move from money to men. We are sometimes astonished that the French bore the burden of military conscription so patiently during the Revolution and thereafter; but it must be remembered that they had been used to it for a long time. Conscription was preceded by the militia, a heavier burden, although the number of men demanded was smaller. Periodically the youths of the countryside were required to draw lots, and a certain number of soldiers were selected, from whom were formed militia regiments where one did six years' service.

Since the militia was a comparatively modern institution, none of the old feudal authorities were involved in it; the whole operation was run solely by agents of the central government. The Council fixed the number of militia for the kingdom and divided it among the provinces. The intendant determined the number of men to be levied in each parish; his subdelegate presided over the lottery, judged the pleas for exemption, chose which militia men could live at home and which had to leave, and delivered the latter to the military authorities. There was no appeal except to the intendant and the Royal Council.

Similarly, it could be said that outside the *pays d'états* all public works, even those of the most local interest, were decided upon and conducted solely by agents of the central power. There still existed many other independent local authorities which, like the lord, the finance office, the grand overseers, could participate in this aspect of public administration. But almost everywhere these old authorities acted little or not at all: the most cursory examination of contemporary government files demonstrates this. All the highways, and even the roads which went from town to town, were constructed and maintained from the national tax receipts. It was the Council which decided on the plans and handled the bidding. The intendant directed the work of the engineers, the subdelegate gathered the corvée which was to execute them. Only the smallest roads were left to the care of the old local authorities, and they remained impassible.

The central government's chief agent with regard to public works was, then as now, the Roads and Bridges Corps. Here everything was like it is today to an astonishing degree, despite the different times. The administration of roads and bridges had a council and a school, inspectors who annually traveled through France, and engineers who lived on-site and under the intendant's orders and were in charge of directing the work. The institutions of the old regime, which, in far greater number than is usually realized, have continued to exist in the new society, have usually lost their names in transition while retaining their form, but this one has kept both—a rare occurrence.

The central government, with the aid of its agents, took upon itself alone the maintenance of public order in the provinces. The mounted police were spread out over the kingdom in small units, and everywhere they were placed under the intendant's authority. It was with the aid of these troops, and if necessary of the army, that the intendant dealt with all unforeseen dangers, arrested vagrants, repressed begging, and put down the endless disturbances caused by the price of bread. It never happened, as previously, that the governed were called upon to help the government in this part of its task, except in the towns, where there usually existed a city guard whose officers and soldiers were chosen by the intendant.

The judiciary had retained the right to make police regulations, and often used it; but these regulations were only applicable over part of the nation, and generally in just a single place. The Council could always overturn these regulations, and very frequently did so when it was a question of lower jurisdictions. It itself made general regulations every day, equally applicable over the entire kingdom, either in regard to matters other than those dealt with by the courts, or even on the same questions previously dealt with by the judiciary. The number of these regulations, or, as they said then, these "decrees of the Council," was immense, and grew immeasurably with the approach of the Revolution. There was almost no part of the social economy or political organization which had not been modified by these decrees during the forty years before the Revolution.

In the old feudal society, if the lord had great rights, he also bore great burdens. It was up to him to help the poor within the bounds of his domain. We find a last trace of this old law of Europe in the Prussian Code of 1795, which says: "The lord must see that poor peasants receive an education. He must, insofar as possible, feed those of his vassals who do not possess any land. If some of them fall into want, he is required to come to their aid."

In France, no such law had existed for a long time. As his old powers were taken from the lord, his old obligations were withdrawn. No local authority, no council, no provincial or parish association took his place. No one was legally obligated to take care of the rural poor any more; the central government had boldly taken it upon itself alone to provide for their needs.

Every year the Royal Council assigned to each province, from the general tax receipts, certain funds which the intendants distributed to help the parish poor. It was to the intendant that the poor peasant turned. In times of food shortage, it was the intendant who had rice or wheat distributed to the people. The council made annual decrees which established, in particular places which they carefully chose themselves, charity workshops where the poorest peasants could find work in return for a small wage. We can only presume that charity given from so far away was often blind or capricious, and always very inadequate.[12]

The central government did not limit itself to coming to the aid of the peasantry in its distress. It also claimed to teach them how to get rich, to help them and if necessary to force them to learn how. For this purpose the government occasionally had its intendants and subdelegates distribute little pamphlets about agriculture, and it founded agricultural societies, promised bounties, and at great expense set up nurseries and distributed their products. It seems that it would have been more effective to reduce the weight and diminish the inequality of the burdens which then oppressed agriculture; but this is not something that was ever considered wise.

Sometimes the Council wanted to make people better-off whether they liked it or not. There were innumerable decrees which forced artisans to use certain methods and make certain products; and since the intendants were inadequate to supervise the application of all these rules, there existed inspectors-general of industry who traveled through the provinces to keep them in hand.[13]

There were decrees of the Council prohibiting certain crops from being sown on land which the council did not think appropriate. One finds decrees where it ordered vineyards torn up that in its opinion had been planted in poor soil. To this extent had the government already exchanged the role of sovereign for that of guardian.

CHAPTER THREE

How What Is Now Called Government Paternalism* Is an Institution of the Old Regime

In France, municipal liberty survived feudalism. When the nobility had already ceased to govern the countryside, the towns still kept their right to govern themselves. Up until around the end of the seventeenth century, we find them continuing to form small democratic republics

---

*I have taken the liberty of translating Tocqueville's *tutelle administrative*, which might be more strictly construed as "wardship" or "guardianship," by the broader term "paternalism," which I think better conveys his meaning to contemporary readers.—Trans.

where the magistrates were freely elected by all the people and were responsible to them, where municipal life was public and active, where the city was still proud of its rights and very jealous of its independence. In 1692, for the first time, elections were generally abolished. Municipal positions were then transformed into offices, which meant that the king sold to a few inhabitants in every town the right to govern all the others forever.

This was to sacrifice, along with the towns' freedom, their economic prosperity; for if the transformation of municipal positions into offices often had useful effects when it was a question of the judiciary, since the first prerequisite of a good judiciary is the complete independence of the judge, it never failed to be disastrous when it was a question of government proper, where above all one needs to have responsibility, subordination, and enthusiasm. The government of the old monarchy did not do this by mistake: it was very careful not to use the method it imposed on the towns on itself, and it made sure that it did not turn the intendants and subdelegates into offices obtainable by purchase.

And what deserves all the contempt that history can bestow, this great revolution was accomplished without any political purpose in mind. Louis XI had limited municipal freedoms because their democratic character frightened him; Louis XIV destroyed them without being afraid of them.[14] What proves this is that he returned their liberties to all the towns that could buy them back. In fact, he wanted less to abolish their rights than to buy and sell them, and if in fact he did abolish them, it was without intending to, purely because it was financially expedient; and oddly enough the same game went on for eighty years. Seven times, in that period, the right to elect their magistrates was sold to the towns, and when they had once again become accustomed to the pleasure, it was taken away from them in order to be sold once again. The motive behind the action was always the same, and often openly admitted. "Our financial needs," it states in the preamble to the edict of 1722, "require us to look for the most secure means of meeting them." The means were sure but disastrous for those who fell under this strange tax. "I am struck by the huge sums which have always been paid to redeem municipal offices," writes an intendant to the controller-general in 1764. "The sum of all that money, expended in useful works, would have been to the profit of the town, which, however, has experienced only the weight of authority and the privileges of the officeholders." I cannot find any more shameful aspect of the old regime anywhere.

Today it seems difficult to say how the towns of the eighteenth century

governed themselves because, besides the fact that the source of municipal power changed constantly, as has just been said, each town also still
retained a few shreds of its old constitution and its own particular customs.[15] There were, perhaps, not two identical towns in all France; rather
there was a false diversity which hid their similarities.

In 1764, the central government decided to make a general law on municipal government. Through its intendants, it had reports sent in on the
way in which things were done in each town. I rediscovered part of that
inquiry, and I ended up being convinced by my reading that municipal
affairs were carried on in the same manner almost everywhere. The differences were purely superficial and in appearance; the reality was the
same everywhere.

Most often the government of the towns was given to two assemblies.
All the big towns followed this pattern and most of the little ones. The
first assembly was composed of the municipal officials, more or less numerous in each town. They were the executive power in each town, the
city council, as it was called. Its members exercised power for a fixed
term, and they were elected, when the king had authorized their election
or the town had been able to repurchase their offices. They performed
their duties for life when the king had reestablished the offices and succeeded in selling them, which was not always the case; for this kind of
merchandise became more and more devalued, as the municipal authority
subordinated itself more to the central power. In either case the municipal officials did not get any salary, but they always received tax exemptions and privileges. There was no hierarchical order within the city
council: government was collective. There was no magistrate who was
particularly in charge of and responsible for it. The mayor was the president of the city council, not the chief executive of the city.

The second assembly, which was called the general assembly, elected
the city council in places where elections were still held and everywhere
continued to take part in the chief business of the town. In the fifteenth
century the general assembly was often composed of everyone; "this
custom," says one of the reports in the inquiry, "was in accord with the
popular spirit of our ancestors." Then the whole population elected their
municipal officials; the general assembly was sometimes consulted on particular matters, and municipal officials were responsible to the whole
people. At the end of the seventeenth century these practices were still
occasionally encountered.

In the eighteenth century, it was no longer the population itself, acting
as a body, that formed the general assembly. The general assembly was

almost always representative, but what one must remember is that nowhere was it elected by the mass of the public or imbued with its spirit. Everywhere it was composed of notables, some of whom appeared by virtue of their own rights, while others were sent by the guilds or trade organizations, each one of whose representatives obeyed the binding instructions given him by his small group.

The later one gets in the century, the more the number of notables by right multiplies in the general assemblies; the deputies of the trade guilds become less numerous or disappear. One meets only official city councilors; that is, the assembly contained only the bourgeois and almost no artisans. The people, who are less easily fooled into being content with the mere appearance of freedom than is often imagined, ceased to take any interest in the affairs of the community, and lived at home as if they were in a foreign country. From time to time the magistrates futilely tried to revive among the people the municipal patriotism which had done such wonders in the Middle Ages; the people remained deaf. The greatest interests of the town no longer seemed to concern them. It was hoped they would vote, in those places where the vain image of a free election still existed. The people stubbornly abstained. Nothing is more common than such a historical spectacle. Almost all the rulers who have tried to destroy freedom have at first attempted to preserve its forms. This has been seen from Augustus down to our own day. Rulers flatter themselves that they can combine the moral strength given by public consent with the advantages that only absolute power can give. Almost all have failed in the enterprise, and have soon discovered that it is impossible to make the appearance of freedom last where it is no longer a reality.

By the eighteenth century, the municipal government of the towns had everywhere degenerated into a small oligarchy. A few families ran everything in their own interest, far from the public eye and without being responsible to it. Throughout the whole of France, urban government was struck by this illness. All the intendants report it, but the only remedy that they can think of is to further subject the local authorities to the central government.

It was difficult, however, to go beyond what had already been done. Independently of the edicts which from time to time altered the administration of all towns, each town's particular laws were often overturned by arbitrary decrees of the Royal Council, issued upon the request of the intendant, without preliminary inquiry and sometimes without notice to the inhabitants of the town itself.[16] "This measure" say the inhabitants of a town which had been effected by such a decree, "has astonished everyone in town from top to bottom, none of whom expected anything like it."

The towns could not establish a sales tax nor levy any other kind of tax, nor mortgage, nor sell, nor sue, nor lease, nor administer, nor use their surplus income, without first obtaining a decree from the Council, after the intendant's report. All their public works were executed according to the plans and budget which the Council had approved by decree. Such works were evaluated by the intendant or his subdelegates, and it was generally the state's engineer or architect who directed them. This is something that will certainly surprise those who think that everything in France is new.

But the central government was even more involved in the towns' government than the above would indicate; its power extended still further than its rights. I found in a circular sent by the controller-general to all the intendants around the middle of the century: "You will give particular attention to everything which goes on in the municipal assemblies. You will make precise reports of what is done and suspend all decisions they take, in order to send them to me immediately along with your opinion."

In reality, one sees through the intendant's correspondence with his subdelegates that the government had its hand in all the towns' business, from the least to the most important. The government was consulted about everything, and it had a firm opinion about everything; it even supervised holiday celebrations. In some cases it was the central government which ordered demonstrations of public joy, set off fireworks, and illuminated houses. I found an intendant who fined the members of the civil guard 20 livres for being absent from the Te Deum.

Furthermore, the municipal officers had an appropriate sense of their place. "We beg you very humbly, my lord," some of them wrote to an intendant, "to grant us your goodwill and protection. We will try not to render ourselves unworthy of it, through our submission to all Your Greatness' orders." "We have never resisted your wishes, my lord," wrote others who still grandly called themselves the lords of the town.

It is thus that the bourgeoisie prepared itself for government and the people for freedom.

If only this strict submission by the towns had preserved their finances! But it did nothing of the sort. It has been suggested that without centralization the towns would have immediately bankrupted themselves. I do not know; but it is certain that in the eighteenth century centralization did not prevent them from going bankrupt. All the administrative history of the period is full of the disarray of their affairs.[17]

If we turn from the towns to the villages, we will find other powers and other forms; but the same subordination.[18] There is clear evidence that in the Middle Ages the inhabitants of each village formed a community distinct from their lord. The lord used it, oversaw it, governed it; but the community possessed in common certain goods of which it was the real owner; it elected its chiefs and it governed itself democratically.

This old parish constitution can be found among all nations that have been feudal, and in all countries where those nations have carried the remnants of their laws. In England we see traces of it everywhere, and it was still alive in Germany sixty years ago, as can be seen by reading Frederick the Great's law code. In France itself, in the eighteenth century, there still existed a few vestiges.

When I was first doing research on the nature of the old-regime parish in the archives of an intendancy, I remember that I was surprised to find, in such a poor and downtrodden community, several striking traits which I had previously encountered in the rural communities of America. They were traits which I had wrongly thought were unique to the New World. Neither community had any permanent form of representation, any municipal council properly speaking, and both were governed by officials who acted independently, under the direction of the whole community. Both occasionally had general assemblies where all the inhabitants, united in a single body, elected their magistrates and dealt with their principal affairs. They resembled each other, in a word, as much as the living could resemble the dead.

These two beings with such different fates had had, in reality, the same birth. Suddenly transported far from feudalism and made absolute mistress of itself, the medieval rural parish became the New England township. In France, separated from the lord, but enclosed in the powerful hand of the state, it became what we will now describe.

In the eighteenth century, the name and number of parish officials varied depending on the province. In old documents one sees that these officials had been more numerous when local life was more active; their number declined as local life became more sluggish. In most eighteenth-century parishes they were reduced to two: one was called the collector, while the other generally called himself the syndic. Usually these municipal officials were still elected or were supposed to be: but everywhere they had become the tools of the state more than the representatives of the community. The collector raised the *taille* under the direct orders of the intendant. The syndic, placed under the daily supervision of the intendant's subdelegate, represented him in all things which had to do with public order or the government. He was the subdelegate's chief agent with regard to the militia, public works, the execution of all the common laws.

The lord, as we have already seen, was a stranger to all the details of government; he no longer even supervised them; he did not help out. Furthermore, the efforts on which his power was formerly based now seemed unworthy to him, to such an extent that it was better for his power to be destroyed. Now one would have wounded his pride by asking him to participate. The lord no longer governed; but his presence in the parish and his privileges prevented a good parish government from establishing itself in place of his. An individual so different from all the others, so independent, so favored, destroys or weakens the rule of law.

As I will show later on, the lord's presence had made almost all the rural people who possessed any property and education flee to town one after another. Beside the lord there remained only a flock of coarse and ignorant peasants, incapable of directing the administration of their common affairs. "A parish," rightly said Turgot, "is an assembly of huts and of inhabitants equally passive." The bureaucratic files of the eighteenth century are full of complaints which arose from the incapacity, inertia, and ignorance of the parish collectors and syndics. Ministers, intendants, subdelegates, even nobles, all constantly deplored it; but none understood its causes.

Until the Revolution, the government of the rural parish in France retained something of that democratic aspect which we have seen in it in the Middle Ages. When it was time to elect the municipal officials or to discuss some common business, the village bell called the peasants before the church door; rich and poor had the right to be present there. The assembly that met, it is true, did not have any formal discussions, or any votes; but everyone could express his opinion, and a notary present for the purpose, writing in the open air, recorded the different views and took minutes.

When we compare these vain appearances of liberty with the real impotence with which they were combined, we already see in miniature how the most absolute government could be combined with some of the most extreme democratic forms, to such an extent that the charade of an apparent freedom was added to oppression. The democratic assembly of the parish could certainly express its wishes, but it had no more right to carry them out than did the town council. It could no longer even talk except when its mouth had been opened for it; for it was only after having asked the intendant's express permission, and, as they used to say appropriately, "under his good pleasure," that the parish assembly was allowed to meet. Even if it was unanimous, it could not tax itself, nor sell, nor buy, nor rent, nor sue, without permission from the Royal Council. It had to obtain a decree to repair the damage the wind had done to the church roof, or to rebuild the rectory's crumbling wall. The rural parish most distant from Paris was as subject to this rule as the closest suburb. I have seen parishes ask the Council for permission to spend 25 livres.

As a rule the inhabitants had kept, it is true, the right to elect their officials by universal suffrage; but it was often the case that the intendant told the little group of voters who it was he preferred, and this candidate was always elected unanimously. Other times the intendant annulled a free election, named the collector and the syndic himself, and indefinitely postponed new elections. I have seen a thousand examples of this.

One could not imagine any fate more cruel than that of these communal officials. The least agent of the central government, the subdelegate, made them obey his smallest whim. Often he condemned them to pay a fine; sometimes he had them imprisoned; for the guarantees which elsewhere still defended citizens against arbitrary power no longer existed here. "I have sent to prison," said an intendant in 1750, "several leaders of the disturbed communities, and I made these communities pay the expenses of the mounted police sent. They have been easily subdued by this means." Thus parish offices were considered less honors than burdens which one sought to avoid by all kinds of tricks.

And yet these last remnants of the old parish government were still dear to the peasants, and even today, of all the public freedoms, the only one they really understand is the freedom of the parish. The sole business of a public character that really interests the peasants is the parish. The same peasant who happily leaves the government of the whole nation in the hands of a master, balks at the idea of not being able to have a say in the government of his village; thus there is still substance to the most hollow forms!

What I have just said about towns and parishes must be extended to almost all bodies that had a separate existence and collective property. Under the old regime as now, there was in France no city, town, or village, no tiny hamlet, no hospital, factory, convent, or college, which could have an independent will in its own affairs, or freely administer its own goods.[19] Then, as today, the government kept the French under its tutelage, and if the insolent word paternalism had not yet been invented, the reality already had been.

CHAPTER FOUR

How Administrative Justice and the Immunity of Public Officials Are Institutions of the Old Regime

There was no country in Europe where the ordinary courts were less subordinate to the government than in France; but there was also no country where extraordinary tribunals were more common. These two things were more related than one might think. Since the king had barely any influence over the judges' fate, since he could neither fire them, nor change their residence, nor as a rule even promote them; since in a word he controlled them neither through ambition nor fear, he soon felt troubled by their independence. This led him, more than anywhere else, to limit their jurisdiction over matters which directly affected his power, and to create alongside the ordinary courts, for his own special use, a more dependent kind of tribunal, which gave his subjects the appearance of justice without making him fear its reality. In countries where the ordinary courts had never been as independent from the government as the French courts then were, as in certain parts of Germany, similar precautions were not taken and administrative justice never existed. The prince was sufficiently master of his judges that he had no need of commissioners.

If you read the royal edicts and declarations published in the last century of the monarchy carefully, as well as the decrees of the Royal Council issued in that same period, you will find few in which the government, after having taken a decision, omits to say that the challenges which might occur and the lawsuits to which they might give rise will be brought exclusively before the intendants and the Council. "His Majesty further commands that all challenges which might effect the execution of the present decree and its attachments will be brought before the intendant, to be judged by him, with right of appeal to the Council. We forbid our courts and tribunals to take note of them." This is the usual formula.

In matters regulated by laws or the old customs where this precaution had not been taken, the Council constantly intervened by means of "evocation" to remove business in which the government was interested from the hands of ordinary judges, and give itself jurisdiction. The registers of the Council are full of decrees of evocation of this kind. Little by little the exception became the rule, and fact was transformed into theory. It was established, not in the laws, but in the minds of those who applied them, as a principle of state, that all trials in which there was a public interest, or which arose from the interpretation of a government act, were not the province of ordinary judges, whose only role was to judge between private individuals. In these matters we have done nothing but find the formula; the idea belongs to the old regime.

From that time on, most legal questions which were raised in reference to tax matters were the exclusive domain of the intendants and the Royal Council. It was the same for everything relating to traffic regulations, public transportation, highways, river navigation, etc. In general, all the trials in which the public authorities were interested took place before administrative courts.

The intendants took great care to see that this exceptional jurisdiction was continually extended. They alerted the controller-general and spurred on the Council. The reason which one of these magistrates gave in order to obtain an "evocation" is worth repeating: "The ordinary judge," he said, "is under fixed rules, which require him to eliminate something that is against the law; but the Council can always depart from the rules for a useful purpose."

In accordance with this principle, one often saw the intendant or the Council take jurisdiction over trials which were related to public administration only by an almost invisible connection, or even that were clearly completely unrelated. A gentleman who had a quarrel with his neighbor, and was unhappy with the decision of his judges, asked the Council to evoke the matter; the intendant who was consulted responded: "Although it is a question here merely of an individual's rights, whose jurisdiction belongs to the ordinary courts, Your Majesty may always, when he wishes, reserve for himself the jurisdiction over any kind of business, without being accountable for Your reasons."

Through an evocation, all lower-class people who disturbed the peace by some act of violence were ordinarily sent before the intendant or the provost of the mounted police. Most of the riots so frequently provoked by the price of grain gave rise to this kind of evocation. The intendant then gathered together a certain number of people of rank, a sort of improvised prefectural council chosen by himself, and acted as a criminal judge. I have found decrees, rendered in this way, which condemned people to the galleys or even to death. Criminal trials judged by the intendant were still frequent at the end of the seventeenth century.

Modern jurists assure us that we have made great progress with respect to administrative justice since the Revolution. "Formerly the judicial and executive powers were confused," they say; "since then we have separated them and returned each to its place." In order to really appreciate the progress of which we speak, one must never forget that if, on the one hand, judicial power under the old regime constantly extended itself beyond its natural sphere of authority, on the other hand, it also never completely filled it. Whoever looks at one of these two things without the other has only a partial and incorrect idea of the subject. Sometimes the ordinary courts were allowed to make rules for public administration, which was manifestly outside their sphere; sometimes they were forbidden to judge real trials, which was to exclude them from their own domain. We have, it is true, eliminated the judiciary from the executive sphere where the old regime had very wrongly introduced it; but at the same time, as we have seen, the government of the old regime constantly intruded into the judicial sphere, and we have left it there: as if the confusion of powers were less dangerous in one direction than another, and even worse; since the intervention of the judiciary in government only hurts efficiency, while the intervention of the government in the judiciary debases people and tends to make them simultaneously revolutionary and servile.

Among the nine or ten constitutions which have been permanently established in France in the last sixty years, there was one in which it was expressly stated that no agent of the government could be sued in the ordinary courts without the government's previous permission. This article seemed so well designed that while the constitution of which it was part was destroyed, it was carefully preserved, and since then it has been carefully sheltered from our revolutions. Government officials are still in the habit of calling the privilege granted them by this article one of the great conquests of '89; but in this they are wrong, for, under the old monarchy, the government took equal pains to keep its officials from the misfortune of having to submit to the law like ordinary citizens. The only essential difference between the two periods is this: before the Revolution the government could protect its agents only through arbitrary and illegal actions, whereas since then they have been legally entitled to break the law.

When the courts of the old regime wished to try some representative of the central government, there usually intervened a decree of the Council which removed the accused from his judges and sent him before commissioners named by the Council; for, as a state counsellor of the time wrote, an administrator thus attacked would have been faced by prejudiced judges, and the king's authority would have been compromised. This kind of evocation did not take place occasionally, but daily, not only in reference to the most important officials, but even to the least. It was enough to be attached to the government by the slightest link to have nothing to fear but the government itself. An agent for the Roads and Bridges in charge of rounding up corvée labor was charged by a peasant with mistreatment. The Council evoked the matter, and the chief engineer, writing confidentially to the intendant, said: "in fact the agent is very reprehensible, but that is not a reason for letting the matter follow its normal course; for it is of the highest importance to the department of Roads and Bridges that the ordinary courts do not hear or take jurisdiction over the complaints of those subject to the corvée against the agents in charge of it. If that was allowed, work would be hindered by constant lawsuits, which public animosity against these officials would create." In another situation, the intendant himself reported to the controller-general about a government contractor who had taken his materials from a neighbor's field: "I cannot stress too much how prejudicial it would be to the interests of the government to abandon its managers to the judgment of the ordinary courts, whose principles can never be reconciled with the government's."

It has been exactly a century since these lines were written, and it seems as if the officials who wrote them could be our contemporaries.

CHAPTER FIVE

How Centralization Had Been Able to Introduce Itself among the Old Powers and Replace Them without Destroying Them

Let us now briefly summarize the three preceding chapters: a single body, placed at the center of the kingdom, which ruled public administration throughout the country; the same minister directing almost all internal affairs; in every province, a single official who dealt with all the details; hardly any lesser administrative bodies or any that could act without previous authorization; exceptional courts which judged matters in which the government was involved and protected all its agents. What is this, if not the centralization we know? Its forms are less obvious than today, its procedures less regular, its existence more difficult; but it is the same thing. We have neither added nor taken away anything important. It has been enough to knock down everything which surrounded it to make it look like what we see today.[20]

Most of the institutions which I have just described have since been imitated in a hundred different places; but at that time they were peculiar to France, and we will soon see what a great influence they had on the French Revolution and its effects. But how were such new institutions able to establish themselves in France amidst the remnants of feudal society?

It was a work requiring patience, skill, and time, more than strength and brute force. When the Revolution arrived, almost nothing of the previous system of government had been destroyed; in effect a new structure had been built underneath it. Nothing indicates that the government of the old regime had followed a plan laid down in advance in order to effect this difficult operation. It had only acted in accordance with the instinct which leads all governments to want to run everything themselves, an instinct which remains constant despite the diversity of its agents. The government had left the old powers their ancient names and honors, but it had little by little removed their authority. It had not eliminated them, but escorted them out of their domains. Profiting from this one's inertia or that one's egoism, to take their place; making use of all their vices, never attempting to correct them but always to supplant them, it finished by effectively replacing almost all the old authorities by a single official, the intendant, whose very name was unknown in the days of their birth.

The judicial power alone had impeded the government in this grand enterprise; but even there the government finally took control of the substance of power, leaving only its shadow to its adversaries. The government had not excluded the parlements from the executive sphere, but it had gradually extended its influence in such a way as to almost entirely replace them.[21] In certain fleeting and unusual cases, in times of food shortage, for example, when popular passions offered support to the magistrates' ambitions, the central government briefly allowed the parlements to govern and let them make a noise which often made a splash in history; but the government soon silently returned to its place, quietly retaking control over everyone and everything.

If we pay close attention to the parlements' struggle against royal power, we will see that it was almost always waged on political rather than administrative grounds. The quarrels usually arose from a new tax; in other words the two adversaries did not dispute about the executive but about the legislative power, over which the parlements had as few rights as they did over the executive. This is more and more the case as the Revolution approaches. As popular passions begin to burn, the parlement becomes more involved in politics, and as, at the same time, the central government and its agents become more experienced and more able, the same parlement involves itself less and less in government proper; every day, it is less an administrator and more a spokesman.

The times, moreover, constantly offered the central government new fields of action where the courts did not have the agility to follow them; it was a question of new matters for which there were no precedents and which were foreign to the parlements' routine. Society, which was making great advances, created new needs every minute, and every one of them was a new source of power for the central government; for only the government was in a position to satisfy them. While the executive authority of the courts remained fixed, the government's was mobile, and constantly extended itself along with civilization.

The Revolution which approached, and began to stir the minds of all the French, suggested to them a thousand new ideas which the government alone could realize. Before it overthrew the government, the Revolution improved it. The government perfected itself like everything else. This is extremely striking when one studies the archives. The controller-general and the intendant of 1780 barely resemble the intendant and controller-general of 1740; government had been transformed. Its agents were the same, but they were moved by a different spirit. As government became more detailed, more extended, it also became more uniform and more knowledgeable. It moderated itself while succeeding in taking over everything; it oppressed less while it controlled more.

The first efforts of the Revolution destroyed this great royal institution; it was restored in 1800. It was not, as has been said so many times, the principles of 1789 which triumphed then and thereafter with regard to public administration, but on the contrary those of the old regime, which were then revived and remain in existence. If you ask me how this part of the old regime was able to transport itself in its entirety into the new society and be incorporated within it, I will reply that, if centralization did not perish in the Revolution, it was because centralization itself was the beginning of that Revolution and its sign. And I will add that, when a people has destroyed its aristocracy, it runs towards centralization as if self-impelled. It then requires far less effort to encourage it down the slope towards centralization than to hold it back. In such a nation's midst all powers tend naturally towards unity, and it is only with great skill that one can succeed in holding them apart.

The democratic revolution, which destroyed so many old-regime institutions, thus had to consolidate this one, and centralization took its place
so naturally in the society which the democratic revolution formed, that
we have easily been able to think it one of the new society's own works.

CHAPTER SIX

On Bureaucratic Habits under the Old Regime

One could not read the correspondence of an old-regime intendant
with his superiors and subordinates without noting how the similarity of institutions makes the officials of that time similar to those of our
own. They seem to shake hands across the abyss of the Revolution which
separates them. I would say the same of the governed. Never has the
power of legislation over people's minds been made more visible.

The minister had already conceived the desire to see every detail with
his own eyes and to decide everything himself in Paris. This passion grew
as time went on and administration improved. Towards the end of the
eighteenth century, not even a charity workshop located in the depths of
a far-distant province could be established but that the controller-general
wanted to directly supervise its expenses, write its regulations, and choose
its location. Did someone want to create a poorhouse? They must report
to him the names of the beggars who came there and tell him exactly
when they entered and when they left. From the middle of the century
(1733), M. d'Argenson writes: "The details confided to the ministers are
immense. Nothing is done without them, everything by them, and if their
knowledge is not as broad as their powers, they are forced to leave everything to commissioners who become the real masters." A controller-
general did not only ask for reports on business, but information about
individuals. The intendant inquired in turn of his subdelegates, and repeated word for word everything they told him as if he knew it himself.

In order to run everything from Paris, and know everything there, it
was necessary to invent a thousand new means of control. The paperwork
was already enormous, and official procedure was so slow that I have
noticed that it always took at least a year for a parish to obtain authorization to rebuild its bell-tower or repair its rectory; usually two or three
years passed before the request was granted. The Council itself remarked
in one of its decrees (29 March 1773) "that official formalities involve infinite delays in business and all too often give rise to very justified complaints; however the formalities are absolutely necessary."

I thought that the taste for statistics was peculiar to present-day bureaucrats, but I was wrong. Towards the end of the old regime, little preprinted forms were often sent to the intendant, which he merely had to have his subdelegates and parish syndics fill out. The controller-general had reports made on the type of land, its use, the kind and quantity of its produce, the number of animals, the work-habits and mores of its population. The information thus obtained was neither less detailed nor more accurate than that which our mayors and subprefects provide today in similar cases. On these occasions the judgment which the subdelegates gave about those they governed was generally unfavorable. They often returned to the refrain that "the peasant is naturally lazy, and only works because he must in order to live." This is an economic doctrine widespread among government officials.

Even the official language of the two periods bears a striking resemblance. In both eras the style is equally colorless, verbose, vague, and flabby; each writer's own character is hidden and loses itself in the common mediocrity. If you have read a prefect you have read an intendant.

Only towards the end of the century, when the individual styles of Diderot and Rousseau had had time to spread and be diluted in ordinary language, does the false sensibility which fills those writers' books win over the government officials, and even spread to the accountants. The official style, whose base was usually very dry, then became mellow and sometimes almost tender. A subdelegate complains to the intendant of Paris "that in the course of his duties he often suffers sorrows heart-rending to a sensitive soul."

The government distributed, as it does today, a certain sum as charity to the parishes, on the condition that the inhabitants also had to make a certain contribution themselves. When the sum the inhabitants had contributed was sufficient, the controller-general wrote in the margin of the documents: *Good, express satisfaction;* but when it was unusually large he wrote: *Good, express satisfaction and sensibility.*

The bureaucracy, almost all bourgeois, already formed a class with its own character, its own traditions, virtues, honor, its own pride. It was the aristocracy of the new society, which was already alive and formed: it was only waiting for the Revolution to make room for it.

Already what characterized government in France was the violent hatred which the government felt for all those outside it, noble or bourgeois, who wanted to concern themselves with public affairs. The smallest independent body which seemed to want to come into being without its permission frightened the government; the tiniest free association, what-

ever its object, disturbed it; it only allowed those which it had arbitrarily
created and governed to exist. It disliked even the great trade guilds
themselves; in a word, it disliked interference by citizens in any way in the
examination of their own business; the government preferred sterility to
competition. But since one must always give the French the pleasure of a
little license, to console them for their servitude, the government permitted free discussion of all kinds of general and abstract theories on questions of religion, philosophy, morals, and even politics. It freely allowed
attacks on the fundamental principles on which society was then based,
and even allowed disputes about God himself, provided that its least
agents were not criticized. The government thought that all the rest was
irrelevant to it.

Although the newspapers of the eighteenth century, or as they were
then called, the gazettes, contained more poetry than polemic, the government already regarded that minor power with a jealous eye. It was
tolerant about books but already very hard on newspapers; not being able
to absolutely eliminate them, it attempted to make them serve only its
own purposes. I found, dated 1761, a circular addressed to all the intendants of the kingdom, where it was announced that the king (Louis XV)
had decided that from then on the *Gazette de France* would be written
under government supervision: "His Majesty wishing," says the circular,
"to make this newspaper interesting and to assure its superiority over all
others. In consequence," adds the minister, "you will send me a bulletin
on everything that happens in your region that might interest the public,
particularly things which relate to natural philosophy and history, or any
unusual and interesting facts." Attached to the circular was a prospectus
which announced that the new gazette, although appearing more often
and containing more material than the newspaper it replaced, would cost
subscribers much less.

Armed with these documents, the intendant wrote to his subdelegates
and put them to work; but they started out by replying that they knew
nothing. Then there came a new letter from the minister, bitterly complaining of the provinces' barrenness. "His Majesty commands me to tell
you that he intends you to take this matter very seriously and give the
clearest possible orders to your agents." The subdelegates then complied:
one of them reported that a salt smuggler had been hung and shown great
courage; another, that a woman in his district had given birth to triplets;
a third, that a terrible storm had taken place, which, in fact, had not
caused any harm. One of them declared that, despite all his efforts, he
had not been able to find anything worth reporting, but that he would

himself subscribe to such a useful gazette and that he was going to ask all good people to imitate him. So much effort, however, appears to have been of little use; for a new letter tells us that "the king, who has the goodness," says the minister, "to personally enter into the details of the measures relative to the improvement of the gazette, and who wishes to give this newspaper the superiority and renown that it deserves, has shown much discontentment that his wishes have been so poorly fulfilled." One sees that history is an art gallery where there are few originals and many copies.

Further, it must be recognized that in France the central government has never imitated those governments of southern Europe, which seem to take over everything in order to do nothing. The French government often showed great intelligence in its task and always great energy. But its activity was often fruitless and even counterproductive, because sometimes it wished to do things that were beyond its strength, or to do something beyond anyone's control.

The government barely undertook, or quickly abandoned, the most necessary reforms, which required perseverance in order to succeed; but it constantly changed some rules and laws. Nothing remained at rest for an instant in the sphere which it inhabited. New rules succeeded one another so quickly that officials, even when given orders, often had difficulty figuring out how to obey them. Municipal officials complained to the controller-general himself of the extreme mutability of secondary legislation. "The variation of financial rules alone," they said, "is such that they do not permit a municipal official, even if he were permanent, to do anything but study the new rules as they appear, to the point of being forced to neglect his own job."

Even when the law was not changed, the way it was applied changed daily. When one hasn't seen the old regime at work, reading the secret documents it has left, one cannot imagine the contempt into which the law had eventually fallen, even in the minds of those who applied it, when there was no longer any political assembly, or newspaper, to slow down their capricious activity and limit the arbitrary and changing whims of the ministers and their departments.

One can hardly find any decrees of the Council that do not mention previous laws, often of very recent date, which have been made but not executed. There was in reality not an edict, not a royal declaration, nor letters patent solemnly registered, which did not incur a thousand modifications in practice. One can see from the letters of the controller-general and the intendants that the government constantly allowed exceptions to its rules. It rarely broke the law, but every day it made it bend in every direction, according to the particular case and in order to make its work easier.

The intendant writes to the minister about a sales tax from which a state contractor wishes to be exempt: "It is clear that to take literally the edicts and decrees which I have just cited, no exemption from this tax exists; but those who are experienced in the matter know that with such laws it is as with the penalties which they impose, and that, although one finds such prohibitions in almost all the edicts, declarations, and decrees relative to the establishment of taxes, that has never stopped exceptions being made." This is the old regime in a nutshell: a rigid rule, lax implementation; this is its character.

Anyone who judged the government of those times by the list of its laws would fall into the most foolish errors. I found, dated 1757, a royal declaration which condemned to death all those who authored or printed writings against religion or the established order. The bookseller who sold them and the merchant who transported them had to bear the same punishment. Have we gone back to the century of St. Dominic? No, this was exactly when Voltaire reigned.

We often complain that the French hold the law in contempt; alas! When could they have learned to respect it? Among the men of the old regime, the place that the idea of the law ought to hold in the human mind was vacant, one might say. Every lawyer asked for a departure from the established rules in his favor with as much insistence and authority as if he were demanding a return to them. And in fact no one ever brought up the law as an objection except when they wanted to politely say no. The people's submission to authority was still complete, but their obedience was the result of habit rather than will; for if by chance they happened to be moved, the smallest excitement could immediately lead to violence, and it was almost always put down by violence and caprice, rather than by law.

In the eighteenth century the central power in France had not yet acquired that healthy and vigorous constitution which we have seen in it thereafter; nevertheless, since it had already succeeded in destroying all the intermediate powers, and since between it and the individual there was nothing but an immense empty space, from a distance it already appeared to everyone as the only location of the social machine, the unique and necessary agent of public life. Nothing shows this better than the writings of its detractors themselves. When the long malaise that preceded the Revolution began to make itself felt, all kinds of new social and political theories blossomed. The purposes of the reformers varied, but their means were always the same. They wanted to borrow the strength of the central power and use it to destroy and rebuild everything according to the new plans they thought up; only the state appeared to be sufficient to accomplish such a task. The power of the state must be as unlimited as its rights, they said; it was only necessary to convince the state to make proper use of that power. The elder Mirabeau, that gentleman so infatuated with the rights of the nobility that he rudely called the intendants *trespassers* and declared that if one left to the government alone the choice of judges, the courts would soon be nothing but *packs of commissioners,* Mirabeau himself had confidence only in the action of the central power in order to realize his dreams.

These ideas did not stay in books; they penetrated all minds, were mingled with mores, infused habits, and spread everywhere, even into everyday life. No one thought that any important business could be well managed without the involvement of the state. The farmers themselves, people ordinarily very impatient of instruction, were brought to believe that if agriculture was not progressing, it was chiefly the government's fault, because it gave them neither enough advice nor enough help. One of them wrote to an intendant, in an irritated tone in which one can already hear the Revolution: "Why doesn't the government name inspectors who would go into the provinces once a year to see the state of the crops, who would teach the farmers how to improve them, who would tell them what to do with their animals, how to fatten them, raise them, sell them and where one ought to market them? These inspectors ought to be well-paid. The farmer who showed the best crops would receive public honors." Inspectors and medals! This is an idea that would never occur to a Suffolk farmer.

In most eyes, there was already none but the government who could assure public order: the masses feared only the mounted police; the wealthy had confidence in them alone. For both, the police horseman was not only the principal defender of order, he was order itself. "There is no one," says the Guyenne provincial assembly, "who has not noticed how the sight of a mounted policeman is enough to restrain the most insubordinate men." [22] So everyone wanted to have a squad on his doorstep. The archives of an intendancy are full of this kind of request; no one seemed to suspect that behind the protector might hide the master.

What was most striking to the émigrés when they arrived in England was the absence of these police. It filled them with surprise and sometimes with contempt for the English. One of them, a distinguished man,

but one whose education had not prepared him for what he was seeing, wrote "it is absolutely true that an Englishman consoles himself for
having been robbed by saying that at least there are no police in his country. He who is angry at everything that disturbs the peace, nevertheless
consoles himself for the sight of seeing the seditious circulate within society with the thought that the letter of the law is more important than
any other consideration." "These false ideas," he added, "are not fixed in
all minds, there are some wise men who are against them, and this wisdom must in time prevail."

That these English follies might have had something to do with their
liberties never entered the writer's head. He would rather explain this
phenomenon by more scientific reasons: "In a country where the climate
is humid and the density of the circulating air gives the temperament a
serious tinge, people are disposed to prefer serious subjects. The English
nation is therefore by nature interested in matters of government, the
French nation distant from them."

The government having thus replaced Providence, it was natural that
everyone invoke it in his own need. One finds an immense number of
requests which, always founding themselves on public interest, nevertheless deal only with petty private interests.[23] The files which contain them
were perhaps the only place where all classes of old regime society mixed.
Reading them is depressing: peasants ask to be compensated for the loss
of their animals or their house; well-off landowners request help in man-
aging their lands; industrialists ask for privileges from the intendant to
guarantee them against any troublesome competition. It is very common
to see manufacturers confide to the intendant the poor state of their business, and beg him to obtain some help or a loan from the controller-
general. An account had been opened, it seems, for this purpose.

The nobility themselves were sometimes great beggars. Their rank
can be recognized only because they beg with a very haughty tone. It
was the tax of the vingtième which, for many of them, was the cause of
their dependence. Their payment of this tax was fixed each year by the
Royal Council on the intendant's recommendation, and so it was to the
intendant that they usually addressed themselves for postponements and
abatements. I have read a ton of these requests made by nobles, almost
all titled and often great lords, requests made because, they said, of the
insufficiency of their income or the bad state of their affairs. Usually,
noblemen called the intendant only "Mister," but I have noticed that in
these circumstances they always called him "My Lord," as the bourgeois
did. Sometimes pride and poverty mingle in these pleas in an amusing

way. One of them wrote to an intendant: "Your feeling heart would never allow a father of my rank to be taxed strictly according to the rules, as a father of common rank would be."

In times of food shortage, so frequent in the eighteenth century, the population of each district turned as one to the intendant and seemed to expect its food from him alone. It is true that everyone already blamed the government for all their problems. The most inevitable things were its fault; it was even blamed for the weather.[24]

Let us no longer be astonished at seeing with what marvelous ease centralization was reestablished in France at the beginning of this century. The men of '89 had knocked down the building, but its foundations had remained in the very souls of its destroyers, and on those foundations it was possible to rebuild it again, and to construct it more solidly than ever.

CHAPTER SEVEN

How France, of All the Countries of Europe, Was the One Where the Capital City Had Already Acquired the Greatest Domination over the Provinces, and Consumed the Entire Country

It is neither the location, nor the grandeur, nor the wealth of a capital city which causes its political predominance over the rest of the empire, but the nature of the government. London, which is as populous as a kingdom, has up to now not exercised a sovereign influence over the destiny of Great Britain. No American citizen thinks that the people of New York City could decide the fate of the Union. Still more, no one, even in the state of New York, thinks that the particular will of that city could control things by itself. However, New York City today contains as many people as Paris did at the outbreak of the Revolution.

Paris itself, even during the Wars of Religion,[†] was by comparison with the rest of the kingdom as populous as it would be in 1789. Nevertheless, it could decide nothing. At the time of the Fronde,[†] Paris was still nothing but the biggest city in France. In 1789 it was already France itself.

Already in 1740 Montesquieu wrote to one of his friends: in France nothing exists but Paris and the distant provinces, because Paris has not yet had time to devour them. In 1750, the marquis de Mirabeau, a dreamer, but sometimes profound, said of Paris without naming it: "Capitals are necessary, but if the head becomes too big, the body gets apoplexy and everything dies. Therefore, what will happen if, leaving the provinces to some kind of direct control and regarding their inhabitants as second-class citizens, so to speak; if, in making no source of recognition and no avenue for ambition available outside the capital, all talent is attracted to the capital city!" Mirabeau called this a kind of silent revolution, one which depopulated the provinces of their notables, their businessmen, and their intellectuals. The reader who has read the preceding chapters carefully already knows the causes of this phenomenon; to note them again here would be to abuse the reader's patience.

The government was not blind to this revolution but noticed it only in its most material form, the growth of the city of Paris. The government saw Paris extending itself daily, and was afraid that it would become difficult to govern such a big city properly. One finds a great number of royal regulations, principally from the seventeenth and eighteenth centuries, whose purpose is to arrest this growth. The rulers concentrated the entire public life of France more and more in or near Paris, and yet they wanted Paris to stay small. It was forbidden to build new houses, or it was required that they be built only in the most expensive way in the least attractive neighborhoods, which were selected in advance. Every one of these ordinances states, it is true, that despite the preceding one Paris has not stopped growing. Six times during his reign, Louis XIV in his omnipotence tried to contain Paris and failed: the city grew constantly, despite the edicts. But its predominance grew still more rapidly than its walls; what assured this was less what happened within its bounds than what happened outside them.

At the same time, in fact, local freedoms were disappearing more and more. Everywhere the vital signs of independent life ceased; the different characteristic traits of the provinces were mixed together; the last traces of former public life were erased. However, it was not that the nation was in decline; on the contrary there was activity everywhere, but its only source was Paris. I will give just one example out of a thousand for this. In the reports made to the ministry on the state of the book trade, I found that in the sixteenth century and the beginning of the seventeenth, there were important publishers in provincial towns which in the eighteenth century no longer had any publishers, or whose publishers no longer did anything. It would be impossible to doubt that infinitely more writings of all kinds were published at the end of the eighteenth century than in the sixteenth; but the movement of thought no longer originated anywhere but at the center. Paris had succeeded in devouring the provinces.

When the French Revolution broke out, this first revolution had been entirely completed.

The famous traveler Arthur Young left Paris a little after the meeting of the Estates-General and a few days before the taking of the Bastille; the contrast he noticed between what he had just seen in the city and what he found beyond it took him by surprise. In Paris, everything was noise and motion, every minute produced a political pamphlet; they were printed at the rate of ninety-two a week. Never, he said, had he seen anything like it, even in London. Outside of Paris, everything seemed silent and inert; few pamphlets were printed and no newspapers. The provinces, however, were roused and ready to burst out, but they were immobile; if the citizens occasionally gathered, it was to learn the news that was expected from Paris. In every town, Young asked the inhabitants what they were going to do. "The response is the same everywhere," he says: "We're only a provincial town, we have to see what they'll do in Paris,"— "These people do not even dare to have an opinion," he adds, "until they know what people think in Paris."

We are astonished at the surprising ease with which the Constituent Assembly[†] was able to destroy, at one stroke, all the old provinces of France, and methodically divide the kingdom into eighty-three separate parts, just as if it was a question of virgin soil in the New World. Nothing was more surprising or even terrifying to the rest of Europe, which was unprepared for such a sight. "This is the first time," said Burke, "that we have seen people cutting their country up into pieces in such a barbarous fashion." It seemed, in fact, that a living body was being torn apart: but only the dead were being dismembered.

At the same time that Paris was thus completing its acquisition of omnipotence with respect to the rest of the kingdom, within Paris another change was being accomplished which was not less worthy of history's attention. Instead of being only a commercial town, a place of consumption and pleasure, Paris had become a town of industry and manufacturing; a second fact which in the end gave a new and more formidable character to the first.

The event had distant origins; it seems that from the Middle Ages Paris was already the most industrial city in the kingdom, just as it was the biggest. This becomes evident as one approaches modern times. As all government business was attracted to Paris, industry rushed in too. As Paris became more and more the model and arbiter of taste, the unique center of power and art, the principal location of national activity, the industrial life of the nation retreated there and became more concentrated.

Although the statistical documents of the old regime usually do not merit much trust, I think that one can safely argue that during the sixty years which preceded the French Revolution, the number of workers more than doubled in Paris, while, in the same period, the general population of the city increased by barely a third. Independently of the general causes which I have just mentioned, there were some very particular ones which attracted workers to Paris from all over France, and gradually brought them together in certain neighborhoods which they ended up occupying virtually all by themselves. The shackles of industry forged by the contemporary tax code were less heavy in Paris than anywhere else in the kingdom: nowhere could one so easily escape the yoke of the guild-masters. In this respect certain suburbs, especially the St. Antoine and Temple districts, enjoyed very great privileges. Louis XVI considerably extended the prerogatives of the St. Antoine district, and did his best to accumulate there a huge population of workers, "wishing," said that unlucky prince in one of his edicts, "to give to the workers of the St. Antoine district a new sign of our protection, and to deliver them from hindrances which are prejudicial to their interests as well as to the freedom of commerce."

The number of factories, workshops, and blast furnaces had so increased in Paris on the eve of the Revolution, that the government finally became alarmed by it. The sight of this progress filled it with several very imaginary fears. One finds among others a 1784 decree of the Council, where it is said that "the King, fearing that the rapid multiplication of manufactures will entail a consumption of wood which would cause harm to the provisioning of the town, from now on prohibits the creation of this kind of establishment within fifteen leagues of Paris." But as to the real danger that such a concentration might provoke, no one feared it. Thus, Paris had become the master of France, and the army that would become master of Paris had already gathered.

We are more or less agreed today, it seems to me, that government centralization and the omnipotence of Paris have counted for much in the fall of all the governments that we have seen succeed one another for the past forty years. I will easily show that we must attribute to the same factor a large role in the sudden and violent fall of the old monarchy, and that we must number it among the chief causes of that first revolution that gave birth to all the others.

CHAPTER EIGHT

That France Was the Country
Where People Had Become Most Alike

Anyone who carefully considers France under the old regime will encounter two very different perspectives. It seems that everyone who lived there, particularly those in the middle and higher reaches of society, the only ones who could make themselves heard, was exactly the same. However, among this uniform crowd, there still obtruded a multitude of little barriers which divided it into many groups, and each of these little sections looked like a separate society, which was concerned only with its own interests and did not take part in the common life.

I think of this almost infinite division, and I realize that in these circumstances nowhere were the citizens less prepared to act together and lend one another mutual support in a time of crisis, so that a great revolution was able to turn this society upside down in a moment. I imagine all those little barriers within society removed by that great outbreak itself; I immediately perceive a mass more compact and more homogeneous than perhaps any the world had ever seen.

I have told how, in almost all the kingdom, independent provincial life had long been extinct; this had greatly contributed to making all the French very like one another. Across the differences which still existed, the nation's unity was already apparent; the uniformity of legislation makes this clear. As one descends the course of the eighteenth century, one sees an increasing number of edicts, royal declarations, decrees of the Council which apply the same rules, in the same way, to all parts of the empire. It was not only the government, but the governed, who conceived the idea of such a general and uniform legislation, everywhere the same, the same for all; this idea is evident in all the projects for reform which follow one another during the thirty years preceding the outbreak of the Revolution. Two centuries before, the very substance of such ideas, if one can speak thus, would have been lacking.

Not only did the provinces resemble one another more and more, but in each province people of different classes, at least those who were placed above the masses, became more and more similar, despite the particularities of their rank. Nothing highlights this more than reading the cahiers presented by the different orders in 1789. We see that those who wrote them varied greatly in their interests but that in everything else they showed themselves alike.

If you study how things happened during the early Estates-General, you will see an entirely different spectacle: the bourgeois and the noble had more common interests, more common business; they gave evidence of much less reciprocal dislike; but they still seemed to belong to two separate races. Time, which had maintained and in many respects aggravated the privileges which separated these two groups, had worked to make them remarkably similar in everything else.

For several centuries the French nobility had constantly impoverished itself. "Despite its privileges, the nobility ruins itself and exhausts itself every day, and the Third Estate[†] acquires its fortunes," sadly wrote a nobleman in 1755. The laws that protected noble property were still the same, however; nothing in their economic situation seems different. Nevertheless, everywhere the nobility were impoverished in direct proportion to their loss of power.

One might say that, with human institutions as with human beings, independently of the organs which carry out the various functions of existence, there exists an invisible central power which is the vital principle. When that vital flame is extinguished, it is in vain that the organs seem to act as they did before; everything slows down at the same time and dies. The French nobility still had entailments (Burke even notes that in his time entailments were more common and more strict in France than in England), they still had primogeniture, perpetual agricultural dues, and all that were called the useful privileges; they had been relieved of the heavy obligation to make war at their own expense, and yet they had retained, and even considerably extended, their immunity from taxation; that is, they had kept the tax-exemption while shedding the burden. They further enjoyed several other financial advantages which their ancestors had never possessed; and yet they were gradually impoverished in proportion to their loss of the exercise and spirit of government. It is to this gradual impoverishment itself that we must partially attribute the great division of landed property that has been noted above. The noble had ceded his land, piece by piece, to the peasants, retaining only his manorial dues, keeping only the appearance rather than the substance of his old position.[25] Several provinces of France, like the Limousin of which Turgot speaks, possessed only a crowd of poor nobles, who owned hardly any land, and lived from seigneurial rights and agricultural dues.

"In this region," says an intendant, since the beginning of the century "the number of noble families still amounts to several thousand, but there aren't fifteen of them who have more than 20,000 livres of income." I read in a kind of instruction that another intendant (of the Franche-Comté) left to his successor in 1750: "The nobility of this region is good enough, but very poor, and it is as proud as it is poor. It is much humbled in comparison with what it once was. It was not bad policy to keep it poor, in order to make it serve, and keep it in need of us. It forms," he adds, "an organization where one must possess at least four quarters in order to be admitted.* This organization does not possess an official permit, but is merely tolerated, and it meets only once a year, in the intendant's presence. After having eaten and heard mass together, these nobles each return home, some on old nags, others on foot. You will see how comic this assembly is."

This gradual impoverishment of the nobility was more or less evident, not only in France but in all parts of the Continent, where, as in France, the feudal system was disappearing without being replaced by a new kind of aristocracy. Among the German peoples who bordered the Rhine, this decadence was visible everywhere and very much remarked. The opposite was noticed only among the English. There, the old noble families that still existed had not only kept but greatly increased their wealth; they had remained first in riches as well as in power. The new families that had arisen alongside them had only imitated their opulence without surpassing it.

In France, the commoners alone seemed to have inherited all the wealth that the nobility had lost. One might have said that they grew solely from the nobility's flesh. However, no law forbade the bourgeois from ruining himself, or helped him get richer; he nevertheless enriched himself constantly; in many cases he had become as rich, and sometimes richer, than the noble. Still more, his wealth was often the same kind: although he usually lived in town, he was often a landowner; sometimes he even bought seigneurial privileges.

Their education and way of life had already created a thousand similarities between the bourgeois and the noble. The bourgeois had as much education as the nobleman, and, as must be noted, his education had often been received in exactly the same place. Both were enlightened by the same sun. For one as for the other, their education had been equally theoretical and literary. Paris, more and more become the only teacher of France, ended up giving the same shape and a similar way of thinking to all minds.

---

*By "four quarters," Tocqueville means four quarters of nobility, that is, one must have had not only noble parents but noble grandparents, which would result in four quarters on one's coat of arms.—Trans.

Doubtless, one could still perceive a difference between the manners of the nobility and the bourgeoisie at the end of the eighteenth century; for there is nothing which equalizes so slowly as those surface mores which we call manners. But, at bottom, everyone above the masses resembled one another; they had the same ideas, the same habits, the same tastes, were inclined to the same pleasures, read the same books, spoke the same language. The only difference between them was in their rights.

I doubt that this similarity existed to the same extent anywhere else in the world, not even in England, where the different classes, although solidly connected to each other by common interests, still often differed in mind and mores; for the political liberty which that admirable power possessed, which created the necessary relations and the mutual links of subordination among all citizens, nevertheless did not always make them the same. It is the rule of a single individual which, in the long run, always has the inevitable effect of making people alike, and of making them mutually indifferent to each other's fate.

CHAPTER NINE

How Such Similar Men Were More Divided than Ever Before, Separated into Small Groups That Were Estranged from and Indifferent to One Another

Let us now consider the other side of the picture, and see how the same French, who were so similar, were, however, perhaps more isolated from one another than could be seen anywhere else, and even more isolated than they had ever previously been in France.

There is much in the notion that, when the feudal system was established in Europe, what has since been called the nobility did not immediately form a *caste* but was composed, in the beginning, of all the leading people in the nation, and was thus at first nothing but an aristocracy. This is not a question I wish to discuss here. It is sufficient to remark that since the Middle Ages the nobility had become a caste; that is, birth was its distinguishing feature. It indeed preserved the true mark of an aristocracy, that of being a group of citizens who govern; but it was birth alone that decided who should be at the head of this body. Everyone who was

not born noble was outside this closed and separate class, and occupied a •
more or less high but always subordinate place in the state.

Everywhere that feudalism was established on the European continent,
it ended up becoming a caste system; only in England did it again become an aristocracy. I have always been astonished that a fact unique to
England among modern nations, and which alone could make sense of
the peculiarities of its laws, its mind, and its history, has not attracted
more attention from philosophers and statesmen, and that habit has made
it invisible to the English themselves. It has often been half-seen, half-
described; never, it seems to me, has it been fully and completely grasped.
Montesquieu, visiting Great Britain in 1739, wrote perceptively: "Here I
am in a country which hardly resembles the rest of Europe"; but he added
nothing more.

It was much less its parliament, its freedom, its press, its jury, which
made England even then so different from the rest of Europe, but rather
something much more effective, and much more peculiar. England was
the only country where the caste system had not been merely changed but
really destroyed. In England, nobles and commoners together engaged in
the same businesses, pursued the same professions, and, what is still more
important, married each other. There the daughter of the greatest lord
could already marry a new man without shame.

If you want to know if caste, and the ideas, habits, and barriers that it
has created among a people have truly been eliminated, consider their •
marriages. Only there will you find the decisive sign that you are looking
for. Even now in France, after sixty years of democracy, you will often
look for it in vain. The old and new families, which seem merged in everything, still avoid joining themselves together in marriage as much as
possible.

It has often been remarked that the English nobility has been more
prudent, more able, more open than any other. What ought to be said is
that there has long been no nobility, strictly speaking, in England, if one
takes the word in the old limited sense which it has kept everywhere else.
This unique revolution is lost in the depths of time, but there still remains one living witness: language. For several centuries the word "gentilhomme" [gentleman] has entirely changed its meaning in England, and
the word "roturier" no longer exists. When Molière wrote the following
line from *Tartuffe* in 1664, "Et tel que l'on le voit, il est bon gentilhomme"
("And, as one sees, he is very much a gentleman"), it would already have
been impossible to translate it literally into English.

If you want to make another application of linguistics to history, follow across time and space the fate of this word "gentleman," of which
our word "gentilhomme" was the ancestor. As ranks became closer and
mixed with each other in England, the definition of "gentleman" was proportionately extended. Every century it was applied to people placed a
bit lower in the social scale. Finally, it traveled to America with the English. There it is used to designate any citizen indiscriminately. Its history
is the history of democracy itself.

In France, the word "gentleman" still remains narrowly restricted to
its original sense; since the Revolution it has nearly disappeared from
use, but it has never changed. We have preserved intact the word used
to designate the members of the caste, because we have preserved the
caste itself, as separate as it has ever been from all others. But I will go
still further, and suggest that the caste has become much more exclusive
than it was at the time when the word originated, and that among us it
has taken the opposite course from that which we have seen among the
English.

If the bourgeois and the noble were more similar, they were at the same
time more and more isolated from one another; two phenomena that
ought not to be confused. The two situations, rather than softening each
other, often aggravated the difference.

In the Middle Ages, and as long as feudalism continued to reign, all
those who held land of a lord (those whom feudal language proper called
his vassals), many of whom were not noble, were constantly associated
with the lord in the government of the manor; this was even the principal
condition of their tenure. Not only did they have to follow their lord to
war, but they were required, by virtue of their concession, to spend a
certain amount of time at his court, that is, to help him render justice
and govern the population. The lord's court was the mainspring of feudal
government; it appears in all the old laws of Europe, and I have encountered very clear vestiges of it even today in several parts of Germany.
The learned feudalist Edme de Fréminville, who, thirty years before the
French Revolution, was preparing to write a great book on feudal rights
and the renewal of terriers, tells us that he has seen in the "title-deeds of
numerous manors, that the vassals were obliged to come every two weeks
to the lord's court, where, being assembled, they judged together with the
lord or his judge, the trials and lawsuits which occurred among the inhabitants." He adds that he has found "sometimes eighty, a hundred and
fifty, or even two hundred of these vassals in one manor. Many of them
were commoners." I have cited this not as a proof—there are a thousand

others—but as an example of the way in which in the beginning, and for a long time thereafter, the rural class was drawn into contact with the nobility, and daily joined with them in the conduct of affairs. What the lord's court did for the small rural proprietors, the provincial estates, and later the Estates-General, did for the bourgeoisie of the towns.

One could not study what remains to us from the Estates-General of the fourteenth century, and above all from the provincial estates of the same period, without being astonished at the place that the Third Estate held there, and at the power that they exercised. As a man, the bourgeois of the fourteenth century is doubtless inferior to the bourgeois of the eighteenth; but the bourgeoisie as a body held a higher and more secure place in political society in the former period. Its right to participate in government was uncontested; the role that it played in political assemblies was always important, often dominant. The other classes always felt the need to reckon with it.

But what is striking above all, is to see how the nobility and the Third Estate found it easier then to run things together or to resist together than they have since. This is noticeable not only in the Estates-General of the fourteenth century, several of which were given an unusual and revolutionary character by the misfortunes of the time, but in the provincial estates of the same period, which were much more ordinary. Thus one sees, in Auvergne, the three orders taking the most important decisions in common and overseeing their execution through commissioners chosen equally from all three orders. The same thing is found at the same time in Champagne. Everyone knows the famous act by which the nobles and bourgeois of a large number of towns agreed, at the beginning of that same century, to defend the nation's freedom and the privileges of their provinces from the encroachments of royal power. One finds several episodes like these, which seem to belong to English history, in our own.[26] Such events were no longer to be seen in the centuries thereafter.[27]

In effect, to the extent that the government of the manor became disorganized, to the extent that Estates-General became rare and then ceased to meet, and as the general freedoms finally succumbed, pulling down local liberties in their ruin, the bourgeois and the noble no longer had contact with one another in public life. They no longer felt the need to come together and reach agreements; every day they were more independent of each other, but also more estranged from one another. In the eighteenth century this revolution was complete; these two never met except by chance in private life. The two classes were no longer merely rivals, they were enemies.

And what seems truly peculiar to France, is that at the same time that the order of the nobility thus lost its political powers, the noble as an individual acquired several privileges which he had never formerly possessed, or increased those which he already had. One might say that the parts enriched themselves at the expense of the whole. The nobility had less and less the right to rule, but the nobles had more and more the exclusive prerogative to be the ruler's chief servants; it was easier for a commoner to become an officer under Louis XIV than it was under Louis XVI. This often happened in Prussia, while it was almost unheard-of in France. Each of these privileges, once obtained, was hereditary. The more the nobility ceased to be an aristocracy, the more it seemed to become a caste.

Let us take the most hateful of all these privileges, that of tax exemption: it is easy to see that, from the fifteenth century until the French Revolution, this privilege did not stop growing. It grew through the rapid increase in government spending. When only 1,200,000 livres were raised from the taille under Charles VII,† the privilege of being exempt from the taille was worth little; when 80 million livres were raised under Louis XVI, it meant a lot. When the taille was the only tax that fell on commoners alone, the nobles' exemption was barely noticeable; but when taxes of this kind were multiplied under a thousand different names and in a thousand forms, when four other taxes had been added to the taille, when fees unknown to the Middle Ages, such as the royal corvée applied to all public works or services, the militia, etc., were added to the taille and its accessories, and were as unequally imposed, the noble's exemption appeared immense. The inequality, although great, was still in fact more apparent than real; for the noble was often struck through his tenant by the tax which he himself escaped; but in this matter the visible inequality was more galling than the inequality that one actually felt.[28]

Louis XIV, pressed by the financial needs which crushed him at the end of his reign, had established two general taxes, the capitation and the vingtième. But, as if tax exemption was in itself a privilege so honorable that it had to be recognized even when it was being attacked, care was taken to make the means of collection different even when the tax was common. For some, it remained harsh and degrading; for others, indulgent and honorable.

Although inequality of taxation was established throughout the European continent, there were very few countries where it had become as visible and as constantly felt as in France.[29] In a great part of Germany the majority of taxes were indirect. As for the direct taxes themselves, the noble's privilege often consisted of a smaller share of a common burden.[30] Further, there were certain taxes which struck only the nobility, and which were intended to replace the unpaid military service which was no longer demanded. But, of all the ways to make distinctions between people and classes, inequality of taxation is the most pernicious and the most apt to add isolation to inequality, and to make both to some extent incurable. Note its effects: when the bourgeois and the noble are no longer subjected to paying the same tax, each year the assessment and levying of taxes marks a clear and precise division between classes. Each year, every privileged person feels a real and pressing interest not to let himself be mixed up with the mass, and makes a fresh effort to hold himself apart. Since there is almost no issue of public interest which does not derive from taxes or end up in taxes, from the moment when the two classes were no longer equally subject to taxation, they had almost no further reason to meet together again, no more reason to experience common needs and feelings; it no longer required any effort to keep them apart: in a sense the motive and desire to act together had been taken from them.

Burke, in the flattering picture that he traces of the old French constitution, counts in favor of the institution of our nobility the ease with which the bourgeois obtained nobility by buying himself an office: this seemed to him analogous to the open aristocracy of England. Louis XI had, in fact, multiplied ennoblements—it was a means of debasing the nobility; his successors were lavish with them as a means of getting money. Necker tells us that in his time, the number of offices which gave nobility had risen to four thousand. Nothing similar could be seen anywhere else in Europe, but the analogy that Burke wanted to establish between France and England could not have been more false.

If the English middle classes, far from making war on the aristocracy, have remained so closely united with it, this has not been primarily because of the openness of their aristocracy, but rather, as has been said, because the English aristocracy's shape is indistinct and its boundary unknown; less because of how easy it is to get there, than because no one ever knows when he has arrived; to such an extent that everyone who gets close can think himself part of the aristocracy, attach himself to its hegemony, and get some glory or profit from its power. But the barrier that separated the nobility from the other classes in France, although very easy to cross, was always fixed and visible, always recognizable to those who remained outside by obvious and hateful signs. Once the barrier was crossed, one was separated from everyone in the circle one had just left by privileges which were painful and humiliating to them.

The system of ennoblements, therefore, far from diminishing the hatred of the commoner for the noble, rather increased it immeasurably; it was sharpened by all the envy which the new noble inspired among his former equals. This is what made the Third Estate, in its cahiers of grievances, always show more irritation towards the newly ennobled than towards the old nobles, and far from asking that the door which led out from the commons be enlarged, the Third Estate constantly asked that it be narrowed.

At no point in our history was nobility so easily acquired as in 1789, and never were the bourgeois and the noble so estranged from one another. Not only did the nobles in their electoral colleges feel nothing of what the bourgeoisie felt, but the bourgeoisie avoided with the same care everything which smacked of nobility. In certain provinces, the newly ennobled were repulsed by one side because they weren't judged noble enough, and by the other because they were found to be too noble already. It is said that this was the case with the famous Lavoisier.

And if, leaving the nobility aside, we now consider the bourgeoisie, we will see an absolutely identical sight, with the bourgeois almost as cut off from the people below as the noble was set apart from the bourgeois. Almost the entire middle class lived in towns during the old regime. Two causes above all had produced this result: the privileges of the nobility and the taille. The lord who lived on his lands usually showed a certain familiar good will towards his peasants; but his insolence towards his bourgeois neighbors was almost infinite. It had constantly grown as his political power had shrunk, and for that very reason; for, on the one hand, ceasing to rule, he no longer had any interest in getting along with those who could help him govern, and on the other hand, as has often been noted, the noble liked to console himself for the loss of his real power by the abuse of his conspicuous privileges. His very absence from his lands, rather than comforting his neighbors, increased their difficulties. The absenteeism did not even serve this purpose; for the privileges exercised by his representative were no less unbearable to endure. Nevertheless, I do not know if the taille, and all the taxes that had been attached to it, were not still more effective causes.

I could briefly explain, I think, why the taille and its attachments weighed so much more heavily on the countryside than on the towns, but perhaps that would seem a waste of time to the reader. Let it suffice to say, therefore, that the bourgeoisie gathered in the towns had a thousand ways of lessening the burden of the taille, and often escaped it entirely, which none of them would have been able to do alone if they had remained on their lands. In this way the bourgeoisie escaped above all the obligation to collect the taille, which they feared still more than the obligation to pay it, and rightly; because there was never, under the old regime nor even, I think, under any regime, a worse situation than that of the parish collector of the taille. I will have occasion to demonstrate this later on. However, no one in the village, except the noble, could escape this obligation: rather than submit to it, the rich commoner rented out his land and left for the nearest town. Turgot is in agreement with all the secret documents that I have consulted, when he tells us "that the collection of the taille transforms almost all commoner rural landowners into townsmen." This is, by the way, one of the reasons why France has more towns, and above all small towns, than most other countries in Europe.

Thus surrounded by walls, the rich commoner soon lost the tastes and ideas of the countryside; he became a complete stranger to the works and affairs of those of his fellows who remained there. His life no longer had any purpose but one: he wanted to become a public official of his adopted town. It is a great mistake to believe that the passion for public employment of almost all the French of our day, and in particular of the middle classes, has been born since the Revolution; it was born several centuries previously, and since then it has grown constantly, thanks to the thousand new incentives which have been carefully fed to it.

Public employment under the old regime did not always resemble our present version, but there was even more of it, I think; the number of petty jobs was almost endless. From 1693 to 1709 alone, it is calculated that forty thousand places were created, almost all within the means of the least bourgeois. I have counted in 1750, in an average provincial town, as many as 109 people employed to render justice, and 126 charged with executing their decrees, all townspeople. The ardor of the middle class to fill these posts was really unrivalled. As soon as one of them felt he had a little capital, rather than employing it in business, he immediately used it to buy a position. This miserable ambition has done more harm to the progress of agriculture and commerce in France than even the guilds and the taille. When jobs were lacking, the imagination of the seekers, putting itself to work, soon invented new ones. A Lord Lemberville published a report to prove that it was completely in the public interest to create inspectors for a certain industry, and ended up by offering himself as a candidate for the job. Who among us has not met a Lemberville? A man with a little education and a little spare time would not think he was ready to die until he had been a public official. "Everyone, according to his means," says a contemporary, "wants to be something by grace of the King." In this matter the greatest difference between the times of which we speak and our own is that then the government sold positions, whereas now it gives them away; to acquire them we no longer offer our money; we do better—we surrender ourselves.

Divided from the peasants by location, and still more by lifestyle, the bourgeois was usually set apart by interest as well. There have been many justified complaints about the tax privileges of the nobles; but what can one say about those of the middle classes? The offices which exempted them from all or part of the public expenses were counted by the thousands: this one from the militia, that one from the corvée, another from the taille. Where is the parish, says one of the writings of the times, which does not number within it, independently of nobles and clergy, several inhabitants who have procured themselves, with the aid of some position or commission, a tax exemption? One of the reasons which occasionally impelled the abolition of a certain number of offices intended for the bourgeoisie was the decrease in tax receipts created by such a large number of tax-exempt individuals. I do not doubt that the number of people exempted was as large, and often larger, among the bourgeoisie than among the nobility.

These miserable prerogatives filled with envy those who were deprived of them, and glutted those who possessed them with the most selfish pride. There is nothing more clear, throughout the eighteenth century, than the hostility of the bourgeoisie of the towns for the peasants of their countryside, and the jealousy of the countryside versus the town. "Every town," says Turgot, "is concerned with its own special interests, and is ready to sacrifice the countryside and villages of its neighborhood to them." "You have often been obliged," he says elsewhere, speaking to his subdelegates, "to repress the constantly usurping and encroaching tendency which characterizes the conduct of the towns towards the countryside and villages of their neighborhood."

The masses who lived with the bourgeoisie within the town walls became estranged from them, almost enemies. Most local taxes that the bourgeoisie established were made in such a way as to fall primarily on the lower classes. I have more than once had occasion to prove what the same Turgot says somewhere else in his works, that the bourgeoisie of the towns had found the means to adjust the sales taxes so that they did not weigh heavily on them.

But what one chiefly sees in all the acts of this bourgeoisie is its fear of seeing itself confused with the masses, and its passionate desire to escape from their control at all costs. "If it please the King," say the bourgeois of a town in a report to the controller-general, "that the position of mayor become elective once again, it would be appropriate to require the electors to choose only among the principal notables, and even among the presidial."[†]

We have seen how the policy of our kings was to successively take their political rights away from the people of the towns. All their legislation from Louis XI to Louis XV reveals this plan. Often the bourgeoisie of the towns joined them, sometimes they suggested it. At the time of the municipal reform of 1764, an intendant consulted the municipal officials of a small town on whether the artisans and *others of the lower orders* ought to keep the right to vote for magistrates. These officials responded that in reality "the people have never abused this right, and that it would no doubt be good for them to keep the pleasure of choosing those who would rule them; but that it would be still better, for the maintenance of order and public peace, to limit the right to vote to the assembly of notables." The subdelegate reported on his side that he had met in secret in his offices with "the six best citizens of the town." The six best citizens were in unanimous agreement that it would be best to restrict the suffrage, not even to the assembly of notables, as the municipal officials had suggested, but to a certain number of deputies chosen from the different groups which made up the assembly. The subdelegate, more favorable to the people's liberty than these bourgeois themselves, while reporting their advice, added "that it was, however, very hard on these artisans to pay, without being able to control their use, the taxes imposed by those of their fellow citizens who because of their tax privileges were perhaps the least interested in the question."

But let us finish the picture; let us now consider the bourgeoisie in itself, separate from the people, as we have considered the nobility separately from the bourgeoisie. We find within this small portion of the nation, situated apart from the rest, infinite divisions. It seems as if the French people were like those supposedly elementary particles inside which, the more closely it looks, modern physics keeps finding new particles. I have found no less than thirty-six different bodies among the notables of a small town. The different groups, although very small, constantly worked at making themselves smaller still. Every day they went about purging themselves of the heterogeneous parts they might contain, in order to reduce themselves to basic elements. In the course of this great work some of them had reduced themselves to three or four members. Their personalities were all the more lively and their attitude the more quarrelsome. Each group was differentiated from the others by a few small privileges, the least fair being nevertheless a sign of honor. There were constant struggles over precedence among them. The intendant and the courts were deafened by the noise of their quarrels. "We have finally decided that the holy water will be given to the presidial before the town council. The parlement hesitated, but the king evoked the matter to his own Council, and decided himself. It was time. The affair has made the whole town boil." If one of the groups was given precedence over another in the general assembly of notables, the latter would cease to appear; it would renounce public affairs rather than see, it said, its dignity raped. The guild of wigmakers of the town of La Flèche decided "that it would in this manner bear witness to the true pain it was given by the precedence accorded the bakers." A portion of the notables of one town obstinately refused to fulfill their office "because," said the intendant, "some artisans have been introduced into this assembly, with whom the leading bourgeois would find it humiliating to be associated"; "if the place of alderman," says the intendant of another province, "is given to a notary, that would disgust the other notables, the notaries here being people of low birth, who are not from notable families and have all been clerks." The six best citizens of whom I have already spoken, who so quickly decided that the people should be deprived of their political rights, found themselves in an unusual quandary when it came to deciding who were the notables, and what order of precedence ought to be established among them. In such a matter they more modestly expressed only their doubts; they feared, they said, "to give too much pain to some of their fellow-citizens."

The natural vanity of the French strengthened and sharpened itself in the continual friction among these groups' self-esteem, and the legitimate pride of the citizen was forgotten. In the sixteenth century most of the groups of which I have just spoken already existed; but their members, after having taken care of the business of their own associations among themselves, constantly met with all the other inhabitants to deliberate together about the general interests of the city. In the eighteenth century, they had almost entirely withdrawn into themselves, for the acts of municipal life had become rare, and were always executed by officials. Every one of these little societies therefore lived only for itself, and was only interested in itself and in matters which directly affected it.

Our ancestors lacked the word "individualism," which we have created for our own use, because in their era there were, in fact, no individuals who did not belong to a group and who could consider themselves absolutely alone; but each one of the thousand little groups of which French society was composed thought only of itself. This was, if one can use the word thus, a kind of collective individualism, which prepared people for the real individualism with which we are familiar.

And what is still stranger is that these isolated people had become so similar that it would have been enough for them to change places to become unrecognizable. Furthermore, whoever could have plumbed their minds would have discovered that, even to them, the little barriers which divided such similar people seemed to be as contrary to the public interest as to good sense, and that already they adored unity in theory. Each of them only held on to his own rank because others divided themselves by rank; but they were all prepared to mingle in the same mass, provided that no one held aloof and that no one was above the common level.

How the Destruction of Political Liberty and the Division of Classes Caused Almost All the Ills of Which the Old Regime Perished

I have just described the most deadly of all the maladies that attacked the constitution of the old regime and condemned it to death. I want to go back again to the origin of this strange and dangerous sickness, and show how many other ills had followed in its wake.

If, after the Middle Ages, the English, like us, had entirely lost their political liberty and all the local freedoms which cannot long exist without it, it is very probable that the different classes which composed their aristocracy would have separated from each other, as happened in France and more or less on the rest of the continent, and that all of them together would have been separated from the people. But freedom always forced them all to stay in touch with one another, in order to be able to reach an understanding when necessary.

It is interesting to see how the English nobility, pushed by its own ambition, has known how to mingle on familiar terms with its inferiors when necessary, and pretend to consider them its equals. Arthur Young, whom I have already cited, and whose book is one of the most instructive works which exist on the old France, tells us that, finding himself one day in the country with the duc de Liancourt, he expressed the desire to speak with some of the ablest and richest local farmers. The duke instructed his intendant to bring them to him. About which the Englishman made the following remark: "With an English lord, we would have had three or four farmers come, who would have dined with the family, and among ladies of the highest rank. I have seen that at least a hundred times in our isles. This is something for which one would search France in vain from Calais to Bayonne."

Certainly, the English aristocracy was more haughty than the French aristocracy, and less inclined to be familiar with those who lived beneath it; but the necessities of its situation required it to do so. It was ready to do anything in order to lead. For centuries no inequalities of taxation had been seen among the English, except those which were successively introduced in favor of the poor. Consider, please, where these different political principles can lead neighboring peoples! In eighteenth-century England, it was the poor man who enjoyed tax privileges; in France, it was the rich.[31] There, the aristocracy had taken upon itself the heaviest public burdens, so that it would be allowed to govern; here, the aristocracy kept its immunity from taxation until the end, in order to console itself for having lost the government.

In the fourteenth century, the maxim "Do not tax those who do not consent" seemed as solidly established in France as in England itself. It was often cited: to break it still seemed an act of tyranny; to obey it, to return to legality. At that period one finds, as I have already said, a mass of analogies between our political institutions and those of the English; but since then the destinies of the two peoples have parted, and are becoming increasingly more different with time. They resemble two lines which, starting from neighboring points, but following slightly different directions, diverge from one another more and more the longer they extend.

I would dare to argue that from the day when the nation, tired of the long disorders that had accompanied the captivity of King John[†] and the insanity of King Charles VI,[†] permitted the kings to establish a general tax without its consent, and when the nobility had the cowardice to allow the Third Estate to be taxed provided that the nobility itself was exempted; on that day was planted the seed for almost all the vices and abuses which affected the old regime for the rest of its life, and finally caused its violent death. I admire the unique wisdom of Commynes[†] when he said: "Charles VII, who won the argument over imposing the taille at his will, without the consent of the estates, heavily burdened his soul and those of his successors, and made a wound in his realm that will bleed for a long time." Consider how the wound was actually enlarged over the course of time; follow its consequences step by step.

Forbonnais rightly says, in his erudite *Researches on the Finances of France,* that during the Middle Ages the kings generally lived on the revenues of their domains: "and since extraordinary needs," he adds, "were provided for by extraordinary contributions, they were borne equally by the clergy, the nobility, and the people." The majority of the general taxes voted by the three orders during the fourteenth century were indeed of this character. Almost all the taxes established at that period were *indirect,* that is to say they were paid by all consumers without distinction. Sometimes the tax was direct: it bore then, not on property, but on income. The nobles, the clergy, and the bourgeoisie were required to give to the king, for example, a tenth of their annual income. What I have said about taxes voted by the Estates-General ought to be extended equally to those which were established at that period by the various provincial estates on their territories.

It is true that, from this time on, the direct tax known under the name of taille was never levied on the nobles. The obligation of unpaid military service dispensed them from it; but the taille, as a general tax, was then of limited use, more applicable to the manor than to the kingdom. When the king later attempted for the first time to raise taxes on his own authority, he understood that it was necessary to choose one which would not seem to strike directly at the nobility; for the nobility, who then formed a rival and dangerous class for the king, would never have accepted an innovation which would have been so harmful to them; he therefore chose a tax from which they were exempt; he chose the taille.

To all the particular inequalities which already existed there was now joined a more general one, which preserved and aggravated all the others. From then on, as the needs of the public treasury grew with the increase in central power, the taille was extended and broadened; soon it was multiplied tenfold, and all new taxes became tailles. Every year, therefore, the inequality of taxation separated classes and isolated individuals more deeply than ever before.[32] From the moment when taxation had as its purpose, not to strike those most capable of paying, but those least capable of defending themselves against it, the monstrous consequence of sparing the rich and burdening the poor was inevitable. We are assured that Mazarin, needing money, thought of establishing a tax on the principal houses of Paris, but that having encountered some opposition from those interested, he limited himself to adding the five millions he needed to the general bill of the taille. He wanted to tax the most opulent citizens; he ended up taxing the poorest. But the treasury lost nothing.

The income from taxes so badly distributed had limits, and the needs of rulers no longer had any. However, they did not wish to convoke the Estates-General to obtain grants from them, nor to provoke the nobility to demand the convocation of those assemblies by taxing them. From this came that huge and monstrous fertility of the financial mind, which so strikingly characterized the administration of public finance during the last three centuries of the monarchy.

One must study the administrative and financial history of the old regime in detail, in order to understand to what violent and dishonest practices the need for money can reduce a government that is well-intentioned but acts in secret, without check, once time has consecrated its power and delivered it from the fear of revolution, that last safeguard of peoples. In these annals one finds at every step royal estates sold, then seized as inalienable; contracts violated, acquired rights ignored, the state's creditor sacrificed at every crisis, public faith constantly deceived. Privileges granted in perpetuity were perpetually taken back. If one can sympathize with displeasures caused by drunken vanity, one could lament the fate of the ennobled unfortunates who, during the whole course of the seventeenth and eighteenth centuries, were required from time to time to repurchase those vain honors or unjust privileges which they had already paid for several times. It was thus that Louis XIV annulled all the titles of nobility acquired in the past ninety-two years, the majority of which had been given by him; one could not keep them except by furnishing a new sum, *all these titles having been obtained by surprise,* says the edict. An example which Louis XV would not fail to imitate, eighty years later.

The militiaman was forbidden to find a replacement for himself, for fear, it was said, of increasing the price the state paid for recruits. Towns, communities, hospitals were forced to fail to meet their obligations, so that they would be in a position to lend to the king. Parishes were forbidden to undertake useful works, for fear that, thus dividing their resources, they would pay the taille less promptly.[33]

The story is told that M. Orry and M. de Trudaine, the one controller-general and the other director-general of Roads and Bridges, had conceived the project of replacing the road corvée by a tax in money, to be paid by the inhabitants of each district for the repair of their roads. The reason that these able administrators had to give up their plan is instructive: they feared, it was said, that the funds having been raised, the public treasury could not be prevented from taking them for its own use, in such a way that soon the taxpayers would have had to bear not only the new tax but the old corvée as well. I do not fear to say that no one could have escaped the law if he had conducted his own business the way that the great king, in all his glory, handled public funds.

If you find some old establishment from the Middle Ages which continued to exist while, in opposition to the spirit of the times, its vices worsened, or some pernicious innovation, dig down to the evil's root: you will find a financial expedient that turned into an institution. To pay the debts of a day you will see new powers founded which last for centuries.

In the very distant past, a particular tax, called the right of franc-fief, had been established on commoners who bought noble estates. The right created the same distinction between lands that existed between people, and they increased in tandem. The right of franc-fief served more than all others, perhaps, to keep the commoner and the noble apart, because it forbade them to mix in that which brings people together faster and better than anything else, landownership. An abyss was thus regularly reopened between the noble landowner and his neighbor the commoner. On the contrary, nothing more encouraged the cohesion of these two classes in England than the abolition, from the seventeenth century on, of all the signs which distinguished the fief from land held by commoners.

In the fourteenth century, the feudal tax of franc-fief was light and only occasionally levied; but in the eighteenth century, when feudalism was almost destroyed, it was rigorously demanded every twenty years, and it represented an entire year's income. The son paid it when inheriting from his father. "This tax," says the Agricultural Society of Tours in 1761, "does infinite damage to the progress of the art of agriculture. Of all the taxes on the king's subjects in the countryside there is unquestionably none whose burden is as painful." "This tax," says another contemporary, "which at first was imposed only once in a lifetime, has since become a very cruel tax." The nobility itself would have liked to see it abolished, for it prevented commoners from buying their land; but the needs of the treasury demanded that it be maintained and increased.[34]

The Middle Ages are wrongly charged with all the evils which the trade guilds could produce. Everything indicates that in the beginning masterships were only means of linking together the members of the same profession, and establishing within each trade a small free government, whose mission was both to help the workers and to contain them. It does not appear that St. Louis† wanted anything more.

It was only at the beginning of the sixteenth century, in the midst of the Renaissance, that for the first time the right to work was thought of as a privilege which the king could sell. Only then did each guild become a little closed aristocracy, and finally we see established those monopolies that were so prejudicial to the progress of the arts and that so revolted our ancestors. From Henry III, who generalized the evil, if he did not create it, until Louis XVI, who eliminated it, one can say that the abuses of the mastership system constantly grew and extended themselves, at the very time when the progress of society made them more unbearable and public reason more aware of them. Each year new professions ceased to be free; each year the privileges of the old ones were increased. Never was the evil pushed further than during what are often referred to as the greatest years of the reign of Louis XIV, because never had the need for money been greater, nor the resolution not to appeal to the nation firmer.

Letrone[†] rightly said in 1775: "The state has only established the trade guilds in order to find resources there, sometimes through the licenses that it sells, sometimes through the new offices that it creates and which the guilds are forced to redeem. The edict of 1673 extended to their logical consequence the principles of Henry III, by requiring all the guilds to acquire letters of confirmation for a sum, and all artisans who were not yet part of a guild to join one. This miserable business produced 300,000 livres."

We have seen how towns' entire constitutions were overturned, not for political reasons, but with the intention of acquiring some money for the treasury. It was to this same need for money, joined with the wish to request nothing from the Estates, that the venality of offices owed its birth, and little by little it became something so strange that nothing like it has ever been seen. Thanks to this institution, created by the financial mind, the vanity of the Third Estate was kept in good shape for three centuries and directed uniquely towards the acquisition of public offices; this universal passion for government jobs was encouraged to penetrate into the bowels of the nation, a passion which became the common source of revolution and servitude.

As financial embarrassments increased, new jobs were created, all paid for by tax exemptions or privileges; and as it was the needs of the treasury, not of government, which determined them, in this way an almost incredible number of absolutely useless or harmful posts were created.[35] As early as 1664, at the time of the inquiry made by Colbert, he found that the capital sunk in this miserable kind of property amounted to nearly five hundred million livres. Richelieu destroyed, it is said, 100,000 offices. They were immediately reborn under other names. For a little cash one thus deprived oneself of the right to direct, to control, and to constrain one's own officials. In this way there was gradually built a bureaucratic machine so vast, so complicated, so hobbled, and so unproductive, that it was necessary to let it spin its wheels, and to construct an instrument of government alongside it which was simpler and more manageable, by means of which one could really do what all those other officials were supposed to do.

We may be sure that none of these detestable institutions could have lasted twenty years, if it had been permitted to discuss them. None of them would have been established or allowed to grow worse if the Estates had been consulted, or if their grievances had been listened to, when by chance they still met. The rare Estates-General of recent centuries did not cease to protest against them. On several occasions one sees these assemblies point out as the origin of these abuses the power which the king had arrogated to raise taxes arbitrarily; or, to reproduce the very expressions which the energetic language of the fifteenth century used, "the right of enriching himself from the people's substance without the consent and deliberation of the three Estates." They did not concern themselves only with their own rights; they forcefully demanded, and often obtained, respect for the rights of the towns and provinces. At each new session, voices were raised within the Estates against the inequality of taxation. The Estates asked several times for the abandonment of the guildmastership system; from century to century they attacked the venality of offices with increasing vigor. "He who sells an office sells justice, which is an infamous thing," they said. When the venality of offices was established, they continued to complain about the abuses that were made of them. They rose up against so many useless jobs and dangerous privileges, but always in vain. These institutions were established precisely against the Estates; they were born of the desire not to convene them, and of the need to disguise from the eyes of the French the taxes which no one dared reveal in their true light.

And note that the best kings had recourse to these practices as much as the worst. It was Louis XII who finally established the venality of offices; it was Henry IV who sold them as hereditary: by so much were the vices of the system stronger than the virtues of the men who practiced it!

This same desire to escape from the tutelage of the Estates made the kings confide most of the Estates' political functions to the parlements. This confused the judiciary power with the executive in a manner very harmful to the proper conduct of affairs. The kings had to appear to furnish some new guarantees to replace those that had been eliminated; for the French, who accept absolute power patiently, as long as it is not oppressive, have never liked its sight, and it has always been wise to put up screens in front of power which, without being able to stop it, at least hide it a little.

Finally, it was the desire to prevent the nation, from which money was asked, from demanding its freedom back, that made the government constantly alert to ensure that the classes remained apart from each other, so that they could neither come together again nor join in a common resistance; thus the government would never have to deal with more than a very small number of men at one time, separated from all the others. During the whole course of the long history of the French monarchy, where so many remarkable rulers appear, some notable for their intelligence, others for their character, almost all for their courage, there is not a single one who makes an effort to bring the classes together and unite them in any way but in submission to an equal dependence. I am mistaken: one alone wanted to, and even wholeheartedly attempted to; and that one—who can fathom the judgments of God!—was Louis XVI.

The division of classes was the crime of the old monarchy, and later became its excuse; for once all those who made up the wealthy and enlightened portion of the nation could no longer agree with one another, and help one another govern, it was virtually impossible for the country to govern itself, and it was necessary for a master to intervene. "The nation," said Turgot sadly in a secret report to the king, "is a society made up of different orders badly united, and of a people whose members have very few ties, where, by consequence, no one cares about anything but his own personal interests. Nowhere is any common interest visible. The villages, the towns have no more contact than do the regions of which they are part. They cannot even agree among themselves to undertake necessary public works. In this perpetual war of claims and counter-claims, His Majesty is obliged to decide everything by himself or through his delegates. They wait for your special orders in order to contribute to the public good, in order to respect someone else's rights, sometimes even to exercise their own."

It was no small thing to bring together again fellow citizens who had lived like this for centuries, as strangers or enemies, and to teach them how to conduct their affairs in common. It was much easier to divide them than it was to reunite them later on. We furnished a memorable example of this to the world. When, sixty years ago, the different classes which made up the society of old France reentered into contact with one another, after having been isolated for so long by so many barriers, they at first only rubbed each other's raw spots, and made contact only in order to tear each other apart. Even today their jealousies and their hatreds survive them.

CHAPTER ELEVEN

Of the Kind of Freedom That Existed under the Old Regime and Its Influence on the Revolution

If one stopped reading this book here, one would have only a very incomplete picture of old-regime government, and one would poorly understand the society which made the Revolution. In seeing these citizens so divided and so withdrawn into themselves, a royal power so strong and wide, one might think that the spirit of independence had disappeared along with political freedom, and that all the French were equally bowed in subjection. But this was in no way the case; the government already managed all common affairs by itself and absolutely, but it was still far from being the master of all individuals.

In the midst of many institutions already prepared for absolute power, freedom lived; but it was an unusual kind of freedom, one which is hard to understand today, and which must be carefully examined in order for us to understand the good and the harm which it has been able to do.

While the central government had replaced all the local powers, and increasingly occupied the whole sphere of public authority, some institutions which it had allowed to survive or which it had itself created, some ancient customs, old mores, even abuses, hindered its movement, and still preserved the spirit of resistance in the depths of the soul of many individuals, and kept for many personalities their consistency and shape.

Centralization already had the same nature, the same procedures, the same ambitions as in our day, but not yet the same power. The government, in its desire to make money from everything, had put most public positions up for sale, and had thus deprived itself of the ability to give them and take them away at will. One of its passions had thus greatly interfered with the realization of another: its greed had counterbalanced its ambition. Thus, in order to act, it was constantly reduced to employing tools it had not made and could not break. Often, therefore, its strongest intentions were watered-down in practice.[36] This harmful and bizarre system of public employment functioned as a kind of political guarantee against the omnipotence of the central power. It was like an irregular and badly constructed dike which divided the central power's strength and dissipated its shock. Also, the government did not dispose of that infinity of favors, aids, honors, and money that it can distribute today: it thus had many fewer means to seduce as well as to constrain.

Further, the government itself did not understand the precise limits of its power very well. None of its rights were formally recognized or solidly established; its sphere of action was already immense, but it still marched with an uncertain step, as if in strange and foggy terrain. If the formidable shadows which then hid the limits of all powers, and hovered about all rights, were favorable to the attempts of rulers against the liberty of their subjects, they were also often useful in their subjects' defense.

The bureaucracy, sensing its own novelty and low birth, always acted timidly, for fear of encountering an obstacle in its path. It is a striking spectacle, when one reads the correspondence of the ministers and intendants of the eighteenth century, to see how this government, so encroaching and so absolute as long as obedience was not contested, backed off at the sight of the least resistance, how the slightest criticism bothered it, how the smallest disturbance startled it, and how it would then halt, hesitate, negotiate, consider public opinion, and often remain well inside the natural limits of its power. The spineless egoism of Louis XV and the kindness of his successor lent themselves to this. These rulers, furthermore, never imagined that anyone could think of dethroning them. They had none of that harsh and worried character that fear has often given those who have governed since. They only trampled on people they didn't see.

Several of the privileges, prejudices, and false ideas which most hinder the establishment of an ordered and beneficent freedom, preserved the spirit of independence among a great number of subjects, and inclined them to stiffen their necks against abuses of authority. The nobles very much despised the administration proper, although they asked its help from time to time. They retained, even in the loss of their old power, something of their ancestors' pride, as opposed to servitude as to law. They were not interested in the slightest in the general freedom of citizens, and were quite willing that the hand of power should weigh upon those around them; but they did not intend that it should touch them, and to make sure of this they were, if necessary, ready to run great risks.

At the moment when the Revolution broke out, this nobility, which was going to fall with the throne, still had an attitude towards the king (and still more in relation to his officials) infinitely more haughty and a language more free than the Third Estate, which would soon overthrow the monarchy. Almost all the guarantees against the abuse of power which we have had during thirty-seven years of representative government were boldly demanded by the nobility.[37] In reading its cahiers, one feels, amidst and beyond their prejudices, the spirit and some of the great qualities of aristocracy. One must still regret that, instead of bending the nobility under the yoke of the law, we have slaughtered it and alienated it. In acting thus, we have deprived the nation of a necessary part of its substance, and given liberty a wound which can never be healed. A class which led for centuries had acquired, during that long, uncontested experience of greatness, a certain pride of heart, a natural confidence in its strength, a habit of being respected, which made it into the most resistant part of the social body. It not only had manly mores, it increased the virility of the other classes by its example. In destroying it, its enemies weakened themselves. Nothing could completely replace it; it could never recreate itself; it could recover the titles and goods but never the spirit of its ancestors.

The priests, whom we have often since seen so slavishly submissive in things civil to the temporal power, whatever its form, the government's boldest flatterers as long as it pretends to favor the Church a little, were at that time one of the most independent bodies in the nation, and the only one whose particular liberties compelled respect. The provinces had lost their freedoms, the towns possessed but their shadow. Ten nobles could not meet to discuss anything without the express consent of the king. The Church of France retained its periodic assemblies until the end. Internally, ecclesiastical power itself had limits that it respected.[38] The lower clergy had real guaranties against the tyranny of their superiors, and they were not prepared by the unlimited arbitrary power of the bishop for passive obedience to the ruler. I am not presuming to judge the old constitution of the Church; I only say that it did not in any way prepare the priest's soul for political servility.

Many clergymen, furthermore, were of noble birth, and brought with them into the Church the pride and insubordination of people of their rank. All, further, had a high rank in the state and possessed privileges. The practice of the same feudal rights that were so fatal to the moral power of the Church gave its individual members a spirit of independence in relation to the civil power.

But, above all, what contributed to giving the clergy the ideas, needs, feelings, often the passions of the citizen, was landownership. I have had the patience to read most of the reports and debates which the old provincial estates have left us, especially those of Languedoc, where the clergy were more involved than elsewhere in the details of public administration, as well as the transcripts of the provincial assemblies which met in 1779 and 1787. Bringing the ideas of my time to that reading, I was astonished to see bishops and abbés, among whom several were as eminent for their sanctity as for their knowledge, make reports on the establishment of a road or a canal, discuss the matter with deep knowledge, and present with infinite skill and art what were the best means to increase agricultural output, to assure the well-being of the population, and to make industry prosper. They were always the equals and often the superiors of the laymen who worked with them on the same business.[39]

I dare to think, contrary to a very widespread and strongly entrenched opinion, that nations which remove the Catholic clergy from any participation whatsoever in landownership, and turn all their income into a salary, serve only the interests of the Vatican and those of the temporal rulers, depriving themselves of a very important element of freedom. A man whose chief devotion is to a foreign authority, and who can have no family in the country where he lives, is in reality linked to the earth by a single solid connection, landownership. Cut that link, and he no longer belongs to any place in particular. In the place where chance has dictated his birth, he lives as a stranger in the midst of a civil society almost none of whose interests can directly concern him. For his conscience, he depends solely on the pope; for his subsistence, only on the ruler. The Church is his only fatherland; in every political event he sees only what can help or hinder it. As long as the Church is free and prosperous, of what importance is anything else? Indifference is his most natural state in politics. An excellent member of the Christian Church, he is a poor citizen everywhere else. Such feelings, and similar ideas, in a body which is the director of youth and the guide of mores, cannot fail to enervate the soul of the entire nation with respect to public life.

If one wants to have a correct idea of the revolutions which can take place in men's minds as a result of changes in their situation, one must reread the cahiers of the clergy in 1789.[40] There the clergy often showed themselves intolerant, and sometimes stubbornly attached to some of their old privileges; but, for the rest, they were as opposed to despotism, as favorable to civil liberty, and as enamored of political freedom as the

Third Estate or the nobility. The clergy proclaimed that individual freedom ought to be guaranteed, not by promises, but by a procedure similar
to habeas corpus. They demanded the destruction of political prisons, the
abolition of exceptional courts and evocations, public trials and meetings,
the irremovability of all judges, the eligibility of all citizens for all employments, employments which should be decided only on the basis of merit,
a system of military recruitment less oppressive and less humiliating to
the lower classes, from which no one should be exempt; the redemption
of feudal dues, which, derived from the feudal regime, the clergy said,
were contrary to liberty. They demanded the unlimited right to work, the
destruction of internal tariffs, the multiplication of primary schools: there
ought to be one in every parish that would be free of charge, they said;
secular establishments for charity throughout the countryside, such as
charity workshops; all kinds of encouragements for agriculture.

In politics proper, the clergy proclaimed more loudly than anyone else
that the nation had the inalienable and imprescriptible right to assemble
to make laws and freely vote taxes. No Frenchman, they affirmed, could
be forced to pay a tax which he had not voted on himself or through his
representative. The clergy further demanded that the Estates-General,
freely elected, meet every year; that they discuss all important business in
public; that they make general laws which could not be escaped through
any custom or special privilege; that they make the budget and even oversee the expenses of the royal household; that their deputies be inviolate
and that the ministers remain permanently responsible to the Estates.
The clergy also wanted assemblies of the Estates to be created in every
province, and municipal governments in every town. Of divine right, not
a word.

I do not know if, all in all, and notwithstanding the shocking vices of
some of its members, there has ever been a clergy more remarkable than
the Catholic clergy of France at the moment when the Revolution over-
took it, one more enlightened, more national, less confined purely to the
private virtues, better provided with public virtues, and at the same time
with more faith, as its persecution well demonstrated. I began the study
of our old society full of prejudices against the clergy; I have ended up
full of respect. In truth, it had only those faults inherent to all groups,
political as well as religious, that are strongly united and well-organized:
the tendency to encroach on other spheres, intolerance, and an instinctive
and sometimes blind attachment to the special rights of their group.

The bourgeoisie of the old regime was similarly much better prepared to show an independent mind than that of today. Even some of the vices of its situation helped it. We have seen that the public offices that it occupied were even more numerous then than now, and that the middle classes showed as much ardor to fill them. But look at the difference in the times. The majority of these offices, being neither given nor taken away by the government, increased the importance of the holder without putting him at the mercy of authority: thus what today completes the subjection of so many people was then precisely what most helped them make themselves respected.

The immunities of all kinds, which so unfortunately separated the bourgeoisie from the masses, also made of them a pseudo-aristocracy which often showed the pride and spirit of resistance of real aristocracy. The general good was easily forgotten in all the little groups which divided the bourgeoisie into so many parts, but there was always concern for the interest and rights of the group.[41] There was a common dignity, common privileges to defend. No one could lose himself in the crowd and hide his cowardly subservience. Every individual found himself on stage, in a very small theater, of course, but a very well-informed one, and there had a permanent audience that was always ready to hiss or applaud.

The art of smothering the sound of resistance was much less perfected then than now. France had not yet become the deaf place where we live today; it was on the contrary very attentive, even though political freedom never showed itself, and it was enough to raise one's voice to be heard far away. What above all assured the oppressed a way to make themselves heard then was the organization of the judicial system. We had become a country of absolute government through our political and administrative institutions, but we had remained a free people in our judicial ones. The judicial system of the old regime was complicated, cumbersome, slow, and expensive; these were doubtless great faults, but one never met servility towards power in it, which is nothing but the worst form of corruption. That deadly vice, which not only corrupts the judge but soon infects the whole people, was entirely foreign to it. The magistrate was irremovable and did not seek promotion, two things equally necessary for his independence; for whom can one not constrain when one has a thousand means of winning him over?

It is true that the royal power had succeeded in stealing from the ordinary courts jurisdiction over almost all matters which concerned public authority; but it still feared them while robbing them. If it forbade them to judge, it did not yet forbid them to hear complaints and give their opinion; and since judicial language then retained all the manners of old French, which liked to give things their proper names, the magistrates often frankly labeled the proceedings of the government despotic and arbitrary.[42] The irregular intervention of the courts in government, which often disturbed the efficient administration of business, thus sometimes served as the guardian of men's liberties: it was a great evil which limited a greater one.

At the heart of these judicial bodies, and all around them, the vigor of the old mores was retained in the midst of the new ideas. The parlements were doubtless more interested in themselves than in the public good, but it must be recognized that they always showed themselves bold in defense of their own independence and their own honor, and they communicated their spirit to all who came near them.

When in 1770 the parlement of Paris was broken up, the magistrates who belonged to it suffered the loss of their status and power without a single one of them personally surrendering to the royal will. Even more, the other kinds of courts, like the tax court, which were neither attacked nor threatened, voluntarily exposed themselves to the same fate, when punishment had become certain. But there is still more: the leading lawyers who pleaded before the parlement willingly associated themselves with its fate; they gave up what constituted their own wealth and glory, and condemned themselves to silence rather than appear before dishonored judges. I know nothing greater in the history of free nations than what happened on this occasion, and yet this took place in the eighteenth century, alongside the court of Louis XV.

Judicial habits had become in many respects national habits. The idea that everything was subject to discussion and all decisions to appeal, the custom of public hearings, the taste for formal procedures, things that were enemies to servitude, had been widely taken over from the judiciary: this is the only part of a free nation's education that the old regime gave us. Government officials themselves borrowed much from the language and customs of the judiciary. The king felt obliged to give reasons for his edicts and to explain them before concluding them: the Council preceded its decrees by long preambles; the intendant had a bailiff explain his ordinances. Among all administrative bodies of older origin, such as, for example, the Treasurers of France or the *Elus,* business was publicly discussed and decided after hearings. All these habits, all these forms, were so many barriers against the arbitrary will of the ruler.

The lower classes alone, above all those of the countryside, found themselves almost powerless to resist oppression other than by violence. The majority of the means of defense I have just mentioned were, in effect, beyond their reach; to make use of them, they would have needed a place in society where they could be seen, and a voice capable of making itself heard. But above the lower classes, there was no man in France who, if he had the courage, could not quibble over his obedience and still resist while bowing.

The king spoke to the nation as a leader rather than as a master: "We consider it to be our glory," said Louis XVI at the beginning of his reign, in the preamble of an edict, "to command a free and generous nation." One of his ancestors had already expressed the same idea in older language, when, thanking the Estates-General for the boldness of their remonstrances, he said: "We would rather speak to free men than to serfs."

The men of the eighteenth century hardly knew that kind of passion for material well-being which is the mother of servitude, a spineless passion, yet tenacious and unalterable, which easily mingles and so to say interlaces itself with several private virtues, the love of one's family, good morals, respect for religious beliefs, and even the lukewarm and regular practice of the established religion, which allows honesty and forbids heroism, and excels at making well-behaved men and slack citizens. Those men were both better and worse.

The French of those days loved joy and adored pleasure; they were perhaps more disorderly in their habits and more abandoned in their passions and their ideas than the French of today; but they were ignorant of that tempered and decent sensuality that we see now. In the upper classes, one was much more concerned with adorning one's life than with making it easy, more interested in becoming famous than in getting rich. Even among the middle classes, one never allowed oneself to become completely absorbed in the search for well-being: one often abandoned its pursuit to pursue higher and more delicate pleasures; everywhere one put stock in something beyond money. I know my nation, writes a contemporary in an odd fashion, but one not lacking in pride: "capable at making and spending its gold and silver, it is certainly not in its nature to honor them with a permanent worship, and it will always be ready to return to its old idols, courage, glory, and I dare say magnanimity."

Further, one must guard carefully against judging the baseness of men by the degree of their submission to the sovereign power: that would be to use a false measure. However submissive the men of the old regime were to the wishes of the king, there was one kind of obedience which was unknown to them: they did not know what it was to bow before an illegitimate or disputed power, one little honored, often despised, but which one served because it was useful or could do one harm. That degrading form of servitude was still foreign to them. The king inspired in them feelings which none of the most absolute rulers whom the world has known since has been able to inspire, and which have even become almost incomprehensible to us, to such a degree did the Revolution extirpate them from our hearts, down to the deepest roots. They had for the king simultaneously the tenderness that one has for a father and the respect that one owes only to God. In submitting themselves to his most arbitrary commands, they gave way far less to constraint than to love, and thus they often kept their soul quite free in the midst of the most extreme subjection. For them, the greatest evil in obedience was coercion: for us, it is the least. For us the worst is the servile feeling which makes one obey. Let us not hold our ancestors in contempt, we do not have the right. May it please God that we may recover, with their faults and prejudices, a little of their greatness!

One would therefore be very wrong to believe that the old regime was a time of servility and subordination.[43] There was much more freedom then than in our day: but it was a kind of freedom that was irregular and intermittent, always contracted within the limits of a class, always linked to the idea of exception and privilege, which allowed one to defy the law almost as much as arbitrary power, and almost never went so far as to furnish the most natural and necessary guarantees for all citizens. Thus reduced and deformed, freedom was still fruitful. It was freedom that, in the very era when centralization worked more and more to equalize, to bend, and to tarnish all characters, preserved their native originality, their color, and their shape for a great many individuals, nourished self-respect in their hearts, and often made the desire for glory predominate over all other passions. Freedom alone formed those vigorous minds, those bold and proud geniuses whom we will see appear, and who will make of the French Revolution the object of the simultaneous admiration and terror of generations to come. It would be very strange if such manly virtues had been able to grow from a soil where freedom no longer existed.

But if this kind of disorderly and unhealthy freedom prepared the French to overthrow despotism, it perhaps made them less capable than any other people of founding in its place the free and peaceable empire of the law.

CHAPTER TWELVE

How, Despite the Progress of Civilization, the Condition of the French Peasant Was Sometimes Worse in the Eighteenth Century Than It Had Been in the Thirteenth

In the eighteenth century, the French peasant could no longer be the prey of petty feudal despots; he was only rarely exposed to violence on the part of the government; he enjoyed civil liberty and owned a piece of land; but all people of other classes were separated from him, and he was perhaps more isolated than anyone has ever been anywhere else. This was a new and unique kind of oppression, whose effects deserve to be carefully considered in themselves.

From the beginning of the seventeenth century, Henry IV complained, according to Péréfix, that the nobles were abandoning the countryside. By the middle of the eighteenth century, this desertion had become almost universal. All the documents of the time note and deplore it: the economists in their books, the intendants in their correspondence, the agricultural societies in their reports. We find the real proof of it in the registers of the capitation. The capitation was paid at one's principal residence: it was paid in Paris by all the greater nobles and some of the lesser.

In the countryside there remained hardly any but the noble whose wealth was too little to let him leave. That kind of person found himself in a position toward his neighbors, the peasants, where never a rich landowner was to be seen, I think. No longer their leader, he no longer had the interest which he formerly had had to get along with them, to help them, to lead them; and, on the other hand, not being burdened with the same public expenses as they, he could not feel very much sympathy with their misery, in which he did not share, nor associate himself with their grievances, which were foreign to him.[44] These people were no longer his subjects, and he was not yet their fellow citizen: a fact unique in history.

This brought about a kind of absenteeism of the heart, if I may put it that way, still more common and more effective than absenteeism strictly speaking. From this it came about that the noble living on his lands often had the same views and feelings that his steward would have had in his absence; like him, he no longer saw in his tenants anything but debtors, and he demanded from them everything which was still coming to him according to law or custom, which sometimes made the payment of what was left of feudal dues harsher than in the feudal era itself.

Often indebted and always in need, the noble usually lived very poorly in his chateau, just trying to save the money he was going to spend in town that winter. The people, whose words often go straight to the heart of things, gave to this kind of petty noble the name of the smallest of the birds of prey: they called him the *hobby-hawk* [*hobereau*].

Doubtless there were individuals who did not fit this description; I speak of classes, they alone ought to interest history. There were, at that time, many rich landowners who without any need and without any common interest were concerned about the well-being of their peasants— who denies it? But those individuals successfully fought against the law of their new situation, which, despite themselves, pushed them towards indifference, as it pushed their former vassals towards hatred.

The abandonment of the countryside by the nobility has often been attributed to the particular influence of certain ministers and certain kings, by some to Richelieu and by others to Louis XIV. It was, in fact, a policy almost always followed by the rulers during the last three centuries of the monarchy, to divide the nobility from the people, and to attract the nobles to court and into government service. This was seen above all in the seventeenth century, when the nobility was still an object of fear to the Crown. Among the questions addressed to the intendants this one was still found: do the nobles of your province like to stay at home or not?

We have the letter of an intendant responding on this subject; he complains that the nobles of his province like to stay with their peasants, rather than fulfilling their duties to their king. But note this well: the province of which he spoke thus was Anjou; later called the Vendée. These nobles, who were criticized for preferring to live with their peasants, who refused, it was said, to do their duty to the king, were the only ones who defended the monarchy in France arms in hand, and were able to die there in combat for it; and they owed that glorious distinction only to the fact that they had known how to keep their peasants around them.

Nevertheless, one must avoid attributing the abandonment of the countryside by the class which then led the nation to the direct influence of a few of our kings. The chief and permanent cause of this fact was not the will of certain men, but the slow and constant actions of institutions; and what proves it is that when, in the eighteenth century, the government wanted to fight the evil, it could not even halt its progress. As the nobility lost its political rights without acquiring any others, and as local freedoms disappeared, the emigration of the nobility increased: there was no longer any need to encourage them to leave; they no longer had any desire to stay home. Country life had become boring to them.

What is said here of the nobles ought to be extended to rich land-owners in general, everywhere: centralization meant countrysides empty of rich and well-educated inhabitants; and I might add centralization meant lands of bad and antiquated agricultural practices. I could comment on Montesquieu's saying, in demonstrating its meaning: "Land is productive less by virtue of its fertility than by virtue of the freedom of its inhabitants." But I do not want to go beyond my subject.

We have seen how the middle class, also leaving the countryside, everywhere looked for refuge in the towns. There is no point on which all the documents of the old regime agree more. In the country one almost never sees more than one generation of rich peasants, they say. If a farmer finally succeeded by hard work in acquiring a little money, he immediately took his son from the plow, sent him to town, and bought him a little office. From this time dates that striking horror which even now the French farmer often shows for the profession that has enriched him. The effect has outlived the cause.

In truth, the only well-educated man or, as the English say, the only *gentleman* who lived permanently among the peasants and remained in close touch with them was the priest. The priest would also have become the leader of the rural population, despite Voltaire, if he himself had not been so strongly and visibly attached to the political hierarchy; by possessing several of its privileges, he inspired some of the hatred to which it gave birth.[45]

Therefore we see the peasant almost entirely separated from the upper classes; he is distant even from those of his neighbors who could have helped him and led him. As they acquired education or wealth, they fled; he remained as if selected and set apart from the rest of the nation.

This was not seen to the same extent among any of the great civilized nations of Europe, and in France itself the fact was recent. The peasant of the fourteenth century was both more oppressed and more helped. The aristocracy sometimes tyrannized him, but they never abandoned him.

In the eighteenth century, a village is a community whose members are all poor, ignorant, and coarse; its magistrates are as unpolished and as despised as the inhabitants: its syndic does not know how to read, by himself its tax-collector cannot balance the accounts on which his own fortune and that of his neighbors depend. Not only does his old lord no longer have the right to govern him, but he now considers it a kind of degradation to take part in the government of the village. To assess the taxes, raise the militia, regulate the corvées, these are servile duties, the syndic's work. There is no longer anyone but the central government which is interested in the village, and since it is very far away, and has nothing to fear from its inhabitants, it is only interested in making a profit out of it.

Come see now what becomes of an abandoned class, which no one has any desire to tyrannize, but which no one is interested in educating and serving.

The heaviest burdens which the feudal system placed on the rural inhabitants had doubtless been lightened or eliminated; but what we hardly know enough about is that others had been substituted which were perhaps still heavier. The peasant no longer suffered all the evils his ancestors had borne, but he endured many miseries they had never known. We know that it was almost uniquely at the peasant's expense that the taille had increased tenfold over two centuries. A word must be said here about the manner in which it was levied, to show what barbarous laws can be created or preserved in civilized centuries, when the nation's most enlightened men have no personal interest in changing them.

I found in a confidential letter written in 1772 by the controller-general himself, to the intendants, a description of the taille which is a small masterpiece of exactitude and concision. "The taille" says this minister, "is arbitrary in its division, and those subject to it are mutually responsible for its payment. It is levied on persons and not on land. In most of France it is subject to constant changes because of all the yearly variations in the wealth of those who pay it." Everything is there in three sentences; the evil from which one profited could not be more cleverly described.

The sum total which the parish owed was set every year. It changed constantly, as the minister said, in such a way that no farmer could foresee a year in advance what he would have to pay the following year. Within the parish, a peasant chosen by lot each year to be tax collector had to divide the burden of the tax among everyone else. I promised that I would describe the situation of this collector. Let the provincial assembly of Berry in 1779 speak; it is not suspect: it was made up entirely of privileged people who were appointed by the king and never paid the taille: "Since everyone wants to avoid the burden of being collector," it says in 1779, "it is necessary for everyone to take turns at it. The raising of the taille is therefore given to a new collector every year, without regard for competence or honesty; thus the makeup of each tax-roll resembles the character of the man who drew it up. The collector imprints it with his fears, his weaknesses, or his vices. How, furthermore, could he do it well? He acts in the dark. For who really knows how rich his neighbor is, and how his wealth compares with that of someone else? However, the collector alone must make the decision, and he is responsible with all his property, and even his body, for the receipts. For two years he usually has to waste half his days running around among the taxpayers. Those who don't know how to read must find someone in the neighborhood who can do it for them." Turgot had already said of another province, a little before: "The job is the despair and almost always the ruin of those who are burdened with it; we thus successively reduce to poverty all the better-off families of a village." [46]

This unfortunate peasant was, however, armed with immense arbitrary power; he was almost as much a tyrant as a martyr. During the exercise of his office, while he was ruining himself, he had everyone else's ruin in his hands. It is again the provincial assembly which speaks: "Preference for his relations, for his friends and neighbors, hatred, vengeance against his enemies, the need for a protector, the fear of displeasing a well-off citizen who can give him work, struggle with the feelings of justice in his heart." Terror often made the collector pitiless: There were parishes where the collector never went out to collect taxes unless accompanied by bailiffs and marshals. "When he goes out without a bailiff," says an intendant to a minister in 1764, "the taxpayers don't want to pay him." "In the district of Villefranche alone," the provincial assembly of Guyenne tells us again, "106 marshals can be counted, constantly at work."

To escape this violent and arbitrary taxation the French peasant, in the middle of the eighteenth century, acted like the Jew of the Middle Ages. He appeared to be destitute, even if by chance he wasn't really so badly off; being well-off made him justifiably afraid. I find very tangible proof of this in a document which is no longer from Guyenne but from 100 leagues away. The Agricultural Society of Maine announced in its report for 1761 that it had had the idea of distributing some animals as prizes and encouragements. "It has been stopped," it says, "by the dangerous consequences that low jealousy could bring down on those who won the prizes, and which, through the arbitrary division of the taxes, could harm them in later years."

In this tax system, every taxpayer had, in fact, a direct and permanent interest in spying on his neighbors and reporting to the collector on the increase of their wealth; everything was listed there, from envy, informing and hatred. Would one not think that these things were happening in the domains of some rajah of Hindustan?

However, there were at the same time in France some regions where the taxes were levied lightly and fairly: these were certain *pays d'états*.[47] It is true that these provinces had been left the right to raise the taxes themselves. In Languedoc, for example, the taille was paid only on land, and did not vary at all according to the wealth of the owner. It was based on a fixed and public land-register that was carefully made up and reviewed every thirty years, and in which land was divided into three classes, according to its fertility. Every taxpayer knew in advance exactly what proportion of the tax he would have to pay. If he did not pay, he alone, or rather his land alone, was responsible. If he thought he had been treated unfairly in the division, he always had the right to have his assessment compared with that of another member of his parish whom he chose himself. It is what we today call the appeal to proportional equality.

We see that all these rules are exactly the ones we follow now; we have hardly improved them since, we have only made them general; for it is worth remarking that, even though we have taken from the government of the old regime the basic shape of our public administration, we have refrained from imitating it in everything else. It is from the provincial assemblies, not from the government, that we have borrowed our best administrative methods. While adopting the machine, we have rejected the product.

The habitual poverty of the rural population had given birth to maxims which were not likely to put an end to it. "If the lower classes were well-off," Richelieu wrote in his *Political Testament,* "they would not stay in line." In the eighteenth century one didn't go quite so far, but it was still believed that the peasant would never work if he wasn't constantly compelled by necessity: poverty seemed to be the only guarantee against laziness. This is precisely the theory that I have sometimes heard professed with regard to the blacks in our colonies. This opinion is so widespread among those who govern that almost all economists have been obliged to formally combat it.

We know that the original purpose of the taille was to allow the king to buy soldiers so as to relieve the nobles and their vassals from military service; but in the seventeenth century the obligation of military service was imposed once again, as we have seen, under the name of the militia, and this time it weighed only on the lower classes, and almost solely on the peasant. It is enough to consider the multitude of police reports which

fill an intendancy's files, all about draft-dodgers or deserters, to see that
the militia was not easy to raise. It seems, in fact, that there was no public
burden more unbearable to the peasants than this; in order to avoid it
they often fled into the woods, where they had to be pursued by armed
men. This is astonishing when one thinks of the ease with which forced
recruitment is carried on today.

The extreme repugnance of the peasants of the old regime for the militia must be attributed less to the principle of the law itself than to the
manner in which it was carried out; it was above all the long uncertainty
with which it threatened those whom it took (one could be called up until
age forty, at least if one was not married); the arbitrariness of the selection
process, which made a good draft lottery number almost worthless; the
prohibition on finding a replacement; the disgust for a profession that
was difficult and dangerous, where all hope of advancement was lacking;
but above all the feeling that this great burden was borne by themselves
alone, and by the poorest of them, the ignominy of the situation making
its hardships more bitter.

I have had in my hands many transcripts from the draft-lottery of 1769,
in a great number of parishes; there one sees the figures for the number
of persons exempt in each parish: this man is the domestic servant of a
noble; that one is the watchman of an abbey, a third is merely the valet of
a bourgeois, it is true, but this bourgeois *lives nobly*. Wealth by itself exempts; when a farmer is numbered among the highest-taxed annually, his
sons have the privilege of being exempt from the militia: this is what was
called encouraging agriculture. The physiocrats,[†] great lovers of equality
in everything else, were not in the least shocked by this privilege; they
asked only for it to be extended to other cases, that is, for the burden of
the poorest and least protected peasants to become still heavier. "The
poor wages of a soldier," says one of them, "the way in which he is
housed, dressed, fed, his complete subjection, would make it too cruel to
take anyone but a man of the lowest classes."

Until the end of the reign of Louis XIV, the highways were not kept
up, or else were repaired at the expense of all those who used them, that
is, the state, or all the landowners who bordered them; but around that
time, they began to be repaired with the aid of the corvée alone, that is,
at the sole expense of the peasantry. This way of having good roads without paying for them seemed such a good idea that in 1737 a circular from
Controller-General Orry applied it to all of France. The intendants were
armed with the right to imprison recalcitrants at will or send marshals to
fetch them.

From then on, every time that trade increased, every time that the need and desire for good roads spread, the corvée was again extended and its burden increased.[48] We find in the report made in 1779 to the provincial assembly of Berry that the works executed by the corvée in that poor province were valued at 700,000 livres annually. They were evaluated in 1787, in lower Normandy, at nearly the same amount. Nothing could better show the sad situation of the people of the countryside: the progress of society which enriched all other classes made them despair; civilization turned against them alone.[49]

In the correspondence of the intendants from around the same period, I read that it was useful to refuse to employ peasants in repairing the roads of their own villages, in order that they be reserved for only the great highways, or, as they said then, *for the king's roads.* The strange idea that it was suitable to have the poorest, and those who were least likely to travel, pay for the roads, this idea, even though novel, entrenched itself so naturally in the minds of those who benefited from it, that soon they could no longer imagine how anything could be done differently.[50] In 1776 the attempt was made to transform the corvée into a local tax; the inequality was immediately transformed with it and went into the new tax.

From the manorial obligation it had formerly been, the corvée, in becoming royal, was extended little by little to all public works. The corvée was used in 1719 to construct some barracks! *"The parishes ought to send their best workers,"* says the ordinance, *"and all other work ought to give precedence to this."* The corvée transported the convicts to the galleys and beggars to the almshouse; it carted military baggage whenever the troops moved: a very heavy burden in a time when each regiment carried heavy baggage with it. A large number of wagons with oxen to pull them had to be assembled from a great distance. This kind of corvée, which was not very important in the beginning, became one of the heaviest when the standing army became bigger.[51] I find government contractors who loudly demand that they be given the corvée to transport wood for construction to the naval arsenals from the forests.[52] The *corvéables* usually received a salary, but always low and arbitrarily set. The weight of a burden so badly placed became so heavy that sometimes the Receiver of tailles became worried. "The expenses demanded of the peasants for road-repair," writes one of them in 1751, "soon leave them unable to pay their taille."

Could all these new oppressions have been established if they had found rich and educated men alongside the peasants who had the desire and the power, if not to defend the peasants, at least to intercede for them with their common master, who already held in his hands the fortune of rich and poor? I have read the letter that a great landowner wrote in 1774 to the intendant of his province to get him to make a road. This road, according to the landowner, would guarantee the prosperity of the village, and he gave the reasons why; then he went on to propose the establishment of a market, which would double the price of grain, he assured the intendant. This good citizen added that, with the help of a small grant, one could establish a school which would make the king's subjects more productive. He had never thought of these necessary improvements until then; they had only occurred to him because for two years he had been confined to his chateau under house arrest. "My exile for the past two years on my lands," he said innocently, "has convinced me of the great utility of all these things."

But it was above all in times of food shortage that one saw that the ties of patronage and dependence which formerly bound the great rural landowner to the peasants had been relaxed or broken. In these moments of crisis, the central government became frightened of its isolation and its weakness, and it momentarily wanted to revive the individual influences or the political associations which it had destroyed; it called them to its aid, but no one came, and it was usually astonished to find that those whom it had murdered were dead.

In this extremity there were intendants in the poorest provinces, like Turgot, for example, who illegally made ordinances to require the rich landowners to feed their sharecroppers until the next harvest. I have found, dated 1770, letters from several priests who suggest that the intendant tax the great landowners of their parishes, both clerical and lay, "those who possess vast estates which they never live on, from which they draw large incomes which they consume elsewhere."

Even in normal times, the villages were infested with beggars; for, as Letrone said, the poor were helped in the towns, but in the country begging was an absolute necessity during the winter. Occasionally these unfortunates were proceeded against with great violence. In 1767, the duc de Choiseul wanted to get rid of begging in France at a single stroke. We can see in the intendants' correspondence how harshly he acted. The mounted police were ordered to arrest at one blow all the beggars to be found in the kingdom; we are told that more than fifty thousand were seized. The real criminals were to be sent to the galleys; for the rest, more than forty almshouses were opened to receive them; it would have been better to reopen the hearts of the rich.

This government of the old regime, which was, as I have said, so gentle and sometimes so timid when it came to men placed above the lower classes, so enamored of forms, of slowness and consideration, was often harsh and always quick when it acted against the lower classes, and above all against the peasantry. Among the documents I have read, I have not seen a single one which describes the arrest of a bourgeois by order of an intendant; but the peasants were constantly arrested, due to the corvée, the militia, begging, crime, a thousand other circumstances. For some, there were independent courts, long debates, a watchful public; for others, there was the magistrate, who gave summary judgment without appeal.

"The immense distance which exists between the masses and all other classes," writes Necker in 1785, helps to turn "our eyes away from the ways in which power can be used against those lost in the crowd. Without the mildness and humanity which characterize the French and the spirit of the century, this would be a constant source of grief for those who can feel a yoke from which they are exempt."

But oppression showed itself less in the evil that was done to these unfortunates than in the good which they were forbidden to do for themselves. They were free, they were landowners, and they remained almost as ignorant and often more miserable than their serf ancestors. They remained without technology in the midst of prodigies of the arts, and uncivilized in a world shining with enlightenment. While keeping the intelligence and shrewdness natural to their race, they had not learned how to make use of it; they could not even succeed at cultivating their land, which was their only business. "I see under my own eyes the agriculture of the tenth century," says a celebrated English agronomist. They excelled only in the profession of arms; there, at least, they had a natural and necessary contact with other classes.

The peasant lived in this abyss of poverty and isolation; he was kept there as if it were sealed and impenetrable. I have been surprised, and almost frightened, to see that the method the government sometimes used to find out the population of each parish was as follows, less than twenty years before Catholic worship was abolished and the churches profaned without resistance: the priests reported the number of those who were present at Easter communion; added to them was the presumed number of sick and small children: the whole was the total of inhabitants. However, from all directions the ideas of the times had already spread to these coarse minds; they got there by crooked and underground paths, and in these small and obscure places sometimes took on strange forms. Nevertheless, nothing seemed changed on the outside. The mores of the peasant, his habits, his beliefs, still seemed the same; he was submissive, he was even merry.

One must distrust the gaiety that the French often show in their greatest misfortunes; it only proves that, believing bad fortune inevitable, they try to distract themselves from it by not thinking about it, not that they do not feel it. Offer this man a path whereby he can get out of this misery which seems to bother him so little, and he will throw himself down it with so much violence that he will walk over you without seeing you if you are in his way.

We see these things clearly from the point where we are now; but his contemporaries did not see them. It is only with great difficulty that the upper classes ever manage to see clearly what is going on in the soul of the masses, and in particular in that of the peasantry. Education and lifestyle put things in a perspective which is particular to the rich and which remains closed to all others. But once the poor man and the rich man no longer have almost any interests in common, no common grievances, nor common business, the shadows which hide the mind of the one from the other become impenetrable, and these two men could live side by side forever, without ever knowing each other. It is curious to see in what strange security those who occupied the upper and middle floors of the social edifice lived, at the very moment when the Revolution began, and to hear them talking innocently among themselves about the virtues of the people, of their mildness, their devotion, their innocent pleasures, when 1793 is already before them: a ridiculous and terrible sight!

Let us stop here before passing on, and ponder for a moment, through all these little facts that I have just described, one of the greatest of God's laws in the conduct of societies.

The French nobility persisted in remaining apart from the other classes; in the end the nobles had exempted themselves from most of the public burdens which weighed on them; they figured that they would keep their greatness better by avoiding these expenses, and at first this seemed to be the case. But soon an invisible internal sickness seemed to be attached to their rank, which was slowly diminished without anyone attacking them; as their immunities grew, they became impoverished. The bourgeoisie, with whom they so much feared to mix, on the contrary enriched itself and educated itself alongside them, without them, and against them; the nobility had not wanted to have the bourgeois either as associates or as fellow-citizens, but they were going to encounter them as rivals, soon as enemies, and finally as masters. An external power had discharged the nobility from the duty to lead, to protect, to help their vassals, but since at the same time it left them their financial rights and their honorific privileges, they didn't think that they had lost anything. Since they still walked first in processions, they thought that they still led, and in fact they continued to have around them people whom they called their subjects, in the notaries' records; other people called themselves their vassals, their tenants, their lessors. In reality, no one followed them, they were alone, and when, finally, some came to overthrow them, the nobility could do nothing but flee.

Although the fate of the nobility and that of the bourgeoisie were very different, they resembled each other in one respect: the bourgeois ended up living as apart from the masses as the noble himself. Far from getting closer to the peasants, he fled from contact with their miseries; rather than firmly uniting himself with them, in order to struggle together against the common inequality, the bourgeois only sought to create new injustices for his own use: we have seen him as avid to create new exceptions for himself as the noble was to maintain his privileges. These peasants, from whom the bourgeois came, had become not merely strangers but in effect unknowns, and only after he had put arms in their hands did he realize that he had excited passions of which he had no idea, passions that he was as powerless to contain as to direct, and of which he was going to become the victim after having been the promoter.

There will always be astonishment at seeing the ruin of that great royal house of France, which had seemed as if it was going to spread itself across all Europe; but those who read its history carefully will understand its fall without difficulty. In fact, almost all the vices, almost all the errors, almost all the fatal prejudices that I have just depicted owed either their birth, or their duration, or their development, to the art which most of our kings practiced, of dividing people in order to govern them more absolutely.

But when the bourgeois had been so well isolated from the noble, and the peasant from the noble and the bourgeois; when a similar process continued within each class, and there was created within each one of them little individual aggregations almost as isolated from each other as the classes were among themselves, then it was found that the whole was no longer composed of anything but a homogeneous mass, of which, however, the parts were no longer linked. Nothing was in a position to hinder the government any longer, and nothing to support it either. Thus the entire structure of the ruler's greatness could collapse at once, in a minute, as soon as the society on which it was based trembled.

And finally this people, who alone would have profited from the faults and errors of all its masters, if it had really escaped from their hegemony, could not avoid the yoke of false ideas, of vicious habits, of bad inclinations which their masters had given it or let it practice. We have sometimes seen it bring the desires of a slave into the very use of its freedom, as incapable of governing itself as its teachers had been of governing it.

Book Three

CHAPTER ONE

How Around the Middle of the Eighteenth Century Intellectuals Became the Country's Leading Politicians, and the Effects Which Resulted from This

I will now leave the long-term and general facts which prepared the great Revolution which I want to paint, to come to the particular and more recent facts which finally determined its place, its birth, and its character.

France had long been the most literary of all the nations of Europe; nevertheless its men of letters had never shown the spirit that they displayed in the middle of the eighteenth century, nor occupied the place that they then took. This had never before been seen among us, nor, I think, anywhere else.

Men of letters were not daily involved in public affairs as in England; on the contrary, they had never been further removed from them. They were never given any authority whatsoever, and never occupied any public office in a society already full of government officials. However, they did not remain, like most of their German counterparts, entirely strangers to politics, confined to the domain of pure philosophy and belles-lettres. They constantly concerned themselves with topics relating to government; in fact, that was their real occupation. Every day they were heard discussing the origin of societies and their original forms, the primordial rights of citizens and those of authority, the natural and artificial relations among men, the error or legitimacy of custom, the very principles of the laws. Thus penetrating every day to the roots of their era's constitution, they curiously examined its structure and criticized its general plan. Not all of them, it is true, made these great problems the object of special and thorough study; the majority treated them only in passing, and playfully; but they all dealt with them. This kind of abstract and literary politics was spread in varying degree throughout the works of the time. There were none, from the thick treatise to the popular song, which did not contain a little politics.

As for the political systems of these writers, they differ from one another so much that anyone who wanted to reconcile them and make them into a single theory of government would never be able to finish his project. Nevertheless, when we leave out the details in order to get to the basic ideas, we easily discover that the authors of these different systems at least agreed on one very general idea, that each one of them seems equally to have thought of, a general idea which seems to precede all the particular ideas in their minds and to be the common source for them. However divided they are in the rest of their thinking, they all start from this same point: they all think that it would be good to substitute basic and simple principles, derived from reason and natural law, for the complicated and traditional customs which ruled the society of their times. In closely examining this, we shall see that what may properly be called the political philosophy of the eighteenth century consisted of this single idea.

The idea was hardly new: for three thousand years it had repeatedly crossed the human mind without being able to find a home. How did it manage to seize all writers' minds at this time? Why, rather than stopping with a few philosophers, as it had so often done before, did it descend to the crowd, and there take on the shape and heat of a political passion, so that abstract and general theories became the subject of the daily conversation of the leisured, and inflamed the imagination of even women and peasants? How did men of letters, who possessed neither rank, nor honors, nor wealth, nor responsibility, nor power, become, in fact, the chief statesmen of the time, and even the only ones, since although others ran the government, they alone had authority? I would like briefly to show why, and to make clear what an extraordinary and terrible influence these facts, which seem to belong just to our literary history, have had on the Revolution, and on down to our own times.

It was not by chance that the philosophes of the eighteenth century had commonly conceived ideas so opposed to those which still served as the base of their society; these ideas had been suggested to them naturally by the sight of this same society that they all had beneath their eyes. The spectacle of so many abusive or ridiculous privileges, whose burden was more and more felt, and whose justification was less and less understood, forced or rather simultaneously encouraged all of them towards the idea of the natural equality of ranks. Seeing so many bizarre and irregular institutions, the offspring of other eras, that no one had attempted to coordinate or accommodate to new needs, institutions which seemed doomed to live forever after having lost their virtue, the philosophes readily acquired a disgust for old things and for tradition, and they were naturally led to want to rebuild contemporary society according to an entirely new plan, that each of them drew from the inspiration of his reason alone.

The very situation of these writers prepared them to like general and abstract theories of government and to trust in them blindly.[53] At the almost infinite distance from practice in which they lived, no experience tempered the ardors of their nature; nothing warned them of the obstacles that existing facts might place before even the most desirable reforms; they didn't have any idea of the dangers which always accompany even the most necessary revolutions. They did not even have the least suspicion of them; for the complete absence of political freedom had made the world of action not merely badly known to them, but invisible. They were not involved in it, and could not even see what others did there. They therefore lacked that elementary education that the sight of a free society, and the noise of all that is said there, gives even to those who are least involved in government. They thus became much bolder in their innovations, fonder of general ideas and systems, more contemptuous of old wisdom, and still more confident of their individual reason, than is usual among authors who write speculative works about politics.

The same ignorance gave them the crowd's ear and heart. If, as formerly, the French had still taken part in government through the Estates-General, if they had even continued to be daily involved in regional administration through their provincial assemblies, we may affirm that they would never have let themselves be inflamed by writers' ideas as they were then; they would have retained a certain practical experience which would have warned them against pure theory.

If, like the English, they had been able, without destroying their old institutions, to gradually change their spirit by practice, perhaps they would not so easily have thought up completely new ones. But every Frenchman felt daily injured in his fortune, in his person, in his well-being, or in his pride by some old law, some ancient political practice, some remnant of the old powers, and he did not see any means available to remedy the particular problem himself. It seemed that one had to accept everything or destroy everything in the country's constitution.

We had, however, preserved one liberty from the destruction of all the others; we could philosophize almost without restraint on the origin of societies, on the essential nature of government, and on the primordial rights of the human species. All those injured by the daily practice of legislation soon took up this form of literary politics. The taste for it spread even to those whose nature or status normally most distanced them from abstract speculations. There was no taxpayer hurt by the unequal distribution of the tailles who did not feel warmed by the idea that all men ought to be equal; no small landowner devastated by his noble neighbor's rabbits who was not happy to hear it said that all privileges whatsoever were condemned by reason. Every public passion was thus wrapped up in philosophy; political life was violently driven back into literature, and writers, taking in hand the direction of opinion, found themselves for a moment taking the place that party leaders usually hold in free countries.

No one was any longer in a position to dispute this role. An aristocracy in its vigor not only runs affairs, it still directs opinion, sets the tone for writers, and lends authority to ideas. In the eighteenth century, the French nobility had entirely lost this part of its empire; its moral authority had followed the fortunes of its power: the place that it had occupied in the government of minds was empty, and writers could occupy it at their leisure and fill it completely. Still more, the aristocracy itself, whose place the writers took, favored their project. The aristocracy had so forgotten how general theories, once accepted, inevitably end up turning themselves into political passions and actions, that the doctrines most opposed to its special rights, and even to its existence, seemed very clever intellectual games; it freely joined in the games, to pass the time, and peaceably enjoyed its immunities and its privileges while serenely discoursing on the absurdity of all established customs.

We are often astonished at seeing the strange blindness with which the upper classes of the old regime thus aided in their own destruction; but where would they have learned otherwise? Free institutions are not less necessary to the leading citizens, to teach them their dangers, than to the humblest, to assure them their rights. For more than a century, since the last traces of public life had disappeared among us, the people most directly interested in the maintenance of the old constitution had not been warned by any clash or uproar of the decay of that antique structure. Since nothing had changed on the outside, they figured that everything had stayed exactly the same. Thus their minds had frozen in their ancestors' point of view. In the cahiers of 1789 the nobility showed itself just as preoccupied with the encroachments of royal power as it might have been in those of the fifteenth century. On his side, the unfortunate Louis XVI, a moment before perishing in the democratic flood, as Burke rightly remarks, continued to see in the aristocracy the chief rival of royal power; he distrusted the aristocracy as if it had still been the time of the Fronde.

The bourgeoisie and the people, on the contrary, appeared to him, as to his ancestors, the surest support of the throne.

But what appears strangest to us, we who can contemplate the remains of so many revolutions, is that the very notion of a violent revolution was missing from our fathers' minds. It was not discussed, it was not even conceived of. The little shocks that freedom continually gives the most secure societies recall every day the possibility of upheaval, and keep awake public prudence; but in eighteenth-century French society, which was about to fall into the abyss, nothing yet warned that it was losing its balance.

I carefully read the cahiers that the three orders drew up before meeting in 1789; I mean the three orders, those of the nobility and the clergy as well as that of the Third Estate. I see that here one asks for the change of a law, there of a custom, and I take note. I continue thus to the end of this immense work, and, when I come to put together all these particular wishes, I realize with a kind of terror that what is demanded is the simultaneous and systematic abolition of all the laws and all the customs in use in the country; I see immediately that it is going to be a question of one of the most vast and most dangerous revolutions which has ever happened in the world. Those who will be its victims tomorrow sense nothing of it; they think that the rapid and complete transformation of a society so old and complicated can happen without a jar, with the aid of reason, and by its means alone. Poor fools! They had even forgotten that maxim which their ancestors had expressed, four hundred years earlier, in the naive and energetic French of those times: *"by demanding too much freedom one gets too much slavery."*

It is not surprising that the nobility and the bourgeoisie, excluded for so long from public life, showed this singular inexperience; but what is more astonishing, is that even those who ran things, the ministers, the judges, the intendants, showed hardly any more foresight. Yet several of them were very able men in their fields; they knew in depth all the details of the public administration of their time; but as for that great science of government, which teaches how to understand the general movement of society, to judge what is going on in the minds of the masses and to foresee what will come of it, they were as naive as the people themselves. There is nothing, in fact, but the play of free institutions which can really teach politicians this principal part of their art.

This can be clearly seen in the report that Turgot sent to the king in 1775, where he advised him to create, among other things, a representative assembly freely elected by the whole nation, to meet for six weeks annually in the king's presence, but not to give it any real power. It would concern itself only with administration and never with government, it would give advice rather than make demands, and, in truth, would be charged only with talking about laws, rather than making them. "In this way, royal power would be informed and not hindered," he said, "and public opinion satisfied without risk. For these assemblies would have no authority to oppose necessary operations, and if, by some remote chance, they did not accept them, Your Majesty would still remain the master." One could not more completely misunderstand the importance of an action and the spirit of one's times. It is true that it has often happened, towards the end of revolutions, that one could do what Turgot proposed with impunity, giving the shadow of freedom without the reality. Augustus attempted it with success. A nation tired of long debates will voluntarily consent to be duped, provided that it is given rest, and history teaches us that to satisfy the nation it is then enough to gather a certain number of obscure or dependent men from all over the country, and in return for a salary make them play the role of a political assembly for the nation. There have been several examples of this. But at the beginning of a revolution these attempts always fail, and do nothing but arouse the people without satisfying them. The least citizen of a free country knows this; Turgot, great administrator though he was, was ignorant of it.

If one thinks now that this same French nation, so estranged from its own affairs and so deprived of experience, so hindered by its institutions, and so powerless to correct them, was at the same time the most educated of all the nations on earth, and the most fond of things intellectual, one will understand without difficulty how writers became a political power in France, and ended up being the most important one. While in England those who wrote about government mingled with those who governed, the one introducing new ideas into practice, the other correcting and limiting theories with the help of facts, in France the political world remained as if divided into two separate provinces without commerce between them. The first governed; the second established the abstract principles on which all government ought to be founded. Here one took the particular actions indicated by routine; there one proclaimed general laws, without ever thinking about the means to apply them: on one side, the conduct of affairs; on the other, the direction of minds.

Above the real society, whose constitution was still traditional, confused, and irregular, where laws remained varied and contradictory, ranks were separated, status was fixed, and burdens were unequal, there was slowly built an imaginary society in which everything seemed simple and coordinated, uniform, equitable, and in accord with reason. Gradually the imagination of the crowd deserted the former to concentrate on the latter. One lost interest in what was, in order to think about what could be, and finally one lived mentally in that ideal city the writers had built.

Our revolution has often been attributed to that of America: in fact the American Revolution had a lot of influence on the French Revolution, but less because of what was then done in the United States than because of what was being thought at the same time in France. While in the rest of Europe the American Revolution was still nothing but a new and unusual fact, among us it only made more evident and more striking what we thought we already knew. It astonished Europe; here it completed our conversion. The Americans seemed merely to apply what our writers had thought of: they gave substantial reality to what we were dreaming about. It was as if Fénelon† had suddenly found himself transported to Salentum.†

This situation, so new to history, in which the entire political education of a great nation was completely shaped by men of letters, was perhaps what contributed most to giving the French Revolution its particular spirit, and made it lead to what we see today.

The writers not only furnished their ideas to the people who made the Revolution; they also gave them their own temperament and disposition. Under this long training, in the absence of any other directors, in the midst of the profound practical ignorance in which they lived, the whole nation ended up adopting the instincts, the attitudes, the tastes, and even the eccentricities of those who write; with the result that when the nation finally had to act, it brought all the habits of literature into politics.

When we study the history of our Revolution, we see that it was carried out in precisely the same spirit in which so many abstract books on government are written. The same attraction for general theories, for complete systems of legislation and exact symmetry in laws; the same contempt for existing facts; the same confidence in theory; the same taste for the original, the ingenious, and the new in institutions; the same desire to remake the whole constitution all at once, following the rules of logic and according to a single plan, rather than trying to fix its various parts. A frightening sight! For what is merit in a writer is sometimes vice in a statesman, and the same things which have often made lovely books can lead to great revolutions.

The language of politics itself then took on the quality of that spoken by authors; it was full of general expressions, abstract terms, ambitious words, and literary turns of phrase. With the help of the political passions which used it, this style spread to all classes and descended with unusual ease even into the lowest. Well before the Revolution, the edicts of King Louis XVI often spoke of natural law and the rights of men. I find peasants who, in their requests, called their neighbors their fellow citizens; the intendant, a respectable magistrate; the parish priest, the minister of the altars; God, the Supreme Being. To become mediocre men of letters, all they had to do was learn how to spell.

These new qualities were so well incorporated into the old foundation of French character that we have often attributed to our nature what derived purely from this unique education. I have heard it argued that the taste, or rather the passion, that we have shown during the past sixty years for general ideas, systems, and big words in political matters, came from I don't know what special attribute of our race, from what is called a bit pompously *the French mind:* as if this supposed attribute could have appeared all at once at the end of the last century, after having been hidden during all the rest of our history.

What is unique is that we have kept the habits we took from literature, while losing almost completely our old love of letters. I have often been astonished, in the course of my public life, to see people who never read the books of the eighteenth century nor those of any other, and who strongly despise writers, preserve so faithfully some of the chief faults which the literary mind produced before they were born.

CHAPTER TWO

How Irreligion Was Able to Become a General and Dominant Passion among the French of the Eighteenth Century, and What Kind of Influence This Had on the Character of the Revolution

Since the great revolution of the sixteenth century, when the spirit of inquiry attempted to distinguish between true and false among the various traditions of Christianity, some bolder or more curious minds have never ceased to contest or reject them all. The same spirit that in Luther's time made several million Catholics suddenly abandon Catholicism, pushed a few isolated Christians out of Christianity altogether every year: unbelief replaced heresy.

We can say, in a general way, that in the eighteenth century Christianity had lost a great part of its power throughout the European continent; but, in the majority of countries, it was more abandoned than violently attacked; even those who abandoned it left it with regret. Irreligion was widespread among the rulers and advanced minds, but it still barely penetrated into the heart of the middle classes and the people; it remained the whim of a few minds, not a common opinion. "It is a generally widespread prejudice in Germany," says Mirabeau in 1787, "that the Prussian provinces are full of atheists. The truth is that if there are a few freethinkers to be found, the people are as attached to their religion as in the most devout countries, and one can even count a pretty large number of fanatics there." He adds that it is much to be regretted that Frederick II never authorized the marriage of Catholic priests, and above all refused to leave those who married the income from their ecclesiastical benefices, "a measure," he says, "that we would have dared think worthy of that great man." Nowhere had irreligion yet become a general passion, ardent, intolerant or oppressive, except in France.

There, something happened which had not yet been encountered elsewhere. Established religions had been violently attacked in other times, but the feeling against them had always been born from the zeal inspired by new religions. The false and detestable religions of antiquity had not had numerous and passionate adversaries until Christianity came forth to replace them; up until then they had died out gently and quietly in doubt and indifference: it was the death of religion from old age. In France, Christianity was attacked with a kind of fury, without even any attempt to put another religion in its place. Many worked constantly and ardently to sever souls from the faith that had filled them, leaving them empty. A multitude of men fervently threw themselves into this thankless enterprise. Absolute unbelief in matters of religion, which is so contrary to the natural instincts of humanity and puts its soul into such a painful position, seemed attractive to the crowd. What had not, up to then, produced anything but a sort of sickly languor, this time gave birth to fanaticism and the spirit of propaganda.

The existence of several great writers inclined to deny the truths of the Christian religion does not seem sufficient to explain such an extraordinary event; for why had all these writers uniformly committed their minds to this side rather than to another? Why among them did there appear none who thought to choose the contrary thesis? And finally, why did they, more than all their predecessors, find the ear of the crowd so open to their message, with minds so inclined to believe them? Only reasons very particular to the times and the country of these writers can explain their enterprise, and above all its success. Voltaire's ideas had long been abroad in the world; but Voltaire himself, in fact, could hardly have reigned anywhere but in the eighteenth century and in France.

Let us recognize, first of all, that the Church was no more vulnerable among us than elsewhere; the vices and abuses which had been mingled with it were on the contrary fewer than in most Catholic countries; the Church was infinitely more tolerant than it had been previously, and than it still was among other peoples. Thus it is much less at the state of religion than at that of society that we must look for the particular causes of the phenomenon.

In order to understand it, one must never lose sight of what I said in the preceding chapter, that the whole spirit of political opposition to which the government's vices gave birth, unable to make itself felt in public affairs, had taken refuge in literature, while writers had become the real chiefs of the great party which intended to overthrow all the social and political institutions of the country. With this properly understood, the point of the inquiry changes. It is no longer a question of knowing how the Church of that time could sin as a religious institution, but how it formed an obstacle to the political revolution which was gestating, and how it had to be specially irritating to the writers who were that revolution's principal promoters.

By the very principles of its government, the Church formed an obstacle to the ideas which the intellectuals wished to see prevail in civil government. It based itself chiefly on tradition: they professed a great contempt for all institutions that were founded on respect for the past; the Church recognized an authority superior to individual reason; they appealed to nothing but that same reason. The Church was founded on a hierarchy: they aimed at the abolition of rank. For the writers to have been able to come to an understanding with the Church, both sides would have had to recognize that political society and religious society were by nature essentially different, and could not be ordered by similar principles; but we were then very far from that idea, and it seemed that, in order to attack the institutions of the state, it was necessary to destroy those of the Church, which served as foundation and model for them.

Further, the Church was then itself the leading political power, and the most detested of all, although it was not the most oppressive; for it had come to join itself with the political powers without being forced to do so by its nature and vocation, and often blessed in politics the vices that it condemned elsewhere, covering them with its sacred inviolability, and seeming to want to make them as immortal as itself. In attacking the Church, one was sure of immediately according with public feeling.

But, beyond these general reasons, the writers had more particular ones, in effect personal ones, for taking on the Church first. The Church represented precisely that part of government which was closest and most directly opposed to them. The other powers only occasionally made themselves felt; but the Church, being specially charged to oversee thought and censor writings, got in the way of the writers all the time. In defending the general freedoms of the human mind against the Church, they fought their own battle, and began by breaking the shackles which chafed them most.

The Church, further, seemed to them to be, and in fact was, the most vulnerable and least defended flank of the whole vast edifice which they attacked. Its power had weakened as the power of the temporal ruler strengthened. After having been superior, then equal, the Church was reduced to becoming the ruler's client; between the rulers and the Church there was established a kind of exchange: the rulers lent the Church their temporal power, the Church lent them its moral authority; they made its precepts obeyed, it made their will respected. A dangerous trade, when revolutionary times approach, and always disadvantageous for a power which is not founded on constraint, but on belief.

Although our kings still called themselves the eldest sons of the Church, they were very negligent in fulfilling their obligations towards it; they showed much less zeal to protect it than they put forth in defending their own government. True, they did not allow anyone to put a hand on the Church; but they allowed it to be attacked from afar by a thousand arrows. This half-constraint which was imposed on the enemies of the Church, rather than diminishing their power, increased it. There are times when the oppression of writers succeeds in stopping the movement of thought, at other times repression precipitates it; but never has a kind of regulation of the press like that which was then exercised failed to multiply the power of the press a hundredfold.

Authors were persecuted only enough to make them complain, not enough to make them afraid; they suffered the kind of hindrance which animates struggle, not the heavy yoke which crushes. The attacks to which they were subjected, almost always slow, noisy, and vain, seemed to have as their purpose less to keep them from writing than to excite them to it. Complete freedom of the press would have been less damaging to the Church.

"You believe our intolerance," wrote Diderot to David Hume in 1768, "more favorable to the progress of the mind than your unlimited freedom; d'Holbach, Helvétius, Morellet and Suard are not of your opinion." However, it was the Scot who was right. Living in a free country, he had its experience; Diderot was judging the question like a man of letters, Hume like a politician.

I stop the first American whom I meet, whether in his country or elsewhere, and I ask him if he thinks religion is useful for the stability of law and the good order of society; he immediately responds that a civilized society, but above all a free society, cannot subsist without religion. Respect for religion, in his eyes, is the greatest guarantee of the stability of the state and the security of individuals. Those least versed in the science of government know this much. However, in political matters, there was not a country in the world where the boldest doctrines of the philosophes of the eighteenth century were more applied than in America; only the antireligious doctrines of the French were never able to make headway there, even with the advantage of unlimited freedom of the press.

I will say the same for the English.[54] Our irreligious philosophy was preached to them even before most of our philosophes were born: it was Bolingbroke who taught Voltaire. Throughout the eighteenth century, unbelief had representatives in England. Able writers, profound thinkers took its cause in hand; they could never enable it to triumph as in France, because all those who had something to fear from a revolution hastened to come to the aid of the established beliefs. Even those among them who were the most connected with contemporary French society, and who did not think the doctrines of our philosophes false, rejected them as dangerous. Great political parties, as always happens among free peoples, found it in their interest to unite their cause with that of the Church; we see Bolingbroke himself become the ally of the bishops. The clergy, inspired by these examples, and never feeling themselves isolated, fought energetically for their own cause. The Church of England, despite the defects of its establishment and the abuses of all sorts which worked within it, victoriously sustained the shock; writers and orators came forth from its ranks, and zealously threw themselves into the defense of Christianity. The theories which were hostile to it, after having been discussed and refuted, were finally rejected by the effort of society itself, without government intervention.

But why look for examples outside France? What Frenchman of today would think of writing the books of Diderot or Helvétius? Who would want to read them? I will almost say, who knows their titles? The incomplete experience of political life which we have acquired over the last sixty years has been enough to disgust us with this dangerous literature. See how the respect for religion has gradually regained its empire among the different classes of the nation, as each of them acquired that experience in the hard school of revolution. The old nobility, which was the most irreligious class before '89, became the most fervent after '93: the first attacked, it was the first converted. When the bourgeoisie felt itself attacked in its supremacy, we saw the bourgeoisie in its turn become reconciled to faith. Little by little, respect for religion spread everywhere where men had something to lose in popular disorder, and unbelief disappeared, or at least hid, to the extent that the fear of revolution appeared.

It was not thus at the end of the old regime. We had so completely forgotten the practice of great human affairs, and we were so ignorant of the role of religion in the government of empires, that unbelief established itself first in the minds of the very people who had the most personal and pressing interest in keeping the state in order and the masses obedient. Not only did they welcome it, but in their blindness they spread it downward; impiety was the pastime of their idle lives.

The Church of France, up to then so fertile in great orators, feeling itself thus deserted by all those who by common interest ought to have been attached to its cause, fell silent. For a moment one could believe that, provided it kept its money and its status, it was ready to condemn its faith.

While those who denied Christianity raised their voices, and those who still believed kept silent, there came to pass what since has been so often seen among us, not only in questions of religion, but in everything else. The men who kept the old faith feared to be the only ones who remained faithful, and dreading isolation more than error, they went along with the crowd, without thinking like it. What was still the feeling of only part of the nation thus appeared as everyone's opinion, and therefore seemed irresistible in the very eyes of those who gave it that false appearance. Without doubt the universal discredit into which all religious beliefs fell at the end of the last century exercised the greatest influence on the whole of our Revolution; it marked its character. Nothing did more to give its features that terrible expression which we have seen.

When I try to disentangle the different effects which irreligion then produced in France, I find that they were much more in disordering minds than in degrading hearts, or even in corrupting mores; that irreligion inclined the people of that time to go to very unusual extremes. When religion deserted souls, it did not leave them, as often happens, empty and debilitated; rather they were briefly filled by feelings and ideas which momentarily took the place of religion, and which at first did not let them be depressed.

If, with regard to religion, the French who made the Revolution were more unbelieving than we, at least there was left them one admirable belief which we lack: they believed in themselves. They did not doubt the perfectibility, the power of man; they readily became impassioned for his glory, they had faith in his virtue. They put in their own strength the prideful confidence that often leads to error but without which a people is capable of nothing but servitude; they did not doubt in the least that they were called to transform society and regenerate our species. These feelings and these passions had become a kind of new religion for them, which, producing some of the great effects which we have seen religions produce, tore them away from individual egoism, encouraged them to heroism and devotion, and often made them seem insensible to all the petty goods which we possess.

I have studied much history, and I dare affirm that I have never met with a revolution where one could see at the start, in so many men, a more sincere patriotism, more disinterest, more true greatness. The nation there displayed the chief flaw, but also the principal quality of youth, inexperience and generosity.

And yet irreligion then produced an immense public evil. In most of the great political revolutions which had appeared in the world up to then, those who attacked established laws had respected beliefs, and, in most of the religious revolutions, those who attacked religion had not tried to change the nature and order of all powers at the same time, and to abolish the old constitution of the government from top to bottom. There had thus always been a point that remained stable in the greatest social upheavals.

But in the French Revolution, religious laws having been abolished at the same time as civil laws were overturned, the human mind entirely lost its orientation; it no longer knew how to hold on, nor where to stop, and revolutionaries of an unknown species appeared, who took boldness to the point of folly, whom no innovation could surprise, nor scruple hold back, and who never hesitated before the execution of a plan. And one must not think that these new beings were the isolated or ephemeral creation of a moment, destined to pass with it; they have since formed a race which has perpetuated itself, and spread among all civilized parts of the earth, which everywhere has kept the same appearance, the same passions, the same character. We found them in the world when we were born; they are still with us.

CHAPTER THREE

How the French Wanted Reforms before They Wanted Freedoms

One thing worth remarking is that, among all the ideas and all the feelings which prepared the Revolution, the idea and the desire for political freedom proper presented themselves last, as they were the first to disappear.

We had long since begun to shake the old edifice of government; it already reeled, and it was still not a question of freedom. Voltaire was hardly interested in it: three years' residence in England had shown him freedom without making him like it. The skeptical philosophy which was freely preached among the English enchanted him; their political system affected him little: he noticed its vices more than its virtues. In his *Letters on England,* which is one of his masterpieces, Parliament is what he talks about least; in reality, he envied the English above all for their literary freedom, but hardly concerned himself for their political freedom, as if the first could ever exist for long without the second.

Around the middle of the century, a certain number of writers appeared who specialized in treating questions of public administration, and to whom several similar principles have given the common name of *economists* or *physiocrats.* The physiocrats have had less renown in history than the philosophes; perhaps they contributed less to the coming of the Revolution. I believe, however, that it is in their writings above all that we can best study the Revolution's true nature. The philosophes hardly went beyond very general and very abstract ideas in questions of government; the physiocrats, however, without separating themselves from theory, came closer to the facts. One told us what we could imagine, the other sometimes showed us what was to be done. All the institutions that the Revolution was going to permanently abolish had been the particular objects of the physiocrats' attacks; none had found grace in their eyes. On the contrary, all those which may pass for the Revolution's own work had been announced in advance and ardently recommended by them; one could hardly cite a single one whose seed had not been sown in some of their writings; we find in the physiocrats all that is most substantial in the Revolution.

Still more, we already recognize in their books the democratic and revolutionary temperament we know so well: they not only hate certain privileges, but diversity itself is odious to them: they adore equality even in servitude. Whatever hinders their plans is worthless. Contracts inspire little respect in them; private rights, no regard; or rather there no longer are any private rights, strictly speaking, in their eyes, but only public utility. These were in general, however, men of mild and peaceful habits, well-off, honest judges, able administrators; but the spirit peculiar to their work led them on.

For the physiocrats the past was an object of limitless contempt. "The nation has been governed by false principles for centuries; everything seems to have been done at random," says Letrone. Starting from this idea, they set to work; there was no institution too old, too well-founded, for them not to demand its abolition, because it was inconvenient to them and disturbed the symmetry of their plans. One of them proposed to eliminate at once all the old territorial divisions and to change all the provinces' names, forty years before the Constituent Assembly did it.

They had already thought of all the social and administrative reforms that the Revolution made, before the idea of free institutions began to dawn in their minds. They were, it is true, very favorable to the free exchange of commodities, to *laissez faire* or *laissez passer* in trade and industry; but as for political freedoms proper, they were hardly concerned, and even when by chance they thought of them, they at first rejected them. Most started by showing themselves hostile to deliberative assemblies, to local and secondary powers, and in general to all the counterweights which had been established, in different times, among all free peoples, to balance the central power. "The system of checks and balances," says Quesnay,[†] "is a fatal idea in government." "The speculations according to which we have imagined the system of checks and balances are fanciful," says a friend of Quesnay.

The only guarantee that they created against the abuse of power was public education; for, as Quesnay says again, "despotism is impossible if the nation is enlightened." "Struck by the evils which the abuse of authority brings," says another of his disciples, "men have invented a thousand absolutely useless means, and have neglected the only truly effective one, which is universal public education, permanent, essentially just, and part of the natural order." It was the force of this literary gibberish that they intended to substitute for all political guarantees.

Letrone, who so bitterly deplores the abandonment in which the government left the countryside, who portrays for us a countryside without roads, without industry, without education, can hardly imagine that things could be done better if left to the inhabitants themselves. Turgot himself, whose greatness of soul and rare qualities of mind ought to set him apart from all the others, does not have much more taste for political freedom than they, or at least the desire only awakens in him very late, when public feeling suggests it. For him, as for most of the physiocrats, the first political guarantee is a certain public education given by the state, according to certain procedures and in a certain spirit. The confidence that he shows in this kind of educational medicine, or as one of his contemporaries put it, in the *mechanism of an education according to principle,* is limitless. "I dare say to you, Sire," he says in a report where he proposes a plan of this kind to the king, "that in ten years your nation will be unrecognizable, and that, by its intelligence, its good mores, by informed zeal for your service and for that of the fatherland, it will be infinitely above all other peoples. The children who are now ten years old will then be men prepared for the State, lovers of their country, submissive to authority not through fear, but by reason, helpful to their fellow-citizens, accustomed to recognize and respect the law."

It was so long since political liberty had been destroyed in France that its conditions and its effects had been almost entirely forgotten. Furthermore, the debris which yet remained, and the institutions which seemed to have been created to substitute for freedom, made freedom suspect and often created prejudices against it. Most of the assemblies of estates which still existed preserved, along with the outdated forms, the spirit of the Middle Ages, and hindered social progress rather than helped it; the parlements, alone charged with taking the place of political bodies, could not prevent the evil that the government did, and often prevented the good that it wanted to do.

The idea of accomplishing the revolution that they wanted with the aid of all these old tools seemed impractical to the physiocrats; even the thought of confiding the execution of their plans to the nation become its own mistress was not very acceptable to them; for how could one make a whole people adopt and follow a system of reform so vast, and so closely linked in its parts? To them it seemed easier and more opportune to make the royal government itself serve their plans.

This new power did not derive from medieval institutions; it did not bear their imprint at all; in the midst of its errors, the economists found certain good tendencies. Like them it had a natural taste for equality of ranks and for uniform rules; it hated as much as they, from the bottom of its heart, all the old powers which were born of feudalism or which tended towards aristocracy. We would look in vain in the rest of Europe for a government machine as well-mounted, as large, and as strong; the occurrence of such a government among us seemed to them a singularly fortunate circumstance: they would have called it providential, if it had been the fashion, then as today, to make Providence intervene in all questions. "The situation of France," says Letrone, "is infinitely better than that of England; for here we can accomplish reforms which will change the whole state of the nation in a moment, while among the English such reforms can always be impeded by the parties."

Thus it was not a question of destroying absolute power but of converting it. "It is necessary that the state govern according to the rules of the essential order" says Mercier de la Rivière,[†] "and when it is thus, it must be 'all-powerful'." "Let the state properly understand its duty," says another, "and then let us leave it free." From Quesnay to abbé Bodeau, you will find them all of the same temperament.

They did not merely count on the royal administration to reform the society of their own day; they borrowed from it, in part, the idea of a future government which they wanted to found. It was in looking at the one that they made themselves a picture of the other. The state, according to the physiocrats, was not only to rule the nation but to shape it in a certain way; it was for the state to form the citizen's mind according to a particular model set out in advance; its duty was to fill the citizen's head with certain ideas and to furnish his heart with certain feelings that it judged necessary. In reality, there were no limits to its rights, nor bounds to what it might do; it not only reformed men, it transformed them; perhaps it concerned the state alone to make different people out of them! "The state makes men whatever it wants," says Bodeau. This phrase sums up all their theories.

This immense social power that the physiocrats imagined was not only greater than any of the powers which they could see around them; it differed from them in its origin and character too. It did not derive directly from God; it was not at all attached to tradition; it was impersonal: it was no longer called the king, but the state; it was not the inheritance of a family; it was the product and the representative of everyone, and must make the rights of each bend before the will of all.

This particular form of tyranny, which we call democratic despotism,

of which the Middle Ages had no idea, was already familiar to the physiocrats. No more hierarchy within society, no more classes, no more fixed
ranks; a people composed of almost identical and entirely equal individuals, this jumbled mass recognized as the sole legitimate sovereign, but
carefully deprived of all the faculties which might permit it to direct
and even to oversee its own government. Above society, a single official,
charged with doing everything in its name, without consulting it. To control it, a public reason without means of expression; to stop it, revolutions, and not laws: in theory, a subordinate agent; in fact, a master.

Not yet finding around them anything which seemed to conform to
this ideal, they sought it in the depths of Asia. I do not exaggerate in
stating that there is not one of them who does not in some part of his
writings give an emphatic eulogy of China. In reading their books one is
sure to encounter at least this; and since China was still very badly known,
there was no kind of nonsense which they didn't speak about it. This
imbecile and barbarous government that a handful of Europeans mastered at will, seems to them the most perfect model that the nations of the
world could copy. It is, for them, what later England and finally America
became for all the French. They find themselves moved, and apparently
entranced, at the sight of a country whose sovereign, absolute but exempt
from prejudices, once a year plows the earth with his own hands to honor
the useful arts; where all positions are obtained through literary competitions; which has for religion only a philosophy, and for an aristocracy
none but intellectuals.

We believe that the destructive theories which are known in our days
under the name of *socialism* are of recent origin; this is a mistake: these
theories were contemporary with the first physiocrats. While the physiocrats used the all-powerful government they dreamed of to change society's form, the socialists in their imagination grasp the same power to
destroy its base. Read the *Code of Nature* by Morelly, and you will find
there, along with all the doctrines of the physiocrats on the omnipotence
of the state and its unlimited rights, several of the political theories which
have recently frightened France most, and which we think we have seen
born: the community of goods, the right to work, absolute equality, uniformity in all things, mechanical order in all the movements of individuals, regulatory tyranny, and the complete absorption of the personality
of the citizens into the social body.

"Nothing in society belongs individually nor as property to anyone,"
says the first article of this Code. "Property is detestable, and he who
attempts to reestablish it will be imprisoned for life, as a dangerous insane

person and an enemy of humanity. Every citizen will be fed, clothed and employed at the public expense," says article 2. "All products will be gathered in public warehouses, to be distributed to all citizens and to serve their needs. Towns will be built according to the same plan; all buildings for personal use will be alike. At age five all children will be removed from their families and brought up in common, at the state's expense, in a uniform manner." This book seems to strike one as if it were written yesterday, but it is a hundred years old. It appeared in 1755, at the same time that Quesnay founded his school: so true is it that centralization and socialism are products of the same soil. Centralization is to socialism what the cultivated fruit is to the wild one.

Of all the men of their time, it is the physiocrats who would seem the least displaced in our own; their passion for equality was so firm and their taste for freedom so vague that they have a false air of being our contemporaries. When I read the speeches and writings of the men who made the Revolution, I feel myself suddenly transported to a place and in the midst of a society which I do not know; but when I examine the physiocrats' books, it seems to me that I have lived with these people, and that I have just talked with them.

Around 1750 the nation as a whole did not show itself more demanding in the matter of political freedom than the physiocrats themselves; it had lost the desire for freedom and, in losing its use, the very idea of it. The nation wanted reforms more than rights, and, if there had then been found on the throne a ruler of the stature and disposition of Frederick the Great, I do not at all doubt that he would have accomplished in society and government several of the great changes that the Revolution made, not only without losing his crown, but greatly increasing his power. We are assured that one of Louis XV's most able ministers, M. de Machault, glimpsed this idea, and suggested it to his master. But such enterprises are not counseled: one is not made to accomplish them except when one is capable of conceiving them.

Twenty years later, it was no longer the same: the image of political freedom had presented itself to the French mind, and became more and more attractive to it every day. This was made clear by many signs. The provinces again began to conceive the desire to govern themselves. The idea spread that the whole people had the right to take part in its government, and swept up public opinion. The memory of the old Estates-General revived. The nation, which detested its own history, remembered only this part of it with pleasure. The new current carried the physiocrats themselves along, and forced them to encumber their unitary system with some free institutions.

When in 1771 the parlements were destroyed, the same public which had so often suffered from their prejudices was profoundly moved at the sight of their fall. It seemed that with them fell the last barrier which could still contain royal absolutism. This opposition astonished Voltaire and made him indignant. "Almost the whole kingdom is in excitement and consternation," he wrote to one of his friends; "the fermentation is as strong in the provinces as in Paris itself. The edict seems to me, however, full of useful reforms. To destroy the venality of offices, to make justice free, to forbid litigants to come to Paris from the ends of the kingdom to bankrupt themselves, to charge the king with paying the expenses of manorial justice, are these not great services rendered to the nation? These parlements, further, have they not often been barbarous and persecutors? In truth, I admire the "radicals" for taking the part of these insolent and insubordinate bourgeois. For myself, I think that the king is right, and, since one must serve, I think that it is better to do it under a well-bred lion, who is born much stronger than I, than under two hundred rats of my own species." And he adds as a kind of excuse: "Imagine how I must infinitely appreciate the favor that the king does all feudal lords, in paying the expenses of their courts."

Voltaire, long absent from Paris, thought that public opinion had remained at the point where he had left it. It had done nothing of the sort. The French no longer limited themselves to wanting their affairs better run; they had begun to want to manage their business themselves, and it was clear that the great Revolution that everything was preparing was going to occur, not only with the people's consent, but by their hands.

I think that from this time on, this radical revolution—which was going to join all that was best and worst in the old regime in the same destruction—was inevitable. A people so badly prepared to act on its own could not attempt to reform everything at once without destroying everything. An absolute ruler would have been a less dangerous innovator. For me, when I consider that that same revolution, which destroyed so many institutions, ideas, and habits opposed to freedom, also, on the other hand, abolished so many others which freedom can hardly do without, I am inclined to believe that perhaps if the revolution had been accomplished by a despot, it would have left us less unfit to become a free nation, some day, than the revolution made in the name of the sovereignty of the people, and by them.

One must never lose sight of this, if one wants to understand the history of our revolution. When the love of the French for political freedom awoke, they had already conceived a certain number of ideas in regard to government which not only did not easily accord with the existence of free institutions but were almost opposed to them. They had accepted as the ideal society a people without any aristocracy other than government officials, a single and all-powerful administration, director of the state, guardian of individuals. In wishing to be free, they did not intend to depart in the slightest from this basic idea; they only tried to reconcile it with the idea of freedom.

They therefore endeavored to mix together unlimited government centralization and a dominant legislative body: administration by officials and government by the voters. The nation as a body had all the rights of sovereignty, each particular citizen was confined to the strictest subjection: from the one, they demanded the experience and virtues of a free people; from the other, the qualities of a good servant.

It is this desire to introduce political liberty among ideas and institutions which are foreign or opposed to it, but for which we had already acquired the habit or conceived the taste, that for sixty years has produced so many vain attempts at free government, followed by such disastrous revolutions. Finally, fatigued by so many efforts, put off by a task so laborious and so sterile, the French abandoned their secondary objective to return to their primary one. Many of them were reduced to thinking that to live as equals under a master still had, after all, a certain attraction. Thus today we find ourselves infinitely more like the physiocrats of 1750 than our fathers of 1789.

I have often wondered where the source of this passion for political freedom is, which, in all times, has made men do the greatest things that humanity has accomplished, in what feelings it is rooted and nourishes itself. I see clearly that, when nations are badly led, they readily conceive the desire to govern themselves; but this kind of love of independence, which takes rise only from some particular and fleeting problems brought on by despotism, is never durable: it passes with the accident that gave it birth; they seem to love freedom, but one finds that they only hated the master. What peoples who are made for freedom hate, is the evil of subjection itself.

I also do not think that true love of liberty was ever born just from the sight of the material goods that freedom produces; for this often succeeds in hiding it. It is certainly true that in the long run, freedom always brings, to those who know how to keep it, ease, well-being, and often riches; but there are times when it briefly hinders the enjoyment of such goods; there are others when only despotism can temporarily afford their enjoyment. Men who prize only these kinds of goods have never enjoyed freedom for long.

That which, in all times, has so strongly attached certain men's hearts to freedom, are its own attractions, its own peculiar charm, independent of its benefits; it is the pleasure of being able to speak, act, and breathe without constraint, under the government of God and the laws alone. Whoever seeks for anything from freedom but itself is made for slavery.

Certain nations pursue freedom obstinately through all kinds of perils and miseries. Then it is not the material goods which it gives them which those peoples love in freedom; they consider freedom itself a good so precious, and so necessary, that no other could console them for its loss, and they console themselves for everything in tasting it. Others tire of liberty in the midst of their prosperity; they let it be taken from their hands without resistance, for fear of compromising by any effort the very well-being that they owe to it. What do they lack to make them free? What? The very desire to be so. Do not ask me to analyze this sublime desire, it must be felt. It enters of itself into the great hearts that God has prepared to receive it; it fills them, it fires them. One must give up on making this comprehensible to the mediocre souls who have never felt it.

CHAPTER FOUR

That the Reign of Louis XVI Was the Most Prosperous Period of the Old Monarchy, and How This Very Prosperity Hastened the Revolution

It is unquestionable that the exhaustion of the kingdom under Louis XIV started at the very time when that ruler was still triumphant over the rest of Europe. The first indications are found in the most glorious years of his reign. France was ruined well before it had ceased to defeat others. Who has not read that frightening essay in government statistics that Vauban has left us? The intendants, in the reports that they sent to the duke of Burgundy at the end of the seventeenth century, and even before the start of the unsuccessful War of the Succession, all refer to the increasing decline of the nation and do not at all speak of it as a fact of very recent date. "The population has greatly decreased in this region over a certain period of time," says one; "this town, which was formerly rich and flourishing, is today without industry," says another. This one says: "there was once some industry in this province, but today it has been abandoned." Another: "the inhabitants formerly derived much more from their soil than at present, agriculture was infinitely more flourishing twenty years ago." "Population and production have decreased by a fifth since about thirty years ago," says an intendant of Orleans at the same time. One ought to recommend the reading of these reports to individuals who prize absolute government, and to rulers who love war.

Since these miseries had their chief source in the vices of the constitution, the death of Louis XIV, and peace itself, did not restore public prosperity. That the provinces did not recover is an opinion common to all those who wrote on government or political economy in the first half of the eighteenth century; many even thought that they were continuing to decline. Paris alone, they said, enriched itself and grew. Intendants, former ministers, and businessmen agreed with the men of letters on this point.

For myself, I avow that I do not believe at all in this continued decline of France during the first half of the eighteenth century; but an opinion so general, shared by people so well-informed, proves at least that no visible progress was being made. All the administrative documents which relate to this period of our history and have passed before my eyes show, in fact, a kind of lethargy. The government does little more than follow old routines without creating anything new; the towns make almost no effort to improve the condition of their inhabitants and make them healthier; even individuals do not take on any considerable enterprise.

Around thirty or forty years before the Revolution broke out, the scene begins to change. One seems to find then, in all parts of society, a kind of internal movement which hadn't been noted earlier. At first only a very careful examination reveals it; but little by little it becomes more characteristic and more distinct. Every year the movement extends and accelerates: finally, the whole nation stirs and seems to be reborn. Beware! It is not its old life which is reborn; the spirit that directs this body is a new spirit; it momentarily revives the corpse only in order to dissolve it.

Everyone is worried and agitated about his situation and makes an effort to change it: the search for something better is universal; but it is an impatient and sullen search, which damns the past and imagines a state of things entirely opposed to what lies before their eyes. Soon this spirit penetrates the heart of the government itself; it transforms it from within, without changing anything on the outside: the laws are not changed, but they are executed differently.

I said elsewhere that the controller-general and the intendant of 1740 hardly resemble the controller-general and the intendant of 1780. The official correspondence shows this truth in detail. The intendant of 1780, however, had the same powers, the same agents, the same arbitrary authority as his predecessor, but not the same aims: the first was not concerned with anything except maintaining his province's obedience, raising troops, and above all bringing in the taille; the second had many concerns: his head was filled with a thousand projects to increase the public wealth. Roads, canals, manufactures, and commerce were the chief objects of his thought; above all agriculture attracted his attention. Sully† became the fashion then among administrators. It was in this period that they started to form the agricultural societies of which I have already spoken, that they established competitions, that they distributed prizes. There were circulars from the controller-general that more resembled treatises on the art of agriculture than business letters.

It is chiefly in the collection of taxes that one can best see the change which had occurred in the minds of those who governed. The law was still as unequal, as arbitrary, and as harsh as in the past, but all its vices were tempered in execution. "When I started to study the fiscal laws," says M. Mollien in his memoirs, "I was frightened by what I found: fines, imprisonments, corporal punishments put at the disposal of special tribunals for simple omissions; tax-farmers who held almost all property and persons at the discretion of their oaths, etc. Fortunately, I did not limit myself to the simple reading of the code, and I soon had occasion to recognize that there was the same difference between the letter of the law and its application, as between the mores of the old financiers and the new. The judges were always inclined to mitigate offences and moderate punishments." "To how many abuses and vexations can the collection of taxes give rise!" said the provincial assembly of Lower Normandy in 1787; "we ought, however, to render justice to the mildness and moderation which we have become used to for some years."

Examination of the documents fully justifies this assertion. Respect for men's life and liberty often makes itself seen. Above all, one sees a real concern for the problems of the poor: up to then, one would have searched for this in vain. The violences of the treasury towards the poor are rare, remissions of tax more frequent, help more common. The king increases all the funds used to create charity workshops in the countryside or to come to the aid of the indigent, and often he establishes new ones. I found more than 80,000 livres distributed in this way in the Generality of Upper Guyenne alone in 1779, 40,000 in Tours in 1784, 48,000 in Normandy in 1787. Louis XVI did not want to leave this part of government to his ministers alone; he sometimes took it over himself. When, in 1776, a decree of the Royal Council fixed the indemnities that were due to the peasants whose fields the king's boar had devastated in the neighborhood of the captainries, and indicated the simple and sure means of obtaining payment, the king himself drafted the preamble. Turgot tells us that this good and unfortunate ruler gave him documents in his own handwriting, while saying, "You see that I do my part over here too." If one were painting the old regime as it was in the last years of its existence, one would make a very flattering portrait that bore it little real resemblance.

As these changes took place in the minds of the governed and the governors, public prosperity increased with a previously unprecedented speed. All signs announce it: population increases, riches increase still faster. The American war did not slow down this take-off; the state was impoverished, but individuals continued to enrich themselves; they became more industrious, more enterprising, more inventive.

"Since 1774," said an administrator at the time, "the different branches of industry, in developing themselves, have increased the base for all the taxes on consumption." When, in fact, we compare the contracts made between the state and the financial companies charged with raising taxes in the different periods of Louis XVI's reign, we see that the price of the concessions increased continually, with an increasing rapidity with each renewal. The lease of 1786 produced 14 million more than that of 1780. "We can assume that the product of the sales-taxes will increase by 2 million a year," said Necker in the *Compte-rendu* of 1781. Arthur Young assures us that in 1788 Bordeaux did more trade than Liverpool, and he adds: "In recent times, the progress of maritime trade has been more rapid in France than in England itself; trade has doubled here in the past twenty years."

If we want to compare different periods, we will be convinced that in none of the periods which followed the Revolution has the public prosperity developed more rapidly than during the twenty years which preceded it.[55] In this regard the thirty-seven years of constitutional monarchy, which were times of peace and rapid progress for us, alone can be compared with the reign of Louis XVI.

The sight of this prosperity, already so great and flourishing, is astonishing, if one thinks of all the vices which confined the government, and of all the difficulties which industry still encountered; it has even been the case that many political commentators have denied the fact's existence because they could not explain it, judging, like Molière's doctor, that a sick man could not be cured against the rules. How can one believe, in fact, that France could prosper and enrich itself despite the inequality of taxes, the diversity of laws, the internal duties, the feudal dues, the guilds, the venal offices, etc.? Despite all this, however, France began to enrich itself and to develop itself in all areas, because behind all these badly built and badly geared wheels, which seemed as if they were intended to slow down the social machine rather than propel it, hid two very simple and very strong springs, which already were enough to hold everything together and make everything tend towards the goal of public prosperity: a government that had remained very powerful while ceasing to be despotic, which maintained order everywhere; a nation which, in its upper classes, was already the most enlightened and freest on the Continent, in the midst of which each man could enrich himself in his own way and keep his fortune once acquired.

The king continued to speak as a master, but in reality he himself obeyed a public opinion which inspired him or carried him along every day, which he consulted, feared, and constantly flattered; absolute by the letter of the laws, he was limited by their execution. From 1784, Necker said in a public document, as an uncontested fact: "Most foreigners can hardly have any idea of the authority that public opinion today exercises in France: they find it difficult to understand what this invisible power is that commands even in the king's palace. However this is the case."

Nothing is more superficial than to attribute the greatness and power of a people to the mechanism of its laws alone; for, in this matter, it is less the perfection of the instrument than the strength of the motors that determines the result. Look at England: how many of its laws today seem more complicated, more diverse, more irregular than ours![56] But is there, however, a single country in Europe where the public wealth is greater, individual property more extensive, more secure, and more varied, the society richer or more solid? This does not come from the bounty of any particular laws, but from the spirit which animates English legislation as a whole. The flaws of certain organs make nothing impossible, because their vitality is powerful.

As the prosperity which I have just described developed in France, minds, however, appeared more unstable and nervous; public discontent sharpened; hatred against the old institutions grew. The nation made visible steps towards a revolution. Still more, the parts of France which were going to be the chief base of that revolution were precisely those where progress was most apparent. If one studied what remains of the archives of the former Generality of the Ile-de-France, one would easily convince oneself that it was in the regions which bordered Paris that the old regime was first and most deeply reformed. There the freedom and fortune of the peasants were already better guaranteed than in any of the other *pays d'élection*. The personal corvée had disappeared long before 1789. The raising of the taille had become more regular, more moderate, more equal than in the rest of France. One must read the regulations that improved it in 1772, if one wants to understand what an intendant could do then, for the common welfare, as well as for the poverty of a whole province. Seen in this regulation, taxation already has a completely different appearance. Government commissioners go to each parish annually; the community assembles in their presence; the value of goods is set publicly, everyone's capacity openly established; the taille finally based on the agreement of all those who had to pay it. No more of the arbitrary will of the syndic, no more unnecessary violence. Doubtless, the taille retains the vices which were inherent to it, whatever the system for its collection; it weighs on only one class of taxpayers, and there attacks industry as well as property; but in everything else it differs profoundly from what still bears the same name in all the neighboring regions.[57]

Nowhere, on the contrary, had the old regime been better preserved than along the banks of the Loire, towards its mouth, in the swamps of Poitou and the marshes of Brittany. It was exactly there that the flame of civil war was lit and fed, and where the Revolution was longest and most violently resisted; so that one would say that the French found their position the more unbearable as it improved. Such a sight is astonishing; history is full of similar spectacles.

It is not always in going from bad to worse that one falls into revolution. It more often happens that a people who have borne without complaint, as if they did not feel them, the most burdensome laws, reject them violently once their weight is lightened. The regime that a revolution destroys is almost always better than the one that immediately preceded it, and experience teaches that the most dangerous moment for a bad government is usually when it begins to reform itself. Only great genius can save a ruler who tries to help his subjects after long oppression. The inevitable evil that one bears patiently seems unbearable as soon as one conceives the idea of removing it. Every abuse that is then eliminated seems to highlight those that remain, and makes them feel more biting; the evil has decreased, it is true, but the sensitivity to it is greater. Feudalism in all its power never inspired as much hatred in the French than at the moment it was about to disappear.[58] The smallest arbitrary acts of Louis XVI seemed more difficult to bear than all the despotism of Louis XIV. The brief imprisonment of Beaumarchais produced more emotion in Paris than the Dragonnades.[†]

In 1780 no one any longer claims that France is in decline; it would be said, on the contrary, that there are no longer any limits on its progress. It is then that the theory of the continual and indefinite perfectibility of man is born. Twenty years before, nothing was hoped from the future; now nothing is to be feared from it. Imagination, taking advance possession of that near and unheard-of prosperity, becomes insensible to the goods that it already has and hurries towards new things.

Independent of these general reasons for the phenomenon, there were others more specific and no less powerful. Although the administration of finance had improved like everything else, it kept the vices which were inherent to absolute government. Since it was secret, and without checks, it still followed some of the worst practices which had been current under Louis XIV and Louis XV. The very effort that the government made to develop public prosperity, the aid and encouragement that it distributed, the public works that it executed, daily increased expenses without increasing income to the same extent; this continually threw the king into still greater difficulties than his predecessors. Like them, he constantly made his creditors suffer; like them, he borrowed with both hands, secretly and without competition, and his creditors were never certain of receiving their interest; even their capital was always at the mercy of the king's good faith alone.

A trustworthy witness, since he had seen with his own eyes and was in a better position to see clearly than anyone else, said in this regard: "The French found only danger then in their dealings with their own government. If they put their savings in government bonds, they could never count on receiving the interest at a fixed date; if they built its ships, repaired its roads, clothed its soldiers: they remained without guarantees for their investment, without a set time for their payment, reduced to calculating the chances of a contract with the ministers like those of a high-risk loan." And he added very sensibly: "In these times when industry, advancing rapidly, had developed in a greater number of men the love of property, the taste and need for wealth, those who had confided a portion of their property to the state bore with extra impatience the violation of the law of contracts by the debtor who should have respected them most." In fact the abuses of the French government criticized here were not at all new: what was new was the impression they made. The vices of the financial system had been even more obvious in earlier times; but since then there had occurred changes in government and society which made them infinitely more sensitive to these vices than formerly.

The government, during the twenty years that it had become more active and involved in all kinds of enterprises which it had not thought of previously, ended up becoming the biggest consumer of industrial production and the greatest undertaker of projects in the kingdom. The number of people who did business with it, who were interested in its loans, lived from its salaries, and speculated in its markets had increased enormously. Never had the fortunes of the state and the fortunes of the individual been so intermixed. Poor financial management, which long had been merely a public evil, then became a personal disaster for many families. Thus in 1789 the state owed almost 600 million to its creditors, almost all of whom were debtors themselves, which, as a financier of the times said, united in their grievances against the government all those whom its slipshod management united in suffering. And note that as malcontents of this sort became more numerous, they also became more angry; for the desire to speculate, the ardor to enrich oneself, the taste for well-being, spreading and growing with commerce, made such evils appear unbearable to the very people who, thirty years before, would perhaps have endured them without complaint.[59]

From this it resulted that the rentiers, the traders, the industrialists, and the other businessmen or bankers who usually form the class most hostile to political innovation, most friendly to the existing government, whatever it may be, and most submissive even to laws for which they have contempt or which they detest, this time showed themselves the most impatient and the most resolute about reform. Above all, they called loudly for a complete revolution in the financial system, without thinking that in profoundly changing this part of government they were going to bring down all the rest.

How could a catastrophe have been avoided? On one side, a nation in whose heart the desire to make a fortune spread every day; on the other, a government which constantly excited this new passion and constantly hindered it, inflamed it and made it despair, thus pushing from both sides towards its own ruin.

CHAPTER FIVE

How Efforts to Help the Masses Radicalized Them

Since the lower classes had not appeared for a single instant on the political scene in a hundred and forty years, we had absolutely ceased to believe that they could ever mount the stage again; in seeing them so insensitive, we judged them deaf, with the result that, when we began to be interested in their fate, they were spoken of publicly as if they were not there. It seemed as if one could not be heard except by those placed above, and that the only danger one had to fear was not being well understood by the upper classes.

In their presence, the people who had most to fear from the lower classes' anger talked loudly about the cruel injustices of which the lower classes had always been the victim; they showed one another the monstrous vices contained in the institutions most burdensome to the people: they used their eloquence to portray the miseries of the poor and their badly paid work: thus in trying to help them they filled the poor with fury. I do not mean to speak of the writers at all, but of the government, of its principal officials, and of the privileged themselves.

When the king, thirteen years before the Revolution, attempted to abolish the corvee, he said in his preamble: "With the exception of a small number of provinces [the *pays d'états*], almost all the roads of the kingdom have been made by the poorest group of our subjects, without pay. All the weight has therefore fallen on those who have nothing but their hands, and are only very remotely interested in the roads; the truly interested are the landowners, almost all privileged, whose property is increased in value by the establishment of roads. In forcing the poor man alone to maintain them, in making him give his time and labor without pay, we take away from him the only resource he has against poverty and hunger, in order to make him work for the profit of the rich."

When there was an attempt, at the same time, to dismantle the hindrances that the trade-guild system imposed on workers, and it was proclaimed in the name of the king "that the right to work is the most sacred of all properties; that any law which diminishes it violates natural law and must be considered null and void; that the existing guilds are, furthermore, bizarre and tyrannical institutions, the product of egotism, greed, and violence," such words were perilous. What was still more dangerous was to pronounce them in vain. Several months later the corvée and the guilds were reestablished.

It was Turgot, it is said, who put such language into the king's mouth. Most of his successors did not make the king speak any differently. When, in 1780, the king announced to his subjects that increases in the taille would be submitted to public registry from then on, he took care to add as a gloss: "The taxpayers, already tormented by the vexations of the collection of the taille, up to now have still been exposed to unexpected increases in it, with the result that the payments of the poorest portion of our subjects increased in a proportion far greater than that of all the others." When the king, not yet daring to make all burdens equal, was at least trying to establish equal collection for those burdens that were already common, he said: "His Majesty hopes that the rich will not feel themselves injured, when, returned to the common level, they will be doing no more than bearing the burden that they should long have shared more equally."

But it is above all in times of food shortage that inflaming the people's passions, more than satisfying their needs, seems to be the aim. An intendant, in order to stimulate the charity of the rich, spoke then "of the injustice and the insensitivity of these landowners, who owe all that they own to the poor man's labor, and who let him die of starvation the minute he has exhausted himself to increase their riches." The king himself, in a similar situation: "His Majesty wishes to defend the people against the maneuvers which expose them to the lack of basic nourishment, by forcing them to work for such a salary as it pleases the rich to give. The king will not allow one portion of mankind to be delivered to the greed of another." Until the end of the monarchy the struggle which existed between the different administrative powers gave rise to all kinds of manifestations of this sort: the two contenders would freely accuse each other of causing the people's miseries. This can be well seen, notably in the quarrel about the grain trade which took place in 1772 between the parlement of Toulouse and the king. "The government, by its mistaken measures, risks making the poor man die of hunger," says the parlement. "The parlement's ambition and the greed of the rich cause the public distress," returns the king. From both sides the people's minds are thus introduced to the idea that their superiors are at the root of all of their problems.

These things are not found in secret correspondence but in public documents that the government and the parlement themselves take care to print and publish by the thousand. Thus the king addresses some hard truths to himself and his predecessors. "The State Treasury," he says one day, "has been mortgaged by the profligacy of several reigns. Many of our inalienable domains have been leased at very low prices." "The trade guilds," he is made to say another time, with more justice than prudence, "are above all the result of the kings' fiscal greed." "If useless expenditures have often been made and the taille raised beyond reason," he remarks further on, "this has happened because the financial administration, finding the increase of the taille, because of its secrecy, the easiest resource, used it, although several others would have been less burdensome to our peoples." [60]

All this was addressed to the educated part of the nation, to convince it of the utility of certain measures which special interests attacked. As for the people, it was well understood that they listened without understanding.

It must be recognized that there remained, in the midst of this benevolence, a great deal of contempt for those miserable ones whose pains one so sincerely wished to ease. It reminds us a little of Mme Duchatelet, who, according to Voltaire's secretary, felt no embarrassment at undressing in front of her servants, not considering it really proven that valets are men.

And let us not think that it was just Louis XVI, or his ministers, who used this dangerous language that I have just reproduced; the privileged groups who were the nearest object of the people's anger did not express themselves before them any differently. It must be recognized that, in France, the upper classes of society began to interest themselves in the fate of the poor before they were afraid of them; they interested themselves in them at a time when they still did not believe that their own destruction could arise from the pain of the poor. This becomes clear above all during the decade preceding 1789: the situation of the peasants is often complained about, they are constantly discussed; means to help them are continually sought; the chief abuses from which they suffer are exposed, and the tax laws which particularly harm them criticized; but the upper classes are usually just as incautious in the expression of this new sympathy as they had for so long been insensitive to it.

Read the debates of the provincial assemblies which met in some parts of France in 1779, and later in the whole kingdom, study the other public documents which remain from them; you will be touched by the good feelings that one finds there, and surprised by the striking imprudence of the language that was used. "We have seen too often," said the provincial assembly of Lower Normandy in 1787, "the money that the king set aside for roads used for the ease of the rich without being useful to the people. It has frequently been used to make it easier to reach a chateau, rather than to improve access to a town or village." In this same assembly, the order of the nobility and that of the clergy, after having described the vices of the corvée, spontaneously offered to devote 50,000 livres themselves to road improvement, in order, they said, that the roads of the province would become passable without any further cost to the people. It perhaps would have been less burdensome for these privileged to substitute a general tax for the corvée, and to pay their share of it; but, in voluntarily giving up the benefit of unequal taxation, they liked to preserve it in appearance. Abandoning the useful part of their right, they carefully preserved the hateful part.

Other assemblies, composed entirely of landowners exempt from the taille, who firmly intended to continue to be exempt, nevertheless painted in the darkest colors the evils that the taille inflicted on the poor. They drew a terrible picture of all its abuses, of which they took care to make infinite copies. And, what is very peculiar, is that to these striking testimonies of the interest which the masses inspired in them, they occasionally joined public expressions of contempt. The lower classes had already become the object of their sympathy, without ceasing to be the object of their disdain.

The provincial assembly of Upper Guyenne, speaking of these peasants whose cause it warmly pleaded, called them "rough and ignorant beings, turbulent people and coarse and insubordinate characters." Turgot, who did so much for the people, hardly spoke any differently.[61] These harsh expressions were found in writings intended for the widest public, and were intended to be seen by the peasants themselves. It seemed as if one lived in one of those regions of Europe, like Galicia, where the upper classes, speaking a different language from the lower, could not be understood by them. The feudal lawyers of the eighteenth century, who often showed a spirit of kindness, moderation, and justice to the peasants little known to their predecessors, still spoke in some places of "the vile peasants." It seems as if these insults were formal terms, as the notaries say.

As we approach 1789, this sympathy for the miseries of the poor becomes greater and more imprudent. I have held in my hands the circulars which several provincial assemblies addressed, in the first days of 1788, to the inhabitants of the various parishes, in order to teach them, in detail, all the grievances which they could complain about.

One of the circulars is signed by an abbé, a great lord, three noblemen, and a bourgeois, all members of the assembly and acting in its name. This commission orders the syndic of each parish to assemble all the peasants and ask them what they have to say against the way in which the different taxes that they pay are set and collected. "We know, in a general way," it says, "that the majority of taxes, especially the taille and the salt tax, have disastrous consequences for the farmer, but we want to know further about each abuse in particular." The curiosity of the provincial assembly did not stop there; it wanted to know the number of people who enjoyed tax privileges in the parish, nobles, clergy, or commoners, and what exactly those privileges were; what the value of the property of these tax-exempts was; whether they resided on their lands or not; if there were many church lands, or as they said then, property in entail, which was out of circulation, and their value. All this was still not enough to satisfy the assembly; it wanted to be told at what sum one might estimate the taxes, taille, other dues, corvée, which the privileged should have paid, if equality of taxation existed.

This was to inflame each and every individual by the recitation of his miseries, to point a finger at their authors for him, to embolden him by the sight of their small number, and to penetrate his very heart to inflame his greed, envy, and hatred. It seems as if the Jacquerie,† the Maillotins,† and the Sixteen† had been completely forgotten, and that it was unknown that the French, who are the gentlest and even the most benevolent people in the world as long as they remain peacefully undisturbed, become the most barbarous nation on earth as soon as violent passions arouse them.

I have unfortunately been unable to acquire all the reports which the peasants sent in response to these deadly questions; but I have come up with a few of them, and that is enough to see the general spirit which dictated them. In these diatribes, the name of every privileged person, noble or bourgeois, is carefully indicated; his way of life is sometimes described and always criticized. The value of his property is sought with interest; the number and nature of his privileges are described at length, and above all the harm that they do to all the other inhabitants of the village. The bushels of wheat which must be paid to him in feudal dues are listed; his income is guessed with envy, income from which no one profits, it is said. The priest's fees, *his salary,* as it is already called, is excessive; it is bitterly remarked that everything must be paid for at church, and that the poor cannot even be buried free of charge. As for the taxes, they are all badly established and oppressive; there is not one which finds grace in their eyes, and they speak of them all in hot-headed language which breathes fury.

"The indirect taxes are odious," they say; "there is no home in which the tax-farm commissioner does not poke around; nothing is sacred in his eyes, or from his hands. The stamp duties are crushing. The taille-collector is a tyrant, whose greed uses all means to torment the poor. The bailiffs are no better than he; there is no honest farmer who is safe from their ferocity. The collectors are forced to ruin their neighbors in order not to expose themselves to the voracity of these despots."

The Revolution does not merely announce its approach in this inquiry; it is present, it already speaks its language and shows its face in full.

Among all the differences which are found between the religious revolution of the sixteenth century and the French Revolution, there is one that is striking: in the sixteenth century, most of the great threw themselves into the change of religion by calculated ambition or by greed; the people embraced it, on the contrary, by conviction, and without expecting any profit. In the eighteenth century, it was not the same; it was disinterested beliefs and generous feelings which then motivated the educated classes and pointed them towards revolution, while resentment of their grievances and the desire to change their position agitated the people. The enthusiasm of the educated classes ended up setting afire and arming the angers and lusts of the masses.

CHAPTER SIX

Some Practices Which Helped the Government Complete the Revolutionary Education of the Masses

The government itself had long worked to make several ideas, since called revolutionary, enter and become fixed in the minds of the masses, ideas hostile to the individual, contrary to private rights, and friendly to violence. The king was the first to show with what contempt one could treat the oldest and apparently most established institutions. Louis XV shook the monarchy and hastened the Revolution as much by his innovations as by his vices, as much by his energy as by his indolence. When the people saw the parlement, almost as old as the monarchy and which had seemed up to then as unshakable as it was, fall and disappear, it vaguely understood that we were approaching those times of violence and chance when everything becomes possible, when there is nothing so old that it must be respected, nor so new that it may not be tried.

Louis XVI, during the whole course of his reign, did nothing but speak of reforms to be made. There were few institutions whose near destruction he did not foresee, before the Revolution came to destroy them all in reality. After having eliminated several of the worst laws, he soon revived them: one might have said that he only wanted to uproot them, leaving to others the task of taking them away.

Among the reforms that he made himself, several changed old and respected customs brusquely and without sufficient warning, and sometimes violated acquired rights. They thus prepared the Revolution much less by knocking down what was an obstacle to it than by showing the people how to act. What increased the evil was precisely the pure and disinterested intentions which motivated the king and his ministers; for there is no more dangerous example than violence exercised for good purposes by people of good will.

Long before, Louis XIV in his edicts had publicly proclaimed the theory that all the lands of the kingdom had been originally leased on terms by the state, which thus remained the sole real owner, while all others were only occupiers whose title remained contestable and whose rights remained limited. This doctrine had its origin in feudal law; but it was only proclaimed in France when feudalism was dying, and the courts had never admired it. It is the mother idea of modern socialism. It is interesting to see it first take root in royal despotism.[62]

In a more practical and more easily comprehensible way, during the reigns which followed that of Louis XIV, the government daily taught the people the contempt that it was fitting to have for private property. When, in the second half of the eighteenth century, the taste for public works, and in particular for roads, began to spread, the government did not make any difficulty about taking all the land it needed for its projects, and knocking down all the houses that got in its way. The administration of Roads and Bridges was then as taken with the geometrical attractions of the straight line as we have seen it since; it took great care to avoid following the existing roads, because they seemed a bit curved, and, rather than make a slight detour, they cut across a thousand inheritances. The proprietors thus devastated or destroyed were always paid arbitrarily and late, and often not at all.[63]

When the provincial assembly of Lower Normandy took over the administration from the intendant, it stated that the price of all these lands seized by authority for roads during the past twenty years was still due. The debt thus contracted, and not yet paid by the state, in that little corner of France, totalled 250,000 livres. The number of great landowners hurt in this way was small; but the number of small proprietors harmed was great, for already the land was very divided. Each one of them had learned by his own experience the little regard which individual rights merited when public interest required that they be violated, a doctrine which he took care not to forget when the time came to apply it to others for his own profit.

There had previously existed, in a very large number of parishes, charitable foundations which, according to their founders' intentions, had as their purpose to help the inhabitants in certain cases and in a certain way which the donor had specified. The majority of these foundations were destroyed in the last period of the monarchy, or diverted from their original object, by simple decrees of the Royal Council, that is, by the purely arbitrary will of the government. Usually the funds thus given to the villages were taken away for the profit of neighboring hospitals. In turn, the properties of these hospitals were, around the same period, transformed for uses which the donor had not intended, and which he would doubtless never have accepted. An edict of 1780 authorized all these establishments to sell the properties which had been left them at various times, on condition that they be held in perpetuity, and permitted them to give the proceeds to the state, which would pay interest on them. This was, it was said, to put ancestral charity to better use than they had put it themselves. It was forgotten that the best means to teach men to violate the individual rights of the living was not to take any account of the will of the dead. The contempt for the dead which the government of the old regime showed has not been surpassed by any of the powers which have succeeded it. Never, above all, did it show the rather meticulous scruples which lead the English to lend all society's force to each citizen to help him keep his last will in effect, and which make them give still more respect to his memory than to himself.

Requisitions, the forced sale of grain, maximum prices are government measures which had precedents under the old regime. I have seen, in times of food shortage, administrators fix in advance the price of grain that the peasants brought to market, and since the peasants, fearing to be forced, did not come, create ordinances to make them come under pain of a fine.

But nothing was a more pernicious education than certain forms taken by criminal justice when it concerned the masses. The poor man was already better guaranteed than one imagines against the attacks of a richer or more powerful citizen than he; but if he had to do with the state, he no longer found, as I have shown elsewhere, any but special courts, judges prepared in advance, a quick or illusory trial, an executive decree by provision and without appeal. "Let the provost of the mounted police and his lieutenant be aware of the disturbances and demonstrations that may take place because of the grain situation; order that trials be performed by them, judged by the provost as final court of appeal; His Majesty forbids all courts of justice to take jurisdiction over them." This edict of the Council was law during the entire eighteenth century. One sees by the transcripts of the mounted police that, in these circumstances, suspect villages were encircled at night, houses entered before daybreak, and the designated peasants arrested, without any question of warrants. The man thus arrested often stayed in prison a long time before being able to speak to his judge; the edicts, however, declared that all accused were to be interrogated within twenty-four hours. This declaration was neither less obligatory nor more respected than in our own day.[64]

It is thus that a mild and well-established government daily taught the people the code of criminal justice most appropriate to revolutionary periods and best adapted to tyranny. Its school was always open. The old regime gave this dangerous education to the poorest of the poor. Up through Turgot there was no one who in this respect did not faithfully imitate his predecessors. When, in 1775, his new legislation on the grain trade gave rise to resistance in the parlement and riots in the countryside, he obtained from the king an ordinance which, putting the courts aside, delivered the mutinous to the jurisdiction of the provost, "which is chiefly designed," he says, "to repress popular movements, when it is useful for examples to be made rapidly." Still more, all peasants who left their parishes without being provided with an affidavit signed by the priest and the syndic were to be pursued, arrested, and tried by the provost's tribunals as vagabonds.

It is true that in the eighteenth-century monarchy, if the forms were frightening, the penalty was almost always tempered. One preferred to frighten more than to harm; or rather one was arbitrary and violent by habit and indifference, and gentle by disposition. But the taste for summary justice grew even greater because of this. The lighter the punishment, the more easily one forgot the way in which it was pronounced. The gentleness of the decree hid the horror of the procedure.

I will dare to say, because I have the proofs in my hand, that a great number of the procedures followed by the revolutionary government had had precedents and examples in the measures taken with respect to the lower classes during the last two centuries of the monarchy. The old regime furnished the Revolution with several of its forms; the Revolution added only the savagery of its spirit.

CHAPTER SEVEN

How a Great Administrative Revolution
Had Preceded the Political Revolution, and the
Consequences That This Had

Nothing had yet changed in the form of government when already the majority of secondary laws which regulated the condition of persons, and the administration of business, were abolished or changed.

The destruction of the guilds and their partial and incomplete reestablishment had profoundly altered all the old relations between worker and master. Relations had become not only different, but uncertain and constrained. The manorial regulations had been destroyed; the tutelage of the state was as yet poorly established, and the artisan, placed in a difficult and doubtful position between the government and the employer, did not know very well which of these two could protect him, or which was supposed to restrain him. This state of malaise and anarchy, into which the whole lower class of the towns was thrown at a stroke, had great consequences as soon as the people began to reappear on the political scene.

A year before the Revolution, a royal edict had completely overturned the judicial system; several new jurisdictions had been created, a multitude of others abolished, all the rules of competence changed. But, in France, as I have already noted elsewhere, the number of those who were employed, either to judge, or to execute the judges' decrees, was immense. In truth, the whole bourgeoisie was more or less closely connected to the courts. The effect of the law was therefore to suddenly disturb thousands of families in their situation and their wealth, and to give them a new and precarious position. The edict inconvenienced the litigants hardly less, who in the midst of this judicial revolution found it difficult to figure out which law was applicable to them, and which court was supposed to judge them. But it was above all the radical reform to which the government proper was subjected in 1787, which, after bringing disorder into public affairs, came to affect every citizen even in his private life.

I said that in the *pays d'élection,* that is in nearly three-quarters of France, the whole administration of each region had been given to a single man, the intendant, who acted not only without control but without a council. In 1787, a provincial assembly, which became the real administrator of the province, was placed beside this intendant. In each village, an elected municipal body also took the place of the old parish assemblies, and in most cases, of the syndic.

Legislation so opposed to that which preceded it, and which changed so completely not only the order of business but the relative position of men, had to be applied everywhere at once, and everywhere in almost the same way, without any regard for past practices or the particular situation of the province. So much had the unitary spirit of the Revolution already possessed the old government that the Revolution was going to bring down.

In such conditions one sees clearly the part that habit plays in the game of political institutions, and how men deal more easily with complicated and obscure laws, which they have been used to for a long time, than with simpler legislation which is new to them. Under the old regime there were all kinds of powers in France, which varied infinitely according to the province, none of which had any fixed or known limits, to such an extent that each one's field of action always overlapped that of several others'. However, in the end a regular and fairly simple order had been established in affairs; while the new powers, which were fewer in number, carefully limited, and similar in form, collided and tangled amidst the utmost confusion, and often mutually reduced one another to powerlessness.

Furthermore, the new law contained a great vice which alone would have been enough, above all at the beginning, to make its execution difficult: all the powers which were created were collective. Under the old monarchy, only two kinds of government had been known: in the areas where power had been given to one man alone, he acted without the help of any assembly; where there existed assemblies, as in the *pays d'états* or in the towns, the executive power was not given to anyone in particular; the assembly not only governed and supervised the bureaucracy but carried out the administration itself or through temporary commissions that it chose.

Since we were only familiar with these two ways of acting, as soon as one was abandoned the other was adopted. It is strange enough that, in the heart of a society so enlightened, where the government had already, for so long, played such a large role, no one had ever thought of combining the two systems, and of distinguishing the executive power from the legislative power without entirely divorcing them. This idea, which seems so simple, never arrived; it was discovered only in this century. It is indeed the only great discovery in public administration that we ourselves have made. We will see the consequences that the opposite practice had, when, obedient to the traditions of the old regime even while detesting it, transporting its administrative habits into politics, we applied the system which the provincial estates and small municipalities had followed in the National Convention.† Thus, from what had up to then been only an administrative embarrassment, one suddenly brought forth the Terror.

The provincial assemblies of 1787, therefore, themselves received the right to govern in most of the situations where, up to then, the intendant had acted alone; they were charged, under the central government's authority, to set the taille and supervise its collection, to decide which public works ought to be undertaken and to carry them out. They had under their direct command all the agents of the Roads and Bridges corps, from inspector down to laborer. They had to tell them what they thought necessary, render an account of the service of these agents to the minister, and suggest to him the rewards that they deserved. The supervision of the villages was almost entirely entrusted to these assemblies; they had to try in the first instance most disputed matters which previously had been brought before the intendant, etc.; functions several of which were inappropriate to a collective and irresponsible power, and which further were going to be exercised by people who were governing for the first time.

What finally confused everything, was that while the intendant was reduced to powerlessness, he was nevertheless allowed to remain in existence. After he was deprived of the absolute right to do everything, the duty of aiding and observing the assembly's actions was imposed on him; as if a fallen official could ever enter into the spirit of the legislation which dispossessed him, and help make it work! What had been done for the intendant was done for his subdelegate. Alongside him, in the place he had just occupied, a local assembly was placed which was supposed to act under the direction of the provincial assembly, and according to similar principles.⁶⁵

All that we know of the acts of the provincial assemblies created in 1787, and their own transcripts, testifies that immediately after their birth they entered into a silent and often open war with the intendants, the latter employing their superior experience only to hinder the movements of their successors. In one place an assembly complains of being able to obtain the most necessary documents from the intendant only with great difficulty. In another, it is the intendant who accuses the members of the assembly of wanting to usurp the responsibilities which the edicts, he says, have left to him. He appeals to the minister, who often does not respond at all, or is in doubt, for the question is as new and difficult for him as for everybody else. Sometimes, the assembly resolves that the intendant has not governed well, that the roads he has made are poorly constructed or badly placed; he has allowed the communities of which he was the guardian to be ruined. Often, these assemblies hesitate in the midst of the obscurities of legislation so little known; they send far-off to consult with one another, and they have advice sent to them from all over. The intendant of Auch claims that he may oppose the will of a provincial assembly, which has authorized a village to tax itself; the assembly affirms that in this question the intendant can only give advice, not orders, and it asks the provincial assembly of the Ile-de-France [†] what it thinks. In the midst of these recriminations and consultations, the progress of government often slowed and sometimes stopped: public life was as if suspended. "The stagnation of business is complete," says the provincial assembly of Lorraine, which is but the echo of several others; "all good citizens grieve over it."

At other times, it was by excess of activity and self-confidence that the new governments sinned; they were all filled with a restless and innovative zeal which made them want to change all at once the old methods and rapidly correct the oldest abuses. Under the pretext that it was up to them now to be the guardians of the towns, they tried to run communal affairs themselves; in a word, wanting to make everything better, they ended up confusing everything.

If we want to properly consider the immense place which the government had already long occupied in France, the multitude of interests which it affected daily, everything that was subject to it, or needed its consent; if we remember that individuals already counted on the government more than on themselves for the success of their own affairs, to favor their industry, assure their subsistence, lay out and construct their roads, preserve their peace, and guarantee their well-being, we will have an idea of the infinite number of people who must have found themselves personally harmed by the evil which was suffered.

But it was above all in the villages where the vices of the new administration were felt; there, it not only disturbed the order of powers, it suddenly changed the relative position of men, and put all classes into confrontation and conflict. In 1775 when Turgot proposed to the king to reform the administration of the countryside, the greatest problem that he met, he tells us, came from the unequal division of taxes: for how could one make people act in common and deliberate together on parish affairs, which were chiefly the division, collection, and expenditure of taxes, when they were not all subject to paying taxes in the same way, and several were exempt from their burden? Every parish contained some nobles and clergy who did not pay the taille at all, some peasants who were partially or totally exempt, and others who paid it in full. They were like three distinct parishes, each of which would have demanded a separate government. The difficulty was insoluble.

Nowhere, in fact, was the difference in taxation more visible than in the countryside; nowhere else was the population more divided into different and often opposed groups. To succeed in giving the villages a collective administration and a small free government, it would have been necessary first of all to subject everyone to the same taxes, and to lessen the distance which separated the classes.

This was hardly what was done when this reform was finally attempted in 1787. Within the parish the old separation of orders was retained, as well as the inequality of taxation which was its chief sign, and, nevertheless, the entire administration was given to elective bodies. This immediately led to some odd results. If it was a question of an electoral assembly which was supposed to choose the municipal officials, the priest and the lord could not appear; they belonged, it was said, to the order of the nobility, and to that of the clergy; but in principle it was the Third Estate which was to elect its representatives here. Once the municipal council was elected, on the contrary, the priest and the lord belonged to it by right; for it had not seemed fitting to render two such notable inhabitants entirely strangers to the government of the parish. The lord even presided over these municipal councilors whom he had not helped elect, but he was unable to participate in most of their actions. When they proceeded to fix the amount and division of the taille, for example, the priest and the lord could not vote. Were they not both exempt from this tax? On its side, the municipal council had nothing to do with the capitation tax; it continued to be determined by the intendant, according to its own special rules.

From fear that this president, thus isolated from the body which he was supposed to direct, would still indirectly exercise an influence contrary to the interests of the order of which he was not part, it was asked that the votes of his tenants not be counted; and the provincial assemblies, consulted on this point, found this request very just and completely in conformity with principle. The other nobles who lived in the parish could not enter this same commoner-run municipal council. As the regulations took care to note, only the Third Estate had the right to be represented there.

The lord, therefore, only appeared there to be entirely subordinated to his former subjects, suddenly become his masters; he was their prisoner rather than their leader. In gathering men in this way, the intention seemed to be less to join them together than to make them see more clearly in what they differed, and how their interests were opposed.

Was the syndic still the discredited official whose responsibilities were only undertaken when forced, or had his situation been improved with that of the community whose chief official he remained?[66] No one knew exactly. I find in 1788 the letter of a certain village bailiff who was indignant that he had been elected syndic. "This," he says, "is against all the privileges of his office." The controller-general responds that the ideas of this individual must be corrected, "and he must understand that he ought to consider it an honor to be chosen by his fellow-citizens, and that furthermore the new syndics barely resemble the officials who up to now bore the same name, and that they may count on more respect from the government."

On the other hand, one sees the wealthy inhabitants of the parish, and even the nobles, suddenly get closer to the peasants, when the peasants become a power. The lord with right of high and low justice over a village in the neighborhood of Paris complains that the edict forbids him from taking part, *even as a simple inhabitant,* in the operations of the parish assembly. Others consent, they say, "by devotion to the public good, to fill even the function of syndic."

It was too late. As the men of the wealthy classes advanced towards the people of the countryside, and attempted to mingle with them, the people retreated into the isolation which had been made for them, and defended it. One finds municipal assemblies which refused to receive the lord in their midst; others used all kinds of tricks to avoid admitting even commoners, when they were rich. "We are informed," says the provincial assembly of Lower Normandy, "that several municipal assemblies have refused to admit commoner proprietors of their parish who do not live there, even though there is no doubt that they have a right to participate. Other assemblies have even refused to admit tenants who do not own any land in their territory."

Thus, all was already innovation, obscurity, and conflict in the secondary laws, even before the chief laws which regulated the government of the state had been touched. What was still standing had been shaken, and in fact there no longer existed a single regulation whose abolition or coming modification the central government had not announced.

This sudden and immense renovation of all rules, and all administrative habits, which preceded the political revolution among us, and which we barely mention today, was, however, already one of the biggest changes which had ever occurred in the history of a great nation. This first revolution exercised a tremendous influence on the second, and made of it an event different from all those of the same kind that had previously taken place in the world, or which have taken place since.

The first English revolution, which overturned the entire political constitution of that country and went so far as to abolish the monarchy, only affected the secondary laws very superficially, and changed almost none of the customs and practices. The judiciary and the government kept their forms and followed the same paths as in the past. At the height of the civil war, the twelve judges of England continued, it is said, to make the round of the assizes twice a year. Thus not everything was changed at the same time. The revolution was limited in its effects, and English society, although disturbed at its summit, remained solid at its base.

We have ourselves seen in France, since '89, several revolutions which have changed the whole structure of government from top to bottom. Most have been very sudden, and have been accompanied by force, in open violation of the existing laws. Nevertheless, the disorder to which they have given birth has never been either long or general; the majority of the country has barely felt them, sometimes barely noticed.

This is because, since '89, the administrative constitution has always remained in force in the midst of the destructions of political constitutions. We changed the person of the ruler, or the forms of the central power, but the daily course of affairs was neither interrupted nor troubled; everyone remained subject, in the little things which personally concerned him, to the rules and the practices with which he was familiar; he was subject to the secondary powers to which he had always had the habit of addressing himself, and usually he had to do with the same officials; for if at each revolution the administration was decapitated, its body stayed alive and intact; the same functions were exercised by the same officials; these officials transported their spirit and their practice across different political systems. They judged and governed in the name of the king, then in the name of the republic, finally in the name of the emperor. Then, as the wheel of fortune turned full circle, they once again began to govern and judge for the king, the republic, and the emperor, always the same people doing the same things; for what did the master's name matter to them? Their business was less to be citizens than to be good administrators and good judges. Once the first shock had passed, it seemed that nothing in the country had changed.

When the Revolution broke out, this part of government, which although subordinate, daily affected every citizen and influenced his well-being in the most constant and most effective manner, had just been turned completely upside down: the public administration had completely changed all its agents and redrawn all its principles. At first, the state did not seem to have suffered a great shock from this immense reform; but all the French had felt a small personal upheaval. Everyone found his position shaken, his habits disturbed, or his business hindered. A certain order continued to reign in the most important and most general affairs, but already no one knew any longer whom to obey, nor whom to address, nor how to act in the petty matters and individual cases that form society's daily course of life.

The nation no longer being secure in any of its parts, one last blow could therefore put the whole thing in motion and produce the greatest upheaval and the most frightening confusion which ever was.

CHAPTER EIGHT

How the Revolution Came
Naturally from What Preceded It

In closing, I want to bring together some of the traits that I have already described separately, and to envision the Revolution emerging naturally, as it were, from the old regime whose portrait I have painted.

If we consider that it was among us that the feudal system had most lost all that could protect it or serve it, without changing what could harm or irritate, we will be less surprised that the revolution which was going to violently abolish the old constitution of Europe broke out in France rather than elsewhere.

If we note that the nobility, after having lost its old political rights and ceased, more than anywhere else in feudal Europe, to govern and lead the population, had nevertheless not only retained but much increased its financial immunities and the advantages which its members individually enjoyed; that in becoming a subordinate class the nobility had remained a privileged and closed class, less and less an aristocracy, as I said earlier, and more and more a caste, we will no longer be surprised that its privileges appeared so inexplicable and so detestable to the French, and that at the sight of these privileges democratic envy was inflamed to such a pitch in their hearts that it still burns.

If we think, finally, that this nobility, separated from the middle classes which it had repulsed from its midst, and from the people whose loyalty it had allowed to escape, was completely isolated within the nation, in appearance the head of an army, in reality an officer corps without soldiers, we will understand how, after having been in existence for a thousand years, it could be overthrown in the course of an evening.

I have shown in what way the royal government, having abolished provincial freedoms, and substituted itself in three-quarters of France for all the local authorities, had attracted all affairs to itself, the smallest and the greatest alike; I have, furthermore, shown how by a necessary consequence Paris had become the master of the nation, when up to then it had merely been its capital, or rather had become the entire country itself. These two facts, which were unique to France, would alone be enough, if necessary, to explain how a riot could destroy from top to bottom a monarchy which during so many centuries had borne such violent shocks, and which on the eve of its fall still seemed unshakable even to those who were going to overthrow it.

France being the European country where political life had been longest and most completely extinct, where individuals had most completely lost the practical skills, the ability to read facts, the experience of popular movements, and almost the very idea of the people, it is easy to imagine how all the French at once could fall into a terrible revolution without perceiving it, those most threatened by it marching in front and breaking the trail that led to it.

Since there no longer existed free institutions, and in consequence no political classes, no living political bodies, no organized political parties with leaders, and since in the absence of all these organized forces the direction of public opinion, when public opinion was reborn, devolved uniquely on the philosophes, it was to be expected that the Revolution be directed less by certain particular facts than by abstract principles and very general theories; it could be foreseen that rather than separate attacks on bad laws there would be an attack on all the laws at once, and that there would be the desire to substitute a completely new system of government, conceived by the intellectuals, for the old constitution of France.

The Church naturally finding itself entangled with all the old institutions whose destruction was in question, it could not be doubted that this revolution would have to shake religion at the same time as it overturned the civil power; from then on, it was impossible to say what unheard-of audacities the minds of the innovators would be led to, liberated at one stroke from all the limits that religion, custom, and law impose on the human imagination. And he who had carefully studied the country's situation could easily have foreseen that there was no recklessness so unheard of that it could not be tried, nor violence that could not be allowed.

"How is it," cried Burke in one of his eloquent pamphlets, "we do not find a single man who can speak for the smallest district; still more, we do not find one who can respond to another. Everyone is arrested in his home without resistance, whether it be for royalism, moderation, or anything else." Burke did not understand very well the condition in which the monarchy he regretted had left us to our new masters. The government of the old regime had already taken away from the French any possibility, or desire, of helping one another. When the Revolution happened, one would have searched most of France in vain for ten men who had the habit of acting in common in an orderly way, and taking care of their own defense themselves; only the central power was supposed to take care of it, so that the central power, fallen from the hands of the royal government into the hands of a sovereign and irresponsible assembly, and changed from good-natured to terrible, found nothing which could stop it, or even briefly slow it down. The same cause which made the monarchy fall so easily, made everything possible after its fall.

Never had religious tolerance, benevolent rule, humanity, and even goodwill, been more preached and seemingly more admired than in the eighteenth century; the laws of warfare, which is the last refuge of violence, were themselves limited and made gentler. From the midst of such mild mores, however, the most inhuman revolution was going to come! And yet, all that civilizing of mores was not a false appearance; for, as soon as the fury of the Revolution was spent, one sees the same mildness immediately spread throughout the law and penetrate all political habits.

The contrast between benign theories and violent acts which is one of the French Revolution's strangest characteristics, will not surprise anyone who notes that that revolution had been prepared by the most civilized classes of the nation, and was carried out by the most coarse and ignorant. The men of the former sort not having any preexisting link among themselves, no practice at coming to an agreement, no hold on the people, the people themselves became almost immediately the directing power, as soon as the old powers were destroyed. Where they did not rule themselves, they gave at least their spirit to the government; and if one thinks of the way which the masses had lived under the old regime, it will not be difficult to imagine what things were going to be like.

The very peculiarities of their situation had given the common people several rare virtues. Long since freed, and long since become owners of a piece of land, isolated rather than dependent, the people showed themselves proud and sober; they were difficult to tire, indifferent to the delicacies of life, resigned to the greatest evils, firm in the face of danger; a simple and virile race which was going to fill the powerful armies under whose strength Europe would bend. But the same reasons made them a dangerous master. Since the people had for centuries borne all the real abuses, since they had lived apart, nourishing themselves in silence on their prejudices, their jealousies, and their hatred, they had been hardened by the rigors of their fate, and they had become capable of both enduring everything and inflicting everything.

It was in this state that, putting their hands on government, the people themselves attempted to finish the Revolution's work. Books had furnished the theory, the people charged themselves with the practice, and they adjusted the writers' ideas to their own fury.

Those who, in reading this book, have carefully studied eighteenth-century France have been able to see two chief passions born and developed in the nation's breast, which were not at all contemporary with one another and have not always tended towards the same goal. One, deeper and coming from further back, is the violent and inextinguishable hatred of inequality. This was born and nourished from the sight of that very inequality, and had long pushed the French, with constant and irresistible strength, to want to destroy to their very foundations all that remained of medieval institutions and, once the space was cleared, to build a society where men were as alike, and conditions as equal, as humanity could admit.

The other passion, more recent and less well-rooted, brought them to want to live not only equal, but free.

Towards the end of the old regime these two passions are equally sincere and seem equally lively. At the start of the Revolution they meet; they mix and join for a moment and then, heating each other by contact, finally inflame the whole heart of France at once. This is '89, a time of inexperience doubtless, but of generosity, of enthusiasm, of virility, and of greatness, a time of immortal memory, to which the eyes of men will turn with admiration and respect when those who saw it, and we ourselves, will long since have disappeared. Then the French were proud enough of their cause and of themselves to believe that they could be equal in freedom. In the midst of democratic institutions they therefore put free institutions everywhere. Not only did they reduce to dust the outdated legislation which divided men into castes, corporations, and classes, and made their rights still more unequal than their situations, but they broke with a single blow all those other laws, the more recent works of royal power, which had taken from the nation its free enjoyment of itself, and had put the government alongside each Frenchman, to be his tutor, his guardian, and if need be his oppressor. Centralization fell with absolute government.

But when this vigorous generation which had begun the Revolution had been destroyed or worn out, there happened what usually happens to all generations that begin such enterprises; when, following the natural course of this kind of event, the love of liberty was discouraged and weakened in the midst of anarchy and popular dictatorship, and when the lost nation began to search gropingly for its master, absolute government found immense facilities for its rebirth and foundation. These were easily discovered by the genius of he who was going to be simultaneously the continuator and destroyer of the Revolution. The old regime contained, in fact, a whole ensemble of institutions of modern date, which, not being at all hostile to equality, could easily take their place in the new society, and which, moreover, offered unique facilities to despotism. We sought for them again amidst the debris of all other institutions, and found them. These institutions had previously created habits, passions, and ideas which tended to keep men divided and obedient; we revived this and encouraged it. We returned to centralization in its ruins and restored it; and since, at the same time that it was revived, all that had formerly been able to limit it remained destroyed, from the very bowels of a nation that had just overthrown the monarchy suddenly surged forth a power more extensive, more detailed, more absolute than that which any of our kings had exercised. The enterprise seemed one of extraordinary boldness and its success unheard-of, because no one thought of anything beyond what they saw, and they forgot what had been seen before. The master fell, but what was most substantial in his work remained; his government dead, his bureaucracy still lived, and every time that we have since tried to bring down absolute power, we have limited ourselves to placing liberty's head on a servile body.

At several repetitions, from when the Revolution began down to our own days, we have seen the passion for freedom extinguished, then reborn, then again extinguished and again reborn; thus this passion will long continue, always inexperienced and badly regulated, easy to discourage, frighten, and defeat, superficial and temporary. During this same period the passion for equality has still retained possession of the depths of the hearts that it first conquered; there it clings to the feelings which are dearest to us; while the passion for freedom constantly changes its appearance, shrinks, grows, strengthens, and weakens according to events, the passion for equality is always the same, always attached to the same purpose with the same obstinate and often blind ardor, ready to sacrifice everything to those who permit it to satisfy itself, and to furnish to the government willing to favor and flatter it the habits, ideas, and laws that despotism needs in order to rule.

The French Revolution will be but a shadow for those who want to look at it in isolation; it is in the time which precedes it that we must look for the only light which can illuminate it. Without a precise understanding of the old society, of its laws, its vices, its prejudices, its miseries, its greatness, we will never understand what the French have done for the sixty years that have followed its fall; but this understanding will still not be enough if one does not penetrate into the very spirit of our nation.

When I consider this nation in itself, I find it more extraordinary than any of the events in its history. Has there ever been any nation on earth which was so full of contrasts, and so extreme in all of its acts, more dominated by emotions, and less by principles; always doing better or worse than we expect, sometimes below the common level of humanity, sometimes much above it; a people so unalterable in its basic instincts that we can still recognize it in portraits drawn of it two or three thousand years ago, and at the same time so changeable in its daily thoughts and tastes that it ends up offering an unexpected spectacle to itself, and often remains as surprised as a foreigner at the sight of what it has just done; the most stay-at-home nation of all and the one most in love with routine, when left to itself; and, when torn despite itself from its hearth and its habits, ready to go to the ends of the earth and risk all; insubordinate by temperament, and always readier to accept the arbitrary and even violent empire of a prince than the free and orderly government of its leading citizens; today the declared enemy of all obedience, tomorrow attached to servitude with a kind of passion that the nations best-endowed for servitude cannot match; led on a string so long as no one resists, ungovernable as soon as the example of resistance appears somewhere; thus always tricking its masters, who fear it too much or too little; never so free that one must despair of enslaving it, or so servile that it may not once again break the yoke; capable of everything, but excelling only at war; a lover of chance, of strength, of success, of fame and reputation, more than of true glory; more capable of heroism than of virtue, of genius than of common sense, ready to conceive vast plans rather than to complete great tasks; the most brilliant and most dangerous nation of Europe, and the best suited for becoming by turns an object of admiration, of hatred, of pity, and of terror, but never of indifference?

France alone could give birth to a revolution so sudden, so radical, so impetuous in its course, and yet so full of backtracking, of contradictory facts and contrary examples. Without the reasons which I have given, the French would never have made the Revolution; but it must be recognized that all these reasons together would not succeed in explaining such a revolution anywhere else but in France.

Here I have reached the threshold of that memorable revolution; I will not cross it this time: soon, perhaps, I will be able to. I will not then consider its causes, I will examine it in itself, and I will finally dare to judge the society that has come from it.

On the *Pays d'états,* and in Particular on Languedoc

M y intention here is not to examine in detail how things went on in each of the *pays d'états* that still existed at the time of the Revolution. I want only to state their number, make known those in which local life was still active, show what their relations were with the royal government, how they departed from the common rules that I have previously described, how they were subject to them, and, finally, to make clear by an example what they could all easily have become.

Estates had existed in most of the provinces of France, that is, each of them had been administered under the royal government by the *people of the three Estates,* as they said then; which means by Estates composed of representatives of the clergy, the nobility, and the bourgeoisie. This provincial constitution, like other medieval political institutions, exhibited the same traits in almost all civilized parts of Europe, at least in all those where Germanic mores and ideas had penetrated. There were many provinces in Germany where Estates persisted up to the French Revolution; and where they had been destroyed, they had disappeared only in the course of the seventeenth and eighteenth centuries. Everywhere, for two centuries, the princes had made war on them, sometimes open, sometimes hidden, but constant. Nowhere had the rulers attempted to improve the institution in accord with the progress of the times, but only to destroy it, or to deform it when opportunity offered and they could not do anything worse.

In France in 1789, Estates still existed in only five provinces of any size, and in a few insignificant districts. Real provincial liberty still existed in only two, Brittany and Languedoc; everywhere else the institution had entirely lost its virility and was nothing but a facade. I will choose Languedoc and make it the object of special examination here.

Languedoc was the biggest and most populous of all the *pays d'états;* it contained more than two thousand towns, or, as they said then, *communities,* and counted more than two million inhabitants. It was, moreover, the best-ordered and the most prosperous of all these provinces, as well as the biggest. Therefore Languedoc is a good choice for understanding what provincial freedom could be under the old regime, and to what point, even in the regions where it seemed strongest, provincial freedom had been subordinated to royal power.

In Languedoc, the Estates could meet only on the express order of the king, after a letter of convocation annually sent by him to each individual member who was to take part; which made a contemporary rebel say: "Of the three bodies which compose our Estates, one, the clergy, is there by the king's nomination, since he names the bishops and the benefices, and the other two are considered to be chosen by him, since the Court can prevent any member it pleases from attending, without any need to exile him or bring him to trial. It is enough not to invite him."

The Estates not only had to meet but to recess on the dates set by the king. By a decree of the Royal Council the ordinary length of their session was fixed at forty days. The king was represented in the assembly by commissioners who had the right to be present upon their request, and who were supposed to present the government's views. The Estates were, furthermore, closely supervised. They could not take a resolution of any importance, decree any financial measure, without their decision being approved by a royal decree; for a tax, a loan, a lawsuit, they had to have the express permission of the king. All their general regulations, even those which concerned the holding of their meetings, had to be authorized before being put into force. The whole of their income and expenditure, their budget, as we call it today, was annually submitted to the same control.

Furthermore, in Languedoc the central power exercised the same political rights that it had everywhere else; the laws that it wished to enact, the general regulations that it constantly created, the general measures that it took, were as applicable in Languedoc as in the *pays d'élection.* It exercised in Languedoc all the natural functions of government; it had the same police and the same agents; it occasionally created in Languedoc, as everywhere, a multitude of new government officials whose offices the province was obliged to buy back at great expense.

Languedoc was governed, like the other provinces, by an intendant. This intendant had subdelegates in each district who corresponded with the heads of the communities and directed them. The intendant exercised government supervision there in absolutely the same way as in the *pays d'élection*. The smallest village lost in the gorges of the Cévennes could not make the tiniest expenditure without authorization from Paris by a decree of the Royal Council. The part of the judicial system that we now call the Department of Private Claims was as extensive in Languedoc as in the rest of France; it was even more so. The intendant decided in the first instance all questions of highways, judged all disputes about roads, and, in general, pronounced on all matters in which the government was interested, or thought it was. This covered all of its agents against whom indiscreet lawsuits had been brought by injured citizens as much as elsewhere.

What, therefore, distinguished Languedoc in particular from the other provinces, and made it the object of their envy? Three things were sufficient to make it different from the rest of France.

1. An assembly composed of important men, in whom the population had trust, which was respected by the royal power, in which no official of the central government, or, following the language of the times, *no king's officer,* could take part, and where annually the province's special interests were discussed freely and openly. It was enough for the royal government to find this well-informed house in its midst for it to exercise its privileges entirely differently, and though it had the same agents and the same instincts the royal government barely resembled what it was everywhere else.

2. There were in Languedoc many public works which were executed at the king's expense and by his agents; there were others where the central government furnished a portion of the funds and in large part directed their execution; but most were done at the sole expense of the province. Once the king had approved the plan and authorized expenditure on it, the projects were executed by officials chosen by the province and under the inspection of their commissioners.

3. Finally, the province had the right to raise part of the royal taxes, and all those which it had been permitted to establish to pay for its own needs, according to its own preferred method.

We will see what Languedoc was able to get out of these privileges. It is worthwhile to examine it closely. What is most striking in the *pays d'élection* is the almost complete absence of local taxes; the general taxes were often oppressive, but the province spent almost nothing itself. In Languedoc, on the contrary, the sum spent by the province on public works annually was enormous: in 1780, it surpassed 2,000,000 livres a year.

The central government was sometimes disturbed by the sight of such a great expense; it feared that the province, exhausted by such an effort, would be unable to pay the portion of the taxes which belonged to the king; it criticized the Estates for not being more moderate. I have read a report in which the assembly responded to these criticisms. What I will quote literally from it will depict better than anything I could say the spirit which animated this little government.

One sees in this report that, in fact, the province had undertaken and continued to undertake immense projects; but, far from making excuses for this the province announced that, if the king did not object, it would follow this course more and more. The province had already improved or straightened the course of the chief rivers which crossed its territory, and was busy adding to the Languedoc Canal, excavated under Louis XIV and inadequate, extensions which would lead across lower Languedoc via Cette and Agde to the Rhone. It had made the port of Cette usable for commerce, and maintained it at great expense. All these expenses, it was noted, were more national than provincial in character; nevertheless, this province, which benefited from them more than any other, had undertaken them. It was equally in the midst of draining and making fit for agriculture the swamp of Aigues-Mortes. But it was above all with the roads that Languedoc wanted to concern itself: it had opened or put in good condition all those which crossed it to lead to other parts of the kingdom; those which only led between the cities and towns of Languedoc had been repaired. All these various roads were excellent, even in winter, and made a complete contrast to the hard, rough, and badly kept-up roads that were found in most of the neighboring provinces, Dauphiny, Quercy, and the Bordeaux region (*pays d'élection,* it was noted). The province was in accord on this point with business opinion and that of travelers; and it was right, for Arthur Young, crossing the province ten years later, put in his notes: "Languedoc, *pays d'états;* good roads, made without corvées."

If the king would allow it, continues the report, the Estates would not stop at this; they would attempt to improve the secondary roads, which were no less important than the others. "For, note that if the produce cannot leave the farmer's granary to go to market, what does it matter that it can be transported far away?" "The doctrine of the Estates with respect to public works has always been," it is further added, "that it is not the size of the projects, but their utility, that ought to be considered." "Rivers, canals, and roads which make the products of the soil available to everyone, and give value to the products of industry by allowing their transport, in all weather and at low cost, everywhere where they are needed, by means of which commerce can penetrate all parts of the province, enrich the land whatever they cost. Furthermore, such projects carefully undertaken simultaneously in different parts of the territory, more or less equally, support the level of salaries everywhere and help the poor." "The king does not need to establish charity workshops in Languedoc at his own expense, as he has done in the rest of France," the province says in closing, with some pride. "We do not ask this favor at all; the useful projects that we undertake ourselves each year take their place, and give everyone productive work." The more I study the general rules established with the king's permission, but usually on their own initiative, by the Estates of Languedoc, the more I examine the part of public administration left to them, the more I admire the wisdom, equity, and mildness that is shown there, and the more the procedures of the local government seem superior to those which I have just examined in the regions governed by the king alone.

The province was divided into *communities* (towns or villages), into administrative districts called *dioceses;* and finally into three large departments called *sénéchausées*. Each of these parts had a separate representation and a small separate government, which acted under the direction of the Estates or the king. If it was a question of public works which were intended to benefit one of these small political bodies, they were undertaken only on their request. If a community project could be useful to the diocese, the diocese had to contribute to its expenses to a certain extent. If the sénéchausée was interested, it in turn had to supply help. The diocese, the sénéchausée, and the province, finally, had to come to the aid of a community, even when it was only a question of the community's particular interest, provided that the project was necessary and beyond the community's own means; for, the Estates say constantly: "The fundamental principal of our constitution is that all parts of Languedoc are in complete solidarity with one another, and must all help each other."

The projects that the province carried out had first to be described in detail and submitted to the examination of all the secondary bodies that had to agree to them; they had to be carried out for cash payments: the corvée was unknown. I said that in the *pays d'élection* lands taken from proprietors were always paid for poorly or late, and often not at all. It is one of the great complaints that the provincial assemblies raise when they meet in 1787. Some assemblies note that they had even been deprived of the ability to pay back debts acquired in this manner, because the object had been destroyed or altered before its value had been estimated. In

Languedoc, every parcel of land taken from the proprietor had to be carefully evaluated before work began *and paid for during the first year of work.*

The regulations of the Estates relative to the various public projects from which I have extracted these details seemed so well made in the view of the central government that, without imitating them, it admired them. The Royal Council, after having authorized their application, had them copied at the Royal Press, and commanded that they be transmitted to all intendants as an example.

What I have said of public works is still more strongly applicable to that other portion, not less important, of provincial administration which relates to raising taxes. It is there above all that after having passed from the kingdom to the province one finds it hard to believe that one is still in the same realm. I had occasion to say elsewhere how the procedures which were followed in Languedoc, to set and collect the taille, were in part those which we now follow ourselves for raising taxes. I will not repeat myself here; I will only add that Languedoc liked its way of raising taxes so much that, whenever the king created new taxes, the Estates never hesitated to buy at great price the right to raise them in their own way and through their own agents.

Despite all the expenses that I have successively enumerated, the budget of Languedoc was nevertheless in such good shape, and its credit so well established, that the central government often had recourse to Languedoc and borrowed money in the province's name that would not have been lent to it on such good terms. I find that Languedoc borrowed, under its own guarantee, but for the king's account, 73,000,000 livres in its final days.

The government and its ministers, however, looked at such special freedoms with a very jaundiced eye. Richelieu first mutilated them, then abolished them. The weak and spineless Louis XIII, who loved nothing, hated them; he held all provincial privileges in such horror, says Boulainvilliers, that merely hearing their name made him angry. We can never understand the energy weak minds put into hating anything which forces them to make an effort. All the virility that remains to them is employed there, and they almost always show themselves strong in this, even when weaklings in all else. Good fortune decreed that the old constitution of Languedoc was reestablished during the infancy of Louis XIV. He, regarding it as his own work, respected it. Louis XV suspended its application for two years, but then allowed it to be reborn.

Languedoc encountered perils less direct, but not less great, from the creation of municipal offices; this detestable institution not only destroyed the towns' constitutions, but further tended to distort those of the provinces. I do not know if the deputies of the Third Estate in the provincial assemblies had ever been elected for the position, but for a long time they had not been; by right the municipal officers of the towns were the only representatives of the bourgeoisie and the people in the provincial Estates.

This absence of a special mandate given with regard to the interests of the moment caused little notice when the towns themselves freely elected their magistrates by universal suffrage and usually for very short periods. The mayor, the consul, or the syndic then represented the wishes of the population in whose name they spoke in the Estates, as faithfully as if they had been expressly elected for the purpose by them. One understands that it was not the same when the municipal officials had purchased, with their money, the right to govern their fellow citizens. These men represented only themselves, or at most the petty interests or petty passions of their set. However, these officials retained the powers which their elected predecessors had had a right to. This immediately changed the whole character of the institution. The nobility and the clergy, instead of having to face the representatives of the people in the provincial assembly, found there merely a few isolated bourgeois, timid and powerless, and the Third Estate became more and more subordinate in government at the very moment when it daily became richer and stronger in society. It was not thus in Languedoc, the province having always taken care to buy back offices from the king as he established them. The debt contracted by Languedoc for this sole purpose amounted to more than 4 million livres in 1773 alone.

Other, more powerful causes had contributed to making the new spirit penetrate these old institutions and give the Estates of Languedoc an uncontested superiority over all the others. In this province, as in much of the south of France, the taille was real and not personal, that is it was based on the value of the property, and not on the wealth of the owner. There were, it is true, certain lands which enjoyed the privilege of not paying it at all. These lands had formerly belonged to the nobility; but, through the progress of time and industry, it had happened that some of these properties had fallen into the hands of commoners; on the other hand, nobles had become the owners of many properties subject to the taille. The privilege thus transported from persons to things was doubtless more absurd, but it was much less felt, because, still harmful, it was no longer humiliating. No longer being linked in an inescapable way to the idea of class, not creating interests absolutely estranged from or contrary to those of others for any individuals, it no longer prevented people from taking part in government together. In fact, in Languedoc more than anywhere else, they mingled there and found themselves on a footing of perfect equality.

In Brittany, the nobles all individually had the right to appear at the Estates, which often made them seem like the Polish Diet.[†] In Languedoc, the nobles participated in the Estates only through representatives; twenty-three of them took the place of all the others. The clergy appeared in the persons of the twenty-three bishops of the province, and what above all must be noted, the towns had as many votes in the Estates as the first two orders.

Since there was only one assembly and the orders did not meet separately, the Third Estate naturally acquired great importance; gradually it made its own spirit penetrate throughout the body. Still more, the three magistrates who, under the name of general syndics, were charged in the Estates' name with the ordinary conduct of their business, were always lawyers, that is, commoners. The nobility, strong enough to maintain its rank, was no longer strong enough to rule alone. On its side the clergy, although composed in large part of noblemen, lived in complete accord with the Third Estate in the assembly. It enthusiastically joined in most of its projects, working together with the Third Estate to increase the material prosperity of all citizens and to favor their trade and industry, and often putting its great knowledge of men and its rare dexterity in the management of business at the service of the Third Estate. It was almost always a clergyman who was chosen to go and debate with the ministers at Versailles the legal questions which put royal authority and the Estates in conflict. One could say that, during the whole last century of the monarchy, Languedoc was governed by the bourgeoisie, who were checked by the nobility and helped by the bishops.

Thanks to the peculiar constitution of Languedoc, the modern spirit could peacefully penetrate this old institution and change everything while destroying nothing. It could have been the same everywhere else. A little of the perseverance and effort that rulers had put forth to abolish or deform the provincial Estates would have been enough to improve them in this way, and adapt them to the needs of modern civilization, if these rulers had ever wanted to do anything but become and remain masters.

Tocqueville's Notes

1. I have made particular use of the archives of several large intendancies, above all those of Tours, which are very complete, and which concern a very large region, placed in the middle of France, and inhabited by a million people. I owe my thanks here to the young and able archivist in charge, M. Grandmaison. Other regions, including the Ile-de-France, have shown me that things worked the same way in most of the kingdom.

2. THE POWER OF ROMAN LAW IN GERMANY— HOW IT HAD REPLACED GERMANIC LAW

At the end of the Middle Ages, Roman law became the chief and almost the only study of German jurists; in this era most of them even pursued their education outside Germany, in the Italian universities. These jurists were not the leaders of political society but were charged with explaining and applying its laws; if they could not abolish Germanic law, they at least distorted it so as to force its entry within the circle of Roman law. They applied Roman law to anything which seemed to resemble it in German institutions, to anything that had any distant analogy with Justinian's law code; they thus introduced a new spirit, new practices into the national legislation; it was gradually transformed in such a way that it became unrecognizable, and in the seventeenth century, for example, one could say that German law was no longer recognized. It was replaced by a *je ne sais quoi* which was still Germanic by name but Roman in fact.

I have reason to believe that, through the jurists' work, many conditions of old German society became worse, notably that of the peasants; many of those who had up to then managed to keep all or part of their freedom or their property lost them then by pedantic analogies to the situation of Roman slaves or hereditary lessors. This gradual transformation of the national law, and the useless efforts which were made to oppose it, can be well seen in the history of Wurtemberg.

Since the birth of the county of that name, in 1250, up to the creation of the duchy in 1495, its legislation was entirely indigenous; it was composed of customs, local laws made by the towns or by manorial courts, statutes promulgated by the Estates; ecclesiastical matters alone were regulated by a foreign law, canon law. After 1495, the character of legislation changes: Roman law starts to penetrate; the *doctors,* as they were called, those who had studied law in foreign schools, entered government and took over direction of the higher courts. During all the early part of the fifteenth century, and up to the middle of it, one sees political society wage the same struggle against them that took place in England at that time, but with very different results. In the Diet of Tübingen in 1514, and in those which succeeded it, the representatives of the feudality and those of the towns made all kinds of protests against what was going on; they attacked the jurists, who were making their appearance throughout the judiciary and changing the spirit or letter of all laws and customs. The advantage at first appeared to be on their side; they obtained from the government the promise that from then on honorable and enlightened people and not *doctors* would be placed on the courts, chosen from the nobility and Estates of the duchy, and that a commission composed of agents of the government and representatives of the Estates would draw up a law code which could serve as a rule throughout the country. Useless efforts! Roman law soon ended up by entirely driving out the national law from a large part of legislation, planting its roots even on the ground where it let the national legislation subsist.

This triumph of foreign law over indigenous law is attributed by several German historians to two causes:

1. To the movement which then led all minds towards the languages and literature of antiquity, and to the contempt which thus arose for the intellectual products of the national spirit.

2. To the idea, which had always preoccupied the whole German Middle Ages, and which was present even in the legislation of that time, that the Holy Roman Empire was the continuation of the Roman Empire, and that the legislation of the latter was the heritage of the former.

But these causes are not sufficient to make it comprehensible that the same law was simultaneously introduced on the whole European continent. I think that this came from the fact that, at the same time, the absolute power of rulers was solidly establishing itself everywhere, on the ruins of the old liberties of Europe, and thus that Roman law, a law of servitude, agreed wonderfully with their perspective.

Roman law, which everywhere improved civil society, everywhere tended to degrade political society, because it had chiefly been the work of a very civilized and subordinated people. The kings therefore enthusiastically adopted it, and established it everywhere where they were the masters. The interpreters of this law became their ministers or their chief agents throughout Europe. At need, the jurists furnished them legal support against the law itself. Thus they have often done since. Alongside a ruler who is violating the law, it is very rare not to see a lawyer appear who assures you that nothing could be more legitimate, and who proves academically that the violation was just and that the oppressed were in the wrong.

3. THE PASSAGE FROM FEUDAL TO DEMOCRATIC MONARCHY

All monarchies having become absolute around the same time, this constitutional change appears to come from some special circumstance which is met with only by chance at the same time in every country. Thus we must believe that all these similar and contemporary events must have been produced by a general cause which acted everywhere at once equally.

This general cause was the passage from one social state to another, from feudal inequality to democratic equality. The nobles were already beaten down and the people had not yet risen; the former were too low and the latter not high enough to hinder the movements of power. There were then a hundred and fifty years that were the golden age of princes, during which they simultaneously had stability and omnipotence, things which are usually exclusive of one another: as sacred as the hereditary chiefs of a feudal monarchy, and as absolute as the master of a democratic society.

4. DECADENCE OF THE FREE CITIES IN GERMANY— THE IMPERIAL CITIES (REICHSSTÄDTE)

According to German historians, the greatest brilliance of these cities was in the fourteenth and fifteenth centuries. They were then the asylum of Europe's wealth, art, and knowledge, the mistresses of its trade, the most powerful centers of civilization. They ended up, above all in the north and south of Germany, by forming independent confederations with the surrounding nobles, as the Swiss towns did with the peasants.

In the sixteenth century they still retained their prosperity; but the time of their decadence had come. The Thirty Years War hastened their ruin; almost all of them were destroyed or pillaged during this period.

However, the Treaty of Westphalia[†] specifically named them and preserved their status as immediate states, that is, states subordinate only to the emperor; but the sovereigns who bordered them, on the one hand, and the emperor himself, on the other, whose power after the Thirty Years War could hardly be exercised except over these tiny imperial vassals, daily confined their sovereignty within very narrow limits. In the eighteenth century they still existed to the number of fifty-one; they occupied two benches in the Diet and had a separate voice there; but, in fact, they no longer counted for anything in the direction of general affairs.

Internally they were all overburdened with debts; this came partly from the fact that they continued to be taxed by the empire according to their former splendor, partly because they were very badly run. And what is very remarkable is that this bad government seems to derive from a hidden illness that is common to all of them, whatever the form of their constitution; whether it was aristocratic or democratic, it gave rise to complaints that if not identical, were at least equally loud: if aristocratic, the government, it was said, has become the possession of

a small number of families: favors, special interests control everything; if democratic, intrigue and bribery appear everywhere. In both cases one complains of
the lack of honesty and disinterestedness on the part of the government. The emperor was constantly obliged to intervene in their affairs to try to restore order.
The towns decline in population, they fall into poverty. They are no longer the
centers of German civilization; the arts desert them to shine in the new towns,
created by sovereigns, which represent the new world. Trade abandons them;
their old energy, their patriotic vigor, disappears; Hamburg, almost alone, remains a great center of wealth and enlightenment, but because of reasons which
are unique to it.

5. THE DATE OF THE ABOLITION OF SERFDOM IN GERMANY

We will see, in the picture that follows, that the abolition of serfdom in most
of the countries of Germany was very recent. Serfdom was not abolished until:

1. In Baden, in 1783.
2. In Hohenzollern, in 1789.
3. In Schleswig and Holstein, in 1804.
4. Nassau, in 1808.
5. Prussia. Frederick William I had eliminated serfdom on his domains from
1717. Frederick the Great's law code, as we have seen, claimed to abolish it
throughout the kingdom; but, in reality, only its harshest form disappeared,
Leibeigenschaft; serfdom was retained in its milder form, *Erbuntertänigkeit.* It
was only in 1809 that it was entirely eliminated.
6. In Bavaria, serfdom disappeared in 1808.
7. A decree of Napoleon, dated from Madrid in 1808, abolished it in the
Grand Duchy of Berg and in various other small territories, such as Erfurt,
Bayreuth, etc.
8. In the Kingdom of Westphalia, its destruction dates from 1808 and 1809.
9. In the Principality of Lippe-Detmold, from 1809.
10. In Schaumburg-Lippe, 1810.
11. In Swedish Pomerania, also from 1810.
12. In Hesse-Darmstadt, from 1809 and 1811.
13. In Württemberg, 1817.
14. In Mecklenburg, 1820.
15. In Oldenburg, 1814.
16. In Saxony, for Lusatia, 1832.
17. In Hohenzollern-Sigmaringen, only from 1833.
18. In Austria, 1811. In 1782, Joseph II had eliminated *Leibeigenschaft;* but serfdom in its milder form of *Erbuntertänigkeit* lasted until 1811.

There are some regions presently German, such as Brandenburg, Old Prussia,
Silesia, which were originally populated by Slavs, and which were conquered and

partially occupied by Germans. In these regions, serfdom had always presented a much harsher appearance than in Germany, and left traces still more marked at the end of the eighteenth century.

6. FREDERICK THE GREAT'S LAW CODE

Among the works of Frederick the Great, the least known, even in his own country, and the least brilliant, is the law code drawn up at his orders and promulgated by his successor. Nevertheless, I do not know if there is anything else that throws more light on the man himself and on the times, and better shows the reciprocal influence of the one on the other.

This law code is a real constitution, in the sense that was then attributed to that word; its purpose was not only to regulate relations among citizens but between citizens and the state: it is simultaneously a civil code, a criminal code, and a political constitution. It is based, or rather seems to be based, on a certain number of general principles expressed in very philosophical and very abstract form, and which resemble in many respects those which fill the Declaration of the Rights of Man in the Constitution of 1791.[†] Frederick's code proclaims that the good of the state and its inhabitants is the purpose of society and the limit of the law; that laws may not limit the freedom and rights of citizens except in the pursuit of the common good; that every member of the state ought to work for the general good in accordance with his position and his fortune; that the rights of individuals must cede to the general good.

Nowhere is there any question of the hereditary rights of the ruler, of his family, nor even of individual rights which would be separate from the rights of the state. The name of the state is already the only one used to designate the royal power.

On the contrary, there is discussion of the general rights of men: the general rights of men are founded on the natural liberty of pursuing one's own good provided it does not interfere with others' rights. All actions which are not forbidden by natural law or by a positive law of the state are permitted. Every inhabitant of the state may demand from the state the defense of his person and property, and has the right to defend himself by force if the state does not come to his aid.

After having laid out these great principles, the legislator, rather than drawing from them as in the constitution of 1791 the dogma of the sovereignty of the people, and the organization of a popular government in a free society, makes a quick turn and heads for another equally democratic, but not liberal, conclusion; he considers the ruler to be the sole representative of the state, and gives him all the rights that were just recognized as belonging to society. The sovereign in the law code is no longer God's representative, he is but the representative of society, its agent, its servant, as Frederick signed himself in all his letters in his works; but the ruler alone represents society, he alone exercises all its powers. The chief of state, it says in the introduction, to whom the duty is given to produce the general good, the sole purpose of society, is authorized to direct and regulate all individual actions for this purpose.

Among the chief duties of this omnipotent agent of society, I find this one: to maintain peace and public safety internally, and to guarantee all against violence. Externally, it is up to him to make peace and war; he alone must make laws and general regulations; he alone possesses the right to pardon and to annul criminal proceedings.

All associations which exist in the state, all public establishments are under his inspection and his direction in the interest of peace and general security. So that the chief of state may fulfill his obligations he must have certain revenues and certain useful rights; he therefore has the power to establish taxes on private wealth, on persons, their professions, their trade, their produce, or their consumption. The orders of the public officials who act in his name must be followed as if they were his own with regard to everything that falls within the scope of their functions.

Beneath this completely modern head we will see a totally gothic body appear; Frederick had only eliminated from it whatever could hinder the action of his own power, and the whole forms a monstrous being which seems to be in transition between one shape and another. In this strange production, Frederick shows as much contempt for logic as concern for his own power, and a desire not to create any useless difficulties by attacking whatever still had enough strength to defend itself.

The inhabitants of the countryside, with the exception of a few districts and localities, are placed in a hereditary servitude which is not limited to corvées and services attached to the possession of certain lands, but which extends, as we have seen, to the person of the possessor. Most of the landowners' privileges are again consecrated by the code; one could even say that they are consecrated despite the code, since it says that, in cases where local custom and the new law code differ, the former is to be followed. It is formally stated that the state may not destroy any of these privileges except by purchase and according to legal forms. The code assures, it is true, that serfdom properly speaking (*Leibeigenschaft*), insofar as it establishes personal servitude, is abolished, but the hereditary subjection which replaces it (*Erbuntertänigkeit*) is still a kind of serfdom, as one may judge by reading the text.

In this same code the bourgeois remains carefully separate from the peasant; between the bourgeoisie and the nobility, there is recognized a kind of intermediate class: it is composed of high officials who are not nobles, of clergy, of professors of higher education, gymnasia,[†] and universities. Furthermore, in order to separate them from the rest of the bourgeoisie, these bourgeois were not confounded with the nobility; they remained on the contrary in an inferior state with respect to the latter. They could not, in general, buy noble lands, or obtain the highest places in the civil service. They were also not *hoffähig,* that is, they could not be presented at Court, except in rare cases, and never with their families. As in France, this inferiority wounded still more as this class daily became more enlightened and more influential, and the state's bourgeois officials, if they did not occupy the most prestigious posts, already filled those where there was the most, and the most useful, to be done. The irritation against the nobility's privileges which, among us, was going to contribute so much to the Revolution, in Germany prepared the approval with which the Revolution was first received. The principal author of the law code, however, was a bourgeois, but he doubtless followed his master's orders.

Despite his contempt for it, the old constitution of Europe was not yet sufficiently destroyed in this part of Germany for Frederick to believe that the time had yet come to sweep away its remains. In general, he limited himself to taking away the nobility's right to assemble and govern themselves as a body, and left to each of them individually his privileges; he only limited them and regulated their use. It is thus the case that this law code, drawn up by the order of a student of our philosophes, and put into practice after the outbreak of the French Revolution, is the most authentic and the most recent legislative document that gives a legal basis to the very feudal inequalities that the Revolution was going to abolish throughout Europe.

The nobility is declared to be the chief body of the state; noblemen ought by preference to be named, the code says, to all honorable posts when they are capable of filling them. They alone may possess noble lands, create entailments, enjoy the hunting rights and rights of justice belonging to noble lands, as well as the rights of patronage over churches; they alone can take the name of the estate that they own. Bourgeois authorized by express exception to possess noble lands cannot enjoy except within the explicit limits of their permission the rights and honors attached to the possession of such properties. The bourgeois, even if he is the owner of a noble property, cannot leave it to a bourgeois heir unless he is heir in the first degree. In the case where no such heirs exist nor other noble heirs, the property must be sold.

One of the most characteristic sections of Frederick's code is the criminal law covering political offenses which is joined to it. Frederick the Great's successor, Frederick-William II, who despite the feudal and absolutist portion of the legislation which I have just given an idea of, thought he saw revolutionary tendencies in this work of his uncle, and who suspended its publication until 1794, was only reassured, it is said, by thinking of the excellent criminal provisions with whose aid the law code corrected the evil principles that it contained. Never, in fact, have we seen even since in this genre anything more complete; not only were revolts and conspiracies punished with the greatest severity; but disrespectful criticism of the government's acts was also very severely repressed. The purchase and distribution of dangerous writings were carefully forbidden: the printer, the publisher, and the distributor were responsible for the author's deed. Balls, masquerades and other amusements were declared to be public meetings; they had to be authorized by the police. It was the same even for public banquets. Freedom of the press and freedom of speech were strictly subject to an arbitrary surveillance. The carrying of firearms was forbidden.

Finally, all through this work, half-borrowed from the Middle Ages, appear provisions whose extreme centralizing spirit borders on socialism. Thus it is declared that it is incumbent on the state to oversee the nourishment, employment, and salary of all those who cannot maintain themselves and who do not have a right to the aid of the lord or the village: they must be assured work appropriate to their strength and capacity. The state must create establishments by which the citizen's poverty may be helped. The state is further authorized to destroy those charitable foundations which tend to encourage laziness, and itself to distribute to the poor the money which these foundations possess.

The boldness and novelty in theory, the timidity in practice which characterize this work of the Great Frederick are to be found in it everywhere. On the one hand, the great principle of modern society, that everyone ought to be equally subject to taxation, is proclaimed; on the other hand, provincial laws which proclaim exceptions to this rule are allowed to persist. It is affirmed that all lawsuits between a subject and the sovereign will be judged in the forms and according to the rules indicated for all other trials; in fact, this rule was never followed when the interests or passions of the king were opposed to it. The mill of Sans-Souci[†] was ostentatiously displayed, and in many other instances justice was made to bend silently.

What proves how this code, which was so innovative in appearance, in reality innovated little, and what in consequence makes it so interesting to study, in order to understand the real state of society in this part of Germany at the end of the eighteenth century, is that the Prussian nation barely seemed to notice its publication. The lawyers alone studied it, and in our own day there are many educated people who have never read it.

7. PEASANT PROPERTY IN GERMANY

Among the peasants there were frequently found some families which were not only free and landowners, but whose property formed a kind of permanent entail. The land owned by these families was indivisible; one son inherited it all: this was usually the youngest son, as in certain English customs. He only had to pay a dowry to his brothers and sisters.

Peasant *Erbgüter* [hereditary lands—trans.] were more or less widespread in all Germany; for nowhere was all the land included in the feudal system. In Silesia, where the nobility until our own day kept immense domains to which most villages belonged, there were however some villages which were owned completely by the inhabitants, and entirely free. In certain parts of Germany, like the Tyrol and Frisia, peasant *Erbgüter* were the dominant form of landholding.

But, in most countries in Germany, this kind of property was only a more or less frequent exception. In the villages where it was found, small landowners of this kind formed a sort of aristocracy among the peasants.

8. THE POSITION OF THE NOBILITY AND THE DIVISION
OF LAND ALONG THE RHINE

From information gathered on the spot and from people who had lived under the old regime, it appears that in the electorate of Cologne, for example, there were a large number of villages without lords and governed by the ruler's agents: that, in the places where the nobility existed, its administrative powers were very limited; that its position was more splendid than powerful (at least individually); that it had many honors, served the ruler, but did not exercise any real and direct power over the people. I am further assured that, in this same electorate, land was very divided, and that a very large number of peasants were landowners, which is attributed particularly to the state of financial need and semipoverty in which a large percentage of noble families had already long lived, a state of financial need that constantly made them sell little parcels of their land which the peasants acquired, sometimes in return for perpetual payments, sometimes for cash down. I have had in my hands a list of the population of the bishopric of Cologne at the beginning of the eighteenth century, which portrays the state of the land at that time; I have seen that already, then, a third of the land belonged to the peasants. From this fact was born a set of feelings and ideas which put these populations much closer to revolution than those which inhabited other parts of Germany where this particular situation was not yet seen.

9. HOW THE LAW ON CHARGING INTEREST ON LOANS
HAD HASTENED THE DIVISION OF THE LAND

The law which forbade charging interest on loans, no matter what the interest rate, was still in force at the end of the eighteenth century. Turgot informs us that even in 1769 it was observed in many places. These laws persist, he says, although often violated. City judges allow interest, while the ordinary courts condemn it. One still sees dishonest debtors suing their creditors in criminal court for having lent them money at interest.

Independently of the effect this legislation could not fail to have on commerce, and in general on the industrial mores of the nation, it had a great effect on the division of land and on its tenure. It infinitely multiplied perpetual payments, both on land and other things. It led the old landowners, rather than borrowing on their land, to sell small portions of it for a price, partly in cash, partly in perpetual payments: this had greatly contributed, on the one hand, to divide the soil, and on the other, to overburden small landholdings with a multitude of perpetual debts.

10. EXAMPLE OF THE PASSIONS WHICH ALREADY AROSE FROM
TITHES TEN YEARS BEFORE THE REVOLUTION

In 1779, a petty lawyer from Lucé complained very bitterly, in a manner which already smelled of the Revolution, that the priests and other big tithe-owners sold to the farmers, at an exorbitant price, the straw that the tithe for procured for them, straw that the farmers had an absolute need for to manure their land.

Example of the Way in Which the Clergy Alienated the People by the Exercise of Their Privileges

In 1780, the prior and canons of the priory of Laval complained that some people wanted to force them to pay sales tax on consumables and on the materials necessary to repair their buildings. They claimed that, sales taxes being representative of the taille, and themselves being exempt from the taille, they owed nothing. The minister told them to apply to the local authorities, with appeal to the tax-court.

Feudal Rights Possessed by Priests, One Example from a Thousand, the Abbey of Cherbourg (1753)

This abbey then owned manorial dues, payable in cash or in kind, in almost all the parishes in the vicinity of Cherbourg; one owed it 306 bushels of wheat alone. It possessed the barony of Sainte-Geneviève, the barony and manorial mill of Bas-du-Roule, the barony of Neuviolle-au-Plein, situated at least ten leagues away. It further received the tithes of twelve parishes of the peninsula, several of which were located very far from it.

II. IRRITATION CAUSED BY FEUDAL DUES AMONG THE PEASANTS, AND IN PARTICULAR BY THE FEUDAL DUES OF PRIESTS

Here is a letter written by a farmer to the intendant himself a little before the Revolution. It is not at all an authority to prove the exact facts that it contains, but it indicates perfectly the state of mind of the class to which its author belonged.

"Although we have very few nobles in this area," he says, "one must not think that the land is less burdened with fees; on the contrary, almost all the fiefs belong to the cathedral, to the archbishopric, to the college of St. Martin, to the Benedictines of Noirmoutiers, of St. Julien, and other ecclesiastics, to whom payments never end, and who for proof constantly bring to light musty old parchments whose manufacture God alone knows!

"All this region is infested with dues. Most of the land owes, annually, a seventh of the wheat grown, others of the wine; this one owes a quarter of the fruit to the manor, another a fifth, always with the tithe taken first; from this one the twelfth, another the thirteenth as tithe. All these dues are so varied that they run from a quarter to a fortieth of the produce.

"What is one to make of all these payments in all kinds of grain, vegetables, cash, poultry, corvée, wood, fruits, candles? I've heard of unusual payments in bread, wax, eggs, headless pigs, rose-wreaths, bouquets of violets, gilded spurs, etc. There are still an innumerable mass of other manorial dues. Why hasn't France been freed of all these extravagant payments? Finally, we are beginning to open our eyes, and there is everything to hope for from the wisdom of the present government; it holds out a helping hand to the poor victims of these exactions of the old fiscal regime, called manorial dues, which can never be bought or sold.

"What can one think of that other tyranny called lods and ventes? A buyer does his utmost to make a purchase and is forced to pay large fees for adjudication, contracts, closing, transcript, stamp, registry, hundredth penny, eight sous per livre, etc., and after all that must show his contract to his lord, who will make him pay the lods and ventes on the price of the transaction. Some claim twenty percent, others twenty-five. Finally, there are even some of them, and I even know who, who demand a third of the price. No, the most ferocious and barbarous nations the universe has known have never invented any extortions like these and in such great number as our tyrants accumulated on our fathers' heads [this literary and philosophical tirade is written without any knowledge of orthography—Tocq.].

"What! The late king allowed the commutation of perpetual payments on city property but not on lands situated in the country? He should have started with the latter. Why not allow the poor farmers to break their chains, to buy back these dues and liberate themselves from the multitude of manorial and agricultural dues which cause so much harm to the vassals and bring so little profit to the lords? One should not distinguish between city and country, lords and individuals.

"The managers of the holders of Church property, at each change of holder, loot and pillage all the tenants and make them pay. We have had a very recent example of this. The manager for our new archbishop upon his arrival announced that all the tenant-farmers of M. de Fleury, the archbishop's predecessor, would be expelled, declaring void all the leases they had contracted with him and throwing out the door all those who didn't want to double their payments and pay large bribes, which they had already paid to M. de Fleury's manager. They have thus been deprived of the seven or eight years remaining on their old leases, perfectly valid ones, forcing them to leave immediately, on Christmas eve, the most critical time of the year because of the difficulty of feeding the animals then, without knowing where or whom to go to. The King of Prussia couldn't have done worse!"

It really seems, in fact, that for the clergy's property the leases of the preceding officeholder did not create any legal obligation for his successor. The letter's author, in remarking that the feudal dues were redeemable in the towns, even though they were not in the country, stated a perfectly true fact. Here is the best proof of that abandonment in which the peasant lived, and on the contrary of the way all those who were placed above him found in him the means for their own advantage.

[The Influence of Feudalism]

All institutions that have been dominant for a long time, after establishing themselves in their natural sphere, go beyond it and end up exercising a lot of influence even in the area of legislation where they do not rule; feudalism, although above all it was a political system, had transformed civil law and deeply influenced the conditions of property and persons in everything which related to private life. It had acted on inheritances through the inequality of their division, from which the principle had descended, in certain provinces, down through the middle class (as Normandy testifies). It had enveloped, one might say, all real property, for there were no lands located completely outside the feudal system or whose owners felt no influence from its laws. It affected not only the property of individuals but that of villages. It influenced manufactures by the fees that it raised from them. It influenced incomes by the inequality of taxation, and material interests in general in almost all their concerns: the landowner, by the fees, payments, the corvée; the farmer, in a thousand ways but among others by the monopolies, perpetual payments, lods and ventes, etc.; the merchants, by the taxes on markets; the traders, by the tolls, etc. In succeeding in knocking it down, the Revolution made itself simultaneously seen and felt at all the sensitive points of individual interest, so to speak.

12. PUBLIC CHARITY GIVEN BY THE STATE — FAVORITISM

In 1748, the king gave 20,000 pounds of rice (it was a year of great distress and scarcity, as were so many in the eighteenth century). The archbishop of Tours claimed that it was he who had obtained this help, and that the rice should be distributed only by him and in his diocese. The intendant affirmed that the aid had been given to the whole region and must be distributed by him to all parishes. After a long struggle, the king, to conciliate everyone, doubled the amount of rice destined for the region, in order that the archbishop and the intendant could each distribute half. Both had agreed that the distributions would be made by the parish priests. It was not a question of either the lords or the syndics. One can see, from the correspondence between the intendant and the controller-general, that according to the former the archbishop wanted to give the rice only to his protégés, and more particularly to have the rice distributed chiefly in the parishes belonging to Madame the duchess of Rochechouart. On the other hand, one finds in this file letters from great lords which ask special favors for their parishes, and letters from the controller-general which indicate the parishes of certain persons.

Legal charity gives rise to abuses, no matter what the system; but it is impractical, thus exercised from far away and in secret by the central government.

Example of the Way in Which This Legal Charity Was Given

We find in a report made to the provincial assembly of Upper Guyenne in 1780: "Of the total of 385,000 livres granted by His Majesty to this region from 1773, the time of the reestablishment of the public relief projects, up to 1779 inclusively, the district of Montauban, capital and seat of M. the intendant, has alone received more than 240,000 livres, most of which sum has been spent within the town of Montauban itself."

13. POWERS OF THE INTENDANT TO REGULATE INDUSTRY

The archives of the intendancies are full of files which relate to the regulation of industry. Not only was industry then subject to the hindrances which were imposed on it by the state bodies, the guilds, etc., but it was furthermore subject to all the government's caprices, usually represented by the general regulations of the Royal Council, and to particular application by the intendants. The latter constantly concern themselves with the length of fabrics, the materials to choose, the methods to follow, the errors to avoid in manufacture. They had under their orders, independently of the subdelegates, local inspectors of industry. On this side centralization was more extensive than in our own day; it was also more capricious, more arbitrary; it made the public officials poke all over, and gave birth to all kinds of habits of submission and dependence.

Note that these habits were above all given to the bourgeois class, to the merchants, the traders, who were going to triumph, more than to those classes which were going to be defeated. Therefore the Revolution, rather than destroying these habits, was to spread them and make them predominant.

All the preceding remarks are suggested by reading the numerous writings and letters titled: "Manufactures and Industries, Cloth—Drugs"; they are found in the papers which remain in the archives of the intendancy of the Ile-de-France. In the same place one finds frequent and detailed reports sent by the inspectors to the intendant about the visits they made to manufacturers to see that the rules laid down for industry were followed; also various decrees of the Council, rendered with the advice of the intendant, to forbid or allow cloth manufacture, whether in certain places, or of certain fabrics, or finally by certain processes.

What predominates in the observations of these inspectors, who treat the manufacturers with disdain, is the idea that it is the state's right and duty to force the manufacturers to do the best possible, not only in the public interest, but in their own. In consequence, they feel obliged to make them follow the best method, and go into the tiniest details of their trade with them, all accompanied by a whole list of violations and enormous fines.

14. SPIRIT OF LOUIS XI'S GOVERNMENT

There is no document in which one may better appreciate the real spirit of Louis XI's government than in the many town constitutions he gave. I have had occasion to study very carefully those which he gave to most of the towns of Anjou, Maine, and Touraine.

All these constitutions are made according to the same model, almost, and the same plans are clearly revealed. A picture of Louis XI appears there that is rather different from the one that we are familiar with. We usually consider this ruler the enemy of the nobility, but, at the same time, the sincere friend of the people, even though a little brutal. In these constitutions he shows the same hatred for the political rights of the people as for those of the nobility. He uses the bourgeoisie equally to diminish those above them and to compromise those beneath them; he is simultaneously anti-democratic and anti-aristocratic: he is the bour-geois king par excellence. He rains privileges on the notables of the towns, thus wishing to increase their importance; he grants nobility to them in profusion, thus lessening its value, and at the same time he destroys the whole popular and demo-cratic character of town government, and restricts government there to a small circle of families allied to his reforms and linked to his power by immense favors.

15. A TOWN GOVERNMENT IN THE EIGHTEENTH CENTURY

I have extracted from the inquiry on town government made in 1764 the file relating to Angers; there one finds the constitution of that town analyzed, attacked and defended alternately by the presidial, the city council, the sub-delegate, and the intendant. Since the same facts are reproduced in many other places, the resulting picture is anything but unique.

Report of the presidial on the current state of the municipal constitution of Angers and on the reforms to be made: "the city council," says the presidial, "al-most never consults the general population of the town, even on the most impor-tant projects, unless they are required to by special orders. This administration is unknown to all those who do not belong to the city government, even the tem-porary aldermen, who have only a very vague idea of it (the tendency of all these little bourgeois oligarchies was, in fact, to consult as little as possible what is here called the general population)."

The city council was composed, according to a decree of 29 March 1681, of 21 officials:

A mayor who acquired nobility, and whose duties lasted four years;

4 temporary aldermen, who served two years;

12 counsellor aldermen, who, once elected, were permanent;

2 city attorneys;

one attorney to whom the office of city attorney reverts;

the clerk of the court.

They have various privileges, among others the following: their capitation tax was fixed and low; they were exempt from providing lodging for troops, or uten-sils, furniture, and food for them; they were exempt from the taxes on double and triple house subdivision, and from the old and new sales taxes, even from the "free gift," which they had found it to be within their own private authority to exempt themselves from, says the presidial; they had, furthermore, allowances of candles, and some of them salaries and free housing.

From these details one can see that it was a good thing to be a permanent alder-man of Angers in those days. Note that always and everywhere this system gave tax exemptions to the richest. As we see further on in the same report: "These posts are intrigued for by the wealthiest inhabitants, who want them in order to get a considerable reduction in their capitation taxes, whose impact is then felt by others. There are presently several town officials whose fixed capitation-tax is 30 livres, who ought to be taxed at 250 to 300 livres; there is one of them who, with respect to his wealth, could pay at least 1,000 livres of capitation." In another place in the same report we find that "among the richest inhabitants there are more than forty officials or widows of officials, whose offices give the privilege of not contributing to the large capitation tax with which the city is burdened; the burden of this tax falls on a large number of poor artisans, who thinking themselves overcharged, constantly protest against their excessive payments, and almost always without reason, since there are no inequalities in the distribution of those taxes of which the town retains control."

The *General Assembly* was composed of 72 people:

the mayor;
two deputies of the cathedral chapter;
one syndic of the clergy;
two deputies of the presidial;
one deputy from the university;
a lieutenant-general of the police;
four aldermen;
twelve permanent aldermen;
one Royal attorney at the presidial;
one city attorney;
two deputies from the Streams and Forests department;
two from the district;
two from the salt monopoly;
two from the tax collectors;
two from the mint;
two from the guild of lawyers and attorneys;
two from the town judges;
two from the notaries;
two from the guild of merchants;
finally two deputies sent by each of the sixteen parishes.

It is these last who were considered to represent the people properly speaking, and in particular the trade guilds. It is clear that things were arranged so as to keep them in a permanent minority.

When positions on the city council became vacant, it was the General Assembly which chose three candidates for the open position. Most of the places on the city council were not reserved for particular groups, as I have seen in several other municipal constitutions, that is, the voters were not required to choose a judge, a lawyer, etc., which the members of the presidial think is very bad.

According to this same presidial, which seems to be inspired by the most violent jealousy toward the city council, and which I strongly suspect of thinking that the only thing wrong with the city's constitution was that they didn't get enough privileges in it, "the General Assembly, too numerous and partly composed of people of little intelligence, should not be consulted except in questions of selling city property, loans, the establishment of sales taxes, and the election of city officials. All other matters could be considered by a smaller assembly, composed only of notables. The only people who could belong to that assembly would be the lieutenant-general of the *sénéchaussée,* the royal attorney, and twelve other notables taken from the six groups of the clergy, the judiciary, the nobility, the university, commerce, the bourgeois, and others who are not members of these groups. The choice of notables, the first time, would be given to the General Assembly, and thereafter to the assembly of notables, or to the group from which each notable is to be chosen."

All these state officials, who would thus enter as officeholders or as notables into the municipal government of the old regime, often resembled today's officials by the titles of the office they exercised and sometimes even by the nature of that office; but they were profoundly different from those of today in their position, which is what one must always pay great attention to, if one doesn't wish to arrive at very erroneous conclusions. Almost all these officials were, in fact, city notables before they acquired public office, or wanted to attain public office in order to become notables; they did not have any idea of leaving the city or any hope of rising higher, which was enough to make them entirely different from what we know today.

Report of the city officials. One sees there that the city council was created in 1474, by Louis XI, on the ruins of the town's old democratic constitution, and always in accordance with the system described above, that is, the restriction of most political rights to the middle class alone, the removal or weakening of the popular element, the creation of a large number of officials in order to interest more people in the reform, the hereditary nobility ignored, and privileges of all kinds given to the section of the bourgeoisie which governed.

One finds in this same report letters patent from the successors of Louis XI which recognize this new constitution, while limiting still further the power of the people. We learn there that in 1485 the letters patent given for this purpose by Charles VIII were contested before the Parlement by the people of Angers, exactly as in England, where one would have brought before a court of justice a suit relating to a town's constitution. In 1661, it was once more a decree of the Parlement which fixed the political rights arising from the Royal Charter. After that, it is only the Royal Council which appears.

It results from the same report that not only for the place of mayor, but for all the other positions on the city council, the General Assembly presented three candidates among whom the king chose, by virtue of a decree of the council dated 22 June 1738. It further results that by virtue of the decrees of 1733 and 1741 the merchants had the right to one place as alderman or counsellor (that is, permanent alderman). Finally, we discover in this report that in those days the city council was in charge of the division of the tax burden for the capitation, military equipment, military lodging, food for the poor, for the soldiers, the revenue service, and the foundlings.

There follows a long list of the services the municipal officials must render, which according to them fully justify their privileges and their permanence, which they are very afraid of losing. Several reasons they give for their work are interesting, among others this one: "Their most essential occupation," they say, "consists in the examination of financial questions, which are continually increased by the constant extension of taxes, the salt tax, the stamp and registry dues, the illegal collection of registry dues and franc-fief taxes. The suits that the tax-collection companies constantly bring in regard to these different taxes have forced the town's officials to defend, on behalf of the city, trials before various courts, the parlement or the Royal Council, in order to resist the oppression which they have been forced to lament. The practice and experience of thirty years have taught them that a man's life is scarcely long enough to avoid the ambushes and pitfalls prepared for the citizen by the agents of the tax-farmers in order to keep their jobs."

What is interesting is that all these things were written to the controller-general himself, in order to make him favorable to the maintenance of the privileges of those who speak, so strong is the habit of regarding the companies in charge of raising taxes as adversaries who may be attacked from all sides without anyone being upset. It is this habit that, constantly extending and fortifying itself more and more, ended up by considering the Treasury a treacherous and hateful tyrant; not everyone's agent but the common enemy.

The same report adds: "All offices were first concentrated in the city council by a Royal Decree of 4 September 1694, in return for the sum of 22,000 livres." This means that the offices were redeemed from the king that year for this sum. By a decree of 26 April 1723, the municipal offices created by the edict of 24 May 1722 were again returned to the city council; in other words the town was allowed to redeem them. By another decree of 24 May 1723, the town was allowed to borrow 120,000 livres for the purchase of the said offices. Another decree of 26 July 1728 allowed it to borrow 50,000 livres for the repurchase of the office of registrar-secretary of the city. "The town," it says in the report, "has paid its money to keep its freedom of election and to allow its elected officials to enjoy, some for two years, others for life, the different prerogatives attached to their offices." Some of the municipal offices having been reestablished by the edict of November 1733, a decree of the Council interposed itself on 11 January 1751, on the request of the mayor and the aldermen, by which the price of the redemptions was fixed at the amount of 170,000 livres, for the payment of which sales duties were suspended for fifteen years.

This is a good sketch of old regime administration relative to towns. They were forced to contract debts, and then authorized to establish extraordinary and temporary taxes to free themselves. To which it must be added that later these temporary taxes were made permanent, as I have often seen, and then the government took its share.

The report continues: "The municipal officials have been deprived of the great judicial powers granted them by Louis XI only by the establishment of royal jurisdictions. Until 1699 the city officials had jurisdiction over disputes between employers and workers. The sales-tax accounts are presented to the intendant, by the direction of all the decrees creating or suspending these taxes."

We also see in this report that the deputies of the sixteen parishes mentioned above, who appeared in the general assembly, were chosen by the guilds, companies, or communities, and that they were strictly the representatives of the small groups which sent them. On every question they had binding instructions.

Finally, this whole report shows that at Angers, as everywhere else, expenditures, of whatever kind, had to be authorized by the intendant and the Council; and we must recognize that, when the government of a town is given to certain men, to be their property, and these men are given, rather than fixed salaries, privileges which make them personally exempt from the consequences that their government could have on the private fortunes of their fellow citizens, central government paternalism might seem a necessity. This whole report, which is furthermore poorly done, reveals an extraordinary fear on the part of the officials that the existing state of things might be changed. All kinds of reasons, good and bad, are accumulated by them in the interest of the maintenance of the status quo.

The subdelegate's report. The intendant, having received these two contradictory reports, wanted to have the advice of his subdelegate. He gave it in his turn.

"The report of the municipal counsellors," he says, "does not merit attention; its only purpose is to validate these officials' privileges. The presidial's is worth consulting; but there is no justification for according to these magistrates all the prerogatives that they demand."

For a long time, says the subdelegate, the town constitution has been in need of improvement. Beyond the immunities which the municipal officials of Angers possessed and with which we are already familiar, the subdelegate informs us that the mayor, during his term, receives housing worth at least 600 francs rent; further, 50 francs in fees and 100 francs for postage expenses; as well as token items. The syndic-attorney was also housed; the registrar too. In order to exempt themselves from duties and tolls, the municipal officials had established for each of themselves a presumed level of consumption. Each one could bring into town, without payment of taxes, so many barrels of wine a year, and likewise for all other articles of consumption.

The subdelegate does not suggest taking their tax privileges away from the city counsellors, but he would like their capitation tax, rather than being fixed and very low, to be set annually by the intendant. He wishes that these same officials be subject to the "free gift" like other people, from which they alone are exempted on who knows what precedent.

The municipal officials, the report says again, are charged with preparing the capitation tax roll of the citizens; they do it negligently and arbitrarily; also there are annually a multitude of complaints and requests, addressed to the intendant. It would be desirable if from now on this division was made, in the interest of each company or community, by its own members, in a general and fixed manner; the municipal officials would continue to be in charge only of the tax-roll of the bourgeois and others who were not part of any guild, like some artisans and the domestic servants of all the privileged. The subdelegate's report confirms what the municipal officials had already said: that the municipal offices had been redeemed by the town, in 1735, for the sum of 170,000 livres.

Letter of the intendant to the controller-general. Armed with all these documents, the intendant wrote to the minister: "It is important," he says, "to the inhabitants and to the public good to reduce the city council, whose too large numbers are an infinite burden on the public, because of the privileges which they enjoy." "I am," adds the intendant, "struck by the enormity of the sums which have been spent, in all periods, to redeem municipal offices for Angers. This amount of money, spent for useful purposes, would have been to the profit of the town, which, on the contrary, has only felt the burden of the authority and the privileges of these officials."

"The internal abuses of this administration merit the Council's full attention," the intendant further says. "Independently of token items and candles, which consume an annual sum of 2,127 livres (this was the total listed for this kind of expense by the standard budget, which had occasionally been imposed on the towns by the king), the public funds are dissipated and employed at the pleasure of these officials for secret uses, and the Royal attorney, who has held his office for thirty or forty years, has made himself so much the master of the government, of which he alone knows all the ins and outs, that it has been impossible for the inhabitants to obtain the least information about the employment of the town's revenues at any time." In consequence, the intendant asked the minster to reduce the city council to a mayor named for four years, six aldermen nominated for six years, one royal attorney nominated for eight years, and a permanent registrar and a receiver-general.

For the rest, the constitution the intendant proposed for the city council was exactly the same as that which this same intendant proposed for Tours. According to him, one needed:

1. To retain the general assembly, but only as an electoral college to elect the municipal officials.

2. To create an extraordinary council of notables, which would fulfill all the functions which the edict of 1764 seemed to give to the general assembly, a council composed of twelve members, whose term would be for six years, and who would be elected, not by the general assembly, but by the twelve bodies considered to be notable (each group would elect its own representative). He lists as the notable bodies:

1. The presidial
2. The university
3. The district
4. The officials of the Streams and Forests
5. The salt monopoly
6. The office of the tax collectors
7. The mint
8. The lawyers and attorneys
9. The consular judges
10. The notaries
11. The merchants
12. The bourgeois

As we have seen, almost all these notables were public officeholders, and all public officeholders were notables; from which we may conclude that, as in a thousand other places in these files, the middle class was as avid for government jobs then as in our own day, and looked as little for a field of activity outside public employment. The only difference was, as I have said in the text, that then one bought the petty importance that places give, and now the seekers ask the favor of being given them free.

One sees in this project that all real municipal power was concentrated in the extraordinary council, which ended up restricting government to a very small circle of bourgeois, since the only assembly where the people continued to appear a little was no longer to be charged with anything but the election of municipal officials and no longer to have any advice to give them. It must be noted again that the intendant was more restrictive and antipopular than the king, who seemed in his chief edict to give the principal functions to the general assembly, and that in his turn the intendant was much more liberal and democratic than the bourgeoisie, at least to judge from the report that I cited in the text, a report in which the notables of another town wished to exclude the people even from the election of municipal officials, which the king and the intendant left to them.

It might be noted that the intendant uses the names *bourgeois* and *merchants* to designate two distinct categories of notables; it is useful to give the exact definition of these two words to show how this bourgeoisie was cut into so many little pieces and by how many little vanities it was worked.

The word "bourgeois" had both a broad and a restricted meaning: it indicated the members of the middle class, and it further designated within that class a certain number of men. "The bourgeois are those whom birth or fortune have put in a position to live comfortably without any gainful employment," says one of the reports produced by the inquiry of 1764. From the rest of the report one can see that the word "bourgeois" should not be applied to those who are members of trade guilds or companies; but to say to whom precisely it ought to apply is more difficult. "For," the same report further notes, "among those who take the title of bourgeois, one often even finds persons to whom it is not appropriate, except for their leisure alone; for the rest, they lack wealth and lead an obscure and uncultivated life. Bourgeois ought, on the contrary, always to be distinguished by their wealth, their birth, talents, mores, and manner of life. The artisans making up the guilds have never been given the rank of notable."

The merchants were, with the bourgeois, the second kind of people who belonged neither to a company nor a corporation; but if only this situation marked the limits of this little class: "Must we," says the report, "mingle merchants of low birth and small trade with the wholesalers?" To resolve these difficulties, the report suggested having the aldermen draw up every year a list of notable merchants, a list that would be sent to their leader or syndic, so that he would summon to city hall only those who were on it. Care would be taken not to mention on this list any of those who had been domestics, peddlers, carters, or any other low functions.

16. One of the most salient characteristics of the eighteenth century, in respect to town government, is less the abolition of all representation and all intervention by the public in affairs, than the extreme instability of the rules to which town government was subject, rights being given, taken away, returned, increased, diminished, changed in a thousand ways, and continually. Nothing shows better the degradation into which these liberties had fallen than this eternal upheaval of their laws, which no one seemed to pay any attention to. This instability alone would have been enough to destroy in advance any special ideas, any nostalgia, any local patriotism, in the institution which however is most suited for them. The great destruction of the past that the Revolution was going to make was thus prepared.

17. The pretext which Louis XIV had used to destroy the municipal liberties of the towns was the bad administration of their finances. However, the same situation, Turgot says with good reason, persisted and became worse after that ruler's reform. Most of the towns are considerably indebted today, he adds, some for the funds which they have lent the government, and others for the expenses or decorations which the town officials, who spend other people's money, and do not have to render account to the inhabitants nor receive instructions from them, multiply with the intent of making themselves known, and sometimes of enriching themselves.

18. A VILLAGE GOVERNMENT IN THE EIGHTEENTH CENTURY, TAKEN FROM THE PAPERS OF THE INTENDANCY OF THE ILE-DE-FRANCE

The situation of which I am going to speak is chosen from many others, in order to show by example some of the forms followed by parish government, to demonstrate the slowness which often characterized it, and finally, to show what a parish general assembly was in the eighteenth century.

It was a question of repairing the rectory and tower of a rural parish, that of Ivry, in the Ile-de-France. Whom to address to get the repairs made? How to determine who was to pay for them? How to find the necessary sum?

1. Request from the priest to the intendant, which states that the rectory and the tower need urgent repairs; that his predecessor, having added useless buildings to the said rectory, had completely changed and deformed the character of the place, and that, the inhabitants having allowed it, it was up to them to bear the expense of putting things in order, with recourse to the heirs of the preceding priest.

2. Ordinance of the lord intendant (29 August 1747) which declares that at the syndic's orders an assembly was to be convoked to deliberate on the need for the work requested.

3. Deliberation of the inhabitants, in which they declare that they are not opposed to the repairs for the rectory but only to those for the tower, given that the tower is built over the choir, and that the priest, since he receives the great tithe, is responsible for the repair of the choir (a decree of the Council, from the end of the preceding century [April 1695], in fact attributed the repair of the choir to whoever possessed the right to receive the parish's tithes, the inhabitants being responsible only for the repair of the nave).

4. A new ordinance from the intendant, who, given the contradictory claims, sends an architect, M. Cordier, to proceed to visit and describe the rectory and the tower, to estimate the cost of the work and make an inquiry.

5. Report of all these operations, which states notably that at the inquiry a number of proprietors of Ivry had presented themselves before the intendant's envoy, which persons appear to be the nobles, bourgeois, and peasants of the place, and have had their say for or against the priest's claims.

6. A new ordinance from the intendant, stating that the proprietors and inhabitants will be informed of the estimates that the intendant's envoy has made at a new general assembly convoked by the syndic.

7. A new parish assembly in consequence of this ordinance in which the inhabitants state that they persist in their views.

8. Ordinance of the lord intendant, which prescribes: That there will be held before his subdelegate at Corbeil, in the subdelegate's offices, the contracting for the work shown on the estimate, contracting which will be made in the presence of the priest, syndic, and chief inhabitants of the parish. Given that the present situation is dangerous, a tax for the entire sum will be levied on

the inhabitants, except that those who still think that the tower is part of the choir and should be repaired by the titheholder may sue him before the ordinary courts.

9. Summons to all parties to meet at the subdelegate's offices at Corbeil, where bids may be made and the contracts let.

10. Request by the priest and several inhabitants, asking that the costs of the administrative procedure not be paid, as was usually the case, by the contractor, these expenses being very high and making it difficult to find a contractor.

11. Ordinance from the intendant which says that the expenses made in arriving at a contract be ascertained by the subdelegate, so that their amount may be part of the said contract and tax.

12. Powers given by several notable inhabitants to M. X, to be present at the contracting and to consent to it according to the architect's estimates.

13. Certificate of the syndic, stating that the usual announcements and advertisements have been made.

14. Transcript of the contract.

For repairs to be made	487 livres
Expenses incurred	237 livres, 18s. 6d.
Total	724 livres, 18s. 6d.

15. Finally a decree of the Council (23 July 1748) to authorize the tax intended to cover this sum.

We might note that several times in this procedure there was question of convoking the parish assembly. Here is the transcript of one of these assemblies; it will show the reader how things generally happened on these occasions.

Notarial Act: "Today after the parish mass, in the usual and customary place, after the bell had rung, there appeared in the assembly held by the inhabitants of the said parish, before X, notary of Corbeil, the undersigned, and the witnesses named thereafter, M. Michaud, winegrower, syndic of the said parish, who presented the intendant's ordinance permitting the assembly, had it read and testified his obedience.

"And at the same time there appeared an inhabitant of the said parish, who said that the tower was over the choir, and, as a result, the charge of the priest; there also appeared (here follow the names of some others who, on the contrary, agreed with the priest's request) . . . then there appeared fifteen peasants, workers, masons, winegrowers, who stated that they agreed with the views of the preceding. And there also appeared M. Raimbaud, winegrower, who said that he was in complete agreement with whatever the intendant would decide. There also appeared M. X, doctor of the Sorbonne, priest, who persisted in the claims and reasons set forth in the request. Of which, and of all the above, those who appeared had knowledge. Done and passed at the said place of Ivry, in front of the cemetery of the said parish, before the undersigned; this proceeding has been attended and transcribed by the notary present from eleven in the morning until two in the afternoon."

We can see that this parish assembly was nothing but a government hearing, with the forms and costs of a judicial inquiry; that it never ended in a vote, that is, with the manifestation of the will of the parish; that it contained only individual opinions and in no manner constrained the government's will. In fact many other documents tell us that the parish assembly was held to inform the intendant's decision, not to be an obstacle to it, even when it was a question that concerned only parish interests. One notes also, in the same documents, that this affair gave rise to three hearings: one before the notary, a second before the architect, and finally a third before two notaries, to find out if the inhabitants persisted in their previous views.

The tax of 524 livres 10 s., ordered by the decree of 23 July 1748, bore on all landowners, privileged or nonprivileged, as had almost always been the case for this kind of expense, but the basis on which the tax was divided among them was different. The nonprivileged were taxed in proportion to their taille, and the privileged with respect to their presumed wealth, which gave a great advantage to the latter over the former. Finally, we see in this same affair that the division of the sum of 524 livres 10 s. was made by two collectors, inhabitants of the village, neither elected nor chosen by lot as most often was the case, but chosen and named to the office by the subdelegate and the intendant.

19. THE STATE WAS GUARDIAN OF THE CONVENTS AS WELL AS THE TOWNS; AN EXAMPLE OF THIS TUTELAGE

The controller-general, in authorizing the intendant to pay 15,000 livres to the Carmelite convent, to which money was owed, recommends that the intendant satisfy himself that this sum, which represents an endowment, will be usefully invested. Similar things happen all the time.

20. HOW IT IS IN CANADA[†] THAT ONE CAN BEST JUDGE THE ADMINISTRATIVE CENTRALIZATION OF THE OLD REGIME

It is in colonies than one can best judge the form of the metropolitan government, because there all its characteristic traits are usually enlarged, and become more visible. When I want to judge the spirit of the government of Louis XIV and its vices, it is to Canada that I must go. There one can perceive the object's deformities as if under a microscope.

In Canada, a crowd of obstacles that past facts or the former social state presented, openly or secretly, to the free development of the government's ideas did not exist. The nobility was almost nonexistent, or at least it had lost almost all its roots; the Church no longer had its dominant position; feudal traditions were lost or obscured; the judiciary was no better rooted in old institutions and old mores. There nothing prevented the central power from abandoning itself to all its natural inclinations and from making all laws in accordance with the views which inspired it. In Canada, therefore, not the shadow of municipal or provincial institutions was permitted, no authorized collective power, no individual initiative. An intendant who had a position much differently preponderant than his colleagues had in France; a government that meddled in still more things than in the metropolis, and even wanted to do everything from Paris, despite the eighteen hundred leagues which separated them. In Canada the government never adopted the great principles which can render a colony populous and prosperous, but, on the contrary, employed all kinds of petty artificial procedures and little regulatory tyrannies to increase and spread the population: forced cultivation, all lawsuits arising from land concessions taken away from the courts and returned to the judgment of the government alone, requirements to farm in a certain way, obligations to live in certain places rather than others, etc.—this happened under Louis XIV; these edicts are countersigned by Colbert. One would think oneself in Algeria,† in the full bloom of modern centralization. Canada is in fact the faithful picture of what we have always seen in Algeria. On both sides one is in the presence of this government that is almost as numerous as the population, dominant, active, regulatory, constraining, wanting to foresee everything, taking everything over, always more familiar with the interests of the governed than they are themselves, constantly active and sterile.

In the United States, on the contrary, the English system of decentralization is exaggerated: the towns become almost independent municipalities, kinds of democratic republics. The republican element which is the base of English mores and the English constitution displays itself without opposition and develops. Government, properly speaking, does little in England, and individuals do much; in America, the government is no longer involved in anything, so to speak, and individuals uniting together do everything. The absence of upper classes, which made the inhabitant of Canada still more submissive to the government than the inhabitant of France was at that time, made the inhabitant of the English colonies more and more independent of authority.

In both colonies one ended up with the foundation of an entirely democratic society; but in Canada, at least as long as Canada remained French, equality was joined with absolute government; in the United States it was combined with freedom. And as for the material consequences of these two methods of colonization, we know that in 1763, the time of the English conquest of Canada, its population was 60,000, and the population of the English colonies 3 million.

21. ONE EXAMPLE, AMONG MANY, OF THE GENERAL REGULATIONS CONSTANTLY MADE BY THE COUNCIL OF STATE, WHICH HAD THE FORCE OF LAW THROUGHOUT FRANCE, AND CREATED SPECIAL OFFENSES FOR WHICH ADMINISTRATIVE TRIBUNALS WERE THE SOLE JUDGES

I take the first thing that I find beneath my hand: a decree of the Council, of 29 April 1779, which establishes that in the future, throughout the kingdom, the shepherds and wool-merchants will have to mark their sheep in a certain way, under pain of 300 livres fine; His Majesty enjoins the intendants to see to the execution of this decree, it is said; from which it results that it is up to the intendant to pronounce the penalties for its violation. Another example: a decree of the Council, 21 December 1778, which forbids carters and haulers from storing the goods with which they are charged, on pain of 300 livres fine; His Majesty directs the lieutenant-general of police and the intendants to see to this.

22. The provincial assembly of Upper Guyenne loudly demanded the establishment of new brigades of mounted police, doubtless as nowadays the general council of Aveyron or the Lot demands the establishment of new police units. Still the same idea: the police represent order and order can be established only by the police and the central government. The report adds: "Every day there are complaints that there aren't any police in the countryside (How could there be any? The noble was not involved in anything, the bourgeois was in town, and the village, represented by a rough peasant, furthermore, didn't have any power), and it must be admitted that, if we except certain cantons in which just and charitable lords use the power over their vassals that their position gives them to prevent those ways of acting to which the inhabitants of the countryside are naturally inclined by the coarseness of their mores, and the harshness of their character, there further nowhere exist almost any means of containing these ignorant, rude, and hot-headed men."

This is the manner in which the nobles of the provincial assembly allowed themselves to be spoken of, and in which the members from the Third Estate, who themselves formed half this assembly, spoke of the people in public documents!

23. Tobacco licenses were in as much demand under the old regime as they are today. The most important people solicited them for their clients. I have found some that were given on the recommendation of great ladies; others were given upon the request of archbishops.

24. This extinction of all local public life had gone beyond anything that we can imagine. One of the roads which led from Maine to Normandy was impassible. Who asked for it to be repaired? The Generality of Touraine, through which it passed? The province of Normandy or that of Maine, so interested in the cattle trade, which followed this road? Some canton finally, especially harmed by the bad state of this road? The generality, the province, the cantons are without voice. It is necessary for the merchants who use the road and who get bogged down in it to themselves attract the central government's attention. They write to Paris to the controller-general, and ask him to come to their aid.

25. GREATER OR LESSER IMPORTANCE OF MANORIAL DUES AND PAYMENTS, ACCORDING TO THE PROVINCE

Turgot says in his works: "I must note that these kinds of payments are of very different importance in most of the rich provinces, such as Normandy, Picardy and the environs of Paris. In these latter, the chief wealth consists in the produce of lands which are combined in very large farms, from which their owners get high rents. The manorial dues of the largest estates form only a very modest portion of their revenue, and this article is regarded almost as honorific. In the provinces that are least wealthy and cultivated according to different methods, the lords and nobles own hardly any land themselves; inheritances, which are extremely divided, are burdened with very large payments in grain, with which all the co-tenants are equally burdened. The fees often absorb the best part of the lands' production, and the lords' income is almost entirely composed of them."

26. ANTICASTE INFLUENCE OF THE COMMON DISCUSSION OF AFFAIRS

We can see from the little publications of eighteenth-century agricultural societies the anticaste influence that common discussion about common interests has. Although these meetings took place thirty years before the Revolution, in the midst of the old regime, and concerned only theory, by the very fact that they debated questions in which the different classes felt themselves interested and that they discussed them together, the rapprochement and mingling of men is immediately felt, the privileged are taken with ideas of reasonable reform like everyone else, and yet it is only a question of conservation and agriculture.

I am convinced that it is only a government which looked for strength solely in itself, and always took men separately, like that of the old regime, which could have maintained the ridiculous and senseless inequality which existed in France at the time of the Revolution; the slightest contact with "self-government" [Tocqueville uses the English word—trans.] would have profoundly changed and rapidly transformed or destroyed it.

27. Provincial freedoms can subsist for some time without the existence of national freedom, when these liberties are old, mixed up with habits, mores, and memories, and when despotism on the contrary is new; but it is unreasonable to believe that one can, at will, create local freedoms, or even maintain them long, when general freedom is eliminated.

28. Turgot, in a report to the king, summarizes in this way, which seems very accurate to me, what the real extent of the nobility's tax privileges was:

"1: The privileged can have a farm of four plows extent completely exempted from taille, which in the neighborhood of Paris would ordinarily pay 2,000 livres in taxes.

"2: The same privileged pay absolutely nothing for the woods, pastures, vines, ponds, as well as for the enclosed lands which belong to their chateaus, no matter how big they are. There are cantons where the chief production comes from pastures or vines; then the noble who registers his lands is exempt from all taxation, which falls on those who pay the taille; a second advantage which is immense."

29. INDIRECT PRIVILEGES IN TAX MATTERS —
DIFFERENCE IN COLLECTION, EVEN WHEN THE TAX IS COMMON

Turgot also draws a picture of this which I have reason to believe is exact, according to the documents.

"The indirect advantages of the privileged with regard to the capitation tax are very great. The capitation is an arbitrary tax by nature; it is impossible to divide it among the mass of citizens other than blindly. It has been found more convenient to base it on the records of the taille, which are already made. A special list has been drawn up for the privileged; but since the latter defend themselves and the taille-payers have no one to speak for them, it has resulted that the capitation of the former has been gradually reduced, in the provinces, to an excessively small sum, while the capitation of the latter is almost equal to the amount of the taille."

Another Example of Inequality in Collection of a Common Tax

We know that for local taxes the tax was raised on everyone; "the said amounts," say the decrees of the Council which authorize these kinds of expenses, "will be levied on all those in this jurisdiction, tax-exempt or not, privileged or nonprivileged, without any exception, conjointly with the capitation, or in proportion to it."

Note that, since the capitation of the taille-payer, joined to the taille, was always proportionately higher than the capitation of the privileged, inequality was found even where it seemed to be most excluded.

Same Subject

I find in a proposed edict of 1764, which was intended to create equal taxation, all kinds of rules whose purpose was to keep a separate position for the privileged in its collection. I note there, among other things, that with regard to the privileged all measures whose purpose is to determine the value of their taxable property can be taken only in their presence or their attorney's.

30. HOW THE GOVERNMENT ITSELF RECOGNIZED THAT THE PRIVILEGED
WERE FAVORED BY THE COLLECTION, EVEN WHEN THE TAX WAS COMMON

"I see," writes the minister in 1766, "that the part of the taxes whose collection is always the most difficult is that which is due from the nobles and the privileged, because of the adjustments which the taille-collectors think themselves obliged to make in their regard, because of which there exist with respect to their capitations and vingtièmes (the taxes which were common to them and the people), very old and much too large arrears."

31. We find, in the *Voyage of Arthur Young in 1789,* a little picture where this state of the two societies is so agreeably painted and so well outlined that I cannot resist the urge to include it here.

Young, crossing France in the midst of the first reactions caused by the fall of the Bastille, was arrested in a certain village by a troop of people who, seeing that he did not wear the tricolor cockade, wanted to put him in prison. To get out of the affair he thought of making this little speech:

"Sirs," he said, "you have just been told that taxes ought to be paid as they were formerly. Taxes ought to be paid, certainly, but not as they used to be. They ought to be paid like in England. We have many taxes that you do not; but the Third Estate, the people, do not pay them; they bear only on the rich. Among us, every window must be paid for; but those who have six windows or less in their house pay nothing. A lord pays the vingtièmes and the tailles, but the small landowner of a garden pays nothing. The rich man pays for his horses, his carriages, his servants: he even pays for the liberty to shoot his own partridges; the small landowner remains a stranger to all these taxes. Still more! We have in England a tax that the rich pay for the aid of the poor. Therefore, if one must continue to pay taxes, they must be paid differently. The English method is much better."

"Since my bad French," adds Young, "went well enough with their patois, they understood me very well; there was not a word of this speech which they did not applaud, and they thought that I might well be a good man, which I confirmed by shouting: Long Live the Third Estate! Then they let me go with a cheer."

32. The Church of X, in the district of Chollet, fell into ruins: it was a question of repairing it in the manner indicated by the decree of 1684 (16 December), that is, with the help of a tax levied on all the inhabitants. When the collectors wanted to raise this tax, the marquis of X, lord of the parish, declared that since he was charged with repairing the choir at his own expense, he did not want to participate in the tax; the other inhabitants replied, with much reason, that as lord and titheholder (he doubtless owned the feudal tithes), he was required to repair the choir alone, and that in consequence this burden could not exempt him from the common charge. At which intervened an ordinance from the intendant which declared the marquis in error and authorized the collectors to sue him. There are in the file at least ten letters from this marquis, each more pressing than the last, asking with great pleas that the rest of the parish pay in his stead, and deigning, in order to obtain this, to call the intendant "My Lord" and even to "beg" him.

33. Declaration of the king which "suspends in time of war the repayment of all loans made to cities, towns, colleges, villages, hospitals, charitable institutions, guild organizations and others, which are paid for by the receipts from duties or sales taxes conceded by us," it is said in this declaration, "with the effect that interest on the loans will continue to accrue."

This was not only to postpone the time for repaying the loan stated in the creditors' contract, but also to attack the collateral made responsible for the debt. Never would such measures, which swarmed through the old regime, have been possible under a government watched over by the public or by assemblies. Let us compare it with what always happened in this kind of thing in England or even in America. The contempt for the law is as flagrant here as the contempt for local freedoms.

34. The case cited here in the text is far from being the only one where the privileged realized that the feudal dues which weighed on the peasant hurt them too. Here is what an agricultural society entirely composed of the privileged said thirty years before the Revolution:

"The irredeemable payments, whether rents or feudal payments attached to the land, when they are considerable become so burdensome to the debtor that they cause his ruin and successively that of the land itself. He is forced to neglect the land, being unable to find the resources with which to get loans on an over-burdened collateral, nor purchasers in a position to pay for both land and dues. One is always comfortable improving and working land of which one is in full possession. It would be a great encouragement to agriculture to find practical means for amortizing these kinds of payments. Many lords of fiefs, persuaded of this truth, would not wait to be asked to consent to such arrangements. It would therefore be very attractive to find and demonstrate practical means for arriving at this liberation from feudal dues."

35. All public functions, even those of tax collector, were compensated for by tax exemptions, privileges which had been accorded to public officeholders by the ordinance of 1681. In a letter addressed to the minister by an intendant in 1782, it says: "Among the privileged, there is no class more numerous than that of the employees of the salt monopoly, of the finances, of the royal domains, of the post office, of the taxes, and other officials of all kinds. There are few parishes where none of these exist, and in several there are two or three."

It was a question of dissuading the minister from proposing to the Council a decree to extend tax exemptions to the employees and domestics of these privileged agents, immunities whose extension is constantly demanded by the farmers-general, says the intendant, in order to exempt themselves from paying that which was paid to them.

Such offices were not absolutely unknown elsewhere. In Germany, some petty rulers had introduced several, but in small number and in unimportant parts of government. The system had not been widely practiced except in France.

36. One must not be astonished, although this appears very strange and in fact is odd, to see in the old regime public officials, several of whom belong to the government proper, sue in Parlement to find out the limit of their various powers. This can be explained when one realizes that all these questions, at the same time as they were questions of public administration, were also questions of private property. What one takes here for an encroachment of the judicial power was nothing but a result of the mistake that the government had committed in turning public employment into a venal office. Positions being held like property, and each officeholder being paid by the number of actions he took, one could not change the nature of the job without harming a right which the officeholder had

bought from his predecessor. One example among a thousand: the lieutenant-general of police of Mans waged a long lawsuit against the financial office of that city, to prove that since he regulated the streets he must also be in charge of making all decisions relative to their paving and entitled to charge a fee for these actions. To which the financial bureau replied that the paving of the streets belonged to it by the very title of its commission. It was not, this time, the Royal Council which decided; since it was chiefly a question of the interest on the capital employed in the purchase of the office, it was the Parlement which pronounced. The administrative problem was turned into a civil trial.

37. ANALYSIS OF THE CAHIERS OF THE NOBILITY IN 1789

The French Revolution is, I think, the only one at the beginning of which different classes were able to separately give authentic testimony of their ideas, and make known the feelings which inspired them, before the Revolution itself had distorted or changed these feelings and ideas. This authentic testimony was embodied, as everyone knows, in the cahiers that the three orders drew up in 1789. These cahiers or reports were written with complete freedom, in the midst of the greatest publicity, by each of the orders concerned; they were discussed at length by those interested and maturely considered by their authors; for the government of that time, when it addressed the nation, did not make question and response simultaneous. At the time when the cahiers were written, most of them were compiled in three printed volumes that could be found in all the bookstores. The originals were deposited in the national archives, and with them can be found the transcripts of the assemblies which wrote them, and, in part, the correspondence which took place at the same time between M. Necker and his agents relative to these assemblies. This collection forms a long series of folio volumes. It is the most precious document that remains to us from the old France, and one which must be constantly consulted by those who want to know what was our fathers' state of mind at the moment when the Revolution broke out.

I thought that perhaps the printed extract in three volumes, mentioned above, had been the work of a party, and did not exactly reproduce the character of this immense inquiry; but, in comparing the one to the other, I have found the greatest resemblance between the large picture and the reduced copy.

The extract from the cahiers of the nobility which I give here makes known the true feelings of the great majority of that order. One sees clearly that they obstinately wished to retain some old privileges, which privileges they were not far from giving up, and what they themselves offered to sacrifice. One discovers above all, in full, the spirit which entirely animated them then with regard to political freedom. A strange and sad picture!

Individual rights. Above all the nobles ask that there be made an explicit declaration of the rights which belong to all men, and that this declaration state their liberties and assure their security.

Liberty of the person. They want serfdom to be abolished where it still exists, and means sought to abolish the slave trade and the enslavement of blacks; that everyone be free to travel or make his home wherever he wishes, whether inside or outside the kingdom, without being subject to arbitrary arrest; that abuses in police regulations be reformed and the police henceforth be under the control of the judiciary, even in case of riot; that no one be arrested and judged except by a jury of his peers; that in consequence the state prisons and other illegal places of detention be abolished. Some of them ask for the demolition of the Bastille. The nobility of Paris insists strongly on this point.

All secret letters or *lettres de cachet*† ought to be prohibited; if the danger to the state makes it necessary to arrest a citizen without his being immediately turned over to the usual courts of justice, measures must be taken to prevent abuses, either by informing the Council of State of the imprisonment, or in some other manner. The nobility want all special commissions, all the special or exceptional courts, all the privileges of *committimus,* decrees of suspension, etc., to be abolished, and the most severe penalties brought against those who give or carry out illegal orders; that in the usual course of justice, the only kind that ought to exist, the necessary measures be taken to assure the freedom of the individual, above all in what concerns criminals; that justice be free of charge and useless jurisdictions eliminated. "The judges are established for the people, and not the people for the judges," it is said in one cahier. It is even asked that there be established in every district a council and public defenders for the poor; that trials be public, and the accused be given the right to defend themselves; that in criminal trials the accused be provided with a lawyer, and that in all proceedings the judge ought to be assisted by a certain number of citizens of the same rank as the accused, who will be charged with rendering the verdict on the crime or violation of the accused (in this respect one returns to the English constitution); that punishments be proportionate to the crime and that they be equal for all; that the death penalty be made less frequent, and all judicial torture be abolished; finally that the situation of prisoners be improved, and above all of those not yet come to trial.

According to the cahiers, ways must be found to make individual liberty respected in the recruitment of the army and navy. Conversion of the obligation of military service into a monetary payment must be allowed, the draft-lottery not held except in the presence of a delegation from all three orders; finally the duties of discipline and military subordination must be combined with the rights of the citizen and the free man. Blows with the flat of the sword are to be eliminated.

Freedom and inviolability of property. They ask that property be inviolable and that it may not be harmed except in cases of indispensable public utility. In this case the government must pay for it at a high price and without delay. Confiscation must be abolished.

Freedom of trade, work, and industry. The freedom of trade and industry must be assured. In consequence masterships and other privileges given to certain companies must be abolished; customs will only be collected at the national frontier.

Freedom of religion. The Catholic religion will be the only dominant one in France, but everyone will be left the freedom of his conscience, and non-Catholics will get back their civil rights and the property that has been taken away from them.

Freedom of the press, inviolability of the mail. Freedom of the press will be assured, and a law will fix in advance the restrictions which may be made on it in the general interest. There will be no ecclesiastical censorship except for theological books; for the rest, it will be enough to take the necessary precautions to know the names of the authors and publishers. Several ask that press offenses be judged only by juries.

The cahiers insist above all, and unanimously, that the mail be inviolate, that letters can become neither the subject nor the means of an accusation. The opening of letters, they say frankly, is the most odious espionage, since it consists of the violation of the public trust.

Teaching, education. The cahiers of the nobility limit themselves to asking that active measures be taken to advance education, that it be extended to the towns and countryside, and that it be directed according to principles in accord with the probable occupations of the children; above all that children be given a patriotic education that will teach them their duties and their rights as citizens. They even want a catechism to be drawn up for the children where they can learn to understand the chief points of the constitution. For the rest, they do not indicate the means to be employed to spread and facilitate education; they limit themselves to demanding educational establishments for children of impoverished nobles.

Attention that must be paid to the people. A great many cahiers insist that more regard must be shown for the people. Several declaim against police abuses which, they say, habitually, arbitrarily, and without regular trials throw a mass of artisans and useful citizens into the prisons, houses of correction, etc., often for misdemeanors or even for simple suspicion, which is a blow to natural freedom. All the cahiers demand that the corvée be definitively abolished. Most districts desire that the redemption of feudal dues be permitted. A great number ask that the collection of several feudal dues be made less oppressive and the tax of franc-fief abolished. The government is interested, says one cahier, in facilitating the sale and purchase of land. This reason is the same one that will be given for the abolition at one stroke of all manorial dues, and for putting up for sale all entailed lands. Many cahiers want the right of keeping pigeon coops to be made less harmful to agriculture. As for the establishments meant to conserve the king's boar, known under the name of captainries, they request their immediate abolition, as detrimental to the rights of property. They desire that new taxes replace the present ones, so that their collection will be less burdensome to the lower classes.

The nobility asks that there be an effort to spread comfort and material well-being in the countryside; that the spinning and weaving of coarse cloth in the villages be established to occupy the country people during the dead season; that there be created in every district public granaries under the inspection of the provincial government, to prevent food shortages and maintain the price of grain at a certain level; that improvement in agriculture and the condition of the country-side be sought; that public works projects be increased, particularly the draining of marshes and flood prevention, etc.; finally that encouragements to trade and agriculture be distributed in all provinces.

The cahiers would like the hospitals to be divided into small clinics created in every district; that poorhouses be eliminated and replaced by charity workshops; that charitable funds be established under the direction of the provincial estates and that surgeons, doctors, and midwives be distributed among the districts, at the expense of the provinces, to treat the poor for free; that for the lower classes justice always be free of charge; finally that thought be given to creating establishments for the blind, deaf and dumb, foundlings, etc.

For the rest, in all these matters the order of the nobility in general limits itself to expressing its desire for reforms, without entering into great detail about their execution. It can be seen that they have lived among the lower classes less than the lower clergy has, and that, less familiar with their misery, they have thought less about the means to remedy it.

On the admissibility to public employment, the hierarchy of ranks, and the honorific privileges of the nobility. It is above all, or rather it is only in what concerns the hierarchy of ranks and differences in status, that the nobility deviates from the general spirit of the reforms requested, and that, while making several important concessions, it clings to the principles of the old regime. The nobility feels that it is fighting for its very existence here. Its cahiers therefore ask insistently for the maintenance of the clergy and the nobility as distinct orders. They even desire that means be found to retain the order of the nobility in complete purity; that therefore the purchase of titles of nobility be forbidden, that nobility no longer be attached to certain jobs, that it be obtainable only by long and useful service rendered to the state. They want false nobles to be sought out and sued. Finally, all the cahiers insist that all the nobility's honors be maintained. Some of them want gentlemen to be given a distinctive mark which will make them recognizable by their clothing.

One could not imagine anything more characteristic than such a demand, or more apt to show the absolute similarity which already existed between the noble and the commoner, despite the differences in rank. In general, in its cahiers the nobility, which shows itself flexible enough about several of its monetary rights, is attached with an uneasy zeal to its honorific privileges. It wants to keep everything that it has, and would like to invent several privileges that it has never had before, so much does it already feel itself carried away by the democratic flood and fear its dissolution in it. How strange! It feels the danger instinctively, but does not perceive it.

As for the distribution of burdens, the nobles ask for the elimination of venal posts in the judiciary; that, when it is a question of this kind of position, the nation may present any citizen to the king, to be named by him regardless of rank, save for conditions of age and capacity. For military positions, the majority think that the Third Estate ought not to be excluded, and that any soldier who had deserved well of his country has the right to reach the highest ranks. "The order of the nobility does not approve any of the laws which close entry into military employments to the order of the Third Estate," say several cahiers; only, the nobles want the right to enter a regiment as an officer, without having passed through the lower ranks, to be reserved to them alone. In addition, almost all the cahiers ask that fixed rules be established for military promotion, equally applicable to everyone, that this not be entirely left to favor, and that one acquire ranks below commanding officer by seniority.

As for clerical offices, they ask that election be reestablished in the distribution of benefices, or at least that the king create a committee which can advise him on the distribution of these benefices.

Finally, they say that from now on pensions ought to be distributed with more discrimination, and that they ought no longer to be concentrated in certain families, and that no citizen ought to receive more than one pension or receive the salary of more than one office at a time; that inheritable pensions must be abolished.

Church and clergy. When it is no longer a question of their particular rights and constitution, but of the privileges and organization of the Church, the nobility no longer look so narrowly at the subject; they have their eyes wide open to spot abuses. They request that the clergy not get any tax privileges and that it pay its debts without the nation's help; that the monastic orders be greatly reformed. The majority of the cahiers think that these establishments have deviated from the spirit of their founding.

Most districts want tithes to made less harmful to agriculture; there are even a large number of them which demand their abolition. "The greatest part of the tithes," says a cahier, "is received by those of the priests who employ themselves least in giving the people spiritual assistance." We note that the second order spared the first little in its remarks. It was hardly more respectful with regard to the Church itself. Several districts formally recognize that the Estates-General have the right to eliminate certain orders of the clergy and to use their property for other purposes. Seventeen districts declare that the Estates-General are competent to regulate ecclesiastical discipline. Several say that there are too many holidays, that they harm agriculture and encourage drunkenness; that in consequence many must be eliminated, that there be a return to just Sunday.

Political rights. As for political rights, the cahiers recognize that all Frenchmen have the right to participate in government, whether directly or indirectly, that is, they possess the right to elect and to be elected, but while retaining the hierarchy of orders; thus no one may choose or be chosen except by his order. This principle fixed, the system of representation ought to be established in such a way as to guaranty to all orders of the nation the means of taking a real part in the direction of affairs.

As for the manner of voting in the assembly of the Estates-General, opinions are divided. Most want separate voting by each order; some think that an exception ought to be made to this rule for voting on taxes; others, finally, ask that things always be done in this manner: "Votes will be counted by head, and not by order," say these, "this form being the only reasonable one and the only one which may avoid and destroy the egoism of groups, the unique source of all our problems, reconcile men and lead them to the results that the nation has a right to expect from an assembly where patriotism and the great virtues will be fortified by enlightenment." However, since this innovation, if made too quickly, could be dangerous in the present state of minds, several think that it should be adopted only with precautions, and that the assembly must judge if it would not be wiser to put off the vote by head until the following Estates-General. In all cases, the nobility asks that each order retain the dignity which is the due of every French-man; that in consequence there be abolished the humiliating forms to which the Third Estate had been subjected during the old regime, for example, of kneeling: "the sight of a man on his knees before another wounds human dignity, and dis-plays, among beings equal by nature, an inferiority incompatible with their essen-tial rights," says one cahier.

Of the system of government to be established, and the principles of the consti-tution. As for the form of government, the nobility asks for the maintenance of the monarchical constitution, the preservation of the legislative, judicial, and ex-ecutive powers in the person of the king, but, at the same time, the establishment of fundamental laws intended to guarantee the nation's rights in the exercise of these powers. In consequence, the cahiers all proclaim that the nation has the right to assemble in Estates-General, composed of a number of members large enough to assure the independence of the assembly. They desire that these Es-tates meet from then on at fixed times, as well as at each new accession to the throne, without there ever being any need for letters of convocation. Many dis-tricts even declare that it would be desirable that this assembly be permanent. If the convocation of the Estates-General did not take place within the period of time set by law, one would have the right to refuse to pay taxes. A small number wish that during the interval that separated one meeting of the Estates from an-other, there be established an interim commission charged with overseeing the government of the kingdom; but most of the cahiers formally oppose the estab-lishment of such a commission, declaring that such a commission would be com-pletely contrary to the constitution. The reason they give for this is interesting: they fear that such a small assembly in face of the government would be seduced by its pressures. The nobility wants the ministers not to have the right to dissolve the assembly, and that they be judicially liable for disturbing its order by their conspiracies; that no officeholder, no person dependent on anything from the government, could be a deputy; that the persons of the deputies be inviolable, and that they may not, say the cahiers, be sued for the opinions that they express; finally that the meetings of the assembly be public, and that, to better inform the nation of their deliberations, they be published.

The nobility unanimously asks that the principles which ought to regulate the government of the state be applied to the administration of the various parts of its territory; that in consequence, in each province, in each district, in each parish there be formed assemblies composed of members elected freely and for a limited period. Several cahiers think that the positions of intendant and of receiver-general ought to be eliminated; all think that from now on the provincial assemblies alone ought to be charged with dividing the taxes and supervising the particular interests of the province. They intend the same for the district and parish assemblies, which will no longer be subordinate to any but the provincial assembly.

Separation of powers; legislative power. As for the division of powers between the assembled nation and the king, the nobility asks that no law may have effect until it has received the consent of the Estates-General and the king, and been transcribed on the registers of the courts charged with its execution; that the exclusive right to establish taxes and set their amount belongs to the Estates-General; that the subsidies to which they may consent only be for the time between one meeting of the Estates and the next; that all taxes which had been collected or constituted without the consent of the Estates be declared illegal, and that the ministers and collectors who had ordered and collected such taxes be liable as embezzlers. That not even a loan could be consented to without the agreement of the Estates-General; there would only be opened a fixed line of credit set by the Estates, which the government might use in case of war or major disaster, with the proviso that a meeting of the Estates-General would be convoked in the shortest possible time. That the entire national treasury be put under the supervision of the Estates; that the expenditures of every department be set by them, and that the surest measures be taken so that the amounts voted could not be exceeded.

Most of the cahiers ask for the elimination of those vexatious taxes, known under the name of rights of insinuation, hundredth penny, ratification dues, and brought together under the name of the *Régie* of the royal domains; "the name *Régie* would alone be enough to wound the nation, since it announces as belonging to the king objects which are really part of the citizens' property," says a cahier; that all the royal monopolies which will not be sold be put under the administration of the provincial Estates, and that no ordinance, no fiscal edict be made without the consent of the three orders of the nation. The evident idea of the nobility is to confer the whole financial administration on the nation, whether in the regulation of loans and taxes, or in the collection of taxes, by the intermediary of the Estates-General and the provincial Estates.

Judicial power. In the same way, in the organization of the judiciary, the nobility tends to make the power of judges dependent, at least for the most part, on the national assembly. It is thus that several cahiers state:

"Let the magistrates be responsible for their positions to the national assembly"; let them not be dismissed without the consent of the Estates-General; let no tribunal be subject, under any pretext whatsoever, to being disturbed in the exercise of its functions without the consent of the Estates; that the abuses of the appeals court, as well as those of the parlement, be judged by the Estates-General. According to the majority of cahiers, judges should be named by the king only upon the nomination of the people.

Executive power. As for the executive power, it is exclusively reserved to the king; but necessary limitations are placed on it to prevent its abuse. Thus, with respect to the government, the cahiers ask that the accounts of the various departments be made public and printed, and that the ministers be responsible to the national assembly; in the same way, that before employing troops for external defense the king make known his intentions in a precise way to the Estates-General. Internally, these same troops may not be employed against citizens except by request of the Estates-General. The number of troops was to be limited, and only two-thirds, in ordinary times, retained on active duty. As for the foreign troops which the government might have in its pay, they were to be removed from the center of the kingdom and sent to the frontiers.

What is most striking in reading the cahiers of the nobility, but which no summary could reproduce, is the extent to which these nobles are really of their time: they have internalized its spirit; they fluently employ its language. They speak of *inalienable rights of man, principles inherent in the social contract.* When it is a question of the individual, they are usually interested in his rights, and when it is a question of society, in its duties. The principles of politics seem to them *as absolute as those of morality, and both have reason as their common base.* If they want to abolish the remains of serfdom, *it is a question of eliminating the last vestiges of the degradation of the human species.* They sometimes call Louis XVI *a citizen king* and speak in several places of the crime of *lèse-nation* which will so often be imputed to them. In their eyes, as in those of everybody else, everything may be expected from public education, and it is the state which ought to control it. *The Estates-General,* say a cahier, *will concern themselves with inspiring a national character through changes in children's education.* Like the rest of their contemporaries, they show a strong and constant taste for uniformity in legislation, except, however, in what concerns the existence of orders. They want uniformity of government, of measures, etc., as much as the Third Estate; they suggest all kinds of reforms and they intend these reforms to be radical. According to them, all the taxes without exception must be abolished or transformed; the whole system of justice changed, except for manorial justice, which needs only to be improved. For them as for all the other French, France was a field for experiment, a kind of political model farm, where everything had to be plowed up, everything tried, except in a little corner where their particular privileges grew; still, it must be said in their honor that even that corner was hardly spared by them. In a word, one may judge in reading their cahiers that the only thing lacking to enable these nobles to make the Revolution was to be commoners.

38. EXAMPLE OF THE RELIGIOUS GOVERNMENT OF AN ECCLESIASTICAL PROVINCE IN THE MIDDLE OF THE EIGHTEENTH CENTURY

1. The archbishop
2. Seven vicars-general
3. Two ecclesiastical courts, called *officialités:* one, called the metropolitan officiality, had jurisdiction over the decisions of the subordinate bishops; the other, called the diocesan officiality, had jurisdiction over:

    1. Personal suits between members of the clergy.
    2. The validity of marriages according to the sacrament.

This latter tribunal was composed of three judges. There were notaries and lawyers attached to it.

    3. Two fiscal tribunals.

One, called the diocesan office, had primary jurisdiction over all questions which arose from the taxation of the clergy in the province (we know that the clergy taxed themselves). This court, presided over by the archbishop, was composed of six other priests.

The other court judged on appeal the suits that had been brought before the other diocesan offices of the ecclesiastical province. All these courts admitted lawyers and held hearings.

39. VIEWPOINT OF THE CLERGY IN THE ESTATES AND THE PROVINCIAL ASSEMBLIES

What I say here in the text about the Estates of Languedoc applies equally well to the other provincial assemblies held in 1779 and in 1787, notably in Upper Guyenne. The members of the clergy, in this provincial assembly, were among the most enlightened, the most active, the most liberal. It was the bishop of Rodez who proposed making the assembly's transcripts public.

40. The priests' liberal political disposition, which is evident in 1789, was not merely produced by the excitement of the moment; it was already apparent at a much earlier period. It was notably displayed in Berry, as early as 1779, by the clergy's offer of 68,000 livres of voluntary gifts, on the sole condition that provincial control be retained.

41. Pay careful attention to the fact that political society was without links, but that civil society still had them. People were connected to one another within classes; there even remained something of the close link which had once existed between the class of lords and the masses. Although this had passed into civil society, its consequences made themselves felt indirectly in political society; the men thus linked formed an irregular and disorganized mass, but a refractory one under the hand of power. The Revolution, having broken these social connections without establishing political connections in their place, simultaneously prepared equality and servitude.

42. EXAMPLE OF THE MANNER IN WHICH THE COURTS EXPRESSED THEMSELVES ON THE OCCASION OF CERTAIN ARBITRARY ACTS

From a report put before the controller-general, in 1781, by the intendant of the Paris region, it is clear that it was the custom in this region that the parishes have two syndics, one elected by the inhabitants in an assembly presided over by the subdelegate, the other chosen by the intendant, the latter being the supervisor of the former. In the parish of Rueil, a quarrel occurred between the two syndics, the elected syndic not wanting to obey the appointed one. The intendant obtained from M. de Breteuil the authority to put the elected syndic into La Force prison for two weeks, and he was was in fact arrested, then deprived of his position, and another put in his place. On this, the parlement, meeting at the request of the imprisoned syndic, started a trial of which I do not have the results, where the parlement says that the imprisonment of the plaintiff and his disqualified election could only be considered *arbitrary and despotic acts.* Justice was sometimes very badly muzzled then!

43. THE REASON WHICH OFTEN FORCED ABSOLUTE GOVERNMENT TO MODERATE ITSELF IN THE OLD SOCIETY

There is hardly anything but the increase of old taxes, and above all the creation of new ones, which can in ordinary times create great embarrassments for the government and upset the masses. In the old financial constitution of Europe, when a ruler had a passion to spend, when he threw himself into an adventuresome policy, when he allowed disorder to creep into his finances, or still more when he had need of money to help him win over a lot of people by large profits or large salaries that were received without having been earned, to keep up large armies, carry out great projects, etc., the ruler immediately had to have recourse to taxes, which at once aroused and agitated all classes, above all the one which makes violent revolutions, the people. Today, in the same situation, one contracts loans whose immediate effect is almost unperceived, and whose final result will be felt only by the next generation.

44. As an example of this I find among many others that the chief estates situated in the region of Mayenne were leased to the farmers-general, who took poor, small sharecroppers as subtenants, sharecroppers who had nothing of their own and who were furnished with only the most necessary tools. One can understand that such farmers-general did not have to accommodate the tenants or debtors of the old feudal lord who had put them in his place, and that exercised by their hand, feudalism could often appear harsher than in the Middle Ages.

The inhabitants of Montbazon had listed on the taille-roll the stewards of a duchy possessed by the prince of Rohan, although these stewards only acted in his name. This prince (who was doubtless very rich), not only had *this abuse,* as he called it, stopped, but obtained the restitution of the sum of 5,344 livres 15 sous which he had unjustly been made to pay and which was to be made up by the inhabitants.

45. EXAMPLE OF THE WAY IN WHICH THE MONETARY RIGHTS OF THE CLERGY ALIENATED THE HEARTS OF THOSE WHOSE ISOLATION OUGHT TO HAVE ATTRACTED THEM TO IT

The priest of Noisai claims that the inhabitants are required to repair his barn and his press, and asks for a local tax for this. The intendant responds that the inhabitants are only required to repair the rectory; the barn and the press remain the expense of this pastor, more concerned with his farm than with his flock (1767).

46. One finds this in one of the reports sent by the peasants in 1788, in response to an inquiry which had been made by a provincial assembly, a report written with clarity and in a moderate tone: "to the abuses of the collection of the taille are added those of the bailiff's agents. They usually come five times during the collection of the taille. They are usually old soldiers or Swiss. Each time they spend about four or five hours in the parish and are charged for by the office of taille-collection at the rate of 36 sous per day. As for the distribution of the taille, we will not discuss the arbitrary abuses too well known, nor the bad effects which tax rolls produced by right by often incompetent and almost always partial and vindictive officials have. They have however been the source of troubles and strife. They have given rise to lawsuits very costly for those concerned and very advantageous to the seats of the courts."

47. SUPERIORITY OF THE METHODS FOLLOWED IN THE PAYS D'ÉTATS RECOGNIZED BY THE OFFICIALS OF THE CENTRAL GOVERNMENT ITSELF

In a confidential letter written 3 June 1772, by the director of taxation to the intendant, it says: "In the pays d'états, taxation being a fixed percentage, every taxpayer is subject to it and really pays it. The percentage is increased in proportion to the increase in the total which must be furnished (one million, for example, instead of 900,000 livres) requested by the king. It is a simple operation, instead of which, in the generality, the division is personal, and to tell the truth arbitrary; some pay what they should, others only half, others a third, a quarter, or nothing at all. How therefore is one to subject the tax to an increase of a ninth?"

48. OF THE MANNER IN WHICH THE PRIVILEGED, IN THE BEGINNING, UNDERSTOOD THE PROGRESS OF CIVILIZATION BY ROADS

The count of X complains, in a letter to the intendant, of the lack of speed with which a neighboring road is being made. This is, he says, the fault of the subdelegate, who doesn't put enough energy into his job and does not force the peasants to do their corvées.

49. ARBITRARY PRISON FOR THE CORVÉE

An example: one sees in a letter of a chief provost, in 1768: "Yesterday I ordered the imprisonment of three men, on the request of M. C., the under-engineer, for not having done their corvée. Upon which there was an outcry among the women of the village, who cried out: "Look at that! They think of the poor people when it's a question of the corvée, but they don't care about giving them something to eat."

50. The resources available for road construction were of two kinds: 1. the chief resource was the corvée, for all large projects which needed only labor; 2. the lesser was taken from a general tax whose income was put at the disposal of the Roads and Bridges Corps to pay for skilled work. The privileged, that is the chief proprietors, more interested than anyone else in the roads, didn't contribute at all to the corvée, and, furthermore, the Roads and Bridges tax being attached to the taille, and raised like it, these privileged were once again exempt.

51. EXAMPLE OF CORVÉES TO TRANSPORT CONVICTS

One can see, from a letter sent to the intendant by a commissioner in charge of chain gangs, in 1761, that the peasants were forced to carry convicts in their carts, that they did so very unwillingly, and that they were often mistreated by the guards, "given," says the commissioner, "that the guards are rough and brutal people, and that these peasants, who are working unwillingly, are often insolent."

Turgot drew a picture of the inconveniences and hardships of the corvée when it was used to transport military baggage, which, after I read the files, does not seem exaggerated to me; he says elsewhere that its primary inconvenience was the extreme inequality of a burden that in itself was very great. The military corvée fell entirely on a small number of parishes exposed to it by their unfortunate location. The distance to travel was often five or six, sometimes ten or fifteen, leagues; then it took three days for the round-trip. The payment made to the owners was only a fifth of their costs. The time of the corvée was almost always summer, harvest-time. The oxen were almost always overloaded, and often sick after having been used, to the point where many owners preferred to pay 15 to 20 livres rather than furnish a cart and four oxen. Finally, an inevitable disorder reigned in the corvée; the peasant was constantly subject to violence from the soldiers. The officers almost always demanded more than was their due; sometimes they forced the drivers to harness saddle horses to the carriages at the risk of laming them. The soldiers had themselves carried on carts already heavily laden; other times, impatient at the slowness of the oxen, they pricked them with their swords, and if the peasant objected he was very badly treated.

52. AN EXAMPLE OF THE WAY IN WHICH THE CORVÉE
WAS APPLIED TO EVERYTHING

The intendant of the navy at Rochefort complained of the peasants' bad will, when they were required by the corvée to cart the construction wood bought by naval suppliers in the various provinces. From this correspondence we can see that in fact the peasants were still forced (1775) to perform this corvée, for which the intendant set the price. The minister of the navy, who sent this letter on to the intendant of Tours, told him that he must furnish the carts requested. The intendant, M. Ducluzel, refused to authorize this kind of corvée. The minister of the navy wrote him a threatening letter, where he announced that he would report his resistance to the king. The intendant responded immediately, 11 December 1775, with firmness, that for the ten years that he had been intendant at Tours, he had never wanted to authorize these corvées, because of the inevitable abuses that they entailed, abuses that the price fixed for the carts did not compensate: "for often," he says, "the animals are lamed by the weight of the enormous loads that they are forced to transport over roads as bad as the weather in which they are driven." What makes the intendant so firm seems to be a letter from M. Turgot attached to the documents, dated 30 July 1774, the time of Turgot's entry into the ministry, where Turgot says that he has never authorized these corvées at Limoges, and approves of M. Ducluzel not authorizing them at Tours.

It results from other parts of this correspondence that the wood suppliers often asked for these corvées without even being authorized to do so by their contracts with the state, because they saved at least a third on transport costs this way. An example of this profit is given by a subdelegate: "The distance to transport the wood from the place where it is cut to the river, by almost impassible roads," he says, "is six leagues; the time employed for the round-trip, two days. In paying the corveables, as their wage, at the rate of six liards per cubic foot, in total 13 francs 10 sous for the trip, it is hardly enough to cover the expenses of the small landowner, his helper, and the oxen or horses which he needs to pull his cart. His effort, his time, the work of his animals, all is lost for him." The king's express command, of 17 May 1776, to perform this corvée was passed on to the intendant by the minister. M. Ducluzel being dead, his successor, M. l'Escalopier, hastened to obey and published an ordinance which stated that "the subdelegate will divide the burden among the parishes, by virtue of which the corveables of the said parishes will be required to present themselves, at the place and time which will be prescribed by the syndics, at the place where the wood is to be found, and to transport it at the price which the subdelegate will set."

53. It is said that the character of eighteenth-century philosophy was a kind of adoration of human reason, a limitless confidence in its omnipotence to transform at will laws, institutions, and mores. It must be properly understood; to tell the truth it was less human reason that some of the philosophes adored than their

own reason. Never has less confidence in common sense been shown. I could cite several philosophes who despised the crowd almost as much as they did God. These philosophes show a rival's pride toward the latter and a parvenu's pride toward the former. Real and respectful submission to the will of the majority was as foreign to them as submission to the divine will. Almost all revolutionaries since then have shown this double character. They are very far in this from the respect shown by the English and Americans for the feelings of the majority of their fellow citizens. Among the English and Americans reason is proud and self-confident but never insolent; thus it has led to freedom, while our kind of reason has only invented new kinds of slavery.

54. Frederick the Great wrote in his Memoirs: "The Fontenelles and Voltaires, the Hobbeses, the Collinses, the Shaftesburys, the Bolingbrokes, these great men have given a mortal blow to religion. Men are starting to examine what they had stupidly adored; reason is knocking down superstition; we are disgusted by the fables that we had believed. Deism makes many converts. If Epicureanism was fatal to the idolatrous worship of the pagans, in our day Deism will not be less so to the Judaic visions adopted by our ancestors. The freedom of thought which reigns in England has contributed much to the progress of philosophy."

One can see from the above passage that Frederick the Great, at the time when he wrote these lines, that is, in the middle of the eighteenth century, still considered England the home of irreligious doctrines. There is something else still more striking that we can see in this passage: a ruler well-versed in the science of man and in that of affairs, who did not seem to think that religion might have any political utility; so much had the intellectual faults of his teachers' minds warped the qualities native to his own.

55. This spirit of progress, which came to light in France at the end of the eighteenth century, appeared throughout Germany at the same time, and everywhere it was accompanied by the same desire to change institutions. Look at this picture made by a German historian of what was then going on in his country:

"In the second half of the eighteenth century," he says, "the new mood of the times was gradually introduced even into the Church states themselves. Reforms were begun there. Industry and tolerance spread everywhere; the enlightened absolutism which had already taken over the large states appeared even here. At no time in the eighteenth century, it must be said, had the Church lands seen such remarkable and impressive rulers as precisely during the last decades which preceded the French Revolution." It must be noted that just as this picture resembled that which France presented, where the movement of improvement and progress started at the same time, in France too the men most worthy of governing appeared at the moment when the Revolution was going to devour everything.

One must also recognize to what point all this part of Germany was visibly involved in the movement of French civilization and politics.

56. HOW THE JUDICIAL LAWS OF THE ENGLISH PROVE THAT INSTITUTIONS CAN HAVE MANY LESSER VICES WITHOUT THAT PREVENTING THEM FROM ATTAINING THE CHIEF PURPOSE FOR WHICH THEY WERE ESTABLISHED

Nations have the ability to prosper despite the imperfections which are found in the secondary parts of their institutions, when the general principles, the very spirit which animates those institutions is fertile. This phenomenon cannot be better seen than when one examines the constitution of justice among the English of the last century, as Blackstone shows it to us.

One perceives there two great striking diversities:

1. The diversity of laws;
2. The diversity of courts which apply them.

I. *Diversity of laws.*

1. The laws are different for England proper, for Scotland, for Ireland, for several little European possessions of Great Britain, such as the Isle of Man, the Channel Islands, etc., and finally for the colonies.

2. In England proper there are four kinds of law: the common law, the statutes, Roman law, and equity. The common law is itself divided into general customs adopted throughout the realm; into customs which are peculiar to certain lordships or to certain towns, or sometimes only to certain classes, such as the customs of the merchants, for example. These customs sometimes differ greatly from one another, as, for example, those which, in opposition to the general tendency of English law, demand the equal division of inheritances among all children (*gavelkind*), and what is still more odd, give a right of primogeniture to the youngest child.

II. *Diversity of courts.* The law, says Blackstone, has instituted a prodigious variety of different courts; we can judge them by the very summary analysis presented here.

1. One first encounters the courts established outside England proper, such as the courts of Scotland and Ireland, which were not always dependent on the English higher courts, even though they were all subject, I think, to the House of Lords.

2. As for England proper, if I am not forgetting something, among the classifications of Blackstone, I find that he counts:

1. Eleven kinds of courts existing according to the common law, of which four, it is true, had already fallen into disuse.

2. Three kinds of courts whose jurisdiction extended throughout the country, but which was only applicable in certain matters.

3. Ten kinds of courts with a special character. One of these kinds is composed of local courts, created by different acts of

Parliament or existing by virtue of tradition, whether in London or in the towns and cities of the provinces. These are so numerous and offer so great a variety in their constitution and in their rules that the author refuses to make a detailed exposition of them.

Thus, in England proper alone, if we can believe Blackstone, there existed in the time when he wrote, that is, in the second half of the eighteenth century, twenty-four kinds of court, of which several were subdivided into a large number of individual ones, each of which had its own special characteristics. If we take away the ones which then seemed to have almost disappeared, there still remained eighteen or twenty.

Now, if we examine this judicial system, we can easily see that it contained all kinds of flaws. Despite the multiplicity of courts, there were often lacking lower courts of the first instance placed near the parties, established to judge small things on the spot at little cost, which made justice slow and costly. The same matters were within the competence of several courts, which threw an awkward uncertainty over how to begin a suit. Almost all the appeals courts judged certain cases in the first instance, sometimes courts of common law, other times courts of equity. The appeals courts were very diverse. The only central point was the House of Lords. Lawsuits against the government were not separated from suits between private individuals, which would seem a great flaw in the eyes of most of our jurists. Finally, all these courts took the grounds for their decisions from four different kinds of legislation, one of which was established only by precedents, and another, equity, was not based on anything in particular, since its object was usually to go against custom or the statutes, and to correct by the arbitrary will of the judge what was outdated or too harsh in statute or custom.

These are a lot of flaws, and, if one compares this enormous and outdated machine of English justice with the modern creation of our judicial system, the simplicity, the coherence, the articulation that is found in ours with the complication and incoherence which is notable in the English system, the vices of the latter appear still greater. However, there was no country in the world where, from the time of Blackstone, the great end of justice was as completely attained as in England; where every man, whatever his rank, and whether he pleaded against a commoner or against the ruler, was more sure of being heard, and found in all the courts of his country better guarantees for the defense of his fortune, his freedom, and his life.

This does not mean that the vices of the English judicial system served what I have called here the great end of justice; it proves only that there are in all judicial organizations lesser flaws which may only moderately hinder this end of justice, and other principles which may not only hurt it but destroy it, even though they are accompanied by many secondary improvements. The former are more easily perceived; this is what usually first strikes vulgar minds. They leap to the eye, as they say. The others are often more hidden, and it is not always the lawyers and other professionals who discover them or point them out.

Note further that the same qualities can be secondary or principal depending on the times, or depending on the political organization of the society. In aristocratic eras, eras of inequality, everything which tends to lessen privilege for certain individuals before the court, to assure there guarantees for the weak against the strong, which tends to make the action of the state predominant, since the state is naturally impartial when it is only a question of a dispute between two of its subjects, all this becomes a principal quality, but diminishes in importance to the extent that the social state and the political constitution turn towards democracy.

If one studies the English judicial system according to these principles, one finds that in allowing the persistence of all the flaws which may render justice among our neighbors obscure, slow, complicated, expensive, and inconvenient, extreme precautions had been taken so that the strong might never be favored at the expense of the weak, the state at the expense of individuals. As we penetrate further into the details of this legislation we see that every citizen has been furnished all kinds of arms to defend himself with, and that things are arranged in such a way as to give everyone the greatest possible guarantee against the partiality, the venality properly speaking of the judges, and against that more common and above all more dangerous kind of venality, which in democratic eras is born of the servility of the courts with respect to public authority.

From all these points of view the English judicial system, despite the numerous lesser flaws which still remain in it, seems to me superior to our own, which it is true is not hindered by almost any of these vices, but which also does not offer to the same degree the chief qualities which are to be found there; our system which, excellent insofar as the guarantees that it offers each citizen with respect to disputes among individuals, is weak on the side which must always be reinforced in a democratic society like our own, that is, guarantees for the individual against the state.

57. ADVANTAGES ENJOYED BY THE PARIS REGION

This region was as advantaged with respect to government charity as it was with regard to tax collection. Example: letter from the controller-general to the intendant of the region of the Ile-de-France, 22 May 1787, which informs the latter that the king has fixed, for the Paris region, the sum which ought to be employed in works of charity during the year at 172,800 livres. A further 100,000 livres are destined for the purchase of cattle which are to be given to farmers. One can see from this letter that the sum of 172,800 livres was to be distributed by the intendant alone, on the condition that he obey the general rules of which the government has informed him, and have the division approved by the controller-general.

58. The government of the old regime was composed of a multitude of different powers, created in different times, most often for financial reasons and not for those of government proper, and which sometimes had the same field of action. Confusion and struggle could not be avoided except on the condition that each acted little or not at all. From the moment when they wanted to shed this lethargy, they hindered each other and got tangled up with one another. From this came the complaints against the complication of governmental wheels and confusion of attribution which are much livelier in the years which immediately preceded the Revolution than thirty or forty years previously. The political institutions had not become worse; on the contrary, they were much improved; but political life had become more active.

59. The Revolution did not happen because of this prosperity; but the spirit which would produce the Revolution, this active, unquiet, intelligent, innovative, ambitious mind, this democratic spirit of new societies, began to inspire everything, and, before overturning society in a moment, was already enough to stimulate it and develop it.

60. THE ARBITRARY INCREASE OF TAXES

What the king here calls the taille, he could have called, with as much reason, the vingtième, as can be shown from the following correspondence. In 1772, the controller-general, Terray, had decided on a considerable increase, 100,000 livres, in the vingtièmes of the Tours region. One sees the pain and embarrassment that this measure caused the intendant, M. Ducluzel, an able administrator and a man of good intentions, in a secret letter where he says: "It is the ease with which the 250,000 livres were given (preceding increase) which has probably encouraged the cruel interpretation and letter of the month of June." In a highly secret letter that the director of taxes wrote to the intendant on the same occasion, he says, "If the increases that are requested seem to you as aggravating, as revolting, with regard to the general poverty as you have so well testified to me, it would be desirable for the province, which cannot find any other defender and protector than your generous feelings, that you at least spare it the supplementary tax roll, a retroactive tax always hateful."

We also see by this correspondence how one lacked any basis and what arbitrariness (even with good intentions) was practiced. The intendant, as well as the minister, put the burden of the surtax more on agriculture than on industry, more on one kind of agriculture rather than another (wine, for example), according to whether they judged that one industry or branch of agriculture needed encouragement.

61. MANNER IN WHICH TURGOT SPEAKS OF THE LOWER CLASSES OF THE COUNTRYSIDE IN THE PREAMBLE OF A ROYAL DECLARATION

"The communities of the country are composed," he says, "in most of the kingdom, of poor, ignorant, and brutal peasants, incapable of governing themselves."

62. HOW REVOLUTIONARY IDEAS SPRANG FORTH ALTOGETHER NATURALLY FROM MINDS, IN THE MIDST OF THE OLD REGIME

In 1779, a lawyer addressed himself to the Council and asked for a decree which would reestablish a maximum price for straw throughout the kingdom.

63. The chief engineer writes in 1781 to the intendant with respect to a request for further payment: "the claimant has not had regard for the fact that the payments which we make are a special favor for the Tours region, and that one is very lucky to get back part of one's loss. If we reimbursed in the manner suggested by the claimant, four millions would not be enough."

64. EXAMPLE OF THE ATTITUDE THAT WAS OFTEN TAKEN TOWARDS THE PEASANTS

1768. The king gave 2,000 francs in remission from the taille to the parish of la Chapelle-Blanche, near Saumur. The priest claimed to have the right to deduct a portion of this sum to construct a bell-tower, to rid himself of the noise of the bells which disturbed him, he said, in his rectory. The inhabitants complained and resisted. The subdelegate took the priest's side and had three of the leading inhabitants arrested at night and thrown into prison.

Another example. Order of the king that a woman who has insulted two horsemen of the mounted police be imprisoned for four days. Another order to imprison for two weeks a hosier who has insulted the mounted police. The intendant responds to the minister that he has already put this man in prison, of which the minister strongly approves. The insults addressed to the mounted police took place on the occasion of the violent arrest of the beggars, a measure which, it seems, disgusted the populace. The subdelegate, in having the hosier arrested, made known to the public that those who continued to insult the police would be still more severely punished.

From the correspondence of the subdelegates and the intendant (1760–70) one can see that the intendant gave them the order to arrest unimportant people, not in order to have them tried, but to have them imprisoned. The subdelegate asks the intendant to have imprisoned for life two dangerous beggars whom he has arrested. A father protests against the arrest of his son, arrested as a vagabond because he was traveling without any papers. A landowner of X asks that a man, his neighbor, be arrested, who has established himself in his parish, whom he has helped, but who has acted very badly towards him and has annoyed him. The intendant of Paris asks the intendant of Rouen to please render this service to the landowner, who is his friend.

To someone who wanted to free the beggars, the intendant responded "that the beggar's compound ought not to be considered a prison, but only a house intended to keep for *administrative correction* those who beg and vagabonds." This idea has even spread into the penal code, so much have the traditions of the old regime, in this respect, been well preserved.

65. STRUGGLE OF THE DIFFERENT GOVERNMENTAL POWERS IN 1787

Example of this: The intermediary commission of the provincial assembly of the Ile-de-France demands control over the beggar's compound. The intendant wants to remain in charge of it, "because this house is not kept up," he says, "with provincial funds." During the debate, the intermediary commission contacts the intermediary commissions of other provinces to get their advice. Among others is found the response which the intermediary commission of Champagne made to these questions, which announces to that of the Ile-de-France that it has met with the same problem and that it is fighting the same resistance.

66. In the transcript of the first provincial assembly of the Ile-de-France, I find this statement in the mouth of a commission spokesman: "Up to now the function of syndic, much more painful than honorable, had to deter all those who combined wealth with intelligence proportionate to their situation."

NOTE RELATIVE TO SEVERAL PASSAGES IN THIS VOLUME

Feudal Rights Still Existing at the Time of the Revolution,
According to the Feudal Lawyers of the Time

I do not wish to write a treatise on feudal dues here, nor above all find out what their origin might have been; I only want to show what those were which were still exercised in the eighteenth century. These dues then played such a large role, and they have since kept such a large place in the imagination of the very people who no longer suffer from them, that it seemed very interesting to me to know what exactly they were when the Revolution destroyed them all. For this purpose, I first studied a certain number of terriers or registers of manors, choosing those which seemed to be of the most recent date. This method led me nowhere; for feudal dues, although regulated by legislation which was the same throughout feudal Europe, were infinitely varied in kind, according to the province, and even according to the district. Thus the only system which seemed to me appropriate to show approximately what I was looking for was the one followed here. Feudal dues gave rise to all kinds of disputes. It was a question of knowing how these dues were acquired, how they were lost, in what exactly they consisted, which of them could not be collected without a royal patent, which could be founded only on a private title, which on the contrary had no need to show a formal title and could be collected in terms of local custom or even by virtue of long practice. Finally, when one wanted to sell them, one needed to know how to value them, and what sum of money was represented, according to its importance, by each kind. All these points, which concerned a thousand monetary interests, were subject to debate, and a whole order of jurists was formed whose sole occupation was to provide enlightenment about them. Several of these wrote in the second half of the eighteenth century, some at the very approaches of the Revolution. These are not jurists properly speaking, these are practitioners whose sole purpose is to show people in their field the rules to follow in this very particular and very attractive part of law. In carefully studying these feudists, one can get a reasonably clear and detailed idea of an object whose extent and confusion is at first astonishing. I give below the most succinct summary of my work that I can. These notes are principally taken from the work of Edme de Fréminville, who wrote around 1750, and that of Renauldon, written in 1765 and entitled: *Historical and Practical Treatise on Manorial Dues.*

The *cens* (that is, perpetual payments in kind and in money which are attached by feudal law to the possession of certain lands) in the eighteenth century still had a profound effect on the condition of a great number of landowners. The *cens* continued to be indivisible, that is, one could go to any one of several owners of property subject to the *cens* and demand the whole amount. It was always imprescriptible. The owner of property subject to the *cens* cannot sell it without giving the owner of the *cens* first option to buy it at the price offered by the purchaser; but this still existed only in certain customs; that of Paris, the most widespread, did not recognize this right.

Lods and ventes. It is the general rule, in lands ruled by custom, that the sale of any property subject to the *cens* produces lods and ventes: these are sales taxes which must be paid to the lord. The taxes are more or less high depending on the customs of the region, but pretty high everywhere; they also existed in regions governed by written law. They usually consist of the sixth of the price; they are called lods there. But in these regions it is up to the lord to prove he has this right. In written and customary regions, the *cens* creates for the lord the privilege of taking precedence over all other debtors.

Terrage or *champart, agrier, tasque.* This is a certain portion of harvest that the lord receives from properties covered by the *cens;* the quantity varies according to contract and custom. It is still found often enough in the eighteenth century. I think that terrage, even in customary regions, always had to be derived from a title. The terrage could be manorial, or connected with the land. The signs which indicate these two different kinds would be pointless to explain here; it is enough to say that terrage connected to the land could be redeemed after thirty years, while manorial terrage was permanent. One could not mortgage land subject to terrage without the lord's consent.

Bordelage. An obligation which did not exist except in Nivernais and Bourbonnais, and which consisted of an annual payment in money, in grain, and in poultry, due from property subject to the *cens.* The due had very harsh consequences; nonpayment for three years gave rise to *commise,* or confiscation by the lord. He who owed *bordelage* was further subject to a crowd of hindrances on his property; sometimes the lord could inherit it, even though the owner had legal heirs. The contract was the harshest in feudal law, and jurisprudence had ended up by limiting it to rural land; "for the peasant is always the mule ready to bear all burdens," says the author.

Marciage. This is a special due collected in very few places, on the possessors of property or land subject to the *cens,* and which consisted of a certain payment which was due upon the natural death of the lord of the property.

Feudal tithes. In the eighteenth century there were still a great number of feudal tithes. In general they had to result from a contract, and did not derive merely from the existence of lordship.

Parcière. The parcières are dues collected on the harvest of fruits produced by the property. Similar enough to the champart or the feudal tithe, they were chiefly in use in the Bourbonnais and in Auvergne.

Carpot. Used in the Bourbonnais, this due is to vineyards what the champart is to other agricultural land, that is, the right to receive a portion of the harvest. It was a quarter of the grapes.

Serfdom. One calls *serf customs* those which still contain some traces of serfdom; they are few in number. In the provinces which are governed by them, there are none or very few where there are not some traces of the former serfdom (this was written in 1765). The serfdom, or as the author calls it, the servitude, was *personal* or *real.*

Personal servitude was inherent to the person and followed him everywhere. Wherever the serf went, wherever he transported his property, the lord could demand it by right. The authors report several decrees which establish this right, among others a decree of 17 June 1760, by which the court excludes a lord of Nivernais from the inheritance of Pierre Truchet, dead at Paris, who was the son of a serf in accordance with the customs of Nivernais, who had married a free woman of Paris and had died there, as well as his son. But the decree seems founded on the fact that Paris was a place of asylum, where the suit could not be heard. If the right of asylum forbade the lord from seizing the goods that serfs owned in the place of asylum, it did not prevent the lord from inheriting the goods left in his lordship.

Real servitude was the result of the occupation of some land, and could end with the abandonment of that land or the habitation of a certain place.

Corvées. A right that the lord had over his subjects, by virtue of which he could use for his profit a certain number of their workdays or those of their oxen and their horses. The corvée *at will,* that is according to the lord's pleasure, had been completely abolished. It had long been reduced to a certain number of days per year.

The corvée could be either *personal* or *real.* Personal corvées were due from the working people who had homes on the lord's land, each man according to his profession. Real corvées were attached to the possession of certain property. Nobles, ecclesiastics, clergymen, judicial officials, lawyers, doctors, notaries and bankers, notables had to be exempted from the corvée. The author cites a decree, of 13 August 1735, which exempts a notary whom his lord wished to force to come, during three days, to record for nothing the acts the lord had passed for his manor, where the notary lived. All corvées had to be established on the basis of a written title. The manorial corvée had become very rare in the eighteenth century.

Banalities. The provinces of Flanders, Artois, and Hainault alone were exempt from banalities [a banality was the lord's right to have a monopoly of mills, bread-ovens, etc., within his domain—trans.]. The customs of Paris were very strict about allowing the exercise of this right only by title. All those who lived within the bounds of the banality were subject to it, usually even nobles and priests.

Independently of the banality of mills and ovens, there were many others:

1. Banalities of industrial mills, such as cloth-mills, cork-mills, hemp-mills. Several customs, among others those of Anjou, Maine, Brittany, establish this banality.
2. Banalities of the winepress. Very few customs mention it; that of Lorraine establishes it, as well as that of Maine.
3. Banal bull. No custom speaks of it; but there are certain titles which establish it. It is the same with the banal slaughterhouse.

In general, the secondary banalities just spoken of are more rare and are viewed with a less favorable eye than the others; they can be established only on a very clear text from the customs, or, lacking this, from a very exact title.

Ban of the grape-harvest. It was still in use throughout the whole kingdom during the eighteenth century; it was purely a police right, attached to the right of high justice. To exercise it, the lord who held high justice did not need any title. The ban of the grape-harvest was obligatory on everyone. The customs of Burgundy give the lord the right to gather his grapes a day in advance of all other vineyard owners.

Right of banvin. A right that *numbers* of lords still have, say the authors, whether in virtue of custom or by special titles, to sell the wine made on their own estates for a certain time (in general, a month or forty days) before anyone else is allowed to. Among the big customs, only those of Tours, Anjou, Maine, and Marche establish this right and regulate it. A decree of the tax-court of 28 August 1751 authorizes, as an exemption, bars to sell wine during the banvin, but only to strangers; and it still has to be the lord's wine, coming from his estates. The customs which establish and regulate this right of banvin usually require that it be founded on a title.

Right of blairie. A payment that belongs to the lord who holds high justice for the permission that he gives the inhabitants to pasture their animals on lands situated within the extent of his jurisdiction or even on wastelands. This right does not exist in regions of written law, but is very well known in regions of customary law. It can be found, under different names, especially in the Bourbonnais, Nivernais, Auvergne, and Burgundy. This right presumes that the lord originally owned all the land, so that after having distributed most of it in fiefs, censives, and other land concessions in return for payments, what still remained could serve only as general pasture for which he conceded a temporary right of use. *Blairie* is established in several customs; but it is only the lord who holds high justice who can claim it, and it must be based on a special title, or at least on old evidence, supported by long possession.

Tolls. There originally existed an enormous number of manorial tolls on bridges, rivers, roads, say the authors. Louis XIV destroyed many of them. In 1724, a commission named to examine all the titles of tolls eliminated twelve hundred, and more were eliminated every day (1765). The first principle in this question, says Renauldon, is that the toll, being a tax, must not only be founded on a title but on a title coming from the sovereign. The toll is entitled: *This by order of the king.* One of the conditions of tolls is to attach to them a list of all the fees that each kind of merchandise must pay. This fee schedule must always be approved by a decree of the Council. The title of concession, says the author, must be followed by uninterrupted possession. Despite these precautions taken by the legislator, the value of several tolls had considerably increased in modern times. I know a toll, the author adds, which was leased for only 100 livres a century ago, and which today brings in 1,400; another, leased for 39,000 livres, now brings in 90,000. The chief ordinances or chief edicts which regulate the rights of tolls are title 29 of the ordinance of 1669, and the edicts of 1683, 1724, 1775.

The authors that I cite, although in general rather favorable to feudal dues, recognize that great abuses are committed in the collection of tolls.

Ferries. The right of ferry differs considerably from that of tollage. Ferry is only levied on merchandise, tollage on persons, animals, carriages. This right, to be exercised, also had to be authorized by the king, and the payments collected had to be fixed in the decree of the Council which established or authorized them.

The right of leyde (it is given several other names, depending on the place) is a tax which is collected on the merchandise brought to fairs or markets. A number of lords regard this right as attached to the right of high justice and purely manorial, say the feudists whom we cite, but this is wrong; for it is a tax which must be authorized by the king. In any case, this right belongs only to the lord who holds high justice, who receives the fines paid to the police. It seems, however, that even though in theory the right of leyde could come only from the king, in fact it was very often founded only on feudal title and long usage.

It is certain that fairs could only be established by royal authorization. The lords, in order to have the right to say which weights and measures their vassals should use at the fairs and markets of the manor, did not need any special title or concession on the king's part. It was enough that the right be founded on custom

and constant possession. All the kings who had successively tried to create uniformity of weights and measures had failed, say the authors. Things have remained
where they were at the time of the drawing up of the customs.

Roads. Rights exercised by the lords over roads.

The great roads, what were called the royal roads, in fact belonged only to the
sovereigns: their creation, their upkeep, the crimes committed there, are outside
the competence of the lords or their judges. As for the particular roads which are
found within their manor, they belong without contradiction to the lord who
holds high justice. These have over them the rights of voirie and police, and their
judges have jurisdiction over all offences committed there. Previously the lords
had been charged with the upkeep of the great roads which crossed their manors,
and, to cover the expenses incurred for their repair, they had been given rights of
toll, boundary, and traverse over them; but, since then, the king has retaken control of the great roads.

Waters. All navigable rivers belong to the king, even if they cross the lord's
lands, without regard to any contrary title (ordinance of 1669). If the lords collect
some duties on the rivers, these are fishing rights, mills, ferries, bridges, etc., by
virtue of concessions which ought to have been given them by the king. There
are lords who still arrogate to themselves rights of police and high justice over
rivers, but this is by virtue of manifest usurpation or extorted concessions.

The small streams belong without contradiction to the lords through whose
territory they pass. They have the same rights of property, police, and justice over
them that the king has over navigable rivers. All lords who hold high justice are
the universal lords of the non-navigable rivers that run through their territory. To
have ownership of them they need no other title than that which gives them the
high justice. The customs of Brittany give this right only to particular nobles. In
general law, it is certain that only the lord who holds high justice has the right to
permit the construction of a mill within the bounds of his jurisdiction. One cannot dam a lord's river, even for the protection of one's property, without the permission of the lord's judges.

Of fountains, wells, flax-steeping pits, ponds. The rainwater which runs along
the great roads belongs to the lords who hold high justice; only they have the
exclusive right to dispose of it. The lord who holds high justice can have a pond
constructed throughout the bounds of his jurisdiction, even on the property of
his subjects, by paying them the price of their submerged property. This is the
precise disposition of several customs, among others those of Troyes and Nivernais. As for individuals, they can make ponds only on their own land; still several
customs require the owner to ask the lord's permission in this case. The customs
which require the consent of the lord require that, when it is given, it be free of
charge.

Fishing. Fishing, in navigable or floatable rivers, belongs only to the king; he
alone can concede it. His judges alone have the right to judge fishing violations.
There are, however, many lords who have the right to fish in this kind of river;

but they hold it by concession from the king or have usurped it. As for the non-navigable rivers, it is not permitted to fish there, not even with a line, without the permission of the lord who holds high justice in the region where they run. A decree of 30 April 1749 condemns a fisherman in this case. For the rest, the lords themselves, in fishing, must submit to the general regulations for fishing. The lord who holds high justice may give the right to fish in his river as a fief or *cens.*

Hunting. Hunting may not be leased like fishing. It is a personal right. It is held that it is a royal right, of which the nobles themselves only make use within the bounds of their jurisdiction or on their fief by the king's permission. This doctrine is that of the ordinance of 1669, title 30. The lord's judges are competent for all hunting violations, with the exception of the hunting of red beasts (these are, I think, the big animals: stags, deer), which are royal cases.

The right to hunt is the one most rigorously forbidden to commoners; even the free-holding commoner does not possess it. The king does not grant it in his pleasures. A lord cannot even grant leave to hunt. Such is the strictness of the law. But every day one sees lords giving permission to hunt, not only to noblemen but to commoners. The lord who holds high justice may hunt within the limits of his jurisdiction, but alone. He has the right to make, within that extent, all the regulations, rules, and prohibitions about hunting. All the lords of fiefs, although they do not have the right of justice, may hunt within the bounds of their fief. The nobles who have neither fiefs nor rights of justice can also hunt on the lands which belong to them in the neighborhood of their homes. It was judged that a commoner who had a park within the limits of someone's high justice had to leave it open for the pleasures of the lord; but the decree is very old; it is from 1668.

Warrens. They cannot now be established without a title. It is permitted to commoners as well as noblemen to open warrens, but nobles alone may have ferrets.

Pigeon coops. Certain customs give the right to pigeon coops only to lords with the right of high justice; others give it to all who possess a fief. In Dauphiny, Brittany, and Normandy, it is prohibited for any commoner to have a pigeon coop or to keep pigeons; only nobles may have pigeons. The penalties pronounced against those who kill pigeons are very severe; often corporal punishment.

Such are, according to the authors cited, the chief feudal dues still collected in the second half of the eighteenth century. They add: "The dues with which we have been concerned up to now are those generally established. There are yet a number of others, less known and less common, which exist only in certain customs or even in a few manors, by virtue of special title." These rare or limited dues, of which the authors speak here, and which they name, total eighty-nine, of which most bear directly on agriculture, in giving the lord certain dues on the harvest, or in establishing fees on the sale of grain as well as on its transport. The authors say that several of these dues were no longer in use in their time. I think, however, that a great number must still have been collected in some places in 1789.

After having studied the chief dues still in use, in the writings of the eighteenth-century feudists, I wanted to know what their importance was in the eyes of their contemporaries, at least from the point of view of the income of those who received them and those who paid them. One of the authors of whom I have just spoken, Renauldon, tells us this in making us acquainted with the rules that the legal profession ought to follow to evaluate in inventories the different feudal dues which still existed in 1765, that is twenty-four years before the Revolution. According to this jurist, here are the rules that ought to be followed in this regard.

Legal jurisdiction. "Some of our customs," he says "estimate the rights of high, low, and middle justice at one-tenth the income of the land. Manorial justice was then very important; Edme de Fréminville thinks that, in our days, justice should only be estimated at the twentieth of the land's revenue; I think this estimate still too high."

Honorary rights. However priceless these rights are, our author, a man who is very positive and for whom appearances count for little, assures us that it is nevertheless prudent for the experts to fix a small value for them.

Manorial corvée. The author gives the rules for the estimation of these corvées, which proves that this right was still occasionally encountered; he values the daily work of an ox at 20 sous, and that of his driver at 5 sous, plus food. This is a pretty good indication of salaries in 1765.

Tolls. With regard to evaluating these tolls, the author says: "There is no manorial due which ought to be estimated at a lower price than the tolls; they are very variable; the upkeep of the roads and bridges most useful to trade now being at the king's and the provinces' expense, many tolls are now useless, and they are daily eliminated.

Fishing and hunting rights. The right to fish can be leased and can occasion expert evaluation. The right to hunt is purely personal and cannot be leased; it is therefore in the nature of an honorary right, but not a useful right, and the experts cannot include it in their estimates.

The author next speaks particularly of the rights of banality, of banvin, of leyde, of blairie, which shows that these rights were the most frequently exercised and those which still kept the most importance, and he adds: "there are a number of other manorial dues, which are found from time to time, which would be too long and even impossible to report here; but, in the examples which we just gave, intelligent experts will find the rules for evaluating the dues of which we do not speak."

Estimation of the cens. Most of the customs intend the *cens* to be valued at one-thirtieth [of the land's income—trans.]. What makes their estimate so high is that this due represents, beyond the *cens* itself, other variable and productive income, such as the lods and ventes.

Feudal tithes, terrage. The feudal tithes cannot be estimated at less than one twenty-fifth, this kind of property requiring neither time, nor care, nor expense. When the terrage or the champart includes lods and ventes, that is, when the land subject to the dues cannot be sold without paying a fee to the lord to whom it is subject, this occasional fee increases their estimated value to one-thirtieth; if not it must be valued like the tithes.

Agricultural fees which do not produce lods and ventes, nor a right of retention (that is, which are not manorial fees) should be estimated at one-twentieth.

Estimate of the Different Kinds of Ownership
Existing in France before the Revolution

We know in France, says the author, only three kinds of property:

1. *Freehold*. This is a free property, exempt from all charges, and which is not subject to any manorial duties or dues, useful or honorific. There are freeholding nobles and freeholding commoners. The freeholding noble has the right of justice, or fiefs dependent on him, or lands paying the *cens* to him; he follows feudal law when dividing them. The freeholding commoner has neither the right of justice, nor a fief, nor lands paying him *cens,* and divides them as commoners do. The author does not recognize as full landowners any but freeholders.

Estimation of freehold property. It must be the highest. The customs of Auvergne and Burgundy value it at one-fortieth. The author thinks that a one-thirtieth evaluation would be correct.

It must be noted that the freeholding commoners situated within the limits of a manorial legal jurisdiction are subject to it. It was not a sign of subjection to the lord but submission to a jurisdiction which took the place of the state courts.

2. The second kind of property was that of property *held as a fief.*

3. The third kind consisted of *property held subject to the cens,* or, in legal language, of commons.

Estimation of the value of fiefs. The evaluation must be lowered according to how high the feudal burdens on it are.

1. In the regions of written law and in several customs, fiefs only owed *the mouth and hands,* that is, homage.

2. In other customs the fiefs, beyond the mouth and hands, were what was called *at risk,* as in Burgundy, and were subject to the *commise,* or feudal confiscation, in the case where the owner took possession without having sworn faith and homage.

3. Other customs, such as those of Paris and many others, subject the fief, beyond the oaths of faith and homage at purchase, to a tax of one-fifth.

4. Finally by others, such as that of Poitou and some others, they are subject to a payment on the oath of fealty, to service on horseback, etc.

Property in the first category must be valued more highly than the others.

The custom of Paris values such property at one-twentieth, which seems, says the author, reasonable enough.

Valuing property held in commons and subject to the cens. To arrive at this estimate, it is useful to divide this kind of property into three classes.

1. Property held in simple *cens*.
2. Beyond the *cens,* property could be subject to other kinds of servitude.
3. It could be entailed, subject to the real taille, or to *bordelage.*

Of these three kinds of commoner property indicated here, the first and the second were very common in the eighteenth century; the third was rare. The evaluations that were made of them, says the author, will be lower as one gets to the second kind, and above all to the third class. The owners of property of the third class are not even, really, owners, since they cannot sell without the lord's permission.

The terrier. These are the rules which the feudists cited above give about the way in which the manorial registers called terriers, of which I have spoken at several points in the text, are drawn up or rewritten. The terrier was, as we know, a single register where all the titles stating the dues that belonged to the manor were listed, whether in property or in honorific rights, real, personal, or mixed. All the declarations of those subject to the *cens,* the customs of the manor, the leases, etc., were inserted there. In the customs of Paris, say our authors, the lords could rewrite their terrier every thirty years at the expense of those subject to the *cens.* They add: "We are nevertheless very happy when we find they have been rewritten every century." One could not rewrite one's terrier (which was a difficult operation for all those who depended on the manor) without obtaining, whether from the grand chancellory if it was a question of manors situated in the jurisdiction of several parlements, or from the parlement in other cases, an authorization which was called *lettres à terrier.* The court named the notary. Before this notary all the vassals, noble and commoner, paying the *cens,* leasing or under the legal jurisdiction of the manor, had to present themselves. A map of the manor had to be attached to the terrier.

Independently of the terrier, other registers called *lièves* were found at the manor, on which the lords or their lessees listed the sums which they had received from their *cens*-payers, with their names and the date of the payment.

Notes and Variants

All remarks by the editor appear in italics. Works cited by the editor appear in italics, underscored. Tocqueville's own words, and those of authors he cites, appear in roman type, underscored only to indicate Tocqueville's own emphasis or underscoring. The translator's occasional remarks are in italics within square brackets and identified as such.

Note on abbreviations: OC stands for the "oeuvres complètes," complete works, of various authors. OC (Beaumont) refers to the edition of Tocqueville's complete works edited and published by his friend Gustave de Beaumont in 1865. MS. refers to Tocqueville's handwritten manuscript of The Old Regime. Copy refers to the printer's copy, which includes considerable handwritten corrections by Tocqueville. Rubbish refers to the plans, sketches, and drafts grouped by Tocqueville under that heading. References to Tocqueville's notes are based either on one of the categories described above, or on Tocqueville's research notes, identified by their source of origin or by the category under which Tocqueville filed them. For further details see the last section of the Introduction, "Tocqueville's Files, Manuscripts, and Proofs," above.—Trans.

Page 84, line 14

The preparatory files for The Old Regime contain three series of notes on the cahiers (Folder C of the research notes): "work on the cahiers," done around 1836; an analysis of the summary of the cahiers from October 1853, the longest set of notes; and, finally, a study of the cahiers done in 1856, based on the original cahiers in the archives, but consisting only of very fragmentary notes on Agen, Aix, and Alençon. This is supplemented by another file in Tocqueville's notes for the sequel to The Old Regime (June 1857), on the cahiers of the three orders of Agen, Aix, Alençon, and particularly Amiens. Before 1856, Tocqueville had also used a copy of the general cahier of the Third Estate of the town and district of Falaise. The 1856 book was therefore based on close study of the summary alone.

Page 85, line 8, after "self"

It was like the eagle in its egg. Break the shell, it will appear. I see there not only what it did in its first effort. —Rubbish.

It was already there like the eagle in its egg. Break the shell, it will appear. —*MS. Copy. Comparison crossed out in proof.*

Page 85, line 20, after "completely"
The purpose of the work that I am now publishing is to show how the old regime can help us to understand this first phase of our Revolution. How, indeed, it was able to give birth to it, facilitate its arrival and direct its course. I admit that in my mind. —*Rubbish.*

Page 86, line 26, after "instructive"
I am not, thank God, among those who think that the disease we suffer from is incurable. With a nation so full of contrasts, of reversals, and of resources as ours, I hold that one must never expect too much or fear too much from the future. —*In the margin of this sentence in the MS., circled.*

Page 86, line 32, after "do"
I throw light on them for the same reason that one puts a lighthouse on a reef. I look with fear and fervor for light on present times. —*Rubbish. The text of the Rubbish continues with a first draft of the "truths." The final text on page 15 uses all their elements and develops them.*

Page 86, line 32
A sketch on a separate page in the Rubbish states Tocqueville's impartiality: I am nothing, and I don't want to be anything. I expect nothing from anyone and it seems to me that I don't fear anything from anyone anymore. I belong neither to a clique nor to a party. I am alone. This isolation in the middle of my country is often cruel. Feeling the pain, I wanted at least to taste the corresponding pleasure, which is to express my thoughts freely, without wishing to flatter, without fearing to displease, concerning myself with the truth alone. —*The MS. shows traces of this idea:* that I pursue. This freedom of expression, furthermore, was easy for me. I am nothing in my country and I do not want to be anything. This sort of isolation has something burdensome in it, doubtless; feeling the pain, I at least wanted to have its pleasure. —*Circled.*
Tocqueville was conscious of the risk of wounding the Legitimists, numerous among his family circle, by "the book's anti–old regime tendency": This kind of harm which the truth does me, gives it an impartial character which seems to me more crushing for that time than everything revolutionary passion would have made me say.—*Letter to Kergorlay, 28 August 1856 (OC, v. 13, t. 2, p. 310).*

Page 87, line 3
From here on Tocqueville very freely summarizes the preface to the first volume of Democracy in America *(1835).*

Page 93, line 4

Frederick II the Great (1712–1786), King of Prussia, ascended the throne in 1740, had contacts with Voltaire, and was an author, most notably of the Antimachiavel (1740). In 1853 Tocqueville had read the Oeuvres historiques of Frederick the Great, doubtless in the 4-volume edition published in 1830 at Leipzig (Brockhaus) and Paris (Rey-Gravier). Here is his judgment on the first two volumes—the Mémoires pour servir à l'histoire de la maison de Brandenbourg and Histoire de mon temps—in a letter addressed to Gustave de Beaumont, 27 October 1853 (OC, v. 8, t. 3, p. 160): What strikes me are the narrow limits in which men's views are confined, even those of great men, where the future is concerned. I have not yet found, in this work of Frederick the Great, a single word which indicates expectation of the great changes which were about to alter the face of Europe. He himself announced the Revolution's approach through his language and ideas, and did not see it coming. Is it not odd that that miserable Louis XV, from the depths of his debauchery, saw what this Frederick, enlightened by all the intelligence of his genius, did not see at all? *See Tocqueville's notes on Frederick's legal code below.*

Page 93, line 23

On 27 August 1791, the Emperor Leopold II and the King of Prussia, Frederick William II, launched a declaration from the castle of Pillnitz near Dresden, announcing that they would intervene in France if they obtained the agreement of the other sovereigns of Europe.

Tocqueville here takes up the analysis of Edmund Burke (1729–1797), the writer and Whig politician. Burke, who had defended the American colonists against the arbitrary power of the British Crown, had, from the publication of his Reflections on the Revolution in France (1790), been a determined opponent of the French Revolution. Tocqueville had read carefully volumes 5–8 of Burke's Complete Works, published in London in 14 volumes beginning in 1815, as well as the Correspondence of the Right Honourable Edmund Burke between the Year 1744 and the Period of His Decease, in 1797, edited by Sir Richard Burke, 4 vols., 1844. Tocqueville's research notes consist of almost nothing but quotations, which are listed in OC, v. 2, t. 2, pp. 338–41. Here he uses mostly the pamphlet "Thoughts on French Affairs," 1791, Works, v. 7, pp. 64–65, which he comments on thus (Folder M): The rulers themselves do democracy's work: through hatred of the upper classes with which they had up to then been in contact and often in conflict, the rulers turned naturally towards the common people [*"the common people" in English in original.—Trans.]* whom they barely knew, whose vices were unknown to them.

But Tocqueville's chief source is above all Burke's 1793 pamphlet "Remarks on the Policy of the Allies with Respect to France," Works v. 7, which he comments on as follows in his notes: The whole purpose of Burke's pamphlet titled "Policy of the Allies," printed at the end of 1793, is to oppose the policy which consisted of attacking France as foreigners and not as the ally of a party in a civil war;

concerning oneself with the old politics of interests rather than seeing that the sole interest at present was the complete destruction of the French Revolution; that this destruction could only be effected by using the party of the old regime, this party alone (he does not imagine the possibility of a compromise), by treating it as the legitimate authority and giving it control over internal matters . . .

Page 94, line 10

Tocqueville here quotes Arthur Young, *Voyages en France pendant les années 1787–88–89 et 90*, 2d ed., Buisson, 1794—Year II, v. 1, p. 216, journal of 17 October 1787. The English farmer and agronomist Arthur Young (1741–1820) made three trips to France in 1787, 1788, and 1789. His narrative, published in English in 1792, was translated into French by 1793.

[Young includes the clergy in the original—Trans.]

Page 94, line 18

Paraphrase of Burke's speech in the debate "On the Army Estimates" (February 1790). In his research notes (Folder M) Tocqueville comments on the idea that France is reduced to long powerlessness: No foresight that the fury which had made such internal destruction could well throw the nation towards the outside, and amidst the destruction of its organized strength multiply its wild and natural force a hundredfold.

Page 94, line 29, after "simple"

Externally the Revolution was an ordinary event; a fact of limited importance. Internally it was a reform, but easy. —*Circled.* This was true of the rulers but not of the peoples. The people immediately had a feeling that what was happening in France was something new. —*Crossed-out remark in the margin.* The reform to make was immense but simple. —*Correction in the margin. MS.*

Page 95, line 10

Joseph de Maistre, *Considérations sur la France*, chapter 5; "There is in the French Revolution a satanic character which distinguishes it from anything that has ever been seen, and perhaps from all that is to come."

The satanic character of the Revolution is also affirmed by Burke; Tocqueville cited, in his research notes, Burke's speech before the House of Commons of 11 May 1791: the revolution is "a shapeless monster born of hell and chaos." Tocqueville also cited the *Reflections on the Revolution in France, Works*, v. 5, p. 173 ("the alembic of hell, which is now so furiously boiling in France").

Page 95, line 13

Salvian, priest of Marseille, author around 450 of *De gubernatione Dei.* Burke, "Letters on the Proposal of Peace," 1796, *Works*, v. 8, p. 8.

Page 96, chapter title

Doubtless Tocqueville is here alluding to the polemics about the freedom of education in which he took part through his parliamentary speeches and his articles published in the newspaper <u>Le Commerce</u> in 1844–45. The Ministry envenomed the religious question in order to make the absence of any electoral or parliamentary reform be forgotten. Thus, wrote Tocqueville, it was a question: in which one can remain the servant of M. Guizot and reanimate a dying popularity; what a lucky combination! It is the dew of heaven which falls at last on a parched earth *(article of 28 November 1844, OC, v. 3, t. 2, p. 563).*

Page 96, after chapter title

Make a strong effort to avoid as much as possible, in <u>all these chapters</u>, the <u>abstract</u> style, in order to make myself fully understood, and above all read with pleasure. Make a constant effort to contain abstract and general ideas in words which present a precise and particular picture. Example: when I say how the Revolution has substituted an immense new social power for the dispersed old powers, recall the destroyed powers by naming them by their names, and in depicting the new social power try to use words which present the picture of government and bureaucracy as we know them and as we see them function daily. This will diminish the absolute value of the sentence in itself, since I am not only talking about France, and the thought extends beyond the space in which these words enclose it. But one writes in order to please, and not to attain an ideal perfection of language. —*Rubbish. Title Page. Last reviewed by Tocqueville, 1856.*

Page 96, line 3, after "religion"

The problem with this is that I am speaking about the subject in general, and of what is proper to the Revolution without regard to France, while this irreligious passion which I am going to talk about is a fact more French than foreign, so perhaps this would go better in the chapter which treats the characteristics and causes of the Revolution in France. —*In the margin of a draft of this paragraph, little different, in a Rubbish file dated from Compiègne.*

Page 96, line 6, after "authority"

The hostility against Religion or even against Catholicism, is it as accidental a thing as I say it is? Isn't there in democratic societies a permanent tendency contrary to observances, to fasts, to mysteries, to confession? —*In the margin of the Rubbish chapters written at Compiègne.*

Page 96, line 20, after "philosophy"

Very important. Highlight this and don't be afraid to extend it. I find our time as blind and stupid in its absolute and systematic denigration of what we call the Enlightenment as the men of the eighteenth century were in their blind infatuation with it. —*In the margin of the Rubbish chapters written at Compiègne.*

Page 97, line 20

Allusion to the rebirth of faith which followed the relaxation of the links be-tween Church and State after the Revolution of 1830. Tocqueville was struck notably by the success of Lacordaire's lectures at Notre Dame in 1835, at which he was pres-ent. See OC, v. 3, t. 2, p. 491.

Page 97, line 23

Tocqueville here takes up again an idea discussed in a chapter of the second volume of <u>Democracy in America</u>, *"On the Progress of Catholicism in the United States."*

Page 97, line 31, after "impiety"

If it is true that the democratic social state and institutions can weaken the religious spirit, in any case this would only be in a very slow and indirect way. Equality of condition gives individual reason a wider field of action and more lively and continuous activity; it pushes all men in general towards the quest for the goods of this world, and leads them to pursue them. One could say that it thus tends to create in people habits of heart and mind which can be harmful to instinctive faith, and dampen the ardor for zeal, but in itself it surely suggests no impious feeling and in no way inspires hatred of religion and its ministers. What I have said of religion, I will say it. *—Rubbish, Compiègne. This continuation no longer figures in the MS. In the margin of this paragraph in the MS:* As Prince Eugène said in a military way, "I have been very fortunate in this world and I hope to be so in the next." All this seems to me to need to be deepened. Indicate the position, tendency of the priests, spirit proper to the clergy.

Page 97, line 36, after "result would be"

As a rule, to abolish traditions, weaken the family, liberate the senses, take from wealth its influence and from truth itself its authority. *—Circled. MS.*

Page 98, line 10

Note to the King of 3 July 1790, <u>Correspondance entre le Comte de Mirabeau et le Comte de la Marck pendant les années 1789, 1790 et 1791 recueillie, mise en ordre et publiée par M. Ad de Bacourt</u>, *Paris, 1851, v. 2, pp. 75–76. Tocqueville changes the meaning of the end of the Mirabeau's text: "The idea of creating only a single class of citizens would have pleased Richelieu. If this level surface was good for freedom, it also facilitated the exercise of power. Several reigns of absolute government would not have done as much for royal authority as a single year of freedom."*

Page 98, line 22, after "or rather"

This new power, an impersonal power, always the same whoever the sovereign was, which bore the abstract name of the State. *—Circled marginal addition. MS.*

Page 99, line 3

In the Rubbish dated from Compiègne, after a draft of the end of the text there is a discussion of the revolutionary disease which no longer figures in later versions of the text: It is true that the French Revolution has left in the world a spirit of uneasiness and anarchy which seems eternal. But even this is an accidental and secondary effect of the Revolution, although more lasting than most of the others. It will come to an end like them. All great revolutions, whatever their object or their character, create a similar attitude, provided that they endure and succeed. When, for whatever reason, laws become fragile and the opinions of men unstable, when men themselves briefly raise and lower themselves by sudden and passing efforts, a taste for violence is always born in certain weak or depraved souls, a taste for instability and risk which often survives the event which created it. It is the passion for gambling transported into politics. *Circled:* This love of change for itself, this contempt for justice and for acquired rights, this attraction to tyranny and this simultaneous disgust at and horror for rules and authority, even for rules one has made and authority one has established, all these things are symptoms of the same illness. This sickness is the revolutionary disease proper, a disease endemic to countries which are in revolution or have just been, and which is born in all of them everywhere, just as typhus is born in all hospitals and ends up being a separate and particular illness, although born from the contagion of a thousand different diseases. If this disease of the human mind seems more terrible this time, and seems more durable than previously thought, this comes from the fact that the French Revolution has been the most violent, the deepest, the most fertile in catastrophes and reversals, and above all the most general revolution that there has ever been. If it had been particular to France, at the end of a certain time, whatever its anarchic violence, we would have seen minds come back to themselves, habit recover its empire and law its power. But the French Revolution struck all the peoples of Europe one after another, and still works on many of them, so that for sixty years there has continued to be a great revolutionary school open in some part of the world, where all violent, insubordinate, or perverse minds go to train and instruct themselves.

In the revolutionary disease of our times, whatever may be said of it, there is certainly something which does not let it be confused with the similar ills that all revolutions create. Above all it can be more widespread, because here the accidental illness finds itself with living roots in the permanent social state, the habits, ideas, and lasting mores that the revolution has founded.

What is or at least seems to be particular to it is its character as a doctrine. The modern revolutionary disease is not only a habit, a tendency of hearts and minds; it is a theory, a philosophy, if one can speak thus, to which one can assign three sources:

1. The democratic character of this revolution, which deprived tradition of its power, many moral rules of their stability, and took from the individual and from individual rights much of the instinctive respect that was given them, even in

revolutionary times, in aristocratic societies. It created a social power which has few natural scruples, little likely to encounter resistance.

2. The triumphant example of the first French Revolution, which, by the sole use of violence, energy, and audacity, without prudence, overthrew the monarchy and conquered Europe. This made superficial minds, who did not pay attention to the particular reasons why violence, energy, and audacity without prudence succeeded that time, this made them believe and teach, I say, that the universal and permanent method for success was energy, audacity, and violence.

3. The essentially theoretical and philosophical character of this revolution, which gave even violent people the habit, and suggested to them the need, to philosophize their violence.

The reasons I have just given explain the particular character the revolutionary disease has this time, and partly explain why to a certain extent and in some of its symptoms it seems to be permanent, since its particular character comes in part from the fundamental characteristics of the society created by the Revolution. Therefore some of it will necessarily remain, even after the revolutionary period is completely over. This something will be a certain disquiet and chronic instability, and a permanent disposition to relapse easily into the revolutionary disease.

All these nuances should be noted somewhere, but where? Here? Shouldn't it rather be at the end of the work when I will try to paint the permanent situation created by the Revolution? I lean towards this latter system. All this furthermore to look at again in revising and reviewing all these chapters, which must still be considered as merely unfinished drafts (15 December 1853); a first effort of thought trying to reveal itself.

Page 99, after chapter title

Of the chapters already done this is the one which has cost me the most work and with which I am the least content. —*Circled.* Take care with what I say about the unitary ideas of the Middle Ages. Ampère thinks that what I say is more true of the fifteenth century than the Middle Ages. Say the same thing but more vaguely, showing in a few words these ideas spread through all history without being too precise. —*Rubbish. Title page last reviewed by Tocqueville in 1856. On a page in the same Rubbish file, Tocqueville notes:* read to Ampère today, 13 December 1854.

A file dated from Compiègne and titled: Rubbish from chapter three. Little to salvage here I'm afraid, *contains plans and thoughts that clearly show Tocqueville's perplexity:*

What makes the Revolution resemble a religion

1. Forms a body of doctrine. A sort of political Gospel or Koran.
2. Inspires proselytism. Not only believed but preached.

3. Spreads outside its own territory.

4. Separates or unites men despite differences of language, race, nationality.

What makes it spread like a religion

1. Bases itself on principles so general, so natural, so much founded on the nature of human society outside any particular society, that it can be understood and adopted by all people.

2. Inspires proselytism.

3. In France in particular and Europe in general finds a social state and an ensemble of circumstances which prepare the minds of different nations to receive it.

If one digs, one finds that what makes the Revolution resemble a religion reduces itself to the general nature of its principles. It is because the revolution has this character that it has been easy to make it into a grand theory all linked together, a sort of political gospel. It is because it has this character that the revolution has been able to aim at conquering not only one people, but all humanity, that it has been able to present not a particular good but an absolute good to its audience and inspire proselytism. It is for this reason finally that it has been able to spread.

Make understood in a quick and striking manner how it resembles a religion.

Then say how this religion found the ease with which it spread itself in the social state and the circumstances of the times.

End perhaps by the sentence: or rather it was a religion . . . which like Islam simultaneously had soldiers, apostles, and martyrs.

Spotlight the trait of proselytism much more, which is crucial, or at least point to it from the beginning as a salient trait. A political revolution preached to nations other than the one which made it. What a novel and unique characteristic!

In general tighten, accelerate. My present chapter is full of meanders. Analysis of the present chapter which shows well that:

1. The French Revolution did not have any special territory of its own. It divided and united men independently of nationalities, of languages.

2. This has never been seen except in religious revolutions and it is only with a religious revolution that it may be compared.

3. The Reformation of the sixteenth century produced notably similar effects.

4. The revolution is therefore a political revolution which acted like and took the appearance of a religious revolution. This is its great novelty.

5. Why the revolution resembled a religion. Way in which religions work. It attached itself to general truths outside the particular condition of a people and could thus spread far. The more religions have had this character, the more in fact they have spread. Politics is the ancient natural religion which has a country.

Christianity which passed through all the barriers that differences of nationality or race raised against it.

The French Revolution is founded on general ideas like a religion, which is what made it possible for it to spread like one.

Comparison with the English Revolution which even though it ended up in the same dogmas, surrounded them with a particular form.

The French Revolution never did that. It inspired proselytism which made it more and more resemble a religion. It formed a coherent theory, a political gospel, which equally made it resemble a religion. It is a religion. However, it required particular circumstances for this religion to spread first in France and then in Europe.

Note: It is very clear, on this page above all, how the thought is deflected and scattered. The comparisons of the revolution with religion come and go. The traits which make it resemble a religion are scattered. It needs: first, everything which gave the revolution the appearance of a religion. Then what produced this resemblance.

Revise this chapter later and redo it quickly as if I had never written it before.

Note In the comparison that I made between the way the French Revolution worked and the way religions work, I based myself on ideas which were not studied carefully enough. I go back to it, not to lengthen this chapter which is already long enough, but to consolidate and delineate the terrain on which I have built.

What I said about the method followed by religions is, in the highest degree, applicable to the Christian religion. But does it apply equally to others? Do all consider man in the abstract? Yes, at least in a certain part of their prescriptions; for all claim to regulate the relations of men between themselves, independently of the positions these men occupy in each society. These are the natural relationships. Those of father to son, son to father, brother to brother, men to men. Even if religions want to regulate relationships which have their foundation in civil or political law, at least they consider these relationships in such a general fashion that their rules are applicable in all societies, such as, for example, the relations between a servant and a master or even those of a superior and an inferior; religion says in a general way that the servant is obliged to serve with honesty and fidelity, leaving the particular civil or political law to say if this man will be a paid servant, a slave, or a serf. Religious codes which try to contain these latter things, like India's, lose part of the expansive properties of religion. All religions want to regulate the natural relationships with God, and this for all men without distinction. In this part of their prescriptions all religions place themselves outside the particular condition of one society and can act on every man's mind in whatever society he lives without distinction.

But alongside this general tendency of religions, which leads them all without distinction to consider man in the abstract, at least in a large part of their prescriptions, they have another part, visible in most, which brings them back to almost the character of political laws, and gives them something absolutely particular and applicable only to certain countries, certain nationalities, certain climates, certain civilizations, certain races. All the religions of the ancients (those to which we give that name par excellence) *[the Greco-Roman world.—Trans.]* had this character in the highest degree. If they saw men as similar beings subject to one and the same law, all having similar rights and duties, these were men confined within the circle of certain particular nationalities. There were, so to speak, as many gods and human species as there were nations. The Jews themselves were like this. Several religions kept particular social or political institutions, or thought them necessary, like slavery, which made them inadmissible in countries which did not accept these institutions. Only the Christian religion has been completely faithful to what I call the philosophical method natural to religions. It has placed itself absolutely outside all particular institutions which can exist among men, social or political, all legal conventions, in order to consider the human species as a single whole composed of similar individuals, all subject to the same moral law and called in the same way to the same fate. Islam itself, which took so much from Christianity, and which coming after it ought to have profited from its example, is full of political prescriptions which are linked to the institutions of certain countries.

It is true that there are in all religions, in their dogmas or observances, some things which differ from what most men consider natural laws. But this has nothing to do with what concerns me at the moment. For these things which separate religions profoundly from one another and which even, if you like, separate all of them more or less from what general reason indicates, these things do not prevent them, ordinarily, from being believed and followed by men of different nations. These things are given by religion not as truths for the use of certain men or laws applicable to certain countries, but as truths and as general laws which must be accepted and followed by the whole species, at least when dogma or practice does not tie them to a certain people or to certain customs, to certain political laws, as for example the religions which mingle religious and political power, in such a way that they demand obedience to the laws of God and those of authority.

Page 99, line 35

Tocqueville's analysis is taken from the first pages of book one of the Histoire de la guerre de trente ans et de la paix de Westphalie *(1791–1793), by Friedrich von Schiller (1759–1805). The library at Tocqueville preserves the French translation by M. A. Mailher de Chassat, Paris, 1820. There are no remaining notes by Tocqueville on this work.*

Page 100, line 6

Tocqueville's analysis owes much to his reading of Burke. See in particular his research notes (Folder M) on Burke's "Thoughts on French Affairs," 1791, Works, *v. 7, pp. 13–17:* The French Revolution acting like a Religion and changing all the relations of Nations.

Well understood by Burke from 1791. The French Revolution, he says, has no resemblance to or similarity with the political revolutions that have already been seen in Europe. It is a Revolution of doctrine and theoretical dogmas. It much more resembles revolutions which were made on religious foundations and for which the spirit of conversion was essential. The last theoretical and dogmatic revolution which happened in Europe was the Reformation. The effect of this Revolution *[was]* "to introduce other interests into all countries, than those which arose from their locality and natural circumstances." *[Tocqueville's notes generally quote Burke in the original English.—Trans.]* The principle of the Reformation was such that it could not be localized and confined within its region of origin. The principle of justification by faith and by works, for example, cannot be true or false depending on the country. The spirit of proselytism therefore spread in all regions with great elasticity, and great divisions were everywhere its result. Divisions which in appearance were purely dogmatic mixed with politics and became still more heated from the contact. For a long time Europe was divided into two great factions under the name of Catholic and Protestant, which divided not only nations, but the citizens within each state. In each state people drew closer "to those of their own doctrinal interest in some other countries than to their fellow citizens or to their natural government when they or either *[of them]* happened to be of different persuasions; these factions, if they did not absolutely destroy, at least weakened and distracted the locality of patriotism. The public affection came to have other motives or other ties . . ." If one looks closely, adds Burke, at the character and spirit of recent events, *[one sees]* that the same effect is now produced for political reasons . . . In the modern world, there has not yet been any example "of this spirit of general political faction, separated from religion, pervading several countries and forming a principle of union between the partisans in each." But the thing is nevertheless part of human nature. The ancient world furnishes a striking example that one can find in politics a reason for establishing factions of this kind as powerful and as dangerous as those which are born of religion. "The ancient factions in each commonwealth of Greece connected themselves with those of the same description in some other states." Secret plots, public alliances took place founded not on the conformity of great political interests, but to lead to the expansion "of the two leading states which headed the aristocratic and democratic factions." The Spartans were at the head of aristocratic opinion and the Athenians of democratic opinion, as in the time of the Reformation the King of Spain represented the Catholic interest and the King of Sweden the Protestant interest.

Commenting on the same pamphlet, p. 18, Tocqueville notes:

Definition of the dogma of the new political religion according to Burke: "that the majority told by the head in every country is the perpetual, natural, increasing, indefeasible sovereign; that this majority is perfectly master of the form as well as the government of the state, and that the magistrates, under whatever names they are called, are only functionaries to obey orders; that this is the only natural government; that all others are tyranny and usurpation." *[This passage is a paraphrase of Burke by Tocqueville.—Trans.]*

Tocqueville cites Burke's "Three Letters Addressed to a Member of the Present Parliament on the Proposals for Peace with the Regicide Directory of France," v. 8, p. 167: "this fanatical atheism left out, we omit the principal feature of the French Revolution." In his research notes Tocqueville comments: Above all it is this trait which turns all the spectators' ideas upside down, and throws so many minds into that sort of religious horror with which one would have examined a stray being from hell, if one had arrived in our world. A party which openly attacked all ideas of religion and the next world, and which, in this enervating doctrine, found the ardor of proselytes and even of martyrs, that previously religion alone seemed able to create! A sight at least as inconceivable as it was frightening. Capable of making the strongest minds lose their grip. Never forget the philosophical character of the French Revolution, its <u>chief</u> although <u>transitory</u> characteristic.

Page 100, line 30, after "religions"

On this point see the chapter of volume 2 of Democracy in America, "How in the United States Religion Knows How to Serve Democratic Interests." There Tocqueville relates the rapid diffusion of Catholic monotheism to the social and political state of the Roman Empire, which had made a large part of the human race "like an immense flock of sheep, under the scepter of the Caesars."

Page 100, line 34, after "race"

In his Rubbish file Tocqueville next sketches a commentary on Islam and on the Reformation as types of Christian universalism, and then interrupts himself. A remark in the margin explains this interruption: The idea goes off track. It must be focused on the general character, the common method of religious revolutions, and not be deflected into particular religious revolutions. Which has the double disadvantage: 1. First of all losing from sight the substance of the thought and 2. To encourage dangerous comparisons between Christianity and the Revolution.

Page 101, line 6, after "places"

Compare the English Revolution to ours. In both places indeed one ends up with the principle [and] practice of the sovereignty of the people. But in England each citizen demanded the right to participate in government by virtue of the country's old institutions and national tradition. Liberty was not a right of man but a particular privilege of the Englishman, his "birthright," as one said. The principle of the sovereignty of the people thus enclosed and hidden within the British Constitution was not exposed outside the British Isles. In France, equal power for each citizen was demanded not as a particular privilege possessed by Frenchmen, but by virtue of a general right which belonged to the species, and which every man brought with him at birth. Thus explained and highlighted the dogma of the sovereignty of the people immediately left France and spread throughout the world. *—Crossed out, Rubbish.* Ampère suggested this cut

13 December 1854, the piece not containing any new ideas. —*Rubbish, last reviewed 1856; the MS. does not bear any trace of this continuation.*

Page 102, after chapter title

How all Europe had had the same institutions and these institutions were everywhere in decay in the eighteenth century. —*Rubbish. Last Reviewed 1856. On a separate sheet from the Rubbish:* Critique by Ampère. Too general. Some medieval institutions of Roman origin even in Germanic countries. The towns above all. Perhaps thus more different among themselves than I say. The criticisms only correct with regard to this first part of the chapter. The viewpoint good. Only perhaps there is more to particularize in speaking purely of central Europe or if, which would be desirable, I keep to the general point of view, not going into so much detail.

Page 102, line 16, after "themselves"

Studying them one quickly realizes that they are adapted to a society different from ours rather than to a barbarous society. *Circled marginal addition, MS.*

Page 102, line 19, after "society"

No legislation had ever penetrated more deeply into all the customs, all the ideas, all the interests of the men who were subject to it, nor was better mixed into all that it effected. In truth there was almost no act of human life that it did not more or less control. —*Circled, MS.*

Page 103, line 37, after "enlightenment"

Tocqueville in fact here relies on the judgment of Edmé de Freminville, who compared the terriers of the fifteenth and sixteenth centuries with those of the seventeenth century in his work La pratique universelle pour la renovation des terriers et des droits seigneuriaux, Paris, 1746–1757. *In his notes Tocqueville comments:* Nothing shows better the institution's decadence than such work becoming worse at the same time as society is improving.

Page 104, line 31

Citation from Stramberg in Ludwig Haüsser, Deutsche Geschichte vom Tode Friedrichs der Grossen bis zur Gründung des deutschen Bundes, *4 vols., 1854–57, v. 1, p. 132. In Tocqueville's notes the quotation is followed by this commentary:* Is it not strange to find again in Germany and in the ecclesiastical states all the precursor signs of the French Revolution: disquiet and vague discontent, hatred of the past, better and more innovative rulers than formerly. What could better demonstrate the generality and the irresistibility of this revolution?

Tocqueville took abundant notes, dated July 1854, on chapters 4–6 of book one of Haüsser's work relative to the social and political situation of Prussia. Haüsser

(1818–1867), professor at Heidelberg from 1840 until his death, disciple of Schlösser, and an important figure in German historiography, was a virulently anti-Catholic and anti-French Prussian patriot.

Page 105, line 17

On the evolution of the feudal system in England, and the effects of the revolution of 1640, Tocqueville used volume 5 of Thomas Macaulay's <u>History of England</u> (1849–1861). He later returns, on pp. 152–53, to the opposition between the English aristocracy and the noble caste in France. Tocqueville asked Macaulay a series of questions on the difference between the aristocracies of France and England by the intermediary of his friend Nassau Senior. See their 1854 correspondence, OC, v. 6, t. 2, pp. 160–63.

Page 105, chapter title

The expression summarizes Tocqueville's notes on Burke's second pamphlet against the Revolution, "Letter to a Member of the National Assembly," 1791, <u>Works</u>, v. 6, p. 83.

Page 105, chapter title

What was the real object of the Revolution? What was its own work? Conclusion of the four preceding chapters. —*Title in the Rubbish, last reviewed 1856.*

Page 106, line 23

Tocqueville interpreted the revolution of 1848 and notably the attacks of the socialists against property as the continuation of the French Revolution. See his <u>Recollections:</u> And here is the French Revolution starting again, for it is always the same. (OC, v. 12, p. 87.)

Page 107, line 3, after "Europe"

Paraphrase of Burke, <u>Reflections on the Revolution in France</u>, v. 5, p. 83.

Page 107, line 4, after "law of Europe"

He touches the event and does not see it. And elsewhere: is it not, he says, absolutely incomprehensible that the clergy's fortune, which persisted over the course of so many centuries and resisted the shock of so many events, is taken, and why? To pay the recent and disrespectable debts that a discredited and overthrown government had contracted.

Burke does not see that the whole spirit of the Revolution reveals itself here. These goods which were violently seized were like plunder from the old world, debris from the old feudal edifice that had been overthrown; that recent and disrespectable debt that one wanted to repay was the result of an ordinary contract. One violated an exceptional and privileged property, one respected an obligation of common law. This seems extraordinary and unnatural to Burke, he doesn't understand anything about what is going on because he is not at the correct point of view for observation. *Circled, then crossed out.*

Page 112, line 9
   Note in the margin in the Rubbish: Check this point exactly in Delisle's work.

Page 112, line 9, after "in Normandy"
   Serfdom had also been abolished in England. But here is an aspect of the condition of the people which is absolutely peculiar to France. *Circled marginal addition.*

Page 112, line 17, after "evidence"
   We can affirm that it liberated, at least for a moment, the soil, but we should not say that it was the Revolution which divided it. *Circled marginal note.*

Page 112, line 22, after "land"
   Oeuvres de M. Turgot, edited by Dupont de Nemours (1808–1811), v. 7, "Report to the King on Local Government," p. 407.

Page 112, line 24
   Oeuvres complètes de Necker, 1820, v. 9, De la Révolution française (1796), p. 90.

Page 112, line 28
   Under the Second Empire (1852–1870), there was concern about the overdivision of landownership, which endangered the profitability of farming and risked the impoverishment of the agricultural population.

Page 112, line 29, after "succeeded"
   Tocqueville's notes on feudal dues contain an analysis of the decrees of 4–11 August 1789; 15–28 March, 3–9 May, and 18–29 December 1790; 28 August 1791; 25–28 August 1792; and 7–18 July 1793, on the abolition of feudal dues. The file then contains a study of two sectional reports of 1791 from the commune of Sainte Geneviève, near the chateau of Tocqueville. Tocqueville tried to establish the distribution of land among the proprietors there and agricultural income in comparison with the situation in the 1850s, and completed this inquiry by questioning the mayor, "a simple and confident soul," on the purchase of the emigrés' lands. He also studied the tax rolls of the communes of Fermanville (1791), Vrasville, Angoville, St.-Pierre Eglise (April 1793), and Réville (1791), of which he consulted the mayor, Count Duparc, on the change in the number of landowners between 1789 and 1852, and the sale of the emigrés' lands. Tocqueville also went through the registers of transcripts of the sale of the lands of the emigrés, established in 1824, which had been given to

him by the director of the registry office of St.-Pierre Eglise and which included all
sales from Year 2 and Year 3 (September 1792 to September 1794).

Page 113, line 7, after "them"

I wanted to find for myself, in the parts of France where a similar study was possible for me, traces of the fact so remarked on by Young. I questioned old farmers and tried to reconstruct with them the old land map of their villages. It will be for those more knowledgeable than I to say what brought about such an odd state of things. I limit myself to stating the fact and I will often have to describe its consequences. —*Rubbish. Crossed-out marginal addition:* At least I have seen that Young was right. A document finally unquestionably establishes the truth of the traveler's assertions, and substitutes certainty for probability in this matter: this is the list of taxpayers drawn up in all parishes, by virtue of a law of the Constituent Assembly (put in a note the exact date of the law). *Marginal note:* which created direct taxation. The lists, drawn up by the inhabitants themselves, had to state the number of landowners the parish contained, and often the extent and nature of the properties they possessed. I have reason to believe that this list has almost always disappeared in consequence of the disorganization of rural mayors, but in several places I have found it and there I have noted several pictures like the following: here introduce the text of the most striking notes. From all this information I can conclude that the chief effect of the Revolution with respect to property was to divide the property of the nobles and the Church among people who for the most part already possessed more or less large portions of the land, and that properties changed hands rather than the Revolution increasing the number of proprietors. I conclude from this, finally, with assurance, that the passion for property —*Rubbish.*

Page 113, line 9

Arthur Young, Voyages en France pendant les années 1787–88–89 et 90, 2d ed., Buisson, 1794—Year 2, v. 3, chap. 12, "Size and Tenure of French Farms." Tocqueville does not quote, but he summarizes Young's comparative study of the size of farms in France and England.

Page 113, line 11, after "frequently"

Tocqueville's information on property in England was drawn from the article by Léonce de Lavergne, "L'Economie rurale en Angleterre," Revue des deux mondes, 15 March 1853.

Page 114, line 10

Tocqueville himself being unable to answer this question in 1852–53 created a method of sifting the archives by analogy with the present. See his research notes (Folder K): The best way of seeing what was happening in the countryside thus seemed to me not to look at what in theory were the rules and organs of municipal administration then, but to take one by one all that today constitutes the chief acts of that administration and to see what existed then for each of these acts.

Page 115, line 7, before "Indeed"
In the pays d'état themselves, that is to say in the small number of provinces which had kept the right to tax themselves and even to dispose of part of their revenues for their own use, the nobility were part of the Estates, but the nobles no longer governed the countryside, its affairs being as foreign to the lord as they could be in provinces that had not retained any privileges. —*Rubbish.*

Page 115, line 13, after "income"
One may be astonished that the kings, who had taken away the nobles' political rights and deprived them of their power to govern, allowed private courts to persist, one of the institutions of feudal law most contrary to general ideas of justice, to the interests of the litigants, and the good of society. This is explained, if one remembers that of all the secondary powers, that which least harms the government is the judicial power, above all when it is exercised only at the lowest level. It is the essence of the judicial power to concern itself only with particular cases. It doesn't give the one who exercises it any general influence on the conduct of affairs, nor a habitual hold on the minds of men. —*In the margin of a first draft in the Rubbish.*

Here in the Rubbish there is a discussion about exemptions and honorific privileges, in the margin of which Tocqueville writes: The hard thing here is: 1) The difficulty of being brief and at the same time sufficiently precise, clear and striking. 2) To avoid becoming boring, because the subject is well known, or is thought to be. Draw the picture, then afterwards get rid of it or shorten it, depending on the effect obtained. Perhaps put it all in a note. *The MS. nevertheless includes a long discussion of feudal dues, replaced in the final text by the paragraphs from "I don't wish to speak" to "the farmer." At the end of this continuation Tocqueville notes in the margin:* Perhaps eliminate all this in order to stick to the main idea: all this is less than in the rest of the continent and yet more hated.

Page 115, last line, after "buy out"
See Tocqueville's research notes (Folder E) on the Mémoire sur l'état des classes agricoles depuis le XII siècle jusqu'à 1789, presented by Dareste de la Chavanne to the Academy of Moral Sciences for the Prize of 1853:

Redemption of Feudal Dues
The ability to redeem feudal dues was never accorded under the old regime, although often demanded.
This was, however, the most orderly and gentle means of transforming the old society into the new. But royal authority would not have gained anything directly

from it, and as a general rule, one can say that in France royal power had only taken from feudalism that which hindered its exercise. The nobles themselves, freely assembled, would have done more and better.

Page 116, line 24, after *"land"*

The expression "servitude of the land" was inspired by reading Boncerf, Les inconvénients des droits féodaux, London, 1776, pp. 13–14, which made the parallel between the abolition of serfdom, already effected, and the freedom of inheritance, which remained to be accomplished. In his notes Tocqueville underlines Boncerf's "already revolutionary fury": Servitude of the land identified with that of men: this absurd idea (which furthermore reigned in all minds during the revolution, and dominated the authors of the law code to the point of restricting landowners' freedom in a thousand ways in order to preserve the freedom of inheritances), this idea, I say, is already axiomatic here: assuredly, there were excesses in the charges imposed on the base; but on the other hand there is extreme exaggeration in the appreciation of the evils which flowed from it. England is clear proof of this.

Page 116, line 28

On the difference between England and France on this point see Tocqueville's notes on Blackstone. [To be included in volume 2 of this translation.—Trans.]

Page 116, line 33

In his notes (Folder E) on Dareste de la Chavanne's report Tocqueville returns several times to the increasing displacement of the taxes. The general purpose of the lord's taille was to provide for local public interests, for local administration; it was, insofar as one can use the same word to apply to such different social conditions, what we today call the "centimes additionels" *[local property taxes.—Trans.],* alongside the royal taille, the tax raised for general purposes. When the lords became virtual strangers to local government, they nevertheless continued to receive more or less large portions of the lord's taille. This at least seems to be the case. It was as if the local property taxes of today, instead of serving to make roads, bridges, schools, and churches, became a salary for the prefects, the sub-prefects, and the mayors. Even if the local taxes were much lower and the income thus created very small, its burden would nevertheless seem a thousand times more unbearable than a much heavier tax spent for public interests.

And the same with respect to the tolls: See the transformation of all things at the expense of the lower classes, and even the blows aimed at the nobility turned against them. Originally the lord received the payment. But he was required to keep up and oversee the road. In the eighteenth century, the fee is still in part collected, and not only is the lord no longer charged with all these things but, by a strange turn of events, he is exempt from taking part in road-building, which falls entirely at the lower classes' expense.

The notes on feudal dues (Folder A) summarize Tocqueville's idea: The whole feudal hierarchy destroyed from above at the time of the Revolution, on top nobles who no longer had any duties nor in truth any rights with respect to one another; preserved below the nobility: not hierarchy, but subjection.

Page 117, next-to-last line

This description of peasant mentality was to become famous. Jaurès notably was inspired by it in 1900 in the chapter dedicated to the causes of the Revolution in his Histoire socialiste de la Révolution française.

Page 118, line 4

On the peasants' hatred growing with the weakening of feudalism see the notes on feudal dues (Folder A): One must not conclude from the fact that a people does not complain about something which they think inevitable, and does not even seem to bear it with impatience, that they do not feel it. Men become impatient of an evil not only in proportion to its size, but still more perhaps in proportion to the possibility that they see of removing it. It is only when one presents people with the hope of getting rid of an evil, and sees how they react to it, that one can get an idea of the weight that they bore.

It is in seeing the peasants run from everywhere against the chateaus and the lords in 1789 that I judge what the peasants suffered from feudal dues in 1788.

I see before my eyes a unique phenomenon: impatient and excited minds, insatiable for freedom, who find themselves constrained by a prudent constitution. A little annoyance overexcites them, great annoyance calms them. I use this word on purpose. They are not only submissive; they are calm. How different I am! A limited freedom is enough for me, and I accept without difficulty great authority under the rule of kings. Complete restriction exasperates me, and despotism gives me revolutionary feelings. A little freedom inflames the spirit of liberty to fury. A despotism which seems solidly established extinguishes it.

Page 118, chapter title

At first Tocqueville had gathered in a single chapter two called "How Government Was More Centralized in France Than Anywhere Else" all of the chapters relating to centralization (chapters 2–5). The chapter two of the final text constituted the first section, which Tocqueville titled "How in Reality the Central Government Ran Everything. Bad title." Rubbish. The MS. bears the final title. The division into sections is maintained in the Copy, the final section beginning after a preamble ("He who considers" to "never before seen in the world").

Page 118, line 7, after "envies us"

The praise of centralization was widespread under the July Monarchy. It is found in Guizot, Thiers, and specialized writers on administrative law like Cormenin, who published a pamphlet, "De la centralisation," in 1842. In parliament, as in his articles in Le Commerce, *Tocqueville denounced government centralization in France. See* OC, v. 3, t. 2, pp. 129–32.

Page 118, line 13, after "created"

In his research notes (Folder F) on old French law Tocqueville dated very precisely, from the edict of April 1683 regulating local communities' debts, "the first establishment of bureaucratic paternalism": This edict was very remarkable. It was the point of departure for centralization. Or rather, centralization was already there in its entirety. The administration of all details was given to the intendants and the Royal Council. We see clearly the character of all government proceedings in France. Municipal freedom was badly established, it gave rise to many abuses; rather than improving and regulating it, it was eliminated.

We see the intendant already become the master of everything, as he still was a century later. The powers delegated to him were even greater, he was less obliged than he would be in the eighteenth century to refer to the Royal Council. It is centralization's first youth. In the beginning all business is concentrated in the hands of the central authority's local representative, then the science of government and general civilization improve, all affairs are attracted into the hands of the central power itself and end up in its offices.

Page 119, line 19

On the Royal Council Tocqueville made notes from the Répertoire universel et raisonné de jurisprudence *of Pierre Guyot, edition of 1784–85, v. 4, and from the* Répertoire universel et raisonné de jurisprudence *of Merlin, 4th ed., 1812–25, article "Royal Council." In August 1854 he also extracted from the* Recueil général des anciennes lois françaises *the various texts concerning the Council. On this question see* Michel Antoine, Le Conseil du Roi sous Louis XV, *Paris, 1970; Roland Mousnier,* Le Conseil du Roi, de la mort d'Henri IV au gouvernement personnel de Louis XIV, *1947, republished in* La plume, la faucille et le marteau, *Paris, 1970, pp. 141–78.*

Page 119, line 32

See the notes taken on Isambert's Recueil des anciennes lois, *v. 23, p. 121. Tocqueville quotes the Remonstrances of 30 December 1774, which remind the King that "the men of the Council by their office are only called on to give simple advice, and cannot, by virtue of their position, have real and effective votes." Tocqueville comments:* We see clearly from this that the Council of State, even when it judged, whether administrative questions or real trials, did not render real verdicts; it was the King who was considered to judge, with the advice of his councilors. Which shows that the same principle established by Napoleon for the modern Council of State, and so beloved by the administrative legalists, is nothing but the principle of the old regime, the prerevolutionary institution carried on afterwards.

Page 120, line 26

A page of the Rubbish bears a crossed-out first draft of this piece on the intendant:
Government action was still more centralized in the provinces than at Paris. We
know that the whole kingdom was divided into 30 parts, called generalities. At
the center of each one of them was the intendant, or, to speak the official language
of the times, the commissioner on dispatch (put a note to indicate what precisely
a commissioner on dispatch was). —*Marginal note.* Certainly there was a great
lord who bore the title of governor of the province, this was the old representative
of the feudal monarchy, but this was no longer anything but an empty title without any function. *Later marginal addition:* He was not merely charged with a
task; he was par excellence, like the prefect of our times, the sole representative
[*"sole"—circled*] of the state. Above him there was only the government, and he
corresponded with each of the ministers. Below him were the various agents of
the bureaucracy of which he was the sole center in the generality. No council,
either appointed or elected, supervised his actions. He owed an account of them
only to the minister and the Royal Council. We are going to see that he exercised
most of the functions of our prefects and in addition several others that the prefects don't have. Let us not forget his irremovability, the mobility of his career,
his desire to advance, his being a stranger to the province. Crucial. *Remark in the
margin of the preceding sentence:* He was always a stranger to the province and
was never there except in passing, he always wanted to be someplace different
and better. *Later marginal note without reference to the text:* was further divided
into a certain number of districts and in each of them was placed a subdelegate.
At the top of the page, circled: All this is jargon. But how to avoid jargon when
one speaks bureaucratic language? See however if the same things can't be said
in French.

Page 120, line 39

*Mémoires du marquis d'Argenson, ministre sous Louis XV, Paris, 1825, p. 180.
The quotation here is cut up. The phrase attributed to Law is: "You have neither
parlement, nor committees, nor estates, nor governors, I would add almost neither
king nor ministers." In his notes (Folder J) Tocqueville comments:* This influence of
the intendants and of the whole system of which they were a part exercised a dominant influence, in my view, on the destiny of France, and it has remained unseen
in history chiefly because 1: the intendants, although very powerful, barely belonged to the aristocracy and made a very small show in the aristocratic hierarchy
(I saw the traces of these impressions in my childhood) 2: their power was only
directly exercised on the lower classes, which was not noticed until the day the
people made everyone tremble.

Page 121, line 35

*The royal taille, at first an exceptional tax, became a permanent and annual
tax in 1439. In principle the Treasurer of France and the Directors-General of the*

Finances, after having received each year from the Royal Council the total for the taille, presided at the division of the taille among the parishes by the Delegates. But after the declaration of 16 April 1643, they worked under the intendant's authority.

Page 121, line 39

For the Capitation, a head tax created 18 January 1695, it was the intendant who set the tax rolls according to the schedule established by the Council, and by virtue of his appreciation of the taxpayers' financial capacity.

Page 122, line 10, after "government"

The militia had been instituted on 29 November 1688 to guard certain places. It was the intendant who was responsible for their equipment, their maintenance, and raising the special taxes necessary for them.

Page 122, line 39

A first design bureau had been created in February 1744 at Paris. But it was the Council's edict of 14 February 1744 which unified the administration of the construction and repair of roads and bridges in the entire kingdom and organized the education of the designers. The school thus created took in 1775 the official title of Ecole des ponts et chaussées. The personnel educated by this school were hierarchized, subject to strict rules, and although the engineers of the roads and bridges were by law commissioners, in practice their status was similar to that of modern bureaucrats.

Page 123, line 30

See below. In July 1854 Tocqueville had taken notes on the Allgemeines Landrecht, issued in 1795.

Page 124, line 1, after "people"

A circled sketch in the Rubbish on the powers of the intendant, briefer, ends with this remark, of which Tocqueville did not take account in his work: What makes this idea lack precision and correctness is that while strictly true for certain places and certain cases, it is exaggerated for certain others. Thus: 1) The courts and above all the parlements often intervened in these matters. 2) In the towns, the city council was the government's intermediary in these same matters. What I say was not strictly true except in the countryside. What I say there is half true, but also half false. This is what troubles me. What also troubles my mind is that it deflects from portraying centralization, which is my real object, and concentrates on portraying the intendant, who should only be an accessory to the chief portrait.

Page 124, end of chapter two

Notes on the arbitrary powers of the intendant.

In May 1855 Tocqueville took notes on the Mémoire concernant MM. les intendants fait par M. Daube, maître des requêtes (1738), at the National Library in Paris.

The author, René-François Richer, seigneur of Aube (1688–1752), was intendant of Caen (1723), then of Soissons (1727–1731). Recalled, he then retired to live with his relative Fontenelle. Of a difficult character, he had reforming views which alienated the privileged. The Marquis d'Argenson described him as follows: "He is an obstinate and stiff-necked man, very honest, and with other virtues of character . . . he was no use at all as intendant of Caen, because he immediately made himself disliked. He did not want to recognize that it was customary, until better times, that all those near the throne receive unjust favors . . . He wanted to change all the usual allocations of the arbitrary taxes, and above all the capitation tax. Those whom he helped did not thank him, thinking this was merely justice as usual, and those whose taxes he increased made such a loud outcry that the Throne and Court rang with their complaints. He was thought to be a bad intendant because he was too good. At Soissons he did almost the same thing." *Journal et mémoire du marquis d'Argenson, Paris, 1859, v. 1, pp. 80–81. The manuscript of the* Mémoire concernant MM. les intendants *remains at the National Library (Mss. fr. 21 812). Tocqueville comments thus in his notes:* The author of this report is evidently a capable man, one who loves justice, moderate, intelligent. He does much honor to the bureaucracy of the old regime. But he is already an administrator of our time, that is, one without the slightest idea of rights, of public opinion, of the participation of the locality. He considers the bureaucracy as being in sole charge of doing what the area needs, in spite of itself if necessary, without owing an account to anyone but its superiors.

Roads and Bridges. Ways. Rivers. Paths.

What is in general striking in this very interesting part of the report (pp. 244–417) is:

1) The absolute absence which seems to be revealed in the report of obligatory rules or laws in this question. The author, a man of good sense, just and humane, indicates the best rules to follow here in order not to take subjects' time or property unnecessarily, in order to sufficiently indemnify those whom one damaged in the name of public utility, how to recognize and describe a sufficient public need . . . But all this is advice which has nothing mandatory about it, which does not even show a general or accepted practice. In this matter the minister and the intendant seem to have absolutely no other limits than their own honesty and intelligence.

2) The absolute absence of even the most indirect local participation in all these operations, almost all of which are basically of local character. Public life is no longer even suspected or imagined in any form.

3) The absence of the idea of possible resistance in any form whatsoever, even complaints and murmurs. One speaks of reason, of justice, of utility, but of public opinion there is no more question than if one acted in a Santo Domingo sugar mill *[i.e., among slaves.—Trans.]*.

Corvée

The use of the corvée to build and maintain roads and to provide, along with the funds of the roads and bridges department, the means which the state wished to use, this use of the corvée was not a common or authorized fact at the time when the author writes (1738), but only a system which was being tried out.

General Remarks about the corvée on pp. 355 and following

About this I ought to note first of all that according to this report:

1) This enormous innovation was not made by virtue of any rule or general law at all.

2) The system was applied according to the intendants' whims, and they were of varying enthusiasm on the question of roads.

3) The author, despite his good intentions, does not even raise the question of whether it is just to burden only those who pay the taille with such a demand.

4) Finally, there is not even the trace of any objection or complaint whatsoever to be seen, raised by anyone, by parlements or writers. One sees only that when the system is attempted with too much rigor, the unfortunates on whom it works (in anima vili) *[the experimental animals—Trans.]* create tensions which require the police to be sent.

5) It is a question of work done for free and without compensation. p. 371.

Administrative Justice

The edict of March 1693 had made inspection, that is, the required registration for a fee of notarized documents in the public registers of the Court Clerks, obligatory. The copying of extracts of the documents into the public register was required by the edict of December 1703 and the declaration of 19 July 1704. Tocqueville quoted the following: "The old taxes, which the King had the tax-farmers collect, were created by laws whose execution, as well as that of their various later regulations, was under the jurisdiction of various kinds of courts, those of the district, of the salt-tax, the judges of commerce, which were responsible to the superior tribunals of the Tax-Court, the Court of Accounts and the Parlement. But taxes whose origin was more recent, such as those on alcoholic drinks, on property transfers, on legal documents, were subject to the jurisdiction of the intendants." p. 572. *Nonliteral quotation. In his notes Tocqueville commented thus in the margin:* Excellent passage to show how the power and jurisdiction of the intendant increased with new things, and how arbitrary authority extended itself little by little in place of old rights and old freedoms. In the beginning, courts; now an independent and irresponsible bureaucrat.

The Intendant's Extraordinary Arbitrary Authority. The Dependence on Him Which This Created

Tocqueville summarized here pp. 594–97 of the manuscript. For d'Aube, "in general it is from the accurate computation of everyone's income and expenses that

decisions should be made about whether he should pay the king more or less in capitation tax." The insistence on the understanding of individual cases is central in d'Aube's report, which argues for educating young intendants by means of internships, where they would learn to understand the national mind and character, and the art of getting along with people. Tocqueville commented: The capitation tax on the nobility was in part personal, in part real. This comes out strongly from the rules stated by the author on pp. 594 and following. The amount of the tax is not to be based solely on income. There are regions where the cost of living is higher than others. He who lives in the country is richer than he who lives in the town. At the same level of income the married man is less wealthy than the bachelor. The father of a family is less wealthy than he who has no children. The age of the children should be considered. Very noble birth imposes expenses that ordinary birth does not impose. The nobleman who has acquired the habit of being overly frugal, which makes him live less honorably than he could and ought, should be taxed to the utmost. p. 596: "What I have just said gives a sufficient idea of the many different respects in which every intendant ought to know his district's nobility."

Page 124, line 12, after "products"
The example is taken from a file titled "letters of the Controller-General to the Intendant, 1781–82, 1783, Tours archives": A nursery of mulberry trees established at La Flèche: this reminds me of Algeria. The government does not do what is useful and does what isn't necessary.

Page 124, line 21
Tocqueville gives several examples of this in his research notes on the Recueil général des anciennes lois françaises. Thus: Manner of encouraging trade. Declaration of 25 September 1694 (v. 20, p. 227). "Aware of the damage which the spreading custom of wearing buttons of the same cloth as the clothing does, instead of silk buttons which was very useful to the silk manufacturers, forbids tailors, under pain of a fine of 500 livres, to put cloth buttons on clothing (note that they were cheaper) and forbids anyone to wear such under penalty of a 300 livres fine of which half should go to the accuser."

Page 124, chapter title
In the Rubbish and the MS. this chapter constituted section 2 of the projected long chapter two on centralization. Two files of extracts from notes in the Rubbish allow us to identify the documents used in this chapter. They are headed: "Administration of Towns and Parishes. Extracts made from the chief notes relative to the matter (December 1854)" and "Parish Government (January 1855)."

Page 125, line 7

Edict of 27 August 1692 replacing elected mayors by hereditary mayors in return for payment in all the cities, with regard to which Tocqueville noted (Folder H): This is Louis XIV's first and greatest attack against municipal institutions. Raynouard (Histoire du droit municipal, v. 2, p. 355) and the authors of the present collection rightly remark that this measure had a purely financial and no political purpose and that the edict of 1692 had no other motivation than to force the towns to buy back their rights!

Page 125, line 19

In his research notes Tocqueville comments (Folder J): I do not know anything more miserable than this seventeenth-century municipal revolution. Everything in it is worthy of contempt: 1) The conduct of the king, which does not even have for excuse a mistaken political idea or an arbitrary passion, but which in changing, in permanently destroying municipal freedoms had regard only for financial expediency. 2) The conduct of the estates, which, while caring much for their own freedom, did not see that one of the roots of those freedoms was the maintenance of the popular spirit of the towns and which, after having bought back the towns' freedom, confiscated it for their own profit. 3) Finally the conduct of the populations (this is the most excusable of the three), which allowed themselves to be deprived of their freedoms with sorrow, but without resistance.

Page 125, line 26, after "years"

In the extracts of his notes conserved in the Rubbish Tocqueville made a list of the general laws relative to the sale of offices: THE SALE OF OFFICES: Laws on the towns which deprive them of their freedoms or make them clearly partial. Edict of July 1690, which begins to establish offices, Same of 1792 *[sic for 1692]*. Declaration of 19 August 1702. Same of 1704, which ends up making everything into an office. Same of 1706, which divides the offices into two, accords exaggerated powers to the mayor by office. Same of 1709, everything down to the town criers an office. Town valets. Same of 1714, authorizes the towns to purchase the offices. Same of 1717, reestablishes elections. Same of 1722, which reestablishes the offices. Same of 1724, which eliminates them. Same of 1733, which reestablishes them. Decree of the Royal Council of 1737, which provisionally reestablishes elections—between 1737 and 1764 there were certainly some measures which reestablished offices since there is an edict of 1764 which reestablishes elections and eliminates all offices. Edict of 1764, on the government of towns. Destroys all offices (crucial). Edict of 1771, which reestablishes offices, still in force at the Revolution. Independently of the edicts the towns' constitutions were often individually changed by decrees of the Council.

Page 125, line 32, after "them"
Nonliteral quotation from the preamble to the edict creating and reestablishing some municipal and other offices, Versailles, 1 August 1722.

Page 125, line 38, after "officeholders"
Letter of the intendant to the minister sending him a project of letters patent for the new constitution of Angers, 1764, Tours archives.

Page 126, line 8, after "town"
Before applying the edicts of August 1764 and May 1765 on municipal reform, the Controller-General, Laverdy, had asked the intendants to lead a major inquiry into the functioning of municipal institutions among all the city councils. In November 1853 Tocqueville studied the results of this inquiry for the Generality of Tours.

Page 128, line 2
Report presented by the officials of the Presidial Court of Le Mans in 1764 (Tours archives). The inhabitants' astonishment derived from a decree of the Council of 22 January 1757, which modified the municipal constitution of Le Mans in favor of the privileged, authorizing the mayor and the town councilors to name six or eight of the leading citizens for important business rather than convoking an assembly of notables. In November 1853 Tocqueville took notes (Folder H) on this report in the archives of Tours and comments thus on the 1757 decree: This example is good to keep to show with what disregard local freedoms and town constitutions were treated. We see that this decree was not brought about by any request, preceded by any inquiry, subject to any opposition, it was the result of an arbitrary wish of the intendant and the Council.

Page 128, line 7
I need to look at the edict of August 1764 again. It is there that all the rules of paternalism are legally set. —*In the margin of the MS., circled.*

Page 128, line 9, after "them"
There are hardly any absolute rules during the old regime. Diversity is its character. But here one departs from character. There are no exceptions to the rule. It is applied without distinction to all towns and in each town to all its business. Louis XIV established it. His successor extended it. —*Circled marginal note, MS.*

Page 128, line 18
Letter from Laverdy, 22 August 1764, to the intendant Lescalopier, Tours archives.

Page 128, line 26
See the notes on the file labeled "town militia" (Tours archives): Required Joy from the Town Militia. Ordinance of the intendant of Tours (1759), which con-

demns to a 20-livres fine, which must be paid under penalty of imprisonment, the tanners of Loudun who had been missing from the company in which they were ordered to bear arms at the occasion of the Te Deum for a victory of His Majesty.

Page 128, line 31
Letter from the Mayor and town-councilors of Loches, 1747, to the intendant. Tours archives, in Tocqueville's file "Town militia, municipal offices."

Page 128, line 32
Correspondence of the municipal officials of Beauvais with the intendant Berthier, 1780, from Tocqueville's notes (Folder I) on the files of the former Generality of Paris.

Page 129, line 6
In his notes (Folder E) on Dareste de la Chavanne Tocqueville is nevertheless less enthusiastic about the medieval commune. <u>Agricultural community of the Middle Ages</u> which must not be confused with the administrative community of the parish in later centuries.

These were associations among commoners (whether subject to main-mort or freed) to cultivate in common the land ceded to them by the lord. These associates lived together, the master they named divided the work, divided the profits. It was a kind of phalanstery as the name given by Beaumanoir (v. 1, p. 305) indicates: "compani" people who live from the same bread, pp. 51 and following.

Nothing shows better how the dreams of the socialists belong to the infancy and not to the maturity of society. The agricultural communities of the Middle Ages (very similar to what is still seen today in the Russian countryside) lose themselves in the night of time; they are preserved longest in the most backward provinces, in regions where serfdom is customary and freedom has most difficulty in being established. They disappear as property and acquired freedom make people feel the desire for individual life and independence. *Tocqueville sees a residue of them in the collective obligation to pay the* <u>cens</u> *which Turgot complained of in the Limousin.*

Page 129, line 9, after "laws"
In the margin of this paragraph a circled note: Consult Delisle on all this. —*MS.*

Page 129, line 16, after "America"
On the American township see <u>Democracy in America</u> *(1835), v. 1, part 1, chap. 5.*

Page 129, line 29
This parallel between France and the American township is the subject of a variant on separate pages in the Rubbish: How one finds disfigured traits of the <u>English Parish</u> and the American Township in the Parish of the Old Regime (August 1853).

When one closely and carefully examines the old-regime parish, one is aston-ished to find in it, among the degraded marks of servitude, a family resemblance to the English parish and the American township. In France as in England and America, the representative system proper was not found in the town. The parish had certain officials elected by it, it did not have a town council. It was the com-munity as a whole, all the inhabitants, which was in charge of all important com-mon business and said how community properties would be administered, if they would be sold or rented, if there were borrowings to make, lawsuits to start or defend, public works to be undertaken. It was the community as a whole which received the accounts of the agents charged with administering its finances and which audited them.

One finds traces of all these old rights in the debris which remain. The Ameri-can township never had more. See now what becomes of this semirepublican con-stitution under the practice of our last kings. Instead of these 22 officials of the American township, each one of whom was concerned with only a single kind of business, and who by their large number attest to the variety and power of municipal existence, in the French township you will find only 2 administrative agents, at most 3. The Syndic, who is a kind of general agent, the Collector of the Taille, and sometimes the Treasurer of the Municipal Funds. In many provinces, these officials were no longer elected; in all, they could be removed at the inten-dant's pleasure and replaced, for an indefinite period, by administrators of his choice. Everywhere, furthermore, these town officials were charged with duties so repulsive, held so low by the authorities, and so low in public opinion itself, that when in 1788 Louis XVI at the request of the Notables reestablished rural townships, the leading inhabitants of the parishes declared that they would not undertake their administration, at least if the job of Syndic was not elevated and the name changed.

The inhabitants still assembled, as in old times, at the church door at the sound of the bell, but they could only do so when the subdelegate or the intendant had authorized them. This assembly had become a sort of open-air inquiry made by a notary, who received the testimony of a certain number of inhabitants and drew up a report of the hearing in legal style. In these assemblies the parish's important business was still discussed. But there was no longer any decision to make. People were only there to give advice. The community could no longer either borrow or sell, or plan the communal works according to its wishes, or sue, or in the end give any sign of life whatsoever, except upon the request and with the permission of the intendant. The community was still allowed to have wishes, but not pow-ers. When it was allowed to tax itself and to execute public works at its own ex-pense, it was the intendant who made the plans, it was before his subdelegate that the contract was made, it was he who prescribed the way in which the tax would be raised and most often named the commissioners to collect it. This is what had become of the old French parish in the eighteenth century, but even in these empty, lying appeals to public opinion on important questions, this representation itself described the old reality. Parish freedom had ceased to be, but its trace was found in the particular way in which it was smothered.

In a later draft in the Rubbish this parallel is put at the end of the description of parish life and ends the chapter: Here I find an exceptional perspective. The old French parish does not resemble at all the township of our own day. The only object of comparison which presents itself is in America. I see some analogy between the constitutions of this miserable and inert community and the constitution of the so active and so prosperous New England township. I will say at length where this resemblance comes from, but my subject takes me elsewhere. *Circled:* In France, as in America, the principle of representation and that of hierarchy are not accepted in the rural community. There the community of inhabitants names a certain number of public officials, who are not at all subordinate to each other and who only execute decisions under their control in their own departments. In America, it is true, everything is alive, and in France everything was dead. But nevertheless it is easy to find in the corpse the form and relationship of the organs which it used in life. This is interesting and sad.

Page 130, line 18, after "passive"
  Oeuvres, Turgot, v. 7, "Report on Local Government," p. 400.

Page 130, line 36, after "oppression"
  Tocqueville's clairvoyance is here sharpened by the experience of the Second Empire. See his research notes (Folder K): How democratic forms can be the cloak of arbitrary government. One could highlight this truth (if it was necessary to highlight it more than by what we see) through the parishes of the old regime, where the most democratic forms were united with the most absolute absence of local freedom, with the most complete bureaucratic arbitrariness, and were only put before them as a screen. What seems new to us is an old practice.

Page 132, chapter title
  Together with chapter five this chapter was section three of the large version of chapter two, devoted to centralization. The first version of it, finished in January 1855, was titled: How administrative law and what in our time is usually called official immunity were institutions of the old regime and were then found only in France. *—Rubbish. The MS. and the Copy furthermore do not diverge from the text of chapters four and five of the final version.*

Page 132, line 27
  Perhaps a decree of the Council of 28 January 1780.

Page 133, line 19
  Tocqueville here uses notes (Folder H) on a suit brought against a manufacturer of Tours who violated the regulations, by his rivals, 1778:

Evocation, administrative law

The master of the guild of silkmakers at Tours seized in a manufacturer's workshop various fabrics which were not made according to regulation. The judge convicted the manufacturer. The condemned manufacturer asked that the affair be evoked by the Royal Council. The intendant, consulted by the Controller-General, gave the following reasons in favor of this solution: The judge is subject to rules which do not permit him to allow a workshop which breaks the regulations whose execution he is required to enforce. It is only the Council which can depart from the rules when it is a question of supporting useful establishments. The ministers wanted to have the intendant make an edict which provisionally ordered the lifting of the seizure of fabric, while awaiting the Council's decree, and the intendant responded: "I must tell you my incompetence is too clear here to risk rendering a decree which could be overturned by the parlement, which already happened to me in 1777. The Controller-General had authorized me to order a release of the same kind; the members of the community concerned appealed my edict to the parlement, where it was overturned. I sent the Royal Council news of this edict and never received any decision." We see that the parlement had first jurisdiction over everything which did not come directly from the Royal Council, which, on the contrary, had priority over the parlement.

It certainly must also be believed that it was not a question here of an action initiated by the public minister, but of a real trial brought by commercial competitors which was taken away from the ordinary judge, even though he was acting by virtue of regulations in force, the State not being interested in the slightest, except through the opinion that it was in the general interest that the regulations be broken.

The silk manufacturers, established at Tours by Louis XI in 1470, had been in trouble since the seventeenth century as a result of competition from Lyons, and were the object of intendant Du Cluzel's concern. See F. Dumas, La généralité de Tours au 18ème siècle, Paris, 1894, chap. 5.

Page 133, line 29

A letter from the intendant of Tours to the Controller of 15 May 1782, on the request by the Marquis de Harcourt for evocation of a case relating to the draining of a swamp. In his analysis of this file Tocqueville notes that the intendant in fact decided to let the courts judge the case.

Page 134, line 2

Tocqueville moved the manuscript of his first work on administrative law, the report made 19 July 1845 to the Academy of Moral and Political Sciences on Macarel's Cours de droit administratif (OC, v. 16, pp. 185–98), to his notes. Administrative law was organized under the July Monarchy thanks to the work of three writers: Cormenin, with whom Tocqueville had very poor relations in 1848 in the constitutional committee; De Gérando, whom Tocqueville had known at the Academy of

Moral Sciences; and Macarel, whose influence was the greatest. Since his 1845 report Tocqueville had insisted on the false character of the "progress" represented by the separation of the judiciary from the administration, or more exactly, of ordinary justice and administrative courts subject to the sovereign's intervention.

Page 134, line 19

In October 1854 Tocqueville consulted the volumes relating to the reigns of Louis XIV, Louis XV, and Louis XVI in the Recueil général des anciennes lois françaises (research notes, Folder P) about the administrative activity of the parlements. But this collection did not allow him to determine the nature and extent of parlementary action: because one finds there only decrees of those regulations which attracted the particular attention of the various compilers, which does not give any fixed rule to the mind and does not permit the drawing of any certain conclusion.

Tocqueville nevertheless drew two conclusions from this study: On the administrative action of the judicial bodies: In general one can say that almost without exception the executive power of the parlement was exercised with respect to particular cases and particular places. This court, even in making administrative decrees, profoundly retained the judicial character, which is only to recognize and pronounce on particular cases. *On the overlapping of jurisdictions: different names and nature of the acts of government power:* We see successively appear in the collection of general laws of France edicts, royal declarations, decrees, letters patent, regulations, edicts of the Council. These are the diverse manifestations of the sovereign's will. But it would be very useful to distinguish them by somewhat characteristic traits and to know which had to be submitted to the courts for confirmation . . . in reality, I think that the question of knowing which were the administrative acts which had to be judicially registered was, like so many others, undecided and left in part at least to the decision of the executive power itself. *Tocqueville also left some equally brief notes on the Arrets de règlement, collected and arranged by Louis François de Jouy, Paris, 1752, relative to the Parlement of Paris.*

Page 134, line 23

Reference to article 75 of the Constitution of 22 Frimaire, Year VIII: "the agents of the government, other than the ministers, cannot be sued for acts relative to their duties, except by virtue of a decision of the Royal Council: in this case, the suit takes place before the ordinary courts." Tocqueville had denounced the irresponsibility of government agents, notably in a series of unsigned articles in the newspaper Le Commerce of 16, 17, and 27 February and 1 March 1845 to support a proposition of reform by Isambert, which failed amid general indifference. See OC, v. 3, t. 2, pp. 155–67. Article 75, theoretically repealed by the decree of 19 September 1870, in fact remains in force today.

Page 135, line 14

Extract from a file containing the correspondence of M. de Trudaine, director of Roads and Bridges, with the intendant of Tours from the 1760s until 1780. Tocqueville comments thus (research notes, Folder H): How much this resembles what the same bureaucrat would say in our day, and how little it resembles the way in which such things have always been understood in England. How far we are from those surveyors *["surveyors" in English in original.—Trans.]* of the English forest laws.

Page 135, line 20

Letter of the intendant of Tours to the minister, July 1783.

Page 135, line 21

1783.

Page 135, chapter title

In the Rubbish, this chapter constitutes chapter three of book two. The draft is titled: "On bureaucratic mores in the old regime or how they made the reestablishment of centralization easy. January 1855." The MS. bears the final title.

An isolated idea on a page from the Rubbish suggests a comparison between this chapter and the analyses of the paternalistic State found in volume 2 of Democracy in America: In our time of great civilization and softened mores, when one wants to get a correct idea of the kind of harm that absolute government can do to men, it is the procedures of the old regime's government, and the long-term effect that they produced, that must be studied: mild, good-natured, regular, pernicious. It was not by tyranny that the old regime degraded the character of the French, it was by paternalism.

Page 136, line 9

Let the reader not be in a hurry to conclude that I am keeping him too long immersed in the details of pre-Revolutionary public administration. From these little facts there will soon arise important consequences when we pass on to the Revolution itself. —*Circled. Tocqueville's hesitation is explained by a circled marginal note:* perhaps finish the section here, the rest could be seen as repetitive. Summarize. —*MS.*

On the same page of the MS., there is a circled continuation in the margin without reference to the text: I do not know any European country where things happened in this way then: administrative law and the guaranty of officials were never known to the English. They have only been introduced in part, and only in our time among the Germans—still to be carefully checked. In old-regime Germany the courts were not as separate from the government as in France, and the judges were not as completely independent of the government there, but nothing escaped from their jurisdiction. The administrative trial did not exist.

Page 137, line 13

In his research notes on the Recueil des anciennes lois françaises *Tocqueville notes this increase with reference to the edict of February 1763, which regulated those colleges which were not part of universities:* As we advance into the eighteenth century we suddenly see the political authority of the king weaken and become more and more limited, and his administrative power at the same time constantly extend itself and become more active and more able. This leads to another remark, that the administrative power also becomes more able, more active, more perfected, at a time when there is no longer a single great minister and when even the majority of the ministers are very mediocre men, thus developing as if by itself due to the effects of general causes. The progress of civilization, that of equality, of the innovating spirit of the times which penetrated everything and turned to everything, the growing impotence of the old secondary powers, the vitality proper to the new hierarchy which without creating a single eminent leader produced more and more experienced agents.

Tocqueville returns to this idea apropos of the conflict between the king and the parlement *in 1774:* I always come back to this idea: the political power of the king is more and more shaken as his administrative power broadens and penetrates. We see the Revolution and centralization approaching at the same time. Two effects which seem opposite and which are produced by the same cause.

The growth of government continues after the Revolution, as Tocqueville remarks in his notes on Necker's Compte Rendu au Roi *(OC, Necker, 1820, v. 2, pp. 98–99).* Function of the intendant or detached commissioners. In fact, the intendant exercised all administrative functions, even those which today are divided between the prefect and the General Council, and if his action was not concerned with so many objects and did not always go into so many details as the prefect's, that came from the state of civilization and the imperfection of administrative science, not from a division, a limit, or a moderation of powers.

Page 138, line 21

A Madame de C who called herself Lady de la Bourre de la Dubriel[?] and other places did not have, says the minister (1773), more than 3,000 livres of net income, but having a carriage at Paris with a negro asked the admission of her daughter to St. Cyr. The Comptroller-General wants to know about the financial state of this lady so rich at Paris and so poor in her domains. *—Marginal addition, circled.*

Page 138, line 23

Mémoires du marquis d'Argenson, *p. 173. The remark was inspired by the incompetence of M. de Maurepas, Navy Minister at the death of Cardinal Dubois in 1723.*

Page 138, last line

Edict of the Council of 29 March 1773, which orders that the upkeep of the buildings serving the administration of justice will be at the expense of the towns in which the courts or jurisdictions are established. Tocqueville here interprets the edict in a questionable manner: the Council judged the edict necessary insofar as operating expenses were paid by the Crown, and the Crown was arguing from a desire for simplification when it charged the towns with the upkeep of the buildings.

Page 139, line 2

The Copy includes a note relative to this discussion, crossed out in the First Galleys: An example of this nascent taste for bureaucratic statistics. In 1783, the intendant wanted to have information on the forests which existed in the different parishes of the Generality of the Ile de France, and addressed himself to his subdelegates to obtain it. The Subdelegate of St. Denis reported to him (15 October 1783) that he had sent a memo to all the syndics of the parish, that few had responded, and that all the responses were insufficient.

Page 139, line 2, after "bureaucrats"

Although it has passed into common usage to use the word "bureaucracy" to abstractly designate all those who administer, it is nevertheless modern jargon which one should try to avoid. *—Marginal note in the Rubbish. Tocqueville kept the word in the final text. [The translator has also frequently been compelled to use the word "bureaucracy" when translating Tocqueville's references to public administration.—Trans.] On the tendency to abstraction of democratic periods, see Democracy in America.*

Page 140, line 29

Circular of 11 August 1761 from the Duc de Choiseul, followed by a letter from the minister of 20 May 1762 and a new letter from the minister (this time the duc d'Aiguillon) of 31 October 1771. In his notes (Folder H) devoted to this affair Tocqueville comments thus on the circular of 11 August: We see that no mention is made of any matter which in any respect deals with public affairs . . . To the minister's letter were attached prospectuses from the Gazette in which we see that to effectively assure the success of the new business against its competitors, the authorities use as in our days means of which the competition cannot avail themselves.

Page 141, line 10

Under the reign of Isabella II (1833–68), measures were taken which tried to restrain the large estates but without making a real agrarian reform. More than an original political analysis, the comparison with Spain is the repetition of a commonplace of historical literature. Guizot had already compared French and Spanish absolutism. In the final text, Tocqueville enlarged his suggestion to the whole of Southern Europe, whose inertia he had deplored as early as his voyage to Sicily (1826–27). See Tocqueville's Oeuvres, Pléiade ed., v. 1, p. 156. He again reflected on the consequences of the inertia of the Italian despotisms during his stay at Sorrento in the Bay of Naples from November 1850 to April 1851. See his letter to Beaumont of 3 December 1850, OC, v. 8, t. 2, pp. 331–32: I can't find anywhere in the whole French language words which sufficiently express my pity and contempt for this miserable nation and, still more, for these miserable governments of Italy, which do not even know how to use the despotism that they adore; which only employ the country's resources to hire more soldiers, and their soldiers only to stupidly repress good passions as well as evil ones, legitimate interests just like disorders, and civilization like freedom.

Page 141, line 11, after "southern Europe"
   First version: these governments of the south. *—Corrected between the lines, MS.*

Page 141, line 27
   Report of the municipal officials of Angers, 1764.

Page 142, line 11
   Nonliteral quotation of a letter from the intendant regarding the request for exemption from sales taxes by the director of works on the bridge of Toure, example taken from notes (Folder F) on "ministerial correspondence," Tours archives.

Page 142, line 19
   Declaration of 16 April 1757. In his notes (Folder F) Tocqueville remarks: Nothing better characterizes the end of the old regime. Legislation that is harsh to the point of atrocity. Practice that is indulgent to the point of impotence, tending to despotism, ending up in anarchy. If there remained only this law from the reign of Louis XV, into what ridiculous mistakes would posterity be precipitated?

Page 143, line 12
   Mirabeau, <u>L'Ami des Hommes,</u> 1756–1758, v. 1, <u>Traité de la population</u>, pp. 44, 47.

Page 143, line 27
   Report of a large farmer from the Soissons region, without date, Tours archives.

Page 143, line 28
   In his notes Tocqueville concludes thus: Inspectors and medals. Assuredly a similar idea of how to make agriculture progress would never have come into an Englishman's head, and a society where one could conceive and express such ideas was very close to resembling our own. Note the word State. The abstract idea of social power. It is no longer the King; it is any government whatsoever.

Page 143, line 30, after "masses"
   Already signs are met of what the mass will do when the chains of tradition are broken. It doesn't riot, but the least arousal leads it immediately to violence.

The punishment inflicted on these obscure criminals is almost never violent but almost always arbitrary; in general exceptional courts decided the verdict and punished the delinquents with complete authority. The parlements usually remained strangers to this part of government. If we often encounter riots during the old regime, we hardly ever see any associations. The French sometimes assembled tumultuously to disturb the peace together, but they never came together peaceably for purposes of public interest. They had not only lost the habit of conducting their own affairs together, they had lost the desire to do so and almost the idea. Rather than destroying the spirit of association, the old regime infinitely fractioned it and thus reduced it to powerlessness. In the eighteenth century many commercial companies were seen, many literary associations were found, but when it came to associations whose purpose was to fill a public need or to concern themselves in common with a public matter, no one [wanted] to speak of it. Although the government was not yet in a position to provide for all public needs, individuals had already entirely lost the habit and even the very idea of helping themselves. Even in times of public disaster people didn't want to make any collective effort. It was for the king or the intendant to come to their aid. To maintain public order from day to day, they never imagined any other means but the mounted police. *Crossed out. The Rubbish gives a shorter later version of this continuation that is not crossed out.*

Page 143, line 31

After having cited the transcript of the assembly of upper Guyenne (research notes, Folder J), Tocqueville refers here to a file titled "Maréchausée" consulted at the archives of Tours, 17 September 1853, about which he remarks in his notes (Folder H):

Taste for the police

I find petitions from the inhabitants of small towns and villages which demand with loud cries the establishment of police units, absolutely like one would do in our days and for the same reasons. We find ourselves very far from the feeling of those English who preferred to be robbed than to see police stations established. Further on, 1784. Indirect request from the inhabitants of Mayenne for the establishment of a provost's court. Nothing more useful, they say, than quick trials, punishment that immediately follows the crime . . . there follow the claims of Mayenne to this lovely court (and these men wanted to be free! They were good for nothing but a change of despot).

Page 144, line 9

The quotations which follow are taken from Tocqueville's notes (Folder J) on the Tableau de l'Ancien Régime, 1796, manuscript possessed by L. D'Aunay, written by an emigré (M. de Galaisière, the grandfather of Madame d'Aunay, former intendant of Alsace, councilor of State, member of the Assembly of Notables, and secretary of one of the committees of that Assembly) in response to Calonne's book Tableau de l'Europe. At the beginning of these notes: Good to consult for the material on institutions, and to show what an abyss existed between the new society and the spirit of these representatives of the old society. Everything is perfect in the old regime and one could not reestablish anything in France but it alone. What is remarkable is less the hatred for free institutions than the impossibility of understanding them, of feeling their advantages, and the taste for absolute monarchy become a way of thinking which was natural and which one did not know how to get rid of. Not an accidental feeling, but a sort of mental temperament.

Page 144, line 18, after "need"
    Example: "The welfare state. A carter who lost a horse because of the collapse of a bridge begs the intendant to give him an indemnity!" *taken from Tocqueville's research notes (Folder H), from a file titled "ministerial correspondence." Another example, taken from a file titled "Intendance, ministerial letters 1766 to 1770":* The government the sole fountain of largesse. A doctor of Tours asks for a sum of money and gets it because he does his job well. 1766.

Page 145, line 3
    Claim against the vingtième tax by M. de Martigny, 1783, notes taken 5 July 1853, Folder H. The vingtième was a taxed based on income and paid by everyone except the clergy. The intendant was judge in the first instance of all disputes relative to this tax and powerful pressures on him were useful.

Page 145, line 6, after "him alone"
    The province then resembled —*Galley* a nest full of baby birds who cried to their mother for the beak. —*MS., Copy, Galley. In the margin, in the MS.:* perhaps eliminate all this? *In the margin in the Galleys in Tocqueville's handwriting:* keep this last metaphor? I doubt it. *In Beaumont's handwriting:* We also have some doubt.

Page 145, chapter title
    This chapter constitutes chapter four of book two in the Rubbish and the MS. In the Rubbish one finds mention of finishing the draft in January 1855.
    Tocqueville hesitated to devote a chapter to Paris, one of the title folders in the Rubbish shows: At first I had the idea of treating this subject as part of the continuation of centralization. But it is too important not to be a separate chapter. Paris is perhaps, after all, the most efficient cause of the Revolution. It is true that Paris was itself only an effect of the chief cause, which was centralization. It is therefore natural to speak of it only after discussing centralization; but it must be discussed in a separate chapter because the preponderance of Paris will be a subject to which I will have to return constantly throughout the course of the book.
    A page of remarks completes this thought:
    Omnipotence which Paris had already obtained. Subordination of the Prov-

inces. This chapter ought to be put here. It cannot and should not be long, but it is very important for explaining the Revolution, because one of the first causes of the subordination of the provinces and the preponderance of Paris was centralization in particular, and in general the government of the old regime, which had the effect of depriving all points on the circumference of public life in all forms, and concentrating it at Paris alone. Picture this gradual extinction not only of the political life of provincial towns, but of their social originality; arts, letters, education, intellect, wealth, taste . . . Good observation to take from the life of Lesueur by Vitet.

Page 146, line 1
Letter of Montesquieu to Abbé Nicolini, Bordeaux, 6 March 1740. Tocqueville's library does not contain any edition of Montesquieu's letters with notes by Tocqueville.

Page 146, line 10
Mirabeau, L'Ami des Hommes, nonliteral quotation.

Page 146, line 24
See above all the declarations of 18 July 1724 and 16 May 1765.

Page 147, line 19
After having been present at the meeting of the Estates-General and noting the extraordinary outpouring of the press, Young left Paris 28 June 1789. Tocqueville cites here statements collected at Nancy on 15 July. Arthur Young, Voyages en France, 1794—Year II, 2d ed., v. 1, p. 429.

Page 147, line 27
Burke, Reflections on the Revolution in France, Works, v. 5, p. 328.

Page 147, line 35
Tocqueville's research notes (Folder R) contain a questionnaire by Tocqueville on the growth of the working-class population addressed to his godson, Alexis Stoffels, and to a scholar, Pétitons: 1) State the increase in the working-class population of Paris, in the 25 years preceding the Revolution of 1789. 2) See if one of the causes of this increase is not to be found in the existence of certain advantages or privileges which certain neighborhoods of Paris offered the lower classes. *Pétitons sent a synthesis based on the Histoire civile, physique et morales de Paris by Dulaure, 1821–25, v. 8; on the Dictionnaire administratif et historique des rues de Paris et de ses Monuments, in 2 vols., by Louis Lazare, 1844–49; on the Dictionnaire géographique, historique et politique des Gaules et de la France, in 6 vols., by the Abbé*

Expilly, 1762–1770; on the guide of the guild of merchants and committees of trades (1766), and on the Encyclopédie.

Page 148, line 22

In August 1776 Louis XVI had issued an edict reestablishing the guilds while lowering the fees to be paid when being raised to master's rank. He reduced these fees by half in favor of the workers and artisans of the Faubourg St. Antoine of Paris by the declaration given at Versailles, 19 December 1776. Tocqueville quotes very freely here from the preamble of this declaration.

Page 148, line 30

Citation of the Council's decree on the privilege accorded to the royal porcelain manufactory, and regulations for the others, Versailles, 16 May 1784. The 1856 edition wrongly states 1782; Tocqueville's notes give 1784.

Page 149, chapter title

(February 1855). Ampère would like this chapter divided into two. —*Rubbish. In the MS. Tocqueville wrote and paginated his text continuously but divided it into chapters. The Copy and the Galleys substitute one chapter with two sections. In the margin of the heading "first section" in the Galleys, in Beaumont's handwriting:* I have great doubts about whether this physical division into two sections is good: 1) You make it in order to highlight two pictures side by side, two remarkable facts; but this division into sections is not used in your book. 2) It is in general used rather in scientific works. 3) It does not seem to me necessary in order to make these two ideas stand out, they strike the reader enough by themselves, without any need for this eccentric form which astonishes him. *It was therefore only at the proof stage that Tocqueville went along with Ampère and Beaumont's suggestion of a division into two chapters.*

A separate page states what is at stake in this chapter:

Men's similarity *[Marginal addition:* "not only the similarity but the feeling of similarity"*]* must be well established; it is this which allowed the democratic Revolution and which explains the ease with which this nation, divided into a million little compartments, suddenly was able to become a blank slate. Their separation and the division of their interests explains: 1) they were so much alike to the point that the social and political system which put so many barriers between such similar people must appear absurd and decrepit. 2) the impossibility of forming centers of government or of resistance with men in the habit of thus always considering themselves separately and never acting in common. 3) the irritation against privileges greater for this reason. 4) preparation for political indifference and above all for individualism. —*Rubbish.*

Page 150, line 5, after "races"

Too strong a picture, I think. —*In the margin in the MS., circled.*

Page 150, line 37, after "intendant"

M. de Serilly. In March 1854 Tocqueville had taken notes on the extract made by M. Droz of the manuscript of the instructions of M. de Serilly written in 1759 for his successor, M. de Beaumont, deposited at Besançon.

Page 152, line 14, after "same"

The problem with the whole first part of this chapter seems to me to be a character which, if not absolutely exaggerated, is at least too absolute. This could give rise to considerable criticism and in any case diminishes the effect I want to produce. It would be more truthful and more efficient to show the differences which still remained, and only describe everything which began to be profoundly or considerably analogous despite these differences. I think the lower classes in the different provinces still differed a lot. What had become homogeneous was the whole social group above them. This was the group which gave the Revolution its powerful unity. —*In the margin of a first version of this sentence in the Rubbish. In the final text Tocqueville did not take this reservation into account.*

Page 152, chapter title

Note to put at the beginning of the chapter

From the Rubbish: Classes. Increasing institutional inequality as it diminished in reality.

A finished piece, where I can find a good version when revising.

Growing inequality in institutions and mores, as it decreased in reality (July 1853).

This idea, which at first sight seems a paradox, seems more and more indisputable to me as I continue to study old-regime France.

If one goes back several centuries, at first one finds what I have called real inequality to be much greater. That is, the difference between the political power, wealth, and education of the nobility, and the power, wealth, and education of the other classes was much greater then than in the eighteenth century, when the nobility and the bourgeoisie were equal in political rights (neither having any), often equal in wealth, and more often equal in education. But yet, if we go back several centuries, we see that there did not yet exist that separate life of the different classes which was characteristic of the eighteenth century. They often met, they touched, sometimes they mingled, all the while remaining distinct. Together they concerned themselves with common business, combined their efforts and their demands. They bore the social burden together. They had an equal right to take part in government, they were represented in a great number of public employments; they contributed equally from their purses. I even think that the ability of a bourgeois to enter the nobility through the possession of lands whose ownership gave political rights was greater. In short, if inequality existed, isolation did not, and even inequality was based less absolutely on the fact of birth.

Little by little the occasions to act in common for the common good disappeared; the need that the noble had of the commoner and the commoner of the noble in both local and national affairs was no longer felt; many jobs, such as the higher positions in the judiciary, for example, that of chancelor, which originally were open to commoners, ceased to be. The Third Estate lost its political importance, at the same time that general political life was extinguished; the nobility as a group also lost its political importance for the same reason, but they found their advantage as individuals. Government positions became, more and more, the exclusive privilege of noblemen, and government positions became, more and more, enviable things.

Taxation finally stopped being common to become, at first exclusively and then primarily, on the person and property of commoners. Even though this inequality ended up being less great when common taxes on the two classes were later established by Louis XIV, it was nevertheless enough to create barriers more insurmountable, differences more marked and more felt, an isolation more complete than had ever existed before between the two classes. In the eighteenth century the privileges, not of the nobility but of the nobles; the separation of classes, their isolation, the exclusive advantages and the unobtainable distinction of birth were greater than they had ever been. Birth played a greater role in the fate of individuals. *In the margin of the two last paragraphs:* It is a commonplace to say that the inequality of rights at the approach of the Revolution, without being greater, seemed more unbearable, because the real equality of conditions was great. I add that the inequality of rights was, in certain respects, much greater, and of a nature much more shocking, than it had been at any previous time.

Page 152, line 27, before "feature"
    distinctive.—*MS.*

Page 153, line 13
    Letter from Montesquieu to Father Cérati, 21 December 1729. The 1856 text gives 1739 by mistake.

Page 153, line 28
    Tocqueville himself had faced the hostility of his family to his marriage in October 1835 to Mary Mottley, a middle-class English commoner. He advised his friend Kergorlay to avoid any mésalliance: There is a general rule from which in your situation I would not vary: it is not to choose a wife except from a family which belongs on both sides to what fifty years ago we would have called our class. *OC, v. 13, t. 2, p. 36.*

Page 153, line 37
    Tartuffe, line 494.

Page 153, last line

The distinction between "gentleman" and "gentilhomme" was a commonplace that Tocqueville had already discussed in his notes on his English trip in 1833 (Oeuvres, Pléiade, v. 1, p. 450) and to which he returned in his correspondence with Nassau Senior. See the letter of 2 July 1853, OC, v. 6, t. 2, p. 161.

Page 154, line 32

Edmé de Freminville, La pratique universelle pour la rénovation des terriers et des droits seigneuriaux, 1746–57, p. 147.

Page 155, line 9, after "exercised"

This would be to make a big mistake, says the Marquis de Mirabeau, whom I love to cite in these matters because he brings into the middle of the eighteenth century some of the ideas, traditions, and passions of the fifteenth. Mirabeau says it would be a mistake to believe that the deputies of the Third Estate appeared in our assemblies like subjects who came to implore clemency and claim their masters' charity: they were received as inferior in dignities and prerogatives, but as equal in substance, and the Third Estate, which by name means nothing but Estate number three, saw no distinction between itself and the nobility other than that which was already accepted between the nobility and the clergy, first among equals.

The same freedom is found in the deliberations, the same competition in the votes with a marked preeminence. —*Circled. In the margin of this paragraph, circled:* perhaps eliminate this quotation. Don't use the elder Mirabeau too much; a discredited authority. —*MS.*

Page 155, line 15

On the Estates-General Tocqueville's notes group remarks based on the compilation of Mayer, Des états généraux et autres assemblées nationales, 1788–89, 18 vols.; l'Histoire des états généraux de France, by E. J. B. Rathery, 1845; and the Histoire complète des Etats Généraux et autres assemblées représentatives de la France depuis 1302 jusqu'en 1626, by M. A. Boullée, ed. Langlois and Leclercq, 1845, two works written for a competition launched in 1840 by the Academy of Moral and Political Sciences and crowned in 1844 on a report by Amédée Thierry; and the Recueil général des anciennes lois françaises and the Recueil général des états tenus en France sous le Roi Charles VI, Charles VIII, Charles IX, Henry III et Louis XII, by Toussaint Quinet, 1651.

The period which Tocqueville privileges in his notes (Folder R) is the fourteenth century: The Estates-General of the fourteenth century are often turbulent and factious, they more or less claim to put royal authority under supervision and to get the whole government into their hands, but one barely sees appear there the war of class against class. The three orders seem to act together voluntarily. The taxes which they vote are either indirect taxes which strike everyone, or taxes on income to which everyone is subject.

As we approach our time in the sixteenth and the beginning of the seventeenth century, the hatred and jealousy of the orders becomes more and more visible, more and more bitter, until finally in 1614 the impossibility of working together seems to be fixed. *Tocqueville made efforts to establish a chronology of the evolution of the Estates-General of the fourteenth and fifteenth centuries based on the Recueil des anciennes lois:*

1355. These are the most famous Estates-General, I think, those which were compared by Voltaire (Essay on Mores) to the English Parliament . . .

1356. Ordinance made in consequence of the Estates-General that met in March. Here it is a question of an income tax and no longer of an indirect tax. 4% of income. Everybody pays. The only privilege is for the poor. Workers who do not earn at least 100 sous do not have to pay. This is the most striking example of the equality of taxation and of the English system in France. How far we are from the seventeenth and eighteenth centuries!

1356. October. These were different Estates from the preceding ones. They took place during the captivity of King John and were composed of 800 members of whom 400 were from the Third Estate. They had a short and troubled existence and they seem like nothing but a revolutionary assembly. They also recognized the principle of equal taxation, in the tax which they proposed. We see that it was a question of forming a grand council of government from the representatives of the three estates. Thus equality even of power . . .

In Tocqueville's notes we find commentary on later Estates: The Estates of 1483 are the most essential to read. We see them having themselves given accounts, voting a real budget, demanding periodicity. This happened during the minority of Charles VIII.

The Estates of 1483, says the author, distinguish themselves from all those which preceded them by the accord of liberal ideas with respect for royalty. They have the remarkable characteristic that there we find everyone—Third Estate, Clergy, Nobility, defending the rights of the people. Political speakers are produced there. But one senses the resolution of the defeated, and above all inexperience . . .

The Estates of 1614. Bad will of the parlement against the Estates which increases as the idea of being a political body and replacing the Estates comes to the parlement. They claim the right to register the Estates' decisions, p. 281. Remark well how these assemblies without experience, assembled at long intervals, merely by the force of their constitution and of their contrary viewpoints, are a hundred times wiser and more politically astute than those learned companies of magistrates . . .

Page 155, line 28

This famous episode is doubtless the manifesto of the League for the Common Good in the course of the year 1314 under Philip the Fair. The movement of resistance led by the nobility would lead Louis the Quarrelsome to the issuance of several provincial charters in April–May 1315.

Page 156, last line

On a separate page in the Rubbish: A Hungarian nobleman, says the Duke of Ragusa in his trip v. 1, does not have to pay any tax.

Page 157, line 27

OC, Necker, v. 9, De la révolution française, 1821, p. 122: In 1789 Necker estimated that half the order of the nobility were families ennobled in the preceding two centuries by the purchase of offices, on which Tocqueville in his notes comments thus: explore the consequences of this special system of ennoblement which was peculiar, I think, to France, at least in this way, by the purchase of offices. I will find, I think, that this simultaneously contributed to diminishing the nobility's moral force, increasing the passions hostile to it, keeping the nobility separate from the other classes and maintaining its privileges.

Page 157, line 34, after "unknown"

I glimpse it and cannot see it, like the farsighted man of W.*[alter]* Scott who saw the man he wanted to meet very well, but only from the rear. *—Above a draft of this passage in the Rubbish.*

Page 158, line 11

See the notes of 1853 on the summary of the cahiers, p. 14. Tocqueville there comments on the wish that "the new nobles and ennobled will always be included with the other nobles":

We will see the Third Estate as concerned with closing the door to nobility as the English middle classes are desirous of opening the doors of the aristocracy. Think well on this and draw the consequences. How Burke is fooled by false analogies when he speaks of the ease with which commoners in France could become nobles, seeing in this something similar to the open aristocracy of England. *[Sieyès:]* "It is by mistake that the Third Estate, which is composed of 99% of the nation, has been described as an order. It is the nation itself."

Commentary on this phrase of Sieyès. How it is not only of the times, but in accord with the temperament of the race, to pass without intermediary, through the imagination, from submission to absurd subordination to the idea of exclusive domination.

This idea is expressed in the cahier of Rennes. This cahier is constantly coming back to mind, and remains in my memory as the one which is the most full of absolute ideas, in fact revolutionary ideas, the boldest in innovation, the most hateful against the privileged, and, in sum, the one where one most detects already the period which is to follow. This doubtless came from the fact that in Brittany the struggle between the orders had already begun violently in '89, above all at Rennes. Is it not odd, however, that this fury against the still-living old regime shows itself in the heart of the province which will take up arms to reestablish the toppled monarchy?

Tocqueville returns to the same theme in commenting on the heading "Nobility": See with what care the Third Estate wants to close all avenues which can lead it to nobility and how instead of wanting to become noble, it seems to consider the nobility only as strange and harmful animals, which it must, insofar as possible, keep from reproducing, if they cannot be destroyed. When one puts together what is said under this heading, with what is scattered elsewhere, one sees that what the Third Estate asked for, all in all, was the pure and simple annihilation of the nobility [and even in truth the aristocracy *crossed out*]. It was not led to this little by little. It wanted this from the first day and before the Revolution began, just as afterwards.

Page 158, line 19

Antoine-Laurent Lavoisier (1743–1794), scientist and administrator, was the son of a procurator of the Parlement of Paris who in 1722 acquired the office of secretary-councilor to the king, an office which gave hereditary nobility. Although noble, in 1787 Lavoisier represented the Third Estate of Romorantin in the provincial assembly of the Orléans region. In March 1789, after having been rejected at Blois by the Third Estate, he was welcomed by the nobility, which elected him an alternate deputy to the Estates-General.

Page 158, line 23

Look in Boncerf (who, it is true, deserves little confidence) how the feudal dues, banalities, corvées, led the rural bourgeoisie to flow towards the towns. —*In the margin of this paragraph, circled in the MS.*

Page 158, line 37

See what Necker said about this. —*In the margin of this sentence, circled in the MS.*

Page 159, line 14

Oeuvres, Turgot, v. 4, p. 125.

Page 159, line 31

Tocqueville made many appraisals of the judicial personnel of provincial towns: the evaluation here relates to the administrative and judicial personnel of the generality of Tours in 1755, as given by the almanac of Touraine, which Tocqueville had consulted at the National Library on 1 November 1853. Tocqueville also considered

the judicial personnel of Angers, based on a speech "on the old institutions of An-
jou" made by Métivier, prosecutor-general at the appeals court of Angers, 7 No-
vember 1851, which listed fourteen different jurisdictions and twenty-nine courts at
Angers, including the seigniorial jurisdictions, which inspired the following obser-
vations by Tocqueville (research notes, Folder P):

1. Except in a few cases all these courts were courts of the first instance. There
was no parlement at Angers.

2. Several of these jurisdictions had the right to judge the same affairs, which
made establishing competence very difficult.

3. All the judges judged by virtue of their office. Which explains in part these
horrible multiplications of judges, the treasury's expedients being the common
source of a crowd of abuses during the old regime.

4. We see that the whole middle class filled the judiciary. Which explains why
the taste for and knowledge of judicial forms was so widespread and still is, and
that judicial language and forms have invaded government proper, administrators
rendering decrees, village assemblies being held before a notary, the acts of the
intendant being judicially registered . . . Which further explains why it is that the
only instinct in conformity with an ordered freedom that the middle classes had
and have retained in France is the taste for legal forms, the only part of the education of a free people that the old regime gave them.

5. It is perhaps in the matter of judicial organization that the Revolution most
truly innovated. It has at least innovated infinitely more with respect to the administration of justice than with respect to administration proper.

6. These abuses of the judicial system were doubtless very great. But one ought
to note that fundamental abuses, the ones truly destructive of the order and morality that a judicial system can represent, that is: the bribing of judges, servility
which is another form of venality, these capital vices which corrupt not only justice, but which effect a nation's whole temperament, were not found there. There
were major problems, justice was complicated, expensive, slow. Great abuses, but
secondary, which would not have been able to last very long faced with public
discussion and the action of a society participating in its own affairs.

7. Such abuses do not prevent a society from prospering. Look at English civil
justice which, still today, presents the same vices in part, in the midst of unprecedented prosperity. It was not to correct such evils that the Revolution was necessary and why it took place.

Page 159, last line

Tocqueville takes this example from his notes on the Mémoire by Dareste: As
early as 1626 Charles de Lemberville sought to demonstrate in his Discours politiques et économiques that the disappearance of forest made peat very precious,
and ended up asking for the appointment of an inspector-general of peat bogs.
Doesn't it seem as if this fact, which is actually 227 years old, happened yesterday
and that Charles de Lemberville was a man we knew?

Page 160, line 4
Mirabeau, L'Ami des Hommes, v. 2, Mémoire sur les états provinciaux, p. 88.

Page 160, line 33
Tocqueville cites here almost literally the "Report to the King on Local Government," Oeuvres, Turgot, v. 7, p. 436. It is the King whom Turgot reminds that he was obliged to repress the usurping tendencies of the towns.

Page 161, line 7
Report of the Municipal Officials of Le Mans on the edict of 1764, Tours archives.

Page 161, line 13
La Flèche. —*In the margin, circled in the MS.*

Page 161, line 19, after "notables"
Report made by the municipal officials of La Flèche in response to a letter from the intendant, 1765, Tours archives.

Page 161, line 29
Letter of the subdelegate to the intendant, 1765, relative to the report made by the municipal officials of La Flèche in favor of the assemblies of notables and the protest of the people of La Flèche against this report, Tours archives.

Page 162, line 10
Decree of 19 March 1785, which by evocation (the question being before the parlement) decided that incense and holy water would be given to the officials of the district of Arnay le duc before the town officials.

Page 162, line 15
Transcripts of the municipal elections of La Flèche, 1754, Tours archives.

Page 162, line 18
Tocqueville's research notes (Folder H), taken in November 1853 at the archives of Tours on the edict of August 1764: letter of the subdelegate to the intendant with regard to the town of Laval based on a petition addressed to the Controller-General by the notaries which showed:

1) That although there were 54 voters *[in the General Assembly]* this only made 18 votes because there were only 18 groups represented, all the deputies of each group voting the same.

2) That all assemblies whose purpose was not elective end up agreeing with the opinions of the mayor and syndics, judges, lawyers, doctors, and deputies of the wholesale merchants (aristocracy), of whom the majority were deputies or

officers and who further only made up 3 or 4 voting groups, although their deputies were the majority in number.

3) That when these members differed over the election of the mayor and town
council, they were at least agreed not to take the town's officials from outside
their own class. And in consequence, they asked that notaries be put in the class
of lawyers and doctors. That they vote by order and not by head.

From this episode Tocqueville concludes: See this noble pride and almost caste
within the heart of the bourgeoisie.

Page 162, line 28

*Notes (Folder H) taken in November 1853 in the Tours archives on the edict of
1764: Letter from the subdelegate to the intendant, 1765, with regard to the town of
La Flèche, after having met with the six leading citizens of the town.*

Page 163, line 6

*The word individualism appeared in the 1820s, at first among the counterrevolu-
tionaries, then among the socialists to stigmatize the atomization of postrevolutionary society. It entered the dictionary of the Académie Française in 1835. Tocqueville
devoted long discussions to individualism in the second volume of Democracy in
America. See Oeuvres, Pléiade, t. 2, pp. 612–20.*

Page 163, chapter title

In the Rubbish the title of this chapter is "How Inequality Was the Source of
Almost All the Ills from Which the Old Regime Died" *and is found mixed in with
the preceding chapter. Tocqueville described his project on separate pages in the Rubbish:* There are two things to distinguish at the end of the chapter.

1) The good effects of political freedom.

I have already discussed them so much in the first part that there are only two
more points to make.

Either extend all these ideas in the first part. Or go back over them only very
lightly and in passing in the second. The first course seems to me difficult to
adopt. These ideas are very necessary in the first part, they are interwoven *["interwoven" in English in the original.—Trans.]* so intimately with the facts, that it
is almost impossible to disengage them.

The second must be attempted: firstly, in supporting them with the English
example and ending up rapidly with the idea *[of]* the English aristocracy having
the privilege of paying, the French of not paying. Secondly, in showing how in
France itself classes came together as soon as freedom appeared. However this
ought to be done very cautiously, for the examples are few in number, not very
significant, and further, there is always the example of the pays d'état to get in
the way, which I cannot dispose of without a very awkward digression.

2) The bad effects of the lack of freedom are proved, in fact, by French history.

What I have put together under the heading of <u>taxation</u>. This discussion is perhaps interesting and is necessary.

But however I do it, I will have a lot of difficulty making sure that the subject of this chapter does not get mixed up with the subject of the preceding one. Therefore, it is necessary to be as short and tight as possible.

The extracts from the notes used for this chapter are grouped in a folder of the Rubbish titled: Awkward Consequences of the Absence of Political Liberty in France. Right to vote taxes taken away earlier in France than anywhere else. Generalizations: taxation source of everything. *In the MS. the chapter is titled:* Book two chapter seven. Continuation of the preceding chapter. How the Absence of Political Liberty in France at the Same Time as the Isolation of Classes Brought About Most of the Ills Which in the End Destroyed the Old Regime.

Page 163, last line

Arthur Young, Voyages en France pendant les années 1787–88–89 et 90, *2d ed., Buisson 1794—Year II, v. 1, pp. 316–17, journal of 10 October 1788. Tocqueville, who in his notes left a file of extracts from the* Voyages *of Arthur Young, particularly appreciated his analysis of the system of landed property, and of the tax burden, and in the journal of 1789 the study of the role of men of letters and the state of the public mind.*

[Young said the incident happened at the estate of the duc de la Rochefoucauld, and in a note remarked that the only time he had seen the English precedent followed in France had been at the estate of the duc de Liancourt.—Trans.]

Page 164, line 8

The anecdote is good but should it be put in? Arthur Young must not be overused. I will have need of him again perhaps in the next chapter. —*In the margin of the MS. In the margin of this paragraph, in an early version of the MS.:* This said many times . . . An idea of Beaumont's: Describe abusive behaviors in England so similar to those of our towns, and show that this remained entirely <u>local</u> and <u>limited</u> thanks to the general freedom.

See that however even in the fifteenth century the upper orders show themselves indifferent to the Third Estate, according to Coquille, and why it was not thus among the English. But among the English themselves it was this way for a long time. Freedom only acts over the long run.

Page 164, line 12

This point is first discussed in Tocqueville's research notes (Folder K): We say: the government must be able to act without obstacle, but that it should only act for the good of the governed. This is a joke. We forget that men, kings or nobles, do what they want or what is in their interest, not their duty. They are not good, taken in the mass and in the long run, except in exact proportion to their need to be. An aristocracy does not become close to the people and only takes care of them when it has need of them; and it only feels this need when there are free institutions.

Do we believe that the English aristocracy would have opened its ranks and concerned itself with guaranteeing the people's rights if there hadn't been any Parliament? That would be a great mistake, the English noble is naturally the proudest, the most exclusive, and often the harshest of all nobles. This is well seen in things where he can dispense with the public. It is political freedom which has softened and bent this iron . . . England has an aristocracy, France had a nobility. The one is a type, the other a separable species. Develop this idea.

Page 164, line 38

Commynes (in 1498), book six, p. 526 of the 1625 edition. Tocqueville cites here approximately and at second hand from the book Doléances sur les surcharges que les gens du peuple supportent en toute espèce d'impots, avec des observations historiques et politiques sur l'origine et les accroisements de la taille, sur l'assujetissement du tiers état au paiement de la totalité de ce tribut, et sur les moyens légitimes de soulager les taillables et de rétablir les finances, sans recourir à des nouveaux impots, *by Gaultier de Biauzat, 1788, p. 114, and comments in his notes on Commynes' text about the wound made by the taille:* It bled up to 1789, and was only closed by opening other wounds from which torrents of blood flowed. What wisdom in this man of power, without morals, but who was placed at the period of transition from feudal freedom to absolute government. He had seen enough of the one and retained enough of the ideas of the other to be able to judge the advantages of free institutions, and the natural and invincible vices of absolute government, better than so many great men born after despotism's maturity. *Commynes' remarks were doubtless inspired by the Estates of Orleans of 25 October 1439, under Charles VII, which voted a tax for the deliverance of the Duke of Orleans. The ordinance of 2 November 1439 which followed organized the general taille and exempted it from Estates' consent to an ordinary and permanent taille, but in his notes Tocqueville dates from 1444 its establishment by Charles VII.*

Page 165, line 4

Véron de Forbonnais, Recherches et considérations sur les finances de France depuis l'année 1595 jusqu'à l'année 1721, *Basel, 1758, v. 1, p. 12.*

Page 165, line 27

Say nothing about the period when the taille was raised without the Estates' consent without having studied the question again more closely. Commynes' text is very clear but I think that M *[blank]* in his report contests it. Turgot himself (who must be reread extensively in all this part) seems to indicate that the arbitrary taille was only generalized by Charles VII. However, who can have more authority than Commynes? — *On a page of ideas at the end of the draft chapter in the Rubbish.*

Page 166, line 2

Tocqueville follows here the account of Louis XIV's regency by Gaultier de Biauzat, pp. 136–37. Emery, the superintendent of finances, had put a tax on houses built in Paris, but the Parlement refused to register this edict. The regent converted the tax into an increase of five to six million in the taille under the name of "soldiers' rations." In 1646 the taille was estimated at 50,284,000 livres.

Page 166, line 23

Edict of December 1692 (Recueil général des anciennes lois françaises de 420 à 1789 by Isambert and Taillandier, v. 20, p. 172) annulling all titles of nobility accorded since 1600 and not registered in the courts, and requiring the payment of a fee to use the titles even if registered. In his notes (Folder F) on the collection Tocqueville comments: Louis XIV's financial robbery: an individual would have been considered the most dishonest of thieves if he had acted thus, and at the same time the most stupid if he still had need of confidence to sell and borrow. When I see all these things, I am frightened by the unlimited ability of the French to accept a bad, tyrannical, and absurd government.

Page 166, line 26

Edict concerning the evaluation of offices, Versailles, February 1771. This edict revoked all heredities and survivances, "except to repay those who hold them who may have paid for them."

Page 166, beginning of line 34

Turgot tells that M. Orry. —*Copy.*

Page 167, line 10

In his notes on the work of Edmé de Freminville (Folder J), Tocqueville comments on Philip the Tall's ordinance of 1320 introducing the taxation of commoners possessing fiefs: Nothing shows better that originally there was not the slightest difference between noble and commoner vassals, any more in France than in England; here we see clearly, furthermore, that government fees came from possession of land and not from birth. From this that all those who owned land ended up being the aristocracy in England. Why wasn't it the same in France?

See also Tocqueville's notes (Folder J) on the article "Franc Fief" from the Encyclopédie: Terrible influence of the tax of franc fief on the division of classes. Perhaps there was no political act which contributed more than this miserable fiscal measure, not only to perpetuate the absolute separation between commoner and noble, but even to aggravate it. I have reason to think that originally considerations of blood did not have the same weight that they have had since, and that the ownership of noble property brought with it a good portion, if not the entirety, of feudal rights, which tended to make an aristocracy rather than a caste. But, the royal treasury coming to distinguish among proprietors those who were noble from those who were not, in order to raise a large sum from the latter, an increasing gap was created between rich nobles and wealthy commoners. And thus here, as in a thousand other cases, the creation or the persistence of the abuses which became the most unbearable of the old regime was derived from royal taxation. Here, notably, the <u>monetary</u> interest of the nobles would have been to <u>destroy</u> the tax of franc fief, in order to give more value to property when it was sold and to receive the fees on property transfer more often. It was the king's interest alone which was opposed to it.

Page 167, line 20

The statute of the twelfth year of Charles II, chap. 24, abolishes distinctions between inheritances, and assimilates the freehold to the military fief. —*MS.* Reread this passage of Blackstone and his commentaries. Do not guess anything on this subject. —*In the margin of the MS.*

Page 168, line 20

Nonliteral quotation from Letrosne, <u>De l'administration provinciale</u>, 1779, book 9, chap. 5, p. 519. Tocqueville gives 1775 by mistake, the date of publication of the Essai sur la liberté du commerce et de l'industrie by Bigot de Sainte Croix, published by Abbé Baudeau, which Letrosne follows in this chapter.

Page 168, line 38

Louis XIV in the first period of his personal reign tried to limit the inconveniences of the venality of offices, whose high price excluded many nobles and deprived the king of the free choice of his officials. In December 1665 the offices were valued and a maximum price was set for them. Tocqueville here bases himself on the estimate made by Colbert according to Letrosne, <u>De l'administration provinciale</u>, p. 187.

Page 169, line 18

The Estates of Tours, which met on 5 January 1483, protested against the taille on the grounds that "the peasants are subjected to the will of those who wish to enrich themselves from the people's goods without the consent and deliberation of the three estates," quoted from Rathery.

Page 169, line 31

On the venality of offices Tocqueville based himself on his reading of Henrion de Pansey, <u>De l'autorité judiciaire en France</u>, 1818, whose 3d edition, published in

2 vols. in 1827, is preserved in his library. It is from the introduction to this work (paragraph 9) that Tocqueville quoted nonliterally from Jean Bodin, The Republic, book 5, chap. 4: "Those who sell situations, offices and benefices, they also sell the most sacred thing in the world, that is, justice." On this point see the classic work of Roland Mousnier, La vénalité des offices sous Henri IV et Louis XIII, 1945 thesis, Paris, 1971.

Page 170, line 34
Turgot, "Report on Local Government," Oeuvres, v. 7, p. 391. Paraphrased quotation.

Page 171, chapter title
From Tocqueville's research notes (Folder K): How the constitution of the old regime was badly put together: Defective, not because it did not have checks and balances, but because the checks and balances were misplaced; not because guaranties did not exist, but because they were combined in a way that imposed harmful obstructions on the government, without protecting the citizens.

It could not be said, even after the virtual destruction of the Estates-General, that the French monarchy was absolute. But freedom was a badly-put-together machine. Royal authority faced very powerful counterweights and citizens had very important guaranties, but the counterweights were badly positioned and the guaranties detrimental to the public good, without being effective for individuals. A much smaller apparatus would have produced greater results.

Oversight and opposition had been moved from political assemblies to judicial bodies. There they were simultaneously more dangerous and less effective. There is nothing more unsuited to government and administration than a court. Most of the good qualities of a judge are defects in a politician. The habit of submitting to forms, of seeing nothing but individual cases, behaving only according to very detailed and very particular fixed rules . . . all these habits make a court composed of the most able judges more unsuitable for the business of government than a political assembly composed of mediocrities would be. Furthermore, it is enough that for legal purposes the essence of a good court is to be always composed of the same irremovable individuals, in order to fill the court with prejudices and self-interest, and make it very dangerous both to the government and the governed.

As the result of all these causes, during the old regime we see the parlement, as soon as it acts politically, create thoughtless opposition, and obstruct the kings almost as much in their good ideas as in their most dangerous; striking almost always off-target, whether in timing or substance. The beautiful remonstrances of M. de Malesherbes at the beginning of the Seven Years War are full of truths; but of irrelevant truths. It was only through its arbitrariness and its folly that the monarchy managed to hide from the people's eyes the sight of the parlement's flaws as a political body, and make this court popular.

This power so obstructive, so dangerous, so noisy, was not protective: jurisdiction over most trials with political significance had been taken away from it. In taking on a political role that a judicial body could not fill, it did not fulfill the only political role of which a judicial body is capable. In fact, we must not think that courts, as people in our day like to say, do not have a natural political function to fill. In a balanced monarchy they have a very great role, one that they alone can play and where nothing can replace them. It is the role of recalling the bureaucracy and the government to the observance of the law in particular cases, particular instances, by their special decrees; to be the general mediator between the sovereign and individuals; there are no freedoms and no serious guaranties without this.

The parlements, which were involved in judging the laws, changing them, reforming them, with making by executive decree real administrative laws, allowed most political crimes and almost all misdemeanors to be judged by royal commissioners. Still more important, jurisdiction over almost all trials in which the government was a party was taken away from them, that is to say they kept the powers which obstruct and disturb government, and did not exercise those which effectively preserve the freedom of individuals. They did that for which by nature they were unsuited, and did not do that for which they were intended by nature.

All this, it seems to me, which has never been seen clearly and in detail as I have just described it, was glimpsed even under the old monarchy. Everything that people could say then and now against the parlements was very well founded. But the service that they rendered was, however, immense. They alone prevented the spirit of independence, the idea of the balance of powers, of limits to absolute authority, from perishing in France as it did throughout the continent at the end of the fifteenth century, and kept our moral level high.

The parlements were poorly constructed instruments of freedom, inappropriate for the use people wanted to make of them. But they were better than nothing. Thanks to them one could almost always (above all among the educated classes) complain, protest; that is, one could always have the honor of resistance even if one rarely profited by it: a situation which is perhaps more effective at keeping hearts high and courage alive than full and complete freedom!

I have said that the parlement was incapable of carrying out the duties of political life well. I add that it was incapable of routinely fulfilling them at all. It always had to tear itself away from its habits for that, force itself to go beyond its own spirit, extend itself outside the ordinary circle of its existence, which could only happen occasionally, in grave and unusual circumstances, according to the parlement's emotions and not according to public needs; which made it easy for the strong power of Louis XIV to expel it from politics and for the weak power of Louis XV to exclude it from administration. During the whole eighteenth century the parlement became more spokesman and less and less administrator. The spirit of the century pushed it to take the first of these two roles, and this very spirit surrendered the other role more and more to the government.

Page 171, after chapter title

There is a first draft of this chapter in the Rubbish composed of several ideas: Note that under the old regime the educated classes enjoyed a freedom that often extended to license, although never extending so far as the regular use of a right; that indirectly, through reading and writing books, through speaking freely of everything, they participated in public affairs more than in any monarchy on the continent; sometimes in resisting, whether it be in the estates, in the parlements, or by the force of opinion and mores. While the lower classes, on the contrary, were the most backward on the earth, without education, without any experience of self-government *[Tocqueville uses the English word.—Trans.],* without any preparation whatsoever nor of any kind for public life: a long habit of obedience never lost, no preparation for the Revolution except material needs and envious and avaricious passions. Easy return from license to obedience; desire for a master never entirely lost and always easily found.

A notation on a title folder in the Rubbish shows that this chapter shifted position: Chapter which was previously intended to go immediately after those on centralization but should, I think, be put between chapters seven and eight because it contains many things which are not easily understood before one has got to that point. *On another title folder in the Rubbish:* Book two chapter five. How on the Continent France Was Still the Country Where One Saw the Most Freedom, and the Kind of Freedom That Reigned There (February 1855). Of the Kind of Freedom Which Was Found under the Old Regime and the Effects It Had. *Above and below these titles, remarks for review:* Bring together all the causes which created freedom and show what kind of freedom. Redo this whole little chapter. Make it a big one where one goes into the phenomenon's details and its causes, rather than only stating them . . . See if this chapter is not too brief and of a nature to confuse the reader after those which precede it. Perhaps it lacks certain nuances. No. I think that the natural place for this chapter is between those which now are numbers seven and eight. After the chapter on collective individualism, the ideas that I describe in the present chapter are easier to understand. *A separate page from the Rubbish shows the connections between chapters 10 and 12:* Perhaps put this chapter after the one on classes, because the distinctions between classes, the individual privileges, the little social groups, at the same time as they encouraged vanity, destroyed common feeling and permitted the government to be master because of the chronic divisions between citizens, also maintained pride, the feeling of personal value, in many individuals, and these are the feelings where independence of mind implants itself. This state of things weakened the mass, but gave color to individuals. Excellent! Good idea. True piece. This leads to going into more detail than I previously have about the feelings of the nobility, and brings me to say of it what I have wanted to say for a long time, and after having portrayed the feelings of the bourgeoisie will lead me down to the people, and will lead me naturally to say more clearly than I already have how the preceding picture only applies to the classes above it.

The big chapter on the people very naturally follows next. Therefore it seems certain to me that this chapter ought to come after the one on classes and before the one on the lower classes. *The MS. gives the final place and title of the chapter.*

Page 173, line 19

On a separate page from the Rubbish, a more developed first draft: There is no fate more sad than that of an aristocratic body which has not wanted to, or has not been able to, raise the democracy *[first version]* bourgeoisie *[correction between the lines]* up to itself, but which has been thrown down despite its resistance and as if drowned in its floods . . . It loses not only its power, but its character . . . and of all the traits which formerly characterized it, in the end it keeps only the distinction of manners.

Page 173, line 33

Tocqueville was indignant at the support given to Napoleon III by the clergy. See his letter to Corcelle of 17 September 1853 (OC, v. 15, t. 2, p. 81), and on the superiority of the clergy of the old regime, see the letter to Corcelle of 23 October 1854 (OC, v. 15, t. 2, p. 125).

Page 173, last line

A remark by Beaumont under the paragraph in the Galleys: "Here are a bunch of bold new ideas on the old clergy. Although you will have against you the liberals of Piedmont and for you the authors of the Austrian Concordat, I am very far from suggesting that you change this chapter: firstly an idea contrary to all received opinion surprises, and it is one of the great merits of your book to often create this impression. Here as always, after surprise comes judgment: at bottom I think that you are right."

Page 175, line 1

In the margin of a page of the Rubbish headed "Liberalism of the clergy" and summarizing the cahiers: Two systems to follow which are not mutually exclusive:

1) Put in my text itself some very salient aspects that I will choose.

2) Do a long note to describe the cahier of the clergy in its entirety;

Certainly do a note for the cahiers of the nobility and perhaps those of the Third Estate.

Try to see the cahiers themselves and extract from them what is most striking;

Perhaps the extended study of these cahiers should be reserved for the second volume? This would not prevent, in any case, some aspects.

The MS. only includes a few lines of introduction up to "the clergy proclaimed." All the analysis of the cahiers on pp. 197 and 198 is a handwritten addition on the Copy.

Page 175, line 11

the multiplicity of primary schools; —*Copy; handwritten passage. The printed text says "private schools," which is doubtless a misprint.*

Page 176, line 12
From Tocqueville's research notes (Folder K):
Privileges of the bourgeoisie

When we speak of the old regime we concern ourselves only with the privileges of the nobility and clergy, but in fact those of the bourgeoisie were immense: the bourgeoisie had a thousand ways of defending themselves against abuse of power that the lower classes lacked, above all the rural population; the bourgeoisie filled the lower courts, the Church, municipal governments, the educated world. One could say of the old monarchy that it was a government which, in regard to the educated and propertied classes, gave the most substantial guarantees and granted, although very irregularly, very great freedoms. For everything was organized so that those who were visible, who could raise their voices and resist, did so successfully. The government's very flaws led to this result. It possessed with respect to power what was superfluous and not what was necessary. It could imprison citizens, raise the taille, make laws without restriction; it could not do the things which were naturally its exclusive domain. The independence of the parlements and their irregular action in the domain of public law and administration; the irremovable and hereditary governments of cities and towns, the thousand customs, the rulers' indolence, the mores of the salon and the academy, gave to all the French situated above the masses more guaranties and effective freedoms than were then to be found in most of the countries of the continent, and which are not to be found in France even today.

The lower classes alone, above all those of the countryside, were abandoned, isolated, without help, without recourse, left to bear not tyranny (there was no tyranny anywhere) but arbitrary authority and the weight of all the public burdens.

Nowhere is this better seen than in the legislation on the draft. In this legislation it was not only the noble, it was the bourgeois, it was the well-off man who was exempted. The burden weighed only on the people, and among the lower classes on the poorest. The government's arbitrariness, which is frightening, since there it acted on men's lives, had only the lower classes for its field. Here it was unlimited.

Page 177, line 26
In March 1771 the parlement of Brittany opened an inquiry on the bribery of witnesses of which four years earlier the duc d'Aiguillon, the commander in chief, had been guilty. D'Aiguillon having asked to be judged by the Court of Peers, the king stopped the trial by a lit de justice of 27 June 1770. The parlement replied on

2 July, excluding the duc d'Aiguillon from the peerage by a decree which was over-
turned on 3 July. After a second lit de justice *on 7 December, the parlement was*
on vacation from 10 December to 7 January 1771, and on 13 January the conflict
reopened. The members of the parlement were exiled to the provinces and the law-
yers ceased to plead. The remonstrances made by Malesherbes, president of the Tax
Court, on 18 February 1771 because of the lawyers' solidarity with the parlement pro-
voked the exile of Malesherbes on 6 April 1771 and the abolition of the Tax Court
by the edict of 9 April. See Jean Egret, Louis XV et l'opposition parlementaire, *Paris,*
1970, pp. 175–78.

Page 178, line 14

Edict abolishing the right of main morte and personal servitude in the king's
domains, Versailles, August 1779. Recueil des anciennes lois françaises, *v. 4, p. 139:*
"constantly occupied with everything that might concern the happiness of our peo-
ples, and putting our chief glory in commanding a free and generous nation, we
have not been able to see without pain the remnants of serfdom which persist in
several of our provinces."

Page 178, line 15

The draft of the discussion which follows is found in the Rubbish in a file titled:
"three sheets to read carefully before doing the final draft of chapter seven." The
text, on unpaginated sheets, bears in the top margin this crossed-out remark: "try
to use part of this piece either in the chapter on the kind of freedom found in the old
regime, or elsewhere." A separate page after this draft explains Tocqueville's hesita-
tion and the late introduction of this discussion in the chapter:

There are two ideas which I have not known how to describe in this chapter,
which however must be put somewhere and which it will be necessary to put elsewhere, if they cannot find a place here directly.

1) The passion for material well-being and the need to obtain it at any price
was much less widespread under the old regime. There were passions close to it,
but of another type, such as the love of pleasure, of luxury, of splendor, of deli-
cacy . . . but that quiet and tenacious passion for material well-being that we
know, which mingles itself among the most honest feelings, which easily interlaces itself with religion, family feeling, this taste for ease, for the conveniences of
life, the idea of increasing one's fortune and employing all one's heart in this was
more rare *marginal addition:* which depraves less, enervates more, brings less disorder and more baseness and which more surely than any other passion delivers
men into the power of any sort of government which does not disturb their peace
and assures the success of their little business . . . was then less general than today.
This can end with the sentence from the Marquis de Mirabeau . . .

2) That the same degree of obedience that debases and depraves us did not produce the same effect on our fathers. Several versions to choose from and try out.

Of these two ideas, the first is in the same family as those of this chapter and can be woven in easily, although this will still be very difficult. The second presents still more difficulty, being of another family than those of the chapter.

To make it easy, in the lower classes they thought little about making their fortune, they despaired of it and directed their imagination elsewhere. *Crossed out:* little to improve in their condition however difficult it was, their imagination directed itself elsewhere. *Correction between the lines:* in the middle classes.— *Rubbish.*

Page 178, line 22
On the desire for material well-being in democracies see Democracy in America, v. 2, pt. 2, chap. 10.

Page 178, line 36
Mirabeau, L'Ami des hommes, v. 1, Traité de la population, chap. "Mores," 1756, p. 79.

Page 179, line 20, after "servility"
Our time is so different from preceding periods that one says something different from what one means when using the same words that our fathers used. Servility is a word too gross for what I would like to portray. When we say servility we mean something cowardly, low, someone who has the consciousness of humiliation, of slavery, and submits himself with a view to the profit gained by servitude. This is the sickness of a few in all centuries. The almost universal disease of our times is different. It does not seem shameful and seems almost natural to those who are struck by it. First difference from servility.

And it can be combined with a certain respect for oneself, a certain feeling of one's own dignity seen in a certain way, a certain disinterestedness, another difference from servility.

It is rather an accepted idea that everything is to be expected from the government; that most honest ways of making a living come from the government, and that it is just to depend on the government, whose wishes and advice must be followed, as long as it does not abuse its power too much.

It is a kind of feeling of a domesticated animal which can be combined with all kinds of private virtues and some public virtues, like the taste for law and order, which servility doesn't permit. In some way it takes the color out of the whole soul.

The one is more contemptible, the other more dangerous. *—On a separate page in the Rubbish. In the margin of this last paragraph:* In fact the change that people accepted then can only be compared to the change which the wild beast made to the state of domestic animal. Unfortunately, I don't know the words to get this idea across. In English one has "tameness."

Page 180, line 9

Tocqueville takes this remark of Péréfix from the work of C. Dareste de la Chavanne, Histoire des classes agricoles en France depuis Saint Louis jusqu'à Louis XVI, *Paris, 1854, p. 89, which he comments on in his notes:* It was above all after the Wars of Religion that the nobility, having lost its feudal independence, and seen the consideration that up to then landed property and the ownership of a castle had given it diminish, let itself be tempted to leave them. Sully already complains of this in his memoirs and, according to Péréfix, Henri IV loudly declared to the nobles that he wanted them to get used to living each from his own estate, living in their house, and ordered them to take care of their land. *In his work* Histoire de Henri le Grand *(1661), Péréfix tells how this advice was given to the nobility by Henri IV in 1598 for the purpose of easing the burden on the public treasury of pensions for the nobility.*

Page 180, chapter title

How the Peasant Was Worse Off in the Eighteenth Century Than in the Midst of the Middle Ages. —*Title page, Rubbish. Another title page from the Rubbish:* How in the Eighteenth Century the French Peasant Was More Isolated, More Abandoned, and to Tell the Truth More Unhappy Than He Had Been in the Preceding Centuries, and Than He Still Was in Most of the Countries of Europe. *The MS. bears the final title.*

On an unpaginated sheet in the Rubbish, there is a discussion on the responsibility of the central power that was not retained: to put somewhere in this chapter.

I know everything there is to say against government charity, but that does not stop me from thinking that it becomes necessary when slavery has been abolished and the common field has disappeared in its turn. From the moment when the rich classes no longer have a direct and permanent interest and a strict duty to come to the aid of the poor classes, and preserve them from the most extreme hardships, it is necessary that the law force them to do so. When next the aristocracy proper itself gives way and in his turn the client disappears as the slave and the serf have disappeared, legislation which provides for the most pressing needs of the poor is still more necessary. And when finally the last traces of the old hierarchy of ranks are eliminated and individuals are isolated from one another, independent and mutually indifferent, such legislation becomes absolutely indispensable. Democratic society, government charity, two things which go together.

It often happens that the rich citizens of democratic countries do not see this truth at all, or don't want to see it, and the fear caused by the needs of the poor and the detestable passions created by those needs make the rich call to their aid a master who, while oppressing them, reassures them; but I dare to predict that in thus sacrificing their freedom to fear and egoism, they will not have put their purses out of danger. For of all the new societies, those which can least avoid government charity are precisely democratic societies where freedom doesn't exist. For in these societies the free institutions which can create habitual relations between rich and poor, give them common interests, *Sentence interrupted:* For this master, whoever he may be, wanting in his turn to protect himself from revolutions, will impose on the rich in one form or another the same poor-tax that they did not want to vote freely. *—Addition without reference to the text, on the bottom of the page.*

Page 181, line 23

In August 1853 Tocqueville had consulted the summary of the reports of the intendants made on the order of the duc de Bourgogne by the comte de Boulainvilliers (1698).

Page 182, line 30

Reading the work of Boncerf, Tocqueville notes (research notes, Folder J) the indifference or silence of the philosophes themselves on the servitude of the land, which he explains thus: On the one hand the grievance in its general form was only really felt later on; and on the other, above all, it was principally felt by the peasants. The writers were almost all nobles or bourgeois. The former always had rights of this sort, and the latter, who very often possessed them *in the margin:* (Voltaire said with much satisfaction "my vassals") furthermore did not suffer from their existence, and since they were almost all (all the bourgeoisie who could write) living in towns, these fees, as we know, weighed little or not at all on urban property. What the philosophes pursued above all was the freedom to think and above all to think about general theories. They were not very interested in the political liberty of individuals and the freedom of property.

Page 183, line 27

Circular of M. Terray, 6 May 1772, with regard to the vingtième. In the analysis he makes of this circular in his notes (Folder H), Tocqueville adds: The minister does not mention the variations coming from the absolute increase in the taille, which was nevertheless a major cause. *And with regard to variations according to the taxpayer's wealth:* If one had been looking for a procedure for making neighbors into jealous mutual enemies, one couldn't have found better.

Page 184, line 12

Oeuvres, Turgot, v. 1, p. 107.

Page 184, line 23

Tours archives, official report of the intendant to the minister, 1764.

Page 184, line 25

Extract from Tocqueville's notes (Folder H) on the transcripts of the assembly of Upper Guyenne: It results from the commission's report that in the district of Villefranche alone, in 1765 there were 10 conveyors of writs, 39 officers, 57 subofficers, and 106 employees, not counting the archers and sheriffs. *Noting the arbitrariness in how each taxpayer's quota was fixed by the tax collectors, Tocqueville commented:* Only the separation of classes and the absence of local public life explain such abuses. Also you see them denounced, as soon as the classes, while remaining separate, deliberate together on the common interests of the province.

Another observation: what widened and generalized the idea of abuses was the secrecy which reigned about the government's actions; the lack of publicity either awakens criticism or puts it to sleep, depending on the state of the public mood. It often prevents suspicion from being born, it increases and exaggerates it when it is born.

Page 184, line 27
From Tocqueville's research notes:
The Tax of the Tenth (October 1853) Action of the Syndic.
The Tax of the Tenth—Examination of the Royal Declaration which reestablished it in 1741. *Declaration for the raising of the tenth of the revenue of the goods of the kingdom, Versailles, 29 August 1741, Recueil général, v. 22, pp. 145–46.*

This was a real "Income Tax" *[original in English.—Trans.]* since the tax bore on income whatever its source, and its only basis was income. In reading the edict we see that it was not only a question of income derived from land, but of that produced by all kinds of feudal dues, loans, commerce and industry, offices, excepting bonds backed by the Hotel de Ville and the tailles, and the finance notes paying 2 percent employed in our budget (I think that this is what we call treasury bonds).

As to the way in which this tax was fixed, in order to really know it in detail, it would be necessary to read the edict of its original creation, I believe that of 27 December 1710, and that which reestablished the tax in 1734. The edict I am examining at the moment, however, gives an idea of it, saying that for the old proprietors the tax would be based on the accounts of 1734, and that new landowners would provide exact declarations to those designated for this purpose, in the form prescribed for them by the intendants. Fifteen days are given for these declarations; if missing, the proprietor will be condemned to pay double the tenth, that is the fifth, and quadruple in case of false declaration.

How should one proceed to check if the owner's declaration is true or false? Not a word is said. One sees that the basis for the amount of tax is the declaration of the owner himself. One sees, at the same time, what an immense amount is left to the intendant's arbitrary decision.

Ordinance of the intendant in accordance with the edict

The ordinance of the intendant of Tours, of 25 September 1741; it says:
1. New landowners will be required within 15 days of the publication of this ordinance to furnish an exact declaration of their properties, signed by those who

know how to sign their names, and with respect to the others certified by the syndic and two of the leading inhabitants.

2. This declaration will be given to the mayor or syndic, who will send it to the subdelegate.

3. The subdelegates will send it to the intendant in order, after the verification which will be performed on the order of the intendant, for it to be used in the tax roll of the tenth.

Role of the Syndic

What must be noted here, among other things, is the role of the syndic. It is the syndic who is the intermediary between the sovereign and individuals, not the lord, even in this case where the lord is as interested as the peasant; the lord is only mentioned in order to say that he can, if he wishes, give his declaration directly to the subdelegate without passing through the syndic. Thus he is isolated as much as possible from the population, which he comes into contact with neither through command nor through a common obedience. He is just left with this useless and harmful privilege.

Note also that while taking the syndic for the sole government agent in the parish, he was degraded by making it seem like an insult to be required to use him as an intermediary with the government.

Page 184, line 31
Report of 1767 of the Agricultural Society of Maine.

Page 185, line 27
Tocqueville's notes (Folder J) here quote Richelieu's Political Testament, *first part, chap. 4, section 5, at second hand and approximately, following Gaultier de Biauzat:* "If the nations were at leisure, if they were not stopped by various necessities, they would with difficulty abide by the rules which are prescribed to them by reason and the laws. They must be compared to mules, which, accustomed to burdens, are spoiled by a long rest more than by work." *Tocqueville comments:* I have heard exactly the same things said of the Arabs, by the generals of the Army of Africa *[that is, of the then French colony of Algeria.—Trans.].*

Page 186, line 18
Tocqueville comments on the tables presented by the syndic for the draft gathered in a file entitled "draft" in the Tours archives. The exemptions cited are those of the parish of Fondettes, near St. Cyr sur Loire.

Page 186, line 31
Oeuvres, Turgot, letter to M. de Monteynard, Minister of War, on the draft, v. 6, p. 414.

Page 187, line 19

In his notes on the Recueil des anciennes lois Tocqueville comments on the edict on the corvée of 24 February 1776, prepared by Turgot:

The reasons given to eliminate corvées were uniquely of a kind to arouse popular passion. We see there: firstly, that with the exception of a very small number of provinces, the roads were all built and maintained by corvées demanded from the poorest portion of our subjects without any pay. Secondly, the whole weight fell on those whose only possession was their labor and who were only interested very distantly and in the long run in the roads. The real interested parties were the landowners whose property increased in value, and yet almost all the privileged did not pay. Thirdly, the state treasury was exhausted by the excessive expenditure of several reigns (it is the king to whom this is said). Fourthly, in some of the pays d'état the roads had been paid for in cash, and this had resulted in better finances and great improvement. Fifthly, since the expenditure was useful to all landowners, it was right that all the privileged participate in it as was the custom for all local expenses. Sixthly, for all the work done up to the present by corvée, it should be done by estimates and detailed accounts . . . the budget decided by the king and his Council, the Royal Council will annually decree a budget for each region, reserving to the king and the Council, as in the past, jurisdiction over the path of the roads, over bidding, adjudications, and all matters which could be contained in them . . . (that is, over all disputes).

Thus inequality was destroyed. But no local authority was created, no participation by the taxpayer of the new tax. Democrat and centralizer, that is the whole Turgot.

The violent resistance of the parlements led to the reestablishment of the corvées by the edict of 11 August 1776: Thus in this matter Turgot's edict was never applied, he did nothing but dishonor the corvée and make its burden more unbearable by officially highlighting how awful it was in the preamble that we read above.

Page 187, line 37

Letter from the road surveyor of Touraine to the Royal Attorney listing the complaints of the taille collectors. This and all the preceding examples are taken from the Tours archives.

Page 188, line 13

Letter from M. D'Armaillé, councilor of the Parlement of Brittany. Tours archives.

Page 188, line 24

On these ordinances of Turgot, see Oeuvres, Turgot, v. 6, pp. 8–9.

Page 188, last line

Decree of the Council concerning vagabonds and disreputable people, Versailles, 2 October 1767. With regard to a similar text, the declaration of 3 August 1764 con-

cerning vagabonds and disreputable people, Tocqueville comments: It was easier to send vagabonds and beggars to the galleys than to seriously concern oneself with poverty.

Page 189, line 17

Necker, OC, v. 5, De l'administration des finances de la France, p. 384, on which in his notes (Folder J) Tocqueville comments: What better example of the way in which arbitrary power, inequality, contempt for men corrupts nations. See a people treated arbitrarily and with contempt, but gently by the most pious rulers, and amidst the most sentimental mores, and which becomes under this regime the nation most apt to violence, to cruelty, and to disorder as soon as the political link is relaxed!

Page 190, line 29

Let us stop a moment here to find and contemplate *—First version* in this long march and get our breath back while contemplating for a moment from this point *—Marginal correction* the general laws to which God has made human societies subject *—First version* which preside over the destiny of our race. *—Correction below the paragraph.* And how in the short space of a human life, it constantly happens that happiness follows vice and success fault or error, so that the image of this great law is confused and hidden from our eyes and it sometimes happens that we deny it *—First version* perceive it badly *—Interlinear correction* but turn yourself away from this little object, in order to look at one more vast, although still small if it is considered in the immensity of things. Take in several generations at a glance, and a great mass of people at once—and several centuries at once *—Interlinear addition* let the ideas, the passions, *[the]* actions, the errors of the times bear their natural fruits and you will find an order as certain and as absolute as that which contains and directs the stars above our heads. View things from this perspective and you will see errors and vices engender by a sort of regular germination, infallible and always the same, miseries and catastrophes, just as the tassel pulls the cord. The law you are looking for will seem to you as incomprehensible but also as certain as that which *—Ellipses in the MS.* The nobles accept tax exemptions, while letting the taxes weigh on their vassals alone. *—Rubbish.*

On a page from the Rubbish headed "variant," another version: We always confuse God's policy, if I may dare speak this way, with His justice. From this come many difficulties in morality and history. *—Circled* These two things are in truth very close; but they are distinct and they must be separated in order to see them better.

Whoever says "justice" says "direct individual responsibility." In criminal law the punishment belongs to the one responsible alone. Is this often the case in this world? Some mistakes have consequences with infinitely greater effects *[?]* than the purest feelings. They make the fortune of those who commit them and the ruin of those who later accept them. There are crimes whose effect is only fully felt a century after the first and chief culprits are dead. A given ruler dies peacefully in his bed, whose passions and vices make his great-grandson mount the scaffold.—No, it is not down below that we must look for the proofs of divine justice. They are elsewhere. And I give thanks to Heaven for this, for he who could manage to produce proof of divine justice in this world, would by the same effort have shaken the strongest proof of the existence of the other world. —*Circled.* No, the field of divine justice is not down here. It must be sought elsewhere. *Marginal correction:*

The sight of this world only teaches us one thing with which we must know how to content ourselves. It shows how in the long run, and by a sort of natural and necessary germination, certain opinions and certain actions always end up by producing certain revolutions in the fortunes of nations, of classes, or of families, so that for one who thus knows how to connect these effects to their causes over time, the plan that Providence follows in the governance of human affairs, whatever it is, manifests itself. History teaches only this; but it is enough. *In the margin of a first draft of this variant:* You say you want to know God's law? Study revolutions, these are the great courts where from time to time the law is made known and the verdict made final.

In the margin of another separate and earlier draft in the Rubbish Tocqueville notes: The word justice *[of God]* is not entirely the right word, because false ideas, foolishness, prejudices also lead to the final catastrophe just as well as vices and crimes. The word law renders the thought better than justice. *A briefer version appears in the MS., where it is crossed out. In the margin of the sentence "but turn yourself away" . . . "the immensity of things," Tocqueville writes: "perhaps a sentence from Pascal. Look." Tocqueville returns briefly to the same theme in a note on the Copy relating to book two, chapter ten, page 187, a note which no longer appears in the final text.*

Page 192, line 7

Tocqueville develops this point on a separate page in his research notes (Folder K): The French peasant has never understood anything of the operation of free institutions. The deputy he himself names has never in his eyes been anything but an envied neighbor who meddles in government without any right.

Page 195, top of page

The separation between books two and three was introduced in the second edition.

Tocqueville put remarks on the folders from the Rubbish file after rereading them. On the folder of the first draft: Chapter six (a chapter which has cost me a lot of effort and which has remained in the state of an unfinished draft).

How the absence of any public life favored the birth and accelerated the development of the philosophical doctrines which produced and characterized the French Revolution.

On the general doctrines which produced and characterized the French Revolution, and why they were developed in France more rapidly than anywhere else, and had more influence on everyone there than in any other country.

Perhaps first do some short chapters titled thus:

1) Of what we call the philosophy of the eighteenth century and why it was born in that century rather than in another, and in France rather than elsewhere.

2) Why the absence of any public life favored the birth and development of that part of the philosophy of the eighteenth century which related to social principles.

3) Of the influence that the philosophes' religious doctrines exercised on the character of the Revolution.

On the bottom of the folio of the next to last version: Book two. Chapter nine. How towards the middle of the eighteenth century, men of letters became the chief politicians of the country. Which had never before been seen in France or elsewhere, and the effects which this had. Marie *[Tocqueville's wife.—Trans.]* thinks this chapter is difficult to understand and boring, which unfortunately seems to me true enough. Chapter redone on several occasions, written without enthusiasm, although the subject originally excited me very much and strongly attracted me (August 1855).

Let it rest for a long time and take it up again for a last effort.

Another folio from the same period bears the following remarks:

1

The chapter nine included here was almost finished when I left Compiègne *[3 April 1853].* Hardly anything was left to do but the end (how the nation ended up making its own the opinions of the intellectuals or the philosophes in political questions, by having a literary politics) . . . the whole ending up with this thought: and it is thus that we happen to see, a thing new and frightening, a great Revolution not merely prepared, but led by intellectuals (or philosophes). It is also here that the sentence about the so-called <u>natural and racial</u> taste of the French for general ideas ought to be found, a racial taste which only appeared after 2,000 years, preceded by a picture of the persistence of this taste, even in practical matters. No one wants to speak of a postal treaty without having first remade all Europe. *Note in the margin:* I really want it, but I surprise myself a little . . .

Having returned to Paris, I'm afraid that in the broken-up life I lead, I won't be able to find my train of thought and the frame of mind to write it down. I will therefore put my work away in order to pick it up again when I'm at Tocqueville. Then, it should be looked at again as a whole and the chapter revised at one go.

2

It seemed to me, afterwards, that it would be good to put a more general view of the subject somewhere, probably immediately before chapter nine. Here is what I would say, according to this plan (which perhaps is not feasible without disturbing chapter nine, which must not be done, for in chapter nine the subject is presented in the form that is the most pleasant and easiest for the average person to understand), this would be the order of ideas:

1) What precisely must be understood by the philosophy of the eighteenth century. How this philosophy was really the natural philosophy of the times. How easy it was to spread in this period, and especially in France, where the sight of so many absurd inequalities pushed the human mind rapidly towards the idea of equality, and where the destruction of all individual existences encouraged people not to recognize any authority.

2) How the philosophes could become the chief political men, real party bosses in France, and what came of this.

3) On the irreligious opinions of the philosophes, of their causes, of the ease with which they spread, of their effect on the Revolution. If I could put here a picture of what there was of greatness in this society which was without mores and without beliefs, greater than any that we have seen since, and show that this greatness was precisely the source of the great things which were done then (of greatness without experience), that would be very good. If this cannot be put in here as a digression, then make it a separate chapter. The book is incomplete without this.

4) At what period the spirit of freedom showed itself in the theories of the philosophes. First race, our centralizers of today. Disappear around 1780 to reappear 20 years later and multiply. *Note beneath the text:* I intended to attribute the whole Revolution to this vice. I have seen people astonished at how from this immoral and irreligious greatness, genius was able to do such great things . . . A good chapter here but separate, after the four chapters above, I think.

Page 195, line 4

And now I find my way again, and, leaving behind the old and general facts which prepared the great revolution which I am going to describe, I come to the particular and more recent facts which succeeded in determining its place, its birth, and its character.

Page 196, line 6, after "project"

A first version of the paragraph filed by Tocqueville in the notes in the Rubbish, headed "to carefully review when the galleys return":

The men to whom in the eighteenth century the common name of philosophes was given were very varied people: their doctrines were often different and sometimes contradictory; for if some brought to light a bold materialism, others showed themselves to be decided and eloquent spiritualists. Some advocated the pleasures of the senses and voluptuousness, others stoic virtue. Here Sybaris, there Sparta. Most attacked Christianity, others made magnificent elegies to it, and as for what regards the conduct of society, we have seen several of them tend towards the government of a single man, imposing equal laws on all, while others only recognized as a legitimate source of power the effective sovereignty of the people. It would be vain to try to gather all these systems into one common idea.

Page 197, line 20

Tocqueville here cites a remark by Burke: "I admit that we too have had writers of that description who made some noise in their day. At present, they repose in lasting oblivion. Who, born within the last forty years, has read one word of Collins, Bolingbroke." Burke, Works, v. 5, Reflections on the Revolution in France, p. 172. *Tocqueville comments on this passage in his notes (Folder M):* These doctrines, however, fill the whole continent more and more, but England which received them first because of its freedom, by the power of that same freedom abandoned them at the time when they made their explosion into practical life in France.

Page 198, line 10

A first sketch of this idea in Tocqueville's notes (Folder K): In all civilized countries writers are the first authors of revolutions. Almost all the agitations of men in civilized countries start in writers' books, and often in their most abstract works; it is among the intellectuals that all revolutions which are actually made are prepared. But in general writers' ideas disappear before being put into practice by politicians.

Page 198, line 18, after "project"

Compare for a moment the English aristocracy and the French nobility during the whole course of that same eighteenth century. The former is always busy defending its rights, inch by inch, not only in fact but in principle, caring more about proving that they are necessary and legitimate than about extending them. The English aristocracy is always worried, with one eye on the people, never allowing a single abstract idea to circulate without exploring its practical effects and, if they appear dangerous, without immediately opposing the idea's practical dangers or problems. The English aristocracy gave way, however, but little by little, and without breaking under the effects of the spirit of the times. The French nobility seems to have entirely forgotten. *—First version on a separate page of the MS. In the margin:* Perhaps eliminate this piece or put it elsewhere. *The piece is eliminated in the paginated version of the MS.*

Page 199, line 12

This remark on the cahiers is made by Tocqueville at the head of his notes on the summary of the cahiers of the clergy (Folder C): When we put together all the abuses noted and all the reforms demanded by the order of the clergy, we see that there is enough here to bring about twenty revolutions.

But see a little the dangers of fixed theories when it comes to a thing as changeable as man. Read the cahiers of the old Estates-General! You will find there almost as many abuses noted, almost as many reforms demanded. These grievances then had absolutely no effect. Impotence was their uniform character. Those of '89 brought about a revolution. In all respects their general character was to go beyond the predictions and desires of those who made them. There is no political science: there is only observation and particular facts.

In the continuation of The Old Regime *Tocqueville was going to develop the different meanings which circumstances give to demands expressed in similar terms. Contemporary historians are sensitive above all to the inscription of the cahiers in the traditional universe of absolutism. See François Furet,* Penser la révolution française, *Paris, 1978, p. 63.*

Page 199, line 26
Tocqueville here quotes the response of the Chancellor to the Estates held at Tours under Charles VIII in 1483, from the Recueil *of Toussaint Quinet (p. 165). But the Chancellor attributed the formula to the* "ancients."

Page 200, line 8
Nonliteral quotation. Oeuvres, *Turgot, "Report on Local Government," v. 7, p. 478.*

Page 201, line 2, after "reason"
Little by little in minds an ideal political world, alongside the reality of things. In describing general principles, the reform of such and such a particular law was soon lost from view, finally imagining a complete and general transformation of all institutions.

I do not know if there is anything more different and often more contradictory than the spirits which direct the philosopher and the statesman. What makes the book's merit is precisely the law's defect. For the one who acts there are almost nothing but particulars, for the one who writes about government, almost nothing but general laws. —*Rubbish.* The writer must chiefly aim at novel views, original details, the greatness of the whole and the strict relation of ideas to each other. To succeed the statesman. —*Marginal addition. The text is interrupted. There follows a first version of the discussion on the habits of literature on page 201, last paragraph, first draft.*

In the notes from the Rubbish, "to carefully review when the galleys return," Tocqueville put a more developed version of this sketch on unpaginated sheets: The man who writes about politics in an abstract manner is naturally not very worried about traditional ideas, established institutions . . . His purpose is precisely to say new things, and his point of departure is his own mind. What is important to him is not so much that his plans agree in detail with the facts, that they be immediately realizable, it is that they contain great and general truths, that they are original —*First version* the views are precisely ingenious and original, bold —*Marginal correction*. The greatest merit of a book of this kind is here. But what the writer loves above all is to create an exact fit between the parts of his book. He can easily get this since he creates it. Logic, so little necessary in action, is necessary in books. It is therefore necessary that the Republic imagined by the writer form a great whole of dispositions which are closely interlaced and compose a well-connected unit in all *[its parts]*. The writer is obliged to show as much respect for logic as the statesman is often obliged to show little regard for it. Although every good law ought to have its origin in an abstract and general idea, most of the things which make a book on legislation succeed would harm the law. What makes the chief merit of one is to please the mind; what makes the success of the other, is to be exactly adjusted to a particular need of the times.

In the margin: They were ignorant of the fact that in the conduct of affairs one must always distrust minds which are too ingenious. They miss what is true in searching for what is original. For usually the world is run with the help of the adapted commonplaces of the times —*First version* one lives —*Sketched interlinear correction.*

The text of the next-to-last version of August 1855 retains only a very short version.

Page 201, line 16

Reference to Telemachus and Mentor's stay at Salentum, in Les aventures de Télémaque by Fénelon, Paris, 1699. In book eleven, Idomeneus, the king of Salentum, reforms his government following the advice of Mentor. Salentum thus offers a model of Fenelonian politics.

Page 201, line 16

The American Revolution produced an immense impression, but that impression was itself an effect, not a cause. A revolution like that of 1640 or even of 1688 would have produced almost no effect. But America's revolution fit into the national ideas of the French of that time. —*On a separate page in the Rubbish.*

Page 201, line 17

In the margin of the penultimate version of this paragraph in the Rubbish, close to the final text: The source of all the problems with this part is that after having pointed out the intellectual habits which belong chiefly to writers separated from politics, like those of the eighteenth century, I finish by speaking in general, which gives the idea some imprecision, it seems to me, and makes it less true. *In the margin of the paragraph which starts "If one thinks" (p. 200) in the MS., there is a similar remark, circled:* That's where the flaw of this chapter is. One goes back to the men of letters only after a too-long detour during which they have been lost from view. *Tocqueville did not take these remarks into account.*

Page 202, line 18

The idea of explaining literary production and mental habits by a national "spirit" is central to Mme. de Stael's approach, but she relates the "French spirit" to political and social institutions, and not to the "race." In the second volume of Democracy in America *Tocqueville had already reflected on the French passion for general ideas (part one, chapters one and four) and had related it to the democratic social state.*

In the margin of the first draft of these thoughts about the taste for theory (pp. 200–202), Tocqueville puts forward an idea about the French temperament which begins this paragraph: The habit of making theories about everything makes us think that all these defects come from our French nature, from our race . . . although we don't see any trace of them in the way in which the French of earlier centuries spoke and acted in public life. What seems hereditary is impetuosity and mobility, which are related, but very different. *—Rubbish.*

Page 202, line 24

A reflection on a separate page in the Rubbish states: I have seen the entire system of Europe rebuilt anew, and new counterweights put in the balance of power, apropos of a postal treaty.

Page 202, chapter title

On the folder of the first draft Tocqueville notes: A chapter which has given me extreme difficulty, above all because of the extreme difficulty of the subject, which in the end I am happy enough with, but yet which still contains some parts which don't absolutely satisfy me. *—Rubbish.*

In the margin of an outline of the chapter: What is most constricting in all this part is my duty and my desire to say nothing which might bear on Catholicism. *—Rubbish.*

Page 202, line 25

In the MS. this paragraph is preceded by a circled discussion: One cannot deny that once the human mind is full of ideas about equality and natural rights, the idea of natural religion will present itself. Once entered into the former ideas, minds go on to the latter voluntarily, if nothing stops them. *In the margin, circled:* All this is true in itself, but of doubtful accuracy for France, where the disgust for religious tradition seems to have accompanied or perhaps preceded the other ideas.

Page 203, line 18

Tocqueville took nineteen pages of notes on the work of Honoré-Gabriel Riqueti de Mirabeau, De la monarchie prussienne sous Frédéric le Grand, *London and*

Paris, Lejay, 1788, 8 vols. These notes were lost in 1862. Tocqueville quotes here approximately from two passages of v. 5, book 8, pp. 22 and 60.

Page 204, next-to-last line

A first sketch of these ideas, in the margin of a first draft of the text of page 205 ("they showed much less zeal") *in the MS.:* Beyond all this there is (which I don't want to say) a natural hostility between the basis of the political principles that the writers wanted to see prevail (principles that were enemies of tradition, of intellectual authority, that were favorable to independent human reason, rooting themselves in natural law, rejecting all conventional or imposed symbols; principles which have remained the same in the new political society founded by them), a natural hostility, I say, between these principles and the natural principles of the Church, a natural antagonism which perhaps can never end, but which in any case can never end until all the ties which linked the political world to the religious world have been cut, and it is recognized that the political principles of the one are different from those of the other.

Page 205, line 30, after "arrows"

Therefore one must not be astonished that those who wanted to overthrow the government first freely attacked the Church. After having sown their ideas in philosophy, little by little they transplanted them into politics, with as much efficiency and less danger than if they had wanted to plant them there right away.

Page 205, line 31, after "increased it"

There is nothing more discussed and more difficult in all of political science than those things which relate to the press, because the rules which ought to direct this part of government are not only different but absolutely contradictory, depending on the times. *—Crossed-out marginal note.*

Page 206, line 1

Furthermore the supervision of the press was then in its first infancy. Governments did not possess any of those improved and clever means that they have gradually discovered since, with whose help the march of ideas is stopped almost as easily as the movement of persons. It would have been very difficult for the government to entirely forbid publication of writings hostile to Christianity if it had wanted to. But, in reality, it didn't want to at all. Here it only acted with a weak and intermittent will. It often raised its hand, but almost never struck. It was enough for it to give the impression of wanting to. *—Circled first version.* less . . . to excite *—Second version on an added sheet. In the margin of the first version, circled, without reference:* It was still ignorant of the art which it has since learned of placing a whole nation in quarantine vis-à-vis the civilized world without doubting itself. *—MS. The Copy bears the final text as a handwritten correction.*

Page 206, line 9

Letter from Diderot to Hume, February 1768, that Tocqueville comments on (research notes, Folder K): How right Hume was and how his good sense and practical experience lead him straight to the truth here!

Page 206, line 20

See on this point Democracy in America, *v. 1, part 2, chapter 9, "The Main Causes Tending to Maintain a Democratic Republic in the United States."*

Page 206, line 26

Henry Saint John, first Viscount Bolingbroke (1678–1751), writer, Member of Parliament (Tory) in 1700, Secretary for War (1704–1708), then for Foreign Affairs (1710–1714), was a friend of Pope and Voltaire. While considering Christianity a fable, he argued that a politician must profess the doctrines of the Church of England.

Page 207, line 15

Tocqueville alludes here to the sudden reversal of the anticlericals after the Revolution of 1848, and above all to the brutal turnabout of Thiers, who worked very actively in favor of the Falloux Law [law establishing Church control of education. —Trans.] for fear of socialist teachers. Tocqueville had already made this parallel between the nobility's return to religion in 1792 and that of the bourgeoisie in 1848 in his Recollections *(OC, v. 12, pp. 121–22).*

Page 207, line 38, after "character"

We have spoken too much, in my view, of the old regime's corrupt mores. Upper-class life was assuredly much more relaxed before the Revolution than it has been since; (and above all vice showed itself there more complaisantly—*marginal addition)* but all in all, however, the Court of Louis XVI was more moral than that of Catherine II, and taking the nation as a whole I doubt that the private morality of today (nor even that which could be noted then in the chief states of Europe —*crossed-out marginal addition.)* It is much less the corruption of mores than the disorder of ideas which produced and characterized the Revolution. —*Folder of drafts and plans, Rubbish. There follows a first version of the next-to-last paragraph of page 208. In the margin of the discussion:* The libertinage of the mind, as Bourdaloue says, in applying these words not only to religious matters, but to everything which may become the object of human thought. *The whole passage is in brackets accompanied by the marginal remark:* to be eliminated I think. In any case to word better. No. *In two later drafts of the chapter, the praise of the relative morality of the French of the eighteenth century is circled, Tocqueville asking himself in the margin about the possibility of transferring it to chapter seven (book two, chapter eleven). The MS. bears the final text. On Tocqueville's hesitations, see the note to page 178, line 15, and the note to page 209, chapter title.*

Page 208, line 24, after "quality"

Have we at least become more sensible than our fathers in becoming more cold? I confess I doubt it. It could well be that our vices and our flaws are only of a different kind. None of our recent revolutions has had a night like 4 August 1789. I see well that we are safe from that kind of folly. But I do not see that for all that we are much more reasonable —*Marginal addition* than to youth, or rather what it had, to wit: inexperience —*First and second editions.*

Page 209, chapter title

At first Tocqueville had planned to put this chapter at the end of the present book two, with the considerations on freedom under the old regime. The first title folder of the Rubbish says: first draft, first throw Chapter eight or nine. How the idea and the desire for political freedom only manifested itself late in the eighteenth century and only at the approach of the Revolution. I do not know if this chapter should be put before or after chapter eight? *The folder "Rubbish from the new draft" bears the notation "chapter eleven" like the folder of the MS.*

Page 209, line 19

Tocqueville's notes contain two pages on Voltaire's stay in England in 1726–29 and on his encounters there. Voltaire's Philosophical Letters (1734) indeed contain a study of the diffusion of materialist ideas ("Letter on Locke"), but Voltaire also defended political freedom in his "Letter on Parliament" and religious freedom in the "Letter on the Quakers."

Page 210, line 4

In his notes on Dareste de la Chavanne (Folder E) Tocqueville comments: The economists end up with freedom, or at least with the abolition of the old servitude, through considerations about the production of wealth; the great writers of the same period through general principles and political theories. It was like two different kinds of workmen, placed one above the other on different floors, but digging the same mine in the same direction, and who will end up coming out of the same hole . . .

Page 210, line 16

Letrosne, De l'administration provinciale, 1779, p. 331: "Everything among us seems to be done by chance," and p. 508, "In a nation governed for centuries by false principles." It was also Letrosne who proposed changing all the names of districts in 1776, forty years before the division into departments, as Tocqueville says a few lines lower down, but Tocqueville emphasizes that the ideas of Letrosne were close to those expressed by Mirabeau in 1750.

Page 210, line 32

Tocqueville quotes here the Maximes générales du gouvernement économique d'un royaume agricole (1758) by Quesnay, according to the collection edited by Eugène Daire, Physiocrates, Paris, 1846, p. 81, first maxim, which he comments on in his notes (Folder D): This is so much more remarkable as the economists, fundamentally, are the greatest, the most active and most effective, the most serious and the most honest revolutionaries of the time. It is frightening and instructive to see in their mind, from the beginning, the germ of the real and final spirit of the Revolution. The sight of the inconveniences created by classes, orders, and inequality leads them through theory to want absolute government (revolutionary in truth), just as the passions born of equality instinctively and practically led the masses to desire that same government.

Page 210, line 36

Quotation from the introductory note by Daire, Physiocrates, p. 17. Daire is commenting here on Quesnay's treatise, Le droit naturel.

Page 211, line 1

Baudeau, Première introduction à la philosophie économique; ou analyse des états policés, 1771, p. 777.

Page 211, line 12, after "spirit"

He proposed to the king establishing a council which would have sole direction of all schools in the kingdom, from high schools down to the smallest village schools, which would establish uniform methods everywhere; which would have textbooks written which would be required for use and which would introduce to everyone the ideas which seemed most useful. *—Marginal addition. —MS.*

Page 211, line 22

Almost literal quotation from the Oeuvres of Turgot, v. 7, p. 399. The quotation is taken from the "Report on Local Government."

Page 212, line 13

Letrosne, De l'administration provinciale, et de la réforme de l'impot, 1779, p. 282.

Page 212, line 32

The quotation is in fact from Letrosne.

Page 213, line 37

Tocqueville had originally acquired a first idea of the "Code de la nature" in 1852–53 from Alfred Sudré's book, Histoire du communisme ou réfutation historique des utopies socialistes, Paris, 1848, whose chapter 13 is consecrated to an analysis of

Morelly's Code, but Tocqueville had also consulted an edition of the Code which he commented on in his notes (Folder R): Absolute and smothering equality, uniformity in all things, the mechanical regularity of all the movements of the social body, regulatory tyranny, everything is there.

At the same time Tocqueville had read the Recherches philosophiques sur le droit de propriété et le vol by Brissot de Warville, in the collection titled Bibliothèque philosophique des législateurs, 1782, v. 6, which he described thus (Folder K): Same character, same folly, but we approach the revolution, more irreligious licentiousness, more violent, still more senseless, destruction of property, of the family, raw advocacy of material passions. Gross materialism and sensualism, furious hatred against religion and religious institutions. Crude rehabilitation of voluptuousness. Cannibalism justified. Paradoxical, impious, and antisocial. But Mirabeau never equaled this work of our days.

Page 213, line 38

To be derived from this idea, which spread under Louis XIV, that the state is the real owner of the land, whose proprietors have only use-rights. An analogous idea is also supported by several economists who say that the state is the co-owner of all land. Voltaire laughs at this doctrine (supported I believe in a work titled "Considerations on the essential and natural order of societies" by Mercier de la Rivière) in "the 40-écu man."—*On a page of reflections in the Rubbish.*

Page 214, line 32

Tocqueville follows here the Mémoires d'un ministre du trésor public 1780–1815 by Mollien, Paris, 1845, v. 1, p. 6. Machault d'Arnouville, the Controller-General of Finances, in May 1749 had instituted a 5 percent tax on incomes, the vingtième, based on the taxpayer's declaration. This tax gave rise to a "tax war" between the privileged, the parlements, and the clergy.

Page 214, line 32, after "later"

This is not very exact. The Social Contract dates, I think, from before 1760. *—In the margin of the MS., crossed out.*

Page 215, line 21

Tocqueville took notes on Voltaire's correspondence chiefly on the period extending from December 1770 to June 1771, when the parlements were fighting Maupeou's reform of the parlement, decreed 27 November 1770 and adopted on 3 December. In the conflict between the King and the parlements Voltaire took the King's side, discrediting the political institution of the parlements by pointing to their condemnation of la Barre and Calas. What Tocqueville presents in the following lines as a quotation is in fact a montage of nonliteral extracts from Voltaire's letters to d'Alembert (8 April 1771), to the duc de Richelieu (29 April 1771), to the marquise du Deffand (1 June 1771), and to d'Alembert (8 December 1772). Tocqueville's library contains an edition of the Oeuvres complètes *of Voltaire in 22 vols., Paris, 1826, but it is not certain that Tocqueville used it.*

Page 216, line 26

We resemble the economists of 1750 much more than the Girondins of 1794. —*Crossed out* Constituents of 1789 —*An isolated idea written previous to the first draft, which contained the final text; Rubbish.*

Page 217, line 7, after "breathe"

without constraint, without fearing the arbitrary will of his fellows, —*Copy, handwritten passage.*

Page 217, line 21

A first sketch of this discussion in Tocqueville's research notes (Folder K): That it is less the advantages that freedom brings which attract men than an instinctive desire for it.

The hatred that free men or men worthy of freedom bear for absolute power is born simultaneously from two things: from a rational idea and from an instinctive feeling. They have learned and remembered that in the long run the arbitrary power of a master never fails to slow or stop the progress of public prosperity, often creates oppression, and always problems, and that it does not even guarantee that material well-being which leads avaricious souls and degenerate nations to accept it. For this reason they reject it. But what makes them flee and avoid it at all costs, is the in some sense disinterested, instinctive, and involuntary desire for independence, it is the manly and noble enjoyment of being able to speak, act, breathe without constraint; it is the desire to feel that one depends not on a man but on God and the law.

Revolutions, poverty can teach the most avaricious and cowardly peoples that despotism has its problems. But who gives men the desire for freedom, if they have not known it or have lost it? Who will make them understand those noble pleasures? Who will make them love it for itself, if this love is not naturally in their heart? Who will even flatter himself that he can make them understand the pleasure it gives, those pleasures which are lost even to the imagination as soon as one has lost their use? You see a free people, do you want to know the probable future of freedom among them? Examine the nature of the link which attaches them to freedom . . . What do they lack to be assured of keeping their freedom? What? The very desire to be free. You see a prosperous and tranquil people under the empire of free institutions. It grows. It becomes wealthy, it shines. Don't swear yet that its independence is lasting if it is material goods that attach it to freedom; for these goods can be momentarily taken away from it, and despotism can for a while procure them for it . . .

Interest will never be visible enough and permanent enough to keep the love of liberty in men's hearts, if desire does not keep it there. There is therefore a rational desire for freedom which is derived from the sight of the good things which it procures. And then there is an instinctive tendency towards freedom, irresistible and seemingly involuntary, which is born of the invisible source of all great passions. Never forget this when you reason . . . A desire which is found, it is true, in all men, but which only holds first place in the hearts of a small number . . . The common source, not only of political liberty, but of all the high and manly virtues . . . One finds that it is less the sight of the advantages which liberty brings than the pleasure of being free which attaches people so strongly to their rights, and makes them so jealous of them.

Page 218, line 6

Tocqueville cites the reports of the intendants and Vauban according to the report of Dareste de la Chavanne, addressed to the Academy of Moral Sciences under the title of Histoire des classes agricoles en France, depuis St. Louis jusqu'à Louis XVI, *Paris, 1854. Vauban claimed in 1698 that the income from inheritances had dropped by a third in thirty years and attributed this decline to the taille. Faced with Dareste's skepticism, Tocqueville notes (Folder E):* One can well contest Vauban's figures, but not admit that a mind as penetrating and as precise as his could be wrong about the general fact of the decline in revenue from land. It is enough to have studied the legislation of the taille, above all at the time when the improvements of the end of the eighteenth century had not been introduced, to understand the effects of which Vauban speaks. We ought to be astonished that a country was not irretrievably ruined by such a system of taxation, which has hardly any analogue except in India.

The decline of French agriculture under Louis XIV was also mentioned by d'Argenson in his mémoires in 1739, but Tocqueville noted (Folder J): This piece has been cited by Lavergne in his work on English agriculture. Do not quote.

Page 218, line 8

In 1854 and 1855 Tocqueville had closely followed the development of the Crimean War, hoping that its cost would detach the French from the imperial regime. See notably his letter to Corcelle of 6 July 1855, OC, v. 15, t. 2, p. 138: The war worries people a little; we fear above all the increase of expenditures; we shiver, when we have the time, over the loss of children departed for the army; but, at bottom, we are so happy to sell our cattle and our wheat at such high prices that all the rest is drowned in a great joy.

Page 218, line 26, after "years"

around 30 or 35 years before *—First Galley, remark by Beaumont beneath the text:* it would be better (at least if you have no special reason) to put a round number: 30 or 40 years. Five years more or less make no difference, and seem to be a microscopic observation that should be avoided in such great studies. *Tocqueville took account of Beaumont's remark in the third edition.*

Page 219, line 11

In the margin of the MS., Tocqueville wrote, then crossed out, some citations taken from the intendants' correspondence, followed by this crossed-out remark: perhaps leave *[these citations]* for the chapters on centralization; their irony disturbs the laudatory intention of the piece. Limit oneself to saying: the letters of the Controller to the intendants are full of agricultural principles.

Page 219, line 15

Tocqueville was inspired to this commentary by the long instruction attached to the Council's decree of 17 May 1785 concerning the rarity of fodder and the means to use it for the preservation of animals (see Recueil des anciennes lois françaises, v. 28, pp. 52–63). In the instruction, a real treatise on agriculture, all the means which can be used to replace grass in the nourishment of animals are discussed, and it is added: it is up to the intendants' wisdom and prudence to choose which appears the most appropriate, according to the nature of the soil and climate of the provinces entrusted to them.

Page 219, line 28

Mollien, Mémoires d'un ministre du trésor public 1780–1815, Paris, 1845, v. 1, pp. 64–65, nonliteral quotation, Tocqueville adding the sentence "I was frightened by what I found," which comes from the context.

Page 219, line 31

Nonliteral quotation. Procès verbal des séances de l'assemblée provinciale de basse Normandie, tenue à Caen en novembre et décembre 1787, Caen, 1788, p. 105.

Page 220, line 1, after "1787"

See the Procès verbal des séances de l'assemblée provinciale de Haute Guyenne, Paris, 1787, v. 1, session of 26 September 1779, p. 95, and the Procès verbal des séances de l'assemblée provinciale de basse Normandie, pp. 105 ff.

Page 220, line 8

Decree of the Council of State of 21 January 1776 for the destruction of rabbits within the domains of the royal captainries, Oeuvres, Turgot, v. 8, pp. 135–43.

Page 220, line 10

In the Copy a note is inserted here which does not appear in the final text: Example of the care that began to be taken of the lower classes at the approach of the Revolution.

Budget of expenses of the Generality (1787). Here there appear 24,931 livres distributed to doctors who had taken care of epidemic diseases; 6,320 livres for aid given to unfortunate or deserving persons.

A correspondent of 1784 who states that the intendant had purchased 159 cows in Normandy, for the sum of 11,026 livres, to be distributed by the syndics to some poor families in the Generality. A large number of receipts and promises had been printed in advance that the syndic had to have signed by the persons to whom he sold the cows.

Page 220, line 19

Mollien, v. 1, p. 101, which dates from 1750 and chiefly from 1774 the growth in income from indirect taxes and notes: "it is the merit of these taxes that they follow in proportion to the new pleasures that increases in income procure for the taxpayers." Tocqueville comments (research notes, Folder J):

1. Note that it was much more difficult with a tax-farm to know and state the growing increase in income from the tax than it would be in our days, when the state collects taxes itself.

2. Note also, in passing, that beyond all the inconveniences of the system of farming out the indirect taxes, this system had the further special drawback that it deprived the state of part of the gradual increase of revenue, and that it was, in consequence, still less appropriate where general causes made that income grow almost limitlessly.

3. Note the date of 1750. All observations concur in giving it, in all respects, as the starting point of progress.

4. Note above all the proof of the growing prosperity of France as the Revolution approached. Derive it from these numbers. They do not prove it for me any more than a thousand other signs that I find, but they will be beyond doubt for a large number of readers.

Page 220, line 25

Tocqueville here compares the numbers given by Necker in his Compte-rendu of 1781 to those Necker gave in April 1787 in his Mémoire en réponse au discours prononcé par M. de Calonne devant l'assemblée des notables, Necker, OC, v. 2, Compte rendu au roi, January 1781, p. 114; and Mémoire, p. 212: the income from the general tax-farm went from 126 million livres in 1781 to 150 million in 1787.

Page 220, line 29

Arthur Young, Voyages en France pendant les années 1787–88–89 et 90, 2d ed., Buisson, 1794—Year II, v. 3, pp. 298–300.

[But Young deplored the vast sums of money wasted, in his opinion, on building magnificent but rarely used roads between insignificant hamlets.—Trans.]

Page 220, line 35

From Tocqueville's research notes (Folder J), from a folio titled: It Was Not the Government's Flaws Which Brought About the Revolution, But Rather the Remedies Which Were Applied to Them. *Remark on the folder:* Democratic despotism. Royal domination. Its picture presented itself to the mind of Frederick the Great amidst the ruins of the Middle Ages.

That we have exaggerated the administrative flaws of the old regime and that it was not these flaws which destroyed it.

There was certainly nothing more confused, more incoherent, more complicated, more irrational, and more badly defined than the old regime's administrative machine, so complicated and confused that no one has ever dared describe it. Its gears were infinite and almost all functioned more or less outside their natural place: courts exercising legislative powers, and on the other hand irremovable and hereditary bureaucrats. There was an enormous diversity of procedures depending on the locale and on the status of the individuals concerned, enormous diversity of authorities who were not necessarily subordinate to one another, of lesser authorities who were all tangled up, badly or not at all defined, and the order always and everywhere invisible. There were a variety of weights and measures, of internal tariffs, of local tolls . . . When this machine is studied piece by piece, without getting to the common motor and the general laws which moved and governed it, it is difficult to understand not only how the machine could function usefully, but how it could work at all.

In fact all these defects in the machinery of government caused considerable problems, and slowed and complicated the government's work. These were problems, but very minor problems. When one pushes below this confusion, this incoherence, this infinite variety, one sees two very simple and very strong connections which hold everything together and make everything work towards the same end:

1. A very centralized and very dominant royal power which was the master in all important things, which possessed powers that were poorly defined but immense, which in fact it exercised.

2. A nation which, among its free and enlightened classes, was as homogeneous and similar in ideas, mores, feelings, civilization, as it was diverse in its governing institutions.

The limbs were imperfect, but the heart was powerful.

Nothing is more superficial than to relate the strength and prosperity of nations solely to the functioning of the administrative machine. One must look not at the perfection of the means of action, but at the internal and central force which makes the machine work. *In the margin: "vague expressions."* Even today our administrative system as a mechanism is much simpler, quicker, more rational than that of the English. Look, however, how public life in England today is still more fruitful, more varied, more energetic than among us. The difference comes from this internal source of strength which is the great cause which makes things work and produce. The limbs can be insignificant when the heart is powerful.

I am very convinced:

1. That the immense flaws of the old regime's administrative system could easily have been corrected little by little, without a revolution and in a way that would have damaged public prosperity very little, if a judicious national representation had been mixed with it, along with time and prudence; that, even such as the flaws were, they harmed public welfare much less than has been supposed.

2. That it was not these flaws which motivated the Revolution and which brought it about, although they facilitated the Revolution when for other reasons it had ripened.

3. That the Revolution was not made in order to change bureaucratic rules, but in order to change the status of individuals. *In the margin:* There are people so infatuated with uniformity and bureaucratic perfection that they voluntarily take the Revolution's side for the sole reason that the meter was substituted for the toise *[an old French unit of length.—Trans.]*.

I am further convinced that in fact, and as a result of the general causes which I spoke of above, the consequences of these administrative flaws were less annoying than it seems they ought to have been. See in the notes which I took on Necker's works *(Necker, OC, v. 5, De l'administration des finances de la France):*

1. How the obstruction imposed on commerce by internal tariffs and tolls was smaller than we think, the amount of money paid for this tax by the taxpayers much smaller than in our day.

2. How the taille itself was lighter and more equitable than we think, weighing still more on vanity than on the purse, and that the expenses of collecting it were very low.

Many similar remarks could be made after studying this document and several others.

Page 221, line 2

Allusion to Molière's The Hypochondriac.

Page 221, line 23

Necker, OC, v. 4, De l'administration des finances de la France, 1784, p. 50. The continuation of Tocqueville's notes on Necker's works (Folder J) qualifies this statement: Public opinion so much the more influential in proportion to the lack of energy of individual opinions.

Necker glimpses here one of the great reasons why in France there is almost never anything but a great current of opinion which overthrows and submerges all. He says: In France, a general tendency to imitation prevents there from being a multiplicity of opinions, and makes all those who are isolated weak; so that united together in common and then forming a sort of impetuous flood, opinions have very powerful force as long as they last. p. 51.

To put it simply, everyone is more afraid of being alone in his opinion than of following bad advice; we march together without thinking the same, but in order to appear to think the same. This means the greatest and apparently most general movements of opinion in France demonstrate neither unanimity nor duration. For in fact we only act in common because of the illusion that the majority is on a certain side, and as soon as that illusion has been dissipated by being closely examined, the movement suddenly stops and we go in another direction, always with the same unanimity and the same violence, founded on the same illusion.

Page 223, line 5

After a lawsuit with the comte de la Blache, who refused to pay a debt, Beaumarchais, falsely accused, was imprisoned at Fort L'Eveque in 1773. This imprisonment and then his condemnation to civil penalties gave him an aura of martyrdom, and he obtained a reversal in 1776.

The "dragonnades" were the persecutions directed by Louis XIV against towns dominated by Protestants at the time of the revocation of the Edict of Nantes (1685).

Page 224, line 1

Tocqueville here quotes Mollien, p. 130, then p. 112. In his notes (Folder J) he comments thus: Certainly here is one of the Revolution's chief causes which, after having been emphasized too much, it has become the fashion to downplay today. One has only to look at our own time (when it is true that sensitivity on these matters has grown with the passion for material well-being and the habit of enjoying it) to see how many crazy ideas, theories, violent feelings, are born immediately, seemingly from nowhere, at the slightest problem in private fortunes.

Note this formidable combination:

1. A social state which is rapidly increasing the desire for material well-being.

2. Financial disorder which is rapidly increasing and interfering with this desire more and more.

Two movements in opposite directions which arouse people and direct their energy against the government.

This same government of Louis XVI, which saw industry, commerce, property, and the taste for material well-being grow rapidly, saw the amount of government debt designated by the name of "callable debt" pass from 250,000,000, which it had already reached in 1785, to 559,202,000 in 1789 (p. 113).

I cannot insist too much on this side of the subject: that the very prosperity, the progress in all senses which marked the reign of Louis XVI, and which in a certain sense made the Revolution inexplicable and more culpable, actually explains it and ought to be considered as what announces it, as one of its chief causes. Men had become developed enough to see what they needed better and to suffer more, although the sum of their sufferings was much less than before. Their sensitivity had grown much faster than their relief. This is true of the grievance about freedom, and of that about equality as well as that about money.

Mine this well, because here there is not only a great perspective on the French Revolution, but an opening on the general laws that rule human societies.

Page 224, line 15
Tocqueville here follows Mollien, v. 1, p. 114.

Page 225, line 27
Royal Edict abolishing the corvée and requiring that work on major roads be paid for, 1776, Oeuvres, Turgot, v. 8. Tocqueville here paraphrases pp. 274 and 280–81.

Page 225, line 34
Edict abolishing guilds, February 1776, Oeuvres, Turgot, v. 8. Tocqueville here paraphrases the preamble, pp. 330–48.
In his notes on the Recueil des anciennes lois françaises, Tocqueville returns to this edict of February 1776:
The whole spirit of the Revolution is already here in the discussions of the Edict. We see among other things: firstly, contempt for the past expressed in the most crude manner, in the name of a ruler all of whose rights were traditional. None of the good sides which the guilds might have had, even if they no longer had them, were shown. They were the product of ignorance, of greed, of violence, above all of the kings' fiscal avarice, bizarre tyrannical creations, contrary to humanity. Everything in them was contrary to good sense, to reason. Secondly, to destroy them one based oneself less on reasons of utility and details, on motives taken from practice, but on very general, very abstract, and very philosophical ideas: the guilds are a violation of natural rights that neither time nor even the acts of authority can consecrate . . . the right to work is the first, the most sacred and most imprescriptible of all properties . . . the guilds are an affront to natural rights . . . This is the more remarkable because Turgot, the author of this idea, was a man of action, who had spent his entire life in business and amidst forms. Nothing proves better how the philosophes had given their mindset to everyone, since the practical men and the detail men spoke their language. Thirdly, the guilds were destroyed everywhere at once, absolutely with a single blow, without transition, without gradation, it was truly a revolutionary reform. Fourthly, in the considerations, the preamble highlights for the king how the tax system has aggravated all the guilds' abuses. One notes well, among other things, how the excess of this spirit led Louis XIV to extend and aggravate this system at the end of the seventeenth century.
We see clearly here the way in which the government created irregular taxes with the aid of offices and privileges taken away from and given to the guilds. Fifthly, one sees the hatred of guilds extending almost to the hatred of associations. The evil, says the edict, is the faculty accorded to artisans of the same profession to assemble, v. 1, p. 370.
On the reestablishment of the edict in August 1776 Tocqueville notes: Even at Paris these effects *[of the edict]* must have been very great. All the old habits of the working classes were disturbed, all traditions broken, all ties relaxed, all discipline relaxed, innumerable difficulties of execution created because the prop-

erty of the guilds had been taken away, the tests abolished . . . from which the inevitable discontent, confusion, disorientation, all still better preparation for the Revolution as the trouble of making was joined to the trouble of partly remaking.

Turgot, in breaking the restraints on trade, in giving the individual his independence, had at the same time left him alone to face the state. He had broken the connection which united as well as the link which strangled. The new edict which reestablished the annoyances and the privileges, also reestablished association, common life, elections . . . less democratic, less economic, more liberal. In this as in all the rest, Turgot is the modern bureaucratic school.

Page 226, line 9

Declaration of the imposition of the taille and the capitation, stating that they could not be changed except by virtue of letters patent registered with the courts, and that measures would be taken to ensure an equal division, Versailles, 13 February 1779.

Page 226, line 14

Paraphrase of the Council's edict concerning the division of the vingtièmes and abolishing the vingtièmes on industry in towns, villages, and the countryside, Paris, 4 November 1777. In the margin of this analysis Tocqueville notes: Boncerf gets a lot from these admissions. To believe that a government can proclaim such truths and live!

Page 226, line 25

Ordinance which enjoins the owners of estates to provide for the subsistence of their sharecroppers and serfs, Limoges, 28 February 1770, Oeuvres, Turgot, v. 6, p. 9.

Page 226, line 33

Citation of the Council's edict of 29 November 1772, overturning the Toulouse parlement's edict of 14 November 1772, which demanded the free circulation of grain according to the principles of the physiocrats. Tocqueville gives nonliteral quotations from these two texts in the following paragraph. The Controller-General, Terray, had taken, in 1772, a series of measures restrictive of the grain trade. The good harvest of 1772 ought to have relaxed the constraints, but the free-traders won their case only in 1786. On this matter see Georges Frèche, Toulouse et la région midi-Pyrénées au siècle des lumières vers 1670–1789, Paris, 1974, pp. 815–18. In his research notes (Folder P) Tocqueville left a more extended commentary on this quarrel, where the King's concern for the kingdom's welfare clashed with the economic presuppositions of the Parlement of Toulouse: Administrative, legislative, and censuring action of the parlements. The government taking all its support from the passion of the lower classes (4 November 1853).

Nothing shows better, on the one hand, the power that the smallest association, the smallest group had in that scattering of men, with regard to all general or local public life, and on the other hand the real weakness of that royal power so absolute in theory, than the cautious language (amidst the most bitter bile) which the King in his Council's decree uses (this passed however for the time of Chancellor Maupeou, a year after the dissolution of the parlement of Paris in 1771): "The King has seen with sadness that the parlement has given itself over to a not very thought-out discussion . . . that if his parlement had carefully examined . . . it would have seen." There follows a modest enough justification of the measure taken by the government: "That if the parlement had seen in the precautions ordered by His Majesty problems harmful to the prosperity of the province of Languedoc, it ought to have addressed itself to His Majesty by other means, and not taken actions which seem to make the King as legislator the opponent of the King as administrator."

See now how the King calls the needs and passions of the lower classes to his aid: "His Majesty has the fortunate advantage that his supreme authority gives him of watching over the subsistence of his subjects, and assuring by a just balance profitable sales of their products to the farmers and the ability to acquire these products at a price proportionate to their abilities to the consumers." (See already how the government poses as Providence and takes on, as the socialists of our days attempt, the regulation of supply and demand) . . . "That the power and bounty of His Majesty impose on him the protection of his subjects in forbidding all maneuvers which tend by hoarding, monopoly, and export to raise the price of grain, and to thus expose his subjects to lack the most necessary food or to deliver themselves up to the rich to work for whatever salary it pleases the rich to give them." (The King defender of the poor—who his government constantly crushed without even paying attention—against the knavishness and tyranny of the rich.) "That the measures taken by the King have already had for result halting the rapid increase in the price of grain and even lowering it, a salutary effect which nevertheless the parlement complains about. (Voilà the parlement which wants to starve the people in the interest of the wealthy and the King who prevents them from dying of hunger.) . . . "The parlement has let itself be seduced by greedy landowners who will never think they get high enough prices for their goods . . ." (Voilà the King inciting class war and inciting people against hoarders). "But the King will not allow any particular court to contradict what he has determined for the general good, and it is enough that the sowing be exposed to the intemperance of the seasons and the lash of heaven without there being surrendered without warning or deliberation the nourishment of one part of humanity to the greed of the other." (In a philosophical, flowery and literary style, that the King will not abandon the people to the evil passions of the rich and the parlement, which meant the people to die of hunger. In form and substance this is very similar to what was said in 1793, thirty-one years later, and which has often been repeated since.)

Page 227, line 1

Tocqueville follows the spirit but not the letter of the Council's edict concerning the mortgaged royal domains, Versailles, 14 January 1781: "His Majesty has been unable to see without pain that this ancient patrimony of the Crown has been so diminished by the liberality of the kings his predecessors, by concessions at very low prices, by disadvantageous exchanges and by usurpations, that there now remains in his hands only the most modest income from this kind of property."

Page 227, line 3

Edict abolishing the guilds, February 1776.

Page 227, line 8

Paraphrase of the preamble of the declaration on the taille and the capitation taxes, 13 February 1780.

Page 227, line 12

A note by Tocqueville (Folder K) gives a much more positive image of Louis XVI's policy: Among the crowd of our kings, I see but one who passionately loved the people for themselves, and did not mingle that feeling with other less high passions, whose heart was completely purged of that pride natural to the hearts of rulers, and that king, who could say it without trembling, that king was Louis XVI. So much are the judgments of God inexplicable, or rather so much is it true to say that it is only the other world which can make sense of this one. Let us recognize that the Divine plans, whose trace we can follow in the conduct of the human race, become hidden and virtually invisible when it is a question of the individual's fate, and that for each man in particular it is only the other world that can make sense of this one.

Page 227, line 15

See Mémoires sur Voltaire et sur ses ouvrages par Longchamp et Wagnière, ses secrétaires, v. 2, Paris, 1826, pp. 119–21. Longchamp, describing how Mme. du Chatelet bathed naked before him, comments: "I have even been able to judge how great ladies regard their servants as nothing but machines."

Page 227, line 18

In the First Galley in the margin of this sentence in Tocqueville's handwriting: "Is this not a little too quick?" In Beaumont's hand: "It is a little too quick but it is so pretty and portrays the idea so admirably that we vote to keep it."

Page 228, line 1

Procès verbal des séances de l'assemblée provinciale de Basse-Normandie, session of 3 December 1787, pp. 233–34. Nonliteral quotation. In his notes (Folder P) Tocqueville comments on the effort by the privileged: Assuredly for some Normans the effort is very great. See, despite this, the class pride. I do not know if in simply allowing equal taxation to replace the corvée, they would have had more to pay (all in all I think so), since through their tenants they already paid it in part. But while accepting the consequences of equal taxation, they could not subscribe to the principle.

Page 228, line 22

Tocqueville uses here the <u>Procès verbal des séances de l'assemblée provinciale de Haute Guyenne, Paris, 1787, v. 1, sessions of 26 and 27 September 1780</u>. A striking picture of the poverty and the nefarious effects of the taille is also painted in the report of 10 October 1782. On the brutality of the peasants see also the note to p. 282, note 22, line 14.

Page 229, line 4

Tocqueville comments here on a pamphlet dated 25 January 1788 coming from the communications commission of Maine and addressed to all the towns of the province.

Page 229, line 26

Tocqueville analyzes three responses sent to a questionnaire of 1788 by the communication commission of Touraine, 5 April 1788. The one cited in the text (not literally) is the transcript of the meeting of the syndics and municipal officials of the parish of Saint Paterne to the northwest of Tours near Chateau-du-Loire (Sarthe), dated 18 May 1788.

Page 229, line 38

In his notes (Folder H) Tocqueville comments on several occasions on the hotheaded and inflated style of the polemics. Thus apropos of the rents due to the Church: "We have not dared say a word of the <u>cents obit</u> (these were the fees due the Church to pray for the dead) and other ecclesiastical <u>salaries</u> which are nothing less than excessive. Their source is sacred, the fathers of the Church have authorized them, we will say nothing about them. What! An unfortunate cannot die without bankrupting his family, without taking into the tomb the fruits of thirty years' labor that he had saved for his children." Note that they don't say anything! Don't you see how the literary and philosophical style has descended into boots, simultaneously crude and ornate. Boots ornamented with lace.

Page 230, line 5

In his notes Tocqueville comments thus: In the midst of this gracious amplification, we see clearly however the real abuse of this collection, and we see that the collector is very much always the same unfortunate, persecutor and persecuted. *After having cited the bitter complaints relative to the taille and the salt tax:* ... One of the causes which made people wonder so freely if there existed abuses, above all in the farmed-out taxes, and that people responded so freely, was the circumstance that they were farmed out. This system, independently of so many other inconveniences, had that of getting people used to complaining about the taxes, despising those who collected them, and dishonoring them and the tax itself.

Page 231, line 10, after "for"

When the evil commit acts of violence a very cruel tyranny results, but one which does not at all demoralize. But if the same actions which people of good will permit themselves to do hurt less, they corrupt more. They teach the doctrine, source of all crimes in times of revolution, that there can be a certain virtue in doing evil, and that there exists a right against Right. —*Crossed out.*

Page 231, line 20

See Tocqueville's notes (Folder K): I asked Lanjuinais (January 1853) if it would not be interesting to research the causes of socialism in France. He gave me this profound and original response: socialism is our natural disease. It comes naturally from our laws, from our ideas in questions of government, from the political and administrative construction of our society. It is to centralization what the wild plant is to the cultivated and grafted tree. Develop this.

Victor-Ambrose Lanjuinais (1802–1869), son of a deputy to the Estates-General, deputy from 1838 to 1848, had been Minister of Commerce in the Odilon Barrot cabinet in 1849 when Tocqueville was Minister of Foreign Affairs, and then like Tocqueville an opponent of the Second Empire.

Page 231, line 38

Procès verbal des séances de l'assemblée provinciale de Basse-Normandie, p. 121. Some incomplete accounts established from the year 1779 indicate that the amount of the indemnities due was 257,441 livres. In his notes (Folder P) Tocqueville comments on this figure: If, in 1789, there were expropriated landowners to whom the price of their property had been owing for eighteen years, judge how things must have happened in 1750 and before? How can one complain about the revolutionary government, which afterwards showed so much contempt for the rights of property, when a government that was old, regular, peaceful, showed so little respect for the smallest interests. See how things have always been done in England.

Page 232, line 19

Edict concerning the expenses of the hospital buildings of the kingdom, Versailles, January 1780.

Page 233, line 12

At the Tours archives Tocqueville had looked through a file on the police, as well as the correspondence of the Controller-General with the intendants, where Tocqueville had noted several orders of arrest followed by detention without trial. The

Edict of the Council that he quotes is doubtless that of 19 May 1739, later published, which he comments on: What contempt for legal forms and for humanity as soon as it is a question of the poor. How this reminds us of the measures taken against the socialists. Still the same spirit and the same bureaucratic mores. Note that a similar ordinance which changed the whole order of jurisdiction in capital cases was not submitted to the courts at all; was not the object of the slightest declaration on their part; a law which effected property would not have happened without being registered by them.

Page 233, line 26

Royal Declaration, which orders that the bandits who gathered to rob the houses and stores of the millers, bakers, and workers will be judged by the Provost-General of the police, given at Versailles 5 May 1775, Oeuvres, Turgot, v. 7, pp. 274–75.

Page 234, line 32

By a series of ordinances of May 1788 the Chancellor Lamoignon de Malesherbes had reformed the whole judicial system: On 1 May he had returned to the ordinary courts all administrative disputes and eliminated the twenty-six finance offices, the elections, the tax boards, the jurisdiction of the officials of the Streams and Forests, and the Salt Board. He had also reduced jurisdictions to two levels, the presidial courts and the grand district courts. Tocqueville comments on this judicial reform in his notes (Folder F) on the Recueil des anciennes lois françaises: Principle of the separation of judicial and executive powers before the Constituent Assembly: Here it is no longer the old regime's principles, but the modern principle of the separation of judicial and executive powers which is followed. The Constituent Assembly did nothing but imitate. The Constituent was much less novel in its work than is supposed; everything was prepared, announced, or tried before it. It is interesting to see how the Empire and we have since returned to the principle of the old regime, only turning it in another direction. The old regime combined the executive power with the judicial power; the Empire combined the judicial power with the executive power. That is the only difference, a difference entirely to the detriment of freedom. Louis XVI alone and the Constituent really applied the principle *[of separation of powers.—Trans.],* since all that was administrative came from the executive, everything that was judicial from the judiciary. It is interesting to see this current of despotism like a river which passes from one side to the other, while disappearing for a moment under freedom in 1789 . . .

But what must be noted here, as in all kinds of institution, is how everything was already ruined before the time of the great earthquake of '89. Judge how many habits changed or were derailed by this ordinance, how many individual positions attacked or disturbed, how many novelties in the things that affect people most. Such a reform would have been enough to take two or three years in a regular state, and the same or greater reforms were in course or finished everywhere. Still more, people foresaw that what was not yet changed was going to change. In the preamble of the ordinance, it is said that it is <u>necessary</u> to subject to a general revision <u>all our civil and criminal laws</u>. Everything that is demanded in the cahiers is indicated or attempted simultaneously by the royal power then, and except for itself it proposes to change everything in France.

Another sign of the times is that Malesherbes clearly indicates that it would be better to modify the organization of the parlements but that he doesn't dare.

Page 235, line 12

The Edict of 17 June 1787 had organized for each region a hierarchy of assemblies: provincial assemblies, department assemblies, district assemblies, municipal assemblies. These assemblies enshrined the power of the notables: of the twenty provincial assemblies which functioned, ten were presided over by bishops or archbishops and ten by members of the high nobility. They opposed themselves very quickly to the ministry so that the reform did not permit an exit to the crisis of absolutism. This attempt nevertheless gave birth among the Legitimists to the thesis of a spontaneous reform of the monarchy, which could have allowed the Revolution to be avoided.

Page 236, line 5

In the margin of this paragraph, crossed out in the MS.: Check all this very carefully in order to say nothing wrong accidentally in a matter which can easily be checked.

Page 238, line 3

Turgot, "Mémoire sur les municipalités," <u>Oeuvres</u>, v. 7, p. 429.

Page 238, line 28

In his notes (Folder P) Tocqueville comments on the system of local assemblies as it came out of the regulations of 15 July 1787: The parish assembly (which must be clearly distinguished from the town assembly) has no other purpose than the nomination of the Third Estate's representatives in the municipal assemblies, which are what we understand today by the term town council. One is the electoral body, the other an administrative body. *Marginal note:* They must also be clearly distinguished from the old parish assemblies. Those were a deliberative body and not an electoral body, except accidentally. The other is nothing but an electoral body and never a deliberative body.

Page 238, line 37

Tocqueville gets this information from the <u>Procès verbal des séances de l'assemblée provinciale de Basse-Normandie</u>, pp. 165–70, and comments (Folder P): What a mess and what inexperience! The nobles themselves who, in 1787, were still afraid of being too powerful in the new municipal assemblies! Like all these efforts which precede the Revolution, they only put the classes face to face, show them their strengths and weaknesses, their inability to live together, and do nothing but prepare and animate the war that is going to break out between them. Free provincial and even national institutions were, at most, compatible with France such as the old regime had made it, but not rural communal institutions. In provincial and national institutions there might be merely conflict. Here, it was necessarily war.

Page 239, line 13
Example taken from notes (Folder I) on the files of the former Generality of Paris at the Hotel de Ville: Complaint of the lords Faguet and Cottin, beadles of the Sainte-Chapelle at Paris (28 March 1788), on having been elected, the one syndic of the municipal assembly of Pantin, the other member of that of La Villette Saint Lazare, the places of their residence. The reference to devotion to the public good is taken from notes on the same file.

Page 239, line 19, after "assembly"
Example taken from notes (Folder I) on the files of the former Generality of Paris at the Hotel de Ville:
As soon as parish rights lead to political importance, the lords start no longer holding themselves apart. But too late. *["Too late" in English in the original. —Trans.]*
Demand (19 November 1788) from the lord who held the right of high justice of the village and parish of Saint Gervais and Saint Protais, who complains that he has been forbidden to preside over the parish assembly, and even to participate as a simple inhabitant.

Page 239, line 20
Quotation taken from the correspondence of the communication commission of the provincial assembly of the Ile de France with the minister in February 1788.

Page 239, line 31
Procès verbal des séances de l'assemblée provinciale de Basse-Normandie, pp. 166–67, report on the regulation of 15 July 1787 presented at the session of 24 November 1787.

Page 241, line 5, after "disturbed"
habits to which humans are ordinarily much more attached than to their rights —*Crossed out.*

Page 241, end of chapter seven
From Tocqueville's research notes:
Government Inquiry on the Uniformity of Weights and Measures, 1764. Signs and Causes of Revolution Which Are Found There (August 1853)
Perhaps good to cite as a dangerous way of preparing reforms.

First sign of the Revolution and its preparation

I see that in 1764 Controller-General Laverdy sent a circular to all intendants, containing a series of questions to ask the leading businessmen of their districts: Would it be useful to reduce all weights and measures to the same scale? What were the advantages and disadvantages of this change? What would be a good way to institute it? . . . There are many things to note here:

1) First, the ideas about reform which began to affect the government itself, however enamored of routine it might be.

2) Next, the new and imprudent way in which the government stirred up public opinion on these questions, addressing itself by circular to all those chiefly concerned, in order to ask them about the reality of the problem and about the remedy for it. If Colbert had had the idea for such a reform (and I think I remember that he had), he would have made up his mind about the idea and decided in secret, then he would have had several able specialists come to him to confer about the means of execution. To make a sort of public inquiry, by appealing to public opinion on an administrative matter, to look for information from the public and to be supported by it, these are the proceedings of free governments, foreign to the nature of absolute governments, and which the latter ought never to use (however useful they may be at a given moment) if they want to remain absolute. It sometimes happens that freedom and despotism can do the same thing, but they can never do it in the same way. One can be easily convinced of this truth by closely studying the history of revolutions. In general, governments meet their downfall less because of the things they do than the means that they use. There are certain procedures that are so much a part of their own nature that they cannot use others, even to do good, without profoundly altering that nature, and as if destroying their own roots. Among the goods that a free government can assure men there are many that it is in the interest of absolute governments to give them, and which they can give without danger to themselves—laws in conformity with the spirit of the times, equal burdens, the security of goods and even to a certain extent that of persons, good use of the taxes . . . But all these things must come on the instructions of the government itself, all these reforms must be the effect of its sole wisdom, the product of its sole will, the work of its own agents. Thus intends the very nature of these governments. It would be better for them to do the wrong thing while remaining faithful to their nature than to do the right thing while forgetting it. If these means seem imperfect and do not allow them to completely achieve their goals, it is a problem with which they must deal and get used to, for there is no solution.

3) The third thing that it is appropriate to consider are the results of this sort of government inquiry. It did not lead to anything. The government recognized the problem, aroused the nation, and then went back to sleep itself, as if it could put the nation back to sleep too.

How many signs and causes of a Revolution!

In the margin in the MS., crossed out: To reread very carefully:

1) The Edict of June 1787 which sets the rules.

2) The Regulation of 5 August 1787 which indicates the means of execution.

Page 241, chapter title

Tocqueville hesitated over the content and position of this chapter, as notes on the successive title folders in the Rubbish show. On the folder for the first draft: Chapter ten. How the French Revolution Came Naturally from All the Facts Which Preceded It. A piece which has cost me a lot of work and which I leave without being fully satisfied. It ought to be carefully examined whether it is appropriate to go into the French character in detail, and if it would not be better to limit oneself to the <u>version</u> which consists of implying only that without the nation's particular character the causes that I have described would still not have been able to produce the Revolution. The picture of a nation is always a vague and indistinct image, when one wants to do it all at once. There is always more pretence than truth in it. A piece for effect, a concession to the <u>false taste of the times</u>. *On a later folder:* Book two, chapter fifteen, How the French Revolution Came Naturally from All the Facts Which Preceded It. I still have some doubts about this chapter and I wonder if a summary doesn't rather weaken more than strengthen the effect produced. If the <u>French character</u> could be enough for a chapter, I think that that would be better.

Page 242, line 3

The old regime, Mirabeau said, will not even have the honor of perishing in a civil war, and he spoke the truth. *—In the margin of a draft of this paragraph in the Rubbish.*

Page 243, line 7

Burke, "Policy of the Allies," 1793, <u>Works</u>, v. 7, p. 135.

Page 243, line 8

This is not entirely true because elsewhere, on page fifteen of my notes, he shows the cause very well. Only he does not see that such a cause proves that the aristocracy was dead before it hit the ground. *—Marginal note crossed out in the MS.*

Page 243, line 37

Sketch of this discussion: Why from mores so gentle, so humane, so well-meaning did there arise a Revolution so cruel? The gentleness was on top. The violence came from the bottom. It was the upper classes who suffered the Revolution, it was the tough ones who made it. Nowhere was the top of society more civilized, and more softened and <u>sweetened</u> by civilization, nowhere the lower part more uncivilized. In countries where, however, the upper classes had in fact lost their empire, and aristocracy its roots, a civilized top and a barbarian bottom had been seen in other times and places. But then the civilized had had, beyond civilization, real power. —*Rubbish.*

Page 244, line 34, after "respect"
   when those who claim credit for its conquests without even being able to understand their spirit will have long disappeared —*Circled. MS.*

Page 246, line 19, after "instincts"
   to the point that it still resembles the portrait Caesar made of it, two thousand years ago, and at the same time —*Rubbish. The reference to Caesar no longer appears in the MS.*

Page 246, line 29, at "citizens"
   Today —*MS., crossed out.* leading citizens —*Interlinear correction in handwriting.* Today —*Copy.*

Page 247, line 1, after "turns"
   An object of admiration, of contempt, of pity —*Rubbish, MS., Copy, First Galley. In the margin of "contempt" in the First Galley there is a remark by Beaumont: "Do you need to leave this word in? This question merits examination. It is a serious thing to say this of oneself. The word is well justified by the facts: but among the traits of this nation you have painted so well are found sensitivity and pride. Now one accepts everything, except the contempt. To replace* <u>contempt</u> *by* <u>hatred</u>*: it is another idea but exempt from problems. Don't leave contempt without consulting." The final text uses Beaumont's suggestion.*
   In the margin of a draft of this portrait, little different from the final text in the Rubbish: Reread a similar piece in The Genius of Christianity *[by Chateaubriand.—Trans.]* in order to avoid imitating him without wanting to.

Page 247, line 2
   A sketch of the portrait of the French appears in the notes of September 1853 (Folder J) on the work of Gaultier de Biauzat, Doléances sur les surcharges que les gens du peuple supportent, *1788:*
      Idolatry of Kings. Character attributed to the French of all times.
   One might believe that it was only after Louis XIV that it was established as an historical and philosophical doctrine that the French naturally and by national character idolized their kings. But we see this same idea expressed very much earlier. The first law of the French, says Sully, book ten, is to want whatever the sovereign wants, and their strongest passion is to please him. Yet Sully had seen the Wars of Religion and in particular the Catholic League; he had heard very

revolutionary and almost republican doctrines preached by both Huguenots and Catholics. He nevertheless retained, through all that, the impression that we have just reported; in effect, these two things can be seen in France in such rapid succession that one could almost say that they are found at the same time. The same souls who are drawn most easily towards rebellion return to servitude by a natural tendency, as a tree bent by the wind stands up straight after the wind stops. This is doubtless seen in other countries; but what is really worth noting, is that the Frenchman has always covered this adoration of power with a sort of passionate attachment for the person who exercises it, of such a kind that he seems less to act from fear and greed than from love, which uplifts his servitude and hides it. The French do not merely bear their chains with patience, they wave them in triumph and kiss them passionately.

A file of diverse notes (Folder K), not dated, also contains, besides a reference to the portrait of the Gauls by Caesar in the Gallic Wars, *several discussions of the French character:*

Why it will always be easier in France to eliminate freedom than to restrain it.

It is not only the influence of Paris, the subordination of the provinces, centralization, which often make the parties among us disappear behind an apparent unanimity of opinion, and show the nation marching on the same footing, all together, successively in different directions. The cause of this phenomenon is still more permanent and deep. It is not an institution, it is a character trait. The need that the Frenchman has of not being alone in his opinion, the fear of isolation, the desire to be part of a crowd. When he perceives that that crowd is forming, increasing, and finally putting itself in motion, he throws himself in and runs to it. This is enough, when passions are not ardent and material interest violently engaged, to make the whole nation run, sometimes this way, sometimes that way, but always to one side.

On another page:

revolutionary and servile France

Louis Napoleon said on I don't know what occasion that he had always known that he would become the leader of France, because France was neither Bourbon nor revolutionary. What must be said is that France is neither Bourbon, nor liberal, but revolutionary and servile.

If the French love freedom, it is like the smallest of their properties, and they are always ready to offer it as ransom in moments of danger.

On another page: The French nation is the nation among whom it is the least permitted to predict its conduct by opinions, by actions, by morality, because in everything it follows its instincts, which are often worth more than its principles, so that it can be very demoralized without becoming very corrupt.

On another page: I have always thought that men do not consistently succeed except in things where their faults are useful to them. For example, the French and war.

Page 249, title

At first Tocqueville thought of inserting his consideration of the freedom of the Estates in chapter nine or ten of book two. A note on a page of the Rubbish for chapter nine is evidence of this initial intention: I have never been able to put conveniently in this chapter, nor in chapter seven, although I've really wanted to, the piece on the advantages which freedom had had under the old regime itself, advantages proven by the Estates and the provincial assemblies. The difficulty comes above all from the fact that the advantages were not always the rapprochement, at least <u>direct</u>, of classes, which however is this chapter's real subject. The classes remained very divided in the pays d'état, in some of them above all, for special reasons which do not destroy my principle but which one cannot give without weakening it, and furthermore distracting from the point. The rapprochement, however, was indirect, in that freedom at least always prevented mutual oppression, and some of the greatest abuses of separation, and sometimes served positively to bring the classes together. Look how taxes are less unequal in the pays d'état. How the lower classes are benefited. Look in the provincial assemblies how the orders voluntarily mingle, how they tend visibly towards equal taxation. See the passionate attachment of the people to these freedoms, even when they have kept more of their old abuses than of their old advantages! All these things are necessary to say somewhere? And if possible in a few words in one of these chapters. Review this again in passing.

Elsewhere Tocqueville thought of devoting a special chapter to the Estates, insisting exclusively on how little real autonomy they had. The draft of the Appendix is in fact brought together in a folder of the Rubbish which bears the following notes: Chapter or <u>note</u> following the chapters on centralization. On the Pays d'État and in particular on Languedoc, book two, chapter three or four-b How the Central or Royal Government Had Taken Control of the Pays d'État Themselves. On Centralization in the Pays d'État. On the Pays d'État. Chapter to be slightly revised, above all in order to better separate the part that relates to Estates in general from that which relates to Languedoc alone. *A separate page of the Rubbish states this project:* The purpose of this work is not exactly to make known all that was done in the pays d'état, but only:

1) To give some idea of the pays d'état, their number, their population, their varying political life.

2) To show, even in those which were most alive, the degree of dependence which existed between them and the central government, and to show what was the real extent of the <u>exception</u> to centralization. *The MS. and the Copy give the title of "Appendix."*

Page 249, line 17, after "centuries"

Tocqueville was conscious of the gaps in his inquiry. See his notes (Folder R) on the Estates of Languedoc: I am weak on all this, because I have not studied any archives from the pays d'état, but many important documents ought to be found at the National Archives. *Tocqueville's chief sources were books: The <u>Mémoire sur les états provinciaux</u> of Mirabeau; J. Albusson, <u>Lois municipales et économiques du Languedoc</u>, Montpellier, 1780–1787, 7 vols., of which Tocqueville consulted only the first three; the <u>Recherches sur la France</u> of Pasquier, books seven and eight, <u>L'Etat de la France</u> by Boulainvilliers, <u>L'Encyclopédie</u>, the OC of Necker, v. 2 (chiefly the <u>Compte-Rendu au Roi</u> of January 1781). Tocqueville also refers to Montalembert's analysis in <u>Des intérets catholiques</u>, 1850–51.*

Page 249, line 22

Note: the estates no longer met in most of the territories belonging to Prussia and Austria. In the Electorate of Saxony, in Bavaria, and in other countries, they were spared only because of their powerlessness. The only countries where they still kept a certain strength were Wurttemberg and Mecklenburg. —*Circled note in the margin of the MS.*

Page 249, line 23, after "size"

Languedoc, Brittany, Burgundy, Flanders, Provence, and in a few small unimportant districts such as the County of Foix, the Marsan, the Four Valleys —*Crossed out. MS.*

Page 250, line 16

Nonliteral quotation from Mirabeau, <u>Mémoire sur les états provinciaux</u>, part two, section one. Appearing anonymously in 1750, this report became the fourth part of <u>L'Ami des hommes</u>, published in 1756–58 in 2 vols. In this edition, used by Tocqueville, the quotation is found in v. 2, p. 86.

Page 251, line 11

Montalembert (<u>Catholic Interests</u> 1852) says: One must read (in the government correspondence of the reign of Louis XIV published by Depping in the collection of unpublished documents on the history of France 1850–51) what was thought of the estates' independence and authority by witnesses worthy of belief, bishops, magistrates. —*In the margin, circled, in the MS.*

Page 252, line 6

"Mémoire presentée au Roi en 1780 par les Etats généraux de Languedoc," published by J. Albusson, <u>Lois municipales et économiques du Languedoc</u>, Montpellier, 1782, v. 2, pp. 352–66. The quotation Tocqueville takes from the report on pp. 354–56, without being literal, does not change the meaning.

Page 253, line 10, after "work"

They add: if the bureaucrats agreed to all the roads that were asked of them, double would have been spent, which would have been voted without regret. —*In the margin, circled, in the MS.*

Page 253, line 31
*This principle of solidarity is affirmed in 1754 in a report by the Estates, and again in the assembly of January 1756 at Montpellier (*Lois municipales et économiques du Languedoc, *v. 2, pp. 297, 338).*

Page 254, line 5
Edict of the Council of 27 August 1766 containing regulations for public works, following a deliberation of the estates, Lois municipales et économiques du Languedoc, *v. 2, p. 455.*

Page 254, line 27
Tocqueville gets his information from the Lois municipales et économiques du Languedoc, *v. 2, pp. 148ff. The work gives for the period from December 1770 to December 1781 a sum of 71,200,000 livres borrowed.*

Page 254, line 32
Summary of intendants' reports made by order of the duc de Bourgogne (1698) by the comte de Boulainvilliers, op. cit., p. 392. Boulainvilliers here treats Languedoc according to the testimony of the intendant Lamoignon de Bevel in 1698. In his notes on this work (Folder J) Tocqueville comments: One sees well in this passion of Louis XIII the opposite of that great seventeenth-century reaction which led all sovereigns towards absolute power and which succeeded everywhere except England.

Page 256, line 25, after "Third Estate"
It is a thing which appears very surprising today to see bishops, and among them several very eminent ones who have been made saints, bishops who make reports on the management of a road or a canal, are masters [of] all the details of the matter, who profess principles which would not be disavowed by the political economy of our day, who adopt with infinite science and art the best means to encourage agriculture and make commerce and industry prosper; always equal and often superior to all the lay people who discuss the same matters with them. *In the margin:* perhaps put this in the chapter on freedom. *Tocqueville went over to this idea: a version of this paragraph that is not very different was added in his handwriting to the Copy at book two, chapter eleven, p. 195 ("and particularly . . . affairs") and the Copy gives on handwritten pages from "how the assembly was unique" to the end of the almost-final text of the Appendix.*

Page 256, line 30, after "bishops"
These facts explain all the preceding. —*First version.* It is this preponderance of the Third Estate which explains how in other parts of France, provincial freedom showed itself sterile and routine, more hostile to the spirit of the times than

the despotism of the central government itself, but the opposite in Languedoc. —*Sketched marginal correction. MS.*

Page 257, line 6

On 1 June 1853, Tocqueville moved to Saint-Cyr-les-Tours on the north bank of the Loire river, in order to benefit from the care of Dr. Bretonneau. Until April 1854 he worked in the nearby Tours archives with the help of the young archivist, Charles de Grandmaison, who completed the classification of the papers of the former intendency of Tours. On his stay see Charles de Grandmaison, Alexis de Tocqueville en Touraine, Paris, 1893. In April 1853 Tocqueville examined the papers of the Generality of Paris at the National Archives.

Page 257, line 18

All the preceding is a transcription of a conversation with Hälschner of 4 August 1854.

Page 257, line 24, after "Wurtemberg"

On Württemberg Tocqueville's chief source was the book by August Ludwig Reyscher (1802–1880), professor at the University of Tübingen, Das gesamte Württembergische Privatrecht, 3 vols., 1837–1848. In September 1854, Tocqueville noted (Folder Q): In reading this work, I was struck by the great analogy which exists between what happened in Wurttemberg in 1836 and what happened in France in 1788, particularly with respect to the position of the peasants and land tenure. To the point that I am convinced that the best way to really understand the state of things in France in 1788 is not to study French documents, which discuss them in old forms and with old ideas, and which relate to institutions so destroyed that what is before our eyes keeps us from comprehending them. Rather it is to study German books of the kind I have just very lightly gone through which, written in our days, with contemporary ideas, even amidst old institutions immediately make the image of the past appear to us and make us understand it. *In this work Tocqueville was above all interested in the introduction of Roman law and the late transformation of the aristocracy into a caste.*

Page 259, note 3

This note is an abbreviated transcription of Tocqueville's notes on Ludwig Häusser's work, Deutsche Geschichte vom Tode Friedrichs der Grossen bis zur Gründung des deutschen Bundes, v. 1, chap. five, on the estates.

Page 260, line 10

In his research notes (Folder Q), Tocqueville follows this analysis with the following commentary: When we look at the picture of Germany, so similar in a thousand details to that which France presents, we are struck by the widespread symptoms of the death of the old society on the one hand, and the signs of the birth of the new on the other. This is true everywhere, to a greater or lesser degree, but true everywhere on the continent. Highlight this. Try to understand this effect of the institutions' old age, which seems independent of their goodness or of their intrinsic flaws. Their life fades whatever the form and nature of their organs. The same institutions which produced life produce death; what made prosperity makes ruin. Things absolutely good in themselves cease to be good when contained in this milieu. Freedom, when it is mingled with these medieval institutions and when it retains the character that freedom had had in that period, rather than producing devotion, the great civic virtues, prosperity . . . leads directly to the contrary. Aristocracy becomes useless, and democracy sterile and venal . . . Look, with regard to this, how towards the end of the old regime, before its outer skin had yet been touched, nothing was alive except what was no longer part of it. Freedom founded on new principles as in England, the bureaucratic and democratic despotism of rulers on the Continent, that which lives and is powerful in this society is that which is foreign to it.

Tocqueville returns to this idea several times, notably with regard to the decline of the estates in the seventeenth century amidst public indifference (Haüsser, v. 1, p. 117): If the estates had thus almost silently disappeared before the new regime, this did not come from the power of this regime alone, but from the fact that they had outlived themselves by defending only the special interests of individuals and groups. They deprived themselves of popular support, which on the contrary went over to the side of absolutism. In obstinately wishing to maintain everywhere the divided powers of the Middle Ages, the estates resisted that unity of government which was not only a conquest of the rulers, but a good and a necessity for the country *(In the margin:* use all this well and above all think on it well to explain the sterility of the estates where they still existed in France*)*. The old estates did not work to eliminate subjects' oppression, serfdom, the tax privileges which no longer had any sense. It was the rulers who did that *(In the margin:* see well the revolutionary character of Frederick the Great's rule*)*.

Page 260, note 5

Tocqueville contents himself here with translating from German a note which had been sent to him in July 1854 by Hälschner at Bonn, and which is preserved among his notes. The printed text gives by mistake the date of 1789 for the abolition of serfdom in Hohenzollern, while the note gives the correct date of 1798. We correct it. Leibeigenschaft or personal servitude had been introduced in the Germanic countries in the fourteenth century. It presents analogies with the servitude of the feudal period and is to be distinguished from Erbuntertänigkeit, which was the servitude of property or of land. See Friedrich Lütge, Geschichte der deutschen Agrarverfassung, Stuttgart, 1963.

Page 261, line 3

Tocqueville transcribed a note taken in the course of a conversation with M. Walter at Bonn, 30 June 1854.

Page 261, note 6

Tocqueville took notes on the <u>Allgemeines Landrecht</u> in July 1854. These indicate that the Frederician Code was only one of the legal documents that he wanted to study: he also planned to read the Bavarian law code (1750) to discover the relationship between classes and the Austrian law code (1811) to follow there the stages of the abolition of serfdom. We do not know if he realized this project, of which the book does not bear any trace. Frederick II (1712–1786), who ascended the throne in 1740, had from 1746 charged the minister of justice, Samuel Baron von Cocceji, to establish a law code founded on reason. Cocceji's project, which was published in 1749–51, did not correspond to Frederick's desire for clarification. He then turned to a Prussian official, Carl Gottlieb Svarez, who despite hostility from conservatives undertook the writing of the code after 1780. In 1791 <u>Das allgemeine Gesetzbuch</u> was published, which was supposed to enter into force from 1 June 1792. But King Frederick William II, who had succeeded his uncle in 1786, in no way shared his admiration for the Enlightenment and notably for Montesquieu. On 18 April 1792 he ordered the suspension of the work. It required the second partition of Poland in 1793, which brought Prussia new territories, for the new law to be applied to all Prussia, but at the price of a conservative revision. It was this revised code which entered into force 1 June 1794 under the title of <u>Allgemeines Landrecht</u>. The <u>Landrecht</u>, which was subordinate with respect to the laws of the different provinces, was also a compromise. The first part, which discussed men in general, followed the conceptions of the Enlightenment, while the second part treated social relations as they were defined through estates in fidelity to the old regime. The <u>Allgemeines Landrecht</u> was to remain in force until the publication in 1851 of <u>Das Preussische Staatsgesetzbuch.</u>

Tocqueville's notes bear on the letters patent of 5 February 1794, which in promulgating the code recalled its subordinate character but also affirmed the necessity of unifying the individual laws of the provinces. Then, ignoring the first part, Tocqueville studied the second (titles 8–10), notably the sections relative to peasants, serfs, bourgeois, towns and urban communities, guilds, substitutions, modes of landownership, and feudal rights, from which Tocqueville concluded: We see that all this does not show a state of things substantially different from that in France. *Finally Tocqueville studied the* liberal principles, traces of the new society, *and notably title 19 on public assistance, which the note discusses. Tocqueville was inspired simultaneously by the Code and by chapter 22 of Karl Adolph Menzel's work <u>Zwanzig Jahre Preussischer Geschichte 1786–1806,</u> which he read with Hälschner's help.*

Page 264, line 8, after "capacity"

See how, at the very moment when the image of democratic monarchy presents itself amidst the ruins of feudal society, there comes to mind the idea of the state charged with the job of subsidizing all needs and obliged to furnish work. —*Crossed out, MS.*

Page 264, line 21

In his notes (Folder Q) Tocqueville returns several times to Frederick's inability to change the existing social state: Frederick's Code is very interesting, above all for making known everything which remained of medieval institutions in the eighteenth century; since its tendency was entirely modern, one can be sure that everything which it retained and consecrated from the old world and from medieval society was imposed on it by the reality of facts and the power which they still retained.

A very good analyst of the Landrecht and its hybrid character, Tocqueville minimizes its influence. The Landrecht, although little read outside specialist circles, played an essential role in the unification of Germany by offering the courts a connecting link of procedure amidst contradictory provincial legal systems. It also favored the passage from a society of orders to bourgeois society and the emergence of egalitarian demands by its filiation with the philosophy of the Enlightenment. See Reinhart Koselleck, Preussen zwischen Reform und Revolution, Stuttgart, 1967.

Page 264, note 7

On the agrarian question, Tocqueville took notes on the work of the Rhenish Catholic conservative Pierre Reichensperger, Die Agrarfrage auf Preussen und die Rheinprovinz, published in 1847. Reichensperger, who gave a moderate doctrine to a then-distressed Catholic opinion, had like the liberals been subject to the influence of the French Revolution, which separated him from the Historical School and gave him a taste for unity. He elaborated a defense of decentralized monarchy by means of a theory of "corporate representation" which borrowed from the historical school the idea of an organic construction of society and from the liberal school the idea of civil equality. Above all he was concerned with the social question, which brought him close to Tocqueville. On Reichensperger, see Jacques Droz, Le libéralisme rhénan, 1815–1848, Paris, 1940, pp. 381–92. Tocqueville had also summarized in September 1854 the volume Agrargesetze des Preussischen Staats, Breslau, 1850, which collected all the laws modifying the Prussian old regime since 1807.

Page 265, note 8

This information is drawn from Tocqueville's notes on Germany: Notes by Circourt "on the political, administrative and social condition of The Electorate of Cologne, at the end of the last century," taken from a conversation with President Wurtzer at Plittersdorf (August 1854) on the situation of the various estates in society *(see this note published in Tocqueville's OC, v. 18, pp. 196–98),* and a list of the distribution of land established by M. Walter in July 1854, according to a description of 1669 from which it appears that a third of the land belonged to peasants. *It is this document which by mistake Tocqueville attributed to the beginning of the eighteenth century.*

Page 265, note 9, line 3
Tocqueville uses here the Mémoire sur les prêts d'argent, Turgot, Oeuvres, v. 5, pp. 262–358.

Page 265, note 10, line 1
Lucé, example taken from Tocqueville's notes from the Tours Archives.

Page 266, note 10, line 5
The "droits de tarif" were a sales tax which the inhabitants of Laval had created in order to exempt themselves from the personal taille.

Page 266, line 12
Cherbourg. Notes taken on an article in the Phare de la Manche, 9 February 1854.

Page 266, note 11, line 3
A first version of this text, very little different, is found in Tocqueville's research notes (Folder H) under the title: Extract from a manuscript in the Tours archives, undated, but relating to the years preceding the Revolution: unsigned and titled "Notes on Agriculture." All the ideas and passions of the times are alive here. The author must be a peasant without money who reads the writings of the times, but himself writes without knowing how to spell. He hates the lords, above all the ecclesiastical lords, doesn't like the bourgeois at all, above all those who want to get involved with agriculture, rails against the new plows, which does not prevent him from being very much the enemy of old institutions outside the profession of agriculture (May 1854).

Page 268, last line
Extract from Tocqueville's notes (Folder J) on the Procès verbaux des séances de l'assemblée de Haute Guyenne, Paris, 1787, v. 1, report for 17 September 1782, p. 46. Tocqueville concludes: We see that it was only in 1773 that the idea of socially helping the poor presented itself. Since there was no social life except at the center, it was naturally there, contrary to all reason, that the idea was put into execution. Condition of aid. To obtain a charity workshop, the community must contribute to the expenses (p. 47) exactly as in our days. One usually contributes two-thirds of the contribution paid (p. 126). There is much less new in our administrative methods than is thought.

Page 269, note 14

This note and the following were written based on notes (Folder H) that Tocqueville took at Tours, 30 November 1853, on the constitutions of the principal towns of Touraine, Anjou, and Maine, in which Tocqueville studied the files established on the occasion of the edict of August 1764, which created a uniform municipal regime. At Tours: The Town Council had been established by Louis XI in 1461. It is said there that the inhabitants will choose one of themselves to be mayor, who will exercise the duties of that office for a year, and 24 town councilors for life. Furthermore, since that time the inhabitants have not ceased to be present at extraordinary assemblies which have common business as their purpose, through the deputies of the 16 parishes of which the town is composed. *At Le Mans the mayoralty was constituted in 1481. Remarking that the majority of the towns of the Generality of Touraine owed their constitutions to Louis XI, Tocqueville noted:* In all these constitutions, if I am not mistaken, the municipal officials control the whole judicial system regarding public safety, and the whole administrative apparatus relating to it, except there was a right to appeal from the mayor to the seneschal, who was doubtless a royal official. City Hall was also charged with the regulation of guilds and trades and the repair of streets. Later some of these rights passed to the lieutenant of police, a royal official, the others to the Finance Office. *At first unsure of the significance of Louis XI's policy, Tocqueville in the end accused him of having destroyed the republican institutions of Tours by according nobility to elected officials:* We see clearly in the constitution of the town of Tours, as in all those which, at the same time, came from Louis XI, this ruler's idea: 1) Abase nobility by offering it to the bourgeois. 2) Destroy the municipal democracy of the towns and their republican institutions. 3) Put power into the hands of the bourgeoisie, creating a kind of town oligarchy.

Page 270, note 15, line 5

The Edict of May 1765 put in place at Angers, as in all towns of more than 4,500 inhabitants, an assembly of guilds and communities, an assembly of notables, and a city council. See Jacques Maillard, Le pouvoir municipal à Angers de 1657 à 1789, *Angers, 1984, v. 1, chap. 6, and Maurice Bordes,* La réforme municipale du contrôleur général Laverdy et son application (1764–1771), *Toulouse, 1968.*

Page 271, line 3, after "livres"

which ought to be —*First and second editions.*

Page 271, line 11

At Angers, a sleepy little town of clerics, rentiers, servants, and artisans without ambition, the absence of large fortunes made the capitation tax's weight particularly heavy. See François Lebrun, Histoire d'Angers, *Toulouse, 1975.*

Page 273, line 3

The printed text bears 1708 by mistake. Tocqueville's notes correctly give 1738. We correct.

Page 274, line 3

Beyond the partial redemptions between 1694 and 1708, the town had proceeded to a general redemption of offices created since 1692 in May 1716. After the reestablishment of town offices in all towns in August 1722, a decree of the Council of 26 April 1723 authorized the Angevins to redeem them for the payment of 796,000 livres, of which 170,000 were borrowed. After the reestablishment of the offices in November 1733 by Orry, to cover the expenses of the War of the Polish Succession, a royal decree of 11 January 1735 (given here by the printed text erroneously as 11 January 1751) permitted the Town Council to purchase the offices for 170,000 livres, assembled thanks to an increase in sales taxes. See Maillard, Le pouvoir municipal à Angers de 1657 à 1789, v. 1, pp. 28–34.

Page 274, line 11

The printed text mistakenly reads 1669. We correct. Tocqueville's notes give the correct date of 1699, at which date the creation of a lieutenant-general of police at Angers deprived the Town Council of jurisdiction over manufacturing and rendered useless the presence of a merchant on the Town Council. In 1732 the community of merchants demanded a town councilor in order to be able to oversee the creation of the tax roll for the capitation, and received satisfaction by an edict of 15 August 1733. A new demand in 1737 was followed by an edict of 15 August 1741 reserving two places for merchants. See Maillard, Le pouvoir municipal, v. 1, pp. 34–37.

Page 274, line 28

The position of subdelegate became permanent at Angers after 1697. In 1764 the subdelegate was Germain-François Poulain de la Guerche, councilor at the presidial court, subdelegate from 1729 to his death in 1769, Mayor of Angers from 1733 to 1739, then town councilor for life.

Page 275, line 16

Gaspard-César-Charles Lescalopier, lord of Liancourt, maitre des requêtes (1733); intendant of Montauban (1740–1756); intendant of Tours from June 1756 to October 1766, then Councilor of State (1766).

Page 275, line 20, after "enjoy"

It is very odd that this thought did not lead anyone to the idea of destroying the privileges, or at least substituting a salary in cash for them, if one did not want to leave the position unpaid. —*Crossed out in this passage in the research notes.*

Page 275, line 24, after "officials"
Whose fault was it? *—Crossed out in this passage in the notes.*

Page 277, line 11
Report presented by the mayor and councilors of the town of La Flèche, 1764, analyzed in Tocqueville's notes.

Page 278, note 18
Tocqueville here reproduces without change his notes (Folder I) taken on the files of the former Generality of Paris at the Hotel de Ville, on the repair of the rectory of Ivry near Corbeil. These notes are titled: Mixture of judicial arbitrariness and pedantry, characteristics of the old French bureaucracy.

Page 280, note 20
Tocqueville had traveled in Canada from 21 August to 3 September 1831.

Page 281, note 21, title
Example of government regulatory power exercised by the Royal Council. Clearly the courts had the right to make police regulations only occasionally and in a limited territory, and the majority of these regulations, the only ones which could have serious effects, emanated under the old monarchy as in our day from the deliberative bureaucratic authorities, or from the Council of State. — *Copy.*

Page 282, line 3
Edict of the Council which orders that workers and merchants of sheep mark them with blood or another material which will not harm the wool, and forbids, under pain of a 300-livres fine, marking them with tar or with anything else capable of changing the quality of the wool, 29 April 1779.

Page 282, line 6
Edict of the Council which forbids wagoners and carters from storing the merchandise they are charged to deliver and ordering them to transport it directly to its destination, in conformity with the bills of lading which they have been given, 21 December 1778.

Page 282, note 22, line 14
Extract from Tocqueville's notes on the Procès verbaux des séances de l'assemblée provinciale de la haute Guyenne, *Paris, 1787, v. 1, report of the committee on public charity, 13 October 1787, p. 216. In his notes (Folder J) Tocqueville concludes:* Always the same thing, for all the classes above them the lower classes are a deaf man of whom one can say anything one likes without his hearing a word.

Page 282, note 24, line 9

Tocqueville takes two similar examples from his notes (Folder H) from a file titled: "letter of the Controller-General to the Intendant," Tours archives. In December 1773 some businessmen asked M. Trudaine to have a road opened between Sablé and Alençon, about which Tocqueville comments: It is instructive to see the lords and businessmen ask with loud cries for a road which must be made at the sole expense of the peasants, and for which neither one will pay anything. *In 1781 the merchants of Normandy made demands with regard to the road from Le Mans to Saumur.*

Page 283, line 9

Consequence of the works relative to the food shortage of the year 1770. Oeuvres, Turgot, v. 6, p. 63.

Page 283, note 26, line 8, after "question"

of conversation and of agriculture —*First and second editions.*

Page 283, note 26, last line

This note reproduces with minor variations Tocqueville's ideas in his notes (Folder H) taken at Tours on the collected deliberations of the Tours Agricultural Society in 1761, and the collection of the Agricultural Society of Maine, one of its branches. The Agricultural Society, founded in 1761, was divided into three sections, Tours, Angers, and Le Mans, and met once a week. In Tocqueville's notes this passage ends with the following crossed-out lines: Strange connection of causes! The same system of government which, the Revolution completed, is the greatest guarantee of a gross and excessive equality, was, before the Revolution, the most efficient cause of maintaining, and even creating, an absurd inequality; the sole difference is that then it worked on classes, now on individuals. Then and now its intention was to isolate.

Page 283, note 27, last line

Tocqueville's research notes (Folder K) present a complementary idea: To want great political freedom without provincial or municipal freedoms, is as if one wanted to make great universities flourish in a country where one had destroyed the elementary and high schools.

Page 283, note 27, end of last line

However, among us it is some people's dream. Pure dream —*Copy.*

Page 283, note 28, line 1

Oeuvres, Turgot, Observations de M. le Garde des Sceaux sur le projet d'édit proposé par M. Turgot pour la suppression des corvées, et réponses de ce ministre, v. 8, p. 196.

Page 284, note 29, last line

Projet d'une imposition territoriale, Oeuvres, Turgot, v. 4, p. 192. In this proposed edict of 1764 to improve the raising of the vingtième, the landowners of the fief elect a representative to be present at the tax department, about which Turgot comments: "It is very inconvenient to remember the spirit of privilege and distinction in the division of a tax in which they are never heard, and to put injustice under the guard of vanity, credit, and power."

Page 284, note 30, last line

Extract from Tocqueville's research notes (Folder H) on a file titled "Intendance. Ministerial correspondence 1766–1770." Colbert was the Controller-General of Finance.

Page 285, note 31, last line

Arthur Young, Voyages en France pendant les années 1787–88–89 et 90, Buisson, 1794—Year II, v. 1, pp. 455–56, journal of 26 July 1789. The quotation is not literal but is faithful to the meaning of the text.

Page 285, note 32, last line

Conflict between the inhabitants of Tigné and the marquis de Beauveau, example taken from a file titled "subdelegation," Tours archives. The example is followed in Tocqueville's research notes (Folder H) by this commentary: We see, for the rest, how from this period on, the agents of the bureaucracy made their rules superior over everyone and subjected everyone to their will, unless however by chance there was a noble with support at Paris who knew how to defend himself against the ministers and their agents.

Page 285, note 33, line 5

In his notes Tocqueville refers to the Declaration of 1763 forbidding organizations of merchants and artisans to borrow money without having been authorized to do so by letters patent.

Page 286, note 34

Analysis taken from the works of the Agricultural Society of Maine, 1761.

Page 286, note 35, line 12

Example taken from a file titled: "letters of the Controller-General to the Intendant, 1781, 1782, 1783," Tours archives.

Page 287, note 37

The analysis of the cahiers of the nobility was given additional proofs through a process of drafting an outline and then filling in details without changing the mean-

ing. For an example of the method, see Tocqueville's note on feudal dues, where the same process is observable.

Page 294, last line

Tocqueville gives an ambivalent interpretation of the summary of the cahiers of the nobility (research notes, Folder C): The nobility participates in the spirit of the times, tending to uniformity and despotism; thus the wish that "the organization and administration of the provincial estates be uniform throughout the Kingdom" (summary p. 83): Remark this invasion by the spirit of the times, this identity between the ideas of the nobles and the ideas of the people who were going to be their opponents, in everything which did not directly and visibly effect the nobility, how this nation of the old regime was already <u>one</u>, how all the differences were only artificial, and how the idea of uniformity, passing through all these apparent differences, had taken root in all minds! What contempt for the past, for tradition, in this class which only lived by virtue of tradition and the past!

But on the other hand Tocqueville insisted on the nobles' traditional attachment to freedom and decentralization, citing the nobility's wish (summary, p. 91): The provincial estates must be given all power to regulate everything which can be favorable to agriculture, commerce, manufactures, poverty, and any other purposes whatsoever, apt to improve the situation of the inhabitants of the provinces, being by their position in a better state to judge the local means appropriate to this end. *Tocqueville comments:* It is easy to see that the best-rooted and most developed ideas of local freedoms and decentralization persisted in the nobility. Much more than the physiocrats, much more innovative however, the nobles were the natural rivals of central authority; they retained better, furthermore, the old spirit of the Middle Ages. See, instead of that, the physiocrats, centralizers, and revolutionaries. New spirit.

In 1857 the reading of the cahiers of the nobility of Amiens inspired the following conclusion in Tocqueville:

<u>Identity of the wishes of the three orders for free institutions.</u> The more I read the cahiers, the more I am certain that in the matter of freedom, of free institutions, of the government of the country by itself, the wishes of the three orders were not merely analogous but <u>identical</u>. If the ideas and the language of one order are more lively in this sense than those of another, it is those of the nobility. Often quasi-republican, <u>vote by head</u>. Here, that is to say on the question of equality, of the relationships of classes to one another, division starts. In the relations of all the classes in general or of the nation with the king, here there is no division at all.

Page 295, note 39, line 5

Jérome-Marie-Champion de Cicé, bishop of Rodez, president of the provincial government, asked that the transcripts be printed to inform the citizens, 5 October 1779.

Page 296, note 42
Taken from Tocqueville's notes (Folder I) on the files of the former Generality of Paris at the Hotel de Ville.

Page 296, note 43, title
This note appears in a slightly different version in Tocqueville's notes (Folder K), under the crossed-out title: That the System of Loans and the Completely Modern Action of Public Credit Facilitate the Establishment and Duration of Despotism.

Page 296, note 43, last line
In Tocqueville's notes (Folder K): The final result will be hardly felt by him and perhaps will never be felt by anyone, if a wise and economical government succeeds his own.

Page 297, line 2
Example taken from a file titled: "Intendance. Ministerial letters 1766–1770," Tours archives. In his notes (Folder H), Tocqueville adds this commentary: How many things escaped the intendants. We see in this same file that the inhabitants of Montbazon abolished the syndic there, elected a Town Council, decided on a tax. All this without the intendant knowing anything, except because of requests for information made of him by the Controller-General. Which proves not freedom, but isolation. Because as soon as he knew he made haste to annul all these acts.

Page 297, note 45
Curé de Noisai, example taken from the file titled "subdelegation," Tours archives.

Page 297, note 46
Report sent in 1788 by some peasants in response to an inquiry made by the intermediary commission of Touraine, example taken from a file titled "Intermediary Commission," Tours archives.

Page 297, note 47
Extract from Tocqueville's research notes of 9 July 1853 taken on the file titled "intendance, correspondence on the vingtièmes," Tours archives.

Page 297, note 48
Extract from notes (Folder H) taken at the Tours archives on the file titled "Intendance. Ministerial letters 1766–1770," letter of January 1775 from the Comte de Vibraye to the intendant.

Page 298, note 51, line 6
Extract from notes (Folder H) taken at the Tours archives on a file titled "militia."

Page 298, last line
Letter from Turgot to the Controller-General, on the corvée for the passage of troops, Limoges, 19 April 1765, Oeuvres, Turgot, v. 4, p. 375.

Page 299, note 52
Example from notes (Folder H) taken at Tours on a file titled "Intendance. Ministerial letters 1766–1770."

Page 299, note 52, line 9, after "king"
He also recommends making sure that the peasants are wrong. In general, as one gets closer to the Revolution, power shows itself more gentle, more concerned with the needs and rights of the lower classes. This comes from all the correspondence. The intendant. —*From Tocqueville's research notes.*

Page 299, note 52, line 18
François-Pierre Du Cluzel, marquis de Montpipeau (1734–1783), councilor of the Grand Council (1755), master of requests (1759), intendant of Tours from October 1766 to 9 August 1783, the date of his death. On the corvée at Tours see François Dumas, La Généralité de Tours et l'intendant Du Cluzel (1766–1783), Paris, 1894, pp. 55–74. There were around 150,000 to 200,000 corvéables in the generality annually.

Page 300, note 54, line 8
Truncated quotation from Histoire de mon temps (1740), Oeuvres historiques of Frederick the Great, 1830, v. 2, chap. 1, p. 67.

Page 301, note 56
Quotation taken from Häusser, Deutsche Geschichte, v. 1, p. 128. If Tocqueville owes to Häusser the remark that the rulers are better than in preceding centuries, he differs from him in attributing to France the merit of this improvement. The author, writes Tocqueville in his notes (Folder Q), like a real German who speaks so often and with reason of the bad influence of France, forgets to say that the majority of these rulers had been more or less influenced by our eighteenth-century philosophy, directly or indirectly.

Page 302, line 5
Tocqueville uses here the notes (Folder Q) taken in June 1853 on Blackstone, Commentaries on the Laws of England. This is similar to Tocqueville's reflections on English law during his second trip to England, Oeuvres, Pléiade, v. 1, pp. 608–9. Neither the MS. nor the Copy of this note has been found.

Page 303, note 56, line 21, after "authority"
In Tocqueville's research notes the following discussion is inserted here: And do not say: this is the result of this or that disposition of English law. No. For that

matter one would not know what in particular to use to show it, just as one would not know what part of the law to detach in order to separate it from the whole, just as one would not know how to say what was the particular source of life in a human body. So much do we perceive that everything here concurs, simultaneously, in the guarantee of individual rights and their free defense against oppression, from whatever side it may come.

The basis, the form, the administrative rules like all the others, everything is in accord. The same idea reigns everywhere. It is in examining the laws and customs of the English in detail, much more than in regarding their great political institutions, that we understand what freedom is, how it is obtained, how it lasts, and that we see clearly how dangerous and absurd it is to believe that one can, in the heart of the same society, seemingly form two regions. In one region self-government, publicity, guaranties; in the other, dependence, secrecy, arbitrariness, and the absence of forms to protect the weak man against the strong. Above all the weak man par excellence in our democratic societies, the individual, against the strong man par excellence, the state. In a word, what a miserable daydream to believe that we can long combine political laws taken from the spirit of the Republic with bureaucratic laws taken from the spirit of the absolute monarchy.

Page 303, note 57
From Tocqueville's notes (Folder I) on the former Generality of Paris, taken at the Hotel de Ville.

Page 304, note 59
This thought was inspired by reading Turgot.

Page 304, note 60, last line
Extract from a file titled "intendance, correspondence on the vingtièmes," Tours archives. In his notes (Folder H), after having cited Terray's circular on the increase of the vingtième of 6 May 1772, where Terray affirms that "the vingtième is a tax proportionate to the income of capital, it can never give rise to arbitrariness. It is not at all communal," Tocqueville comments: This is very nice, but the problem was to find a way for the government to evaluate income exactly. The minister refused to give a general method to follow. This is what makes the enormous arbitrariness, above all when one asked for an increase . . . The arbitrariness was not in the nature of the tax, but in the uncertainty of its base. Nothing can replace a cadaster . . . We see that the Revolution only generalized, perfected, and increased the tax of the vingtièmes, established by Louis XIV, and whose excellence was recognized 20 years before the Revolution by the minister, who wanted to make it the chief territorial tax.

Page 305, note 61
*Oeuvres, Turgot, v. 7, Mémoire de M. Turgot au Roi, pour lui proposer l'aboli-
tion des contraintes solidaires pour le paiement des impositions royales, pp. 124–25.*

Page 305, note 62
Example taken from a file titled "administrative correspondence," Tours archives.

Page 305, note 64
*Extracted with few modifications from Tocqueville's notes (Folder H) taken at
the Tours archives on a file titled "Intendance. Ministerial letters 1766–70."*

Page 305, note 64, line 21
*M. de Pasdeloup, whose request is supported by the intendant of Paris to the
intendant of Tours and not of Rouen. This example and the discussion which precedes it figure in the notes Tocqueville took at Tours (Folder H) on the "letters of
the Controller-General to the Intendant, 1781, 1782, 1783."*

Page 307, line 8, after "very"
special and so little attractive —*First and second editions.*

Page 307, line 14
*The note which follows in fact reproduces notes Tocqueville took on the work of
Renauldon, lawyer at the court of Issoudun, Traité historique et pratique des droits
seigneuriaux, Paris, 1765. Tocqueville had further consulted the Dictionnaire de droit
et de pratique by Ferrière (3d ed., 1749), L'Encyclopédie (article "franc-fief"), Le
Traité des rentes foncières by Henrion (1828), the Collection de décisions nouvelles
by Denisart (1754–56), and Les inconvénients des droits féodaux, by Boncerf (1776).
He also made an oral inquiry among his Norman friends, archivists, and scholars
like Delisle, and at Paris the lawyer Freslon, who advised him to consult the terriers
of some great houses deposited at the National Archives. Tocqueville's inquiry was
voluntarily partial, as his research notes state:* What interests me above all are the
effects of feudalism on the bourgeoisie and the lower classes (the commoners)
and not the effects which feudalism produced between noble and noble and fief
and fief.

Page 315, last line
Tocqueville's notes on Feudal Law (Folder O) show his persistent perplexity:
After having studied this whole subject of the feudal system there still remains
this obscure area: In a seigneurie—what is the seigneurie? The land owned or
the whole parish in which it is found? I see well all those to whom the lord has
ceded some land, large or small, in return for some advantages which he retained:
to one a domain in fief, to another a censive, but the other inhabitants of the

lordship to whom he had given nothing, by virtue of what were they obliged to furnish him, some of them corvées, others a percentage of the fruits of their harvest, these others to pay a market fee, to have their grain ground at the lord's mill . . . ? It is this point that I cannot clear up for myself.

This can only be explained by saying that in the beginning one of two things must have happened:

1) Either all the land of the parish had originally belonged to the lord, who had not accepted anyone, even as an inhabitant without possessions, except in return for certain conditions.

2) Or, which would be simpler, violence or the need for protection had established these customs which time had then legitimized.

Let us suppose a parish like Tocqueville under the old regime, and myself the lord. I suppose that an average proprietor like Roussel holds from me, as feudal lord, the lands that he possesses under the condition of faith and homage, and is in general covered by the feudal condition. I suppose again a small landowner like Doublet, who equally holds from me as a censive the piece of land which he possesses. Further as owner, and by civil and not feudal law, I could have rented the farm of le Pourg to Birette for a perpetual rent, that of La Valette to Lehot under an ordinary lease. Independently of these four men who all hold land from me, whether by feudal or civil title, there would be the mass of inhabitants, not possessing any land or possessing only land that they hold from others or do not hold from anyone. All those there, as inhabitants of the parish, would be required to grind their grain at my mill, to bake at my oven, to accept my right of pigeon-keeping, and to pay me certain fees.

Glossary

Algeria. Algeria was a French colony 1830–1962.

cahiers. The lists of grievances drawn up separately by each of the three orders, clergy, nobility, and commons, before a meeting of the Estates-General. They were written up in each locality, and then those of the Third Estate were edited and combined to form cahiers at the regional and provincial levels.

Canada. By "Canada" Tocqueville does not mean the modern nation but the French colony, which consisted largely of the area that is the present-day Canadian province of Quebec.

capitation. A personal tax designed in theory to strike everyone except the clergy, whether they paid the taille or not.

Charles VI. King of France from 1380 to 1422, he suffered frequent bouts of insanity.

Charles VII. King of France from 1422 to 1461, he recovered most of France from the English with the aid of Joan of Arc.

Commynes, Philippe de (c.1447–1511). The author of celebrated memoirs, he was the adviser of both Duke Charles the Bold of Burgundy and later of King Louis XI of France.

Constituent Assembly, National Assembly. June 1789–September 1791. The successor of the Estates-General after the Revolution had broken out in earnest.

Constitution of 1791. First French constitution after the Revolution.

corvée. Traditionally, forced labor that the peasant or artisan was required to provide for his lord, without payment. More broadly, any kind of forced labor, paid or unpaid, whether performed for a lord or the king.

Dragonnades. The persecution of French Protestants by Louis XIV.

Estates-General. The meeting of the representatives of each of the three orders, traditionally convoked by the king in order to receive approval for new taxes. None had been held, however, since 1614. The Third Estate declared itself to be the National Assembly in June 1789 (see *Constituent Assembly*).

Fénelon/Salentum. Abbé Fénelon (1651–1715) was a bishop, a member of Louis XIV's court, later disgraced for his Jansenist religious opinions. He was the author of the *Adventures of Telemachus,* a work very popular in the eighteenth century, in which Salentum figured as a Utopia.

Fronde (1648–1651). Party of opposition to the royal government led by elements of the nobility and culminating in a revolt by the city of Paris and portions of the nobility.

Generality. An administrative division of old-regime France, directed by an intendant.

Gymnasia. Elite German high schools.

Ile-de-France. The region surrounding Paris.

Jacquerie. Great peasant rebellion of 1358.

John II. King of France from 1350 to 1364, he was captured by the English at the battle of Poitiers in 1356 and ransomed at great price.

Letrone, Guillaume-François (1718–1780). Physiocratic publicist.

lettres de cachet. A document issued by the king with which anyone could be imprisoned without trial and held indefinitely.

Maillotins. Name given to the 1382 rebellion of Paris against new taxes.

Mercier de la Rivière (1720–1793). Important physiocrat and enlightened man of letters.

Mill of Sans-Souci. Frederick had a palace at Potsdam called Sans-Souci. Frederick wanted to buy a windmill from the local miller, who refused to sell. When Frederick threatened him, the miller told the king he should obey the law, and Frederick backed down. The story is probably apocryphal.

National Assembly. See Constituant Assembly.

National Convention. Name of the French parliament from September 1792 to October 1795.

pays d'élection. Those provinces of France, the majority, where provincial assemblies of Estates no longer existed.

pays d'états. Those provinces of France which still possessed traditional provincial assemblies, known as provincial Estates, some of which, e.g., Languedoc and Brittany, had considerable rights and privileges. See the Appendix.

parlement. Not to be confused with the Estates-General, the parlement was the chief court of each region. In addition to its judicial functions it also had certain administrative powers. The parlement of Paris had primacy over the other parlements. Most important, the parlement of Paris was supposed to register royal edicts, including tax edicts, in order for them to have the force of law.

philosophes. Term used to describe the philosophers and men of letters of the eighteenth-century French Enlightenment.

physiocrats. A group of French economists and social reformers in the eighteenth century who were united by the belief that land was the only true form of wealth. Leading members included Letrone, Mercier de la Rivière, Quesnay, and Turgot.

Polish Diet. The medieval Polish legislature, in which a single negative vote could veto any proposal. It persisted until the eighteenth century.

presidial. Appeals Court. Established in 1551 in certain towns to be the final court of appeal for less important cases. In other matters, verdicts of the presidial were subject to appeal to the parlement.

Quesnay, François (1694–1774). Leading physiocrat, author of the influential *Tableau économique.*

Salentum. See Fénelon.

Sixteen. Name of the Paris city council which ruled the city, largely independent of outside authority, during the Wars of Religion.

St. Louis. King Louis IX of France (1214–70). He died while on Crusade in Tunisia, after having done much to consolidate royal authority.

Sully, Duc de (1560–1641). Minister under Henry IV, undertook financial and tax reforms and attempted to encourage trade and above all agriculture.

Swiss. The French army in 1789 included a number of units of foreign mercenaries, both Swiss and German, who were collectively known as the "Swiss."

taille. The fundamental personal tax of eighteenth-century France. It was based on a total amount to be raised from the whole kingdom. In most of France individuals contributed to it in proportion to their supposed total wealth, but in some *pays d'états* it was a land tax. Nobles, clergymen, and others who possessed privileges were largely exempt from paying the taille and the other taxes based on it.

Third Estate. The commons. The clergy were the First Estate and the nobility were the Second Estate. Everyone else was a member of the Third Estate.

Thirty Years War (1618–48). Period of general warfare in Europe, triggered by conflict between Protestants and Catholics.

tithe. A payment, proportional to one's harvest or income, typically owed to the Church, but also often to one's lord.

Treaty of Westphalia. Signed in 1648, it ended the Thirty Years War, and formed the diplomatic basis of Europe until the French Revolution.

Vendée. Region of western France which was a center of royalist opposition and revolt against the Revolution.

vingtième. A 5 percent income tax imposed on both nobles and commoners.

Wars of Religion. Sixteenth-century struggles between French Catholics and Protestants, which ended with the Protestant claimant to the throne converting to Catholicism as Henry IV (1589).

Index

This index covers the Introduction as well as Tocqueville's text. The Notes and Variants have not been indexed. See under S for 1787, 1788, 1798, 1791, and 1793; see under E for 1848.

Absolute government
  accepted by the French, 170
  aristocracy needed to avoid, 87
  in Canada, 281
  cannot be combined with consent, 127
  and centralization, 245
  China as ideal type, 213
  combined with democracy, 130
  destroys economy, 218
  encouraged by revolution, 85, 98
  encourages social homogenization, 29, 31,
    152, 191
  enlightened absolutism, 300
  inherent vices, 223
  physiocrats and, 212–13
  taxes and, 296
absolute monarchy
  and aristocracy, 32, 34
  and bourgeoisie, 99, 199
  centralized, 28
  created civil society, 30, 34
  defined as old regime, 23
  destroyed itself, 53
  divided people, 191
  and equality, 34, 35, 38, 211–13
  and freedom, 38–39, 171–72, 176
  hatred of peasant for, 8
  inherited older elements, 15
  intermediate social state, 32
  necessary, 6
  parlements' last opposition to, 215
  practice and representation, 10
  Roman law and, 258
  unlike medieval monarchy, 104
  when created, 259
Algeria, 26, 273

Allgemeines Landrecht. See Prussian Code
America
  absent in The Old Regime, 30
  archetype of democracy, 20
  compared to Canada, 281
  contrasted to France, 15
  decentralization in, 281
  definition of "gentleman" in, 154
  editions of The Old Regime, 75
  English influence, 26
  example of peaceful equality, 5, 6
  ideal liberal society, 74
  influence of American Revolution, 201
  lacked old regime, 14–15
  model, 213
  New England township, 129
  possible future of France, 11
  religion in, 45–47, 206
  respect for majority, 300
  Revolutionary War, 220
  role of cities, 145
  role of individual, 31, 281
  rule of law, 285–86
  state subject to courts, 66
  taste for generalization, 43–44
Ampère, Jean-Jacques, 9, 69
Anarchy
  not favored by Revolution, 105
  popular dictatorship and, 245
  of urban lower classes, 234
Argenson, R. L. Voyer d', 120, 138
Aristocracy
  absence of real, 42, 43
  absolute monarchy and, 4, 24, 32, 33, 34, 35,
    50, 54, 98, 115, 131, 143, 156, 173, 181–82, 191,
    198, 269, 270, 272

Aristocracy (*continued*)
  Arthur Young on, 94
  Austria and, 115
  beggars, 144
  bourgeoisie and, 29, 31, 38, 151–54, 155, 157, 158, 190–91
  bourgeoisie as pseudo-, 176
  bureaucracy as, 139
  cahiers of, 287–94
  Canada without, 280
  as caste, 29, 30, 32, 33, 37, 38, 152–53, 156, 241
  centralization and, 37, 115, 124, 137, 182, 293
  collective individualism, 32
  destruction of, 32, 35, 50, 87, 106
  in 1848, 5
  England and, 3, 17, 30, 33, 105, 153, 157, 163–64
  Estates-General and, 94, 150, 249, 293
  freedom and, 36, 37, 39, 87, 163, 172–73, 216
  guild as, 168
  hated by physiocrats, 212, 213
  ideal type, 25
  ideas and, 198
  impoverishment of, 4, 29–30, 150, 151, 283
  intendants recently ennobled, 120
  isolation of, 190–91, 241, 282
  judicial powers of, 115, 154
  peasantry and, 41, 181–82
  language and, 153–54
  Languedoc, 256
  medieval, 16, 104, 259
  obsessed with privilege, 2, 7
  officers without troops, 241–42
  physiocrats hate, 212, 213
  political inexperience of, 199
  political prerogatives of, 4, 23, 27, 29, 30, 32, 114, 115, 117, 124, 156, 238, 272
  prestige of, 121
  Prussian Code and, 263–64
  purchase of, 32, 34, 53, 157–58, 290
  recent, 33
  return to religion, 207
  in Rhineland, 265
  similarity to commoners, 290, 294
  social state, 4, 12, 14, 22, 23, 32, 103, 259, 303
  tax-exemptions, 32, 115, 156–57, 158, 164, 165, 167, 186, 198, 229, 241, 283, 284, 309
  urbanization of, 29, 31, 180–81
  Vendée, 181
  view of history, 2
Artisans
  excluded from city government, 127, 161–62
  guilds and, 168, 234, 275, 277

  imprisoned without trial, 289
  taxation of, 271
Association
  charitable, 123, 188
  conflict among associations, 161–62
  free, 139
  political, 188
  Prussian Code on, 262
Austria, 111, 115, 260

Barante, Guillaume, 1
Barruel, abbé, 41, 42
Beaumarchais, P. A. de Caron, 223
Beaumont, Gustave de, 9, 63, 70, 73, 74, 76
Beyle, Henri. *See* Stendhal
Blackstone, Sir William, 69, 301–3
Blank slate
  Burke on, 18
  fiction, 15
  created by Louis XIV, 54
  Revolution as, 13, 25, 34, 48
Bolingbroke, Henry Saint John, 206
Bonaparte, Bonapartists. *See* Napoleon I; Napoleon III
Bourgeois, bourgeoisie. *See also* Absolute monarchy; Aristocracy; Lower classes; Peasants
  bureaucrats, 139
  connected to judiciary, 234
  control urban government, 127, 161, 162, 269, 270, 272, 276
  desire for independence, 37, 175–76, 178
  desire for public employment, 159
  as dominant, 38
  enrichment, 4, 29–30, 151
  excluded from political power, 139, 199
  governing Languedoc, 256
  habit of submission, 128, 269
  in Estates-General, 150, 155
  in Prussian Code, 262–63
  internally divided, 34, 161, 176, 276–77
  isolated from peasants and lower classes, 32, 34, 40–41, 127, 158, 160–61, 162, 176, 191
  not irreligious outside France, 203
  as office-holders, 32, 66, 159
  political inexperience of, 199
  return to religion, 207
  soft, 37
  tax exemptions, 32, 159, 160
  urbanization of, 31, 40, 182, 282
Boutmy, E., 12

Brittany
  backward, 52, 222
  Estates, 256
  retained provincial liberty, 249
  and Vendée, 52
Bureaucracy. *See also* Absolute monarchy;
  Centralization
  absolute monarchy and, 32, 38
  antithetical to freedom, 245
  aristocracy and, 33, 115, 172
  class, 139
  confused with government, 28, 51
  creation of old regime, 24
  defeated aristocracy, 27
  despotic, 26
  dominates local powers, 104, 114
  effects of 1787 reform, 238
  habits, 138
  incarnated in intendant, 234
  independent of society, 24
  judge of society, 34
  language of, 139
  love of progress, 52
  love of statistics, 139
  modern derived from old regime, 8–9, 27, 185
  omnipresent, 25
  and paternalism, 43, 50
  in *pays d'états*, 235, 252, 254
  physiocrats rely on, 212, 216
  and rationalism, 48
  timidity of, 172
Burke, Edmund, 13, 18–19, 54, 77, 94, 95,
  106–7, 147, 150, 157, 198, 243

Caesar, Julius, 94
Cahiers
  demand a revolution, 199
  fear of Swiss, 94
  of the clergy, 68, 78, 174
  of the nobility, 78, 173, 198, 287–94
  of the Third Estate, 158
  show little fear of populace, 94
  show similarity of French, 149
  Tocqueville analyzed summary of, 68
  Tocqueville's notes on, 76, 78
  Tocqueville's use of, 84
Canada, old-regime centralization of, 26,
  280–81
Caste. *See* Aristocracy, as caste
Catholicism, Catholic Church. *See also*
  Religion
  cahiers of the clergy, 68, 78, 174

  cahiers of the nobility and, 288–89, 291
  civil society and, 174
  and democracy, 46, 97
  freedom desired by, 37, 68, 173, 174–75, 295
  in Germany, 300
  independent, 37, 68, 173–74
  landownership, 40, 113, 173, 174
  in Languedoc, 256
  leading tithers in Europe, 116
  marriage of priests, 203
  and monarchy, 47, 205
  at outbreak of Revolution, 175, 204
  part of old regime, 45, 47, 97, 116, 204–5, 242
  peasants alienated by, 265–67, 297
  and Protestantism, 44–46
  public opinion opposed to, 45
  servility, 47, 173
  Tocqueville deplored Revolution's break
    with, 42
Causes
  of democracy unknown, 19
  of end of feudalism, 259
  of French irreligion, 204
  of French Revolution, 19, 41, 42, 43, 72, 93,
    96–97, 163, 164, 243
  of hatred of feudalism
  of importance of capital, 145–46, 148
  independent of intentions, 7
  of old regime, 25
  of rural ignorance
  of successful revolutions, disappearance
    of, 95
  Tocqueville's search for historical, 3, 7, 8, 10
  of triumph of Roman law, 258
  of upper-class urbanization, 158, 173–74
Centralization
  administrative, 1–2, 20, 23, 28, 118–24
  in Canada, 26, 280–81
  of charity, 124, 138, 268
  continuity, 1–2, 39, 55, 67, 118, 145, 171, 245
  democracy and, 23
  effect on urban government, 128
  in 1836 Essay, 23–24
  encourages urbanization, 182
  freedom and, 37, 51, 55, 216, 245
  government, 148, 171, 216
  imperfect in old regime, 23, 27, 28, 171
  increases after destruction of aristocracy, 137
  industry and, 269
  intellectuals and, 42
  leads to equality, 98, 179, 245
  Napoleonic, 55

Centralization (*continued*)
origins, 135–38
product of civilization, 67, 137
in Prussia, 70
Revolution and, 28, 39, 42, 47, 51, 137, 216, 245
survives Revolution, 27
Charity
in cahiers of the nobility, 289–90
central government control of, 124, 138, 268
clergy favor public, 175
increases near Revolution, 219–20
in Languedoc, 253
at Paris, 303
Charles VI, 164
Charles VII, 156, 164
Charles VIII, 272
Chateaubriand, François-Auguste-René de, 1
Church. *See* Catholicism; Religion
China, 48, 213
Circourt, Adolphe de, 11, 59
Civil society
becoming enlightened, 103
Catholic clergy and, 174
created by absolutism, 30, 34
determines political change, 23
disassociated from politics, 30
incomplete in old regime, 34
linked individuals, 295
nobility in, 32
Roman law and, 258
Civilization
breaks down barriers, 103
French, 300
German, 70, 259–60, 300
hindered by provincial assemblies, 104
led to centralization, 67, 137
literary, 43
monarchy and, 53
not changed by Revolution, 105
parlements condemned by, 67
peasants not helped by, 180–92
providential meaning, 17
provincial estates adaptable to, 256
roads and, 297
rulers act in name of, 16
sense of movement, 40
Tocqueville's use of term, 27, 52
universal path of, 5
Classes. *See also* Aristocracy; Bourgeoisie; Bureaucracy; Lower classes; Peasantry
abolition of privileges, 96
alone interest history, 181

in cahiers, 287
division of, isolation of, 39, 41, 163–71, 189, 191, 238, 239
freedom within, 179, 295
hatred among, 35, 38
legal barriers between, 35
nonrural, 37
Old Regime not history of, 62
only one class, 98
physiocrats on, 213
relations among, 84
similarity of, 103, 149–52
struggle of, 24
Clergy. *See* Catholicism; Religion
Colbert, Jean-Baptiste, 26, 168, 280
Commynes, Philippe de, 164
Comte, Auguste, 41
Conscription
accepted during and after Revolution, 122, 186
in cahiers of the nobility, 288
how carried out, 186
humiliating to lower classes, 175
old-regime militia worse than modern, 122
peasants hid from, 40, 186
Tocqueville's study of, 66
Constant, Benjamin, 41, 67
Constituent Assembly
destroyed old provinces, 147, 210
end of Revolution, 50
ordered creation of land registers, 61
repeated in 1848, 5
Constitution
administrative, 54, 63, 240
ancient, or old, of Europe, 16, 17, 103, 104, 105, 106, 157, 198, 241, 263, 296
aristocratic, 58
in cahiers of the nobility, 288, 289, 292
constitutional monarchy, 220
of 1848, 58
English, 17, 105, 288, 303
of France, 134, 168, 242
German town, 259
of Languedoc, 253, 254, 256
national, 101
old regime as semiconstitutional, 54
parish, 129
political, 54, 100, 118, 240, 261
provincial, 72, 104, 249
Prussian Code as, 261
of 1791, 261
taught to children, 289

of town, 103, 119, 126, 254, 269, 270–77
vices, 218
of the Year VIII, 26
Convention, 68, 236
Corcelle, 10
Corvée
  applied widely, 156, 187, 298–99
  arranged by subdelegate, 122
  attacked, 228
  attempt to abolish, 225
  cahiers of the nobility demand abolition,
    289
  case of mistreatment evoked, 135
  Church, 116
  in Ile-de-France, 222
  imprisonment for, 298
  manorial or seigneurial, 111, 115, 303, 313
  none in Languedoc, 252, 253
  peasants and, 40, 189
  project of replacing with tax, 166–67, 187
  Prussian Code and, 262
  for road repair, 186, 298
  Syndic and, 183
Courts
  administrative, 133
  bourgeoisie's involvement in, 234
  in cahiers of the nobility, 288
  conflict with executive, 66
  confusion in 1787, 234
  English, 301–3
  executive usurped authority, 176
  extraordinary, 132, 135
  extraordinary, and clergy, 175
  extraordinary, and poor, 189, 232–33
  guardian of liberty, 176–77
  independent, 132, 177
  mixture of judicial and executive power,
    134, 169
  outstripped by executive, 137
  protests of, 296
  role in legislation, 119, 123
  Royal Council as, 119
  sole opposition to centralization, 136
  Tocqueville's research and notes on, 66, 77
  unchanged in English Revolution, 240
  venality sometimes useful for, 125, 176
  in Württemberg, 257–58

Declaration of the Rights of Man
  Prussian Code resembles, 261
  Tocqueville's love of, 38
Deism, 300

Democracy
  as abstraction, 13
  America as pure type of, 5
  American and Canadian, 281
  American compared to French, 14–15, 30
  attracted to general ideas, 43
  centralization and, 23, 138
  and despotism, 48, 212–12
  and envy, 241
  favors imagination, 53
  at flood tide, 1
  forms of combined with absolutism, 130
  history ends with, 5
  idea of freedom, 36
  and individualism, 32, 35
  limited suffrage denies, 22
  of medieval parish, 129
  and monarchy, 259
  need guaranties for individual against state,
    303
  origin incomprehensible, 19, 20
  Prussian Code democratic but not liberal,
    261
  religion and, 45–47, 97
  rural government retained elements of, 130
  social state, 31–32
  temperament, 210
  tends to social homogenization, 31, 88
  Tocqueville annoyed democrats, 75
  Tocqueville studied in America, 3
  transition to, 1
  tyranny, 5
Despotism
  bureaucratic, 26, 55
  clergy opposed, 174
  democratic, 36, 48, 87–88, 212–13, 246
  first stage of Revolution opposed, 38
  French tolerance for, 6, 50, 56, 245, 246
  imperial, 39, 55
  physiocrats and, 210, 212–13
  royal, 223, 231
  Russian, 70
Diderot, Denis, 139, 206
Doctrinaires, 41
Draft. See Conscription
Dragonnades, 223

Economists. See Physiocrats
Edict of Nantes, 44
Education
  in cahiers of the nobility, 289, 294
  clergy and, 68

Education (*continued*)
  controlled by men of letters, 201, 202
  of a free nation, 177, 195
  physiocrats and, 210–11
  in Prussian Code, 123
  revolutionary, 53, 230–33
  same for aristocracy and bourgeoisie, 31, 151
  and the state, 68, 294
1848
  affected Tocqueville's views, 24, 40
  justified Tocqueville, 5
  replay of the French Revolution, 3, 5
England, the English
  absence of police, 143–44
  always different, 17, 30
  aristocratic, 17, 30, 33, 151, 153–54, 157, 163–64
  attitude to majority, 300
  class divisions, 152
  constitution, 17, 281
  effects of freedom, 163–64, 200, 209, 285–86
  intellectuals and politics, 195, 200
  irreligion, 206, 209, 300
  landowners govern, 115
  laws, 221, 240, 301–3
  libertarian spirit, 26, 281
  pay feudal dues on land, 116
  physiocrats condemn, 212
  political experience, 94, 200
  Poor Law, 23
  really modern, 17, 105, 240
  respect for dead, 232
  Revolution, 17, 54, 240
  role of comparison, 30, 69, 74
  Tocqueville's 1836 essay for English readers, 3
  Tocqueville's note on, 77
  views of French Revolution, 94
Enlightenment. *See also* Intellectuals;
  Physiocrats
  abstraction, 15
  attitude to religion, 44
  confident in ability to alter mores, 300
  encouraged centralization, 27
  fascinated by politics, 43, 44, 52
  influenced both aristocracy and bourgeoisie, 31
  influenced peasantry, 196, 202
  Revolution blamed on, 41
  Tocqueville influenced by, 42
  Tocqueville's interpretation of, 73
Equality
  absolute monarchy and, 34, 35, 38, 211–13

  civil vs. political, 22
  despotism and, 88
  encourages centralization, 98, 179, 245
  Europe tends towards, 4, 18, 259
  France desires, 3, 50, 51, 85, 244, 245–46
  France typical of trend towards, 5
  freedom and, 2, 38, 49, 50, 85, 244–46, 281, 295
  philosophes and, 96
  physiocrats and, 48, 186, 210–14
  religion and, 45, 47
  Revolution acceleration of trend, 4
  Revolution as religion born of, 13
  social, 13, 22, 106
Estates-General
  brought together nobility and Third Estate, 155
  in cahiers, 94, 175, 291–94
  called in 1789, 38
  destroyed everywhere, 249
  fourteenth-century, 32, 150, 155
  gave political experience, 197
  imposed equal taxation, 165
  kings avoided calling, 166, 168, 169
  memory of, 214
  protests of, 169
Europe
  America and, 11
  Christianity in retreat throughout, 44, 45–
  46, 203
  eighteenth century compared to fifteenth,
  101
  England and, 17–18, 30, 97, 153
  evolution of, 4
  France and, 18, 19, 20, 29, 45–46, 59, 72, 85,
  107, 116, 118, 132, 145–48, 156, 159, 182, 195,
  241, 242, 249
  Germany and, 11, 103
  old constitution of, 16, 17, 103, 105, 107, 123,
  241, 263
  providential history, 17
  revolutionary tradition, 69
  Roman law in, 258
  shared major historical characteristics, 16,
  102–5, 106, 116, 152–53
  southern, 141
  Tocqueville's analysis European, 75

Fénelon, abbé, 201
Frederick II (the Great), 21, 70, 77, 93, 111, 129,
  203, 214, 260, 261–64, 300
Frederick William I, 260

Frederick William II, 263
Freedom
under absolutism, 34–35, 37, 49–50, 51, 72,
125, 130, 171–79, 242
America and, 14, 74, 281, 300
aristocracy and, 36, 37, 39, 87, 163, 172–73, 216
aristocratic and democratic, 36
cahiers of the nobility and, 287–94
charade of, 127, 130, 199
desire for, 2, 38, 49, 50, 55, 67, 68, 72, 85, 96,
209–17, 244–46
England and, 94, 152, 163, 206, 300
Enlightenment and, 73
equality and, 2, 38, 49, 50, 85, 244–45,
281, 295
French inexperience of, 43, 44, 49, 197,
198–99, 206
history of, 6
local, 74, 146, 163, 182, 242, 249–50, 283, 286
lower classes and, 125, 128, 177
medieval, 36
parish, 131
paternalism and, 26, 50
political, 31, 39, 49, 51, 104, 152, 163–71, 197,
209–17, 287
1789 and, 38, 86
Tocqueville's hopes for, 6, 74
Tocqueville's love of, 86–88
urban, 124, 125
Freslon, Pierre, 8, 11, 61, 67
Fronde, 145, 198

Germany. See also Frederick II; Frederick
William I; Frederick William II; Prussia
absolutism, 69
anti-aristocratic feeling, 263
corvée, 116
delayed France, 70
destruction of Estates, 249
England and, 21
Free Cities, 259–60
free peasants, 113, 264
irreligion in, 203
living old regime, 11, 21, 71, 154
nobility, 115
point of reference, 71
reformism in late eighteenth century, 300
Roman law in, 257–58
serfdom, 111–12, 260–61
similarity to medieval Europe, 102, 103–4
taxation, 156–57

Tocqueville studied German, 70
Tocqueville's notes on, 77
Government. See Absolute government
Guardianship. See Paternalism
Guizot, François, 1, 4, 5, 6, 16, 18, 19, 23, 24, 25,
27, 30, 56, 58

Helvétius, Claude Adrien, 206, 207
Henry III, 168
Henry IV, 169, 180
Holbach, Paul H. D. d', 206
Homogeneity
absolute government encourages, 29, 31,
152, 191
class division encourages, 152–63, 191
democracy tends towards, 31, 88
of French society, 141–45
Hume, David, 45, 206

Independence
aristocratic freedom and, 36
democracy tends towards, 43
democratic freedom and, 36
endurance of, 171–79
of English colonies, 281
vs. freedom, 7
government hatred of, 139–40
judicial, 125, 132–35, 177
leads to isolation, 87
mutual, of nobility and bourgeoisie, 32,
154–55
peasant passion for, 21, 117
state independent of society, 24
venal offices source of, 37
Individualism. See also Individuals
centralization smothers, 55
collective, 32, 35, 162–63, 191
democratic, 31, 32, 35, 87
democratic idea of freedom and, 36
physiocrats and, 48
smothers public virtues, 87
Tocqueville planned section on, 72
Individuals. See also Individualism
don't effect history in democratic eras, 43
freedom of, 68
isolation of, 33, 39, 152–63, 165, 191
nothing between state and, 142
rights of, 38, 232, 261, 287–94
Inequality. See also Equality
absolute government preserved, 35, 283
absolute monarchy created, 34

Inequality (*continued*)
 aristocratic, 303
 bourgeoisie supported, 191
 civil, 22
 feudal, 259
 hatred of, 244
 more apparent than real, 156
 political, 22
 of taxation, 156–57, 165, 169, 191, 238, 268, 284
Intellectuals
 abstraction, 56
 added to 1840 analysis, 44
 adore reason, 299–300
 all political in Enlightenment, 42, 44, 52, 195–202
 aristocracy favored, 198
 conflict with Church, 41, 45, 57, 72, 96, 97, 202–9, 300
 control political education, 201, 242
 desire simplicity and logic, 42, 196–97
 direct public opinion, 242
 free discussion permitted, 139–40, 197–98
 have unique place, 195
 influence aristocracy and bourgeoisie, 31
 leading politicians, 43, 195–202, 242
 lower class adjusts ideas, 244
 political inexperience and, 42, 72, 195, 242
 political systems differ widely, 196
 provinces lost, 146
 revolution and, 20, 96
 society celebrates, 42, 195, 197
 Tocqueville and German, 70–71
 Tocqueville's drafts on, 73
 Tocqueville's notes on, 77
 two aspects of, 96–97
Intendants
 administered draft, 122
 aristocracy refused to be, 121
 cahiers of the nobility and, 292
 controlled parish government, 114, 129–31, 278–80, 296
 controlled police, 122
 controlled town government, 126–27, 128, 161, 162, 270, 275–76
 description of, 120–22
 directed charity, 123–24, 145
 displaced traditional powers, 136
 elder Mirabeau disliked, 143
 France ruled by, 120, 121
 judicial role, 132–33, 305
 in Languedoc, 250–51
 made exceptions to rules, 141–42
 more progressive as Revolution approaches, 137, 219, 222
 never venal office, 125
 pivotal to bureaucracy, 25, 26
 political inexperience, 199
 provincial assemblies and, 53–54, 234, 306
 Royal Council and, 119, 120
 set taxes, 121, 144
 similar to modern bureaucrats, 138, 139
 supervised industry and crafts, 124, 142, 269, 281–82
 Tocqueville emphasizes role of, 24
 Tocqueville studied documents of, 25, 65
 Tocqueville's notes on, 77
Irreligion. *See also* Religion
 common in Europe, 45
 due to social situation, 96, 204–5, 242
 in eighteenth-century France, 45–46, 202–9
 of intellectuals, 57
 new character of, 203
Islam, 101

Jansenism, 44
Joseph II, 260
Judiciary. *See* Courts

Kergorlay, 1, 54, 56, 57, 60, 61
King John, 164

Landowners. *See also* Landownership
 bourgeoisie often, 151
 cens and, 307
 clergy as, 97, 174
 dependent on government, 144
 in 1848, 40
 England and Germany administered by, 115
 France not administered by, 21, 116–17
 peasants as, 21, 40, 112, 113, 116–17, 189, 264, 265
 in Prussian Code, 262
 Revolution's effects on, 113
 rich isolated from poor, 180–82, 187–88
 state of in 1789, 60, 77, 112
 Tocqueville's experience as, 61
Landownership. *See also* Landowners
 brings people together, 167
 Tocqueville defines feudalism as government based on, 21
 Tocqueville gives political interpretation, 29

Languedoc, 7, 74, 174, 185, 249–56, 295
Lavoisier, Antoine Laurent, 158
Law, John, 120
Letrone, G.-F., 76, 168, 188, 210, 211, 212
Liberalism
  clergy among most liberal, 295
  dilemma of, 22
  Enlightenment in liberal critique of Revo-
    lution, 41
  incompatible with paternalism, 26
  intendant more liberal than bourgeois, 276
  Malesherbes', 2
  Prussian Code not liberal, 261
  of Restoration historians, 6, 38
  Revolution liberal and illiberal, 38
  right to sue government index of, 66–67
  spirit of Revolution, 96
  Tocqueville desired, 74
  Turgot as liberal, 49
Liberty. See Freedom
Louis XI, 64, 125, 157, 161, 269, 272
Louis XII, 169
Louis XIII, 23, 254
Louis XIV, 24, 44, 51, 54, 64, 66, 125, 146, 156,
  166, 168, 181, 186, 217, 218, 223, 231, 252, 254,
  277, 280, 281, 310
Louis XV, 2, 9, 41, 140, 161, 166, 172, 177, 214,
  223, 230, 254
Louis XVI, 2, 23, 43, 148, 156, 168, 170, 178, 198,
  202, 217, 220, 223, 227, 230, 284
Louis-Philippe, 26
Lower classes. See also Peasants
  in cahiers of nobility, 289–90
  comprise all village inhabitants, 182
  contempt for, 185, 225–30, 305
  democracy and, 97
  drafted, 185–86
  estranged from bourgeoisie, 32, 34, 160–61,
    176, 191
  fear only police, 143
  gained from Revolution, 8, 60
  given revolutionary education, 53, 230–33
  government charity for, 123–24, 138, 264
  government harsh towards, 189, 232–33, 298
  hate medieval institutions, 18
  invest in land, 113
  long absent from politics, 225
  most harmed by feudal dues, 115
  new concern for, 219
  radicalized, 53, 225–30
  rulers incite against rich, 78–79

    tax system and, 164–65, 285
    at time of Revolution, 243–44
    upper classes' incomprehension of, 190, 199
    urban, and reforms, 234
    violent resistance to oppression, 177–78
Luther, Martin, 202

Maistre, Joseph de, 13, 95
Malesherbes, C. G. de Lamoignon de, 1, 2, 67
Maria-Theresa, 111
Marx, Karl, 5, 24, 40, 58
Masses. See Lower classes
Material well-being, passion for
  of bourgeoisie, 37
  civilization encourages, 52
  eighteenth century exempt from, 178
  freedom alone limits, 88
  mother of servitude, 178
Maupeou, R. N. de, 49
Mazarin, Cardinal de, 165
Men of letters. See Intellectuals
Mercier de la Rivière, L. S., 76, 212
Michelet, Jules, 1, 13, 14, 19, 52
Middle class. See Bourgeoisie
Mill, J. S., 3, 5
Mirabeau, G. R., the elder, 67, 143, 146
Mirabeau, G. R., the younger, 76, 97–98, 203
Molière, 153, 213
Mollien, F. N., 219
Monarchy. See Absolute monarchy
Montesquieu, Charles de Secondat de, 22, 42,
  56, 145, 153, 182
Morellet, A., 206, 213
Mores
  aristocratic, 31, 37, 173
  bourgeois, 31
  bureaucratic, 72
  Church and, 47
  effects of centralization on, 39, 143
  English, 152, 280–81
  Enlightenment belief concerning, 300
  freedom based on, 283
  Germanic, 249
  hindered centralization, 171
  industrial, 265
  of old regime invested in new world, 13
  of parlements had independent, 177
  peasants', 190
  and physiocrats' ideas, 49
  primacy over laws, 10, 27
  real basis, 84

Mores (*continued*)
Revolution made laws accord with, 4
softening of, 16, 52, 219, 243

Napoleon I, 8, 9, 38, 40, 50, 55, 57, 58, 96, 260
Napoleon III (Louis-Napoleon Bonaparte), 5,
8, 41, 58
National Assembly, 98
Necker, Jacques, 63, 77, 112, 157, 189, 220, 221,
287
Nobility. *See* Aristocracy

Pantheism, 47
Paris
became industrial, 147, 148
as center, 138
chapter on, 72
effect on Revolution, 148
growth, 146
home of leading nobles, 180
impotent during Wars of Religion, 145
omnipotence, 28, 31, 145–48, 151, 242
relative prosperity, 218
swallows provinces, 145–46, 147
Parish
controlled by central government, 26, 114,
131, 138, 278–79, 292
democratic before Revolution, 130
example of government, 288–89
forbidden to undertake public works, 166
ignorance of officials, 130
impotent, 130
intendant, taxes set by, 121
like American township, 129
lord in, 114, 130
New England township compared to, 129
officials of, 114, 129
old constitution of, 129
peasants attached to freedom of, 131
reform of in 1787, 234–35, 238–39
resemblance to American township, 129
Tocqueville studies government, 63
Turgot's proposed reform, 237
Parlements
defended their freedom, 177
destruction harmed monarchy, 230
given Estates' political functions, 169
government replaced, 136, 137
incite lower classes, 226
popularity, 49, 215
rebellions, 38

Tocqueville praised, 66–67
unable to keep up with society, 67, 137,
211
Voltaire's attack on, 215
Paternalism
abolished in 1789, 245
contrast with America, 43–44
created by old regime, 124–31
desire for, 50
equality and, 50
France subject to, 2
freedom and, 51
necessity, 274
restored, 245
shaped French, 26
state as, 26, 124, 216, 245, 278–80
Peasantry
attached to parish freedom, 131
contempt for, 40, 66, 130, 139, 305
corvée and, 186–87, 297, 298, 299
draft and, 185–86
English, 113
Enlightenment ideas and, 196, 202
estranged from bourgeoisie, 160, 191
German, 111–12, 113, 257, 264, 265
hatred of aristocracy and feudalism, 22, 60,
111–18, 266–67
incited by rulers, 99
isolated, 29, 34, 39–40, 72, 182–83, 185, 187–
88, 189, 191, 239, 267
as landowners, 21, 29, 75, 112–14
medieval, 103
oppressed by lords, 21–22, 113, 114
parish officials elected by, 114
Prussian Code, 123, 262
radicalized, 225–33
in 1789 and 1848, 40–41
state power over, 39–40
tax burden, 183–85, 297
urbanization of well-off, 182
worse off in eighteenth century, 180–92
Philosophes. *See* Intellectuals
Physiocrats
administrators and writers, 43, 48
China as model, 48, 213
favor absolute state, 48, 211, 212
favor drafting poorest peasants, 186
first socialists, 213–14
imagine democratic despotism, 48, 212–13
influence on Revolution, 48, 209
love equality, 186, 210

modern people similar to, 51, 214, 216
oppose individual rights, 210
philosophes and, 73, 209
saw intellectuals as aristocrats, 213
Tocqueville read, 67
Tocqueville's notes on, 76
uninterested in political freedom, 211, 214
Pilnitz, Declaration of, 93
Pitt, William, 94
Polish Diet, 256
Poor, the. *See* Lower classes
Press
    censored by Prussian Code, 264
    power of, 205
Proletariat. *See* Lower classes
Protestantism
    Jansenism an aborted, 44
    Reformation, 99
    Tocqueville silent on, 46
Provincial assemblies
    call for more police, 143, 282
    clergy in, 295
    complaint of, 183, 184, 253
    destroyed old regime, 53, 234–37, 306
    had best administrative methods, 185
    hindered progress, 104
    inquiries radicalize masses, 229
    new ones created in 1787, 53
    radical language, 227–28, 282
    Tocqueville read transcripts, 68, 84, 174
    Tocqueville's notes on, 77
Prussia
    atheists uncommon in, 203
    centralization, 70
    commoners as officers, 156
    law code, 123, 261–64
    lords required to aid peasants, 123
    nobility in administration, 115
    serfdom eliminated, 260
    Tocqueville read about, 70
    Tocqueville's notes on, 77
Prussian Code, 123, 261–64
Public opinion
    blank slate idea in 1789, 48
    braked authority, 36, 172, 221
    desire for self-government, 214–15
    directed by intellectuals, 242
    king obeys, 221
    led state and bureaucracy, 52, 172
    past devalued by, 17, 20
    physiocrats obey, 49

political sensitivity grows, 52
Voltaire ignorant of, 215

Quesnay, François, 48, 76, 210, 212, 214
Quinet, Edgar, 44

Religion. *See also* Catholicism; Irreligion
    Aim of Revolution not to destroy, 96–99, 105
    Americans support, 206
    in cahiers of the nobility, 288–89, 291
    Christianity's fate unclear, 47
    Church government, 295
    Church of England, 206
    determined by society, 47
    English support, 206
    Frederick the Great on, 300
    free discussion allowed, 140, 142
    irreligion of intellectuals, 57
    no more proselytizing, 44
    pagan, 100
    vs. philosophy, 41, 42, 213
    revives in nineteenth century, 46, 207
    Revolution a new kind of, 13, 46, 96, 99–101, 187
    Revolution borrowed ideas and feelings from, 18, 19, 28
    Revolution unlike, 16, 230
    spread of Christianity, 100
    Tocqueville's view on, 41, 45–47
Richelieu, Cardinal de, 66, 98, 168, 181, 185, 254
Robespierre, Maximilien de, 41
Roman Empire
    concentration of power in, 98
    decadence full of good Christians, 88
    feelings of independence, 36
    Montesquieu's history Tocqueville's model, 56
Roman law
    feudal law not imitation of, 102
    law of servitude, 258
    power in Germany, 257–58
    spread throughout Europe, 258
Rousseau, Jean-Jacques, 40, 41, 42, 139
Royal Council
    description of powers, 119–24
    destroyed charitable foundations, 232
    justifies bureaucratic delay, 138
    and Languedoc Estates, 250
    made exceptions to rules, 141
    made uniform national rules, 149
    power to evoke court cases, 132–35

Royal Council (*continued*)
  regulated industry, 269, 281
  set tax of nobles, 144
  supervised parish, 131
  supervised towns, 127–28, 272–73
  Tocqueville disliked judicial role of, 67
  Tocqueville studied, 66
Royer-Collard, P.-P., 10
Russia, 69, 75, 77

Saint-Simon, duc de, 41
Salentum. *See* Fénelon
Say, Jean-Baptiste, 48
Schiller, Friedrich von, 99
Scott, Sir Walter, 1
Serfdom
  Church had serfs, 116
  disappeared in France, 21, 112
  in Germany, 21, 111, 260
  nobility want to abolish, 287–88
  peasants compared to serfs, 189
  in Prussian Code, 262
1787
  provincial assemblies of, 166, 187, 219, 227,
    236, 253, 295
  reform of government in, 53, 234, 238, 306
1788
  Bordeaux's trade in, 220
  German peasants in, 111
  position of syndics in, 239
  provincial assemblies' circulars of, 228, 297
1789
  as continuity, 5, 83, 85, 13
  combined liberty and absolutism, 50
  easy acquisition of nobility in, 34, 158
  1848 and, 5, 40
  end of history, 9
  feudal dues in, 115, 312
  freedom and, 38, 86
  glory of, 7, 36
  government debt in, 224
  physiocrats and, 48, 51, 216
  provincial estates in, 241
  as rupture, 13, 54, 83, 85
  rural government in, 114
  two phases of Revolution in, 38–39
  what the French wanted in, 13, 14, 53
1791
  Constitution of, 261
1793
  aristocracy returns to religion after, 207

survivor of, 11
  Terror, 170
Sieyès, E. J., 33
Socialism
  centralization and, 214, 264
  first roots in absolute monarchy, 231
  physiocrats and, 213
  small peasants support, 260
St. Louis, 167
Staël, Mme. de (Germaine Necker), 30
Stendhal, 33, 42
Suard, Jean-Baptiste, 206
Sully, duc de, 213
Syndics
  degraded position, 183, 239, 306
  description of, 129–30
  illiterate, 182
  quarrel between, 296
  replaced by assemblies in 1787, 235
  rival, not delegate, 39
  role in parish government, 278–80
  tools of state, 26

Tabula rasa. *See* Blank slate
taxes
  advantages of Paris region, 303
  based on communities, not individuals, 32
  bourgeois control, 161
  in cahiers of the nobility, 287–94
  capitation, 121, 238, 270, 271, 275
  change in temperament of collection, 219,
    227, 228
  clergy protest, 175
  destroy old regime, 164–66
  English, 105, 164, 285
  Estates protest, 169
  exemptions and privileges, 32, 126, 142, 150,
    156–57, 160, 164, 168, 228, 229, 237, 266, 270,
    275, 280, 283, 284, 285, 286
  in fourteenth century, 165
  franc-fief, 167, 289
  increase in sales, 220, 222
  increases upset masses, 296
  industry shackled by, 148
  inequality in Europe, 156–57
  intendant and, 144
  in Languedoc, 251–52, 254
  lower classes crushed by, 66, 160, 165
  monarchy multiplied, 32
  parishes and, 114, 131
  in *pays d'états,* 185

in Prussian Code, 264
Revolution eliminates, 60
role in countryside, 39
Royal Council fixed, 119, 121, 133
1787 reform and, 53–54, 236–38
taille, 121, 156, 158–59, 164, 165, 183–84, 185, 198, 222, 226, 229, 237, 266, 280, 297, 298, 304
towns need state consent to, 128
urbanization and, 158–59
vingtième, 144, 304
Terror, the
administrative habits and, 236
June 1848 insurrection mimicked, 5
Tocqueville's family and, 2
Thierry, Augustin, 1, 6
Thiers, Adolphe, 6, 7, 55
Third Estate. *See* Bourgeoisie
Thirty Years War, 99, 259
Tocqueville, Alexis de, works
Democracy in America, 4, 5, 6, 7, 10, 12, 17, 20, 30, 31, 43, 47, 54, 56, 66, 70, 74
Recollections, 1, 3, 5, 7, 54, 58
"Social and Political State of France before and after 1789," 1, 3, 23, 36
Tocqueville, Hervé de, 2, 3
Towns. *See also* Urbanization
in America, 281
Angers as example, 270–77
assemblies governed, 235
bankrupt, 128, 277
bourgeois estranged from lower classes, 180–82, 270–77
constitutions of, 103, 119, 126, 168, 270–77
decline of democracy, 126
freedom lost, 173
freedom survives feudalism, 124
German Imperial Cities, 259–60
government by notables, 126–27, 270–77

hostility to countryside, 160
Louis XI and, 269–70
monarchy deprives lower class of rights, 167
political instability, 277
sale of offices, 125, 126, 247
state control, 26, 127, 128
taxes, 128
Tocqueville studied administration, 66
two assemblies, 125
Turgot, Anne Robert Jacques, 25, 43, 49, 76, 112, 130, 150, 159, 160, 170, 184, 188, 199, 200, 211, 220, 226, 228, 233, 237, 265, 277, 282, 283, 284, 298, 299, 305

Urbanization, 130, 158–59, 182. *See also* Towns

Vendée, 52, 181
Virtues
bureaucratic, 139
of a free people, 51, 216
freedom allows one to judge, 88
French retained aristocratic, 37
German cities no longer inspire, 104
individualism smothers public, 87
Languedoc's history has political, 74
of the lower classes, 190, 243–44
manly, 37, 86, 104, 179
old-regime clergy had public, 175
private, 88, 178
Revolutionary faith in human, 208
Voltaire, 41, 44, 45, 77, 142, 182, 204, 206, 209, 215, 227, 300

Wars of Religion, 145
Writers. *See* Intellectuals

Young, Arthur, 77, 94, 113, 147, 163, 220, 252, 284–85